CLASSROOM LEARNING

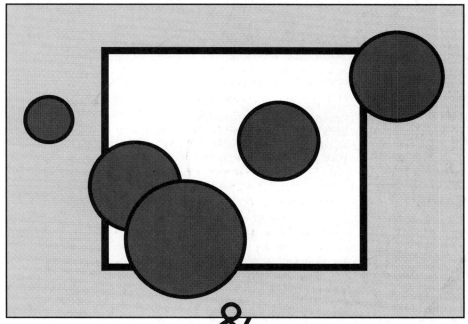

& TEACHING

Robert L. Hohn
University of Kansas

Longman *Publishers USA*

Classroom Learning & Teaching

Longman, 10 Bank Street, White Plains, N.Y. 10606

Associated companies:
Longman Group Ltd., London
Longman Cheshire Pty., Melbourne
Longman Paul Pty., Auckland
Copp Clark Longman Ltd., Toronto

Acquisitions editor: Virginia L. Blanford
Production editor: Linda W. Witzling
Cover design: Bob Crimi
Text art: FineLine
Production supervisor: Richard Bretan

Library of Congress Cataloging-in-Publication Data
Hohn, Robert.
    Classroom learning & teaching / Robert Hohn.
        p.   cm.
    Includes bibliographical references and index.
    ISBN 0-8013-0879-8
    1. Learning. 2. Learning, Psychology of. 3. Teaching.
I. Title.   II. Title: Classroom learning and teaching.
LB1060.H64 1994
370.15'23—dc20   94-4817
                                                     CIP

12345678910-MA-9897969594

Contents

PART III   LEARNING AND TEACHING   227

Preface

I wrote this text to help teachers and others in related roles to develop personal theories of learning and teaching that will contribute to their effectiveness as educators. This is an applied text, designed to convert psychological concepts, principles, and theories into useful policies and procedures for the solution of instructional problems.

Recent research and theory building has led to a merger of traditional behavioral and cognitive theories of learning that can be directly applied to instructional issues. Teachers can benefit from the insights derived from both psychological orientations, and both are stressed in this book. There has also developed a new understanding of the learner and the biological, psychological, and cultural influences that contribute to learning potential. This text provides the background information necessary to understand the learning of all individuals, rich or poor, able-bodied or not, male or female.

I have found through conversations with teachers over the years that whatever their level of experience, they prefer educational psychology texts that make direct application to the learning of the subject matter content and skills they are responsible for delivering. For that reason, this text devotes specific chapters to the learning of core curricular areas, to the learning of prosocial values and commitment, and to the acquisition of learning strategies and problem-solving skills—all of which contemporary teachers are expected to foster in their students. These components have been delivered, I believe, in an interesting, informative manner, one that reveals the study of educational psychology as rewarding and stimulating.

FEATURES OF THIS TEXT

I've tried to incorporate into the writing of the text many of the components of effective instruction the book discusses. For example, because examples and applications help us to recall and understand new ideas, I have included numerous illustrations of teacher behavior and curriculum materials to demonstrate how content discussed in the text can be translated to the classroom. Some other features that improve learning are highlighted briefly in the sections that follow.

Chapter Outlines and Objectives

Each chapter begins with an outline of major topics and a list of learning objectives for these topics. Read the outline and objectives to familiarize yourself with what is to come and to discover what content is most important. Exams are often constructed from chapter objectives, so it is to your advantage to formulate possible responses to questions about each objective.

Introductory Vignettes

All chapters begin with short vignettes or anecdotes about particular instructional situations. Vignettes also occasionally appear within chapters. These features serve as examples of major ideas and are frequently referred to in the text, to link content with practical application.

Margin Notes

Research has demonstrated that notes written in the margin of a text are most effective in aiding recall and understanding. By writing down your own notes as ideas occur to you, you will facilitate later study of the text. To foster this process, I have written my own notes in the margins. Some are summary statements of what has been described; others are questions you might consider about the application of the content. Be sure to add your own notes, as well. Pausing in your reading to consider my notes or to construct your own will make it much easier to process the text, as well as to review material later.

Practical Examples in Tables

Wherever possible, I have provided practical examples. In many cases, these appear in the form of tables or figures that summarize techniques and materials, or research findings that have direct application to instruction. Seeing the material in tabular form should allow you to organize and subsequently retrieve desired information. Tables will also be useful when you consider your own instructional role in relation to the text content.

Concept Maps

Students have told me often that it is difficult to keep straight all the material in a lengthy chapter before it has been properly assimilated. To remedy this problem, I developed concept maps illustrating the organization of each chapter. These schematic devices for representing a set of concepts in a hierarchical form have been found to aid organization and integration. By reviewing the concept map that accompanies each chapter summary, you will see how the material you have just read fits together. Each concept map is designed to demonstrate how the chapter material can fit into your personal theory of learning and teaching. You might try constructing your own maps, or adapting mine to reflect your ideas and interests.

Exercises

Each chapter contains one or more exercises to aid you in applying the material and to help you become an active learner, capable of utilizing text information for your own purposes.

Suggested Readings

I have selected reference items that were prominent in the chapter and listed them after the exercises. These suggested readings will allow you to study text topics in greater depth. Of course, all the references mentioned in the text are listed in the back of the book.

ORGANIZATION OF TOPICS

This book is arranged to present the information an effective teacher needs to understand learning and teaching in a particular sequence. First, we must *understand the learner,* and this goal is the focus of the first three chapters. Chapter 1 concentrates on basic definitions and historical ideas about psychology and learning. Chapter 2 discusses the learning process from a biological and physiological point of view. Chapter 3 considers such developmental influences on learning as language, cognitive skills, culture, gender, and learning style.

The second section examines three major *learning theories* that are particularly applicable to educational practice: operant learning (Chapter 4), social learning (Chapter 5), and cognitive information processing (Chapter 6).

When we understand how individuals learn and what important theories have to say about the learning process, we can consider the learning of specific types of content. The third section of the text, which covers *learning and teaching,* examines various educational outcomes in terms of how the learning takes place. Educational practices that can contribute to the acquisition of instructional content are emphasized. Chapter 7 addresses the subject matter areas of reading, writing, mathematics, science, and social studies. Chapter 8 considers motivation and its role in learning. Chapter 9 analyzes the learning of values, and Chapter 10 focuses on the acquisition of learning strategies and problem-solving skills. In Chapter 11 I give special consideration to the learning needs of students who are disabled. Finally, in the last section of the text, Putting It All Together, Chapter 12 summarizes major ideas and identifies common threads of the text.

ACKNOWLEDGMENTS

Although I am listed as the sole author of this text, I did not write it alone. Many people have helped with the writing itself or provided ideas, inspiration, and wisdom that shaped the content. In addition, I received emotional support and encouragement when I needed it. I would particularly like to thank Dr. Virginia Blanford, my editor at Longman, who despite arriving after the book had begun, provided steady support and guidance and encouraged me to choose my own path; and Linda Witzling, my production editor, who time and again rescued me. I would also like to thank:

J'Anne Ellsworth, Northern Arizona University

William J. Gnagey, Illinois State University

Sharon McNeely, Northeastern Illinois University

Sarah Peterson, Northern Illinois University

Elizabeth Popiel, University of Idaho

Albert E. Roark, University of Colorado at Boulder

who reviewed earlier versions most thoroughly and whose suggestions have greatly improved the final product, and my fine colleagues at the University of Kansas, who either read parts of the text, stimulated the growth of ideas contained within it, or offered words of encouragement—in particular Robert Harrington, Peter Johnsen, William LaShier, Neil Salkind, Everlyn Swartz, and Dick Tracy. Thanks to those who labored to decipher my often impenetrable handwriting in order to type the manuscript—Peggy Billings, Jan Maltby, Maria Martin, Debra Rhoton, and Judy Turner.

Many thanks to my parents, Walter and Marjorie, who taught me long ago to love to learn but also to love life, and to my wife, Norma, and my sons, Robert and Keith, who not only gave unconditional love and encouragement but serve every day as examples of how effort and patience lead to success, and my students over the years, who have taught me far more than I have taught them.

part **I**

Understanding
the Learner

chapter 1

Learning and Teaching

OUTLINE

Value of Learning Theories to Educators

Learning and Teaching
   Why Study Learning?

Components of Learning

Why Study Learning Theories?
   What Is a Theory?

Early Learning Theories
   Philosophical Roots
   Early Research on Learning
   Structuralism vs. Functionalism
   The Emergence of Behaviorism

Thorndike and the First Learning Theory

The Rise of Cognitive Theories: Gestalt Psychology
   Gestalt View of Learning
   Gestalt and Behavioral Explanations of Learning

CHAPTER OBJECTIVES

1. Explain why learning theories can be useful to educators. *p.5 — help solve problems with students*
   — growth
2. Derive a definition of learning that distinguishes this phenomenon from development, performance, and thinking.
   James   p.9 — use skills already learned

3

3. Justify the use of theory in explaining how individuals learn. *p.11*
4. Describe the philosophical explanations of learning in the positions of Plato, Aristotle, Locke, Kant, and Mill. *p.12-13*
5. Compare the structural and functional views of learning. *p.16*
6. Explain Thorndike's laws of learning and their educational relevance. *p.19-22*
7. Contrast the behavioral and Gestalt views of learning. *p.27*

VALUE OF LEARNING THEORIES TO EDUCATORS

As you begin to read this text, you are probably shaking your head and saying to yourself, "Why am I studying this? All we are going to cover is a lot of theories that don't even agree with one another. I don't need them to be a good teacher." If you feel this way, you are not alone. You are expressing the sentiments of a good many teachers when they begin to study learning. The perceived irrelevance of theories was best summarized by a successful teacher I encountered in class a few years ago. We were about to consider early theories of learning. Our conversation went something like this:

> *"Dr. Hohn, psychology is interesting and all, but I don't think this class will be useful to me."*
> *"Why is that, Bill?"*
> *"Well, first of all, I teach social studies and all these theories seem to talk about is how chimps learn to get a banana or how somebody solves a math problem."*
> *"Hmmm, anything else?"*
> *"Yeah, a lot. I teach eighth graders in a little farm town. I have enough to do to keep them interested. All the students mentioned in these theories seem to like to learn and always seem to get the right answers. It's not like that in my class or with other teachers I know. Do you want me to go on?"*
> *"Don't stop while you're on a roll."*
> *"OK, I already know how to teach, and besides, the teacher's manual for the textbook I use gives me a lot of ideas about how to teach the content. I don't see what these theories are going to tell me that I can't get from the manual."*
> *"I see. Go on."*
> *"Every theory seems to explain just one type of learning, or a single component. It seems that they're all describing part of the elephant, so to speak. It's like each one has something to sell."*
> *"Perhaps, but don't you think there may be reasons for that?"*
> *"Maybe, but I wish the academics would work it all out and come up with one theory I can really use. Right now, I guess all I need to know is who my kids are, what the course content is, and what the school wants them to learn."*

Mercifully, we were interrupted and the conversation ended before my blood pressure reached a dangerous level. My initial reaction was anger and frustration at being unable to clarify, or "sell," as my student had put it, the value of studying learning theories. I could not be terribly angry at this young man because I sensed he had expressed what others were afraid or too polite to say out loud. I did feel, however, that his comments revealed considerable misunderstanding, not only of learning but of teaching as well.

That conversation and other similar interchanges over the years have been partially responsible for the development of this book. I believe that it is *only* through understanding how people learn that we can be effective teachers. Moreover, rather than seek to rely on one theory to provide all the answers, we must recognize that at present, *there is no one best description of the learning process, just as there is no one "best" way to teach.* Educators can benefit from knowing various learning theories, because each position adds to their views of how to engage in this very complex process.

Everyone has personal theory of learning

The suggestion that successful teachers don't need theories to operate ignores the personal, or *implicit,* theory about learning that every teacher possesses. An implicit theory is a set of beliefs and hypotheses that serves to guide our actions but may not be readily apparent to us (Gage, 1963). While not necessarily verbalized in an orderly fashion as one might expect of traditional theories, these unstated beliefs nevertheless affect how we function in a variety of situations. Implicit theories are constructed from past experiences. If I ask you to "teach something you know," you will immediately draw on the appropriate implicit theory. To ensure a correct choice, you might identify a topic you think will interest me. You might consider what you can say or demonstrate, the availability of instructional materials, how I might respond, and how you would evaluate my learning and provide feedback. Whatever you decide will be guided by your personal theory of how people learn, not by chance. Your implicit theory will guide your thoughts.

my implicit theory is how I decide to teach.

Learning theories not only help us to develop more useful and accurate implicit theories, they also provide the context from which we observe and interpret events. Teachers who possess theoretical understanding can approach novel situations from a frame of reference that provides clues to appropriate action. Faced with a student who is suddenly disruptive, a teacher who understands the operant learning theory of B. F. Skinner (1953) might attempt to identify the events in the environment that are reinforcing the child's behavior, and then consider modifying certain aspects of the environment. Other teachers might approach the problem from a different theoretical stance; there are several alternatives. Understanding at least one theory provides a base from which to view a problem. A good theory—one that suggests explanatory mechanisms for learners' behavior—increases the probability that a teacher can develop appropriate strategies to rectify problems or reach goals.

Theoretical understanding can help me with students from different angles

LEARNING AND TEACHING

Does teaching exist independently from the learning of students? Can we say that teaching has occurred if no one learns from the presentation? I remember an American history professor in my undergraduate days whose only instructional method was to read his notes to our class of approximately 60 sophomores. At precisely 9:00 A.M. he would enter the lecture hall, take his place behind the lectern, arrange his notes in

professor who read his notes

their proper sequence, and begin to read. He invariably kept his eyes on his material, making no eye contact with the members of the class. One spring morning a mischievous student passed around a note asking everyone to begin to leave at 9:20, as quietly as possible. After some initial giggling and hesitation, we all left, taking about 15 minutes to empty the hall. Our professor, totally immersed in the Reconstruction Era, never noticed the gradual attrition of his class. A lingering student, stationed outside the room, noted the professor's somewhat red-faced departure about 10 minutes after everyone had gone. During the time in which the room was devoid of students, was the oblivious professor "teaching"?

This rather extreme example illustrates the *interaction* of teaching with learning. Probably we would all say that without students to listen, my history professor was not teaching—he was talking to himself. The word *teach* is defined as "to cause someone to learn by example or experience" (*American Heritage Dictionary,* 1985). This definition implies a relation between the act of teaching and student behavior. Teaching and learning are inextricably bound. To think of ourselves as teachers without considering the nature and amount of learning that is occurring would be presumptuous. Teaching occurs only through the mutual interplay of an instructional medium and the efforts of learners to acquire information, principles, or skills.

Teaching inter-
acts with learn-
ing

Why Study Learning?

With the relationship of teaching to learning in mind, it becomes readily apparent why those who are interested in teaching must consider how students learn. If we do not understand the learning process, our teaching may very well resemble the behavior of the inattentive college professor.

what makes them tick?

I once asked 160 teachers what they hoped to gain from taking a course on classroom learning. The following questions, which are representative of the kinds of information teachers can obtain from studying learning, are the 10 most frequently posed. After reading this list, you might note which of these questions you have asked yourself.

How can I get students to pay attention to my presentations? To their reading assignments?

How can I manage my classroom so that students don't interfere with one another's learning and do assume individual responsibility?

How can I ensure that my students don't show up on those national surveys indicating that some high school students don't know where Mexico is and can't place the Civil War in the right century?

How can I help my students to write clear sentences?

Why is it so difficult to get students to cooperate with one another?

How can I interest my students in learning?

What can I do to help my students use what they have already learned when a new learning problem occurs?

Why don't my students understand what they read?

Why are some of my students so low in self-esteem?

Would you add
any questions?

mine → How can I aid my students to have confidence in their own abilities?

As the questions indicate, learning in the classroom is multidimensional. Traditional academic skills are important of course; but the learning of social behaviors, respect for oneself and others, and interest in school and what it offers also demand high priority. If we were to attempt to identify all the different kinds of learning that occur in schools, our list would be considerably longer. It is sufficient to say that teachers are responsible for a large number of learning outcomes, and these must be understood before they can be influenced.

Learning is believed to begin before birth, when a fetus involuntarily moves in the uterus as a result of changes in stimulation such as pressure or temperature (Barclay, 1985). Learning does not cease until death. In between birth and death, the amount and variety of learning acquired by a single individual could fill a library. To understand the breadth and complexity of human learning, we must consider the factors that affect it and the theories that attempt to explain it.

[handwritten margin note: We teach more than our subject matter! Scary! Be on best behavior + set example.]

[handwritten margin note: Learning from birth to death]

COMPONENTS OF LEARNING

No definition of learning is accepted by all psychologists, educators, theorists, and researchers. Most would agree that learning involves the acquisition of new elements of knowledge, skills, beliefs, feelings, and specific behaviors, as well as change in existing elements. Learning depends primarily on some type of external stimulation or experience. The acquisition of learning, the factors that effect changes in learning, and the nature of the external stimulation that induces it may be hotly debated. As we review various learning theories in future chapters, answers to these distinctions will become evident. For now, it is important to identify the most basic characteristics of the learning process.

Learning involves either a change in behavior or the capacity to change one's behavior in the future. When Charles becomes able to demonstrate all the steps necessary to change an automobile tire, we can say definitively that he has learned to change a tire. In this case, we can say that learning is overt; that is, we can directly observe its presence. Suppose that in his driver's education class Charles watched a film on how to change a tire and read about the task in his car manual but never demonstrated the behavior to his instructor. We would say that learning had occurred on the basis of evidence that there had been a change in the capacity to behave. Of course if Charles later dropped and lost the lug nuts, could not operate the car jack, and eventually had to call a service station to get a tire changed, we would have to revise our belief that he had learned this skill.

[handwritten margin note: Behavioral theory?]

We often acquire knowledge and skills without immediately exhibiting them in a manner observable to others, as you may be doing as you read this text. In certain situations, we simply observe someone engaging in an action that we can perform for ourselves when the appropriate time arises. This type of learning, known as *observational learning,* is a key concept of *social learning theory* (Bandura, 1977), which we shall discuss in detail in Chapter 5.

Learning must be followed by a relatively permanent change in behavior. This dimension of learning excludes changes in behavior that are temporary or due to extraneous factors. For example, even the most skilled musicians report days on

[handwritten margin note: Behavioral theory again?]

which their performance is filled with errors and lapses in concentration. It would be inaccurate to describe this decrement as due to "unlearning." It is likely to be attributable to such factors as fatigue, illness, the presence of drugs or alcohol, or even lack of motivation. Behavioral changes do not have to be maintained for a lifetime; after all, we do forget some things over time. While no one has established a fixed time period to clarify the notion of permanence, modification of behavior lasting only a few seconds is not defined as learning.

Learning is a process, the existence of which we infer from changes in performance. Learning is an internal process that others cannot directly observe. What can be observed is a change in behavior, from which we may *infer* learning. The behavioral change may be an increased capability for *performance*. For example, as we practice the addition of single-digit numbers, our scores on a test of addition might progressively increase. Notice the number of addition problems Sarah and Edwin each solved correctly over a five-week period.

	Week 1	*Week 2*	*Week 3*	*Week 4*	*Week 5*
Sarah	13	17	16	19	23
Edwin	14	15	17	18	22

If we assume that the same type of addition problems was tested each week, we can infer that both children were learning how to add. Their scores gradually improved over five weeks. The scores represent the performance from which a teacher can infer learning progress. Note also that the scores did not increase uniformly; Sarah's score actually declined on one week's test. Unevenness in performance is not uncommon in the learning of most skills. We all can recall tasks on which our performance not only failed to improve but seemed to get worse. The author produced uneven results while learning to drive a golf ball, an experience that led, for a short period of time, to more hooks and slices than ever occurred before the instruction.

Since we infer learning from performance, it is helpful to have a predetermined standard, or *criterion,* in mind when we have to judge whether a behavior change is sufficient to indicate learning. Should Sarah and Edwin's teacher cease providing instruction in adding numbers on the assumption that learning is complete? Would your opinion change if you learned that the scores in the preceding chart were based on a 50-item test? The issue of how to define and assess learning based on performance indices is discussed in later sections of this text.

Learning occurs through practice or experience. This characteristic suggests that genetically determined changes in behavior and changes that accompany growth or aging should be distinguished from learning. One early spring day, the author's six-year-old son proudly directed his father to "look at what I learned to do," whereupon he chinned himself on a low-hanging tree branch. Noting that the boy had grown three inches in the past few months, I authoritatively declared, "I think you've grown bigger and stronger, too." While this distinction was probably ignored by my six-year-old, the incident reminds us that the process of human maturation also produces changes in behavior.

This learning–development dichotomy, however, is not straightforward. Adoring parents often believe that they are teaching their infant to talk by repetitively saying

Margin notes:

A learner's performance tends to vary (due to illness, etc.)

Learning definition requires criterion

growing to reach tree limb not learning

"Mama" or "Dada," which the child echoes in a babylike voice. More neutral observers might note the spontaneous verbalizations of infants in the crib, in which a wide variety of sounds emerge without any apparent external stimulation. The human vocal apparatus matures so that it can produce sounds, but actual words are learned from the interactive instruction of parents and other caregivers. As we will discuss in Chapter 3, language is one example of behavior in which both learning and maturation play major roles.

Development and learning produce change

Learning is not the same as thinking. While most learning psychologists recognize the relation of thinking to learning, they are careful to emphasize that learning involves an outcome, while thinking is a process that uses skills already learned. We *learn to think* by improving skills, such as how to search our memory, how to follow sequential steps in solving problems, or how to critically analyze information presented to us. We *think to learn* by attending to, analyzing, and judging new experiences so that new or potential behaviors can be acquired. As we mature, more and more of our new learning results from thinking about past learning.

Learning can occur spontaneously. Recognizing that learning can occur without the learner deliberately setting out to learn, psychologists attempt to distinguish between *intentional* and *incidental* learning. Intentional learning refers to learning that is directed toward a goal—to master the backhand or to be able to recite the 50 American states on command, for example. Incidental learning applies when we acquire knowledge or skills without an intention to do so. If you shut your eyes and think about the physical characteristics of this text—its color, the design on the front cover, the look and feel of the pages—you probably will be surprised at your ability to recall information you do not remember having planned to learn. Some learning occurs without our conscious awareness, though it may not persist without directed attention and practice. One of the difficulties in studying incidental learning is the tendency of learners to switch attention from what they were instructed to do to other aspects of a task, with the result that a component of the task that was originally incidental becomes central to the learner's efforts (Travers, 1982).

incidental learning - osmosis

Incidental learning is important to the process of teaching in two ways. First, we must recognize that students are acquiring all sorts of information that may not be germane to the lesson being taught—that the girl in the next seat wears a certain brand of perfume, that the teacher rarely gets his sports jacket cleaned, that this topic is dull. Second, students may learn the wrong information without realizing it. In teaching a golfer how to swing, for example, professional instructors are often amazed at the bad habits amateurs acquire incidentally. Instruction that includes continual evaluation of a student's progress is necessary to detect errors in incidental learning.

Beware of incidental learning.

Now that we have examined the basic characteristics of the learning process, it is possible to cite one well-known definition: "Learning is a change in disposition or capability that persists over a period of time and is not simply ascribable to processes of growth" (Gagné, 1985, p. 2).

Defn!

This definition is broad enough to allow for the differences in interpretation of various learning theories, yet it recognizes characteristics common to all positions. Like other psychological definitions, each critical term requires further clarification. As we progress through the text, we will further refine our understanding of this complex term.

WHY STUDY LEARNING THEORIES?

Have you ever thought about how you came to know something? Pick a skill or set of facts you possess, and think about how and where you acquired it. More than likely, you acquired that particular piece of learning from one of four basic sources: personal experience, folklore, research, or theory.

Let us first consider *personal experience.* If you teach, you have probably learned a number of skills associated with teaching merely by doing them. Many skills require frequent practice—the only way they can be acquired is to engage in the process directly. Monitoring the progress of students is a good example. With experience, a good teacher learns how to keep "mental notes" on how students are performing, often seeming to attend to many stimuli all at once. Jackson (1968) observed that teachers may make close to a thousand interactions with students each day. Being able to manage such continual activity, while still maintaining a direction for the total class, becomes easier over time through repeated experience.

Unfortunately, we cannot personally experience all the knowledge we need to succeed in life. Often we must rely on a second source of knowledge—the experience and wisdom of others. Traditional wisdom, or *folklore,* is usually passed down to us by parents, teachers, authorities, and even newspaper columnists such as Ann Landers. A lot of useful information is acquired in this manner. Folklore is often dispersed in glib phrases, however, which leave out important details. A broker's advice to "buy low and sell high" if you want to make money in the stock market is valid, but difficult to implement without additional information. The title of a widely read book on classroom management, *Don't Smile Until Christmas* (Ryan, 1970), reflects the traditional wisdom about teaching often imparted to new teachers. It suggests establishing appropriate routines of student conduct by maintaining a firm, relatively uncompromising approach to disruptive behavior in the first few months of school, then relaxing the standards and becoming "nicer" as the year progresses. While such advice may be useful in many situations, as a generalization, it tends to ignore the specifics of the policy's extent, and the steps required for implementation. It also may be incorrect, as in the case of immature or dependent students who require a more nurturant atmosphere for learning.

A third source of knowledge is *research,* in which scientific procedures are followed in attempts to validate certain beliefs or procedures. Much of what is known about effective teaching has been demonstrated through the research efforts of numerous investigators. In analyzing and observing the conditions under which the "Don't Smile Until Christmas" policy is implemented, for example, researchers can clearly describe when, how, and with which students it is most effective. Research often serves the purpose of operationalizing, or putting into precise terms, a procedure being studied, so that those who wish to adopt it can do so more specifically. This text describes many instructional techniques, policies, and curricular materials that have undergone extensive research. A problem with relying exclusively on research as a source of knowledge, however, is that educational research progresses slowly. Research studies must be replicated (repeated), so that the effects of new innovations can be observed in settings other than the laboratory or classroom where the research first occurred. Many initially promising educational fads of the past few decades, such as the "new" mathematics, values clarification activities, and pro-

Folklore often overgeneralized

grammed texts, turned out to possess important limitations when assessed exhaustively.

Relying on research findings entails a related problem: Many phenomena known to be important to learning are difficult to operationalize and study. For example, while most educators recognize the significance of the "self-concept" in learning, its very nature renders the construct difficult to measure and employ in valid scientific endeavors. Many aspects of human behavior do not lend themselves to the demands of scientific analysis as easily as the components of natural sciences.

A fourth source of knowledge is *theory*. Good theories incorporate elements of the other three sources: (1) they serve to explain the events individuals have experienced, (2) they expand and clarify the truisms of folklore, and (3) they are based on and modified by the findings of empirical research. In effect, a theory acts as a systematic organization of various knowledge sources. This text presents a variety of theories devoted to organizing what is known about learning. Knowledge of learning theories allows those interested in the topic to go beyond personal experience, to analyze traditional wisdom, to understand and interpret research evidence, and to develop more systematic ways of thinking about how people learn.

What Is a Theory?

In the broadest sense, a theory is an organized attempt to explain a set of observed events. Marx (1970) defines it more formally as a

> provisional explanatory proposition, or set of propositions, concerning some natural phenomena, and consisting of symbolic representations of: 1) the observed relationships among independent and dependent events, 2) the mechanisms or structures presumed to underlie such relationships or 3) inferred relationships and underlying mechanisms intended to account for observed data in the absence of any direct empirical manifestation of the relationships. (p. 5)

Note the use of the word "provisional," implying that theories have a temporary or developmental dimension. Theories are always in flux, changing as new sets of facts or observations become known. The big bang theory of the creation of the universe, for example, has been modified frequently in this century as astronomers gain new knowledge about the most distant galaxies and the radiation emitted from their stars. As new technology and observation techniques yield new data, space science theories inevitably must be revised. As we shall soon see, theories of learning also undergo continual revision as research evidence accumulates.

Theories do not typically spring fully developed from the fertile minds of theoreticians. They often emerge when an individual forms a mental *model* of a set of events. A model is "a conceptual analogue that is used to suggest how empirical research on a problem might be pursued" (Marx, 1970, p. 71). It may consist of an analogy the theoretician believes can be used to relate one situation to another. For example, neuropsychologists at one time thought of the nervous system as a telephone switchboard. That view is now considered incomplete, but the model served to give direction and guidance to subsequent research on the human nervous system and its relation to behavior.

Next, theories are developed through a progression of steps that combine empirical research, personal experience, and sound reasoning. The formation of theories is aided when an individual notes the existence of certain *facts* that are agreed on by objective observers. For example, "water freezes at 32°F or 0°C" is a scientific fact. Unfortunately, facts that can be universally agreed on are not as easily found in education. An example that seems to possess substantial consensus, however, is one we have already noted: External stimulation is necessary for learners to change their behavior.

In an attempt to explain one fact, a theoretician might note the relationship between it and other facts. If such a relationship is consistently supported by research, we can use the term *principle*. In education, we have the "feedback principle," according to which external stimulation creates behavior change by providing information, or feedback, to the individual. Principles that survive repeated analysis over time become known as *laws*. For example, Edward Thorndike (1874–1949) identified a number of psychological laws in his study of learning. According to the *law of effect,* a "satisfying state of affairs following a response strengthens the connection between a stimulus and the behavior, whereas an annoying state of affairs weakens the connection" (Thorndike, 1913).

Theories are more than integrated sets of facts, principles, and laws. As Marx suggests in his definition, theories include presumptions and inferences, which are assumed to explain the relationships in question. Psychologists refer to these assumed relationships as *constructs.* Usually symbolic representations of complex relationships, constructs may be observed only indirectly. For example, many learning theories use the construct "motivation" to refer to an inferred condition of the learner that accounts for variations in effort or interest. While motivation is not directly observed, changes in behavior presumed to reflect it, such as an increased number of attempts to solve a task, can be seen. As you might imagine, the more constructs, or assumed relationships, a theory relies on, the greater the difficulty in communicating from the theorist to others. Freud's psychodynamic theory of personality, which consists of a number of constructs such as "id," "ego," "superego," and "repression," has not been universally accepted because of the difficulty in establishing a consensus as to what the constructs represent.

Theories = facts + principles + constructs

measure motivation by behavioral chg

EARLY LEARNING THEORIES

Now that some basic definitions and the role of theory in the learning process have been introduced, it is time to explore those positions and ideas in greater detail. We shall begin with the learning theories that established the base from which modern positions have evolved. Early theories initially defined the major issues that have challenged students of the relationship of learning to teaching. As later sections reveal, many of those issues remain with us.

Philosophical Roots

It has frequently been said that almost all modern thought is a refinement of the epistemology of the Greek philosophers Plato and Aristotle. Plato (427–347 B.C.) believed that there were two kinds of knowledge—that which is acquired from the senses,

#4

such as knowledge of physical objects, and knowledge gained by reason, such as ideas. One's senses thus provide information about the material world, while rational thought leads to the discovery of ideas. Ideas were believed to be *innate,* or present at birth. To access innate ideas, the individual simply recalls what exists in the mind and makes a rational analysis of it. Plato's position was called *rationalism,* and it is generally taken to imply that rational thought about our memories is the key to learning abstract ideas. As he explained to a student in the *Meno,* "All research and all learning is thus nothing but reminiscence. In our researches, we are not looking for what we do not know, we are looking for what we do know but have forgotten" (quoted in Grote, 1975, p. 14).

Plato's rationalist philosophy was extended by later philosophers René Descartes (1596–1650) and Immanuel Kant (1724–1804). Descartes asserted a separation between the mind and the body, or *dualism.* The body was viewed as a machine, and although the mind was free of the mechanical characteristics of the body, it could decide the body's actions. The body, however, provided sensory experiences for the mind. Both mind and body can initiate behavior: the body through *reflex actions,* the mind through deductive reasoning. Descartes is well known for his statement "cogito, ergo sum," or "I think, therefore I am," which he used as his proof of the existence of the mind. Descartes arrived at this conclusion through inquiry or, in his terms, through "doubt."

Kant attempted to clarify the concept of mind-body dualism by noting that the mind imposes order on the external world. It alters information acquired from the senses according to a subjective process, dependent on innate laws, which he called *faculties.* In his *Critique of Pure Reason,* first published in 1781, Kant identified 12 of these innate faculties, including causality, reciprocity, and unity. As a result of these innate faculties, the world can never be known as it is, but only as it is perceived. Kant, like Descartes and Plato before him, argued that the mind is the major source of knowledge and that the external world is at best only a beginning point in the mind's reasoning.

Other philosophers, led by Aristotle (384–322 B.C.) and later John Locke (1632–1704) and John Stuart Mill (1806–1873), viewed the role of experience in a much different light. These *empiricists* believed that experience is the only source of knowledge. Observation of physical and biological phenomena is thus crucial. Aristotle is known for his collection of facts and his detection of lawful patterns among them. In the field of psychology, Aristotle postulated the *laws of association,* in which certain factors were found to influence memory: for example, the recall of one event that brings about the recall of similar events (law of similarity), the recall of opposites (law of contrast), and the recall of events that were experienced at the same time or place as the original event (law of contiguity). The more often events are recalled together, the more likely it is that recall of one will evoke recall of the other (law of frequency). These laws gave rise to a philosophical position known as *associationism,* which in turn became one of the pillars of modern psychology. The laws of association and other laws governing the empirical world are not knowable through sensory information alone. Rather, they must be discovered through active reason. Aristotle believed that sensory experience and thinking were necessary for the acquisition of knowledge.

Locke extended empiricism by stating that there can be nothing in the mind that does not originate through the senses. He viewed the mind as a blank tablet, or *tabula rasa,* on which sensory experiences cumulatively left their mark. More complex ideas were merely the recombination of simpler ideas according to the laws of association. On this view, therefore, the mind could be understood by analyzing it into simpler units.

Mill refuted the notion that complex ideas merely recombine simpler ideas, while still recognizing the laws of associationism. He believed that simple ideas can produce a complex thought that might be quite different from its parts. For example, the combination of blue and yellow yields green, a color uniquely different from its antecedents. Mill's emphasis on a new totality emerging from its parts was a forerunner to the belief held by the more recent school of Gestalt psychology that *the whole is greater than the sum of its parts.*

We can see a basic division—the separation of empiricism from rationalism—in the earliest philosophical analyses of learning. Is learning based entirely on sensory data, or does it require an original contribution from the mind of the learner? This issue continues to be of major interest.

Early Research on Learning

The establishment of psychology as a science marked the next step in thinking about human learning. Drawing on the experimental techniques of physics and other natural sciences, psychology began to view learning as a process that could be explored scientifically. The work of two German scientists, Wilhelm Wundt (1832–1920) and Herman Ebbinghaus (1850–1909), illustrates this movement to an experimental approach. Wundt is credited with creating, in Leipzig, Germany, one of the first psychology laboratories. He believed the mind could be studied by carefully controlling stimuli and measuring responses. Wundt studied mental processes such as perception, verbal association, feelings, and emotions. A technique known as *introspection* arose from his lab. Subjects were trained to report their immediate impressions, not their interpretations, as they inspected various objects. Wundt was interested in the learners' sensory experience, not in what they had learned about their impressions. This emphasis was in keeping with the empirical tradition. For example, in reporting their immediate impressions of a table, subjects were supposed to describe the hardness, color, and size of the object. Wundt believed that by avoiding labels, such as "table," learners could more scientifically report the most basic elements of the mind, which he held to be the contents most worthy of study.

Ebbinghaus also employed a scientific methodology to study learning, namely, the recall of *nonsense syllables,* unfamiliar consonant–vowel–consonant combinations such as "rok" or "gef." By using meaningless verbal material, Ebbinghaus believed that past learning could be controlled; he also hoped to be able to study objectively the processes of learning and remembering as functions of the simple ideas of the empiricists. He often used himself as a subject, a procedure frowned on by most modern researchers, although it did yield Ebbinghaus some valid findings.

Ebbinghaus would develop a list of 12 nonsense syllables, and conduct a series of *trials* in which he looked at the list, wrote down as many syllables as possible in what he thought was the right order, checked his results, and repeated the procedure until he could reproduce the list correctly. He would then note how many trials it had

Introspection: objective or subjective?

taken to learn the list perfectly. In his studies, Ebbinghaus found that as the number of nonsense syllables to be learned became longer, more time was required to commit them to memory; also, the more frequently he studied a list, the better his learning (Ebbinghaus, [1885] 1964). Although with time he forgot lists that had been learned perfectly, it did not take Ebbinghaus as many trials later to relearn them. This difference in number of trials was called *savings*. Ebbinghaus recorded his learning and savings scores in graphic form, thus creating the first learning curve (Figure 1.1).

Forgetting was minimized when Ebbinghaus practiced a list beyond the point at which he could recite the nonsense syllables perfectly. This phenomenon, known as *overlearning*, addresses the usefulness of practice of some learned material, even after one has apparently learned it. The music teacher who required you to play the scales "just one more time" was perfectly correct in requiring extra trials, boring though it might have been.

Ebbinghaus can be called the first psychologist to study learning and memory by analyzing observable behavior; his results have been replicated many times. An incidental finding of the memory studies was that Ebbinghaus learned poems much more rapidly than nonsense syllables, even though the nonsense syllable lists contained fewer items. This finding anticipated the significance of *meaningfulness* as an important variable in memory. Poems are easier to remember because they possess a structure made up of words, rhymes, and meter, and because unlike nonsense syllables, they make sense. The relation of meaningfulness to learning is discussed extensively in later chapters.

Meaningful vs. non-meaningful material

FIGURE 1.1 Learning curve of Ebbinghaus depicting the repetitions required for the first errorless reproduction of a list as a function of the number of syllables in the series. A lengthy list requires more repetition.

SOURCE: H. Ebbinghaus, *Memory: A contribution to experimental psychology*, H. A. Tuger & C. E. Bussenius, Trans. (New York: Dover, 1964). (Originally published by Dunker and Humboldt: Leipzig, Germany, 1885.)

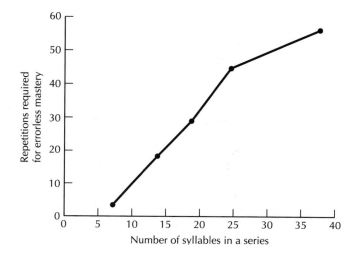

Structuralism versus Functionalism

The focus on identification of the basic elements of human consciousness as exemplified by Wundt and an emphasis on scientific procedures as demonstrated by Ebbinghaus gave rise to an early school of psychology known as *structuralism*. This school of psychology reached its greatest level of influence under Edward Titchener (1867–1927), a student of Wundt's. The structuralists believed that all entities, even those as complex as the human mind, could be broken down into simpler elements, thus revealing their structure. The idea was considered to be the simplest element of consciousness; it was believed that an idea could be made more complex by associating it with others. The structuralists relied on interpretation to study the association of ideas.

structuralism – break things down into simpler elements

A strong alternative to structuralism was developed in the late 1800s by those who believed that consciousness cannot be reduced to basic elements. This view, first advocated by William James (1842–1910) in his book *The Principles of Psychology* (1890), is based on the belief that man adapts to his environment, rather than remaining dependent on it.

Functionalism was influenced by the naturalist Charles Darwin (1809–1892), whose writings on biological evolution changed the way in which our role in the world was defined. If all living creatures were subject to the same evolutionary processes, psychologists were justified in using data from experiments with animals to derive models for human learning. Darwin saw no sharp boundary between "higher" and "lower" animals; all living creatures are inherently biologically equipped to survive in their environment by adapting to its demands. James and other functionalists believed that mental processes had evolved to serve various useful functions for animals just as physical characteristics had evolved. Refuting the dualism of Plato and Locke, the functionalists believed mental processes cannot be considered apart from the environments in which they occur. Structuralism also failed to adequately describe the mind: A model in which the mind is reduced to its most common element will not be helpful in investigating mental functions that contribute to survival and adaptation. Introspection was considered an inadequate experimental technique, because studying an event in isolation ignores its effects on the organism's survival. James agreed that psychology should follow scientific principles, but should be approached in a way that allowed a broad view of human behavior. Psychology should study how people adapt to their environment and how the processes that lead to successful adaptation contribute to it. Functionalists, therefore, chose to study how mental processes operated, what they accomplished, and how they varied with environmental conditions. Processes such as motivation (why people behave as they do), productive thinking, and the effects of emotion on behavior were considered worthy of study.

Functionalists emphasize adaptation

John Dewey (1867–1949) extended the functionalist argument against the reductionist view of human behavior in a famous article, "The Reflex Arc Concept in Psychology" (1896). He believed that the purpose of behavior is overlooked in studies of isolated units. Human behavior, unlike that of animals, is much more than sensory responses and should be studied in its totality. Because Dewey believed that psychology's goal was to determine the significance of behavior in adapting to everyday life, it was logical for him to recommend the application of psychology to areas such as education and industry. He believed that education should be a vehicle for change in society, that schools should be concerned with the larger community's needs and values. He argued for the inclusion of the world of work in school curricula. Later movements to "experience-based education" were prompted by Dewey's suggestions. We can see that up until the early part of this century, the psychological study of learning was an integral part of the study of psychology in general. Structuralists, functionalists, and those who preceded them struggled with basic questions about the nature of human behavior and thought. The scientific study of learning occurred only as a related aspect of these more fundamental issues. A historical record describing these early schools of thought about psychology, as well as behaviorism and the cognitivist approach known as Gestalt psychology, which we consider in the remainder of the chapter, is provided in Figure 1.2.

The psychology of learning became a field of study in its own right when two competing views of psychology rose to prominence. The two families of theory, *behaviorism* and *cognitive–Gestalt psychology,* reflect dissatisfaction with explanations offered earlier such specific psychological processes as learning.

FIGURE 1.2 Historical record of schools of thought about learning

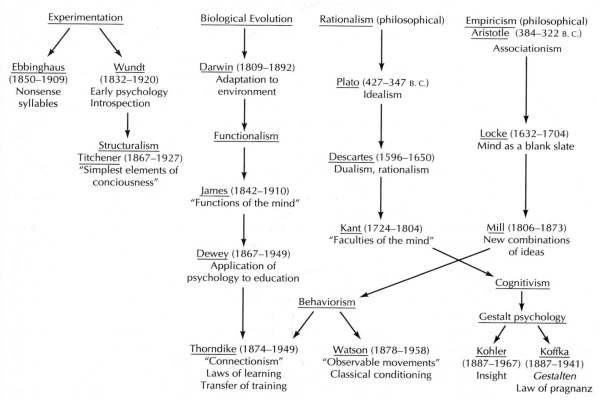

The Emergence of Behaviorism

The attempt to identify the basic concepts of human behavior did not cease in the face of the functionalists' argument. In fact, during the early years of this century there was renewed emphasis on observable behavior as the unit of study for psychology, rather than the broader totality of consciousness. As one might surmise from the name, the school of psychology that became known as *behaviorism* argued that psychologists should study behavior only, avoiding analysis of subjective interpretation of mental processes. As John B. Watson (1878–1958) stated in his book *Behaviorism* (1925), "Behaviorism claims that consciousness is neither a definable nor a viable concept. The behaviorist, who has been trained always as an experimentalist, holds further, that belief in the existence of consciousness goes back to the earliest days of superstition and magic" (p. 2).

In effect, Watson was attempting to finally disassociate psychology from the philosophical tradition of examining the nature of knowledge. He believed psychology could become a science in its own right only by concentrating on phenomena that could be observed directly, such as movements and utterances and their relation to environmental stimuli. We can see the empirical tradition in Watson's emphasis on the role of sensory experience. His rejection of any consideration of the mind and unobservable mental processes, however, clearly marked a break with introspection.

Watson was influenced by the Russian physiologist Ivan Pavlov (1849–1936). Does the name ring a bell? Pavlov had studied reflexive actions produced in dogs in response to environmental stimuli. He had observed that dogs salivate when stimuli such as the ringing of a bell, the footsteps of a caretaker, or other sounds were introduced just before or contiguous to the presentation of food. He realized that these sounds, which were not natural stimuli for producing salivation, took on this power as a result of their close proximity to the presentation of food. Pavlov called naturally occurring responses such as salivation in the presence of food *unconditioned reflexes;* instances of salivation in response to associated stimuli such as bell ringing were called *conditioned reflexes.* Conditioned reflexes can be considered to be learned, although Pavlov did not use that term in his research. This type of learning, known as *classical conditioning* (because it was described in several classic experiments), applies to learning in which contiguity and repetition of stimuli aid learners to generalize an existing stimulus–response association to a new stimulus. Whenever we employ flash cards to teach math facts or vocabulary words and their definitions, we are inducing the acquisition of classically conditioned responses. Classical conditioning may also occur as incidental learning during traumatic experiences in which fears or prejudices are established. The author, who became violently ill after eating salami as a child, still reacts with nausea every time that particular meat is encountered. Many such fears, anxieties, and emotional responses are learned as a result of classical conditioning. Can you identify behaviors of yours that may have been acquired in a similar fashion?

Watson believed that the substitution of new stimuli for existing ones was the kind of experimental manipulation that could be used to build a behavioral science of psychology. His own research extended to the conditioning of humans, as illustrated by the notorious experiment in which little Albert, aged eleven months, was conditioned to fear a small furry white rat (Watson & Rayner, 1920). The infant's fear was later generalized to a rabbit, a dog, and a furry coat. As a result of this kind of research, Watson came to believe that the conditioning process could be used to establish and develop the abilities and personalities of young children. He backed this belief with the following claim:

> Give me a dozen healthy infants, well-formed, and my own specified world to bring them up in, and I'll guarantee to take any one at random and train him to become any type of specialist I might select—a doctor, lawyer, artist, merchant-chief, and yes, even into beggar-man and thief, regardless of his talents, penchants, abilities, vocations, and race of his ancestors. (Watson, 1930, p. 103)

A rather extreme position, you say? Can we control the learning of human beings so that they become exactly what we wish them to be? This question is central to the debate over the possibilities and limitations of behaviorism that continues to the present. Watson himself was aware of the controversial nature of his statement when he continued:

> I am going beyond my facts and I admit it, but so have the advocates of the contrary and they have been doing it for many thousands of years. Please note that when this experiment is made I am to be allowed to specify the way they are to be brought up and the type of world they have to live in. (p. 104)

The practical relevance of Watson's ideas and the straightforwardness of his procedures made behaviorism immensely popular. All that was needed to explain learning was to identify new associations that are conditioned to older ones. Later psychologists such as Edwin Guthrie (1886–1952) and Clark Hull (1884–1952) established more sophisticated associationistic learning theories, attempting to explain more complex learning outcomes. Other behaviorists, mindful of functionalist concerns for the role of purpose and survival in human behavior, took a different approach. The most significant of these behaviorists was Edward Thorndike, introduced earlier in connection with the psychological laws of learning.

Behaviorism = control?

THORNDIKE AND THE FIRST LEARNING THEORY

Thorndike believed that learning involves the formation of connections between sensory experiences (stimuli) and neutral impulses to action (responses). This *stimulus-response (S–R)* theory was referred to as *connectionism* because of the close connections or bonds that formed between stimuli and responses. Compare earlier associationistic theories, which focused on the linking of ideas, rather than observable events such as physical stimuli and behavioral responses.

Through his research with animals, Thorndike observed that connections were acquired gradually. For example, in one of his early experiments, an animal was placed in a boxlike apparatus so designed that when the animal made a specific kind of response, such as tripping a lever or pulling a chain, the box opened, allowing the subject to escape to reach food. At first the animal subjects—dogs, cats, and monkeys—bit, scratched, clawed, and rubbed against the sides of the box. Sooner or later, however, the correct response occurred. Each animal was placed in the "puzzle box" again and again. As trials increased, the time needed to produce the correct response shortened, and eventually, some animals were able to immediately escape. A typical learning curve for Thorndike's animals is found in Figure. 1.3.

The successive decreases in the time required to escape suggested to Thorndike that learning is *incremental;* that is, connections are formed in small steps over time. Successful responses become established—"stamped in," to use Thorndike's term—and unsuccessful ones are abandoned ("stamped out"). The selection of a particular response is based initially on a random set of choices, which Thorndike referred to as a "trial-and-error" process. The correct choice of response was described as being *instrumental* in obtaining success, and thus Thorndike's position has become known as instrumental learning or *instrumental conditioning.*

Instrumental conditioning leads to success

Because Thorndike based his description of animal learning on research and because he was able to explain the relationships of events he observed in an organized way, we can call Thorndike's theory the first theory of learning. The constructs of connectionism, trial-and-error behavior, and instrumental conditioning were blended to provide a systematic account of how animals learn relatively simple tasks. Thorndike realized that human learning is more complex than that of dogs, cats, and monkeys, but he believed that humans learn in the same basic way. He went on to state and support three major and five subsidiary *laws of learning,* which were particularly relevant to education. One of these, the law of effect, was briefly mentioned on page 12. Thorndike's laws are referred to frequently in later chapters. Table 1.1 summarizes each law and provides an example of its educational relevance.

FIGURE 1.3 Improvement in speed of escape from Thorndike's puzzle box

SOURCE: Adapted from E. L. Thorndike, *Animal intelligence: Experimental studies* (New York: Macmillan, 1911).

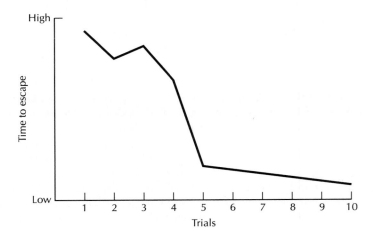

TABLE 1.1 Thorndike's laws and their relevance in education

Law	Relevance
Major Laws	
Law of effect: If an S-R connection is made that results in satisfaction, the strength of the connection is increased; if the connection is followed by annoyance or pain, its strength is decreased. This law was later revised to indicate that reward increases the strength of a connection, whereas punishment does nothing to the strength of a connection (1932).	Behavior that is followed by a pleasant event, such as a smile, a compliment, or a privilege, tends to be repeated. Behavior that is followed by punishment, such as criticism or removal of a privilege, may initially suppress a response, but the suppressed response may eventually reappear.
Law of readiness: When an organism is prepared to act, to do so is satisfying, and not to do so is annoying (1913).	Interfering with someone's intended behavior, or forcing people to do something they are not ready to do, is frustrating.
Laws of exercise: When a connection is made between a situation and a response, that connection's strength is increased (*law of use*). When no connection is made between a situation and a response during a length of time, that connection's strength is decreased (*law of disuse*) (1914). Thorndike renounced this law in 1932 after research indicated that mere repetition did not necessarily strengthen a response, nor did disuse weaken it.	"Practice makes perfect." Many teachers of Thorndike's day required their students to repeat aloud and write again and again basic facts of reading, writing, and arithmetic. We now know that repetition without corrective feedback does not necessarily improve learning and that some learning stays with us even though we fail to practice it. Remember having to write "I will not talk in class" 100 times (all the while talking to your neighbor)? Yet after not riding a bicycle for years, you were able to perform this skill easily, as an adult.
Subsidiary Laws	
Law of multiple response or "trial and error": If our first response does not solve a problem, we try other responses until success is obtained. This law is a good example of Thorndike's functionalist views—we respond in order to adapt to our environment.	Children are encouraged to "try and try again, if at first they don't succeed." Many an educational task is mastered because a student continues to try until getting it right.
Law of attitudes or *set:* One's experiences, beliefs, and preferences predispose one's actions.	Students respond to tests based on how they are set to respond. When we say, "Clear your desks and take out a piece of paper," the general groans indicate a set toward test taking.
Law of partial activity or *prepotency of elements:* We can choose among the many elements of a situation and respond to only the features that lead to adjustment.	We selectively respond to specific stimuli and ignore others. During a boring lecture, the class observes the coffee stain on the instructor's tie and notes how many times he says "er" or "uh."
Law of response by analogy: "To any new situation, man responds as he would to some situation like it, or some element of it" (1914, p. 28).	We are able to adjust to a novel situation by finding common elements between it and past situations. The beginning student of French, in attempting to pronounce a new vocabulary word that looks like an English word, is likely to say it as if it were English.

(continued)

TABLE 1.1   (Continued)

Law	Relevance
Law of associative shifting: A conditioned response can be substituted for an unconditioned response when stimulus elements from the original situation are gradually eliminated and elements not part of the original situation are gradually added.	Responses learned to one situation can be shifted to others. Advertisers pair a celebrity with a product as often as possible, to establish the same positive reaction to the product that at first is elicited by the celebrity alone.

Thorndike's ideas were so prolific that he published more than 500 articles and books on topics such as educational practice, testing, statistics, learning, and how to teach specific subject matter. He is considered to be the first educational psychologist because so many of his recommendations and applications of his learning theory were directed toward education. Two additional concepts that Thorndike studied in the later years of his career were *transfer of training* and *mental discipline.*

"Transfer" refers to the extent to which strengthening or weakening of one connection produces similar changes in another connection. Thorndike believed that transfer occurs only when two connections are in part identical—that is, the stimuli initiating the connections have *identical elements* and call for similar responses. His law of response by analogy suggests that a person will respond similarly upon recognizing identical elements. In a series of studies with R. S. Woodworth (1901), Thorndike found that teaching students a specific skill in a particular context does *not* produce gains in their ability to apply that skill in a different context. For example, learning to add a column of figures and then subtract from a larger figure does not automatically lead to the ability to balance a checkbook, as we may know from personal experience. Although both skills may appear to have identical elements, teachers are well advised to assign practice in checkbook balancing, rather than assuming that transfer will occur automatically. While providing checkbook practice, teachers can point out the similarities between balancing and other math problems students have done.

A related issue is that of *mental,* or *formal, discipline*—the belief that learning certain subjects such as Latin or mathematics enhances mental functioning better than learning other subjects. Remember our earlier discussion of Kant's notion of "faculties" of the mind? The mental discipline view held that faculties were strengthened by studying subject matter that related more directly to theory (e.g., practicing mathematics should improve the faculties of memory, reasoning, etc.). It is as if the brain were a "muscle" that can be strengthened by appropriate practice. In an extensive study to analyze this belief Thorndike (1924) administered IQ tests to 8,564 high school students and retested the group a year later. The classes these students took during the year were noted, in the hope that Thorndike could determine whether certain classes produced greater intellectual gains on the second intelligence test. The results of this study yielded no support for the mental discipline position. The students with greater ability to begin with performed the best regardless of what they studied. Thorndike said:

Can we exercise the mind?

Just because can add colm of numbers, doesn't mean can balance checkbook. Need to point out similarities

The chief reason why good thinkers seem superficially to have been made such by having taken certain school studies, is that good thinkers have taken such studies, becoming better by the inherent tendency of the good to gain more than the poor from any study. When the good thinkers studied Greek and Latin, these studies seemed to make good thinking. . . . If the abler pupils should all study physical education and dramatic arts these subjects would seem to make good thinkers. (1924, p. 98)

Thorndike contributed to our understanding of many issues of education and psychology, and he is referred to repeatedly throughout this text. Perhaps his most lasting legacy is the belief that research should serve as the basis for determining whether practices such as mental discipline should be followed. As a result of his own research on transfer and mental discipline, Thorndike was able to influence educators of his day to design curricula to include subjects that would have utility when students leave school. The study of mathematics, for example, was to be included in the curriculum not merely because it strengthens the mind, but because students can use mathematics when they leave the classroom. Moreover, Thorndike recommended that curricular areas be integrated so that transfer can be maximized. Knowledge and skills that cut across a variety of subjects need to be identified and presented in correspondence with one another. For example, while a science class studies a unit on whales, math classes could have students solve problems concerning the size of whales and the distances they travel, language arts classes could assign students to read and write about whales, and social studies units could determine the economic value and geographic location of whales.

[handwritten margin note: interdisciplinary study]

THE RISE OF COGNITIVE THEORIES: GESTALT PSYCHOLOGY

Have you ever watched an advertising sign that indicates in moving lights where to go to eat or get gasoline? As individual bulbs go on and off in a sequence, the lights appear to be moving toward a desired area. The viewer's perception of movement is known as the *phi phenomenon,* and it was first demonstrated by German psychologist Max Wertheimer (1880–1943) in 1912. The phi phenomenon indicates that just knowing about individual stimuli does not allow us to predict the totality of what we perceive. Even when we are able to isolate the different lights that are turning on and off in succession, the entire image does appear to be moving. This analysis of visual perception led to the view that the *"whole is greater than the sum of its parts,"* or that there is essential unity in many natural phenomena that cannot be subdivided. This is the major assumption of *Gestalt psychology.*

[handwritten margin note: blinking lights + moving signs]

The gestaltists, including Wertheimer, Wolfgang Kohler (1887–1967), Kurt Koffka (1887–1941), and Kurt Lewin (1890–1947), viewed learning as more than the addition of different sense impressions, or the formation of associations as the behaviorists contend, but as the grasping of complete meanings. "Meaningful configurations" (*Gestalten* in German) are acquired in all sensory areas. Melodies are more than their individual musical notes; great paintings are pleasing to the eye in their totality;

[handwritten margin note: music more than notes, paintings more than dots, ice cream more than cream + sugar]

poems are understood not simply as a function of their meter or rhyme; and ice cream is tasty beyond what we would expect of the combination of sugar plus cream. It is these organized and meaningful events that the gestaltists believed should be the subject matter of psychology. Rather than employ introspection to divide experience, as the structuralists had done, the gestaltists felt it was important to study how individuals view whole, meaningful experiences.

Gestalt concepts and principles were initially developed in the field of perception (Koffka, 1935). For example, an object on which we focus our attention in the environment (or the *perceptual field*) is known as the *figure*, while the surrounding setting is called the *ground*. If we switch our attention, figure and ground can be reversed, as the gestaltists demonstrated. In Figure 1.4, we see either a vase (in white) or two faces (in black), depending on whether white is the figure and black the ground, or vice versa. The figure–ground relationship illustrates the difficulty of treating stimuli as distinct and separate from the surrounding perceptual field.

Gestaltists said that perceptions are organized according to several of these principles of perception. Some other important ones are:

Proximity. Stimuli that occur closely together tend to be grouped together in our perceptual field. •• •••• • ••• Here 10 dots are seen as a group of 2, 4, 1, and 3 dots.

Continuity. Elements in a field that appear to represent a pattern or flow in the same direction are perceived as a figure: •• •• •• ••

Closure. We strive to fill in or complete missing elements to form a unitary whole. Items that are not quite finished are perceived and remembered as complete. Thus C will be recalled as **C** . The principle of closure influences not only our perceptions, but our motivation as well. One of Lewin's students, Bluma Zeigarnik (1927/1968), found that unfinished tasks not only were recalled better than completed ones, but there was a tendency for people to want to complete an assigned task if provided an opportunity. This so-called Zeigarnik effect perhaps partially explains why so many adults become hooked on serial dramas or soap operas.

Similarity. Objects that are perceived to be similar in form or color tend to be organized in groups. For example, the following units are viewed and recalled as groups.

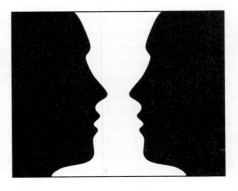

FIGURE 1.4 The vase–faces illusion

```
:: S S | | O O
:: S S | | O O
:: S S | | O O
```

Inclusiveness. The figure we are most likely to see is the one that contains the most stimuli. The "embedded figures" task in which we are asked to find objects hidden amidst a set of larger objects is an example. The larger figure tends to mask the presence of smaller ones. Camouflage appears to function according to this principle—animals whose coats blend in with the coloring of the surrounding trees or brush are difficult to locate.

All these laws, and many others identified by the gestaltists, can be summarized by a basic principle known as the *law of pragnanz,* or "good form": "Psychological organization will always be as good as controlling circumstances permit" (Koffka, 1935, p. 10). Perception always moves toward economical completion, toward the essence of what is to be perceived. Koffka compared the law of pragnanz to the principle of equilibrium in physics—the notion that physical events take the simplest and most regular pattern possible under the circumstances. The law of pragnanz was thus a basic assumption for the gestaltists' later study of the process of learning.

Gestalt View of Learning

According to Gestalt theory, learning consists of the formation of new perceptions when the learner is confronted with problem situations. Problems create a state of cognitive disequilibrium, which generates tension and motivation to solve the problem in order to regain equilibrium. In solving a problem, the individual moves initially according to natural laws, such as the law of pragnanz. The solution will emerge as the individual perceives the appropriate Gestalt, and hence is able to impose a meaningful configuration on the problem. When the solution occurs, it will come in a sudden flash of *insight,* "a special kind of neural organization that is established as soon as the organism achieves its purposes" (Hartmann, 1942).

Learning: a change in perception

Insight was demonstrated in 1925 in Kohler's famous research with Sultan, a chimpanzee. When presented with a banana hanging from the ceiling of his cage, Sultan would first leap for it. This did not work. After growing tired of leaping and missing, the chimp appeared to lose interest and sat in the cage, barely responding to the banana. After some time, Kohler observed Sultan take a pole that had been left in the cage and swing at the banana, knocking it down. On another occasion, Sultan was able to put two sticks together to reach a banana, after having failed to reach it with either stick separately. The animal accomplished a more difficult task by suddenly placing a box under a banana to use as a step stool. In each of these events, Kohler described Sultan's behavior as demonstrating insight. It was as if the tools necessary to solve the problem were always present, but the emergence of a solution required a reorganization of Sultan's perception of the problem. Gestaltists believe that this type of problem solving arises after mental rehearsal or hypothesis testing, rather than through the trial-and-error approach favored by Thorndike.

A concept central to Gestalt views of learning was that of *understanding* or *meaningful learning.* Consider a typical second-grader, arriving home from school:

TOM: I think our teacher is crazy.

MOTHER: Why do you say that, dear?

TOM: Well, yesterday she told us that 5 plus 5 equaled 10. That's OK, but today she said it could be 7 plus 3, 6 plus 4, 8 plus 2, or 9 plus 1! If she can't make up her mind, how am I supposed to?

Has Tom "learned" to add to ten? A gestaltist would say he has learned by memorization, with no understanding of the underlying concept of addition. Since our world follows organized rules, learning must consist of acquiring those rules so that the structure of various subject matters can be understood. Memorization without understanding does not necessarily allow us to remember rules for long periods, or to transfer them to new learning situations. Wertheimer (1945) urged teachers to de-emphasize drill and practice techniques and to focus instead on instruction that teaches the meaning of rules. He offered the example of students attempting to determine the area of a parallelogram ⟋▭⟋ . Under a traditional format, students are first instructed to find the area of a rectangle through the formula A = length × width, then relate this formula to a parallelogram by drawing in dotted lines to make the parallelogram appear as a rectangle ⟋▭⟋ . Students then computed the area using the same formula on the new sides. Students learning by this method, however, had difficulty in determining the area for other four-sided figures. For the trapezoid, ⬭ for example, students who were taught the traditional method dropped parallel lines externally ⬭ and wound up with an answer that was too large. By guiding students' understanding of what was actually involved in determining the area of irregular four-sided figures, Wertheimer observed that students could easily handle area problems. If students were taught to recognize that a rectangle is actually a balanced figure that can be divided into columns and rows of small squares, they were well on their way to "understanding" area. Determining the area of a parallelogram, then, was simply a matter of rearranging the squares so that they could be more easily counted. Students exposed to this way of teaching were able to find the area of a much wider variety of geometric shapes once understanding had been acquired. Wertheimer believed that to be able to apply learning when they are removed from the memorized instructions of a teacher or text, students must be assisted to see the structure of problems. His position continues to be relevant today, with discussion focusing on how students can achieve this deeper understanding of structure.

Gestalt and Behavioral Explanations of Learning

Clearly, Gestalt psychology was at odds with the behavioral ideas of Watson and Thorndike. It is useful now to summarize and compare the major beliefs and assumptions about learning of these two learning theories (see Table 1.2).

Until approximately 1950, Thorndike's behavioral views and the gestaltists' position dominated discussions of how people learn. While both positions remain viable today, they have been incorporated into other, more extensive theories. Much of this

Gestaltists emphasize meaningful learning

TABLE 1.2 Comparison of behavioral and Gestalt learning theories

Belief About	Behaviorism	Gestalt
Nature of the learner	Passive; depends on environmental stimulation	Active; possesses innate perceptual facility to interpret environment
What is learned	Stimulus–response connections	Meaningful wholes are acquired through perceptual reorganization
How learning occurs	Gradual acquisition of new associations through practice	Student insight is achieved when mental structures are reorganized
Role of previous learning	Transfer due to similarity of stimuli	Provides structure for understanding new situations
Role of external rewards	Stamp in or strengthen new associations	Directs attention and confirms solutions to problems
Educational implications	Arrange new stimuli so that correct associations are made by student; drill and practice	Presents content so that meaningful relationships are perceived; fosters discovery

text is devoted to recent developments in which these ideas have been applied to educational practice.

SUMMARY

We began this chapter by noting the interaction of teaching with learning. Many kinds of learning are expected of students in school, and teachers are responsible for the occurrence of such learning. Learning was defined as a "change in disposition or capability that persists over a period of time and is not simply ascribable to processes of growth." Learning is an inference from performance; it occurs primarily through experience but may reflect biological predispositions. Learning occurs incidentally as well as with intention.

Our study of learning is aided by the existence of a number of learning theories. A theory is an organized attempt to explain a set of related events. It allows us to go beyond the limits of personal experience, to avoid the simplification of traditional wisdom, and to examine research findings from a broader point of view. Theories are built from facts into principles, or relationships, and often they require additional assumptions known as constructs. Research findings establish the basic facts used in the development of theory.

Early learning theories grew from the philosophical analysis of knowledge either as a rational identification of innate ideas (Plato), or as the accumulation of associations through experience (Aristotle). Another early view that influenced the growth of theories was Darwin's view of animal species as evolving in an attempt to adapt to their environment. Adaptation was at the heart of the functionalist movement, which applied psychology to human functions such as education (James and Dewey). The development of learning theories was also affected by a tradition of experimentation, as illustrated by the study of memory by Ebbinghaus, the laboratory studies of introspection by Wundt, and the structural approach to consciousness pioneered by Titchener.

Two dominant learning theories of recent times are behaviorism and cognitivism. The behavioral tradition evolved from the empirical, associationist tradition of Aristotle, as well as the contributions of Locke and Mill, who argued that human learning consists of forming new combinations of ideas. Early behaviorists such as Watson described learning as occurring through a conditioning process, in which certain stimuli are paired with others through contiguity. Little Albert's learning to fear furry objects when they were presented with an accompanying loud noise is an example. Thorndike and other behaviorists emphasized the instrumental role of purpose in forming connections and argued that there are additional learning laws that govern their formation. Thorndike's description of learning as being determined by primary laws, such as the law of effect, and subsidiary laws, such as response by analogy, led to the formulation of what is considered the first true theory of learning. Thorndike's research on transfer and mental discipline established psychology as an important contributor to educational practice.

Cognitivism grew as a reaction to what was perceived as overreliance on stimulus–response theories in explaining learning. Originated by gestaltists Wertheimer, Koffka, and Kohler in their research on perception, this approach came to emphasize the development of the "organized whole" as the unit of learning. Organized wholes, or *Gestalten,* emerge through sudden reorganization of the surrounding psychological field. As a result of the insight that prompts reorganization, a new configuration occurs, which is greater than the sum of its parts. This reorganization was believed to produce meaningful learning or understanding, which gestaltists argued should be the goal of education.

The debate between the behaviorists and cognitivists continues to inform our views of learning, as later chapters reveal. Both traditions should contribute to the development of an implicitly useful theory of learning, which it is hoped will be acquired by all readers of this text.

A concept map for this chapter appears on page 29.

EXERCISE

Now that you have encountered a number of early psychological theories of learning, write your own! Don't feel compelled to be scientific; merely state how you believe learning occurs. You can probably do this in two or three paragraphs. After you've finished, put your theory away until you have finished reading this text. In the last chapter, I will ask you to write your own theory again. It should prove interesting to see how your ideas have changed!

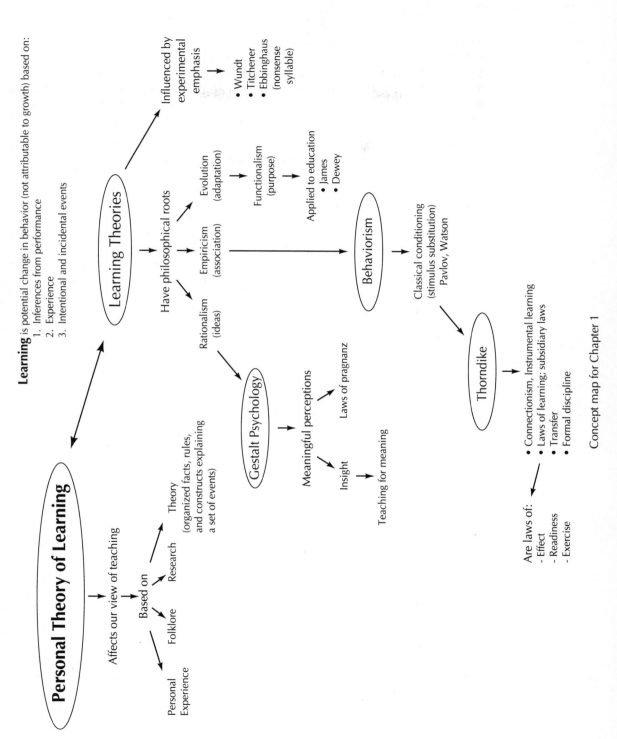

Learning is potential change in behavior (not attributable to growth) based on:
1. Inferences from performance
2. Experience
3. Intentional and incidental events

Personal Theory of Learning

Affects our view of teaching

Based on
- Personal Experience
- Folklore
- Research → Theory (organized facts, rules, and constructs explaining a set of events)

Learning Theories

Influenced by experimental emphasis
- Wundt
- Titchener
- Ebbinghaus (nonsense syllable)

Have philosophical roots

Evolution (adaptation) → Functionalism (purpose) → Applied to education
- James
- Dewey

Empiricism (association)

Rationalism (ideas)

Gestalt Psychology

Meaningful perceptions

Laws of pragnanz

Insight → Teaching for meaning

Behaviorism

Classical conditioning (stimulus substitution)
Pavlov, Watson

Thorndike

- Connectionism, Instrumental learning
- Laws of learning; subsidiary laws
- Transfer
- Formal discipline

Are laws of:
- Effect
- Readiness
- Exercise

Concept map for Chapter 1

SUGGESTED READINGS

Gage, N. (Ed.). (1963). *Handbook of research on teaching.* Chicago: Rand McNally.

Gagné, R. M. (1985). *The conditions of learning* (4th ed.) New York: Holt, Rinehart & Winston.

Koffka, K. (1935). *Principles of Gestalt psychology.* New York: Harcourt, Brace & Company.

Marx, M. H. (1970). *Learning theories.* New York: Macmillan.

Thorndike, E. L. (1932). *The fundamentals of learning.* New York: Teachers College Press.

Watson, J. B. (1925). *Behaviorism.* New York: Norton.

Wertheimer, M. (1945). *Productive thinking.* New York: Harper & Row.

chapter 2

The Human Learning System

OUTLINE

CHAPTER OBJECTIVES

p.33 1. Explain why it is important to understand the biological basis of human behavior.
p.35 2. Describe the structure of the neuron and how messages move along neural pathways.
3. Summarize the major structures of the brain involved in learning.
4. Evaluate arguments that learning is reflected in changes in the neuron, the brain, or brain structures.
5. Describe the role the hippocampus is believed to play in long-term memory.
6. Distinguish between the functions ascribed to the left and right hemispheres, and cite supporting evidence.
7. State a position you can defend on the implications of hemispheric specialization in educational practice.
8. Describe how visual and auditory information is processed and translated by the brain.
9. Highlight important stages in the development of motor control.
10. Explain how the autonomic nervous system functions in responding to stress.
11. Describe three ways to cope with stressful objects or events.
12. Explain how drugs impair learning and behavior.
13. Describe the possible effects of maternal drug use on drug-exposed children.

Mrs. Davenport left her desk and noticed Ricky, who was sitting on the floor beside his seat. The seven-year-old appeared to be playing with his pencils, lining them up in rows.

"Ricky, get back in your seat and finish your assignment. You've been wasting time all morning."

Just five minutes ago, Ricky had been up looking at the clock, watching the hands move. Twenty minutes ago, he was talking to Billy Hoffman and teasing Jenny Lattner. When Mrs. Davenport came into the room after lunch, there was Ricky ripping up paper in the corner. He is constantly on the go. Even when seated at his desk, he twists around, fidgets, plays with objects, or curls his hair. He never seems to pay attention and almost never gets his work done.

"I wonder what his problem is." said Mrs. Davenport to herself. "What am I going to do with him?"

Maureen maneuvered her way down the hospital hallway, and the head physical therapist, Mrs. Gomez, turned to watch. Maureen was a special case. Her legs had been severely damaged in an auto accident and she had endured three operations and four months of hospitalization. Now all the staff orthopedic specialists agreed that the broken bones finally healed and Maureen was ready to resume normal functioning. Unfortunately, the girl was having difficulty walking and continually complained about pain in her legs.

Just then Maureen stumbled into a hospital laundry cart and fell to the floor. "How can I help her to walk easily again?" thought Mrs. Gomez.

Mr. Chenowsky examined the three test booklets again. They were the state competency exams in eighth-grade mathematics. The tests were important because the results would be used to judge the level of math courses appropriate for students in high school.

"I never would have believed it," he said to himself. "Lee Ann is my best student and she got an average score. I wonder why. She seemed awfully uptight before the test . . . kept asking me questions about when to begin and if this test was important. I never did calm her down.

"Steve didn't do well either, though he seemed to be calm enough. In fact, he didn't seem to care how well he did. Simone, on the other hand, did much better than I thought she would. She wasn't too excited; she seemed to just plug along, staying on task right up to the bell.

"There must be something to this stress business after all. I'd like to know why everyone responded differently to it. And what can I do about it?"

WHY STUDY BIOLOGY?

As the preceding cases suggest, there is much we do not understand about learning and behavior. All three situations depict events of learning that are partially attributable to factors that are not psychological. Each case demonstrates the effects of biological states on behavior. Ricky's inability to concentrate, Maureen's difficulty in walking, the math students' reactions to stress accompanying an important test—all are affected in some way by biology.

biological states on behavior

Many of us may not like to think of ourselves in biological terms. It is often difficult to believe that we behave the way we do because our body or our brain functions the way it does. It is too simplistic to try to explain human behavior in biological terms alone, ignoring psychological and social influences. It would be equally simplistic, however, to ignore basic facts about our sensory, nervous, and muscle systems in seeking to explain behavior.

This chapter examines the biological and physiological bases of the human learning system. *Physiology* is a subdivision of biology dealing with the vital processes, activities, and functions of an organism. Knowledge of the physiology of the nervous system (neurophysiology) is useful in explaining psychological phenomena, particularly such complex processes as language. For instance, damage to a specific part of the brain can cause specific linguistic impairments. The nature of these impairments provides clues to the organization of linguistic skills. When a part of the brain known as *Wernicke's area* is damaged, not only is the ability to recognize a spoken word impaired, but so is the ability to spell. Apparently, in recognizing a spoken word and in spelling it, we use similar brain mechanisms.

Neurophysiology also sheds light on the basic mechanisms of learning. For example, studies of neurological activity indicate that in the early stages of learning a skill, the brain works much harder than it does when it performs that skill at an advanced level. Brains that have "learned" use fewer neurons or combinations of neurons, while brains still in the process of learning apparently use larger or inefficient neural circuits (Haier et al., 1988). This finding was obtained through the use of a technique known as positron emission tomography (PET). In a PET scan, volunteers are injected with harmless, slightly radioactive glucose. Active neurons must consume glucose to obtain energy, and the more active a part of the brain is, the more glucose it consumes. PET sensors arranged around the head of the subject pinpoint the concentrations of radioactivity and send the emissions to computers, which produce two-dimensional drawings showing the neural activity. Haier and his colleagues observed PET diagrams while subjects played a computer game requiring them to rotate squares to form different shapes. Neural activity actually decreased as subjects became skilled at this task. Moreover, individuals with higher IQs were found to burn less energy when performing difficult abstract reasoning tasks than did individuals with lower IQs. Haier concludes that to be intelligent is to be efficient, and that learning may actually involve determining which brain areas *not* to use.

Do PET scans indicate brain efficiency?

Recent technology has permitted us to acquire many insights into brain functioning, some of which could not have been predicted just a few years ago. By studying the brain and the entire nervous system, it is possible to better understand the process of learning. We shall begin with the structures themselves.

PHYSICAL STRUCTURE OF THE NERVOUS SYSTEM

The basic unit of the nervous system is the *neuron,* or nerve cell. There are approximately 100 billion of these specialized cells within the brain. According to one projection, the number of possible interconnections between all the neurons in a single human brain exceeds the total number of atoms in the known universe (Thompson, 1985). Doesn't that number boggle the mind! The main function of the neuron is to process and transmit information. Each neuron is estimated to have the processing capacity of a computer; working together, neurons produce more computational power in one brain than in all the computers of the world (Anderson, 1990).

There are many varieties and sizes of neurons. Each type contains a cell body or *soma, dendrites,* an *axon,* and *terminal buttons.* The soma contains the nucleus of the cell, which holds the chromosomes, made up of deoxyribonucleic acid (DNA). Dendrites, thin branches extending from the cell, serve to link neurons together. Messages passing from neuron to neuron are transmitted across *synapses,* which are junctions between the terminal button of a sending cell and the dendrites of the receiving cell. Communication at a synapse proceeds in only one direction, from terminal button to dendrite. Messages are initially sent down the axon, a long slender tube that carries information from the soma to the terminal buttons. Figure 2.1 illustrates the path a message travels in passing from one neuron to another.

Neurotransmitters = chemical conductors

Messages are exchanged from a terminal button to a dendrite via chemicals called *neurotransmitters,* secreted by the terminal button. There are many neurotransmitters, including *acetylcholine, norepinephrine, dopamine, serotonin,* various *amino acids,* and *neuropeptides.* It is not known why there are so many, but it is speculated that neurons of different types require different types and combinations of neurotransmitters. Neurotransmitters affect receiving cells, by either *exciting* or *inhibiting* them. Excitatory effects increase the probability that the receiving neuron will continue to send the message on to the neurons to which it can transmit. Inhibitory ef-

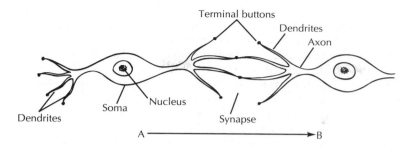

FIGURE 2.1   Message transmission from neuron A to neuron B

fects decrease that probability. Too much of one neurotransmitter or not enough of another can therefore change your mood, your thinking, or your energy level by altering excitatory or inhibitory effects.

Researchers have discovered that certain drugs containing chemicals found in neurotransmitters can be used to treat mental conditions. For example, clozapine inhibits dopamine and serotonin and has been used to reduce the effects of psychoses. The neurotransmitter acetylcholine has been found to build up at the synapses, then decline, resulting in forgetting in rats (J. A. Deutsch, 1971). A deficiency in being able to produce acetylcholine has also been noted in the brains of Alzheimer's disease patients when compared to control subjects (Coyle, Price, & DeLong, 1983). Treatment of Alzheimer's, a disease involving progressive memory loss, has therefore focused on increasing the level of acetylcholine in the nervous system through drug therapy (Davis & Mohs, 1986). The benefits of drugs of another type, the so-called smart pills or mental cocktails, are not supported by research, however. Sorry, those of you who are looking for a quick way to a high GPA! Most likely, these supplements are either excreted or simply stored in the body, and the user merely thinks he is smarter.

PHYSICAL STRUCTURE OF THE BRAIN

Suppose I were to tell you that the ink used to produce 100 randomly selected copies of this text will leave an indelible mark on the hands of those who read it. Neurophysiologists know that for the few (I hope) who believed me, an organ in the brain named the *amygdala* was briefly very active, alerting many parts of the body to this perceived threat. This is known because in recent years scientists have been quite successful in beginning to create a *map* of the functions of many brain components. For example, neurophysiologists have identified the *hippocampus* (residing right next to the amygdala); it plays an important role in converting recently acquired information into long-term memory. What we know about the brain, however, is still less than what we do not know, for as James Watson (1992) states: "The brain is the last biological frontier . . . the most complex object yet discovered in our universe" (p. 7). Let us briefly examine its identifiable components.

The base of the brain is essentially a continuation of the spinal cord, containing the _medulla,_ which regulates autonomic functions such as respiration, blood circulation, and digestion. The _cerebellum_ lies just above the medulla and serves to integrate motion and positioning information from the inner ear and muscles, thus controlling motor coordination and balance.

The largest and most complex part of the human brain is the _forebrain,_ containing the _thalamus,_ the _hypothalamus,_ the _cerebral cortex,_ and the _neocortex._ The thalamus serves as a relay station for sensory pathways carrying visual, auditory, and somatosensory messages to the neocortex. Smell is the only sensation that does not go through the thalamus. The thalamus is composed almost entirely of projection fibers, which extend to all parts of the cerebral cortex. Lying beneath the thalamus is the hypothalamus, the seat of emotions and motivation. Damage to the hypothalamus produces major changes in drinking and eating behavior, temperature control, sexual activity, and emotions such as rage and fear. An animal with a defective hypothalamus might eat enormous amounts of food, then suddenly eat nothing, eventually starving to death; or it might expand its sexual activity to include inanimate objects, then suddenly refuse to copulate at all (Levinthal, 1990). The insertion of electrodes into the hypothalamus of a laboratory animal produces an attack response of great intensity (Flynn, Vargas, Foote, & Edwards, 1970). In addition to its effect on motivation and the emotions, the hypothalamus appears to play a role in the release of hormones from the _pituitary gland,_ which stimulates the _adrenal glands_ to release adrenalin, an important step in energizing the body for emergency situations. We will revisit the hypothalamus later in this chapter when we discuss the endocrine system.

Human memory requires a large neocortex

The cerebral cortex is only a few millimeters thick and covers the left and right hemispheres of the brain. The neocortex is the most recently evolved portion of the brain; it is not present in the brains of nonmammals. Jastrow (1981) relates our heightened demand for memory circuits to the increased size of the cerebral cortex and its wrinkled, folded topography, which permits a great many circuits to fit into a small space. Its area, enlarged by all the folds, encompasses 400 square inches and contains approximately 75 percent of the brain's neurons (A. Smith, 1985). Because nerve cells predominate, the neocortex has a grayish brown appearance, giving rise to the reference to the "gray matter" of the brain. Because the neocortex resembles a walnut in its shape and its wrinkles, physicians used to prescribed walnuts as a medicine for what were believed to be diseases of the brain (Teyler, 1975).

Fissures or crevices in the brain serve to divide the neocortex into four regions, or _lobes,_ named after the bones of the skull that overlie them. Since the neocortex is _bilateral_ (extending across both hemispheres), lobes extend to both sides of the brain. Thus we possess a left and a right frontal lobe, a left and a right parietal lobe, and so on. The different locations and functions of each lobe are identified in Table 2.1.

Localization of motor function

Localization of these functions was discovered by observing individuals with damage to a particular lobe and by noting the changes that occurred as a result of electrical stimulation at different locations. The frontal lobe is so specialized that different parts of the body are linked to different parts of a band that stretches across this lobe. Stimulation of any portion of this band causes muscles, even one particular muscle, to twitch in the appropriate bodily region (see Figure 2.2). Other parts of the frontal lobe yield more general movements when activated. Similar localization oc-

TABLE 2.1   Major lobes of the brain: Their location and function

Lobe	Location	Function
Frontal	Front or anterior part of brain	Body movement; language
Parietal (two)	One on each side of brain, behind frontal lobe	Perception of heat, touch, and taste; spatial processing; music
Temporal (two)	One on each side of brain in front of occipital lobe	Audition, recognition of objects, and memory
Occipital	Back of brain	Vision

curs on the parietal lobe, in which exact stimulation of its sensory band determines the feeling of appropriate heat or touch sensations in different parts of the body.

Cognitive functions are not easily localized. We do know that certain areas in the left frontal lobe control language functions, namely, Wernicke's area (mentioned previously) and *Broca's area.* Damage to Broca's area reduces ability to write and speak, although comprehension of written and spoken language remains unimpaired. The symptoms of this condition, *expressive aphasia,* confirm the hypothesis that the

FIGURE 2.2   Stimulation of the frontal lobe causes specific muscles to react

SOURCE: FAR SIDE copyright FARWORKS, Inc./Dist. by Universal Press Syndicate. Reprinted by permission. All rights reserved.

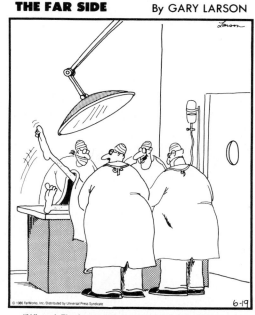

"Whoa! *That* was a good one! Try it, Hobbs — just poke his brain right where my finger is."

motor aspect of speech production is partially distinct from the processing or understanding of speech. Individuals with expressive or Broca's aphasia can sing without difficulty, implying that nonverbal musical ability is localized separately, perhaps on the right hemisphere.

The complexity of the brain should be obvious by now. I have discussed only some of the distinct areas that neurophysiologists have identified. It is entirely possible that future research will discover other areas or structures that affect behavior in some heretofore unsuspected way. Figure 2.3 illustrates the structures and areas of the brain introduced to this point.

THE NEUROPHYSIOLOGY OF LEARNING

Does learning alter the brain visably?

Learning, as defined in Chapter 1, is a change in capability not ascribable to processes of growth. From the physiological point of view, we ask, What has changed in the nervous system as change in capability has occurred? Does the brain itself change in weight, size, or complexity? Has there been a biochemical change at the level of the neuron? Could there be an alteration in how the brain, or one of its structures, functions? If so, which structures relate to different kinds of learning? There are many possibilities, all of which are being actively examined.

FIGURE 2.3 View of the human brain, showing major structures and areas on the left side. (The temporal lobe and auditory cortex are viewed from the right side of the brain only.)

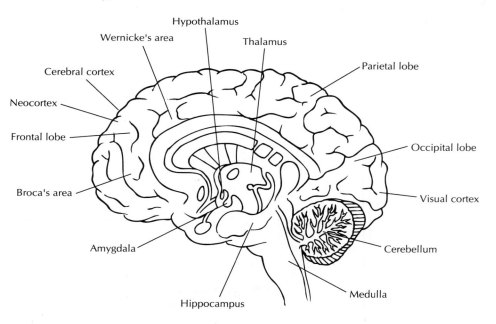

Changes in the Brain

Many of the attempts to answer physiological questions are based on studies of animals. There are two reasons for this type of comparative research: (1) analysis of brain structure often requires intrusive procedures not tolerable in humans, and (2) animal brains are less complex and can be examined with greater confidence that interacting variables have been minimized or controlled. The assumption, of course, is that we can generalize from animals to humans. When clear anatomical differences exist, as in studies of the neocortex, this assumption is less valid.

Generalizations have in fact been made in studies of the effects of enriched environments on brain structure. In research continuing for 30 years, Rosenzweig (1984) studied rats raised in a stimulating environment and animals not receiving the enrichment. Enriched rats were housed in groups in cages equipped with platforms, wheels, ladders, slides, and other manipulable objects. They were also exposed to an open field containing a series of barriers, which changed daily. Control rats were raised in single, dimly illuminated cages where they could neither see nor touch other animals. To test the hypothesis that rats raised in the enriched condition were learning more, the rats were placed in complex mazes. The enriched rats were found to be quicker learners than the control rats apparently because the former made better use of cues outside the maze. At the end of the observation period, all the rats were sacrificed, to permit examination of their brains.

What is a "stimulating environment"?

Many differences in the brains of these two groups of rats were reported and have been replicated over the years. The brain of a typical enriched rat had a thicker and heavier cortex, a richer blood supply, higher protein content, and more acetylcholine. In addition, there were neuronal differences: Enriched rats had more dendrite spines, providing a greater area of contact at the synapses.

These studies indicated that a stimulating environment was associated with specific behavioral and physiological characteristics. As Carlsen (1986) notes, however, the enriched laboratory environment may be more normal for wild rats than the artificial situation of being raised alone in cages. It is perhaps more accurate to say that an impoverished environment leads to a lighter cortex, a less rich blood supply, and so forth. Moreover, as Rosenzweig himself points out, the demonstration that changes in brain size and complexity can be produced in rats as a result of learning does not prove that the effect is generalizable to humans.

Evidence derived from PET scans also suggests that as learning occurs, there are changes throughout the brain. Scans reveal that separate regions of the cerebral cortex harbor the small fragments of a larger idea. The appearance of a baseball, for example, evokes visual and tactile representations of its shape, color, and feel, as well as the grip and arm movements necessary to throw it. Damasio and Damasio (1992) have demonstrated that these representations are re-created in separate brain regions at the same time, but not in the same place. When thinking about a baseball, for example, a particular "convergence zone" on the cortex activates all the relevant storage sites. Simultaneously, it receives neural messages in return that indicate the attributes of a baseball, such as "white" or "round" or "seamed." As new, more complex learning occurs—the grip required to throw a curve ball, for example—Damasio and Damasio believe that other areas of the brain become connected to the main convergence zone. The concept of an object and all its attributes is thus stored as a kind of dormant record dispersed in fragments throughout the brain. The location of the fragments that define *baseball* are stored near the fragments of other ball-like objects, and are closest to those with common attributes. This hypothesis explains why we are able to move rapidly from idea to idea when considering a familiar topic. It also suggests that while aiding students to learn new concepts or processes, it may be helpful to have them first review ideas that are similar to the new material. In this way, the old associations that are activated can help in understanding new information that shares common attributes.

Changes in the Neuron

Experimental techniques have been developed to detect changes in the neuron during learning. One of these techniques involves the insertion of very thin electrodes directly into the neuron itself. A record of *electrical activity* can be recorded, showing neurons periodically "firing" (discharging) or not firing. This electrical activity is believed to accompany the chemical effect of the neurotransmitter received at the synapse. When stimuli are presented, different patterns of firing and not firing can be observed. For example, Morrell (1967) presented a visual stimulus (a picture of a dark bar on a light background) and an auditory stimulus (a click noise) to cats with electrodes implanted in the visual cortex. Each stimulus was found to elicit a unique firing pattern, which decreased in intensity as the stimuli became more familiar. When the stimuli were presented together, a different pattern was observed. The results indicated that a kind of conditioning occurred, with the animal learning to attend to these stimuli while, simultaneously, change in the electrical activity of the neuron occurred.

A recently developed technique uses a SQUID (superconducting quantum interference device) to detect changes that occur in the brain's magnetic field when a neuron fires. Kaufman, Curtis, Wang, and Williamson (1992) aimed a SQUID at the brain of a subject listening to various musical notes. They determined that not only does the brain hear loud sounds and quieter sounds in different areas, but also that the areas that hear tones are laid out like a keyboard, with different neurons activated for different sounds. In fact, the distance between the brain areas that hear low C and middle C is the same as the distance between the areas for middle C and high C, just like on a piano!

Neurons change as learning occurs

A third technique begins with the assumption that learning at the neuronal level is accompanied by a change in the amount of neurotransmitters released at the synapse. Research with *Aplysia californica,* a shell-less sea slug about the size of a squirrel, revealed that simple responses such as withdrawal of a gill or tail are accompanied by chemical changes in the sensory neurons. The snail is initially shocked in the tail section, an event that causes withdrawal from the point of contact. Interestingly, subsequent touches to the snail's siphon (the breathing organ on top of the gill) lead to withdrawal and an increase in the neurotransmitter chemicals in associated neurons of this area of the snail's body, as well. A type of learning known as *sensitization* has occurred. According to the researchers, increases in neurotransmitter chemicals change the way in which sensory neurons function (Kandel & Schwartz, 1988).

Changes in the Functions of Different Structures

While it is useful to understand what is occurring among the neurons, it is clear from recent research that learning occurs on a global level in the brain, not in discrete pockets. Barring traumatic brain injury, we are able to relearn or recall much of what would have been lost if memories were indeed strictly localized. The brain is extremely resilient. No better example exists than the case of Phineas Gage, who in the late 1800s had a 13.5-pound tamping iron blasted into his brain in an industrial accident. Gage lost consciousness but recovered and lived 12 years with the iron bar (the width of a coin) buried in his head—a century ago, medical science could not safely remove it. Although the injury affected Gage's job performance (what a surprise!), this unusual man was able to function in most situations, and even had the foresight to sell his skeleton, cash-in-advance, to several medical schools (A. Smith, 1985).

Gage was obviously fortunate that no critical areas of his brain were destroyed, as specific deficits arise when discrete structures or localized areas of the brain are impaired. We will examine the effects of injury to certain critical structures.

Frontal Lobes.   The large human frontal lobe was once presumed to be a source of our superiority in higher level functioning. Research has demonstrated, however, that this portion of the brain plays a less important role than expected. Early research by Teuber (1959) indicated that men who had received an injury to the frontal lobe were no different from uninjured men in intelligence test performance. More recent studies have revealed that a more specific type of deficit occurs as a result of frontal lobe injury. Individuals with frontal lobe injury cannot make sudden switches in tasks. They also do not perform well on the Stroop Test, a task requiring one to name the color in which a word is printed. The catch is that each word represents a color, and the color of the ink never matches it (e.g., the word "red" might be printed in blue). These results illustrate the difficulty in separating action from knowledge and in understanding expected action (Stuss & Benson, 1984).

Temporal Lobes.   Earlier we identified the role of the temporal lobe in the recognition of objects. The temporal lobe is also apparently involved in memory, and injury to it contributes, along with injury to other structures, to severe *anterograde* or *post-traumatic* amnesia—that is, loss of memory in connection with learning occurring after the injury. *Retrograde* amnesia refers to loss of events occurring prior to the injury. Anterograde amnesia has been vividly studied in the case of H.M., a man who had parts of his temporal lobe removed in the treatment of severe epilepsy. Immediately after his operation in 1953, he was unable to recognize the hospital staff and could not find his way to the bathroom or recall anything else related to the hospital. He never regained his ability to recall events after they had occurred, but his long-term memory of events prior to 1953 was not lost. Milner (1985) reported that forgetting occurred the instant the focus of H.M.'s attention shifted, although in the absence of distraction he was quite capable of learning. Thus, H.M. was able to retain the number "584" for 15 minutes by continuously rehearsing it with an elaborate memory scheme; but one minute after the topic had shifted, he was unable to recall either the number or the strategy used to retain it. In fact, he did not remember that he had been given a number to memorize in the first place. Material that H.M. read, details about his job, and how to find his house all had to be rehearsed daily.

Milner was able to train H.M. to acquire some new knowledge by using tasks that required repeated practice. One task, called mirror drawing, required him to draw a line tracing a star, while seeing his hand and the star only through a mirror. H.M. was able to improve his performance on this task with each day's practice—as most subjects do—even though each day he had no memory of practicing the day before! In other motor tasks requiring little verbal analysis of the necessary performance, and thus no conscious memory, H.M. was again successful after considerable practice. Milner concluded that the temporal lobe plays a significant part in the learning and recall of knowledge and skills of different types, but that deficits in procedural knowledge (how to do something) can be overcome only after considerable practice. It is also apparent that there is a clear distinction between how short- and long-term memory are processed, since H.M. could actively follow and engage in the immediate requirements of short-term learning, but was unable to recall what he had learned after a longer time delay.

Hippocampus and Amygdala.   Animals with lesions in the hippocampus–amygdala area have difficulty orienting themselves spatially. In humans, the hippocampus has been linked to long-term memory, in which it serves as a kind of index. When messages are sent through the hippocampus, the electrical activity of neurons throughout the entire structure is evoked and remains ready to be accessed for long periods of time. This effect, known as *long-term potentiation* (Berger, 1984), is believed to parallel the storage of learned associations. Since the hippocampus has extensive fibrous projections into other areas of the neocortex, it may be that long-term potentiation in the hippocampus is in effect the beginning of stored memories. Memory retrieval begins with hippocampal activity, which then activates zones in the neocortex (Teyler & DiScenna, 1986).

In summary, it appears that both individual neurons and specific areas and organs of the brain undergo consistent modification when learning occurs. As research continues, it is likely that some of the changes within neurons, as well as within larger structures, will be found to be increasingly related, and a clearer picture will emerge. Better understanding of how information is stored within the neuron, how it is transmitted to other nerve cells, and how it is stored in various structures and locations will eventually result in more integrated theories applying to a broader range of learning and memory processes.

Hemispheric Specialization

The cerebrum is divided into two parts by a long *fissure,* or crevice, known as the *superior longitudinal fissure.* This fissure creates two separate hemispheres, each capable of administering bodily functions. Curiously, the left hemisphere controls the right side of the body, while the right hemisphere controls the left side. Thus, when you decide to move your right hand, it is the left side of your brain that sends the command. Messages from one hemisphere react to the other through *commissures* (cross-hemisphere connections) such as the *corpus callosum,* the largest commissure. The two hemispheres are also specialized, or *asymmetrical,* in functions. The left hemisphere seems to be associated with symbolic functioning (e.g., language), while the right deals more with perceptual and spatial processing.

Much recent physiological research (and, as a result, some educational practice) has responded to the issue of hemispheric specialization or asymmetry. The implication is that if the brain is asymmetrical in function, educators need to ensure the provision of appropriate stimulation to both hemispheres. Critics charge that our educational system places too heavy an emphasis on verbal and analytical skills, the province of the left cerebral hemisphere. A balanced curriculum, they argue, should stimulate the right hemisphere as well, through the provision of artistic and spatial content. Let us examine the basis of this argument.

The existence of hemispheric asymmetry seems to be well documented. As Ornstein (1977) observed, "the basic dichotomy of function in left and right hemispheres is mirrored in a wide range of scientific, historical, philosophical and religious writings" (p. 79). In most people, the right hemisphere has been found to weigh more than the left. The left hemisphere, on the other hand, is larger and more convoluted in a section of the temporal lobe dealing with language function (Gerschwind & Levitsky, 1968). Asymmetry is not limited to the brain; it has long been known that in females the right breast is slightly larger, and in males the right testicle is higher as well as larger than the left.

The left hemisphere, which controls the right side of the body, is most frequently the dominant hemisphere. The majority of people in all ethnic groups are right-handed. As a result, many cultures have endowed left-handedness (and therefore presumably right-brained individuals) with sinister or abnormal characteristics. For example, the French word *gauche* (left) is used to describe awkward or erroneous behavior. At one time, our educational system attempted to retrain left-handed writers by restraining their use of the left arm. In fact, left-handers often have a dominant left hemisphere, and the proportion of people whose brains are found to be right-dominated is much smaller (A. Smith, 1985). It should be noted, however, that these data are not conclusive, since the size of a person's dominant hemisphere is not ordinarily known, and the population that *has* had brain scans or brain surgery during life, or autopsy after death, is not uniform.

What evidence exists for the assignment of different cognitive functions to each hemisphere? O'Boyle (1986) summarized the physiological literature by identifying three types of research studies suggesting differences in specialization. One type employs subjects who have suffered unilateral damage to one hemisphere. As we have already observed, damage to Broca's area or Wernicke's area in the left hemisphere leads to language impairment, while damage to the right hemisphere results in visual–spatial deficits. This type of research, however, sometimes fails to specify the nature of the damage: Was only one hemisphere affected? Was the damage a result of surgical intervention to treat a more fundamental neurological disorder? In addition, subjects might have been different in some way prior to the surgery. This type of research emphasizes only what the subject can do after the damage; it does not examine what each hemisphere does during normal functioning.

A second set of research findings relies on evidence derived from so-called split-brain studies. Consider again the corpus callosum, the major commissure, or interconnecting pathway, between the two hemispheres of the brain. The corpus callosum is sometimes severed in the treatment of epilepsy, with the result that the hemispheres are isolated from each other, but fundamentally undamaged. In research on patients with isolated hemispheres, visual information presented to only one side of the brain produces interesting results. A picture of an object such as a cup could be identified when presented to the left hemisphere, but not to the right. That is, the left hemisphere was capable of eliciting a verbal response, while the right hemisphere was not. If the patient were asked to reach under a screen and select by touch the object that had been presented to the right hemisphere, the object would be selected correctly, but the patient could not verbally label it. Thus in this study the right hemisphere permitted expression of an object's name in a nonverbal way only, demonstrating the functional asymmetry of the brain (Sperry, 1974). Again, however, the methodological issue of representativeness arises: All these subjects were epileptic before the experiment, and there may have been other neurological abnormalities.

Research of a third type, involving normal individuals and employing techniques that simulate the split-brain condition, avoids the neurological concerns just mentioned. An auditory task called *dichotic listening* is used. This situation is similar to responding to two people speaking to you at the same time, one on each side. As predicted from our knowledge of cerebral dominance, left hemisphere dominant individuals will attend to and recall information presented to the right ear more effectively (Geffen & Quinn, 1984). In the visual area, the same type of specialized effect occurs. Verbal information is identified more quickly and accurately when presented to so-called left-brain people in the right visual field (Bradshaw & Gates, 1978).

The assumed abilities and disabilities of the right hemisphere have been studied extensively. In general, evidence appears to be emerging that the right hemisphere contributes to the processing of information, including verbal information, in its own way. It appears to be capable of handling nonliteral meanings. Right hemisphere damaged patients in one study showed a cognitive deficit in dealing with metaphoric sentences such as "He is turning over a new leaf," but they were able to process literal sentences like "He's chasing after a white duck" (Kempler & Van Laucker, 1987). Reading a text in braille appears to be easier with the left hand (Harris, 1980), while using sign language is linked to the left hemisphere (Damasio, Bellugi, Damasio, Poizner, & Van Gilder, 1986). Right hemisphere damage has also been related to the emotional expression of speech. Ross and Mesulam (1979) reported the case of a schoolteacher who was not able to express her feelings after a stroke damaged the right hemisphere of her brain. She had difficulty in maintaining classroom discipline because her speech had become so flat and unemotional that the students would not take her seriously. She tried to overcome this failure to communicate by adding phrases such as "I am angry and I mean it!" to convey her feelings. The disorder represented by these symptoms is known as *aprosodia*. The term reflects the inability to express the emotional dimensions, cadence, and melody of speech—all characteristics of language referred to as *prosody*. This important part of communication seems to be controlled by the right hemisphere.

Both hemispheres contribute to linguistic skill

Based on these research findings, it appears that the two cerebral hemispheres contribute in different ways to cognitive functioning. In very few of the areas studied do the hemispheres seem to act independently. For example, as noted, the right hemisphere is utilized in reading braille and the left hemisphere is active in decoding sign language. Such findings indicate that statements that the left hemisphere controls language and the right hemisphere is in charge of visual–spatial tasks are oversimplified. Linguistic skill is composed of a number of factors, and both hemispheres appear to contribute to its expression. Moreover, a related set of research findings provides support for a possible "takeover" effect in language for younger individuals. Zaidel and Sperry (1972) reported relative improvement in linguistic function in a thirteen-year-old following surgery to the left hemisphere, while much less improvement occurred for a person undergoing the same surgery at age thirty.

In terms of educational application, it does not appear to be necessary to reorganize curricular offerings and instructional practice to teach the right side of the brain. We must remember that content areas such as reading and mathematics include complex, multidimensional skills. Each subject matter requires the unique processing contributions of both hemispheres. For example, mathematics requires visual–spatial skill in recognizing numbers, objects, and symbols, as well as skill in linguistic analysis to convert the symbols to a mathematical operation. Both hemispheres directly contribute to eventual success in performance.

math uses both

Rather than abandon traditional approaches to focus on right hemisphere functioning, a more reasonable approach would emphasize the contributions of each hemisphere to the acquisition of a particular skill. For example, reading can be taught using a technique combining linguistic clues (e.g., phonics) with a visual–spatial orientation such as that incorporated in a whole-word approach. Instruction in artistic areas, rather than ignoring the linguistic skills of the left hemisphere in favor of maximizing the visual–spatial capacities of the right, might encourage students to consider the meaning of their creative work. Such an approach would utilize the analytic properties of the left hemisphere. Caine and Caine (1991) note that too often teaching consists of presenting bits and pieces of content that are perceived as fragmented by the learner. But when the brain receives stimulation that is processed by both hemispheres, it can make meaningful connections, thus enhancing learning. Integrated experiences that invoke the world outside the classroom, require group work, employ varied stimulation, allow choices among selected activities, and present instructional units that combine content from several academic areas are more likely to teach the whole brain.

Whole-brain curricula useful?

SENSORY SYSTEMS

Next we will briefly examine the physiological bases of sight and hearing. These two senses contribute much to our learning, and consequently, more is known about them. This is not to say that other senses do not contribute to learning. In fact, educators often are criticized for not adequately using the kinds of learning experience that can occur through other sensations. Nevertheless, analysis and understanding of the visual and auditory systems will be the most useful to us in examining learning processes and instructional procedures in later chapters.

sight + hearing contribute much to learning.

Vision

Vision begins when light passes through the lens of the eye and falls on the *retina* located at the back of the eye. The retina contains light-sensitive cells called *rods* and *cones* because of their respective shape. Cones are involved in color vision, while rods process less sharp, black-and-white images. Cones are concentrated in the *fovea,* a central area of the retina, while rods are located at the retinal periphery. Thus astronomers learn to observe distant stars out of the corners of the eyes, where greater concentrations of rods are located and faint black-and-white images can be sharpened.

The nerve fibers carrying information from the retina are bundled into the optic nerve. The optic nerves from both eyes meet at the *optic chiasma* at the rear of the eye. In each eye, nerves from inside the retina cross over to the opposite side of the brain, while nerves from outside the retina travel to the same side of the brain. As a result, information about the left part of the visual field travels *from both eyes* to the right hemisphere, and vice versa. One effect of this arrangement is the establishment of binocular depth perception. It also allows the anomaly noted earlier in split-brain patients, namely, information eliciting different responses depending on the hemisphere to which it is presented.

The optic nerve sends visual sensations to the *striate cortex,* which lies within the occipital lobe and receives input much as a television set does. Every region on the surface of the retina is connected by the optic nerve to a corresponding region on the surface of the striate cortex on the occipital lobe. If the eye sees a spot of light in one corner of the visual field, there will be electrical activity in a corresponding area of the striate cortex. The striate cortex acts to "interpret" the signal. The process of converting chemical stimulation into recognizable patterns involves specialized cells on the striate cortex, each acting to identify individual visual features, such as edges and corners, color, movement, depth, and distance (DeValois & DeValois, 1980). In essence, it appears that visual information does not travel along a single pathway; rather, different features of a single perception seem to be processed along parallel pathways, leading to a different visual center on the striate cortex. While this is a description of how visual information is acted on as it travels to the cortex, we are still far from understanding how these parallel paths are integrated to permit extraction of visual meaning. The process of seeing cannot easily be separated from the process of understanding (Zeki, 1992).

Hearing

Sounds are funneled through the outer ear by way of the *external auditory canal* to the *tympanic membrane* (eardrum), which vibrates with the sound. The *ossicles,* three bones in the *middle ear* known as the *hammer, anvil,* and *stirrup,* are set to vibrating by the tympanic membrane. This vibration is transmitted to the *inner ear,* containing the spiral shaped *cochlea* (the Greek word for "land snail"). In the cochlea, sound waves are transformed into electrochemical energy. This energy activates the neurons that compose the *auditory nerve,* leading to the *cochlear nucleus* of the medulla, and eventually to the part of the neocortex, the *auditory cortex,* surrounding the temporal lobe.

Possessing two ears allows us to locate and perceive sound waves. If you have ever experienced blockage in one ear, you understand how locating sounds and coping with reduced sound levels become problems. Localization of sounds seems to be accomplished by identifying delays in when sound waves are detected at either ear. The smallest differences in times of arrival at the auditory cortex apparently allow us to discriminate location. Differences in intensity of waves also are utilized to locate the source of sounds.

At the auditory cortex, different cortical neurons appear to respond to messages representing sound waves of different frequency and intensity. The sound "m," for example, varies in the frequency and intensity of the sound waves it produces, and like all sounds, it is presumed to be converted at the cochlea to a different message for transmission to the cortex. The various sounds we hear all produce a "signature," allowing recognition at the cortical level. Selection of which sounds to respond to, the process of attention, is discussed in Chapter 6.

MOTOR CONTROL

Every step we take, every move we make, requires the integration of millions of muscle fibers as well as sensory neurons carrying tactile, visual, and gravitational information to the brain. While it is easy to admire the achievement of a ballet dancer, the movements of a toddler learning to walk or of Maureen struggling to regain balanced mobility in our opening anecdote are equally admirable. Learning motor control is a complex procedure involving all components of the nervous system and encompassing behaviors ranging from holding a pencil to executing a triple somersault. In fact, in terms of the sensorimotor integration required, writing is no less intricate a motor skill than doing the pole vault.

Learning that involves skills requiring motor responses seems to be localized separately from other kinds of learning. It is fitting that in this type of learning several parts of the brain must work together, since the acquisition of motor responses requires practice and integration. Memories related to motor skills have long been thought to be seated in the cerebellum. Recent evidence, however, suggests that the cerebellum acts as a coordinator, sending signals that guide the learning process; the true center for storage of motor memories is now thought to be the brain stem (Levinthal, 1990).

Many unanswered questions remain concerning the way in which motor control is established. The basic act of walking, for example, involves a patterning of brain activity that remains a mystery. As Levinthal states, "It is as if we know how to describe the major ingredients that must be involved in the final result of an expertly baked cake, but have yet to understand the way these ingredients are to be combined" (Levinthal, 1990, p. 280).

No wonder Mrs. Gomez feels frustrated in her attempts to help Maureen walk steadily again. Certain aspects of motor behavior cannot be easily described and communicated to a learner. Physical support and actually placing the limbs in the correct position can help, but continued practice is necessary for relearning.

Motor Development

The rate of motor development varies across individuals and skills. The same child may develop quickly at certain ages and slowly at others at least partially because body growth interacts with motor control. The developmental sequence of the various components of a motor system may also differ among individuals. For example,

Practice allows integration of motor skills

Motor learning skill different from other l

children raised in institutions may not walk until age four, skipping the creeping stage (Dennis & Najarian, 1957). Psychophysiologists are becoming increasingly aware of the contribution of perception and sensory feedback to motor development. Rate and sequence of motor development thus are affected by development of the sensory system. Finally, environmental influences such as available nutrition, medical care, and parenting practices affect motor functioning as well.

Nevertheless, relatively consistent patterns can be observed. As early as 1931, Shirley described the steps and ages of typical occurrences leading to walking: raising the head from the prone position (9 weeks), sitting alone (31 weeks), crawling (37 weeks), standing while holding on (42 weeks), creeping (44 weeks), standing alone (62 weeks), and walking alone (64 weeks). *Prehension,* or grasping, involves the coordination of visual, motor, and tactile systems. At two months, "swiping" movements toward visual and auditory stimuli are first observed. At four months, children attempt to grasp a cube placed before them on a table. At 20 weeks, they reach for and successfully grasp an object in one quick, direct motion. At 28 weeks, they begin to oppose the thumb to the palm. Finally, at 36 weeks they are able to coordinate grasping between the tip of the thumb and forefinger. Hofsten and Ronnqvist (1988) have demonstrated that by six months, children can purposefully plan to reach and grasp an object, indicating the developing relationship between thinking and movement.

After locomotion and prehension have been established, children acquire a large number of other motor skills. During the preschool years they learn to walk backward and up stairs; to jump, hop, and skip; to ride a tricycle; and to throw, catch, and bounce a ball. By four years, most can button, unbutton, and dress themselves. Handwriting begins with simple marks at age two, the use of lines and symbols at ages three to four, and the formation of letters by age five. Drawing skills also develop sequentially from scribbling at age two to producing recognizable objects and figures at age four.

Motor skills improve with maturation

In later childhood, old motor skills are refined and new ones are added. Changes reflect increased strength, speed, precision, and smoothness. Strength has been found to double from age six to eleven, and improvements in eye–hand coordination, reaction time, running speed, and accuracy in throwing are also considerable. Fine motor skills also improve, as demonstrated by ease in writing letters, numbers, and words. Writing capability seems to be acquired by age eight or nine (Ilg & Ames, 1955).

Intercorrelations among various motor abilities tend to decrease with increasing age (Bayley, 1935), suggesting that motor abilities may be specific in their development, rather than depending on some general "motor intelligence." Differences that emerge during late childhood and adolescence appear to be more closely related to opportunities to practice or learn than to development. Even gender differences tend to disappear under conditions of relatively equal opportunity for practice (Munn, 1954). During adolescence, males score higher on tasks that demand strength and tolerance for physical exertion, but this result may reflect differential participation in athletic activities (Ausubel, 1954).

Teaching Motor Skills

Many motor skills such as prehension develop in a relatively uniform sequence despite differences in experience. An enriched environment does not accelerate their development, and a lack of opportunity (within reason) does not retard it. Development is dependent primarily on inherited tendencies and normality of the sensory and motor systems. Rate and extent of development of other, more specialized skills are largely determined by motivation and opportunity to practice. For example, climbing behavior in preschool children can be increased when it is encouraged by adult attention (Harris, Johnston, Kelley, & Wolf, 1964). Musical performance improves throughout the school years when special programs following a planned instructional sequence are instituted (E. E. Gordon, 1989). It appears that given adequate time, resources, and opportunities, specialized motor skills can be taught directly.

Specific motor skills are also acquired incidentally in a peer group context, as students participate in games or athletic activities. To foster motor learning, physical education programs at the elementary and middle school levels should be designed to include as many students as possible. Intramural leagues and intragrade tournaments are more likely than interscholastic competitions to maximize student involvement in motor activities. One middle school sponsors a schoolwide "fun run" twice a year in which not only students but teachers, parents, and community members take part. Students are challenged to better their times from fall to spring, as are other participants, and prizes are awarded based on improvement rather than relative standing.

Guided practice, or coaching, is particularly effective in instruction of relatively complex, specialized activities such as throwing a baseball, playing a trumpet, or performing a gymnastic routine. In these cases, verbal instruction can be used as an adjunct to actual demonstrations: that is, as motor movements are repeated and observed, feedback is available to direct correction of inappropriate responses. One advantage of early coaching is that since the movements involved in specialized skills are learned correctly from the beginning, opportunities for erroneous movements to become highly practiced are reduced. The author, for example, frequently regrets ever having learned the traditional one-handed backhand in tennis because the movements are incompatible with a two-handed top spin shot. Old habits are difficult to break, or as physiological psychologists might describe it, sensorimotor pathways are too well integrated!

Coaching = demonstration + feedback

STRESS AND COPING

So far we have described the physiological systems that control the cognitive and psychomotor dimensions of behavior. Little attention has been directed toward affective or emotional responses, which are also accompanied by physiological changes. In this section, we examine the autonomic nervous system (ANS), the part of the body that controls our emotional reactions.

The ANS has two major divisions: the *sympathetic nervous system* and the *parasympathetic nervous system*. In general, the sympathetic system is activated to deal with emergencies (states of stress or arousal), while the parasympathetic system is oriented toward internal maintenance and acts to slow down many bodily functions without conscious effort on our part. The 22 nerve centers of the sympathetic nervous system lie close to the spinal cord, from which *axonic fibers* are distributed to all parts of the body. Whenever an emergency is sensed (your boss threatens to fire you, a large vicious-looking dog confronts you, you prepare to push your damaged car off a busy freeway), the sympathetic nervous system swings into action. The heart

Sympathetic–parasympathetic balance

pumps more blood to your brain and muscles and to the surface of the skin, breathing becomes rapid and deeper, perspiration increases, your mouth becomes dry, and your scalp may tingle. In short, you are prepared for increased physical exertion.

The parasympathetic nervous system connects to most of the same parts of your body served by the sympathetic, except for the *adrenal glands,* located on top of the kidneys. Parasympathetic stimulation produces physiological effects that are the opposite of those induced by sympathetic stimulation. The heart rate decreases, breathing slows, salivation increases, and so forth. In many situations, the parasympathetic system checks the activities of the sympathetic system—a valuable feature, since if a high level of arousal is permitted to continue for too long a period, damage to the organism could result.

Much of the sympathetic system's work is furthered by stimulation of the adrenal glands. The adrenals produce two arousal *hormones*—adrenalin (*epinephrine*) and noradrenaline (*norepinephrine*). The release of these two hormones triggers increases in blood pressure, heart rate and breathing, pupil dilation, and perspiration. These physical changes also occur when strong emotions such as fear, rage, and sexual arousal are experienced. By controlling the adrenal glands, the sympathetic nervous system stimulates organs involved in emotional reactions not only directly via axonic fibers, but indirectly (by causing the adrenal glands to pump hormones).

The adrenal and other glands are referred to as endocrine glands because they secrete hormones directly into the bloodstream and affect their target organs via the circulatory system. There are at least 10 endocrine glands secreting more than 35 hormones (Vincent, 1990). They affect such biological processes as metabolism (the thyroid gland), the digestion of sugar (the pancreas), growth (the pituitary gland), and primary and secondary sex characteristics (the gonads). The hormones of most interest to us are epinephrine, norepinephrine, and *adrenocorticotropic hormone* (ACTH); these substances play important roles in the body's stress reaction, a process that affects learning and performance.

Stress Reactions

Physiologists view stress as a series of bodily reactions which, if prolonged, can have deleterious effects. The process begins with the introduction of a *stressor* (the source of an emotional reaction). Stressors may be internal, as in diseases directly affecting the body, or external, as in psychological guilt feelings or anger at being thwarted in some pursuit. Three types of physical response to stress then ensue: (1) neural responses through the hypothalamus, (2) glandular responses through the pituitary and adrenal glands, and (3) hormonal production through the release of adrenaline. Selye (1953) described a *general adaptation syndrome,* or pattern of reaction to stress, in which all three types of physical response occur. There are three phases.

1. *Alarm reaction.* At the first appearance of a stressor, the body marshals defensive resources and makes self-protective adjustments, as when you jump back from the curb and feel a sudden queasy sensation in your stomach if a bus passes by too close. If defensive reactions are successful,

the body returns to normal activity and the alarm ceases. Most short-term, or *acute,* stress is resolved in this phase.

2. *Resistance.* If stress continues because the first reaction failed to remove the emergency or because of factors outside the individual's control, the body mobilizes further. More and more hormones are produced. If the emergency continues for too long, all the energy available in the sympathetic nervous system may be expended, and the counterbalancing effects of the parasympathetic nervous system are commenced. Such a prolonged reaction takes a toll on the body; resistance decreases, and physical symptoms such as ulcers may result.

3. *Exhaustion.* If the stressor is unusually severe or continues for a long period, the body's reserves of energy become depleted or totally exhausted. Psychological disturbances, more severe physical reactions such as hypertension, and even death may result.

The effects of stress, particularly if prolonged through the exhaustion stage, are found in both biological functions and psychological states. People differ, however, in how stress affects them. Predispositions in individual perceptions and responses to stressors seem to make a difference. Spielberger (1966) points out that stressful situations occur throughout life; indeed, dealing with stressors successfully provides richness and challenge to our lives. When stressful events occur, it is natural to experience a rise in transitory anxiety, which Spielberger calls an *A-state,* with all the accompanying physiological reactions we have discussed. A sudden announcement that the country was at war, for example, would provoke a stress reaction in almost all of us. Some people, however, possess a predisposition to interpret more events as stressful and to experience stress reactions more frequently (Spielberger, 1972). Spielberger refers to this stable personality characteristic as trait anxiety or *A-trait.* Individuals high in A-trait appear to be most adversely affected by perceived stress.

One effect of prolonged stress is hypertension, or high blood pressure, a precursor to coronary disease. Individuals displaying a lifestyle pattern referred to as type A behavior, characterized by extreme competitiveness, impatience, and a high commitment to work and achievement, are prone to hypertension (Williams, Lane, Kuhn, Melosh, White, & Schanberg, 1982). Other physical effects that appear to be stress-related are certain ulcers (Gross, 1958) and changes in the immune system. Stress may lower the resistance to infection by suppressing the body's reaction to invading agents. Research by Levy, Herberman, Lippman, and D'Angelo (1987) has demonstrated that women with breast cancer who suppressed their anger and lacked social support (conditions presumed to enhance stress reactions) produced fewer of the specialized cells that can attack and kill malign tumors.

Psychological states such as depression have also been attributed to stress reactions. It has been noted that feelings of depression are reported more frequently in the morning and seem to be less likely in the evening. This variation seems to correlate with levels of *corticoid,* another hormone produced in the adrenal gland. Corticoid levels, which are high in the early morning and lower in the late evening, also seem to correlate with feelings of anxiety or fear in other settings. For example, in a study by Francis (1979), the corticoid levels of college freshmen were measured on

Physical effects of stress

the first day of a new semester and again at midterm examination time. Corticoid levels were six times higher during the exam period, and students reported greater feelings of anxiety and depression at that time. Does this report surprise you?

Coping with Stress

What implications can be derived from understanding the physiological basis of stress? Obviously, there is a chain of events from stressor to physiological responses to psychological feelings. By recognizing the internal, intermediary stage of physiological reactions occurring between the appearance of the stressor and our response, we may be more able to cope with the stresses we encounter. I used to experience all the physical signs of a stress reaction when I listened on the radio to games featuring my favorite basketball team. My heart would pump, my breathing would deepen, and I would moan, complain, and gripe if the game didn't go well. Attending a game or watching it on television did not elicit these reactions. It seems that listening to a radio broadcast without the visual input created uncertainty for me that proved stressful. Consequently I stopped listening to the games, although I occasionally ask the score of others who are. If the team is doing well, I may turn the radio on, but only for a minute or so. Much emotional arousal can be averted in this manner.

How do you handle stress?

Identifying stressors and taking steps to avoid them still constitute a key method in reducing stress in our lives. I know someone who leaves for work an hour early to avoid rush hour on the Long Island Expressway; someone else takes the train rather than fly. Planning is one way we can reduce stress.

Unfortunately, many stressors cannot be avoided. The college freshmen mentioned previously could not skip their midterm exams on the plea that tests made them depressed. In these situations, *coping strategies* become necessary. Folkman (1984) distinguishes between coping strategies designed to regulate feelings of arousal and emotion accompanying stress (*emotion-focused*) and those aimed at redefining the problem causing the distress (*problem-focused*). Emotion-focused strategies generally consist of avoidance behaviors such as purposely not thinking about the cause of the stress, keeping busy, or taking tranquilizers. The use of relaxation techniques such as selecting a favorite place and visualizing yourself facing the stressful event in that location is one example. Interrupting a stress reaction through physical movements, such as stretching, head rotations, and purposeful, relaxed breathing, is another. While these strategies may be helpful in the short run, long-term resolutions require focusing on the problem and altering one's perceptions of the situation and its value.

One type of problem-focused strategy is exemplified by telling oneself that failing an exam is not the end of the world or saying "I've failed, but I can learn from this." Another useful approach is to obtain social support by drawing on the experiences of others. Feelings of "We're all in this together" or "Others have gotten through it, so can I" can help in putting the particular stressor in proper perspective. If we can view a stressor as more commonplace and less threatening than originally perceived, the body's response to its presence may be diminished.

A number of organized programs to manage stress have been developed. One attempt, utilizing both emotion-focused and problem-focused coping strategies, is referred to as *stress inoculation training* (Meichenbaum, 1977; Meichenbaum & Turk, 1976). This approach proposes to teach individuals to use a three-phase procedure to cope with stressors on the cognitive, physiological, and behavioral levels. The first phase is *educational;* it consists of discussions of the nature of the stress reaction, how the stressor is experienced, and what the individual is thinking when confronted by it. Models of alternative thoughts and behaviors following the stress reaction are presented. In the second or *rehearsal* phase, specific coping strategies are taught, including relaxation techniques to combat the physiological reaction. Self statements designed to help redefine the meaning of the stressful event and indicate effective functioning in a different manner are introduced. Self statements, which serve to aid in the reevaluation of the threat, lead to more adaptive actions. The third phase, *application,* involves trying out the new strategies on actual stressors, usually progressing from least distressing to most distressing events. Meichenbaum (1977) and his colleagues report a number of studies supporting the effectiveness of this approach in reducing anxiety and pain.

Desensitization is another approach to dealing with ongoing stress (Wolpe, 1958). Knowing that the two branches of the autonomic nervous system inhibit each other, Wolpe believed that relaxation could be used to turn sympathetic arousal off. He also reasoned that when a feared object is presented at low levels of imagery, its ability to produce anxiety or fear can be controlled. If a person relaxes while imagining the object, the object will become associated with relaxation rather than fear. Gradually more intense representations of the feared object can be presented, and eventually the person should be able to stay relaxed while imagining the most feared object. Desensitization is thus the removal of the anxiety-producing power of the feared object. Three elements are required for desensitization to occur: (1) the ability to relax, (2) the construction of a hierarchy of feared objects and events, and (3) the ability to call up images of the feared objects while in a state of relaxation.

Feared objects are identified according to a *stimulus generalization gradient,* a scale describing objects in terms of degree of similarity. Deffenbacher and Suinn (1988) describe this gradient as a hierarchy, with steps leading from the most feared object at the top to the least stressful object at the bottom. In between are steps that become progressively more like the target stressor, and therefore more stress-inducing. For example, if you were terrified at the thought of giving a speech, the hierarchy might be identified as follows: being asked to give a speech, preparing the speech, rehearsing with your family, giving the speech to two or three friends, giving the speech to strangers, making a public speech to a larger group, making an unplanned speech, and finally, giving the most feared speech you can conceptualize, such as speaking to an audience of speech critics.

Once each step has been identified, the individual practices relaxation while imagining the situations on each step from least to more feared. In a book edited by Wolpe, Lang (1964) reported the successful application of this technique to the reduction of stress reactions to a wide variety of objects and circumstances, such as snakes and parachute jumping.

Stress is not always counterproductive; in fact, a certain degree of stress facilitates learning and performance on a wide variety of tasks. Psychologists have long been aware of the inverted U curve displayed in Figure 2.4, which graphs the relationship between efficiency of performance and level of arousal (Hebb, 1972). Moderate

Progressive
desensitization

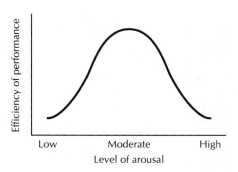

FIGURE 2.4 Efficiency of performance as a function of level of arousal.

SOURCE: Adapted from D. Hebb, *A textbook of psychology,* 3rd ed. (Philadelphia: Saunders, 1972), p. 199. Reprinted by permission of the publisher.

arousal generally leads to the most efficient performance. A higher level of arousal is helpful in simple tasks (e.g., reciting memorized information such as a childhood poem), but lower levels of arousal are better for complex tasks, such as composing an essay answer (Spence & Spence, 1966).

In addition, higher states of arousal during learning are associated with better long-term memory. Kleinsmith and Kaplan (1963) presented subjects with an eight-item, paired associate task. Subjects heard an emotionally loaded word ("rape") paired with a digit (68). Later they were given the word, then asked to repeat the word and recall the number that went with it. Arousal was determined from galvanic skin responses (GSR) recorded during the presentation of each original pair. Responses to low-arousal items were best retrieved within 45 minutes, then were progressively less easily recalled as days and then weeks passed. High-arousal items, on the other hand, were not only better recalled at longer delays than low-arousal items, but actually were remembered better after longer delays than shorter ones (known as *reminiscence*). This surprising result has been replicated several times, although the more usual finding is that long-term recall is only slightly better for high-arousal items (Walker & Tarte, 1963). Kleinsmith and Kaplan explained the reminiscence phenomenon by arguing that arousal lessens activation of the memory during initial acquisition, but during later recall, when arousal is reduced, the memory is more readily accessible.

Optimal levels of arousal

In general, individuals differ in the level of arousal at which they perform most efficiently. The test performance of Mr. Chenowsky's three students in our opening anecdote is illustrative. Simone functioned well under high stress levels, while Lee Ann did not. It is important for Mr. Chenowsky to recognize the optimal level of arousal that elicits the best performance from each student. This will help determine whether some students require a reduction in stress and will indicate whether others may require additional motivation to perform at maximum efficiency.

IMPAIRMENT OF THE LEARNING SYSTEM

When functioning efficiently, the nervous system, aided by intact sensory, motor, and autonomic connections, provides an opportunity for the individual to acquire a multitude of learning outcomes. There are a number of ways, however, in which the learning system can become impaired. Obviously, physical damage to any subsystem, or structure within a system, creates specific learning problems, which can be readily observed. Damage can be prenatal, as a result of a genetic defect, or postnatal, as a result of traumatic injury or disease. In some cases, the nature of the impairment may not be obvious. Two major learning problems that frequently occur and are presumed to be due to an impairment of the nervous system are *attention deficit disorder* and *learning disabilities.* Ricky, the active little boy who was last seen ripping up paper at the opening of this chapter, may suffer from one or perhaps both of these disabilities. At one time such problems were attributed to "minimal brain dysfunction" involving some type of undetected damage to the sensory or cortical areas of the brain (Chalfant & Scheffelin, 1969). Failure of researchers to adequately locate such damage has led to the abandonment of the neurological explanation, although future research may yet shed light on the biological base of these disorders. Educational treatment of disabilities is discussed in Chapter 11.

Drug Impairment

A major impairment to the learning system is the prolonged and extensive use of drugs. A *drug* is any chemical that does at least one of the following:

1. affects a person's physiological condition, including activity level, consciousness, or coordination
2. alters the individual's pattern of incoming sensations
3. distorts or changes the person's perceptions or ability to process sensory information
4. changes an individual's mood or emotions. (McConnell, 1974, p. 56)

Table 2.2 lists common drugs, their effects, and potential complications.

The most significant fact about drugs is that in *all* cases complications of some description accompany habitual use or overdosage. The popularity of drugs stems from their initial effects, such as euphoria or alertness, or feelings of bravado, relaxation, or sensitivity. These states are fleeting, however, and create a false sense of security and an impression of power that is short-lived. An example is found in studies of marijuana and short-term memory. Subjects taking this drug begin memory tasks with better than average performances and strong feelings of confidence. The task ends, however, with subjects forgetting what was required or failing to attend to relevant stimuli (Weil, Zinberg, & Nelson, 1968). Drugs also affect motivation to achieve, as addicts lose track of traditional achievement goals. Pursuit of the chosen drug replaces other motives, to the long-term detriment of the user.

Drug-Exposed Children

Of recent concern to society in general, and to the educational system in particular, is the increasing number of schoolchildren born to drug- or alcohol-addicted parents. Unfortunately, most chemicals ingested by the mother readily cross the placenta and

TABLE 2.2 Common drugs, their effects, and some common complications

Drug	Type	Immediate Effects	Most Common Complications
Alcohol	Mood enhancer	Muscle relaxation, depression, intoxication; impaired motor control, memory, and judgment.	Dehydration, hangover; permanent liver, heart, and brain damage. Overdose or mixing with other depressants can cause respiratory failure.
Amphetamines	Stimulant	Euphoria, talkativeness. Increased adrenaline and stimulated heart rate prevent user from sleeping.	Nervousness, paranoia, hallucinations, dizziness. Overdose can result in decreased mental abilities, sexual impotence, seizures, and death.
Barbiturates	Tranquilizer	Reduced heart rate, respiration; sleep.	Inability to respond to an emergency; death.
Caffeine	Stimulant	Increased mental alertness, blood pressure, and respiratory rate.	Difficulty concentrating; nervousness, insomnia; stomach irritation; fatigue; heart palpitations.
Cocaine	Mood enhancer	Brief euphoria, increased energy and sense of power; restlessness; suppressed appetite for food.	Tremors, nasal bleeding, toxic psychosis, seizures, depression. Death from overdose or impure supply.
Lysergic acid diethylamide (LSD)	Hallucinogen	Hallucinations; distorted perception of time and distance; depression; nausea; disorientation; panic.	Paranoia, physical exhuastion, psychosis ("freaking out"); body and body part distortion; fear of death; flashbacks.
Marijuana	Mood enhancer	Relaxation; altered sense of hearing, time, and vision; increased heart rate and appetite; dilated pupils.	Impaired driving ability; possible lung damage; reduced sperm count and sperm motility; lack of motivation; memory impairment.
Nicotine	Stimulant	Relaxation; increased confidence, metabolism, and heart rate.	High blood pressure; emphysema; bronchitis; heart disease; cancer of lungs, lips, mouth, cervix, and bladder.
Anabolic steroids	Hormones	Increased muscle mass.	Blood disorders, liver problems, cancers; aggressive behavior; growth of body hair, deepening of voice, menstrual irregularities, enlargement of breasts (men), and decrease in sperm production.

SOURCE: Adapted from *Beak Healthy Newsletter*, 1991, *5*(2). Reprinted by permission of the University of Kansas.

enter the embryonic sac. The three classes of drugs most frequently abused by pregnant women are alcohol, opiates (e.g., heroin), and cocaine.

Alcohol. Jones and Smith (1973) described a set of problems among infants born to chronically alcoholic women. The *fetal alcohol syndrome* (FAS) includes pre- and postnatal retardation of growth, craniofacial abnormalities, depression, irritability, jitteriness, mental retardation, and poor coordination. The full-blown symptoms of FAS occur infrequently, in approximately one in a thousand births. However, a less severe form of the syndrome known as *fetal alcohol effects* (FAE), characterized by the same symptoms but to a lesser degree, occurs approximately five times more frequently (Abel, 1982). Heavy alcohol use during pregnancy has been documented as a causal agent, with milder effects associated with moderate drinking (Streissguth, Barr, & Martin, 1983). In addition, other research indicates that a reciprocal interaction between mother and child after birth may account for the behavioral symptoms. Parents of irritable, jittery, poorly coordinated infants are less likely to spend very much time with their offspring and may neglect to provide the kind of stimulating environment necessary for later cognitive or emotional growth (Olson, Bates, & Bayles, 1984). A chain of events has been hypothesized, beginning with maternal alcohol consumption leading to FAE symptoms in infants, which in turn influence the amount and quality of environmental stimulation and support in the child's early years (O'Connor, Sigman, & Haiseri, 1993). If parents of FAE children are helped to (1) recognize the symptoms, (2) not feel that they have caused a destructive and irrevocable condition in their child, and (3) take steps to provide a suitable environment despite an inclination to avoid or punish perceived deficiencies, perhaps later difficulties in learning and social interaction can be reduced.

Opiates.   In 1987 it was estimated that there were 500,000 opiate addicts in the United States and that 4 percent of the infants born in New York City hospitals (3,000/year) were passively addicted to heroin or methadone, a synthetic form of heroin (Hutchings, 1987). These infants showed signs of acute opioid withdrawal: tremors, irritability, high-pitched crying, and disturbed sleep. In a long-term study, 22 high-risk children who had exhibited the foregoing symptoms at birth were found to consistently demonstrate poor performance on several measures through six years of age. The children showed deficits in general cognitive ability and on visual, auditory, and tactile tasks, reflecting impaired organizational and perceptual processes. They were rated as having greater difficulty in social adjustments, including uncontrollable temper, impulsiveness, poor self-confidence, and difficulty in making friends (Wilson, McCreary, Kean, & Baxter, 1979). Hutchings reported (1987) results of Lodge, who in 1976 studied 29 children from birth to four years, born to mothers enrolled in a program for recovering heroin addicts. While these children did not differ from others in cognitive ability, they were found to be active, energetic, and distractible; they tended to have difficulty on fine motor tasks such as drawing. Based on these studies, Hutchings (1987) concluded that children born of heroin- or methadone-addicted mothers are at risk during the school years for attention deficit disorder and learning disabilities involving perceptual processes. He cautioned, however, that attribution of these deficits to mothers' prenatal drug use alone may not be warranted. Genetic factors (perhaps responsible for the drug abuse itself), environmental factors existing in the home during the preschool years, and other medical problems of the child may account for or contribute to learning problems. Analysis of the effects of continued use of drugs in the home, the child's interactions with parents and other family members during the preschool years, and consideration of more specific components of intellectual functioning seem to be needed. For example, Ricciutti and Scarr (1990) studied two-year-olds deemed to be at risk because they had been below average in birth weight. These investigators found that an additional factor contributing to poor cognitive development at that age was the absence of the father from the home. It is no doubt true that factors that led to parental drug abuse, as well as its physiological consequences, all affect children's learning potential. Nevertheless, the existence of a common pattern of neurological and behavioral indicators shared by drug-exposed children must be recognized as part of our understanding of later learning difficulties.

Cocaine.   This drug has become widely available, and its long-term effects, including harm to exposed children, are potentially the most troublesome. Cocaine-exposed infants are more likely to be premature; they have low birth weight, are easily excited or depressed, and demonstrate significant impairment in orientation, motor ability, and alertness (Chasnoff, Griffin, McGregor, Dirkes, & Burns, 1989). These effects may

Does cocaine exposure alone account for deficits?

be noted not only among children whose mothers used cocaine throughout pregnancy, but also in children whose mothers used the drug in the first trimester only. The authors believe that cocaine constricts a pregnant woman's blood vessels, restricting blood flow to the fetus. The use of street cocaine, which may possess unknown impurities, may add additional health risks. Coles, Platzman, Smith, and James (1992) studied 67 healthy, full-term infants born to mothers who used cocaine at least once a week during pregnancy. Though these cocaine-exposed babies were smaller than average, they were free of problems typically blamed on the drug, including gastrointestinal upset, hyperactivity, and tremors. Cocaine appeared to have a less serious impact on infant behavior than alcohol, tobacco, or marijuana. Coles et al. cautioned that these relatively normal infants were carried to term; those who are

Is amount of exposure critical?

born prematurely ordinarily demonstrate the most adverse symptoms. Woods, Eyler, Behnke, and Conlon (1993) observed mothers and infants both before and one month after birth. Although cocaine-exposed infants had lower birth weights and shorter gestation periods, there were no differences in cognitive performance one month after birth. Apparently, not all infants exposed to cocaine during pregnancy automatically demonstrate certain deficits. Recent research by Lester et al. (1992) suggests that the pattern and frequency of cocaine use by the mother during pregnancy may be critical. For example, consistent cocaine use throughout the term may stunt a child's growth and produce a continued pattern of later symptoms, while reduced use in the later months may result in withdrawal symptoms of newborns, followed by a less dramatic expression of symptoms.

The long-term effects of cocaine exposure on children's learning potential are not precisely known, primarily because addiction to this drug among women of childbearing age is a recent phenomenon. Preliminary reports indicate that cocaine-exposed preschoolers exhibit patterns of abnormal behavior similar to those seen in emotionally disturbed children, but no unique crack cocaine behavioral syndrome is apparent. Poor motivation to learn, difficulty in organizing thoughts, sudden mood swings, and slow language acquisition characterize these children. They are likely candidates for special education when they reach school, where they soon will be arriving in large numbers. For example, the number of disabled preschoolers in Los Angeles and Miami doubled from 1986 to 1991 (Schipper, 1991).

Programs designed to aid the learning and development of cocaine-exposed children have followed two forms of intervention typically employed with other at-risk children. First, support for parents is provided through a caring, nonjudgmental environment in which basic health care, safety, nutrition, and skills for interacting with children are taught (Tittle & St. Claire, 1989). Second, children are instructed in intensive, one-on-one programs. These highly structured programs employ cues from more than one sensory modality, and they stress organization and emotional control (Singer, Farkas, & Kliegman, 1992). More complete descriptions of instructional techniques utilized in the education of handicapped children are presented in Chapter 11.

SUMMARY

This chapter described the biological and physiological bases of the human learning system, on the assumption that knowledge of the processes, activities, and functions of the body and its structures will help us to understand learned behavior and the theories that explain it. We first explored the organization and role of the neuron, with attention directed toward the mutual excitation and inhibition of neurons, as mediated through neurotransmitter activity at the synapses. Then we analyzed the organization of the nervous system, including the major structures of the brain.

The forebrain contains the structures that are most responsible for thinking and learning: the thalamus, our relay station for sensory input, and the hypothalamus, which influences motivation and emotion. The large human neocortex is responsible for higher level processing and language; it is divided into left and right hemispheres and four major lobes. Each lobe is somewhat specialized in function: the frontal lobe in movement and language, the parietal lobe in somatosensory reception, the temporal lobe in audition and memory, and the occipital lobe in vision.

The question of what changes in the nervous system as a result of learning was examined from three different viewpoints: changes in the brain, changes in neuronal activity, and changes in the functions of different structures. There is evidence that changes in all three sources occur. Changes at the neuron level were considered in terms of electrical potential, neurotransmitter release, and use of glucose. Changes in the frontal lobes, the temporal lobes, the hippocampus, and the amygdala were found to relate to learning and memory functions.

Research and speculation about specialized roles for each hemisphere were reviewed. While the left hemisphere is more heavily involved in verbal and analytical processes, and the right hemisphere in visual–spatial activities, there is considerable overlap and interaction in hemispheric functioning. Efforts to redesign school curricula to enhance right-brain processing ignore the requirement by most school tasks for multidimensional skills to which both hemispheres contribute.

The visual and auditory sensory systems were examined with particular attention to the conversion of stimuli to brain activity. Motor control was also discussed. Despite considerable understanding of the mechanics of muscular functions, coordinated and controlled movements remain difficult to explain. We considered trends in the developmental acquisition of various motor skills, as well as instructional procedures useful in their learning, such as coaching and feedback.

In addition, we reviewed the nature of stress and its effects on the sympathetic and parasympathetic nervous systems, and we described Selye's general adaptation syndrome. Individual differences in reactions to stress and several procedures for stress reduction and coping were examined. Moderate stress was viewed as a necessary element in learning, and teachers were encouraged to determine optimal levels of stress for their students.

The concluding section focused on impairments to the learning system, with particular emphasis on the effects of drugs on behavior. The effects of drug abuse on exposed children was described as an expanding problem. Specific effects of alcohol, opiate, and cocaine abuse during pregnancy were identified in terms of their impact on children's physical and cognitive development.

A concept map for this chapter appears on page 61.

EXERCISES

1. Interview both parents about the course of a child's sensory and motor development. To guide your interaction, you might compose a series of questions, such as: When did your child first walk? Ride a tricycle? Recognize colors? Note major trends and any differences in the observations made by mothers and by fathers.

2. Make a list of as many of the stressors in your life as you can identify. Can you reduce or eliminate their effects in any ways? Select one stressor and develop a plan to rearrange your environment or develop self statements that might lessen its effect. What new behaviors will be required?

SUGGESTED READINGS

Damasio, A., & Damasio, H. (1992). Brain and language. *Scientific American, 267*(12), 88–109.

Folkman, S. (1984). Personal control and stress and coping processes: A theoretical analysis. *Journal of Personality and Social Psychology, 40*(4), 839–852.

Haier, J. R., Siegel, B. V., Nuechterlein, K. H., Hazlett, E. H., Wu, J. C., Pack, J., Browning, H. L., & Buchsbaum, M. S. (1988). Cortical glucose metabolic rate correlates of abstract reasoning and attention studied with positron emission tomography. *Intelligence, 12,* 199–217.

Levinthal, C. F. (1990). *Introduction to physiological psychology* (3rd ed.). Englewood Cliffs, NJ: Prentice-Hall.

O'Boyle, M. (1986). Hemispheric laterality as a basis of learning. What we know and don't know. In G. D. Phye & T. Andre (eds.), *Cognitive classroom learning* (pp. 21–48). New York: Academic Press.

Singer, L., Farkas, K., & Kliegman, R. (1992). Childhood medical and behavioral consequences of maternal cocaine use. *Journal of Pediatric Psychology, 17*(4), 389–406.

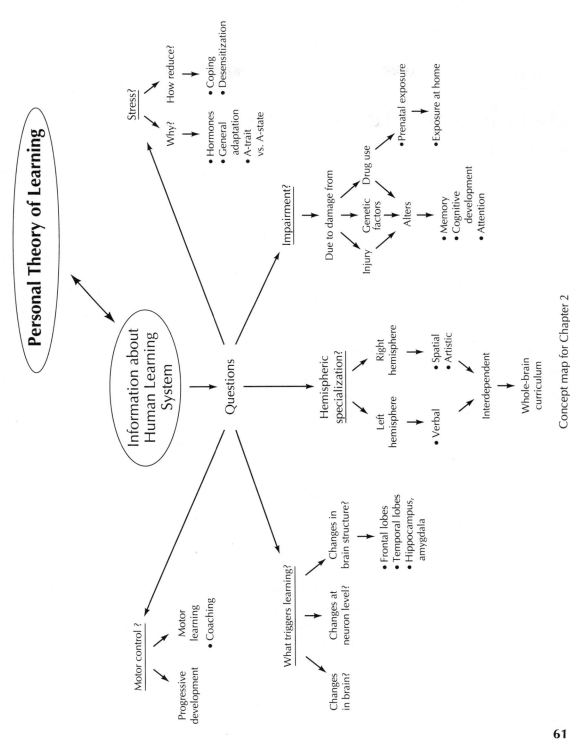

Personal Theory of Learning

Information about Human Learning System

Questions

Stress?

Why?
- Hormones
- General adaptation
- A-trait vs. A-state

How reduce?
- Coping
- Desensitization

Impairment?

Due to damage from

Drug use
- Prenatal exposure
- Exposure at home

Genetic factors

Injury

Alters
- Memory
- Cognitive development
- Attention

Hemispheric specialization?

Left hemisphere
- Verbal

Right hemisphere
- Spatial
- Artistic

Interdependent

Whole-brain curriculum

Changes in brain?

What triggers learning?

Changes in brain structure?
- Frontal lobes
- Temporal lobes
- Hippocampus, amygdala

Changes at neuron level?

Changes in brain?

Motor control ?

Progressive development

Motor learning
- Coaching

Concept map for Chapter 2

Developmental Factors in Learning

OUTLINE

Gender
What Factors Explain Gender Differences?
What Should Be Done to Reduce Gender Bias?

Learning Style
Application of Information about Learning Styles

CHAPTER OBJECTIVES

1. Explain why understanding human development is important in understanding how people learn.
2. Criticize the extreme nativist and extreme environmentalist positions on development.
3. Distinguish between competence and performance.
4. Describe competing theories of language acquisition.
5. Suggest several recommendations for facilitation of the language development of preschoolers.
6. Provide recommendations for instruction of language skills during the school years, including bilingual instruction.
7. Describe the constitutional and environmental factors that affect cognitive development.
8. Summarize major recommendations for the facilitation of cognitive development.
9. Develop a plan you would follow in enriching the education of gifted children.
10. Describe the cultural factors that affect learning.
11. Explain the instructional interventions requiring remedial efforts or adaptation of teachers to culturally diverse students.
12. Describe major gender differences in learning and discuss the factors that appear to explain their occurrence.
13. Outline a program you would follow if you were attempting to reduce gender bias in teaching.
14. Discuss the five major learning styles and their implications for learning.
15. Defend your position on whether teachers should match students according to learning style information.

Mr. Posner was interested in finding out whether eight-year-old Eric was as slow in solving school tasks as the boy's teacher had reported. To help in making that judgment, Posner, the school psychologist, had arranged two balls of clay of similar size and shape in front of Eric. He then asked Eric, "Can you tell me if there is as much clay in this ball as in that one, or are they both the same?"

"They're both the same."

"Okay, now watch what I do." Mr. Posner rearranged one of the lumps into a larger, flat pancake. "Now, is there more clay here, or here, or are they both the same?"

"There's more over here," stated Eric as he pointed to the flat pancake.

> *"Why do you say that?"*
> *"Because this one is bigger."*
> *"Where is it bigger?"*
> *"Here and here and here," said Eric, pointing to the edges of the clay pancake.*
>
> *Mr. Posner sat back and thought. He was beginning to understand the concern Eric's teacher had expressed: "What should I tell her?"*

CHAPTER OVERVIEW

The difficulties in performance experienced by Eric in the preceding anecdote is not surprising. It indicates how the presence of cognitive differences influences the process of learning. Apparent errors can be explained by developmental factors, rather than a failure to learn. This chapter analyzes developmental factors that affect the human capacity to learn. We begin by examining basic concepts and issues that have arisen in studying the developmental process. Then we will review five developmental factors that affect learning: (1) language, (2) cognition, (3) culture, (4) gender, and (5) learning style. Analysis of each factor includes suggested responses to student differences to enhance learning.

CONCEPTS AND ISSUES IN HUMAN DEVELOPMENT

In Chapter 1 we distinguished between learning and development by reserving the term *development* for changes in behavior that are genetically determined and accompany the process of growth. This distinction requires further explanation. We must first differentiate between development and change or growth. *Development* implies a progressive improvement or increase in complexity. We can *change* for the worse, as we do during a progressive illness, and we can *grow* without developing, as we observe when sadly assessing the additional pounds acquired over Christmas vacation. Most developmental psychologists accept a description of development as proceeding "from a state of relative globality and lack of differentiation to a state of increasing differentiation, articulation, and hierarchic integration" (Werner, 1957, p. 126). This view of development is analogous to the embryonic development of an organism, in which a single-celled egg eventually becomes an entity consisting of many, more complex cells.

Development = an increase in complexity

Neural Development

How do differentiation, articulation, and integration come about? As we observed in Chapter 2, the brain undergoes considerable growth in the early years after birth. Not only is there an increase in brain mass, but the synaptic connections also rise rapidly in number and complexity. In fact, there is some evidence that the density of synaptic connections increases until age two, after which there is a decrease. It is believed that the loss is due to the disuse, or "pruning," of unused connections, allowing for more efficient processing in the future (Black & Greenough, 1986). The selective retention and elimination of synaptic connections appear to result in a brain that becomes increasingly differentiated and organized over time.

The apparent overproduction of synaptic connections in the brain is genetically regulated, but the pruning depends on experience (Greenough, Black, & Wallace, 1987). Experiences that are normal for all children in the early years, such as encountering visual stimuli (e.g., patterns) or auditory stimuli (e.g., voices), result in neural activity that maintains synaptic connections. There is an optimum time or sensitive period for these stimuli to have their impact. Greenough et al. (1987) used the term *experience expectant* to designate the processing of this information. It is hypothesized that the development of cognitive ability in children is defined by the occurrence of experience-expectant processing.

Greenough et al. (1987) also described an experience-dependent process that is involved in the storage of information and is peculiar to each individual. The details of such experience differ in both timing and character and therefore are not common to all children. It might include exposure to unique vocabulary words such as "hampa"—my family's way of referring to one grandfather. Experience-dependent information generates new synaptic connections in response to the occurrence of a remembered event. The experience-dependent process appears to correspond to the neural activity that results when *learning* occurs. Further research is needed to determine whether the neural changes associated with experience-expectant information continue in the same manner and degree during later years.

Neural development and learning related to synaptic change

Nature versus Nurture

By now, you are well aware of the *interactive* aspect of the two basic causes of human behavior—maturation and experience. Early philosophical and psychological theories continually debated nativist-versus-environmentalist issues. Obviously, extreme positions that attribute development to the one or the other have little to recommend them. An extreme environmentalist position is flawed because it cannot explain how behavior begins. Nature must provide the capacity to process environmental information and respond appropriately. Moreover, research indicates that infants have a wide range of perceptual skills and understanding of the world. For example, when two-week-old infants observe an adult sticking out his tongue, they imitate the behavior (Meltzoff & Moore, 1983).

An extreme nativist view is equally untenable, in that it ignores the many ways in which experience (or lack of it) contributes to subsequent behavior. Infants existing in restricted environments where they receive little stimulation other than basic sustenance fail to develop normal cognitive skills (Dennis & Najarian, 1957; Deutsch, 1963). Some infants raised in environments where intellectual stimulation is explicitly planned surpass the level of learning they might ordinarily be expected to achieve (Moore & Anderson, 1968). These findings indicate that the most important issue is not whether one or the other set of factors influences development, but how and when nature and nurture, for example, are most likely to interact. The timing of both external stimulation and an individual's physical maturation becomes critical.

Readiness

The suggestion that there is a sensitive period during which experience will have its optimum impact on neural growth introduces an important concept in developmental psychology. *Readiness* is the concept that "attained capacity limits and influences an individual's ability to profit from current experience" (Ausubel, Sullivan, & Ives, 1980, p. 63). It is common to speak of children who are "ready to learn" or "ready to read." Many school districts hold "kindergarten roundups," to assess young children on a wide variety of dimensions to determine their readiness for school. The term is controversial in psychology because it is often misinterpreted.

Readiness is often erroneously believed to be predetermined by genetic factors, thus to be unaffected by environmental influences. Most educators view a state of readiness as a cumulative event reflecting the influence of prior incidental and intentional learning, as well as developmental maturation. It is affected by both experience-expectant and experience-dependent information, as well as by the individual's genetic potential. Readiness may be general, as in the sense of a child's school readiness. It may also be limited to highly specific cognitive capacities necessary for the learning of new skills: Children, for example, must understand quantities before they can learn to add.

Readiness was traditionally studied in the area of motor functioning in behaviors such as walking or toilet training. The role of maturation places severe limits on behaviors of these types because there are relatively clear muscular and structural requirements for such learning. Without appropriate physical maturation, even the best training cannot satisfactorily aid children to walk or control their bladders, as many frustrated parents have discovered.

The area of *cognitive readiness* is somewhat different because the neurological limitations are not clear at all. Ausubel et al. (1980, p. 63) defined cognitive readiness as "the adequacy of existing cognitive processing equipment, or capacity for coping with the demands of a specified cognitive learning task." Individuals demonstrate cognitive readiness when the outcomes of learning activities are reasonably commensurate with the amount of effort and practice involved. In other words, when Mary attempts to read her primer for the first time and, after guidance and a reasonable effort, is able to identify a few words, we can say that she has demonstrated readiness to read. As we will see in Chapter 7, reading is a tremendously complex task to which Mary must be able to apply a number of cognitive skills, including attention, visual discrimination, and concept formation. To be able to understand the meaning of what she has read, she must possess an adequate memory span, patience, and some knowledge of the world. In addition, Mary must have matured physically to the point of being able to focus and refocus on visual cues (e.g., letters) and to sit at her desk and concentrate. All these abilities underlie readiness to read. If Mary has not developed these prerequisites before being introduced to reading, she not only will have difficulty in reading, but will most likely come to dislike it. On the other hand, failure to provide the chance to learn to read once Mary had demonstrated prerequisite skills would be a waste of a valuable opportunity, as well as the child's time in school. Clearly, correctly matching the cognitive readiness of a learner with the demands of a given learning task is a critical dimension of effective teaching.

To summarize, maturation is not the same as readiness; it is a component of it.

Readiness is a sign of experience and maturation

Cognitive readiness = coping with specific tasks

The other major factor is past learning. The existence of readiness does not necessarily depend on maturation alone; it most frequently requires varying proportions of both maturation and learning (Ausubel et al., 1980). Thus, since learning experiences or their absence, as well as genetic factors, contribute to an individual's readiness for a particular task, age is a limited indicator of readiness.

Age versus Stage

If age is not a reliable indicator of readiness, what other markers are available? Some developmental psychologists advocate the use of *stages,* or general characterizations, of children's cognitive abilities to describe their level of competence. As the individual moves from one stage to another, there is a qualitative change in the structures and processes of their thought. Jean Piaget's *stage theory* is the most notable example of this position (1963).

Piaget believed that we continually construct and reconstruct our knowledge, trying to organize it more efficiently and coherently. In doing so we are influenced by biological maturation, environmental factors, and our ability to regulate and modify existing knowledge, or *schemes.* Schemes are potentials to act in certain ways. Infantile schemes are reflected in actions such as sucking, grasping, and looking. The schemes available to an individual will determine how that person responds to the physical environment and also will permit generalization to new objects. With experience, schemes evolve into more abstract rules, or *operations,* which regulate what actions can be performed. As children act on their environment, they observe the changes that occur within it. If these changes fail to match existing schemes, the schemes are likely to be modified. In our opening anecdote, Eric has not observed the discrepancy between his perceptual scheme and the fundamental properties of the rearranged clay balls. It is as if from his view, the difference does not exist. Piaget pointed out the importance of understanding that children do not always possess the same schemes or operations used by adults.

Piaget's schemes are potential actions

Modification of cognition requires a change in available schemes. This occurs through two interdependent functions: *adaptation* and *organization* (Flavell, 1963). Adaptation has two component functions: *assimilation* and *accommodation.* Assimilation involves the integration of new information into an existing cognitive structure. By identifying a penguin as a "bird," a child is assimilating that instance of bird into a personal bird scheme. The creature is a bird because it has wings, feathers, and birdlike feet. At the same time, the child's bird scheme is modified to include animals with wings and feathers, which often fly but sometimes don't, and hang out at the North Pole. Here the accommodation process is concurrent with assimilation. Accommodation is the adjustment of a scheme to particular characteristics of the environment. As a child's experience broadens, accommodation and assimilation constantly interact to promote the development of new schemes and operations.

Assimilation and accommodation are concurrent

The other invariant function, organization, serves to tie schemes together to produce a totality. Schemes become more integrated and organized with experience. Piaget believed that there was a genetic tendency to organize schemes into higher-order systems or structures. This integration results in the coordination of schemes, which permits individuals to master more complex cognitive tasks. The functions of adaptation and organization allow the child to resolve conflicts between existing schemes and environmental realities. Resolving conflict leads to a state of equilibrium. This state is temporary, however, because as new schemes evolve, new aspects of the external world are observed, creating what Piaget referred to as *disequilibrium.* Thus, as individuals strive to attain higher levels of adaptation and organization, cognitive development continues. These higher levels of adaptation and organization comprise the cognitive stages Piaget identified.

Stages are higher levels of adaptation and organization

Each stage builds on and is derived from its predecessor. Although the stages occur in a sequential order, children move from one to another at different ages; therefore the ages commonly used to pinpoint their onset are only approximations. Table 3.1 summarizes the child's thinking according to Piaget's four stages of cognitive development.

Other developmentalists are less enthusiastic about the notion of distinct, qualitative stages creating a *discontinuous* path of cognitive development. They cite evidence that suggests a more incremental, linear path of cognitive growth. They view

TABLE 3.1 Summary of Piaget's stages of cognitive development

Stage	Description
Sensorimotor (birth to 2 years)	Intelligence based on *schemes* such as grasping and sucking. Initial behavior is reflexive, but becomes increasingly goal oriented. Perception is *egocentric;* the psychological world of the child is the only one that exists.
Preoperational (2–7 years)	Mental representation of objects occurs. The child can think about objects not present in the immediate environment (e.g., being able to locate a toy put away the day before) and performs delayed imitation (e.g., copying a response made by the mother at another time). Thought continues to be bound by perception, and concepts are based on physical similarities. Reasoning is often contradictory, and the child has difficulty classifying things into more than one category.
Concrete operation (7–11 or 12)	The child can manipulate concrete events and can solve problems using them. Thought becomes *decentered.* The child can focus attention on several attributes of an object simultaneously and understands relationships among attributes (e.g., a balloon is big but light, a bowling ball is small but heavy). Cooperation is demonstrated. Game rules are followed, and the child can plan activities with others. *Operations* emerge (i.e., cognitive structures are used to transform information).
Formal operation (12–14 to adulthood)	The child can deal with hypothetical situations. Schemes are not tied exclusively to what is immediate and real. There is logical thought; inductive and deductive reasoning occurs. The child can "think about thinking." Higher-order operations emerge in which abstract rules are used to solve problems. For example, algebra rather than a trial-and-error procedure is used to solve the problem: "What number, if multiplied by 3 and reduced by 4, equals 20?"

development as a *continuous,* step-by-step process. Stages of thought can be by-passed or advanced through directed experience, often of a tutorial nature (Brainerd, 1978). What are believed by strict Piagetians to be qualitatively distinct phases in thinking are said to be, instead, short-term problems in understanding the demands and procedures to be followed on a task. For example, Rose and Blank (1974) showed that the inability of some young children to conserve number (to recognize that five things arranged close together are no different from five things spread out) can be improved by changing the way in which the task is conducted. Repeating the question "Are they the same?" apparently communicates to children that the adult believes they are not, thereby influencing the youngsters' judgment. Errors on conservation tasks were halved when the question was asked only once. Let's return to the anecdote about Eric. Would you say that he erred in deciding whether the two clay shapes were the same because his thinking was not at the appropriate stage? Or had he failed to understand the question? Your answer will identify you as an adherent of the "age" or "stage" outlook.

> Is development continuous or discontinuous?

Figure 3.1 tracks the development of cognitive ability according to those who believe that cognitive growth is characterized by discontinuous stages and contrasts this irregular line with the scheme of those who advocate a continuous pattern of growth.

Competence versus Performance

A major problem in understanding developmental change is the determination of whether what a child does is the same as what he or she is capable of doing. We discussed a similar issue in Chapter 1 when distinguishing between learning and performance. In this case, *competence* refers to what a child is capable of doing and *performance* is the observable behavior, from which we may make an inference about competence. Just as in judging learning by observing behaviors such as recall of words or successful problem solution, developmental psychologists infer competence by observing performance on a specific task. Problems arise in making a correct inference when performance is affected by more than one process, when there is

> Competence not necessarily indicated by performance

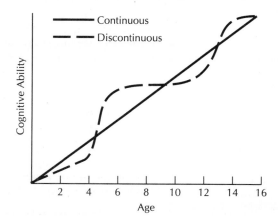

FIGURE 3.1 Continuous and discontinuous patterns of growth in cognitive ability

more than one way of assessing success on a task, or when different tasks might be used to evaluate competence in a particular area of cognition. Thus poor performance on a task might occur for reasons other than lack of competence, and successful performance does not necessarily indicate competence.

The author remembers laboriously memorizing 10 poems for a college class in English literature. The poems were taken from a list of 12, from which only 1 was to be selected for the exam. Sure enough, the test featured 1 of the 2 poems that I believed *never* would be selected. Was my poor performance in attempting to reproduce Keats's "To a Nightingale" evidence of a lack of competence in mastering poetry? I did not think so; unfortunately, my instructor believed it was and graded accordingly.

Developmental examples of the competence/performance distinction are found in a number of cognitive areas. A two-year-old friend of one of my sons once announced: "Santa is brown like reindeer." A few minutes later she was observed drawing Santa in red in her coloring book. Did the little girl believe Santa was brown, or was she responding to the brownness of the reindeer?

Now consider an 18-month-old child who took a black magic marker and produced a circle of dots when asked to draw a rabbit. When asked what the drawing was, she replied, "Rabbit goes hop-hop" (Winner, 1986, p. 26). This child was symbolizing the rabbit's motion, not its size, shape, or color. Someone who noted only the dots would not see a rabbit. The child, however, was definitely aware that markings on a page can represent things in the world.

Finally, a four-year-old was shown four toy garages, three containing toy cars and the fourth empty. He answered "no" to the question "Are all the cars in the garages?" (Mussen, Conger, Kagan, & Huston, 1990, p. 264). At first glance, it would appear that the child did not understand the word *all*. Other questions revealed an alternative interpretation, however. The child had initially assumed that if there were four garages, there must be four cars and one was somewhere else. He understood the meaning of *all*, but was operating from an assumption the adult had not anticipated.

These examples (and others you will have encountered in your interactions with young children) indicate that we cannot easily conclude that a child lacks competence solely on the basis of performance. True competence can be masked by too many other factors in the task itself, in the explanation of the task by the examiner, and particularly in the knowledge, beliefs, and inferences of the child. Indeed, as research data on the development of children accumulate, it is becoming clear that we have long underestimated competence; even infants possess capabilities that are not easily reflected in performance. It is important for educators to base assessments of children's competence on a number of factors, rather than on performance only.

LANGUAGE

Early Language and Thought

Language is a prerequisite for learning about the elements of one's culture. Without language, the sharing of meanings, values, and traditions would be impossible. In fact, as language develops, language and thought about one's culture become closely intertwined. Patterns of thought in a particular culture affect the nature of the language that develops. Language, in turn, affects the type of thinking in which individual members of a culture engage (Vygotsky, 1962). For example, providing the names of objects improved the ability of some preschool children to group objects into categories, while prior practice in grouping the objects into categories improved the learning of the objects' names (Kuczaj, Borys, & Jones, 1989). In other words, learning relevant language influenced thinking about the objects, and thinking about prior experience with the objects helped in learning their names. As we develop understanding of our world, we can be more precise in our language, and language in turn becomes more effective in directing our thought. As Vygotsky (1962) argues, language and thought increasingly influence each other to the extent that much of our thought eventually becomes internalized language. Furthermore, our language becomes the main "window" by which others gain access to our thoughts, foggy as they may at times be.

Language and thought interact

When my older son was 16 months old, and again at 22 months, I secretly placed a tape recorder under his crib to record his speech before he fell asleep. Following are some of the words and phrases revealed by our informal investigation:

16 months	*22 months*
Mama, dada	Play toys
Yellow	Grandpa C. loves Bobby
Zoom, zoom bicycle	Dada read book
Nudie	Bobby sleep now
Where shoes	
Peekaboo, peekaboo	

A number of observations about a child's early language and the relationship of language to thought can be made about these innocent vocalizations. First, language is intrinsically interesting to infants. Our son was alone, and there was no chance of anyone's responding to his speech. He was apparently talking because he enjoyed the act of speaking, not out of expectation of some sort of reinforcement.

Second, although the words and phrases were not organized according to sophisticated grammatical rules, one can derive meaning from them. Phrases such as "Zoom, zoom bicycle" and "Play toys" can be understood, if the listener is willing to make inferences about their intended meaning.

Third, developmental change in performance can be clearly identified. In the course of six months, phrase length increased, ideas became linked together, as in "Grandpa C. loves Bobby," and spoken words became more recognizable. Finally, the words and meanings of what adults say are reflected in the child's language. "Peekaboo" and "nudie" were words used by Bobby's parents (don't tell anyone, please). The youngster was attempting to make sense of what was said to him and was trying to incorporate his perceptions of adult speech into his language system.

These special characteristics of the development of language have sparked considerable debate about its acquisition. One view, based on the behavioral positions of B. F. Skinner (1957) and Mowrer (1958), conceives of language learning as an example of how all learning occurs: through *reinforcement*. Sounds that adults make during caregiving have reinforcement value and are repeated by the child. If the child's

Speech develops through reinforcement

approximation of the sounds is understood, parents are likely to reinforce the speech (e.g., by hugs, kisses, smiles, and statements such as "Isn't baby *sooo* smart?"). Vocalizations that do not approximate the child's primitive language are not reinforced and thus are less likely to be repeated. Parents not only serve as models and reinforcing agents of speech, they also correct their children, providing what Slobin (1964) referred to as *expansion.* For example, a mother might say, "Does Billy want milk?" Billy says, "No milk." If the mother then says, "Billy doesn't want any milk," Billy might respond, "Billy no milk." In this way the child's language is being slowly expanded, becoming more similar to adult speech. Reinforcement, modeling, and expansion are the main components of the environmentalist view of language acquisition.

An alternative position has been vigorously advocated by the linguist Noam Chomsky (1959, 1972). Chomsky believes that the rapid rate of production and comprehension of language observed in most children cannot be explained by reinforcement and modeling alone. That only humans naturally acquire language suggested to Chomsky that language learning is unique, following its own biological and psychological constraints. He believes that people are born with an innate knowledge of language and its rules which permits infants to generalize beyond the words they hear. Chomsky distinguishes between *surface* and *deep structure* of language to illustrate this point. Consider these two sentences:

1. Sandy is easy to ride.
2. Sandy is eager to ride.

They are similarly composed, indicating a similar surface structure, but their meaning is quite distinct. If we paraphrase the sentences, this becomes obvious:

1. It is easy to ride Sandy (the horse).
2. Eager to ride is Sandy (the rider).

Deep structure = meaning?

The deep structure or underlying meanings of the two sentences are quite dissimilar. Chomsky argues that children could not manage these translations from surface structure (what they hear) to deep structure (what the sentences mean) through observation or imitation alone.

Chomsky further notes that information about the structure of language is not directly taught to children. Children simply hear strings of sounds from which they somehow deduce the complex rules of the language being spoken. If language environments do not particularly influence some aspects of a child's linguistic development, and if the structure of language is not directly taught, then the behavioral view of language is limited in its explanation.

There appears to be considerable evidence supporting some of Chomsky's ideas. As we discussed in Chapter 2, one of the major functions of Broca's and Wernicke's areas, in the left hemisphere of the brain, appears to be control of language functions. These areas of the cerebral cortex are not specialized in other species, indicating a possibly unique biological basis for human language. Second, analysis of the errors children make in forming plurals and other word endings suggests that there is a logic to their attempts, as if an unstated linguistic rule was being extended. It is common for children to say "sheeps," mouses," and "childs," even though they have not heard their parents say these words. Third, while many parents who know how can expand their children's language, they do so only rarely, suggesting that children develop language competence in ways not directly related to training.

On the other hand, support for the nativist dimension of Chomsky's view of language acquisition is lacking. Chomsky argued that infants possess a "prewired" mechanism for acquiring language. All that was needed was the availability of a *corpus* of linguistic utterances from which the child could generalize. From the start, this concept was unclear in that it seemed to imply language content as a beginning rather than a result. If innate competence exists, one would expect greater similarity in the early grammatical productions of children, and perhaps greater similarity in structure from language to language. In fact, there appears to be more diversity than similarity in the languages of the world, and it is difficult to find much commonality in the early grammars of children from different language communities (Slobin, 1986).

Corpus required for generalization

It appears that language acquisition is a more complex process than either competing theory would admit. It seems to require both specific language ability (which may be innate) and a wealth of linguistic data provided from models. Occasional newspaper accounts of young children raised in restricted learning environments, who communicate only by grunts, serve as anecdotal examples of what happens to language development in the absence of an adequate corpus from which learners can extract linguistic rules.

Children generate their own language rules?

Most contemporary views of language acquisition incorporate ideas from both theoretical positions. These views agree on several points, paraphrased from observations of Small (1990).

1. Children are sensitive to orderly patterns in the language they encounter, and they form and evaluate hypotheses about language.
2. Children's hypotheses about language are constrained by innate characteristics. (There is, however, disagreement on whether these constraints are specific to language or are general.)
3. Linguistic experience is used by children to confirm or reject their developing hypotheses about language.

Language Structure

Language can be broadly conceived of as the transmission and understanding of messages. It can occur in any one of four channels or combinations: a vocal–auditory channel, which we call speech; a visual–motor channel, which comprises reading and writing; a tactile channel (e.g., that used in braille); and a psychomotor channel (e.g., in American Sign Language, body gestures, facial expressions). That language includes so many "sending and receiving" channels is indicative of its psychological complexity as well as its diversity. As a response to this complexity, educators in recent years have advocated a more integrated approach to the teaching of language. The major skills of speaking, reading, and writing are increasingly viewed as complementary, and instruction in one skill is often supplemented by instruction or practice in others. A writing exercise might begin with students verbally describing what they want to

Language instruction as integrated activities

write, then writing the text, and then presenting it orally to the class. Activating several channels is assumed to facilitate the use of each one.

To understand such a complex system, it is useful to identify its component parts. The study of language is generally subdivided into *phonology,* which refers to the sounds that compose spoken language; *semantics,* which is the meaning of words and sentences; and *syntax,* which consists of the set of grammatical rules used to express meanings. A fourth subdivision, *communication,* which includes all the channels, is the integration of all the parts of language to convey or interpret messages. In many cases, there is more to language than the spoken or written word. For example, the old phrase "your lips are saying no, but your eyes are saying yes" implies that there is more to communication than the literal interpretation of what is said.

Communication = verbal + physical

Early Language Instruction

Based on our knowledge of language acquisition, we can identify a number of procedures and strategies that can be used by parents and teachers of young children.

Offer good examples of correct usage of the language. While few adults possess perfect grammar, precise pronunciation, or the vocabulary of Noah Webster, most can effectively guide the language acquisition of a child. As indicated, children will generate phonological and syntactical rules from the most meager language corpus; thus no adult should feel inadequate as a teacher. All that is needed is clear pronunciation, appropriate volume and emphasis, and the use of common words as labels for objects and actions.

Children need models of correct language

Practice the expansion technique of communication described earlier (Slobin, 1964). When an adult restates a child's phrases in a longer, more grammatical, and more complete syntactical form, the child's efforts are both rewarded and refined. Corrections do not have to be labeled as such; there is no need to say, "No, say it this way." A more effective technique seems to be to repeat the phrase, adding the missing ingredients.

Ask questions requiring more than simple "yes" or "no" answers. Rather than say, "Does Billy want to go to the bathroom?" when Billy is wiggling in his seat, try asking, "What does Billy want to do?" In this way, Billy must express the thought.

Use the principle of contrast in directing questions. D. B. Clark (1988) believes that children assume that words contrast in meaning and that they learn rapidly when new words are contrasted to old ones. The sentence "Would you rather read the fat book, not the thin one?" contrast the properties of two books, hence can be used as a clue to the meaning of "thin." Clark also believes that children strive to fill in gaps in their linguistic knowledge. When they encounter an unfamiliar word and two objects to which the word might refer, they are likely to guess that the new word refers to the object whose name they do not know. In this way, children develop an ever-expanding semantic system. Asking whether Anne likes the "banana food" (which Anne can say) or the "pineapple food" (which she cannot) will help Anne distinguish between the two tastes and acquire a new word as well.

Discuss interesting new words that might appeal to the child. Consider the following interchange between a father and a six-year-old.

DAD: Do you see the crosswalk sign?
SON: Why is it called a crosswalk? Is it a place where you can walk when you're cross?
DAD: No, Joey, it's the place where you walk . . . across. Crosswalk, get it?

As illustrated here, analysis of a new word not only can reveal its pronunciation and meaning, but can point to other words either within it.

Provide a rich linguistic environment that stimulates children to think about, use, and "play" with words. From alphabet and picture blocks that can be arranged to form words and sentences, to interesting tape-recorded stories that children can hear, to storytelling and reading by adults, language is a central part of a child's early environment. Songs have long been employed as language aids, with familiar pieces such as "The Alphabet Song" and "Old McDonald" serving as practice for listening and pronunciation. Games stressing language skills, such as "Simon says" and "I went to the market and bought a . . . ." (requiring recall and production of what has already been said) are also beneficial. Mechanical toys and computers with voice components are additional means of stimulating language responses from children, particularly those who might be reticent to speak out in large groups.

Harness television to induce children to increase their language production. Television is a good source of phonemic and morphemic information for children, particularly programs such as *Sesame Street*. In a study of the effect of television on children's language, the families of 261 children, ages three and five, kept diaries for two years recording the preschoolers' naturally occurring viewing habits (Rice, Huston, Truglio, & Wright, 1990). It was found that watching *Sesame Street* predicted enhanced vocabulary development, while watching other shows did not. The vocabulary-enriching effects were not related to parent education, family size, gender of child, or, most interestingly, whether parents and children viewed the show together. These findings are important because they indicate that children's language development can be aided by watching television without the presence of parents and without parental control of the pace, sequence, and content of the broadcast material. Apparently, the appealing visual and auditory effects of television, coupled with redundancy and humor, as incorporated in *Sesame Street,* can command attention and result in significant language learning.

Practice expansion, contrast, and vocabulary use

Television can aid vocabulary growth

Language Development during the School Years

As formal schooling progresses, linguistic development is closely tied to curricular content, and children acquire words and concepts associated with specific bodies of knowledge. Additional linguistic knowledge acquired during the elementary school years consists of *pragmatic* rules (Dale, 1980). Pragmatics concerns the social use of language, with all its sometimes subtle requirements. For example, when addressing one's elders, it is better to say "May I have some cookies, please?" than "Give me cookies!" Both requests convey the same message, but pragmatic rules allow the speaker to express the meaning required by social context. Knowing when to use slang or informal speech and when to be more formal, as in applying for a job, is an example. Learning not to make critical albeit truthful comments is another. The frankness often found appealing in the six-year-old who calls his father "Fatty" would be inappropriate if spoken by the same child 10 years later.

Teaching comprehension and communication of ideas through different language skills is a major task of the school. In the preschool years, children's comprehension of language is influenced most by their general knowledge of events and the context in which the language occurs. As the school years pass, syntax comes to exert a larger influence over comprehension. The importance of syntax increases as children are required to understand and produce sentences that describe past and future events, hypothetical situations, and alternative explanations of events—all constructions that require more than simple, factual statements. The child must learn to use and understand passive as well as active voice, subjunctive and conditional clauses, and other modes of sentence transformation. Sentence structure as revealed through syntax interacts with semantics and context to expand the individual's ability to convey and receive meaning.

At the secondary level of education, additional linguistic skills become important to learning—the use of metaphor, analogy, satire, humor, irony, and other ways of representing complex ideas. In addition to knowledge of semantics, syntax, and the pragmatic use of language, these skills require *cultural literary* and the ability to represent ideas abstractly. Cultural literacy, or knowledge of a society and the individual's role in it, provides meaning beyond the semantic translation of a sentence. Consider the following riposte of a politician intent on stirring up the townspeople against his opponent: "My opponent is a hopeless extrovert, a confirmed carnivore, and even has a sister who is a terpsichorean in New York."

Vocabulary and semantic knowledge alone would not allow full appreciation of all the humor of this situation. One must also know something of politicians, of the sociocultural status of New York City, and perhaps of the reputed ignorance of the voting public. As we shall see in later chapters, the use of complex linguistic forms can be a valuable aid to learning. For students to benefit from its nonliteral dimension, however, they must possess cultural literacy.

Margin note: Use of syntax and cultural literacy at secondary level

Language Instruction during the School Years

A number of practices and procedures can be followed by teachers to advance the language skills of their students. Some of these are listed next, with brief illustrations.

Utilize classroom experiences that require student verbalization.   Discussions, games, group reports, "show and tell" times, songs, and other traditional activities all provide opportunities for children to use oral language. Not only can the teacher serve as a source of corrective feedback to student speech, but other peers will act as language models. Teachers can draw attention to new or unusual words appropriately used by students, and both praise their use and suggest additional words or phrases.

Stress alternative ways of expressing specific thoughts as a means of revealing pragmatic uses of language.   Questions directed to students such as "How else might we say this?" or "How would your father (or a teacher, principal, sports announcer, politician, or used car dealer) say that?" can stimulate thought about alternatives.

What type of puzzle fosters alternative phrases?

Provide practical applications of grammatical rules.   Working at mastery of grammar skills probably ranks very low in our personal lists of pleasant remembrances of school. Nevertheless, competence in using the many transformations required by our language is a basic skill. Accurate use of grammatical rules serves primarily to express more precise meaning. Instruction in grammar should emphasize the value of good grammatical expression. For example, a lesson on conjunctions might begin with a discussion of things used to join other things together. The teacher can then note that certain words and phrases perform a similar function in sentences and ask the class for examples. By comparing conjunctions to "things that join other things together," the student can see the necessity for the appropriate use of these parts of speech.

Enhance student vocabularies by explaining the derivations of new words.
A lesson about the formation of new words might begin with selected sentences about a moon landing. For example, "The lunar excursion module (LEM) has landed on the moon. The commander uses his microphone (mike) to radio the news to Earth. The crew heard the steady thrum of the engines. Their voyage had been an eye-opener." The teacher then discusses how new words originate through acronyms (LEM or RADAR), through clipped words (mike for microphone), through imitation of sounds (thrum), and through metaphor (eye-opener). The lesson could be expanded by analyzing *microphone* into its constituents: "micro" meaning small and "phone" meaning sound. Other words such as "microscope" and "megaphone" could be introduced, and speculation about their meanings and the meaning of the new constituents "scope" and "mega" could be encouraged. This type of lesson illustrates not only how new words enter our language, but how we can use our general knowledge of words to increase our vocabulary and understanding of the words we use.

Old words reveal new vocabulary

Point out phonological, syntactic, and pragmatic uses of English that may differ from usages in other languages.   The language encountered by many children at home or in their community does not help them to generate the same linguistic rules developed by children from Standard English backgrounds. Not only are different vocabulary words learned, but standard pronunciations and syntactic transformations may not be available. Teachers will need to take advantage of opportunities to compare and contrast standard English with nonstandard dialects or other languages. In Spanish, for example, the equivalents of the comparative and superlative suffixes -er and -est are placed before the adjective. In addition, descriptive adjectives follow the noun, rather than preceding it as in most cases of English. Teachers of students with limited English proficiency should be aware of these potential trouble spots and should provide guidance to correct usage.

Bilingual Instruction

Students whose first language is not English present a unique challenge to their teachers and the educational system. Being raised in a bilingual environment has little effect on the initial acquisition of a first language, but it does lead to later difficulties in vocabulary, syntax, and idea–word relationships in both languages (Carrow, 1957). Parents can work to minimize these effects, and some children are able to acquire two languages in such a way that they actually supplement each other. In most cases, however, special training at school is required for full development of a second language.

Most educators advocate an instructional approach commonly referred to as *bilingual education* as a way of providing language skills to children from bilingual backgrounds. The approach, however, differs widely in implementation. Bilingual education programs generally provide instruction in both English and the home language, in a manner that permits English to be taught as a second language. Programs differ in their purpose and in the extent to which each language is emphasized. In the so-called *transitional* programs, the development of English skills is paramount; instruction is offered in two languages only until children have acquired enough English to allow learning to occur exclusively in English (Fishman & Lovas, 1970). Other programs assume that children learn a second language in the same way they learn the first, that is, the new language is presented in its native form and in contexts that motivate students to learn it (Lambert, 1984). This approach, known as *immersion,* employs only the second target language. The learning of the language is incidental to the learning of new ideas and skills found in the content area. Immersion has been effectively used in Canada to teach French to Anglophone children (Genesee, 1987).

Bilingual immersion—emphasis on new language

A variation of immersion is called *bilingual immersion.* In this approach, classes composed of 50 percent language minority and 50 percent language majority students are taught using *only* the minority language in first grade, except for 30 minutes of English language arts. In grades 2 and 3, English language arts is expanded to 60–90 minutes per day. In grades 4, 5, and 6, there is equal use of English and the minority language. Long-term evaluation of a bilingual (English–Spanish) immersion program in San Diego, California, revealed that by the end of sixth grade, both language majority and language minority students performed well above grade level on tests of reading and math in Spanish. On the English versions of these tests, the language majority students scored well above grade level, while language minority students scored above grade norms in math and near grade level in reading (Lindholm & Fairchild, 1988). The success of this program is attributed to the presence of classmates who are native speakers of another language and to the competence of the instructor. Language minority students also benefit because they can use their native language for all subjects except English (Cziko, 1992).

Maintenance programs, on the other hand, are designed to promote literacy in both languages. In these programs the first language is viewed as more than a temporary medium of instruction allowing preliminary benefits while students learn English. This approach is considered a legitimate alternative contributing to mastery of school subjects, even after English has been acquired. Full bilingualism is the goal of maintenance programs (Fillmore & Valadez, 1986). One procedure followed in maintenance programs is *language alternation,* in which teachers switch back and forth between the two languages as needed, often from sentence to sentence. Jakobson (1981) claims students can separate the new language from the old, provided the switch is made at a logical break. Indeed, code switching is a socially acceptable form of communication in many bilingual communities. Language alternations are made for purposes of communication whenever the teacher perceives that students are having difficulty comprehending what is being taught. Obviously, the decision to adopt a maintenance program depends on the social goals of the community and, more fundamentally, on the presence of a competent bilingual teacher. For the program to be successful, the bilingual teacher not only must devote adequate time to instruction in each language but also must know when to switch from one to the other and how to help children appreciate both languages.

Deciding which approach is most effective is very difficult. Much of the research evaluating techniques and programs has been inadequate—failing, for example, to compare students in bilingual programs to students with similar characteristics in control programs (Willig, 1985). Techniques are frequently poorly described, and in many cases it is impossible for other researchers to determine their reliability because programs were not conducted in a standardized way. Effectiveness also depends on the goals of the program. Immersion programs, for example, are interested in second language competence only, while other programs emphasize different language skills or skill maintenance in the first language as well. Factors such as the amount of deficit in the second language, the social status of the first language group, that group's willingness to maintain its cultural identity, and the group's experience with school and education are all pertinent. It is a mistake to assume that English-speaking children of upper-middle-class families learning Spanish are directly comparable to Spanish-speaking children of poor families studying English because both groups are participating in bilingual education programs.

Some characteristics of effective bilingual instruction seem to be independent of the program utilized. Competence of the bilingual teacher as a user of instructional skills, as a speaker of both languages, and as one who values the cultures underlying the languages being taught is most critical. A teacher with competence in these areas can (1) identify Manuel's problem in understanding a concept presented in English, (2) think of an example of the concept from Latino culture, and (3) present the concept in Spanish as appropriate for the boy's age and level of accomplishment. Manuel will be able to learn the content and may see similarities between language referents, thus enhancing his confidence in his ability to use both languages.

Effective programs also seem to communicate that the first language is only different, not wrong or inferior. Even immersion programs that emphasize second-language acquisition can draw on first-language words, phrases, and cultural events to expand understanding of second-language concepts. Fluency in a second language can be achieved without alienating children from the language and culture of their families and community. The understanding of already acquired rudiments of a first language should be used to aid acquisition of the second.

Finally, much content can be taught nonlinguistically through pictures, diagrams, physical activities, gestures, and a wide variety of nonverbal instructional aids. The author once observed an African soccer player who spoke little English demonstrate and coach an entire team of American ten-year-olds in the art of "heading" a soccer ball. Mathematical properties also can be illustrated in the early stages of learning math through the arrangement and manipulation of objects and symbols. Resourcefulness in presenting concepts in non-language-dependent ways is a mark of good teaching. Once a particular skill has been mastered at a nonverbal level, it can be refined and expanded using appropriate second-language terminology.

As with all children, enrichment of the language skills of bilingual students who are deficient in English requires a clear intent to help, planned input, and patience. Research is still needed to determine the optimal conditions for language development of all learners. It is clear, however, that this is one of society's most important missions, and training those charged with aiding language growth is crucial.

COGNITIVE DEVELOPMENT

This section examines *cognitive development,* the gradual changes by which mental processes become more complex and organized. To begin, let us consider the results of two experiments with children of different ages. Both experiments illustrate the impact of cognitive development in the learning of school-related tasks.

In the first experiment, Murray and Mayer (1988) asked three- and four-year-olds who could count to 10 to compare the numbers 1 through 9. The children were asked to indicate which of two stuffed animals—Teddy and Freddy—had more grapes on its plate. For example, Teddy might have 4 grapes and Freddy 5. The number comparisons went up through 8 versus 9. Other three- and four-year-olds were asked to sort flash cards containing the numbers 1 through 9 into three categories: "little," "middle-sized," and "large." The results of both tasks indicated that children of this age had difficulty in making judgments about the magnitude of single-digit numbers. Three-year-olds seemed to know that some numbers (such as 1) were small, and other numbers (7, 8, and 9) were large, but they could not discriminate among numbers within categories. At best, they understood two categories: small, which consisted of the number 1, and large, which contained all other numbers. Four-year-olds had begun to understand the relative magnitude of the digits but had difficulty in finer judgment, particularly when asked to compare larger numbers (7 versus 8).

The results indicated that in and of itself, the ability to count to 10 should not be interpreted as a sign that a child is ready to learn mathematics. Procedures such as single-digit addition require understanding of the nominal, ordinal, and interval properties of numbers. Emphasis should be placed on diagnosing and fostering children's understanding of number magnitude, perhaps through tasks such as those employed in the experiment, before proceeding to further instruction.

Magnitude concept—a prerequisite to addition

The second experiment illustrates how children from four age groups approach problems requiring the balancing of weights on a scale (Siegler, 1976). A balance scale looks something like this:

Doughnut-shaped metal disks of different weights can be placed on any of the upright pegs protruding along the arm of the scale. The problem solver's task is to predict which side will go down as disks of varying weight are placed in different locations along the scale. There are two dimensions that determine balance—amount of weight and distance of the weight from the center. Problems in this experiment required the solver to coordinate information about these dimensions in order to predict whether the scale would balance, or would go down at one end. Siegler hypothesized that children would solve such problems by using one of four rules of increasing sophistication:

1. If weights are the same, then the scale will balance; if weights are different, the side with more weight will go down.
2. If the weights on both sides are equal, the side with weight placed a greater distance from the center will go down.
3. If both weight and distance are equal, the scale will balance; but if one side has either more weight or more distance, and the two sides are equal on one dimension, then the side with the greater value on the unequal dimension will go down. If one side has more weight, and the other more distance, then guess.
4. Use rule 3 unless one side has more weight and the other more distance. Then multiply weight times distance on each side. The side with the greater total will go down.

By generating six increasingly difficult problems for which different rules yielded specific patterns of answers, Siegler developed a method to determine which rule a child would select. Problems ranged from those in which no dimensions were varied to those in which both dimensions varied. Children using different rules to solve the problems always produced different patterns of responses. For example, children using rule 1 could successfully solve problems in which weight was varied and distance irrelevant, but they solved other problems incorrectly. Those using rule 3 could accurately solve problems in which either dimension was varied, but they did no better than chance when both were varied.

Results indicated that five-year-olds most often used rule 1, nine-year-olds most often used rule 2, and thirteen- and seventeen-year-olds usually used rule 3. Few children of any age used rule 4. Performance on the six problem types was related to the type of rule used and was independent of age. In some cases, younger children surpassed older ones. For example, five-year-olds who used rule 1, which attributes imbalance to weight only, were correct on 89 percent of problems in which there was a conflict between weight and distance and weight was greater. In contrast, seventeen-year-olds using rule 3, guessing when there is a conflict, were correct only 51 percent of the time on similar conflict problems. Percentage correct was found to decrease from age five to age seventeen on all six conflict–weight problems, but on none of the other 24 problems. As Siegler points out, *decreases* in accuracy with age are extremely rare, supporting the conclusion that type of rule determines accuracy, *not* age or experience.

In complex problems, variables interact

This finding would not ordinarily be expected by educators. In fact, Siegler (1991) later related that he was advised by a school superintendent not to use seventeen-year-olds as subjects because they had learned about balance scales and would all perform perfectly! Retesting the seventeen-year-olds on a pan balance scale rather than on an arm balance scale indicated, however, that the high school students could solve weight–distance conflict problems on the original equipment only. This troubling inability to generalize specific problem solving to other materials is unfortunately found in many complex learning situations.

What do these studies tell us? Clearly, performance on school tasks is affected by more than practice alone. In the first experiment, repeated practice in counting did not ensure the ability to make judgments about the relative magnitude of numbers. In the second experiment, experience with a scale did not ensure that children of different ages could solve related problems. Furthermore, behavior in one learning situation does not necessarily allow us to predict how learners will perform on tasks that appear logically similar. Although most adults would assume the contrary, knowing that 8 comes after 7 does not guarantee that a child will be able to state which number is larger. Recognizing that the variables of weight and distance must be coordinated to maintain balance on a scale does not routinely lead to an attempt to establish the basis of that coordination, a thought process one might expect from high school students.

Perhaps most importantly, these studies demonstrate the role of cognitive development in children's learning. Many educators agree that we must understand how the development of thinking skills, such as estimating magnitude or manipulating two variables simultaneously, affects and modifies the learning of school content. Without that understanding, we will not sufficiently aid the learning of our students. Teaching should be related to the child's cognitive level, not to adult conceptions. Consider five-year-old Carmine, who believes that dinosaurs roamed the earth "long ago, back when Grandpa lived." Dinosaurs, of course, are associated with the Mesozoic era, some 150 million years ago. Lacking a mature perspective on geologic time periods, Carmine is severely restricted in his understanding of a term like "the Age of Dinosaurs." Lessons about prehistoric reptiles that take into account the cognitive development of kindergarten children, for example, should focus on broad time distinctions such as "dinosaurs lived before there were people on the earth." A more precise understanding is not consistent with the cognitive level of five-year-olds.

Content presentation must consider cognition

What Variables Contribute to Cognitive Development?

Psychologists have studied for many years the nature of the interaction of maturation and experience to effect cognitive development. One model that summarizes the relative contributions of each dimension has been proposed by Horowitz (1987). In this model, children are placed on two continua: *constitution* (consisting of both genetic and biological factors) and *environment*. Constitution ranges from vulnerable to invulnerable; environment varies from facilitative to nonfacilitative. Children raised in facilitative environments fare well even when they have vulnerable constitutions. Children who are relatively invulnerable (no one is completely invulnerable) are more likely to develop normally even in nonfacilitative environments. The greatest risk occurs for children who both are biologically vulnerable (e.g., as a result of birth defects, cocaine exposure, etc.) and are raised in a nonfacilitative environment. Unfortunately, children living in poverty are most likely to fall into these categories.

Constitutional factors = internal and physical

The list below summarizes environmental and constitutional risk factors that have been suggested as contributing to differences in measured intelligence.

Environmental

Home environment
Excessive noise and distraction (Wachs, 1979)
Lack of play materials
Unpredictable daily routine (Bradley, Caldwell, & Elardo, 1977)

Parental interation
Aloofness, lack of attention (Estrada, Arsenio, Hess, & Holloway, 1987)
Low expectancy of success
Authoritarian or permissive parenting style (Baumrind,, 1973)
Failure to question, provide feedback, or offer guidance (Moore, 1986)

Family structure
Absent father, excessively large family, later-born siblings
Lack of early educational experiences
Low socioeconomic status (SES)
Poverty; uneducated parents
Membership in disadvantaged ethnic group
Reduced school expectations

Constitutional

Premature birth, low birth weight
Prenatal environmental factors
Drug dependency
Fetal alcohol syndrome
Nicotine
Blood incompatibility, Rh factor
Complications at birth
Anoxia, injury
Infections
Viral diseases (rubella)
Sexually transmitted diseases
Chromosomal abnormalities
Down's syndrome
Fragile-X syndrome
Inherited disabilities
Nutritional deficiencies

Several of the environmental factors require further explanation. It appears, for example, that the behaviors most likely to facilitate cognitive development are typical of parents who are affectionate and interested in their children, express positive expectations about each child's potential, stimulate their children through questioning and praise for good performance, and follow an authoritative parenting style (Baumrind, 1973). An *authoritative* parent maintains clear standards, explains the rules, and enforces them consistently and fairly. Important issues, rules, and ideas may be discussed. *Authoritarian* parents, on the other hand, punish misbehaving children without identifying the fault at issue. *Permissive* parents allow children to govern themselves and make few demands with respect to juvenile behavior. Neither authoritarian nor permissive parenting encourages the necessary questioning and safe exploration of possibilities that seem to be necessary for cognitive growth.

> Authoritative parenting is not authoritarian

Family structure variables, such as presence of the father in the home, size of family, and birth order, yield small, positive correlations of intelligence. Baumrind suggests that the *quality* of the interaction between parent and child is more important than structural factors. Single parents who provide a supportive, stimulating home environment, following an authoritative parenting style, can compensate for departures from the traditional, nuclear family.

Early educational experience—whether in preschools attended by children of middle-class and wealthy families, or in programs such as Head Start for economically disadvantaged children—contributes to cognitive development. Long-term studies of a variety of preschool intervention programs indicate that enrolled children not only perform better on IQ and achievement tests shortly after they leave preschool, but graduate more frequently from high school, and attain higher levels of employment (Haskins, 1989; Lazar, Darlington, Murray, Royce, & Snippes, 1982). A major assumption of preschool programs is that enrolled children will benefit from a facilitative environment not necessarily available in the home. The most successful programs, however, directly involve parents, either training them to become more effective teachers at home by using learning activities (I. Gordon, 1970) or employing techniques of behavioral change (Kramer, 1989). If parental involvement and a stimulating educational environment are not continued through the elementary school years, many of the gains derived from preschool programs may be lost (Haskins, 1989).

Parent involvement is important after preschool as well

Reduced expectations inhibit intellectual development during the school years. Knowing that Charles has an IQ of 86, that he comes from an economically disadvantaged family, and that his older brother Richard achieved at a low level in the same school can influence educators to assume that Charles is incapable of learning much. Charles may be called upon less frequently, asked only easy questions, and excused from certain assignments because they might prove too difficult. Charles, who initially may have been interested in tackling the tougher questions or assignments, soon realizes that he is not expected to do so. Consequently, his performance falls to the level his teachers had expected. This negative form of the *self-fulfilling prophecy* (Rosenthal & Jacobson, 1968) has been demonstrated to affect children's school behavior and, eventually, their cognitive growth. For children who arrive at school eager to learn and without labels, on the other hand, a more challenging academic environment is provided, because teacher expectations are higher. One reason for the long-range cognitive effects of successful preschool experiences such as Head Start may be that graduates of these programs demonstrate the positive attitudes and skills that elicit higher expectations from teachers in later grades.

FACILITATING COGNITIVE DEVELOPMENT

The following ideas and recommendations can be applied by parents and educators to foster the cognitive development of children.

Use and refinement of mental processes such as memory and attention, which are required for continued cognitive development. Attempting to cram facts into the minds of children may temporarily increase their achievement in certain areas but will not contribute to long-term competence. It is far better to provide opportunities and materials that encourage children to exercise cognitive processes in a number of domains.

Adopt an authoritative style when relating to young children.   The authoritative parenting style seems to facilitate healthy emotional growth as well as cognitive development. Techniques that seem to be effective include maintaining positive expectations, identifying through discussion the rules and standards children should follow, encouraging exploration of new activities, and questioning children in a nonthreatening way so that thinking is provoked. Communication that takes the form of "I wonder what would happen if . . . " or "Let's see where this goes" serves to alert children to the acceptability and value of risk taking and inquiry.

The constructed nature of knowledge as described by Piaget suggests that facilitation of intellectual development requires interaction with the environment.   The instructor's role is to create and present situations that allow the student to discover knowledge by acting on available content. In the type of situation most likely to facilitate progress, the student is allowed to recognize conflict between present levels of thought and succeeding ones. To resolve disequilibrium, children will engage in personal research.

At the preschool level, Kamii and DeVries (1978) recommended the selection of materials and activities that will produce immediate and observable effects when children act on them in different ways. For example, children can use straws to blow across a pan of water such objects as Ping-Pong balls, bars of soap, Tinkertoy pieces, and crayons. The diversity of objects allows children to determine the properties that favor movement across the water. The relation between the variables of blowing effort, angle of straw, surface area of object, and weight of object can be examined as well. The teacher's role is to lay out the materials, encourage the use of different materials, and ask "What if . . . ?" questions to help children see how relevant variables are related.

At the elementary school level, materials and activities should facilitate the development of such concrete operations as classification, seriation, and conservation. Kamii (1985) has developed a math curriculum for first-graders composed of games and everyday situations. Rather than emphasize drill and practice of math facts, children participated in group activities designed to allow them to invent and use their own mathematical skills. For instance, they held elections, keeping track of votes and calculating how many each side would need to win. They played card games like war and go fish, which require children to sort their cards into suits and rank them, discussing how many cards have been played, how many remain, and so on. Kamii noted that children introduced to this approach not only enjoyed the activities but performed as well as other students on math achievement tests. Rather than directly teaching concrete operations of mathematics, this approach focuses on the child's active construction of the knowledge underlying cognitive structure and academic content.

At the secondary level, activities and materials must contrast the real with the possible, centering on abstract relationships that not only explain but can be recombined to make predictions. Active research efforts, both in the laboratory and in the library, should be frequent activities for children at this level. Rather than follow the steps of a lab manual to complete an experiment, research work should allow individual or group innovation. In the author's high school chemistry class, each lab began with observation of a chemical reaction. Students were then presented a variety of materials from which to re-create the reaction. Other than safety controls, and an occasional reminder of relevant past learning, the instructor offered no direct guidance. Although chemistry was the subject, underlying operations (e.g., combining and manipulating variables) were being practiced in an interactive, exploratory manner.

There are many cognitive skills, all of which can be practiced in an integrated manner. Departing from traditional views of intelligence as a unidimensional construct, Howard Gardner (1983) believes that individuals are capable of independent cognitive functioning in at least seven areas of competence: *(1) linguistic, (2) musical, (3) logical–mathematical, (4) spatial, (5) bodily–kinesthetic, (6) interpersonal, and (7) intrapersonal.* Departing from the "mental faculties" theory of Kant (Chapter 1), Gardner conceived of each of these seven "intelligences" as a potential, not as a given. Thus musical competence will not flower unless adequate stimulation is available. Gardner believes that each intelligence is best developed when knowledgeable adults encourage and stimulate intellectual activity in an interdisciplinary fashion. At least one public school has been designed to provide such an integrated environment. Through a variety of special classes (e.g., bodily–kinesthetic activities, computing) and enrichment experiences such as apprenticelike pods, all the children are given the opportunity to discover their areas of strength and to develop the full range of their capacities (Gardner & Hatch, 1989). At other schools, a "Spectrum" classroom is equipped with "intelligence fair" materials, including miniature replicas and props that stimulate children's writing and household objects that can be reassembled to challenge spatial skills. Creative movement sessions and discovery areas where small experiments can be conducted are part of the Spectrum classroom (Wexler-Sherman, Feldman, & Gardner, 1988). Preliminary results indicate that such an approach affects different intelligences independently, that relative strengths and weaknesses among cognitive areas can be identified, and that cognitive growth in each area of competence correlates with scores on traditional forms of intelligence assessment (Gardner & Hatch, 1989). While additional research is needed before such an approach can be widely implemented, a more coherent and systematic means of developing cognitive abilities seems to have been proposed.

The development of cognitive skills occurs in unplanned as well as planned activities. The author fondly remembers an incident in his brief, but illuminating career as a preschool teacher. I was attempting to help four-year-olds stop saying "poopsie-peepsie" to designate bodily functions. A strict prohibition on saying these words had resulted in considerable tattling, in which individuals would solemnly tell me that "Billy said poopsie-peepsie." The children's game was to get to say this taboo term, yet have the blame fall on someone else. Relying on my fledgling knowledge of psychology, I decided to have everyone say the word over and over, hoping to exhaust my charges' desire to use the term by creating what behavioral psychologists would describe as satiation. We said "poopsie-peepsie" over and over for a full min-

(margin note:) Gardner's multi-factor theory of intelligence

ute, to the wild glee of the class, and the surprise of the head teacher who happened by at that moment. Needless to say, the attempt utterly failed; the children now believed that the term was acceptable and continued to use it. The point of this anecdote is that later one of the four-year-olds asked why some words were "bad," and the question evoked great interest. A fascinating discussion ensued, in which we examined "good" words and "bad" words. The children were able to recognize that certain words hurt others or were inaccurate, and they concluded that they might as well use the good or right ones. We started to identify words that were better than some we did use, and I was amazed at the level of the discussion. Moreover, the preschoolers continued their attempts to use good words on succeeding days. What had started as a futile, perhaps silly attempt to proscribe language turned into a memorable success at influencing the cognitive skills of young children.

Be alert to the misconceptions students may have acquired.   Flavell (1963) warns of "misacquisitions" children may develop when ideas are encountered that rely on operations not yet acquired. As indicated earlier, for example, it is a mistake to insist that children practice adding single-digit numbers when they have not yet mastered relative magnitude. Learning will be incomplete and the ideas poorly understood. As researchers study the learning of specific content, it is becoming clear that existing knowledge structures influence performance. Without understanding the knowledge structure of individual students, it is easy for teachers to assume that errors can be remediated by more practice, when in fact the cure lies in clearer explanations of the underlying operations. In the area of subtraction for instance, Brown and Burton (1978) have identified 110 consistent errors, or *bugs*. These bugs are not random; they are systematic errors that reflect a student's misacquisition of some component of subtraction. A common bug involves "borrowing" as in the problem of subtracting 43 from 92. Those who understand the process know that you are not really subtracting 3 from 2, but a 3 in the unit place from a 2 in the unit place, which entails borrowing from the 10s place. A frequent bug consists of avoiding the borrowing operation by taking the smaller unit's digit from the larger, so that 92 − 43 comes out as 51. Errors of this type are likely to result when a prerequisite concept is missing and the child thinks of subtraction as a repetitive procedure that can be performed successfully without understanding the underlying structure of individual problems or the meaning of what is being done.

> Bugs are mistaken beliefs we all possess

Interaction with peers is central to the acquisition of social knowledge. "One can learn the meaning of perspective—and thereby acquire the rationality and objectivity which only a multiperspective view can confer—only by pitting one's thoughts against those of others and noting similarities and differences" (Flavell, 1963, p. 360). Group projects, class discussions, role-taking activities, debates, and "speech and feedback" reports all require the clash of perspectives so valued by Flavell. Simulations such as model United Nations meetings or political party conventions, in which students take the roles of different members with different agenda, are particularly useful in revealing the value of cooperation, as well as illustrating diversity of opinion. The development of social knowledge, required for understanding our environment and social condition, is advanced by the conflict one may experience when personal ideas are compared to those of someone else.

Enriching the Learning of Gifted Children

Providing for the continued cognitive growth of exceptionally able, or *gifted,* children presents a unique challenge. Gifted children often are identified because they outperform others on school tasks. Ideally, enrichment of the home and school learning environments should widen, rather than narrow, the differences between these students and their peers. The focus of enhancement is to help them to attain the rich potential indicated by their standardized test scores (Jenkins-Friedman & Nielsen, 1990).

Gifted children possess traits in common with other children. Nevertheless, researchers have attempted to identify traits that are most representative of gifted people. For example, Bloom (1985) analyzed the case histories of 120 adults who had attained status in cognitive/intellectual fields (neurology or mathematics), the arts (piano performance or sculpture), and athletics (tennis or diving). Table 3.2 lists the cognitive and affective traits these authors found to be most characteristic of gifted children.

Gifted children possess both unique and common traits

This wide range of representative behaviors can either support or interfere with continued development of an individual's particular abilities. For example, curiosity, a habit of pursuing logical answers, as well as flexibility and creativity in thinking may characterize a student who is excited about learning, good at critical thinking, and stimulating to have in a classroom. But these qualities also may indicate a confronta-

TABLE 3.2   Cognitive and affective characteristics of gifted children

Cognitive	Affective
1. Displays a high level of curiosity.	1. Has an advanced sense of right and wrong; is concerned about ethical issues.
2. Pursues logical answers and solutions; applies logic when evaluating self and others.	2. Is willing to take risks to achieve goals or find answers.
3. Is flexible in thinking, is capable of seeing things from an unusual perspective.	3. Possesses unusual insight.
4. Is able to generate original and unique ideas and solutions.	4. Has high energy levels.
5. Is developmentally advanced in language and reading.	5. Has a long attention span and superior ability to focus on a topic.
6. Is extremely generalized; has a variety of interests.	6. Possesses an advanced, mature sense of humor.
7. Has extremely specialized interests.	7. Is independent and autonomous.
8. Understands complex, abstract concepts; sees the relationship among ideas.	8. Is unusually sensitive and empathetic.
9. Learns and retains basic information easily.	

SOURCE: R. Jenkins-Friedman and M. Nielsen, Gifted and talented students. In E. Meyen (Ed.), *Exceptional children in today's schools* (Denver, CO: Love Publishing, 1990), pp. 466–467. Adapted with permission of the publisher.

tional person who is critical of others and bored by everyday class work. To ensure that development is positive, it is necessary to carefully consider the kinds of instructional and home support that are needed.

Experts recommend that instructional interventions for gifted students include at least three components: (1) *enrichment activities,* (2) *accelerated classes,* and (3) *extension of learning beyond the classroom* (Treffinger, 1986). Programs occurring within the traditional school program are therefore vital to their education. Classroom teachers can provide for these students by (1) identifying the level of instruction they require, (2) creating flexible ability groups for the pursuit of special projects with students of similar ability, (3) individualizing assignments and activities, and (4) modifying the curriculum by allowing gifted students to take pretests to determine competency in a certain area or to work at their own pace. Gifted students may also be enrolled in classes in which they work with other students of similar abilities under the direction of a specialist in gifted education. At the middle school and high school levels, students can participate in honors courses and advanced placement classes. Whenever possible, these students should have the opportunity, through an internship arrangement, to work with mentors or experts in their areas of interest. For example, one high school student who was extremely proficient in writing completed a sports-writing internship with a local newspaper. As technological advances become part of our society, gifted students are likely to become not only users of technology, but producers of it. Therefore, it is desirable to provide opportunities for them to utilize available computer applications and other equipment, as well as opportunities to gain experience in skills such as programming or using computer networks to go beyond the classroom (Jenkins-Friedman & Nielsen, 1990).

How are gifted children taught in your school?

THE ROLE OF CULTURE

Differences among children's cultural environments are also responsible for differences in learning. This view has been traditionally applied to explain failures in school of minority children and those born into poverty. It used to be said that these children had not acquired the values and skills necessary for learning in school because of a cultural background that did not stress learning. The children were therefore classified as *culturally disadvantaged,* and it was assumed that some of the values of the majority culture needed to be absorbed for the children to learn. Recent research, however, has focused more on *conflicts* between cultural beliefs. It is no longer assumed that there is one cultural environment that best fosters learning. Rather, there is emphasis on *cultural diversity,* to acknowledge that all cultures contain elements of value.

The role of culture is difficult to determine precisely, however, because no one is the product of a single cultural group. Children are not just Latino, or poor, or female; they are multifaceted human beings. Culture refers to "all the beliefs, norms, values, and premises which underlie and govern the conduct of a particular group" (Krech, Crutchfield, & Ballachey, 1962, p. 380). Since everyone is a member of many groups, everyone is influenced by many different cultures. The African-American daughter of a dentist in Chicago and an African-American girl born to a rural Missis-

Culture diversity implies no one best culture

sippi farmer belong to different cultural groups. A white, male Catholic growing up in Boston and a white, male Mormon raised in Salt Lake City are exposed to two different cultures. Banks (1988) identified eight major groups to which each of us belong: (1) gender, (2) social class, (3) race, (4) nationality, (5) ethnic group, (6) religion, (7) presence of ability/disability, and (8) geographic region. To understand cultural differences that affect learning, we must attempt to isolate each of these distinct influences, recognizing that each acts in combination with others.

Three cultural influences that have received considerable analysis are *social class, race,* and *ethnicity.* Social class is a major dimension, often overcoming the effects of other factors. For example, students from three racial groups of differing social class levels were compared on achievement. In the mathematics performance of higher social class students, 54 percent of Asian-American students, 40 percent of white students, and 21 percent of African-American students were judged to be high achievers. For low social class students, only 18 percent of Asian Americans, 7 percent of white students, and 2 percent of African Americans were identified as high achievers. On the basis of these results, Hodgkinson (1991) suggests that social class is more useful than race as a predictor of educational achievement.

Income levels define social class. According to the 1990 U.S. Census, 23 percent of children live in families where income is below the $15,000 poverty line. Children raised in a financially impoverished environment are said to be *at risk* for educational, social, and physical problems. According to Garcia (1991), the probability is high that children of poverty will:

receive less prenatal care

be born into families troubled by drug dependency

be born prematurely or have low weight at birth

be exposed more frequently to crime and child abuse

experience interruptions in their schooling due to parental job loss and relocation

be denied education opportunities because of discrimination.

Despite these potential obstacles, many lower social class children still manage to learn successfully. What actually seems to differentiate low and high social class is not disparity in income but the attitudes and behaviors relative to the educational process that are communicated to children (White, 1982). Parents who have had some educational success are the most likely to contribute to the learning of their children. A comparison of achievement levels of nine-year-olds whose parents went to college with those of children from families in which parents had not completed high school reveals significantly higher levels of achievement in science, math, and reading for children of college graduates (Barton & Coley, 1991).

Importance of Parents' Education

Well-educated parents are more likely to show interest in their children's school progress because these parents understand how learning occurs in school. They understand their role in their children's cognitive growth and provide the kinds of enriched

What cultural group best represents you?

Social class can be determined by income level

stimulation described earlier in the chapter. These parents are more likely to read at home, to watch educational television shows, and to visit museums and zoos. Parents with little schooling, on the other hand, while perhaps recognizing the value of education and respectful of teachers, may not be knowledgeable about schools or feel comfortable about them. If they have experienced academic failure themselves, they may expect the same for their children. Less flexible work schedules and a lack of leisure time may not allow them opportunities to visit school or participate in their children's activities. They are more likely to "tell rather than teach" their children (Hess & McDevitt, 1984), and they may be less sensitive to such indications of emerging literacy as pretend reading of environmental print such as road signs and advertisements (Goldenberg, 1989). As a result, their children are likely to have fewer occasions to practice using their linguistic and cognitive skills, to the detriment of educational achievement (Ogbu, 1987).

Parental education contributes to student success

Race and Ethnicity

While social class is the major factor accounting for differences in educational achievement, differences attributable to race and ethnicity must be recognized as well. In a recent national assessment, for example, 39 percent of African-American children read at a basic level compared to 68 percent of white children (Mullis & Jenkins, 1990). Asian-American students, on the other hand, outperformed other racial and ethnic groups in most academic areas even when social class was controlled.

Most educators agree that the differences just noted are due to the effects of: *differential racial discrimination, specific ethnic influences,* or *relegation to minority status.* Discrimination based on racial and ethnic characteristics is unfortunately commonplace in our society. African-American and Latino children are far more likely to be identified as learning disabled or to be tracked into basic skills classes. Students in low-ability tracks reported more isolation, alienation, and punitiveness in relationships with teachers and peers, had limited expectations about their future success; those in high-ability tracks reported more enthusiasm, autonomy, and self-direction (Oakes, 1985). Tracking, while designed to provide the appropriate level of instruction for all students, has in fact been found to *increase* achievement gaps between high- and low-ability groups (Sorenson & Hallinan, 1986). In essence, both student and teacher expectations are reduced; hence less work is required, and students in low-ability tracks receive less attention and feedback (Eccles & Wigfield, 1985). Flanagan (1993) believes that the high number of minority students in low-ability tracks provides an unequal and therefore discriminatory educational experience.

Differential treatment of minority students

Some ethnic influences enhance school learning, while others hinder advancement. For example, the traditional role of Japanese mothers—namely, to assume personal responsibility for their children's learning—has been correlated to the high achievement levels of Japanese and Japanese-American students (Stevenson, 1992). In another cross-cultural study, 57 percent of Japanese and Chinese parents reported supplementing their students' math homework with additional practice at home, while only 28 percent of American parents did so (Stevenson, Lee, & Stigler, 1986). In other cases, ethnic factors contribute to misunderstandings between teacher and student, with the result that relationships and trust are strained. In a study of counselors working with students from either the same or different cultural backgrounds, Erickson and Shulz (1982) found that mismatches in culture produced different interpretations of another's abilities and motives. U.S.-born counselors expected students from other cultures to nod, smile, or otherwise indicate understanding. When no such cues were provided, the counselors repeated their instructions in simpler language. In interviews after the sessions, counselors rated the culturally diverse students as less bright, requiring many trials to learn the simplest information. The same students reported that the counselors, by repeating simple information over and over, as if it hadn't been understood, made the students feel inadequate. Not sharing expectations about proper behavior, each party acquired misperceptions of the other. Similar misunderstandings probably occur in a number of exchanges between teachers and students of dissimilar ethnic or cultural backgrounds.

Ogbu (1992) has argued that there are three types of minority groups, and membership in each affects performance.

1. Autonomous minorities (e.g., Mormons in the United States) are minorities in number only; on most dimensions they fit easily into the majority culture.

2. Immigrant or voluntary minorities have moved to America to seek advantages not available at home (e.g., Koreans, Vietnamese). They expect to encounter cultural differences and are willing to attempt to overcome them for the sake of advancement.

3. Involuntary minorities are descendants of people who were brought into the United States against their will. Often they have been relegated to inferior positions and denied true assimilation into the mainstream.

Type of minority status makes a difference

Ogbu (1992) contends that involuntary minorities may develop a new sense of social or collective identity in opposition to the majority group. Rather than viewing barriers to assimilation and acceptance as challenges to overcome, involuntary minorities see them as markers of their own identity. School learning is equated with agreeing with the majority culture or regarded as something to be avoided, not acquired. Past experiences have suggested to involuntary minorities that acceptance of the standards of the majority culture will not result in a payoff later. Thus there is social pressure within the racial or ethnic group not to assume the majority's values. As a result, there may be little family and community support for engaging in practices that lead to academic achievement.

Minority students require coping strategies

Involuntary minority students who attempt to succeed academically often adopt strategies to shield them from the criticism of their group. One strategy is to "accommodate but not assimilate" by adopting the behaviors of the majority culture at school and return to the culture of the minority at home. Another is to camouflage or disguise one's academic attitudes by pretending not to care about school work or by engaging in the more conventional activities of the minority culture, all the while studying in secret. Other strategies include becoming closely involved in school activities that have appeal to the minority culture, such as sports or music, seeking protection from stronger individuals in return for doing homework, or joining special programs (Ogbu, 1992).

Research is needed to determine whether the beliefs described by Ogbu are extensively held by members of involuntary minorities and how the coping strategies he describes are acquired and modified. His views have direct implications for teachers and community members considering interventions to adopt to aid minority status students.

Interventions

Interventions designed to aid culturally diverse students to learn require either attempted **remediation** of behaviors, values, and beliefs that interfere with successful learning or **utilization** of these beliefs and behaviors as a vehicle to enhance learning.

Remediation.　　Community programs designed to instruct parents in the behaviors and strategies that stimulate cognitive growth can be effective. For example, Parents as Teachers provides instruction in nutrition, child care, and parenting techniques (Meyerhoff & White, 1986). Ogbu (1992) has stressed that the involuntary minority community must play a role in the educational system by teaching children to separate attitudes and behaviors that lead to academic success from those that lead to a loss of ethnic identity. This dual outlook can be achieved when successful members of the group retain their membership in the community and indicate to the children that attaining superior academic performance is desirable, not hypocritical.

The educational setting must feature coordinated, multiyear programs beginning in the preschool years. A good example is "Success for All," a schoolwide restructuring program for inner-city children (Madden, Slavin, Karweit, Dolan, & Wasik, 1993). Important components of the program include one-to-one reading tutors, who daily review materials read in the regular classroom, a family support team providing parent education, and in-class special education service where needed. Comparisons with matched students in matched schools who did not receive the program indicated considerable improvement in reading, a reduction in failure rates, and an increase in attendance for children who were in the program from its inception.

Other restructuring efforts require teachers to assume a more positive attitude about the achievement potential of their culturally diverse students. If school faculty and staff believe in their ability to motivate and help students learn, even schools heavily populated with minority learners can reach high achievement levels (Bandura, 1993). Studies of African-American students who received support from parents, teachers, and other school personnel indicated that these young people achieved at higher levels and had higher self-concepts of ability (Pollard, 1993).

Linking education to the home community, so that the functions of the school are viewed as related to one's ethnic and cultural background, appears to be critical to fostering the academic achievement of culturally diverse students. Newman and Roskos (1993) attempted to create this link at the preschool level by establishing in several Head Start classrooms an office play setting that contained print items from an office (a telephone book, calendars, magazines, charts, signs, etc.). The "office" was staffed by community and parent–teacher volunteers, and inner-city children were encouraged to play in it during their free time. Adults assisted in the children's free play by using the literacy items for such functional purposes as looking up telephone numbers to order pizza or taking messages. Children's play was videotaped. After five months, their ability to read words from the labels and signs placed around the "office" and to identify the objects by name had significantly improved. The authors believed that the presence in a literacy-enriched play setting of familiar adults assisted minority children to think, speak, and behave in more literate ways.

Utilization. Educators can affirm beliefs and behaviors that contribute to each individual's sense of personal and cultural identity, while at the same time helping students acquire new values that can be assimilated. To do so, it is necessary for teachers to learn about students' cultures. Knowing something about cultural, racial, and ethnic values, teachers can more easily help involuntary minority students separate attitudes and behaviors that enhance school success from those that threaten the students' social identity and sense of security.

Utilization of beliefs and behaviors also implies a need for teachers to modify their instructional practices to incorporate demonstrated techniques for providing support and clear communication to culturally diverse children. Many such students learn more effectively when competition is reduced, group activities are employed, and peers serve as models and tutors. In a review of teacher behaviors found to improve the academic performance of low-achieving students, Brophy and Good (1986) found the following to be effective:

Support is important with minority students

1. Structured lessons following an active instruction format.
2. Redundancy in content coverage with smaller steps and high success rates.
3. More low-level cognitive questions, review, and practice.
4. Emphasis on mastery of material, not exposure to large amounts.
5. Clear expectations that students can succeed.
6. Warmth and support, encouragement for good effort, and credible praise for successes.
7. Requirement that students respond overtly when asked questions.

Active instruction with structure is valuable

Finding the time, materials, and support staff to accomplish these modifications is a challenge, particularly for teachers who instruct many students a day. There must be collaboration between pairs of teachers, between teacher and parent or aide, and between teachers and support staff. There is reason to be optimistic that differences in students' ability to learn can be accommodated and that achievement can be enhanced, however. Some research indicates, for example, that as greater numbers of at-risk students move through our educational system, college and graduate school admission score averages do not decline, indicating that these students are having some success (Hodgkinson, 1993). Rather than face the learning difficulties of children from culturally diverse backgrounds with trepidation and lowered expectations, it is important for educators to be optimistic about the rewards that can come from success with these students.

GENDER

Miss Appleton entered her first Calculus 100 class with great anticipation. She had worked hard to become a teacher of calculus in high school, and she was eager to spread her love for mathematics to students, particularly to females who might not have been encouraged to study math.

A quick look at the room indicated that she would not have many fe-males to encourage. There were 14 in the class (a nice teachable group), but only three were female. These students were huddled anxiously in the front. The bravest one approached her: "Are you Miss Appleton?"

"Why yes."

"Uh, are you going to be teaching Calculus 100 or business math? We heard that maybe you wouldn't be teaching calculus if there weren't enough students."

"No, sorry, this will be calculus."

"Oh, . . . Well, I guess we're in the wrong class." The three girls gathered their books and hastily exited, to the accompaniment of snickers from the remaining students.

"My goodness, it's going to take awhile," thought Miss Appleton.

This section examines gender and its influence on learning. At first glance, success in learning wouldn't seem to be affected much by the sex of the learner. After all, sex is a matter of chromosomes and anatomy, not cognitive skill. It is easy to see how a particular student not provided adequate linguistic or cognitive stimulation might fail to develop cognitive skills. But how can the mere fact that one is a male or female have much effect on learning?

There do appear to be differences in how males and females perform and achieve that are not easily explained by cognitive or linguistic variables. After examining differential performance according to the kind of content that was learned, Maccoby and Jacklin (1974) concluded that girls were better in verbal skills, while boys did better on visuospatial tasks and mathematics. More recent comparisons have indicated that most differences have declined to almost zero, although boys perform better on tests of general knowledge, mechanical reasoning, and mental rotation, while girls score higher on language usage and perceptual speed (Feingold, 1992). There is great variability across groups, however (Feingold, 1992; Friedman, 1989; Linn & Hyde, 1989). Males are more likely to be either very high achievers or very low achievers in math, for example (Dorans & Livingston, 1987). Differences of other kinds are observed in school. Girls earn better grades throughout school, even in classes such as math and science (Sadker, Sadker, & Steindam, 1989). Boys are much more likely to have difficulty in reading or to be diagnosed as learning disabled or behavior disordered (Harvey, 1986). In addition, males are observed to be more aggressive (Hyde, 1986), as well as more confident in their math and science abilities (Eccles, Adler, & Meece, 1984) and more interested in those subjects at the high school level (National Science Board, 1987).

Gender differences in cognitive skills are declining

What Factors Explain Gender Differences?

While biological explanations have been offered periodically—for example, Benbow (1986) attributed male dominance in mathematics to endocrine differences—most researchers emphasize the critical role of socialization and *sex role stereotyping*. Gender differences, therefore, are said to be due to a particular kind of cultural influence. Differential treatment aimed at ensuring that boys and girls conform to family and society views of "appropriate" role behavior begins very early. Parents traditionally have promoted independence, aggressiveness, and an action orientation in boys and passivity, nurturance, and empathy in girls (Kagan, 1971). The author recalls selecting just the right toy truck for a son and just the right doll for a niece, for example.

In the classroom, boys are expected to be more independent, are likely to interact more with their teachers, and are punished as well as rewarded more frequently (Sadker & Sadker, 1985). Certain content areas such as math and science have been viewed as more appropriate for males, while social science courses are valued for females. As a result, it has been hypothesized that differential course work is a major contributor to differences in achievement and choice of math or science as a major (Friedman, 1989)—exactly the situation faced by Miss Appleton. Thus, according to this hypothesis, if females were encouraged to take the same number of math and science courses, differences in these subjects would be reduced. When girls do take math and science classes, however, there is evidence that they are differentially treated. Boys are questioned about the subject matter 80 percent more frequently (Baker, 1986) and called on to perform 79 percent more of the classroom demonstrations in science classes (Tobin & Garnett, 1987), for example.

Differential interaction communicates different expectations

What Should Be Done to Reduce Gender Bias?

Select curricular materials that do not reflect sexual bias in their content. Texts, videos, computer software, and supplementary materials should be screened to select items in which boys and girls alike are seen to be participating in a variety of interesting occupations and activities. Stories about females in roles in which they perform scientific procedures or utilize mathematical principles are needed to counteract stereotypes about female occupations. By the same token, when males are introduced to stories with exciting male characters and intriguing plots, gender differences in reading favoring females are reduced (Asher & Markell, 1974). It is assumed that selecting more balanced materials influences students' incidental learning of sex role expectations.

Provide equal opportunities for both sexes in all class activities. Communicating that one sex or the other is supposed to act in a certain way or to assume certain roles but not others does not promote equal opportunities. The author recalls being irritated in junior high school by a teacher who said, "The president [of the history club] is a boy and the vice-president is a girl, so now the treasurer should be a boy and the secretary should be a girl." Not only does such a statement support gender stereotypes, it suggests that competence and interest are less important than some kind of sex-based allocation system. Both boys and girls may be capable physical education aides, may be able to play the drums or the flute (two musical instruments that have been gender stereotyped), or may have prepared the toughest math homework problem correctly. By providing opportunities for students based on interest and skill, not on gender, teachers will be supporting equality of treatment.

Differential coursework and opportunities create expectations

Encourage cooperative activities in which both sexes have a chance to achieve. It seems too obvious to say that we live in a world in which the sexes constantly interact, and therefore educational practice should encourage such interaction. Nevertheless, in many schools girls and boys are separated for reasons of administrative convenience. Maccoby (1990) suggested that segregated play groups serve a socialization function, leading children to acquire distinctive interaction skills that are adapted to same-sex partners. It is within this context that both sexes acquire additional gender-biased information about their respective sex roles.

Should traditional same-sex segregated groups be altered in some way to promote gender equity? An answer is not yet available. One approach has been to establish cooperative mixed-sex learning groups to teach students to value the contributions of the other sex. Peterson and Fennema (1985) found that cooperative learning enhances math achievement for girls at both beginning and advanced levels. Unfortunately, boys' participation in these groups was negatively related to achievement. The inverse relationship was found when groups were competitively structured—boys performed well, but girls did not. It would appear that a mixed-sex structure that encouraged cooperation but also allowed individuals to compete would facilitate learning for both sexes. Design and implementation may pose problems here.

Do same-sex environments facilitate equal opportunity?

Others recommend promoting same-sex environments, hypothesizing that equitable treatment will be forthcoming and that participation rates and achievement scores will be enhanced. In general, research indicates that there are some academic advantages for girls in single-sex settings, but the advantages for boys are mixed when performance is compared to that of other students in coeducational settings (Riordan, 1990). Longitudinal study of girls in selective, single-sex schools indicated that initial advantages decline during adolescence (Gilligan, Lyons, & Hammer, 1990). Bailey (1993) suggested that without clear policy statements, as well as commitment to and implementation of procedures that advance equitable instruction, it does not matter what organizational formats or grouping strategies are employed. Further research is called for, to reveal how such policies and procedures can be implemented.

LEARNING STYLE

Many educators believe that *learning style* influences learning itself. Although defined in a variety of ways, the term is generally assumed to refer to beliefs, preferences, and behaviors used by individuals to aid their learning in a given situation. Learning styles appear to occur in three areas: cognitive, physiological, and affective (Reiff, 1992). Cognitive styles have been defined in terms of the way a person perceives, remembers, thinks, and solves problems (Messick, 1976). Physiological styles are biological and include reactions to the physical environment that may affect learning (e.g., being a "night person" or preferring to study in a warm vs. a cold room). Affective styles include personality and emotional characteristics such as persistence, preferring to work with others or alone, and rejecting or accepting external reinforcement. Various learning styles may include one or some of these dimensions.

One widely accepted cognitive style is *field dependence–field independence,* or *psychological differentiation* (Witkin, Dyk, Faterson, Goodenough, & Karp, 1962). Field-dependent learners are easily affected by manipulations of the surrounding environment, while field independents are less influenced by changes in the field and tend to approach tasks more analytically. The style is typically identified by presenting learners with an embedded figure task. Field-dependent students have more difficulty in selecting hidden objects.

Why is the embedded figures task difficult?

This difference in cognitive style influences how students respond to classroom tasks, although there are few differences found in general achievement. Field-independent learners prefer to work alone, are able to more effectively organize their efforts in working on projects and problem-solving tasks, and prefer to set their own goals. Field-dependent learners, on the other hand, prefer to learn in groups, prefer to interact frequently with the teacher, and require more external reinforcement and teacher structuring of tasks (Witkin, Moore, Goodenough, & Cox, 1977).

Another cognitive style entails *conceptual tempo* (Kagan, Rossman, Day, Albert, & Phillips, 1964); here speed of response is the critical variable. Impulsive children (quick responders) work fast to get an answer, are more easily frustrated and more distractible, and are more likely to take risks than reflective children who work more slowly to avoid errors. Neither impulsivity nor reflectivity has been judged to be a superior tempo for all tasks, although reflectives appear to have an advantage in reading during the early grades and are more adept at using specific learning strategies (Pratt & Wickens, 1983). Most complex tasks require elements of both styles of responding, however, so it is necessary to encourage students at one extreme to incorporate elements of the opposite style. Would you like your airline pilot to be impulsive in making judgments about the plane's operation? What if the pilot were extremely reflective?

A third cognitive learning style is Gregorc's *thinking style* (Gregorc & Butler, 1984). Gregorc categorizes thought into two dimensions: *concrete-abstract* and *sequential-random*. Individuals may display any combination of four possible styles: (1) concrete-sequential, in which direct experience with materials is preferred, (2) concrete-random, in which a more experimental approach to activities is preferred, (3) abstract-sequential, in which learners are skilled at using symbols, and (4) abstract-random, in which learners prefer unstructured learning environments and enjoy using the imagination to solve problems. Gregorc believes that student behaviors of frustration and avoidance can result when learners are mismatched for too long a time (i.e., placed in classes with teachers possessing a different thinking style).

Two other learning styles, describing a more affective dimension, are *learning style elements* (Dunn & Dunn, 1978) and *modalities* (Barbe and Swassing, 1979). The former approach uses the Learning Style Inventory (Dunn, Dunn, & Price, 1985) to assess preferences for environmental stimuli of different kinds (sound, light, etc.), social settings (working by oneself, in pairs, etc.), and physical stimuli (working under time constraints, needing an opportunity to move while working, etc.). It is argued that students achieve best when their learning preferences are matched to teaching methods (Carbo, Dunn, & Dunn, 1986).

In assessing preference for modalities, Barbe and Swassing make the same kind of recommendation. Visual learners prefer to learn by seeing, while kinesthetic learners prefer tasks that require the physical manipulation of objects. While most students learn by using all modalities, some have unusual strengths in learning through a particular sensory pathway.

Application of Information about Learning Styles

In general, those who advocate attention to learning styles recommend that teachers determine through observation or standardized tests the learning style most predictive of a student's best performance. Selection of appropriate materials, environmen-

Do you prefer reflective or impulsive people?

What particular learning preferences do you have?

tal modifications suiting their preferences, and adjustment of tasks where possible would follow. It would be good educational practice to identify and accommodate preferred styles and to present content in a way designed to maximize student strengths.

Critics argue, however, that learning style descriptions and their implications require more careful and extensive comparisons of student performance in the classroom. Some have charged that many styles have been operationalized only vaguely (Curry, 1990). For instance, how frequently must a particular preference or behavior occur for it to be considered a style? Don't we all occasionally engage in some particular way of learning, only to use another way later? Others have emphasized the low reliability and validity of the instruments designed to assess learning styles (Stahl, 1988). A third criticism is that even if learning styles are validly and reliably assessed, it is impractical to try to construct enough adaptations to meet each possible learning style effectively.

Is it possible to teach to every learning style?

Reliability and validity are issues

Learning styles call for *aptitude-treatment interaction.* That is, an individual's characteristics or aptitudes must be matched to a specific treatment or instructional adaptation to result in an outcome more effective than otherwise would have been obtained. Research generally fails to reveal significant aptitude-treatment interactions, however (Cronbach & Snow, 1977; A. Miller, 1981). Instead, relationships tend to be found between more general learner characteristics such as intelligence or achievement and aptitudes. Differential treatments thus do not seem to make too much difference in performance when general abilities are taken into account.

Student = teacher style → better results

what are general abilities?

The desirability of matching students' styles with curriculum or methods has also been challenged. Shipman and Shipman (1985) argued that students need to become proficient in a wide variety of educational environments, since different learning outcomes may occur in each. Kirby (1988) believed that the best learning style to acquire is the *absence* of any particular one. Flexibility to deal effectively with instructional situations of all kinds is most important. Curricula designed to maximize students' strengths may not be what students need. For instance, recommending the use of whole-language approaches with students who have difficulty reading may harm the students who require, in particular, more opportunity to practice decoding skills. In some cases, only one way of responding to an assignment will lead to success, and to attempt to provide a substitute based on learning style differences does the student a disservice.

Match or mismatch, depending on task

Attending to differences among learners that involve their preference or habitual way of responding would appear to be desirable in many cases, insofar as such approaches employ additional ways of presenting content or structuring the task environment. Making decisions based on learning style information alone may be unwise, however, especially if the approach selected restricts students in some manner.

SUMMARY

This chapter described how the development of five factors—language, cognition, culture, gender, and learning style—contributes to the capacity to learn. We began with consideration of basic concepts and issues of interest to developmental psychology, defining development as proceeding from a state of globality and lack of differentiation to a state of increasing differentiation, articulation, and integration. Then we discussed such issues as experience-expectant versus experience-dependent neural development, nature versus nurture, whether cognitive growth follows a stage sequence, discontinuous versus continuous patterns of growth, and competence versus performance.

Language was viewed as a prerequisite for the learning of one's culture. The behavioral view of language acquisition was contrasted with Chomsky's nativist view. The centrist view adopted holds that (1) children form and evaluate hypotheses about language, (2) these hypotheses are constrained by innate characteristics, and (3) linguistic experience is used by children to confirm or reject their hypotheses. To aid children in the acquisition of phonology, semantics, and syntax, it was recommended that adults do the following: provide examples of correct usage, employ the techniques of expansion and contrast, ask questions requiring more than a one-word answer, discuss new words, provide a rich linguistic environment, and harness the drawing power of educational television to enhance early language learning.

Language instruction during the school years centers on vocabulary development, pragmatic rules, and grammatical refinements. Teachers need to identify how Standard English corresponds to or differs from nonstandard dialects or the first language of bilingual children. Several approaches to the delivery of bilingual education, including transition and immersion programs, were reviewed.

Differences in cognitive development were related to a number of constitutional and environmental factors. The home situation, parental interaction, family structure, early education experience, socioeconomic status, and school and teacher expectations were identified as environmental factors that influence individual growth. A set of recommendations for the facilitation of the development of cognition and suggestions for enriching the learning of gifted students followed.

Conflict between the majority culture and other, diverse cultures may impede learning. Social class, race, and ethnicity all impact achievement. Social class is defined by income and parent's educational level and is a significant factor. Racial discrimination, unfavorable ethnic influences, and type of minority status were described as contributing to achievement deficits. Implications for educational and community adaptations were discussed in terms of remedial programs and utilization of students' values and beliefs.

Differences in performance attributable to gender were examined in terms of the effect of sex role stereotypes. Strategies designed to reduce gender bias, such as selection of balanced curricular materials, promotion of equal opportunities in the classroom, and use of activities designed to foster achievement for both sexes were discussed. Learning styles—differences in beliefs, preferences, and behaviors that individuals employ to aid their learning—were reviewed. Field differentiation, conceptual tempo, thinking style, preferences for environmental stimuli, and modalities are related topics. Whether learning style differences can be reliably assessed and accommodated was discussed.

A concept map for this chapter appears on page 101.

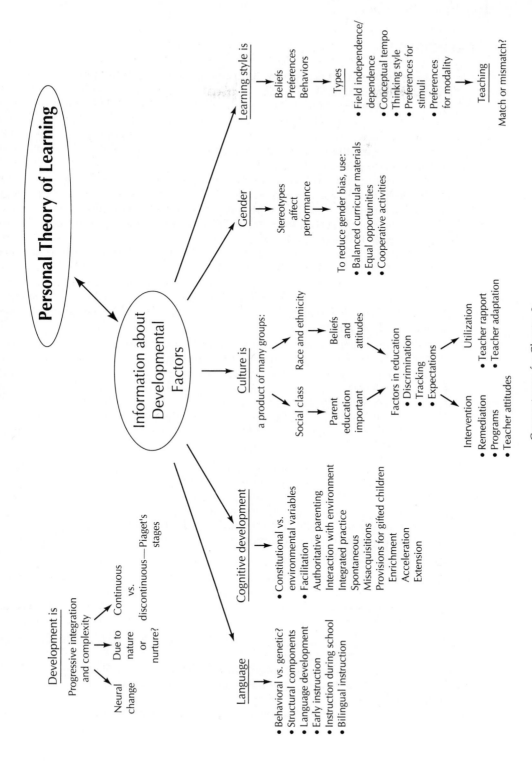

Personal Theory of Learning

Information about Developmental Factors

Development is

Progressive integration and complexity

Neural change

Due to nature or nurture?

Continuous vs. discontinuous—Piaget's stages

Language

- Behavioral vs. genetic?
- Structural components
- Language development
- Early instruction
- Instruction during school
- Bilingual instruction

Cognitive development

- Constitutional vs. environmental variables
- Facilitation
  Authoritative parenting
  Interaction with environment
  Integrated practice
  Spontaneous
  Misacquisitions
  Provisions for gifted children
  Enrichment
  Acceleration
  Extension

Culture is

a product of many groups:

Social class

Race and ethnicity

Parent education important

Beliefs and attitudes

Factors in education
- Discrimination
- Tracking
- Expectations

Intervention
- Remediation
- Programs
- Teacher attitudes

Utilization
- Teacher rapport
- Teacher adaptation

Gender

Stereotypes affect performance

To reduce gender bias, use:
- Balanced curricular materials
- Equal opportunities
- Cooperative activities

Learning style is

Beliefs
Preferences
Behaviors

Types
- Field independence/ dependence
- Conceptual tempo
- Thinking style
- Preferences for stimuli
- Preferences for modality

Teaching

Match or mismatch?

Concept map for Chapter 3

101

EXERCISES

1. Observe and record speech samples obtained from preschool children. Any of the basic dimensions of language—phonology, semantics, syntax, or pragmatics—could serve as a focus. You might record grammatical mistakes involving plurals or tense endings, use of dialects or slang terms, or the occurrence of particular vocabulary words. If possible, interview children at different ages to obtain a developmental sample and record samples from children from different linguistic backgrounds for comparison.

   When conducting language assessment of this type, it is best to prepare a standard list of sentences, phrases, or words to serve as stimuli for children's responses. You might want to use pictures with preschool children. For example, the following items (taken from Berko, 1958) can elicit an appropriate response without tipping off the best answer.

   "In another country, this thing is called a wug: O[]O. Here are two of them: O[]O O[]O. What would they be called?"

   The response of /wugz/ will be elicited if the child has learned the appropriate rule for producing a plural for words ending in /g/. Be imaginative in developing such test items, and make sure they are designed to elicit linguistic responses as objectively as possible.

2. Consider the cognitive stimulation you receive from your environment in terms of the kinds of factors listed on page 83. You might construct a recording sheet to facilitate your evaluation, with space for rating from 1 (excellent) to 5 (poor). Include in your evaluation each of the subcategories under Home environment, Parental interaction, and Family structure. Where do particularly high or low ratings occur? Then select a child, student, or other person you know well. Can you conduct a similar rating of this individual's educational environment? What factors are difficult to identify and assess?

3. Have you ever been treated differently because of gender, social class, or racial or ethnic differences? Be sure to think of instances of differential treatment that were to your advantage as well as to your disadvantage, and consider social as well as academic situations. Can you recall how you felt as a result and what the outcome was? How should the individual(s) who treated you differently have behaved to avoid the biased interaction? Have you responded to others in a way that reflects biases on your part?

SUGGESTED READINGS

Bailey, S. M. (1993). The current status of gender equity research in American schools. *Educational Psychologist, 28*(4), 321–339.

Chomsky, N. (1972). *Language and mind.* New York: Harcourt Brace, Jovanovich.

Garcia, R. L. (1991). *Teaching in a pluralistic society: Concepts, models and strategies.* New York: HarperCollins.

Gardner, H., & Hatch, T. (1989). Multiple intelligences go to school. *Educational researcher, 18*(8), 4–10.

Ogbu, J. U. (1992). Understanding cultural diversity and learning. *Educational Researcher, 21* (8), 5–14.

Piaget, J. (1963). *Origins of intelligence in children.* New York: Norton.

Pollard, D. S. (1993). Gender achievement and African-American students' perceptions of their school experience. *Educational Psychologist, 28*(4), 341–356.

Siegler, R. S. (1991). *Children's thinking* (2nd ed.). Englewood Cliffs, NJ: Prentice-Hall.

Witkin, H., Moore, C., Goodenough, D., & Cox, P. (1977). Field-dependent and field-independent cognitive styles and their educational implications. *Review of Educational Research, 47,* 1–64.

part II

Learning Theories

chapter **4**

Behavioral Approach
to Education

CHAPTER OUTLINE

CHAPTER OBJECTIVES

1. Explain the basic concepts and processes of operant conditioning, including positive and negative reinforcement, punishment, extinction, schedules of reinforcement, and shaping.
2. Summarize the operant principles that apply to classroom management.
3. Describe how you would use operant techniques such as contingency contracting, token economies, behavior reports, assertive discipline, and classwide peer tutoring.
4. Explain the four essential components of instructional design: defining the terminal behavior, priming, prompting, and programming.
5. Describe how you might apply CAI to your teaching.
6. Discuss the use and value of new technologies such as interactive video and hypermedia.
7. Describe the five factors that influence how CAI is employed in the classroom.
8. State the major criticisms of operant conditioning and discuss how they might be resolved.
9. Explain how operant principles can be utilized in teaching.

During World War II, the Soviet army trained dogs to search for food under tanks by keeping the animals hungry and allowing them to find food, upon release from their cages, only near the treads of old, obsolete vehicles. After training, dogs were fitted with small bombs, designed to explode on impact. The plan was to release the dogs at the front lines when attacking German tanks were near. It was expected that the canine suicide squad, seeking food, would run under the panzer units, make contact, and detonate the bombs attached to their backs, with predictable consequences.

Fortunately for the dogs, the plan went awry and was soon abandoned. When released, the dogs ran immediately to the first objects they recognized as potentially marking a food supply. The objects, however, were the latest model Soviet tanks, which resembled those that had been used in training.

After a Psychology 100 lecture on operant conditioning, several students designed a plan to have some fun in class. The instructor had lectured about how smiles, attentive nods, and facial expressions of interest could serve as positive reinforcers of desired behavior. The students agreed to divide into two groups: Those seated on the instructor's left in the lecture room would smile, nod, and look extremely interested, while those seated on his right would frown, look bored, and express obvious lack of interest in the presentation. Two students seated in the middle were assigned to keep records of exactly where the instructor stood while lecturing. Rather than remaining behind a podium, this particular professor was known to roam around in front of the class.

After two weeks of classes, the group reconvened and received the recorders' report. On the first day, the instructor stood on the right and left sides of the room in a seemingly random fashion, approximately 50 percent of the time in each section. By the end of the first week, he spent approximately 60 percent of the time on the left side. At the end of the second week, he was moving to the left side of the room almost 75 percent of the time. The results of the experiment were gleefully reported to the instructor, who said he had sensed that "something was going on." Not surprisingly, in subsequent classes the instructor was particularly sensitive about where he stood to lecture.

Ann spent very little time interacting with other children at nursery school. Typically, she played alone in a quiet area of the classroom or play yard, or interacted only with the teachers. Her isolated play usually attracted the attention of a teacher, whereas social play with other children did not.

It was decided to increase Ann's rate of playing with other children. A plan was initiated in which the teacher was to provide attention if Ann approached other children but to ignore the child if she engaged in isolated play. First, attention was given when Ann merely stood by watching other children, then when she played beside another child, and finally when she interacted in play with the other children. The teachers used two techniques to "provide attention." First, a teacher commented to the other child or children, including Ann as a participant in the play project—for example, "That is a big building you three are making. Bill, Ted, and Ann are all working hard." The second technique entailed keeping accessory materials on hand so that a teacher could bring a relevant item for Ann to add to the play: "Here's another plate for your tea party, Ann."

This approach produced the desired result. Isolated play declined markedly, while social play increased considerably. As a check on the procedure, conditions were reversed after a week. The teacher no longer attended to Ann's interactions with other children, but instead gave attention to her

when she was alone. Within a week isolated play became dominant. The for-
mer contingencies were then reinstated—that is, attention was directed to
social interaction and isolated play was ignored. Again, isolated play de-
clined sharply and social play increased. Only about 15 percent of Ann's play
time was spent in social play as long as the teacher attended primarily to her
isolated play. Interacting behaviors rose to 60 percent of total play time when
the teacher attended only to social play. Subsequently, adult attention was
gradually reduced to the usual amount. Ann's social behavior maintained its
frequency, evidently becoming self-determined. Four checks were made at
later dates to see whether the reinforced pattern of social behavior persisted.
The change appeared to be durable (Allen, Hart, Buell, Harris, & Wolf, 1964).

The foregoing anecdotes have much in common. They are examples of the application of behavioral principles to specific types of behavior. As with other psychological approaches, behavioral procedures rely on certain assumptions or ways of con-
ceptualizing the nature of learning and instruction. They have also been established
on the basis of considerable amounts of research data collected in laboratories, classrooms, and other field settings. Ann's case, for example, is illustrative of many similar
training episodes.

This chapter examines how behavioral principles are utilized in a wide variety of
learning situations. As you will recognize, behavioral ideas and assumptions underlie
much of our educational system as well as other aspects of our society. In our discussion, we shall identify the issues accompanying this approach, as well as the limitations of its application. By the close of the chapter, it is hoped that the reader will
have gained an understanding of the behavioral approach and how it can be wisely
applied to educational problems.

OPERANT LEARNING

Many of the basic principles of behavioral psychology were established through the
early work of theorists such as Pavlov, Watson, Guthrie, Hull, and Thorndike. Some of
these principles were discussed in Chapter 1. Behaviorists believed that psychologists
should study behavior that could be observed directly, avoiding analysis of subjective
interpretations of mental processes. Learning consists of new stimulus–response connections, gradually acquired through practice and strengthened through associations
with external rewards. Some learning occurs through classical conditioning, as in the
case of little Albert (Watson & Rayner, 1920), mentioned in Chapter 1. Albert was an
infant who would spontaneously reach for a tame white rat. When Albert reached for
the rat, the experimenter (J. B. Watson) produced a startle reflex in the baby by hit-
ting an iron rail with a hammer. After six trials of presenting the rat and then the
noise, Albert began to cry and to show avoidance behavior at the mere presence of
the rat. This effect generalized to dogs and white rabbits (and, a humorist once said,
an older Albert even shook with fear when passing a Playboy Club).

Behaviorism received a major transformation, however, when Burrhus Frederick

Skinner (1904–1990) began to expound his version of it. Skinner departed from the behavioral theories of his time in several ways:

1. There are two kinds of behavior: *respondent* (as in classical conditioning) and *operant.* Skinner agreed with Watson that reflexes, and conditioned emotional reactions, as in little Albert's learning of fear, can be adequately characterized as respondent reactions. These are acquired through the substitution of one unconditioned stimulus for another. Thus Skinner used the label *type S* to represent the substitution component of respondent learning. Few human behaviors are acquired in this way, however, according to Skinner. Most behaviors, such as talking or singing, act on the environment to produce consequences. Skinner defined these behaviors, which he designated as *type R,* to emphasize the response component, as operant. That is, they "operate on" the environment to produce an effect.

   Operant behavior affects the environment

2. A scientific explanation of behavior must determine the functional relationships between behavior and physical events in the environment. Environmental events or conditions should be thought of as independent variables and behavior as a dependent variable. It is not necessary to construct theories to determine these relationships. In fact, a preexisting theory may tempt the scientist to assign functions that have not been directly observed, thus perhaps obscuring lawful relationships that have yet to be discovered (Skinner, 1950).

3. A functional analysis of behavior does not need to resort to explanations relying on neurological functioning or on constructs such as abilities or drives. Hull (1943), for example, had theorized that the energizing source of behavior consisted of "drives," the reduction of which served as a goal or motive to behave in a certain way. In a few famous lines, Skinner (1953, p. 31) expressed his disbelief in the explanatory value of drives:

   A single set of facts is described by the two statements: "He plays well" and "He has musical ability." The practice of explaining one statement in terms of the other is dangerous because it suggests that we have found the cause and need search no further.

   In other words, we do not need constructs such as "ability" or "motivation" to understand behavior. Skinner also rejected the notion of mediating events to mental processes or thoughts. While he did not deny their existence, he said that "the private world within the skin is not clearly observed or known" (1953, p. 31). He believed it was better to examine overt responses than to rely on private events to establish a functional analysis of behavior.

   Internal events not necessary

4. Type R learning is defined not by the magnitude of the response, but in terms of its probability. Skinner suggested that it should be measured by its frequency of occurrence, or *response rate.* Response rate is preferable to other learning measures because it can be clearly specified, because it

Learning = change in response rate

provides a continuous record of behavioral change that is free of arbitrary and subjective criteria, and because it can be applied to a wide variety of behaviors. Of the following statements about student's learning—"The student types 35 correct words per minute" and "The student has demonstrated marked improvement"—Skinner preferred the former type.

Basic Processes in Operant Learning

Reinforcement. In analyzing the concept of reinforcement, Skinner began with Thorndike's law of effect, which links the individual's behavior to its subsequent effects. Terms such as "satisfaction," "reward," and "stamped in," however, were viewed as nonbehavioral because they imply some kind of internal reaction. Skinner instead chose to emphasize the consequences that could be linked to the occurrence of a response. When a consequence serves to increase the probability of the recurrence of a response, it is said to act as a *reinforcer,* and the act of producing that consequence is called *reinforcement.* Increases in the recurrence of a response constituted learning for Skinner; he referred to the training that must precede such changes in behavior as *operant conditioning.* Operant responses are considered to be spontaneously *emitted* by the individual, unlike responses in classical conditioning, which are said to be *elicited* by conditioned stimuli. The original stimulus that gave rise to the emitted response is simply not observable or cannot be known, according to Skinner.

Let us consider this last idea in a specific context. When discussing a child's learning with a group of educators, have you ever head the remark "Of course William can't learn—look at his home life." Perhaps someone in the teacher's lounge had said that William was "emotionally disturbed" or "retarded" and that typical learning should not be expected. The assumption inherent in these statements is that some unspecified set of previously experienced stimuli affects the child's present behavior in such a way that learning is not possible or will be limited. Skinner would have vigorously disputed that assumption. Since behavior is determined by reinforcing consequences occurring *after* a response, the issue of presumed stimulation occurring at some time in the past is irrelevant.

Sd is a signal

This is not to say, however, that operant responses cannot become related to a particular stimuli in the future. A response may even become partially controlled by a stimulus, in which case it is called a *discriminative stimulus (Sd).* A discriminative stimulus is any stimulus that was consistently present when a particular response was reinforced. It serves to signal the individual that reinforcement for the emission of a specific operant is forthcoming. In our earlier example of dogs trained to carry bombs under German tanks, the tanks of the Soviet army served as Sds. Traffic lights, cursors on computers, and verbal statements such as "Get ready for a test" or "The sugar, please" are examples of familiar discriminative stimuli. In Skinner's view, they have acquired behavioral control because they just happened to be present when reinforcement for responses occurred. Skinner points out that people can often construct their own Sds, as in the case of making resolutions or developing plans (Skinner, 1963). By making our plans visible, as we do when we write little memos to ourselves, these self-generated stimuli can effectively serve as reminders of behaviors to perform.

Types of Reinforcement.   *Primary reinforcers* increase response rates because of their inherent value. Food is an example of a primary reinforcer because it does not have to be taught; any learner will increase responses to obtain it. *Secondary, or conditioned, reinforcers,* on the other hand, do require instruction, usually through being paired with primary reinforcers, before they can be used to increase response rate. Pictures of enticing foods, for example, can acquire reinforcing value of their own by being associated with the food. Secondary reinforcers possess symbolic rather than intrinsic value, as in the case of coupons or tokens that can be accumulated for conversion into more primary reinforcement. Money is another example of a conditioned reinforcer, but it has been paired with so many primary reinforcers that it has become a *generalized reinforcer*—a special case. Approval, attention, recognition, and smiles are other examples of generalized reinforcers that exist in social situations (Skinner, 1953). Originally, conditioned reinforcers like money, which have little tangible value themselves, increase behavior because they represent primary reinforcers. Only Scrooge McDuck, who in the Walt Disney cartoons bathes and plays with cash in his money bins, treats money as a primary reinforcer! With time, however, generalized reinforcers become effective even though the primary reinforcement on which they are based no longer is present. As Skinner (1953, p. 81) said: "We play games of skill for their own sake. We get attention or approval for its own sake. . . . A miser may be so reinforced by money that he will starve rather than give it up."

Another example of a generalized reinforcer?

Reinforcers can also be positive or negative. Skinner called reinforcers that increase behavior subsequent to their presentation *positive;* those that increase behavior when they are removed were defined as *negative.* Money, praise, smiles, toys, pats on the back, grades of A, prizes, candy, and extra recess time are all positive reinforcers. When parental nagging, class tests, an uncomfortable chair, extreme cold, or a tedious homework assignment serve to *increase* behavior if taken away, they are said to exemplify negative reinforcement. For example, if students increased the time they spent working on daily assignments so that they completed all the questions in a workbook and the teacher subsequently canceled a scheduled test, the reprieve from the exam would be called negative reinforcement. Adolescents who quickly clean their rooms to avoid parental criticism are demonstrating the effect of negative reinforcement by increasing a particular behavior in order to remove the occurrence of the criticism. Skinner (1953) called criticism or nagging, class tests, and comparable unwanted events *aversive stimuli.*

Negative reinforcement is not punishment

The concept of negative reinforcement is probably the most misunderstood of Skinner's terms, perhaps because it appears to combine two terms that are generally considered antithetical. Negative reinforcement is often confused with punishment, and it occasionally appears in popular jargon as equivalent to that term. In fact, *punishment* is quite distinct from positive or negative reinforcement in the phraseology of operant conditioning. "Punishment" entails *decreasing* the probability of an event's occurrence. Punishment can occur in two ways: (1) by presenting aversive stimuli (physical contact, such as spanking a child; criticism; loud noises; long periods of confinement to one's room, etc.) and (2) by taking away positive reinforcers.

Figure 4.1 summarizes the pairings of these different types of consequences. In analyzing this diagram, which is called a truth table, the terms "reinforcer" and "aversive" are defined after the fact. In other words, we know that something is pleasant if, when it is presented, there is an increase in behavior. Likewise, something is aversive

Stimuli

	Reinforcer	Aversive
Present	Positive reinforcement	Punishment
Take away	Punishment	Negative reinforcement

FIGURE 4.1 Positive and negative reinforcement, and punishment

if, after its presentation, there is a decrease in behavior. Since behavior is influenced by its consequence, it is the consequence that gives a response its particular significance. Some events do not produce a consequence; that is, they do not change response rate. Therefore they are considered *neutral* stimuli in Skinner's terminology. We can know whether an event is nonneutral only by observing its effect on subsequent behavior. Skinner referred to this circumstance as the *empirical law of effect,* implying that the effect of a stimulus can be determined only by empirical verification.

Many have charged that this description is circular; that is, it suggests that a reinforcer is an event that affects behavior affected by reinforcers! We cannot define a reinforcer independently from the behavior it reinforces. Malone (1991), one of those who argued that the explanation is circular, nevertheless points out that the observation of the existence of relationships between classes of behavior and specific consequences is sufficient for our purposes.

Moreover, it is important to recognize that what serves as a reinforcer or aversive stimulus for one individual may not function in the same way for someone else. It may not be possible to classify a particular event as one or the other before observing its effect. This was brought home to the author several years ago when a teacher told the following story. In an attempt to control the misbehavior of a sixth-grader, the teacher, in frustration, often sent the boy to the principal's office. For most students, the threat and eventual act of being sent to the principal's office sufficed to decrease disruptive behavior. Not so for this lad, however. A trip to the office seemed to lead to a deterioration in behavior rather than an improvement. One day, the teacher followed the student to the office. It soon became apparent that the principal was not there, and the boy was free to sit in a comfortable chair and read car and sports magazines. When his detention time was up, he returned to class. In effect, being sent to the principal's office had functioned as a positive reinforcer (the student's disruptive behavior was increasing), not as a punishment designed to decrease behavior.

The moral of this story is that we cannot define an event as reinforcing or punishing until its effect has been observed and any change in behavior recorded. In fact, an important function of teachers is to continually observe and record behavioral changes so that alterations in the provision of reinforcers can be arranged (Skinner, 1953).

Punishment and Extinction.   Although by definition punishment reduces undesirable responses, Skinner did not advocate its use to control behavior. In the Middle Ages, it was popular to cut off the hands of people caught picking pockets. Did this

Usefulness of reinforcement determined by its effect

punishment decrease pickpocketing? Obviously—just as capital punishment puts a stop to the criminal activity of those so disciplined. The problem is that undesirable side effects accompany punishment. Here we mention several that were identified by Skinner (1953).

1. Punishment reduces the occurrence of behavior but does not eliminate it. Punished responses may cease temporarily, only to recur in a different setting or at a different time. Many teachers have noted students who, despite having been punished for inappropriate activities in mathematics class, resume them later in the day, in language class.
2. Punishment produces emotional predispositions such as guilt, which are conditioned to the setting in which the punishment occurs. On subsequent occasions, the individual feels guilty in that particular place.
3. Any behavior that reduces or allows avoidance of punishment will be reinforced. Lying, for example, is likely to increase when it makes possible the avoidance of punishment.
4. Punishment does not illustrate the desired behavior; it just draws attention to the undesirable response. The emphasis is on what the individual did wrong, rather than what should be done that is correct.

Other disadvantages of punishment exist as well. Not only is guilt a likely emotional reaction, but feelings of anxiety and hostility may also be elicited by punishment. The author remembers a student colleague in a particularly difficult graduate course. This young man shook with fear when entering the classroom, for the instructor was known to humiliate and threaten with promises of failure and disgrace students who did not measure up to his standards. My fellow student had been treated in such a manner on many occasions. He eventually took revenge by surreptitiously letting air out of the tires of the instructor's car.

Punishment clearly jeopardizes the relationship between student and teacher or parent and child. Whatever feelings of trust and affection may have been established can be eradicated through punishment that is perceived as unfair and too severe. In addition, research demonstrates that those who are punished tend to use punishment in their treatment of others. Child abusers, for example, consistently report having been abused by their own parents (Conger, Burgess, & Barrett, 1979). For all these reasons, it appears that an emphasis on positive reinforcement for appropriate behavior is a more desirable form of behavioral control than punishment of inappropriate responses.

Negative effects of punishment

Elimination of reinforcement will also decrease behavior and can act as an alternative to punishment. When reinforcement is withdrawn completely, the resulting diminution of a behavior is called *extinction* (Skinner, 1963). Clearly, much of what we did as children has been extinguished because reinforcement for childlike or immature behaviors was long ago removed.

Extinction can be expedited by firmly and consistently refusing to reinforce behaviors that are deemed inappropriate, a procedure Kounin (1970) referred to as *planned ignoring*. A teacher once used a form of planned ignoring to extinguish crying in a first-grader. This six-year-old would cry at any pretext and had learned to use tears to control others, including her parents. She had found that most adults bestowed considerable attention on crying children. Many adults were initially taken in but soon realized that the little girl would cry at the slightest provocation, usually to gain attention or to get out of completing a distasteful task. The problem was resolved by the teacher's announcement to the entire class that the plants along the window-sills were not getting enough water. If anyone felt like crying, he or she should go and cry over the plants, because in that way the water from the tears would be put to good use. There was no need to inform the teacher.

Ignoring can lead to extinction

When the student next chose to cry, the teacher did not respond, other than to point to the plants. Other episodes of crying were met in the same way. Needless to say, the girl's parents telephoned promptly to complain that the teacher had been "mean" to their daughter. After a discussion of the approach, however, the parents realized that the procedure was aimed at extinguishing an inappropriate behavior. With their support, planned ignoring continued, and the crying ceased in a number of days.

Skinner recommended the pairing of extinction by withholding reinforcement for undesirable behavior with positive reinforcement of desired behavior that might take its place. The idea here is to establish a situation eliciting *incompatible responses*. Since it is not possible to do two things at once, the reinforced behavior will eventually take precedence. In this way, the student will learn to behave more adaptively. The teacher provided praise, smiles, and physical comfort for desirable behavior worthy of attention at the same time that she was ignoring crying. The child soon learned that the best way to get attention was to engage in behaviors that would be positively reinforced, not only by her parents and teacher, but by peers as well. Obviously, not all attention-getting behaviors can be ignored as a way of withholding reinforcement. A habit of hurling objects at others, for example, must be extinguished in a different manner.

Schedules of Reinforcement.

Our discussion so far has dealt with consequences or contingencies as all-or-none events. That is, behavior either was followed by a reinforcer or it was not. In the real world, however, reinforcement is a sometime thing, particularly social reinforcement. The physical world is much more likely to provide *continuous reinforcement*—that is, an environment in which every response is reinforced. If we turn on a light switch, unlock a door, blow into a trumpet, or pedal a bicycle, reinforcement will occur each time. In fact, when reinforcement for such actions is not forthcoming, we are inclined to find the situation strange, disturbing, or even humorous. How would you feel if your water faucet failed to deliver when you turned it on in the morning?

Intermittent reinforcement maintains behavior

Social reinforcement, on the other hand, seldom is provided continuously. Our loved one does not always say "I love you," friends don't always smile, and teachers unfortunately cannot praise or recognize every good response in the classroom. Reinforcement that occurs sporadically is referred to as *intermittent*. Of course, if reinforcement is sporadic to the point of almost never occurring, the related behavior will eventually be extinguished. If the loved one never says the three little words, the friend never smiles, and the teacher never recognizes a particular student, the person so treated is very likely to stop responding as he or she had done in the past.

One finding in psychology that some might consider as counter to common sense, however, is the discovery that when reinforcement is discontinued, responding continues for a longer time if reinforcement had been provided intermittently rather than continuously. Humphreys (1939) demonstrated that the extinction process was more rapid for college students following 100 percent reinforcement than for students who had been reinforced only 50 percent of the time. Intermittent reinforcement thus results in greater *resistance to extinction* or less chance that a behavior will be extinguished. This so-called *partial reinforcement effect* can be observed in situations such as playing video games, gambling on the lottery, going hunting or fishing, and playing golf. In all those situations, infrequent success suffices to maintain the behavior for long periods of time. The author played golf for many years, with limited success—a few 250-yard drives, one or two 20-foot putts that fell in, and an occasional chip shot that rolled up to the cup. Ignored were the many hooked drives, 5-foot putts that were missed, and chip shots that rolled over the green into the sand trap on the other side. While we will maintain behavior for surprisingly long periods of time under conditions of partial reinforcement, however, there is a limit: When in three golfing outings there were no 250-yard drives, 20-foot putts, or successful chip shots, the golf clubs were violently thrown in the lake and golfing was extinguished.

Skinner carefully studied partial reinforcement effects for a number of years, identifying what he referred to as *schedules of reinforcement,* each capable of differentially affecting behavior (Ferster & Skinner, 1957). He described five useful schedules: continuous, fixed interval, fixed ratio, variable interval, and variable ratio.

Continuous.   Every correct response is reinforced. A continuous schedule is particularly effective in the early stages of training when you want the learner to experience success and recognize that learning is possible. While rapid acquisition occurs under continuous reinforcement, *satiation* is also more rapid. That is, learners are more likely to stop responding when they have received so many reinforcers that interest in the activity is lost. Even the most avidly candy-loving child will cease to be interested in candy after receiving it as a Halloween treat at 100 successive houses.

Schedules
imply planning
of reinforcement

Fixed Interval.   In a fixed-interval schedule, a set period of time must pass before reinforcement occurs. For example, one might decide to provide reinforcement only after a child has remained seated for the fixed interval of minutes. The author's first job was selling baseball scorecards and peanuts in Ebbetts Field in Brooklyn, New York. At the end of each game, the amount of sales was computed, and commissions were doled out. Although in some cases there were few dollars earned, the reinforcement received was enough to ensure my return the next day. Most of us are now on fixed salary intervals, such as every other week or every month. One frequent effect of the fixed-interval type of schedule is a decline in appropriate responding right after reinforcement has been earned. If you have ever met a particularly demanding deadline and then had to return to work the next day, you may be able to appreciate this effect.

Fixed Ratio.   A fixed-ratio schedule is based on a constant number of discrete responses made, not on the time spent responding. If Esther is reinforced every time she completes five math problems successfully, she is being exposed to a fixed-ratio schedule. After the final correct response has been made, it is common to observe a decrease in response rate, as in the case of the fixed-interval schedule. Skinner makes special use of the fixed-ratio schedule in explaining complex behavior. He argues that each of the responses leading to the final one that is reinforced becomes a discriminative stimulus for the next response. Those further from the eventual reinforcement are successively weaker, but they are bound together in that each leads to the next and thus takes the individual one step closer to reinforcement. Skinner referred to this linkage as a *response chain.* Complex sequences of behavior can be trained by beginning with the response leading directly to primary reinforcement and adding new behavioral "links" to the chain (Hilgard & Bower, 1975). We shall examine the application of this approach to instruction in a later section.

Variable Interval.   In a fourth type of schedule, time intervals of variable duration are permitted to elapse before reinforcement is forthcoming. Perhaps reinforcement occurs after 15 minutes of one activity, 30 minutes of another activity, and 20 minutes of another. A steady, moderately high response rate is produced under this schedule, and resistance to extinction is high. Without knowing when reinforcement will occur, the learner keeps on responding for fear of missing out. In trying to reach by telephone someone who is rarely at home, for example, you are likely to maintain the behavior (i.e., redialing) off and on for a long period of time because you realize that success in reaching the party is unlikely but may occur at any time.

Variable Ratio.   In the last type of schedule we consider, the ratio of number of responses to reinforcements is varied. The individual may receive two reinforcements in a row or may have to make 10 or 20 responses in a row before receiving any reinforcement. Variable-ratio schedules produce the highest rates of any of the schedules. Have you ever watched habitual slot machine players in a gambling hall? Since payoff is variable, they know that the more times they pull the handle, the greater the chance of being rewarded. Consequently, they often sit at a favorite machine constantly feeding it coins, ignoring their occasional small winnings.

In the classroom, children should learn that some tasks are more time-consuming than others and may require more responses to complete them. Reinforcement for these tasks will come, but it will require patient, consistent patterns of responding. Proofs of theorems in geometry are good examples of tasks that require a variable number of responses for successful completion.

Superstitious Behaviors.   In addition to identifying the planned schedules just described, Skinner noted that reinforcers not presented contingent upon the occurrence of a particular response may still come to control behavior. This occurs when a reinforcement that follows a desired behavior purely by chance nevertheless becomes conditioned to it. Skinner referred to this sequence of events as *superstitious behavior* (1948) and observed that the random pairing of an event with subsequent reinforcement can form a very powerful type of variable-interval schedule. The baseball manager who never steps on the first base foul line when coming to take out a pitcher is demonstrating superstitious behavior. Perhaps on one occasion the manager happened to notice that he hadn't touched the line and the relief pitcher pitched extremely well. That dramatic coincidence may have created an indelible bond between line-missing and successful relief pitching. Many of our irrational behaviors are accounted for through the establishment of a superstitious schedule, according to Skinner. The author begins every automobile vacation by recording the mileage on a piece of paper, remembering a successful trip taken long ago that had begun with this act. Obviously, all the not-so-successful trips before which recording also occurred are forgotten or ignored.

Shaping.   If reinforcement acts to increase the probability of responses that have already occurred, how can an individual acquire totally novel behavior? Moreover, how do we learn complex behaviors and skills, which require organized sequences of responses? Skinner (1963) used the term *shaping* to explain these kinds of learning.

Shaping involves two components: *differential reinforcement,* in which some responses are reinforced and others are not, and *successive approximation,* in which only responses that become more and more similar to the *target behavior* are selected for reinforcement. Shaping of certain behaviors occurs as a natural consequence of interaction with the environment, as in Skinner's view of language acquisition. Other behaviors can be directly trained, by means of identifying and demonstrating the desired behavioral steps. In the earlier example of encouraging Ann to play with other children, in which the child was reinforced only for social interacting, the teachers followed a shaping procedure.

Shaping: behavior progresses toward goal

Suppose we wanted to teach a child to tie a shoe with the traditional bow knot, using praise as the positive reinforcement. Initially, the child would be praised for grasping the two ends of the shoestring and making an overhand loop, as demonstrated by the teacher. Then praise would be withheld until the loop had been tightened. The next step might entail forming the bows, and praise would again would be withheld until that behavioral step had been demonstrated. Finally, the child would have to complete all the steps in tying a shoe knot before reinforcement was provided.

Skinner (1963) believed that shaping allows the production of complex behaviors that were not likely to occur naturally in their final form. All that is needed is a *program,* which includes a planned series of responses that combine to form the terminal response, and reinforcers that can be supplied to establish each step in the chain. We shall encounter several examples of shaping in later sections of this chapter.

Operant conditioning has had profound effects on contemporary educational practice. The remainder of this chapter is devoted to three major applications: (1) individual and classroom applications, (2) task analysis and instructional design, and (3) educational technology.

INDIVIDUAL AND CLASSROOM APPLICATIONS

Although there is no one "right way" to utilize operant procedures to ameliorate individual or classroom problems of behavior, several guidelines and techniques have been extensively investigated and verified. The following general guidelines should be recalled when operant procedures are applied to the classroom.

1. *Emphasize positive reinforcement to increase the frequency of desired behavior.* Skinner suggested establishing environments in which people behave in personally and socially beneficial ways because they have been exposed to positive reinforcement. He believed that most social institutions, including those of education, tend to resort to aversive techniques such as threats, penalties, and reprimands to control those who fail to meet expected standards. The occurrence of positive reinforcement, however, should not be left to chance.

2. *Positive reinforcement must be provided in a planned, consistent, and systematic manner.* Teachers should avoid giving students inconsistent messages about a specific behavior. If going to the bathroom without verbal permission is allowed on Monday, but not on Tuesday, children will not be able to determine the consequences of their own actions. Desirable and undesirable behavior must be clearly indicated through a consistent set of rules and clearly stated consequences of their violation.

3. *Specify, praise, and ignore.* Becker, Engelmann, and Thomas (1971) suggest three steps as basic to operant procedures in the classroom: Specify the behavior you desire, praise children who demonstrate it, and ignore those who do not. Praise, which is a positive reinforcer for most children, should be directed toward the behavior, not the child. For example, the comment "That's a good answer. You listened very closely to my question" ties the desired behavior to its consequence. By focusing attention on appropriate responses, you will prompt the correct behavior from the students you are ignoring.

4. *When a desired terminal behavior is not currently attainable, reinforcing successive approximations to it will produce the desired result.* If Jack is out of his seat 90 percent of the time and completes only 10 percent of his work, a terminal goal may be for him to be seated 90 percent of the time and complete 90 percent of his work. To expect him to attain that criterion without intermediate goals is inviting failure. If past observation indicates that the student can remain seated 10 consecutive minutes, reinforcement should be provided after that initial length of time. When he is able to stay seated and can complete work for a longer period of time, the criterion for reinforcement should be expanded. With success at each interim level, the criterion should be expanded until the terminal objective is reached.

5. *Identify stimuli that may serve to control the occurrence of critical behaviors.* If Jane has formed a habit of behaving in a certain way whenever she is in the presence of a certain stimulus, that stimulus will elicit that behavior whenever it is present. Similarly, if Jane acts in a certain way only when in the presence of a particular stimulus, she will cease responding when the controlling stimulus is no longer present.

   Stimulus control procedures have been used to increase studying by having a person designate certain locations and times in and at which he will be sure to study; they have been used to reduce the frequency of undesirable behaviors such as smoking or overeating by changing the stimuli present when these behaviors occur (M. B. Harris, 1972). The author once rearranged furniture in his family room so he could not see the kitchen refrigerator during the evening when he was watching TV or reading. The refrigerator had served as a controlling stimulus by "speaking" to the author of its delectable contents. Removing it from sight resulted in a decrease of late night snacking for at least two weeks!

6. *To ensure that positive reinforcement can occur, vary the kinds of reinforcement available.* As we progress through life, the events and objects that influence our behavior change considerably. As children, we respond to pennies, but most adults will not stoop to pick up pennies lying in the street. To utilize the power of positive reinforcement, it is necessary to have available a number of different reinforcers to be employed when others lose their reinforcing value.

   Becker et al. (1971) identified three kinds of conditioned reinforcer that can be used in classroom settings: *social, token,* and *activity reinforcers.* Social reinforcers include praise, attention, smiling, being near, touching, and gentle verbal expressions provided by teachers and others. Token reinforcers consist of symbols or markers such as points, gold stars, stamps, or chips that have been made valuable by being paired with other reinforcers. Activity reinforcers are preferred behaviors the child enjoys, such as drawing, listening to music, shooting free throws, or going to recess. Effective classroom management makes use of all three kinds of reinforcer.

7. *Proceed from a continuous to an intermittent reinforcement schedule.* When a behavior identified as valuable to the individual or group has been isolated, it should be reinforced initially at a 100 percent rate to establish its importance and to encourage high rates of responding. As the behavior becomes more frequent, teachers can change to a ratio or interval schedule with little resistance by the target group or individual. If schedules of reinforcement do not sustain high rates of responding, they can always be adjusted toward lower ratios or intervals per reinforcement.

8. *When used appropriately, punishment can have immediate effects.* Punishment can be used as an agent of behavior change, *if* positive reinforcement has not worked and the side effects accompanying its use would not outweigh the anticipated benefit. Givner and Graubard (1974) provide the following guidelines for the appropriate use of punishment in educational settings: It should be reserved for severe disturbances that are resistant to change from extinction procedures; it should be administered consistently and immediately contingent on the target behavior, to ensure that the child is aware of the cause of the punishment; it should be administered in a matter-of-fact manner without any undue demonstration of emotion (in the presence of negative affect, such as rage or hysteria, the punishment will be seen as a personal reaction of the teacher, rather than a direct and automatic consequence of the inappropriate behavior). Finally, reprimands should be delivered softly and privately, to allow the child to save face and to short-circuit any emotional reaction that might occur after a public reprimand; an alternative to punishment referred to as *time out* should be considered initially, to refocus concern on the

production of appropriate behavior, rather than what was wrong. Time out is a period of time during which a student is not able to earn reinforcement, often through being isolated from the rest of the class for a specified period. He or she is allowed to return to the class only after having met a stated criterion of appropriate behavior. Time out is most effective when the reasons for its administration are known by all students well in advance and the punishment is automatically invoked for all whenever merited.

CLASSROOM MANAGEMENT TECHNIQUES

Now we review the techniques that have been evaluated and found to be effective in managing classrooms from an operant point of view. In general, they incorporate the guidelines just discussed.

Contingency Contracts

Contingency contracts are designed to rearrange the reinforcement contingencies in the environment to modify a particular behavior. Often this technique is directed at behaviors that are reinforcing only in the long term, such as cessation of smoking to extend one's life. In the short run, the presumed pleasure derived from nicotine is more rewarding than the delayed reinforcement of a longer life. Immediate reinforcers for not smoking are needed to maintain the decrease in behavior until long-term effects are more obvious. The contractual component stems from the agreement that is made (often in the form of a signed and witnessed document) that certain actions that might not ordinarily be reinforced will indeed elicit reinforcement as long as the learner keeps his end of the bargain by increasing appropriate responses (Homme, Csanyi, Gonzales, & Rechs, 1970).

Contracts can be simple, covering short-term outcomes such as completing class or homework assignments; or longer periods of time can be specified. In this approach, students and teachers can jointly decide what type of reinforcer will be forthcoming for what specific behaviors. College courses have been conducted in this way, with grades as reinforcers. One graduate student, unable to sustain the effort needed to complete his doctoral dissertation, gave $100 to his adviser, to be returned in amounts of $20 for each chapter completed by a certain date. If a deadline was not met, the $20 would go to a charity. Although the first $20 was forfeited, the experience of having to part with cash prompted the student to complete the remaining chapters on time.

Contingency contracts are often written in "if-then" form, as in "If I clean my room every day, then I will get to use the car on Friday night." They may reflect continuous reinforcement provided immediately after the behavior or intermittent schedules: "If I turn in three straight homework assignments on time, I can turn in one late." They are applicable to groups as well as to individuals, particularly when disruptive behavior has been reinforced by peer recognition. Class parties that are contingent on appropriate behavior by all class members for an established time is an example. Bushell, Wrobel, and Michaelis (1968) used special events such as trips to a park, short movies, or art projects as reinforcers for active study during a Spanish lesson. Results demonstrated that studying was contingent on having a special event be contingent on it.

Premack Principle

The search for reinforcers is a continuous one. The approach to their identification through the Premack principle, named for David Premack (1959), is also referred to whimsically as "Grandma's rule" (Becker et al., 1971). Premack suggested that any response that occurs with a fairly high frequency can be used to reinforce a response that occurs at a lower frequency. In other words, preferred activities will reinforce less preferred activities. For the child who prefers listening to music to reading, time spent listening to music may be made available contingent on increased time spent reading. "Grandma" employed this principle more informally when she said, "First you work, then you play," or "You do what I want you to do, before you get to do what you want to do" (Becker et al. 1971, p. 28). To enact the Premack principle, one simply determines high-frequency behaviors by observing and recording what children do.

High-frequency behavior as reinforcement

Premack demonstrated the validity of his principle when he observed 31 first-graders who were free to play a pinball machine or operate a candy dispenser as frequently as they wanted. The children who spent most of their time playing the machine were called "manipulators," while those who preferred the candy dispenser were called "eaters." These two groups were further subdivided according to whether manipulating or eating was contingent on the other behavior. In both cases, children were perfectly content in the condition in which they were expected to do their preferred activity to receive the less-preferred activity as a reinforcer. They simply continued high rates of playing pinball or eating candy. Those who had to perform the less-preferred activity to obtain time spent in the preferred activity, however, dramatically increased their rate of producing the less-preferred response. Eaters increased their pinball playing significantly to get at the candy, and manipulators increased the rate at which they operated the candy dispenser to have an opportunity to play pinball.

The Premack principle demonstrates that what acts as a reinforcer becomes a very individual matter, and continuous change can be expected. Moreover, this principle offers a useful method of determining potential reinforcers, a task that is often difficult at the secondary level in particular.

Token Economies

A token economy system involves the entire classroom: All students, in exchange for emitting specific behaviors, earn tokens or points, which can be exchanged later for more tangible reinforcers (called *backups*) (Birnbauer, Wolf, Kidder, & Tague, 1965). Tokens are used because they can be manipulated quite easily, can be accumulated, and can be provided in any setting. Moreover, they can represent a direct relationship between the amount of effort or performance and the amount of reinforcement. For example, one token can represent one math problem completed, or two or five, and so on. Since tokens can be exchanged for backup reinforcers, individual preferences of children for a variety of activities may be expressed, thus ensuring that the system is truly reinforcing for each student.

To use a token system successfully, a teacher must identify the behaviors to be changed, to be sure that they are measurable and that both students and teacher know when changes have occurred and reinforcement is due. The ability to apply tokens at the appropriate time, the ability to identify reinforcers that will increase behavior, and the ability to adapt the technique to curricular sequences are all necessary components of token economies (Givner & Graubard, 1974). Tokens should be utilized in conjunction with social reinforcers so that performance of the desired behavior becomes linked to forms of reinforcement other than the token itself. Disadvantages of a token economy are the expense, time constraints, and complexity of keeping track of all contingencies (Kuypers, Becker, & O'Leary, 1968).

Daily Behavior Reports

The system of daily behavior reports has the advantage of involving the home in the reinforcement system. Based on a daily report sent to parents, reinforcement is administered at home, typically because the reinforcer is most available in that setting. Daily behavior reports both make students aware that parents are keeping track of their daily work and help parents find out about their child's school performance. The report should be related to specific behaviors in keeping with a behavioral system—for example, "Clara solved five of ten problems in math seatwork" or "Bill remained in his seat for the entire geography lesson of 25 minutes' duration." Special check sheets can be devised, to be signed by parents and returned by students for in-class reinforcement on the following day.

Assertive Discipline

The assertive discipline approach incorporates positive reinforcement techniques with the view that teachers should exert control over their classrooms through the use of punishment for inappropriate behavior. There appear to be certain basic premises followed by practitioners of this technique, initially described by Canter and Canter (1976).

1. Students will not stop teachers from teaching.
2. Students will not prevent other students from learning.
3. Students will not engage in behavior that is not in their best interests or the best interests of others.
4. Whenever a student chooses to behave appropriately, that behavior will be recognized and reinforced.
5. Students must receive negative consequences when they behave inappropriately.
6. Assertive teachers have the skill and confidence to take charge in their classroom.

7. Teachers must meet their needs, while in no way violating the best interests of students.

The program uses teacher-dispensed reinforcers as in token economy and contingency contract systems. Aversive stimuli such as placing misbehaving students' names on the board for a first offense, adding check marks for additional disturbances, and finally removing children from the classroom are also utilized. Loss of privileges and other consequences are also employed. Canter (1989) argues that rules, positive reinforcers, and disciplinary consequences are most effective when used in combination and believes that assertive discipline teachers should use all three consistently. Misbehavior is dealt with firmly and calmly because it is assumed that teachers and students have a right to a disciplined classroom and misbehavior cannot be entertained.

Evaluations of the effectiveness of assertive discipline generally have been supportive, although much of this material has been in the form of testimonials and unpublished work. A few published studies do support the effectiveness of the technique. For example, Mandelbaum (1983) found that assertive discipline reduced out-of-seat behavior from 96.3 percent to 44.7 percent and inappropriate talking from 98.9 percent to 53.8 percent. Critics argue that such findings would occur from any systematic approach used to deal with a classroom so out of control (Render, Pedilla, & Krenk, 1989) and point out that other supportive findings fail to provide clear comparisons of assertive discipline and alternative techniques in the same study. These critics contend that there has been a surprising lack of investigation of a program that is being so widely used and believe that its effectiveness has yet to be proven. They also argue that a management approach that stresses discipline and conformity tends to be too authoritarian, and they are concerned about long-term effects on students.

Observation of classrooms in which assertive discipline has been employed reveal that it is a potentially useful technique that does decrease disruptive behavior. Teachers need to communicate the expectations of the school and classroom, and to support their fulfillment with appropriate measures. It is very easy for poorly trained teachers to emphasize the punitive aspects of the approach, however. There is a tendency to forget to incorporate the elements of positive reinforcement that most advocates of operant techniques believe should be the primary focus in classroom management.

Classwide Peer Tutoring

Recent applications of operant procedures have emphasized the role of peers in determining group-oriented consequences to improving classroom behavior. Rather than focus on inappropriate behaviors alone, this approach recognizes that the issue of compliance in the classroom is not separate from academic behavior. Students are less likely to be disruptive when they are actively engaged in academic work. Behavior management and instruction need to be coordinated, and other operant procedures fail to provide adequate integration.

Greenwood, Certa, and Hall (1988) believe that other operant procedures are often too narrow and too inflexible to accommodate adaptations to changes over time. Attempts at decreasing undesirable behavior may fail because a desired behavior may not be available for differential reinforcement. Reliance on a small number of reinforcers may be disappointing as satiation reduces their effectiveness. If delays between token earning and receipt of a backup reinforcer are too prolonged, a token economy system will fail to establish or maintain desired behavior. In addition, operant procedures in their traditional form are not acceptable to many school personnel and parents, who disagree with the underlying philosophy and goals of the approach. For these reasons, Greenwood et al. (1988) recommend peer-oriented procedures, which satisfactorily overcome the foregoing objections while at the same time aiding academic learning and improving social behavior.

Peer influence
as reinforcement

The technique utilizes peer influence strategies and cooperative rewards, and a group member's reward is determined entirely or partly by the efforts of others. Groups of students may receive rewards based on the average academic performance of all its members or on the performance of a single target student. Peer influences include spontaneous prompts, reminders, and encouragements, as well as help to improve a specific member's performance and sharing of required work (i.e., members perform the subtasks in which they are most skilled, leading to a group product) (Greenwood & Hops, 1981). In addition, peers serve as tutors, providing direct instruction, monitoring the tutees' responses, correcting errors, and supplying reinforcement through praise and encouragement.

This approach has been found to produce desirable changes in social behavior as well as improvements in academic achievement. In one study, peer tutoring increased the number of social contacts and reduced the frequency of negative social interactions among high- and low-status subjects (Mcleady & Sainato, 1985). Students' inappropriate and off-task behaviors decreased from a rate of 25 percent under conventional teaching to 9 percent during classwide peer tutoring, while academic talk increased from 1 percent to 17 percent (Greenwood et al., 1984).

Classwide peer tutoring, which is one form of cooperative learning, is described more extensively in Chapter 9. Its value appears to lie in the use of social reinforcement, which is an inherent component of any classroom situation. Teachers who can capture the power of social reinforcement derived from peer influence will not have to employ other perhaps coercive forms of control that may not be effective over the long term. This approach represents a recent trend in operant classroom management toward reliance on naturally occurring reinforcers, avoiding issues of cost and appropriateness.

TASK ANALYSIS AND INSTRUCTIONAL DESIGN

The second major application of operant conditioning is in the planning, design, and sequencing of curricula. Skinner believed that learning in the classroom is no different from learning in the laboratory or other settings. It depends on manipulable, observable factors. The typical classroom, however, seemed to violate many of his learning principles (Skinner, 1954) in that positive reinforcement is provided infrequently and inconsistently, there is often a long period of time between behavior and reinforcement, and there are few organized programs that allow a learner to progress through a series of successive approximations to the terminal behavior. Skinner believed that instruction should be designed and sequenced to remediate the foregoing deficiencies in typical educational settings. To that end, he identified four components of instructional design that are acknowledged as valid in most respects by instructional designers today: *defining terminal behavior, priming initial responses, prompting,* and *programming.*

Defining Terminal Behavior

Skinner insisted that the terminal behavior one intends the student to acquire be completely specified in behavioral terms before the commencement of instruction. If a lesson is planned to help students analyze literature, there should be a description of exactly what the students are doing when they "analyze" literature. The goal of "understanding" Newton's laws should be accompanied by a precise definition of how such understanding is demonstrated. Lately, these operational definitions of terminal behavior have come to be called *educational objectives* or *instructional objectives.*

If an educational objective such as having students "understand Newton's laws" is not defined behaviorally, teachers will not be able to determine whether they have helped students accomplish what they had intended. Measurement of improvement will not be possible. Similarly, the learner will not be able to determine what is expected or whether progress toward the objective has been made. Very few present-day educators would argue about the value of defining educational objectives in precise terms, although some might caution that objectives themselves can limit the range of content that teachers and students will select (Eisner, 1969).

Developing educational objectives is not always achieved, however, for a number of reasons. One is that objectives are often confused with *goals,* which are more general or abstract statements of intent. Goals have a place in providing a context, in inspiring dedicated effort, and in establishing a broad direction. Statements such as "The Utopia School District would like all its students to be computer literate" and "All students should learn to be good citizens" are broad goals, not objectives. A goal can be made more useful and more challenging by including a behavioral component that all can recognize and anticipate. John F. Kennedy's famous statement "By the end of this decade [the 1960s], America will put a man on the moon" is an example of a goal statement that effectively defined and directed action because of its behavioral component.

Another reason for the frequent substitution of goals for objectives is that the desired terminal behavior is difficult to define clearly. What behaviors, for example, clearly describe the ability to analyze literature, to produce a creative work of art, or to be a good citizen? There probably would be considerable debate about each. Mager (1972, p. 11) referred to these vague goals as "fuzzies" because they sound nice but don't tell us how to "know one when we see one." To clarify fuzzy goals, Mager recommends (1) writing them down, (2) identifying the performances that, if achieved, would indicate that the goal has been attained, (3) writing a complete statement for each performance, listing the nature, quality, and amount of performance you will accept, and (4) testing the statement by asking yourself a question: "If someone demonstrated each of these performances, would I be willing to say he or she has reached the goal?" For instance, my personal definition of "analyzing literature" focuses on the ability to read a novel and then describe in one's own words the main characters, the problems they face, the moral issue or theme the novel explores, and

Objectives are more behavioral than goals

how the problems are resolved. Other definitions may differ, of course, and performances in the analysis of novels may differ from analyses of poems or satirical essays. The point, however, is that I have translated my goal into a set of terminal behaviors that, if I were teaching literature, could be observed, measured, and communicated to students as appropriate instructional objectives.

Simply defining a terminal behavior does not open the way for instruction to begin immediately. It is also necessary to identify the sequence of responses leading to the terminal objective. This process, known as *task analysis,* involves not only breaking down the task into its constituent parts but considering how the parts are related and organized. In a complete task analysis, one must describe the terminal behavior, isolate the steps leading to it, identify the conditions under which the behavior occurs, and determine a criterion of acceptable performance. Davies (1973) identified three types of task analysis, each serving different purposes: *topic, job,* and *skill.* Topic analysis involves intellectual tasks specific to subject matter content, such as learning to read, solving math problems, and diagramming sentences. We shall consider topic analyses more thoroughly in Chapter 7, when we examine the learning of subject matter. Job analysis concentrates on the global physical movements that constitute a particular job or task. For example, changing the engine oil of a car includes jacking up the car, locating the oil plug, placing a container under the plug, removing the plug, allowing the oil to drain, replacing the plug, pouring in new oil, and disposing of the used oil, all in the proper sequence. Skill analysis is concerned with *how* a task is accomplished, focusing on hand–eye coordination, positioning, and other more precise physical skills. Planning instruction in painting, for example, would require careful skill analysis of the movements involved in holding a brush, dipping it into paint, executing various strokes, and so on. All task analyses are undertaken to identify the sequence that must be mastered for the eventual acquisition of the terminal behavior.

Priming the Initial Response

Simply waiting for initial responses in a sequence to occur so that they can be reinforced is inefficient, according to Skinner. Pure shaping, moreover, through reinforcement of successive approximations, may be tedious and time-consuming. Skinner (1968) dealt with this "problem of the first instance" by priming initial responses, which he achieved by *encouraging imitation* or *providing verbal instructions.* Skinner believes we learn to imitate. Teachers can encourage imitation by demonstrating critical behaviors and then reinforcing legitimate attempts at a response. Verbal instructions can serve to direct attention to initial behavior that is deemed appropriate by the instructor. Once the student has emitted the initial response in a sequence by attempting to imitate or by following directions, the shaping process can begin.

Prompting

Prompting cues responses

Prompting, to establish discriminative stimuli, which serve to control the occurrence of a desired behavior, is necessary for a response to be emitted under the right stimulus conditions. A *prompt* is a learned stimulus that the teacher can use to produce a specified response in the presence of a new stimulus. Skinner used the term because the activity of prompting "encourages the prompt appearance of behavior which already exists" (Skinner, 1968, p. 214).

Every task requires two kinds of response: an attending response to the critical aspects of the task and the required task response. Prompts that aid in directing attention to correct stimuli are called S-prompts, and prompts that help to produce the right target response are referred to as R-prompts. Table 4.1 provides examples of both.

Skinner did not consider a response induced through prompting to constitute learning. A prompt must be gradually removed so that the new stimulus alone produces the correct response. Skinner (1968) called this process "vanishing"; the term *fading* is now used (Becker et al., 1971). Many examples occur in teaching: slowly withdrawing the prompt in successive practice trials; saying the whole word a child is trying to read, then later saying just the first sound, then making the lip movements without the sound; gradually removing the visual supports for forming words as follows:

1. Trace and complete the word C a n
2. Trace and complete the word can C a –
3. Trace and complete the word can C – –

Programming

Skinner felt that complex behavior cannot be reinforced all at once, nor can it simply be divided and reinforced part by part. It must be programmed. The steps in a program must be of appropriate size, and they must be arranged in an effective sequence. In a Skinnerian program, a verbal sequence composed of a stimulus phrase, a required response by the student, and confirmation of the response is supplied for each step

TABLE 4.1 Examples of S- and R-prompts

S-Prompts	R-Prompts
Verbal instructions: "This is a *b* and this is a *d*. See how they are different. Think of the *b* as having a belly in front."	*Verbal instructions:* "Around a tree, around a tree, makes a three" can be used to prompt the writing of the number 3.
Nonverbal: Place an arrow under key letters or use bold type for printing.	*Nonverbal:* Point to the appropriate place to respond (e.g., on the first line to the left).
Physical prompting: Move the child's body through a desired motion, as in touching or tracing a letter.	*Physical:* A tennis coach takes a player's hand, turns the wrist and spreads the fingers to form the backhand grip.
Added cue: Make stimuli less similar by adding a cue. Silent letters can be printed or written smaller than others to cue their silentness (e.g, **kit**e, **bas**e, etc.).	*Added cue:* A child is directed to place one thumb on the paper and write an 8 so that points of the 8 touch his thumb.

SOURCE: Adapted from W. C. Becker, S. Englemann, and D. R. Thomas, *Teaching: A course in applied psychology* (New York: Macmillan Publishing Company, 1971).

or content component. These sequences, known as *frames,* are arranged to progress from basic or most elementary responses to more advanced ones. This gradual progression, as well as built-in priming and prompting, was most likely to produce relatively *error-free learning* (i.e., responses that were highly likely to be correct). A high probability of being correct maximizes the likelihood that positive reinforcement will occur after the response, which in turn should promote further advancement through the program. Confirmation of one's answers (or *knowledge of results*) was presumed to be a positive reinforcer. Skinner believed that by producing responses that were immediately confirmed and reinforced, learning could be individualized—that is, learners could move through programs at their own pace. Materials could be presented in booklet form or on simple paper roll devices known as *teaching machines,* which permit individuals to work on their own, receiving instruction and feedback from the program only. It was not necessary for students to sit and wait for the teacher to get around to them. Skinner's intent was to ensure that the learning environment was controlled and organized so that learning could be "teacher-proof" and "student-proof." An example of an early program is presented in Figure 4.2.

In the programmed text, the correct response to each item appeared on the next page, along with the next frame in the sequence. Learners were to read the item, write the answer on a separate sheet, and turn the page to see the correct response. Note the priming on the last item and the recognition that there is more than one correct response. In this particular program, which represents the *linear programming* mode, learners are to respond to each item in its proper turn at their own pace.

FIGURE 4.2 Example of programmed frames from a programmed text

SOURCE: J. G. Holland and B. F. Skinner, *The Analysis of Behavior* (New York: McGraw-Hill, 1961), pp. 54–55. Reprinted with permission of the publisher.

Set 9	Operant Conditioning: Elementary Concepts **Positive and Negative Reinforcement**

Estimated time: 14 minutes   Turn to next page.

Turning off a television commercial is reinforced by the *termination* of a(n) (1) _____ reinforcer; turning on a very funny program is reinforced by the presentation of a(n) (2) _____ reinforcer.

   (1) negative (2) positive

A man turns his face away from an ugly sight. Turning away is reinforced by the _____ of the ugly sight (a negative reinforcer).

   termination, removal, end

"What does he see in her?" might mean: "How does she _____ his courting behavior?"

   reinforce

A stimulus is called a negative reinforcer if its _____ -tion reinforces behavior.

   termina-, elimina-

Other programs permit students to jump ahead if they have answered correctly a specified number of responses in a row, or go back to earlier pages if too many mistakes or particular errors have been made. That form of programming is known as *branching* because it directs the student along different "branches" of the material (Crowder, 1959). Some branching programs attempt to diagnose student difficulties by analyzing the erroneous choices made under a multiple-choice format. Others attempt to "reteach" the content by explaining it again.

Evaluation of programmed learning revealed that in general, the technique is as effective as or slightly better than other approaches to presenting the same kind of material. Schramm (1964) reviewed 36 studies that compared the results of learning from programmed materials and from traditional presentations: 17 found programmed instruction to be superior in aiding recall and 18 found no differences; only one favored traditional techniques. Bangert, Kulik, and Kulik (1983) found that use of individualized systems had only a small effect on achievement in secondary school courses, although the review did not include studies in which programmed instruction was examined in isolation from other individualized components. Four interesting findings are derived from these reviews.

Organized content is best for programming

1. Most programs dealt primarily with content that lends itself to sequential arrangement. It is clear that such material is learned most efficiently when structure, practice, repetition, and feedback (as required in programmed instruction) are all present. Programs are not easily developed for nonhierarchical material. Consequently, programmed learning usually is not available for the kind of academic content that is most prevalent in such secondary school courses as literature.
2. Factors that affect performance include student familiarity with the programmed material and whether users must construct their own answers or may merely read their way through the program. Abramson and Kagen (1975) found that constructing one's own response is most effective in learning novel material, while reading and mentally responding to the program is sufficient when studying material that is somewhat familiar. Apparently, learners who already possess some understanding of programmed content find it tedious to be obliged to make overt responses, and performance is affected.
3. A well-ordered sequence of frames does not appear to be necessary for learning to occur. In Schramm's review (1964), learning was superior for the ordered sequence in only one of five studies in which an ordered sequence of frames was compared to a random sequence.
4. Many students report negative reactions to programmed materials, complaining about the intense concentration that is required, the often tedious step-by-step review involved, and the feeling of isolation that accompanies working alone with programmed materials.

Critics of programmed instruction argue that imposing a prescribed sequence on certain content detracts from students' ability to organize information, leading to passivity and boredom. Several of these concerns have been addressed by recent technological innovations, as we shall see in the next section.

As a review of what we have discussed so far, recall that Skinner recommended a series of basic components to instruction based on operant principles. Instruction begins with a clear definition of the terminal behaviors that are desired as a result of learning in an area. Objectives that reflect desired behavior, conditions under which behaviors are to occur, and criteria describing acceptable performance are initially established. Material is then presented in a stepwise sequence, proceeding from the simple to the complex, with immediate reinforcement available for intermediate responses. To expedite the production of certain responses, priming and prompting cues might be provided and withdrawn gradually as performance improves. The gradual withdrawal of these cues is known as f _____ .* Content can be arranged to permit individual students to learn at their own pace, following programmed texts or materials presented by machine. Many of these principles have been incorporated in recent technical advances in educational technology, to which we now turn.

EDUCATIONAL TECHNOLOGY

A half-century ago, Skinner suggested that a true technology of education could be developed based on his work in the experimental analysis of behavior: "We will use instrumentation to equip students with large repertoires of verbal and nonverbal behavior. Even more important, the apparatus will nurture enthusiasm for continued study" (Skinner, 1954, p. 91). The author vividly remembers reading a late-1950s account of the "school of the future" in which each student would have a personal workstation and would be able to learn independently, from programmed materials. It was even suggested that students could learn at home, with no teacher present—a rather appealing idea to a sixteen-year-old!

Technological advance is slow

The technological revolution in education has not yet come to pass, at least as educators of the 1950s and 1960s envisioned it. Why not? One set of explanations cites the lack of interesting and challenging programs, the social isolation experienced by learners, and failure to direct attention toward students' contributions to their own learning. In addition, available technology was not widely accepted by teachers as an alternative to traditional instruction. As Cuban (1986) observed, educators adopt technological innovations whenever they offer genuine improvement and fit effectively and economically within the organizational structure of the school. The innovation must make life easier for all concerned. Cuban believes that rejected technical innovations of the past have failed the "practicality ethic" (Cuban, 1986, p. 67). If and when computer-based education meets this standard, it is more likely to become commonplace in public schools.

Part of the practicality concern, of course, is based on financial considerations—it is clear that without monetary support, no innovation will progress very far. It is not our purpose to examine that issue, however. The next section will focus instead on learning and instruction concerns, as we attempt to identify technological advances that not only appear to be supported by research but are practical enough to be employed by educators.

---

*The correct term is "fading." Remember?

Traditional Computer-Assisted Instruction (CAI)

Skinner (1986) viewed the computer as the "ultimate teaching machine," capable of providing all the steps necessary for programmed instruction, administered with infinite patience. Early CAI efforts generally followed the principles of carefully defining objectives, establishing a step-by-step sequence, providing knowledge of results as feedback, and structuring required responses according to restrictive formats such as multiple-choice or true–false items. Preparing CAI became a matter of developing all possible frames of information and anticipating branches that might be needed between the frames to accommodate student needs. More recent approaches to the design of CAI programs are more flexible. Merrill (1987), for example, argues that content structure and task level should be considered in determining appropriate presentation modes for different types of learning. Thus sequential frames might be best for mastery of basic mathematical skills, but the learning of social studies concepts might require a more divergent approach.

There are five major uses of traditional CAI programs, each serving different functions and goals of the classroom: *tutorials, drill and practice, instructional games, simulations,* and *problem-solving tools* (Roblyer, 1986).

How can we use CAI?

Tutorials.   Tutorials are self-contained programs that take the learner through a complete unit or module of instruction on a well-defined topic. They appear to be most useful as follow-up lessons for topics that cannot be covered in depth because of time constraints, as catch-up instruction for students who have missed earlier coverage, or as a replacement option when no teacher is available and students are capable of self-instruction.

Drill and Practice.   Drill and practice programs display items to elicit student response and provide feedback on correctness, but their explanatory component is minimal. Designed to take the place of traditional practice activities such as worksheets and homework, these programs save time for the teacher in preparation of materials and evaluation and deliver feedback with a short "turnaround" time. Kinds of feedback not typically available can be given (speed of response, how well the learner performed in relation to a class or norm group, how performance compares to a child's prior efforts, etc.). New problems can be based on the computer's memory of problems mastered or errors made earlier, thus affording the learner highly individualized practice.

Tutorials and drill and practice software constituted more than half the applications of computers in schools, according to a national survey reported by Becker and Moursund (1985). Some educators recommend even greater use of drill and practice programs, particularly at the first-grade level, believing that the computer is best designed to provide and reinforce the kind of sustained rehearsal that is necessary for mastery of basic skills (Gagné & Merrill, 1991). Research on the effectiveness of these programs tends to find significant but small advantages. For example, Burns and Bozeman (1981) found that CAI mathematics tutorials raised achievement an average of 0.45 of a standard deviation and CAI drill and practice math programs an average of 0.34 of a standard deviation, roughly equivalent to an improvement of 15 percentile points. A review of 42 studies of secondary school classes found an increase of 0.4

standard deviation attributable to tutorial and drill and practice CAI (Bangert-Downs, Kulik, & Kulik, 1985). In a similar review of studies, Kulik, Bangert, and Williams (1983) found, in addition to increased achievement, a general gain in positive attitudes toward the content being learned and toward computers in general, as well as a reduction in the time needed for learning. R. E. Clark (1983) argues, however, that many of the reported studies failed to assign equivalent instruction or practice to control groups, a serious flaw, since in essence the studies so criticized compare CAI to nothing. In studies designed to include adequate controls, researchers noted far fewer comparisons in favor of CAI, and high-ability subjects profited the most.

Instructional Games.   Instructional games presented via computer can stimulate children's interest in content as well as encourage or enhance learned skills by adding motivational and/or competitive elements. Some games present problems in entertaining ways that capture a child's interest in fantasy and make-believe. Consider, for example, a straightforward problem such as "How do you determine the length of the hypotenuse of a right triangle, given knowledge of the length of both sides?" Davis, Dugdale, Kibbey, and Weaver (1977) borrowed from the cast of the original *Star Trek* to formulate a question in which students were asked to help Captain Kirk determine the distance the tractor beam would have to travel to reach the dilithium crystals, knowing the distance from Kirk to the crystals and to the *Enterprise* directly overhead. The addition of *Star Trek*–like graphics further enhanced the interest of this problem for Trekkies and non-Trekkies alike. Although the formal mathematical problem was the same in both instances, Davis et al. (1977) found that the tractor beam problem was solved more accurately and more rapidly. Games also can be created in which an imaginary situation sets the stage for problems that naturally arise, requiring the use of a particular academic skill. For example, customers in a pizza parlor run by the student must be served differing numbers of pizza slices costing different amounts. Other games add competitive elements that allow individuals or groups to demonstrate their superiority by rewarding the attainment of a performance standard. Common video games employ this technique, reinforcing successful players by displaying their initials prominently on the screen. Will students show greater interest in a subject matter when instructional content and an imaginary situation are integrally related, as in the pizza example, or in games utilizing extrinsic reinforcement for reaching an academic goal? This is an interesting research question.

Computer Simulations.   Computer simulations are attempts to create models of real systems to promote a clearer understanding. Although real materials are usually superior, it is often too time-consuming, dangerous, expensive, or otherwise unfeasible to employ them. Simulations allow the learner to perceive relationships by observing actions and outcomes built into the simulation. Abstract principles of relevance to the real-world environment can then be discovered. Simulations differ from games primarily in that they allow more choice of variables that can be manipulated by the learner, and thus are particularly suited to the capabilities of a computer (Lepper, 1985). In the simulation *Odell Lake* (Minnesota Educational Computing Corporation), each student takes the role of a particular fish and faces a series of choices (whether to attack, flee, or ignore fish of a different species). The consequences of the choices are projected to reflect the likely results. Eventually, the student obtains understanding of the relation between predators and their prey and other ecological aspects of North American lakes.

Simulations and games depart from more traditional forms of CAI in that they assume that learning is more meaningful when students discover relevant ideas on their own. Chapter 6 examines this assumption in more detail. For now, it is important to recognize that there is some research support for this position when certain kinds of educational content are to be learned. Woodward, Carnine, and Gersten (1988), for example, found that a health simulation program was an effective way of teaching students with learning disabilities. The program had students manipulate such health variables as stress levels, tobacco and alcohol use, and dietary factors to determine optimal life expectancy. Both short- and long-term recall of health facts and the ability to solve related problems were superior among students who had learned through a computer simulation as opposed to a more traditional, structured presentation of this content. The authors noted that their findings not only supported the use of computer simulations, but demonstrated that students with disabilities can learn abstract concepts meaningfully from CAI presentations as well.

Problem Solving.   Another traditional CAI use of computers has been in problem solving—where the goal is to provide exploration in how to learn, not to master a specific set of content objectives (Roblyer, 1986). Advocates claim that such an approach contributes to creativity and aids in the development of generalized strategies that can be applied to a wide variety of more specific areas. When using problem-solving programs, the act of programming is viewed as an end in itself, and the learner becomes computer literate. Learning to program may lead to the acquisition of valuable planning skills that should increase the individual's ability to function in different content areas. Moreover, learning to program encourages children to engage in active, self-directed learning, allowing examination of areas of personal interest and the testing of personal hypotheses. An example of a problem-solving approach that permits this kind of exploration is that of Logo, a programming language designed to teach young children to program (Abelson & diSessa, 1980). Using only a few commands (Forward, Back, etc.), a learner is able to control the movements of the "turtle" (a cursor displayed on the monitor). Exciting graphic effects can be created, and the student obtains feedback concerning efforts to control the turtle's actions. By putting themselves in the turtle's place, children can make use of their knowledge to design and improve their programs. In some respects, the approach incorporates much of Piaget's model of active learning. Its authors believe that Logo may promote a deeper understanding of the physical world and fundamental concepts of mathematics and physics (Lawler, 1981). Two outcomes of Logo instruction appear to be significant. First, social interaction among children using the Logo program appears to increase as they share knowledge of how to produce certain graphic effects (Weir, 1989). In addition, awareness of what one does or does not understand (metacognitive ability) also increases as a result of Logo training (Clements, 1986).

Two innovations are particularly relevant to CAI—interactive video and hypermedia.

Interactive Video (IV).   Interactive video comes in two forms: a computer linked with a videocassette recorder or with a videodisc player. The major advantage of both types is that computer-based instructional frames can be augmented with enhanced visual and sound accompaniment. For example, a CAI tutorial on oil painting could include a visual demonstration of a master painter using the technique being discussed. Drill and practice questions could be accompanied by a picture of the appropriate technique. An advantage of interactive videocassettes is that most classrooms require only an interface and software, allowing the teacher to create the computer-based lessons.

Videodisc equipment has the added feature of random access. Any segment can be called up to the screen at any time, unlike a videotape, which must be played in the same order every time. A student could study the solar system by looking at any of the nine planets, moving back and forth, spending as much or as little time on each one as desired. Branching, based on student need and interest, is thus easily accomplished.

In a review of existing studies, Bosco (1986) found 24 of 39 statistical comparisons favoring IV. About half the studies reporting positive results found an increase in achievement; other significant differences involved positive attitudes and decreased learning time. Balson, Ebner, Mahoney, Lippert, and Manning (1986) found that videodisc-trained learners acquired new information more rapidly, reported greater satisfaction with their experience, and noted less stress in completing the program. Miller and Cooke (1989) successfully used a videodisc program to teach a main-streamed class of 23 fifth-graders, including 8 students with learning disabilities. The program employed 35 lessons introduced by an actor and accompanied by colorful graphics and sound effects. While most of the content was individual drill and practice, the students spent some time responding orally, in unison. The mean scores on the posttest were 78 for the regular education students and 72 for the learning-disabled students—close enough to be considered as reflecting similar performance. Students reported enjoying the videodisc medium and feeling that "it didn't treat me different." Moreover, the learning-disabled students made no more errors requiring remediation during the program than did regular education students, suggesting that the program could be run efficiently with handicapped learners.

Hypermedia.   In traditional learning, finding out about a topic usually involves reading general books or encyclopedia articles, using references to more specific materials, viewing films if available, and generally browsing through material until one is satisfied that all pertinent material has been considered. This technique has certain inherent limitations, however. Most written and visual materials are meant to be read or viewed from beginning to end. Switching from one medium to another requires abandoning one piece of equipment or location for another, as in moving from the card catalog to the film library. In the process of searching for specific information, you might have to wade through much irrelevant material.

Hypermedia systems eliminate these inefficiencies. Advances in information storage technology allow whole libraries of documents, sounds, and video and graphic images to be placed on laser discs, accessible by a computer. Special software programs allow learners to make nonsequential browsing expeditions through large amounts of information stored electronically in a single location. A school assignment on African elephants, for example, might be prepared by calling up stored articles on the animals' habits, a visual diagram of the regions in Africa where they can be found, a sound recording of their trumpeting, and a clip from the film *Out of Africa* (Trotter, 1989). Rather than assemble this assortment of input into a written report, the student might make a presentation in the form of a *hyperdocument*, or set of written and visual references to the topic. Moreover, the "report" may be sent via networking or modem to the computers of the instructor or of other students. In school districts with extensively networked computer installations, different classes are already communicating with one another. Salomon (1991) described a pilot project in which separate classrooms studied environmental pollution from their respective curricular emphases and reported from one classroom to another using hypermedia technology. Biology classes studied the effects of pollution on the ecological system, physics and chemistry classes investigated the chemical and physical reactions comprising the pollution process, and social studies classes reviewed environmental laws, relevant history, and political and economic effects. Reports were transmitted electronically from one classroom to another and synthesized to form a complete, multidimensional treatment of the issue by English classes. Salomon reported an increase in cooperation as a result of this project, both within and between classrooms.

Hypermedia technology has provoked considerable interest because of its ability to facilitate individual student control of what is learned, to enhance group interaction, to provide instantaneous access to a rich database of materials, to encourage personal construction of unique forms of communication, and to allow immediate input. Whether this technology will become a broad-based instrumentality of effective instruction or will be prove to be a fad that is soon forgotten depends on a number of issues, however. The next section examines these issues in detail.

ISSUES IN THE USE OF CAI

Recent investigations of the effects of CAI have addressed several practical concerns affecting how teachers use computers in the classroom to aid learning. We will discuss five: (1) learner control of CAI, (2) group use of CAI, (3) effects on motivation to learn, (4) gender differences in computer use, and (5) classroom infusion.

Learner Control

Delegating some decision making to learners is a desirable instructional design option that can be exercised using computers. It allows teaches to direct their attention to other instructional methodologies, yet ensures that students can focus on their individual needs. It may increase learners' feelings of control and motivation (Lepper, 1985). Merrill (1987) believes that learners can derive self-determined instructional strategies for learning a variety of skills when given an opportunity to choose among them.

Giving learners control of instruction raises several questions, however. Who should be given what kind of control for which types of instructional task? What if students choose to waste time by playing, rather than working, or spend their computer time on the wrong content? Freedom of choice may contribute to cognitive

New technology allows learner control

overload, in which the learner is overwhelmed by possible choices (Marchionini, 1988). All learners may be allowed to make choices, but not all will choose effectively.

Reinking and Schreiner (1985) studied students' ability to recognize when they had successfully learned from their efforts. They found that the benefit derived from control of computer options may not suffice for some students. These investigators suggested that such a skill may be a prerequisite to effective use of learner-controlled software. Prior instruction in self-questioning, reviewing, and summarizing may be necessary, and students who lack self-monitoring skills may fare better with CAI programs that do not permit large amounts of learner control.

The type of learning activity and the amount of prior knowledge a student possesses about the content to be learned may also determine the value of learner-controlled CAI. Lee and Lee (1991) found that high school chemistry students profited from learner control of a program in reviewing content; initial learning, however, was greater for a program-controlled presentation. That these differences disappeared for students who had greater prior knowledge of chemistry suggests that familiarity with content enables students to select more sensibly what they should study within a program.

A number of factors inherent in programs themselves may determine how learner control affects performance. Having to make many complex decisions about what to study may be frustrating for many students. Subjects not organized in a particular hierarchical sequence, such as social studies, may favor learner choices, allowing students to freely follow their interests, whereas mathematics requires that a definite sequence be followed. Labels used in program "menus" may also affect learner control because they identify content to be viewed, hence may suggest material different from what the learner expects. Making choices of content that do not turn out as desired may serve not only to discredit a particular program, but to convince students that such choices are fruitless. It is clear that learner control of CAI offers potential benefits in efficiency and in the possibility of more meaningful learning for students. Differences in learners' preferences and in choices available require further study, however, particularly as interactive and hypermedia applications become more prevalent.

Individual preferences + knowledge affect use

Group Use

It is unlikely that students in our public schools will have access to individual personal computers. Probably, they will share computers in the classroom, learning in pairs or small groups. For this reason, there is considerable research that examines CAI learning for groups. The major finding is that group learning does not diminish achievement and does increase peer interaction. Clements and Nastasi (1988) observed 48 children working in pairs on either Logo or a traditional CAI program. Children trained on Logo exhibited higher percentages than CAI controls of three social behaviors that would be expected to occur in problem-solving situations. The three behaviors were conflict resolution, rule determination, and self-directed work. Logo subjects also made more metacognitive references in their discussions ("This is what we have to do," "We've already tried that," etc.). Differences can be partially explained by the drill and practice character of much of the traditional CAI training, which re-

Group use is not a hindrance

quires less social interaction, but the researchers still feel confident that group work facilitated social interaction.

Because no differences in achievement have been found between students learning in pairs or larger groups and those working individually, most researchers argue for the efficiency of group use of CAI. Justen, Waldrop, and Adams (1990) found no differences in achievement between individuals and pairs of college students studying research methods. Cockayne (1991) compared single students, groups of two or three, and groups of four or five students who were using videodiscs to study a program on biological development. Students could review video information about biological processes, and they received differential feedback on test performance. Larger groups took more time to complete the program, but there were no differences in achievement. Achievement score multiplied by number of students divided by time spent yielded an efficiency ratio. On this basis, Cockayne concluded that the larger groups were the most efficient.

It seems safe to say that students can learn to share access to a computer. Children who work together at a computer are routinely observed to correct each other's mistakes, cooperate in the completion of assigned tasks, and discuss the assignments in ways that clarify the task even when neither partner appears to understand it at the outset. Some partners divide the tasks according to individual interests and skills, while others take turns at the computer for specified periods (Laboratory of Comparative Human Cognition, 1989). If achievement does not suffer, then not having a workstation for each student in the classroom does not seem to be a major obstacle.

Effects on Motivation to Learn

Like most educational innovations, computers have a built-in advantage in that their novelty in many classrooms creates increased interest and positive evaluations when they are introduced. As we have observed, well-designed, interactive CAI has demonstrated enhanced motivational effects over longer periods of time. What we do not know is what effects prolonged use of CAI will have on children's later intrinsic interest in learning specific content. As Lepper (1985) puts it:

> From one perspective, the use of technical devices to "fool" the child into thinking that this work is fun may prove effective in the short term, but in the long run this strategy of sugarcoating learning will backfire. . . . Children will come to find routine classroom work dull and boring. They will persist less, show decreased attention spans and learn less from traditional classroom instruction. From the other perspective, . . . children should come to like the subject more and should prove more, rather than less, attentive and interested when the subject arises in other domains. . . . One may be able to build generalized positive attitudes toward learning, even among children who have not previously been successful in their regular classroom. (p. 13)

Probably neither position is totally correct—differences in children's established interests and out-of-classroom experiences, as well as the skill of subject matter teachers and, quite obviously, the quality of the programs themselves will eventually affect long-term motivation. As the use of CAI expands in the coming years, it will be necessary for educators to consider both sides of this important issue.

Gender Differences

Female students typically demonstrate less involvement than male students with computers in schools, irrespective of social class or ethnicity (Laboratory of Comparative Human Cognition, 1989). The reason for this discrepancy appears to entail the context and the manner in which computers are introduced into educational settings. When computers are introduced in programming courses, boys demonstrate a higher level of interest and achievement (Hawkins, 1985). In contrast, when they are portrayed as tools for writing and word processing, boys and girls are equally involved (Kurland & Pea, 1983). It appears that girls become readily involved with computers when the software and learning context reflect their interests, as well as those of boys. Girls tend to enjoy the opportunity for collaborative and cooperative learning experiences, rather than isolated and competitive ones. When the computer is presented as a flexible tool for solving problems of interest to them, they become eager to use it, even in courses such as math and science, which traditionally have enrolled fewer females. It has been argued that the appropriate use of computers can overcome the "male" aura of math and science, as well as aid females to benefit from the potential of the electronic devices (Laboratory of Comparative Human Cognition, 1989).

Females prefer cooperative computer use

Classroom Infusion

A major challenge for educators is to incorporate CAI methodology into the classroom, to make it an integral part of the regular instruction and curriculum. Without such infusion, computers may remain novelties, rare rewards, or the focus of after-school activities. While evidence indicates that children's learning can be enhanced by CAI, its potential will be realized only if it is consistently employed. Successful infusion requires compatibility between the instructional objectives required by the teacher or curriculum and the purpose for which the software is designed. Without such a match, it is unlikely that there will be transfer from the software to long-term learning and retention. Compatibility can be fostered by the following procedures (Anderson-Inman, 1987):

1. Choose software that has specific and clearly stated objectives.
2. Examine software to ensure that actual objectives match the stated objectives.
3. Consider software that is designed for use with specific texts or other classroom materials.
4. Evaluate software by determining whether its use results in improved performance on tasks within the existing curriculum.

Choosing compatible software requires careful examination of the materials. First it must be determined which basic goal of CAI is to be met: drill and practice? tutorial instruction? game? simulation? problem-solving experience? One can then evaluate computer software systematically by means of a checklist that covers such educational and practical concerns as whether a particular level of reading ability is required to run the program, whether the time allotted to complete the program can be altered by the teacher to adapt to individual learners' needs, and whether the program can be run without distracting others nearby (Schwarz & Lewis, 1989).

Bell (1985) argues that what is known about learning theories and instructional design should also be factored into choices of courseware. CAI programs of different types not only are directed at different skills, but should follow the instructional rules and procedures that we know from theory and research to be most effective for the teaching of each skill. Bell proposes alternative instructional criteria for each type of CAI program, as presented in Table 4.2.

Infusion of computer technology will occur when teachers can match computer software to their instructional objectives, recognize good courseware that meets instructional criteria, and make a commitment to a more interactive learning process in the classroom. Assuming an adequate financial base and continued research on the effectiveness of new CAI applications, these prerequisites should lead to significant use of educational technology in the future.

TABLE 4.2 Evaluation criteria for microcomputer software

Software	Type of Skill Taught	Instructional Criteria
Drill and practice	Recall, mastery	Presents a variety of examples, provides positive reinforcement, provides immediate feedback.
Tutorial	Concepts	Provides links to prior learning, as well as examples for each defining characteristic, nonexamples, and comparisons and contrasts with other concepts.
	Rules	Provides recall cues for relevant concepts (e.g., verbal cues that permit students to combine concepts into a new rule) and asks students to give a new example.
Simulation	Problem analysis	Presents a novel and complex task that changes as a result of the learner's actions. Provides an opportunity for learners to draw on a range of skills.
Problem solving		Provides cues for recall of prerequisites. Presents new problem. Helps learner reduce hypotheses. Redirects learner when needed.
Exploratory learning		Provides opportunity for experimentation. Includes peer interaction. Provides teacher support activities such as questions or follow-up.

SOURCE: M. Bell, The role of instructional theories in the evaluation of microcomputer software. *Educational Technology, 25* (3), 36–40 (1985). Adapted with permission of the publisher.

CRITICISMS OF OPERANT CONDITIONING

A number of criticisms of operant conditioning and its application to educational practice have been expressed over the years. Some are restatements of issues that have divided psychology since its earliest days—for background information, review the objections to behaviorism by gestaltist psychologists described in Chapter 1. Other criticisms have arisen more recently in response to specific procedures and their effects.

Failure to Recognize the Role of Biological Factors in Learning

Skinner de-emphasized biology's place in human learning, other than to recognize the role of the organism's genetic endowment in accounting for individual differences in intelligence (Skinner, 1953). In all other respects, learning was seen as a function of an individual's history of reinforcement and present contingencies. On this view, factors such as chronological age, readiness, or maturation are of little help in determining why an individual learns or does not learn a new skill.

Nature vs. nurture?

One biological area Skinner tends to ignore is the existence of "prewired" mechanisms that contribute to behavior. We noted in Chapter 3 the Skinner–Chomsky debate on the existence of a genetic predisposition in humans to acquire and process language. Other theorists have pointed to the selective effects of evolution in preparing organisms to associate some stimuli more easily than others: It is argued that different species have different innate tendencies, which may interact with or even negate the laws of learning. Thus some behavior may not be capable of being conditioned in the way trainers expect. An example is provided by Breland and Breland (1961). Raccoons had been conditioned to drop single coins into a box to receive food. In a later stage of conditioning, however, the animals would not release pairs of coins—they would rub them together, or dip them into the box and then remove them, even though such behaviors delayed or prevented reinforcement. Apparently, certain innate raccoon behaviors, such as washing and manipulating food while eating) interfered with learning the conditioned response of dropping a coin. The authors concluded, based on a number of other, similar failures to condition animals, that the behavior of a species could not be understood or controlled without considering its natural behavior patterns and evolutionary history. While few psychologists today are willing to apply the discredited term "instinct" to this finding, particularly in generalizing to human behavior, many are beginning to believe that an organism's evolutionary past may serve to limit the impact of new learning through conditioning.

Few of the techniques for neurophysiological research described in Chapter 2 were available when Skinner did his early work. Evidence that processing of incoming stimuli by the central nervous system affects response selection, rate, and magnitude was not considered in the formulation of his views on learning. Greater understanding of neurological functioning may produce new insights into why conditioning sometimes fails, what factors affect extinction and memory, and why certain objects or events are reinforcing and others are not.

Lack of Concern for Cognitive Processing

Mental events are not considered in operant conditioning unless they are observable as identified behaviors. Note taking, for example, might reflect internal processing or thinking, but Skinner would recognize only the note-taking behavior itself as worthy of consideration. He believed that if it can be consistently shown that particular environmental events have predictable behavioral outcomes, there is no good reason to assume that human behavior is guided by thought. Thinking may be going on, but which is affecting behavior—the thinking or the environmental event? Thoughts have no causal status in Skinner's system of psychology (Nye, 1992).

We discussed in Chapter 3 the role of cognition in children's development. Research in that area indicates that a child's interpretation of the environment and the demands of a task determine the nature of whatever response is produced. The information-processing view of cognition, discussed in Chapter 6, argues that expectancies established through previous learning affect not only how we respond, but what environmental events elicit responses in the first place. Recent advances in educational technology draw on the individual's ability to make decisions, express preferences, and determine what is needed for personal learning. Based on these arguments, it would appear difficult to ignore cognitive mechanisms in developing a comprehensive view of human learning.

Most modern behaviorists are willing to compromise on this point. According to Rachlin (1991):

> Cognitive psychology asks *how* people behave as they do; behavioral psychology asks *why* people behave as they do. These two approaches are complementary rather than competitive. The sharpest picture of the workings of humans is achieved when we use *both* of these perspectives; the better we know how behavior occurs, the more we need to know why it occurs and vice versa. (p. xiii)

Insufficient Description of Complex Behavior

Skinner described the acquisition of complex human behavior such as problem solving as advancing through a shaping process in which responses become more and more refined. Behavior that initially may have a zero probability of occurring can be generated through progressive shaping. Acts often referred to as "creative" by others because they appear suddenly and do not seem to resemble past responses are viewed as a result of special events experienced by the individual, which combine with genetic background to produce the new behavior. An individual who has a large repertoire of responses will try out various behaviors until one emerges that is apparently new. The learner has merely responded to subtle common elements between old and new stimuli. In essence, novel behavior is no more than stimulus generalization.

Complex skills are cumulative

Critics contend that complex behavior is rarely demonstrated in such a linear fashion, nor is it predicted by the frequency of responses emitted previously. Problem solving requires a shift in the individual's perception of the problem and the use of relevant knowledge and skills in a way that may be unexpected. There may be several steps backward before reorganization occurs. It is true that problem solving is more likely to be successful when an individual has a large knowledge base, but an openness to related ideas and a willingness to change one's approach seem to be needed as well. Expert problem solvers reject superficial characteristics of the problem and readily extract critical features to examine. Such strategies do not seem to be produced by shaping but rather through experience in exploration and decision making. This is one of the reasons for the modification of CAI software to include elements of learner control, providing options to be explored, chosen, or rejected. We discuss the acquisition of problem-solving skills and educational procedures designed to advance their learning more thoroughly in Chapter 10.

Overemphasis on External Control as Opposed to Personal Responsibility

Skinner was a *radical determinist:* He believed that behavior is determined by genetic endowment and environmental contingencies only. This position runs counter to the American ideal of the independent individual who makes free choices and takes responsibility for his or her actions. Most of us believe that what we do depends on our personal decisions, that we determine our own fate. Thus when Skinner says that our accomplishments are a function of factors outside our control, and that environmental factors influence us no matter how independent we may feel, we tend to object. Not only is Skinner's position too extreme to account for the individuality of adults, say many critics, but the implementation of operant conditioning appears to reduce students to robots, constantly reinforced to produce the behavior that has been deemed appropriate by controlling adults.

Such an indictment, although based on admirable attachment to the ideals of democracy and equality, seems to be both misplaced and too severe. Most of us would agree, after reflection, that many institutions do not allow free choice and responsibility and that we are controlled by our environment whether we like it or not. We have been taught that we are what we make of ourselves through our own will power,

Determinism vs. free will

fortitude, and ingenuity, but since we will not necessarily have the same opportunities and advantages as others, we shouldn't expect to get everything we want. Moreover, despite our best efforts, sometimes success is more a matter of external factors such as luck or "the breaks" than personal endeavors.

Even if we were to agree that freedom of choice is always possible and cannot be restricted, we would have to recognize that sometimes it is necessary to give up our priorities for the sake of others. We are not free to drive cars at any speed and in any place we would like. Similarly, children are not free to sing out or shout in a classroom whenever they feel so inclined. Socialization of children inevitably involves learning when to suspend personal freedoms for the good of others. Teachers play a critical role in the socialization process and are expected to control the behavior of individuals so that many may benefit.

A more critical issue may be the nature of the behavior that is to be conditioned. No one would argue against the desirability of preventing kindergarten children, forcibly if necessary, from running into traffic, but what about coercing them to be perfectly quiet in the classroom or to wear certain clothes to school? We would probably say that the teacher who trains children not to run into the street is proceeding correctly, but the one who attempts to extinguish all noise in kindergarten class is being punitive (if not wildly optimistic). Which behaviors require the control that operant conditioning can provide?

Gordon Allport (1961) used the term *functional autonomy* to refer to behaviors that became independent (developed autonomy) from their original purpose. An action becomes functionally autonomous when we no longer perform it to obtain the original reward, but because it is rewarding in and of itself. Many children initially learn to read to be like big brother or like daddy, thereby gaining reinforcement. Eventually, however, as the child experiences its value, reading itself becomes the reinforcement and is no longer performed to gain a more primary reinforcement. A teacher who attempts to condition inherently valuable behaviors to the point, eventually, of functional autonomy is not behaving coercively. Rather, the conditioning is contributing to an appropriate educational goal. Attempting to eliminate behaviors that do not have the potential to become functionally autonomous is more problematic. In that case, indeed, it can be more fairly said that external control is too restrictive. A proper test of whether conditioning is appropriate would depend on the eventual value of the behavior to the individual, and that decision requires an objective judgment by the teacher.

Establishing Behavioral Outcomes in Advance Trivializes Education

Critics contend that the act of translating educational goals into instructional objectives in which learner behaviors are predefined reduces learning outcomes to a series of discrete, unrelated items that may border on the trivial. What is the point, they ask, of being able to recite the names of the first 13 American states if the learner cannot explain why each original colony was founded? These critics fear that recall of facts that are most easily defined and observed will become the predominant focus of education. Broader issues and conceptual skills that are less easily objectified will be ignored. Emphasis on students attaining precise objectives will narrow instruction to focus on classroom activities that contribute to the learning of those limited objectives. Opportunities to explore content that arise spontaneously will be lost, and incidental learning of related information and skills will be reduced.

To the extent that objectives are narrowly defined, the foregoing criticism may be valid. If an instructor decides that students can demonstrate mastery of a given subject matter simply by recalling related facts, then defining instructional outcomes in those terms probably will reduce the scope of the curriculum. Since views of what constitutes a fact are frequently revised in some areas, the student's competence may soon be obsolete. Consider, for example, the revision of the number of basic food groups. The author recalls being told as a child that there were seven food groups. Since those far-off days, as nutritionists have learned more about food sources, the descriptive categories have changed several times. At last count, there were four. A more comprehensive objective might be to explain the nutritional basis for forming a food group, so that any subsequent changes in number can be more easily understood. Another example consists of objectives designed for handicapped learners.

One plan contained 31 objectives, such as "The student will reduce fractions to lowest terms up to eighths." An objective at that level of behavior tends to downplay the importance of the student acquiring a broader understanding of fractions in general.

While there is clearly a danger in setting objectives that may restrict learning, such restriction does not have to occur. Objectives can be identified within a context that allows more meaningful learning, if that is what the curriculum requires. It is possible, for example, to develop units of instruction on topics such as the American colonies that coordinate objectives at all levels of thinking (Treffinger, Feldhusen, & Hohn, 1990). Developing a brochure in which the colonies are visited by a "travel agent," who describes each one for potential tourists, not only allows students to master objectives calling for recall of information such as colony names, but also requires the more complex skills of analysis and synthesis. Objectives can be written that define behaviors that reflect the broader purposes of education.

We Learn by Observing Others as Well as by Gaining Reinforcement for Our Behavior

Skinner utilized operant principles to address the issue of how we learn from others. Another person's behavior is observed, the observer matches the response, and the matching response is reinforced. The other person's behavior acts as a discriminative stimulus, indicating which actions will result in reinforcement.

Bandura (1977) points out that this explanation does not account for how learning occurs when neither the *model* (the other person) nor the observer is reinforced; nor does it account for the learner who responds much later in ways similar to those observed earlier. He believes that in addition to learning acquired through classical and operant conditioning, there is a third kind: *observational learning*. The learner must observe a model's response, be aware that reinforcement is contingent on that response, and believe that reinforcement will be forthcoming to anyone who engages in similar behavior. This model of observational learning expands our understanding of what Rachlin (1991) referred to as "rule-governed" behavior (1969), or behavior that is not immediately reinforced. Rule-governed behavior is derived from descriptions of contingencies that are transmitted verbally to individuals, as teachers might do. Laws, ethical principles, and social conventions are probably acquired in this way.

While using behavioral principles as a basis, Bandura introduces internal processes such as awareness and cognition, which Skinner did not recognize. As we shall see in Chapter 5, Bandura's criticism serves to extend behavioral principles and builds a bridge to cognitive views of learning. His ideas serve as an important contribution to the psychological area of *social learning*.

Intrinsic Motivation Is Supplanted by Extrinsic Reinforcement

"Intrinsic motivation" refers to the performance of certain actions because a behavior itself is rewarding. Meeting the challenge involved in solving difficult math problems, browsing through a new book just to see what's in it, and attempting to establish a personal best time in running the mile are all examples of the effects of intrinsic motivation. Individuals will engage in these kinds of behavior not for external rewards, but because they find inherent value in performing them.

Critics of operant conditioning argue that reliance on extrinsic reinforcers reduces intrinsic motivation. This idea is reflected in the statement "Sure, I like to do it, but I tend not to do it, unless I get paid for it." Once introduced, extrinsic reinforcement becomes the controlling factor in the behavior's recurrence, and students do not engage in the activity for its own sake. Deci (1975), for example, has demonstrated that games children typically play spontaneously will be played only for rewards such as prizes and championships after the rewards have been introduced. Another example is found in the well-intentioned efforts of a national pizza chain to provide pizzas for students who read a certain number of books, in which emphasis is placed on the number of books read, not on enjoyment or understanding.

This final criticism suggests that it is a mistake to use extrinsic reinforcers to increase an activity that already is controlled by intrinsic factors. Operant procedures should be applied only to behaviors for which motivation does not already exist. In addition, it appears that classroom-wide programs that reinforce a large number of behaviors would benefit from careful observation and determination of which behaviors actually need to be included. The institution of extrinsic reinforcement may not be necessary and may even be counterproductive. Another way to reduce reliance on extrinsic reinforcers is to move as rapidly as possible from primary to more secondary reinforcers, provided after long-term schedules have been met.

Intrinsic vs. extrinsic motivation

EFFECTIVE TEACHING

This chapter has covered considerable ground, from the earliest studies of reinforcement by Skinner and other behaviorists to the most recent applications of educational technology. It is time now to summarize what has been discussed, with the goal of identifying basic assumptions that contribute to effective teaching from a behavioral point of view.

Operant principles can be applied to a wide variety of settings in which control is important. In many situations the planning of environmental conditions will yield behaviors beneficial to individuals and society. While behavior is often unpredictable because certain environmental and biological factors cannot be managed, the likelihood of obtaining desired outcomes is nevertheless increased when the more manageable conditions are controlled. Many of the examples of classroom management presented earlier demonstrated the value, to both individuals and groups, of reducing classroom disturbances by establishing reinforcement contingencies for appropriate behavior. In programmed instruction, successful learning is identified, rewarded, and corrected if necessary through the feedback mechanism of the program or computer. Planning of the environment has served to modify or reinforce desired behavior in both cases.

Environmental design can occur in a number of situations, to the advantage of individuals. For example, behavioral principles can be utilized in a practical fashion to ameliorate the effects of old age. B. F. Skinner, at age seventy-nine, coauthored a book containing suggestions of a number of ways to simplify and manage one's life so that the decline in abilities accompanying old age is less troublesome (Skinner & Vaughan, 1983). The recommendations include eliminating things that can cause trouble because you don't see them well, or making them easier to find by attaching highly visible markers or tape. It is also advisable to do as much as possible when each chore occurs to you, to minimize later forgetting—get out of bed and put the Internal Revenue forms on the breakfast table, for example, if you happen to recall during the night that your taxes are overdue. Another way to cut down on forgetting is to attach to the handle of your toothbrush a small pill case containing the medicine you have trouble remembering to take so that something you do routinely will serve as a prompt. Similarly, you can use an alarm clock to alert you to significant events occurring throughout the day, or develop a fixed routine of daily behavior (e.g., taking care of household matters between nine and ten, walking just after dinner). You might also set goals and keep a highly visible chart to record your successes and failures in remembering, reinforcing strings of success with a particularly desirable treat. Finally, when the behaviors of your younger days are no longer reinforced, it is necessary to devise new ways of responding. Skinner would argue that every field of human endeavor can be arranged so that appropriate behaviors are maximized, as long as obvious physical deficits possessed by the learner are considered.

Reinforcement should be provided in a clear, consistent, and contingent fashion.   Observation of any classroom reveals areas in which reinforcement is either extremely rare or irregularly provided. Frequently, too, punishment is delivered in an inconsistent fashion, typically when the last straw has been added, and tempers erupt. It is often argued that teachers are only human, and whether they reinforce or punish at a particular time is likely to reflect individual moods. The "only human" truism should not be accepted as an excuse for failure to control how and when reinforcement is provided, however.

In reviewing the role of praise in the classroom, Brophy and Good (1986) find that teachers judged as effective tend to use praise that is *specific, contingent,* and *credible.* Praise should be linked to specific behavior, as in "I like the way you wrote that summary paragraph, Fred." It should be contingent on successful completion of a task. It should also be credible—that is, it should come only after praiseworthy effort; and it should be sincere and not too frequent. Have you ever known a teacher who said "Good" or "Fine" all the time, even when there was nothing good or fine about the situation? The words quickly lose their reinforcing value.

The same criteria can be applied to the use of punishment, as well. If punishment is necessary, it should be administered directly following the unacceptable behavior, and it should be related to a specific offense. Punishment should be consistently applied to all transgressors to the same extent, to ensure that it is linked to the behavior, not to a personal relationship between teacher and student.

Teaching should be structured, following a planned sequence leading to a terminal set of demonstrable behaviors.   A planned lesson with a predetermined organization and measurable outcomes to aid in deciding when learning has been acquired is desirable for most academic content. Behaviorists recommend following a simple-to-complex sequence, as envisioned in Skinner's view of programmed instruction. Priming, prompting, and fading techniques may be used, and reinforcement should be withheld for responses successively approximating the final objective. Recent technological innovations such as interactive video allow the learner to depart from a step-by-step sequence. No matter what sequence is employed, its planning should reflect a clear understanding of the desired outcome.

Whenever possible, instruction should be individualized, to leave students free to choose the pace and format they prefer.   Skinner (1968) envisioned programmed instruction as a method for individualizing education. Reinforcement could be frequent and directed specifically toward each student, immediately contingent on mastery of a step in the instructional sequence. Teaching machines would allow students to establish their own pace, choosing to review materials or advance more rapidly depending on their success in moving through the program. Students would be free to choose among available materials, when alternatives were identified. Students would not have the option of individualizing objectives, for Skinner believed that the teacher was responsible for determining appropriate content. In most other respects, he was a strong proponent of individualization.

A number of individualized instructional plans have been developed over the years, and many of them incorporate Skinner's ideas. One widely adopted plan is described as a *personalized system of instruction* (PSI). Used frequently at the college level, PSI includes organization of courses into appropriate units, creation of alternative ways for students to acquire course content (hearing lectures, viewing videotapes, discussing content in small groups, etc.), evaluation of each unit, and student determination of pace in mastering objectives. Students are free to retake exams, redo papers, and so on, to complete course objectives and improve their performance. Consequently, final grade distributions are skewed heavily toward A, but advocates argue that the grades more accurately reflect mastery of content than do those that follow a normal distribution. A review of research by Glick and Semb (1978) confirmed that students achieve at superior levels under PSI, as opposed to more traditional lecture–discussion formats, and rated the independence provided as highly desirable.

> Have you experienced self-paced college instruction?

Two concerns arise in implementing PSI. One is that students often procrastinate, particularly if other courses being taken do not follow an individualized format. Options to delay taking exams are more likely to be chosen if other courses have more restrictive deadlines, and students fall behind. Bonus points added to test scores for on-time completion appear to reduce procrastination (Glick & Semb, 1978). Of course, with added inducement for early completion, the self-pacing component becomes more restrictive.

The other problem is more fundamental. It involves a basic decision on whether certain content areas or courses adequately lend themselves to this approach. A decision to individualize should be made only after the following questions have been resolved: Is the content clear and are subcomponents easily sequenced? Do alternative instructional formats really provide the same content, or should all students be exposed to the same experiences? Can evaluation techniques adequately assess course mastery, particularly if different options are chosen? Are students ready for the responsibility of working independently, particularly with content that may be difficult or tedious?

Teaching is an experimental process, in which all techniques should be examined routinely and revised if necessary.   That Skinner referred to his model of learning as the *experimental* analysis of behavior reveals one of its most important contributions to effective teaching. There should be a commitment to the continual analysis and evaluation of instructional procedures designed to foster learning. Not only should reinforcers be reviewed frequently to determine whether they still increase desired behaviors, but the organization and sequence of content to be presented should be examined periodically to determine whether students are progressing toward terminal objectives. Alternative instructional formats such as CAI or PSI should be considered as possible substitutes. Perhaps, for example, the ability of CAI to enable students to reinforce their own efforts to learn should be considered. The power of contemporary technology to enrich learning, not just provide drill and practice, should also be examined. It may be possible to refine and improve behavioral techniques by exercising an attitude of experimentation.

Teaching as an experimental process

SUMMARY

After examples of some applications of behavioral principles, this chapter described Skinner's operant learning methodology. Operant behavior produces consequences that come to control the future appearance of such behavior. Consequences that increase the probability of a response—reinforcers—can be primary or secondary (conditioned), positive (presenting something pleasant) or negative (taking away something unpleasant). Punishment, a consequence that decreases the probability of a particular response, can occur either through removal of a positive reinforcer or through presentation of an aversive stimulus. Skinner preferred to employ reinforcement as the predominant way of controlling behavior, to avoid the excessive number of negative side effects associated with punishment. Ignoring can also be used to extinguish certain responses.

While continuous reinforcement may be necessary initially to reinforce behavior, intermittent reinforcement following various schedules can maintain it for long periods of time. Fixed-interval, fixed-ratio, variable-interval, variable-ratio, and superstitious schedules have different effects on behavior. Skinner believed that withholding reinforcement until successively accurate approximations of the desired terminal behavior have occurred (shaping) leads to the acquisition of complex behaviors.

Operant principles have been applied to three areas of educational practice: classroom behavior, instructional design, and educational technology. The approaches recommended were systematic use of positive reinforcement to increase desired behavior, shaping to produce more complex responses, ignoring of undesired behavior, identification of stimuli to control response patterns, selecting effective reinforcers, proceeding from continuous to intermittent schedules, and using punishment only if positive reinforcement fails. These principles are incorporated into classroom management techniques such as contingency contracting, token economies, behavior reports, assertive discipline, and classwide peer tutoring.

Instructional design from an operant point of view requires task analysis in which specific substeps leading to instructional objectives are identified. Instruction then follows a programmed procedure of priming, prompting, and fading, all with the goal of eliciting responses that can be positively reinforced. Programs can be either linear or branching. Research on early attempts at programmed instruction indicate some advantage in learning for basic skill areas, although students do not always enjoy the overt responding or relative isolation accompanying individualization.

Recent educational technology has extended principles of programmed instruction by adding the capacity of personal computers, videodiscs, and electronic linkages. Computer-assisted instruction has been found to be effective in providing tutorial assistance, drill and practice, games, simulations, and problem-solving activities. The effectiveness of these forms of instruction seems to increase when learners are able to exert control over the pace and sequence of materials, particularly when students possess the metacognitive ability to do so. Group use of computers does not appear to have a negative effect on achievement, and females profit as well as males from computers when the technology is introduced appropriately. Problems in the use of CAI include the infusion of useful software, the assessment of long-term motivational effects of its use, and the matching of software to relevant objectives.

Operant conditioning has been criticized for failing to recognize the role of biological factors in learning, ignoring cognitive processes, insufficiently describing complex behaviors, overemphasizing external control, trivializing educational outcomes, failing to account for observational learning, and supplanting intrinsic motivation. Nevertheless, many of these objections can be resolved, and operant principles can be applied to a wide variety of educational areas and settings. The use of these principles assumes an emphasis on consistent, planned reinforcement, structured presentations, appropriate use of individualization of pace and format, and a continual, experimental approach to educational practice.

A concept map for this chapter appears on page 152.

EXERCISES

1. Select someone whose behavior you would hypothetically like to change (yourself, for example). Describe the final goal, the specific target behavior, the techniques you would use (shaping, positive/negative reinforcement, punishment, extinction, etc.), and a schedule of reinforcement/punishment.

2. Choose a specific educational context (e.g., a third-grade classroom, a band room, a middle school gym class, a recreation center, a senior services center).

   a. Identify a clearly defined academic behavior you would like to increase for either an individual or a group of students (e.g., improving word recognition skills in reading).

   b. Describe a shaping procedure for reaching the desired behavior, emphasizing the component parts to be taught sequentially.

   c. Describe instructional procedures (prompting, fading, etc.) that you might use to facilitate the process.

   d. Identify reinforcers and draft a schedule of their occurrence, which you would employ to reward successive approximations.

Personal Theory of Learning

Criticisms Entail
- Biological factors
- Cognitive processing
- Complex behavior
- External control
- Trivialization
- Observation of others
- Intrinsic motivation

Operant Learning

Basic processes

Reinforcement
- Positive
- Negative
- Punishment
- Extinction

Schedules
- Continuous
- Intermittent
- Interval
- Ratio
- Fixed
- Variable

Shaping
- Successive approximation
- Target behavior

apply to:

Classroom Behavior

Specific techniques
- Contingency contracts
- Premack principle
- Token economy
- Daily behavior reports
- Assertive discipline
- Classwide peer tutoring

Instructional Design

Task analysis leads to
- Instructional objectives
- Priming
- Prompting
- Programming

Educational Technology

Traditional CAI
- Tutorials
- Drill and practice
- Games
- Simulations
- Problem solving

New technology
- Interactive video
- Hypermedia

Issues
- Learner control?
- Group use
- Effects on motivation
- Gender differences

Concept Map for Chapter 4

SUGGESTED READINGS

Becker, W. C., Engelmann, S. & Thomas D. R. (1971). *Teaching: A course in applied psychology.* Chicago: Science Research Associates.

Bell, M. F. (1985). The role of instructional theories in the evaluation of microcomputer software. *Educational Technology, 25*(3), 36–40.

Lepper, M. R. (1985). Microcomputers in education: Motivational and social uses. *American Psychologist, 40*(1), 1–18.

Premack, D. (1959). Toward empirical behavior laws: I. Positive reinforcement. *Psychological Review, 66,* 219–233.

Rachlin, H. (1991). *Introduction to modern behaviorism* (3rd ed.). New York: Freeman.

Skinner, B. F. (1953). *Science and human behavior.* New York: Macmillan.

Skinner, B. F. (1963). Operant behavior. *American Psychologist, 18,* 503–515.

chapter 5

Social Learning

CHAPTER OUTLINE

CHAPTER OBJECTIVES

1. Identify the factors that explain social learning and determine how they influence behavior.

2. Describe the characteristics of effective adult models and describe how they influence the behavior of observers.
3. Explain the development of social learning ability in children.
4. Define self-efficacy, explain the sources of information that contribute to its development, and describe how perceptions of self-efficacy can be enhanced in students.
5. Explain the components of self-regulation and describe the strategies students can use to regulate their own behavior.

Before the recess buzzer had stopped its droning, Damon was out of his seat and running toward the door.

"There he goes," thought Mrs. Espinoza. "It's the boys against the girls in kickball today and Damon wants to be the first out. I've told him a thousand times not to run, though."

Before Damon could reach the door, his feet seemed to fly out from under him. He had slipped on water spilled during art class. Damon fell on his backside, bumping his elbow as his body made contact with the hard, tiled floor.

Almost everyone in the class saw the accident. When Damon fell, a sudden quiet came over the room. Damon was a likable boy and no one wanted to see him hurt. When he got up, sobbing "I-I-I hurt m-m-myself," you could see concern on the other children's faces.

"I bet this group won't run in the classroom again soon," thought Mrs. Espinoza as she hurried to comfort the crying boy. "I just hope the lesson lasts."

"Today you are going to learn how to safely operate the jig borer," Mr. Lathrop announced to his metal finishing class. "Watch closely, so you can do it right when it's your turn."

Mr. Lathrop carefully inserted the metal plate to be drilled on the platform under the barrel of the borer. Turning on the machine, he expertly guided the plate as the borer began to punch holes in the heavy metal. When the six predetermined holes had been bored, he extracted the plate and addressed the group: "OK, who would like to have a try?"

No one in the group of 14 raised a hand. "I bet if it was a new video game they'd all jump at the chance," the instructor said to himself. Finally, Albert, one of the more self-confident of the industrial education students, ventured forth. "I'll try, I guess," he said as he seized the metal plate, carelessly stuffed it under the barrel, and reached for the on switch.

"Watch it, you haven't set the safety guides. Don't you guys ever pay attention?" Mr. Lathrop complained. "Now, look again."

What do these incidents have in common? Other than the likelihood that both would tax the stamina of the strongest teacher, they demonstrate that much of our learning stems from observing others. In many instructional situations, learned responses are not directly performed but are mentally "filed," only to be demonstrated later when the individual is called on to produce a response. Many of Mrs. Espinoza's students will think twice before running in a similar situation. Mr. Lathrop showed his students what they were expected to learn to do and then elicited a response (albeit an unsatisfactory one). Both situations required learners to develop a response to be produced on demand in appropriate situations.

Social learning = potential responses

Behavioral theories, such as operant conditioning, traditionally explain learning from others as an imitative response in which the observed behavior serves as a discriminative stimulus. *Imitation* occurs when the observer performs the same response and receives reinforcement. Learning is not complete until the child has been reinforced for his or her behavior. Other behavioral views stress the instrumental nature of imitation, in which the imitator copies an observed behavior by trial and error until reinforcement is attained (Miller & Dollard, 1941). Neither explanation allows subjective analysis of the situation by the observer.

As early functionalists such as James and Dewey first pointed out, individuals adapt to their environment, and psychology must study the nature of this adaptation. Learning by observing others appears to be a good example of how adaptation affects later behavior. The *social learning* theory of Albert Bandura (1925–) attempts to take into account mental processes leading to adaptation when explaining how we learn from others.

BASIC PRINCIPLES OF SOCIAL LEARNING

Observation

We learn by observing the actions of others, just as we learn through classical or operant conditioning of our behavior.   Bandura does not deny that we learn to substitute new stimuli for old ones as in classical conditioning or that we learn through the consequences of our actions as in operant conditioning. An additional source of learning for Bandura (1962) is the ability of individuals to gain information from what others do, to make decisions about which observations are worthy of adoption, and to utilize that information in later situations that require a response.

Bandura (1977) believes that this third type of learning, initially referred to as *observational learning,* differs from imitation in several ways:

1. Learning often occurs without reinforcement being delivered to the *model* or to the *observer.* Young children often produce behaviors they have observed in adults in the absence of direct reinforcement. The author's son Keith was once observed wearing his baseball cap slightly askew, as his father does, with no apparent reinforcement forthcoming for such an act.

2. Imitation explanations do not account for responses that are delayed until a later time. In Mrs. Espinoza's class, what Bandura (1971) calls *delayed matching* is expected to occur when pupils who observed Damon's slip "remember" the consequences of his running in the classroom and choose

not to reproduce this behavior, perhaps days or weeks later. This is a good example of the learning/performance distinction we discussed in Chapter 1. A social learning perspective requires a separation of what learners learn from what they do—to understand learning, one makes an inference from performance rather than automatically equating the two. Operant theory, of course, makes no such distinction: The performance of a response *is* learning, and observers must make the response immediately so they can derive direct reinforcement.

3. Imitation does not explain the emergence of novel responses. Rather than ape the exact behaviors of a model, observers are likely to modify their own responses in light of the model's behavior or to perform responses that are combinations of behaviors observed in more than one model. In an early study, Bandura, Ross, and Ross (1963a) found that when left alone in a playroom, three-year-olds adapted and combined the play behavior of two recently observed adult models into their own form of amusement. It appears that learners extract information from what they observe and act on this information in an adaptive way. Knowing that observational learning is a cognitive process, Bandura (1977) recognized that without knowledge of the aspect of a model's behavior that is being reinforced, observers in complex behavioral situations may have difficulty identifying the link between specific responses and reinforcement. The young ballplayer, attempting to reproduce the batting stance of a baseball hero, may select the most discernible aspects of the hero's behavior to model (spitting, swaggering, scowling?) rather than the characteristics that are most likely to lead to reinforcement (holding the bat level, standing square to the plate, etc.).

Social learning involves adaptation

Interaction

Social learning is determined by a three-way interaction among personal factors, the environment, and behavior.   Bandura does not believe that the variety of behaviors we learn can be explained by simple relationships between the individual and the environment. The environment does not unilaterally determine individual behavior, as operant theorists might contend, because individuals are capable of creating and activating their own environment (Bandura, 1978). On the other hand, advocates of personal determination of behavior through free choice ignore the role of the environment in determining what we attend to, perceive, and think. Bandura instead believes that the person, the environment, and the person's behavior all interact to produce subsequent behavior. None of the three components can be considered as a determiner of behavior independently of the others. Bandura refers to this position as *reciprocal determinism* and represents it schematically as in Figure 5.1.

Behavior is a result of interactions

The *triadic reciprocal interaction* concept illustrates the interaction of the three sets of factors. Personal factors include not only the physical characteristics of the individual (age, sex, race, etc.) but the person's beliefs and expectations as well. The environment affects behavior through the intermediary cognitive processes that de-

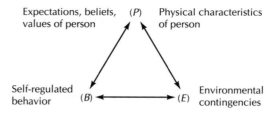

Figure 5.1 Schematic representation of three-way relationship among personal factors, the environment, and behavior

SOURCE: A. Bandura, The self system in reciprocal determinism. *American Psychologist, 33* (4), 344–358 (1978). Adapted by permission of the publisher.

termine what external events are observed, what their consequences are, and how that information can be used in the future. As Bandura (1978) puts it:

Another example of reciprocal interaction?

> The extraordinary capacity of humans to use symbols enables them to engage in reflective thought, to create, and to plan foresightful courses of action in thought rather than having to perform possible options and suffer the consequences of thoughtless action. By altering their immediate environment, by creating cognitive self-inducements, and by arranging conditional incentives for themselves, people can exercise some influence over their own behavior. An act therefore includes among its determinants self-produced influences. (p. 345)

Each set of factors will vary in the extent of its influence on different individuals in different situations. For example, environmental conditions can exert an overriding influence in life-threatening situations, such as the sudden announcement that there is a fire nearby. Self-regulated behavior is often dominant in situations that produce desirable sensory states. You may know people who run or jog long distances regularly, despite weather conditions or the skepticism of others, to achieve a feeling of euphoria or relaxation. They are creating their own environment, rather than reacting to the existing one. Personal cognitions are dominant in other instances, too, where strongly held beliefs or emotions are involved. Adolescents concerned about their physical appearance, for example, often deny or ignore external evidence or the judgment of others to engage in all sorts of beautifying schemes.

In many other instances, the three factors determine behavior in a mutually interdependent fashion. Bandura (1978) provides the example of television viewing. Personal preferences influence which programs we choose to watch from all the many available alternatives. Although the potential television environment is the same for all viewers, the actual environment depends on individual preferences. In turn, selections determine what will be shown in the future, as ratings are fed back to television producers. Since, in addition, production costs and advertising requirements also determine what shows are made available, our preferences are partially shaped by what is available. In effect, viewer preferences, viewer behavior, and the television environment exert reciprocal effects. Bandura believes that this triadic interaction must be considered before human functioning can be understood.

Learner Capabilities

Learners possess several capabilities that allow them to profit from social learning.   As we discussed in Chapter 3, a number of cognitive capabilities develop that contribute to enhanced judgment and problem-solving skills. Bandura (1986) assumes that these capabilities permit social learning to occur most efficiently. They are summarized in Table 5.1

Potential Behavioral Changes

Social learning results in different potential changes in behavior.   As a result of observing the behavior of models, learners acquire either a verbal or a visual symbolic representation of behaviors that may or may not be performed at a later time (Bandura, 1977). These representations affect future behavioral outcomes in at least five ways (Bandura, 1986):

1. They may lead to *observational learning:* the acquisition of completely novel responses that were not in the learner's repertoire prior to observing a model. Whenever a new skill, such as changing the oil in a car or learning how to diagram a sentence, is demonstrated by a model, the learner is engaging in observational learning. Pronouncing a French

> Observational learning of new behavior

TABLE 5.1   Cognitive capabilities that allow us to profit from social learning

Capability	Description	Example
Symbolization	Encoding our observations into symbolic images that allow us to consider past and future events	"I wonder what would have happened if I had been driving that car?"
Forethought	Anticipating possible future actions	"I'll have to study even harder in college."
Vicarious capability	Learning from the experiences of others	"Mr. Jones just chewed out Billy for forgetting his homework. I'd better remember to turn mine in."
Self-regulation	Using personal standards to manage our own behavior	"I know everybody cheats in Mrs. Simmons's class, but if I did it I just wouldn't feel right."
Self-reflection	Thinking about our own experiences and thoughts	"I wrote that the British navy defeated the Spanish Armadillo. I wonder if that's spelled right."
Self-efficacy	Judging how effective we are in dealing with our environment	"I'm no good at statistics. I should put off taking that stat course until I have more time to study."

vocabulary word as a result of hearing the teacher say it is another example. In that case the learner is reorganizing previously acquired phones into a new sound pattern.

2. Internal representations allow us to *disinhibit* or *inhibit* learned responses. In one study, children observed a model punching, kicking, and in general abusing a large inflatable doll (Bandura, Ross, & Ross, 1963b). Ordinarily, these children did not treat dolls roughly. After observing the model, however, they inflicted considerably increased amounts of physical abuse on the doll, when the opportunity arose. It was assumed that children had already learned to kick and punch. What was learned through observation—namely, that these responses could occur in a particular setting—resulted in disinhibition of the traditional command to the contrary. Inhibitory effects, on the other hand, occur when the consequences of a model's behavior are observed to lead to punishment. This condition of vicarious punishment serves as a restraining influence on the observer's future behavior. In the study just cited, some models were chastised for mistreating the doll. Observers consequently did not increase their aggressive behavior toward the doll when they were allowed to play with it.

   Some advocates of televised coverage of capital punishment assume that the inhibitory effects of observing what happens to a convicted felon will be sufficient to cause a decrease in criminal actions. Just as in the case of punishment administered directly to the learner, however, vicarious punishment may not lead to inhibition if the conditions under which the observer is likely to produce the observed response differ substantially from the situation observed.

Response facilitation = prompting

3. *Response facilitation* or *exemplification* (Bandura, 1986) results when learned behavior is prompted by the model's actions. It is as if the model indicates that it is acceptable to engage in a particular behavior already known to the observer. Telethons utilize this type of facilitative effect by having callers state how much they are going to pledge for a particular cause, often "challenging" others to top their contribution.

4. A model's actions also serve to direct our attention to aspects of the environment that we may have been ignoring. This *environmental enhancement* effect is important in instruction because it alerts observers to critical elements that generally go unobserved. Teachers can direct attention to critical features of the student's learning environment in a number of ways.

5. A final type of learning outcome that results from observing a model is *arousal.* Emotions expressed by a model can change an observer's level of physical arousal, although not to the same extent or even with respect to the same emotion. Teachers who display enthusiasm for a topic or idea, for example, may arouse excitement in their students, but students will rarely attain the level of arousal characteristic of the committed teacher. Moreover, in many situations, it cannot be predicted what emotion will be aroused in the observer. Encountering a homeless person looking for food in an alley may evoke feelings of sympathy, disgust, fear, or anxiety,

depending on the observer's predisposition. In this case, social learning has resulted in the creation of an emotional state that affects the probability of subsequent behavior.

Cognitive Processes

Learning by observers from models entails some or all of four cognitive processes: attention, retention, production, and motivation.

Attention.   Attention determines what is selectively observed from among the many actions of a model. Without attention to relevant dimensions of the model's behavior, learning will not occur. Instructors who accentuate critical components of a task or behavior to be learned, subdivide complex activities into substeps, serve as or employ others to be competent models, and emphasize the functional value of a particular behavior that may be observed can enhance learners' attention. Instructors must also remember that many observers, particularly young children, may have short attention spans and may focus on features of a modeled behavior that are *salient* (distinctive, eye-catching) rather than relevant. The author was vividly reminded of this limitation when after demonstrating how to handle a pocket knife to a group of Cub Scouts, he was asked why his knife was red and the questioner's was blue.

Retention.   To be useful, information gained from observation must be retained. In describing the *retention* process, Bandura (1977) noted that observed behavior is preserved through storing it either as a set of images or as verbal descriptions. Images are particularly useful for storing complex activities not easily described in words, such as swinging a golf club. The learning of many cognitive skills, such as proving a geometry theorem, relies more on coding of the steps of the proof into a series of verbal statements or rules. For both types of representation, rehearsal is necessary for retention over a period of time. Rehearsal can be *overt,* as in traditional practice where the learner performs the behavior repeatedly, or *covert,* as in mentally going through the steps of an activity. Athletes, for example, prepare themselves not only by practicing their chosen sport, but by visualizing themselves performing the correct behavior successfully.

Mental practice, as this type of covert rehearsal is known, is believed to help athletes to code their movements into symbolic components, which make the movements more familiar and perhaps more automatic (Vealey, 1986). One specific approach is referred to as visuo-motor behavior rehearsal (VMBR) (Suinn, 1984). Three stages are involved: progressively relaxing different parts of the body, mentally rehearsing the steps of the sport, and using imagery to mentally practice a specific skill in a lifelike, stressful environment. The imagery is believed to generate localized large-muscle responses such as flexing and stretching (Hale, 1982).

In a review of studies of mental practice including VMBR, Orestak (1991) concluded that such imaging appears to be most effective in improving the performance of athletic skills having a large cognitive component (e.g., diving, high-jumping, putting a golf ball). It is most effective when employed by highly skilled athletes who have already mastered basic movements of the sport, however, and may produce a decrease in performance when the imagined behavior has an unsuccessful outcome. Visualizing oneself successfully completing a task to the accompaniment of cheers was found to be the most efficient approach.

Production. Visual and verbal conceptions of the modeled event are translated to action by the learner in the *production* phase. The learner compares the responses produced to the mental version of what he or she retains of the model's actions. Questions such as "Am I holding the racquet the way the coach did?" or "Do I twist my head coming out of a roll or going into it?" are likely to be asked. Problems arise at this phase when the observer has not accurately coded the model's actions into appropriate verbal or visual representations. For this reason, instructors who serve as models must provide corrective feedback, directed at individual learners during their first attempts to produce the response on their own. Deficiencies in observing and representing the modeled behavior can thus be quickly remediated. At later phases of practice, learners should be able to correct their own performance.

Model feedback promotes behavior production

Motivation. The motivational process is presumed to depend on the reinforcement that occurs during observation. Reinforcement can be *direct* (i.e., the learner produces the observed behavior and is reinforced for it), *vicarious* (the model is reinforced for the observed behavior), and *self-produced* (the learner employs internalized standards to evaluate personal performance). Learners do not always need to be reinforced directly, nor to observe someone else being reinforced for particular responses they might emit at a later time. They can derive reinforcement from their own satisfaction in doing something, regardless of the consequences to themselves or others.

This view of reinforcement is a departure from traditional operant theory. For Bandura, reinforcement acts as an incentive for translating observational learning into performance when there is a reason for emitting a particular behavior. It also serves to create an expectation in observers that if they respond in a manner that matches the behavior of a reinforced model, they will be reinforced also. Reinforcement is therefore informational, creating a motive for utilizing what has been observed.

CHARACTERISTICS OF A GOOD MODEL

Consider the following events in which models are employed to facilitate observational learning. Think about why they produced the effects described.

1. "Look how well Danny has organized his literature notebook, class," said Mrs. Stillman. "He has all our readings in order, with the characters identified and theme and plot summarized. He has even used different colored ink to highlight important implications of each work. I wish each of you would try to follow his example."

    There was a muffled moan from the back of the class: "Do we have to hear about that twerp Danny again? He's always perfect in class. I don't want anything to do with him. Who wants to be like him?"

2. "Class, I would like to introduce Charles Jackson. Six years ago he sat right here in this room, but he was arrested for possession of narcotics and spent six months in a juvenile detention center. Now Mr. Jackson is a successful businessman and is here to tell you how he got his life back on track. Give him a listen, will you?"

As the visitor rose, all eyes in the eighth-grade social studies class were on him. Charles Jackson was from the neighborhood; many knew his brothers. He had been just like them—poor and scraping to get by. The students wondered what he would have to say.

The selection of a model is an important component of effective instruction. As the examples indicate, not all models command attention and respect; hence models are not equally useful in presenting behaviors and beliefs that students might acquire. Although Danny demonstrates desired behaviors and is obviously reinforced for them from the teacher, Mrs. Stillman might have chosen a more effective model in an attempt to influence the behavior of her literature students. Charles Jackson, on the other hand, not only promises to command attention, but may by example serve to inhibit undesirable behaviors of some of his middle school observers. In this section, we examine the characteristics that determine whether models will be effective in influencing the behavior of young observers. As we shall see, the characteristics of effective peer models may not be the same as those that describe successful adult models, because effectiveness is partially dependent on the perceptions of the observer.

Effective Adult Models

Competence.   Models who demonstrate behaviors that successfully deal with the environment attract more attention than models who do not display such competence. Students attend to teachers because forethought tells them that they will have to perform the same skills themselves, and they want to be successful when it is their turn. Young children automatically assume that their parents and teachers are competent, as evidenced by their imitation and copying, for better or worse, of what mother, father, or kindergarten teacher does or says. As a learner matures, however, perceptions of competence on the part of adults must be continually demonstrated. Perceptions of a teacher's competence can quickly be revised if glaring errors are detected. The author still recalls the look of disapproval on the face of one of his sons when the first backhand shot that was demonstrated bounced off the court fence.

Prestige or Status.   Models who have achieved a high level of status are more likely to be attended to than those of lower prestige. Status is ordinarily acquired by distinguishing oneself in a certain field, in which case competence is also present. In other cases, however, status is derived from expertise in additional areas, in which the observer presumes competence to be present as well. In our society, professional athletes, pop music starts, and actors are often represented as competent to make judgments about the foods we should eat, the cars we should buy, and the politicians we should elect, despite an absence of any particular qualifications to make recommendations in these areas. The influence of parents and teachers extends to a wide variety of children's behaviors because the adults' perceived status is assumed to generalize to other areas. Bandura (1971) points out that when the consequences of novel behaviors are unknown, the behaviors of prestigious models are likely to be emulated, even in areas outside the models' competence. It is as if the observer assumes that there is less risk in copying what the high-status model might do, since the model is usually successful. Charles Jackson would be an effective model not only because of perceived competence in understanding the problems of the eight-graders, but because of the prestige attached to his success in business.

High-status models tend to attract attention to their behavior when compared to other models, as illustrated by the effectiveness of celebrity endorsements in advertising. If the modeled behavior does not lead to success for the observer, or if the model loses status, however, the behavior is likely to be rapidly abandoned by the observer. This change reflects the observer's reevaluation of the competence of the model. Sales of athletic shoes endorsed by professional athletes have been found to plummet when a particular athlete's scoring average declines.

Control of Reinforcement.   Bandura (1969) maintains that the model who controls dispensation of reinforcers can overcome deficiencies in status or competence. Models who not only are reinforced for their observed behavior but are in a position to provide incentives for those who observe them are most effective. A competent model such as one's boss is often in such a position, in which case modeling is extensive. Even when one's superior is perceived as incompetent, the boss's control of the dispensation of reinforcement will produce an increase in modeled behavior. Providing reinforcement for modeled behavior is one way in which adults gain status according to the judgment of observers.

Do your models possess these traits?

Effective Peer Models

Peer models function in the same social environment and are roughly equivalent in development to the learner. The major factor in peer modeling appears to be *perceived similarity* between the model and the observer (Schunk, 1987). Observers evaluate themselves by comparison with others, believing that the more similar they are to models on a particular characteristic, the more accurate their evaluation will be. Individuals who perceive themselves to be similar to a model tend to use the model's behavior as a basis for assessing whether their behavior is appropriate or their expectations about a situation are correct. In essence, an observer in reflection is saying: "Billy is like me, and it works for him so it must be OK for me to do it, too." Danny is rejected as a model in the literature class example because he is perceived to be so dissimilar to his classmates that they will not apply to themselves the standards represented by his behavior. On the other hand, Charles Jackson is viewed as possessing many of the characteristics the observers see in themselves.

Perceived similarity to a model is particularly influential when the observer has little information concerning appropriate or expected behavior in a situation or task

(Akamatsu & Thelen, 1974). Bandura (1986) additionally believes that similarity to a model helps individuals who lack confidence in their ability to perform adequately on an unfamiliar task, for example, or one on which they have experienced difficulty before. Performance by a similar model serves as evidence that the observers may be able to do well on the task also.

A number of factors contribute to perceived similarity. Based on a review of research, Schunk (1987) has examined four attributes of similarity: age, gender, competence, and background. *Age* of the model seems to be most influential when the observer is trying to judge whether a particular social behavior is appropriate, as in deciding whether it is acceptable to talk out in class. We have all observed children who are reluctant to speak out, even on a topic of interest, until one brave soul makes a response, precipitating a deluge of comments. Age is also salient when children know they are less competent than adults on a particular skill. Much to the chagrin of many an instructor, children tend to pay more attention to what age peers of comparable ability are doing during group lessons in skills such as swimming or driving an automobile.

Gender similarity seems to affect behaviors having to do with sex role stereotypes of proper conduct for boys and girls. For example, Wolf (1973) had children observe a male or female peer playing with a traditionally sex-inappropriate toy (e.g., girls playing with trucks, boys with dolls). When the observers were allowed to play with the toys, those who had been exposed to the same-sex model played longer with the sex-inappropriate toy. Boys rated the male model higher than the female model in attractiveness, although girls did not. Observers may have altered their opinions about sex appropriateness when they saw same-sex models engaging in an activity not traditionally associated with their gender.

Schunk reports a consistent finding that peer models perceived as *competent* enhance the observational learning of children. Observation of competent models leads to better performance on subsequent tasks, and indeed, children have learned to attend to the actions of those who are successful. Brody and Stoneman (1985), for example, found that without competence information, second-graders were more likely to model the responses of same-age peers. When competence information was available (e.g., "When Mary worked the puzzles, she did as well as the second-graders."), modeling was directed toward whichever child was described as competent in doing the puzzles, even a younger kindergarten child.

Similarity in *background* has also been found to influence children's modeling, particularly when little information about appropriate behavior is available. Rosenkrans (1967) had 90 Boy Scouts, ages eleven through fourteen, view a film in which a peer was playing a war strategy game. Subjects who were told that the model had similar interests to theirs, attended a similar school, and lived in the same town judged themselves more similar to the model, produced more modeled behaviors, and recalled more of what the model did during the game than did subjects who were told that their interests were dissimilar to those of the model, who also came from a different town.

Status, or the prestige of a peer model, is important to student observers, as in the case of Danny. In a famous study of classroom management practices (Kounin & Gump, 1962), it was found that if a teacher intervened to induce a student to decrease an inappropriate behavior, and the intervention was successful, the behavior of the

Who were your peer models?

whole class would improve as well. A decrease in inappropriate behavior of all students, even though intervention was directed at only one, is an example of *ripple effect.* This effect was greater when the student who was disciplined possessed higher status than other students. Observers say to themselves, in effect, "I would like to be like Jenny. Jenny got punished for doing that, so I shouldn't do it either." An important implication of this finding is that teachers can have greater impact in affecting the behavior of the larger group by intervening when high-status students misbehave. Low-status students are viewed by peers as dissimilar and therefore are less likely to serve as models when they are punished or reinforced.

Ripple effect = spread of inhibition/disinhibition

DEVELOPMENT OF SOCIAL LEARNING ABILITY

The cognitive abilities presumed to underlie effective learning from models do not arise spontaneously; they must develop as other skills do. Social learning theory has been criticized for ignoring developmental issues in the acquisition of these abilities (Yando, Seitz, & Zigler, 1978). Bandura (1986) attempted to address this oversight by analyzing the role of the four cognitive processes (attention, retention, production, and motivation) in children's developing ability to learn from models.

As discussed previously, young children have difficulty in attending to modeled events for long periods of time, in distinguishing relevant from irrelevant dimensions of a modeled task, and in simultaneously processing multiple sources of information. With experience in social and academic situations, however, most can learn to deploy their attention more selectively to relevant factors and to maintain focus despite the presence of distractions. Children who have difficulty in developing these attentional skills may require additional training involving shaping of responses to relevant stimuli as well as prompting and fading techniques (Schover & Newsom, 1976). The ability to symbolically represent and retain vicarious experiences also improves with development. A more extensive knowledge base contributes to understanding of new information, and the acquisition of memory strategies, such as rehearsal, permits more effective storage and retrieval of modeled events. The ability to recognize the value of memory, practice it efficiently, and monitor its use progresses gradually through the elementary school years (Flavell, 1979).

Social learning skills develop steadily

Physical maturation is obviously required for the motor production of modeled behaviors. The ability to translate into action information that is stored in memory, compare one's own responses with recollections of a model's, and correct subsequent performance also develops progressively. Production of correct ethical or moral behavior is even more problematic. The self-regulatory capability of creating and employing internal standards to evaluate the outcomes of our own behavior becomes easier with experience, although some people never completely free themselves from reliance on external social pressures. Indeed, one of the signs of maturity on the road from adolescence to adulthood is the ability to establish a sense of one's unique identity (Erikson, 1968).

Motivational factors that influence the use of modeled knowledge undergo significant developmental change as well. Perhaps the most necessary change is that children learn to delay gratification, or wait for reinforcement that cannot be expected until the future. The essence of vicarious learning is recognizing that reinforcement to the model can be gained by the observer only when future conditions require him or her to respond in a similar manner. Moreover, the events that possess reinforcing value also change with experience. Young children are motivated primarily by immediate sensory and social effects of their actions. Symbolic incentives and the opportunity to master certain tasks by themselves assume an increasing motivational function as development occurs. As Bandura (1986, p. 91) states, "After children discover that modeling is a good way of improving their capabilities, they adopt the modeled skills for the sense of self-efficacy and the personal satisfaction that it brings them."

Another critical skill in the development of social learning is the ability to make social comparisons of one's behavior to the actions of relevant others. Information about how one compares to others on a particular task is necessary for self-evaluation and the eventual development of internal standards. It is important to locate the point at which social comparison information begins to have an impact on children's learning. Research by Ruble, Boggiano, Feldman, and Loebl (1980), for instance, indicates a well-defined developmental pattern in children's use of comparative information about the success of peers. Children in kindergarten and first, second, and fourth grades were observed performing two tasks. In one they were to arrange five picture cards to tell a story, and in the other they were to throw four balls over a curtain at a concealed basketball hoop. The children could not directly determine the results of their efforts but were told that they had either succeeded or failed. Some were told that other children their age had been more successful than they, while members of a second experimental group were told that peers had been less successful. When asked to predict their future success in competing on these tasks, only the judgments of the fourth-graders were consistently and systematically influenced by the social comparison information. Kindergartners and first-graders made virtually no use of the comparative information, and second-graders were inconsistent and unpredictable. The researchers believe that the subjects' own performance was more salient to the younger children, who seemed to use the comparative information only to determine whether they were doing as well as their peers. Ruble et al. concluded that until children recognize that the outcomes of comparisons have implications for self-evaluation, providing competitive feedback in tasks such as these will have little impact.

With the development of linguistic skill and the ability to read meaningfully, learners are able to rely less on live models and more on those presented through the media. Bandura (1971) believes that *symbolic models,* such as characters in literature or on television shows, are powerful influences on learning. Advances in communications technology such as interactive video (Chapter 4) will enable people to observe on request almost any desired activity. Unlike direct learning, in which behavior is shaped through repeated experiences, in observational learning a single model can transmit new ways of thinking and behaving simultaneously to many people at once. Bandura (1986) cautions that for many people, symbolic modeling takes the place of real life, and social reality is conceived in terms of vicarious experiences. The more people's images of reality depend on the symbolic environment presented by the media, the greater will be the social impact of television, films, and so on. As learning through observation of others expands, it is imperative that we carefully monitor the symbolic modeling that is occurring.

Vicarious learning requires forethought

SELF-EFFICACY

The effects on behavior of our self-referent thought have been studied extensively in recent years, often from different theoretical perspectives (Bandura, 1977; DeCharms, 1978; Rotter, Chance, & Phares, 1972). Of central concern, no matter what the perspective, is people's sense of being able to control events that affect their lives. Bandura uses the term *perceived self-efficacy,* which he defines as "a judgment of one's capability to accomplish a certain level of performance" (Bandura, 1986, p. 391). He distinguishes self-efficacy from outcome expectations, which have more to do with our predictions of the consequences of our behavior. Self-efficacy relates to our feelings of confidence that we can achieve a desired outcome. In a classroom situation, for example, knowledge that well-written essays will be read to the class and thus receive praise is an outcome expectation, while the belief that one can produce such an essay is an efficacy judgment. Yet even students who know how writers of good essays will be reinforced may not work very hard to produce such an essay if they doubt their ability to do so. Students who believe themselves to be capable of producing an essay worthy of recognition, on the other hand, are more likely to perform well. Understanding the mechanisms that determine self-efficacy judgments is therefore important in understanding motivation and school achievement.

Self-efficacy is not to be confused with the more global term "self-concept," which refers to a more extensive view of the self, acquired from experience and the evaluations of others (Damon & Hart, 1982). Self-efficacy judgments are specific to certain domains in which we judge ourselves to possess competence. We describe ourselves, for example, as "good in writing but not so good with numbers."

As you might expect, ability affects feelings of self-efficacy; high-ability students rate themselves as more efficacious than low-ability students (Bandura, 1977). Individuals who judge themselves high in efficacy tend to select challenging tasks, while those with low perceptions of personal efficacy shield themselves from expected failure by avoiding stimulating environments (Bandura, 1986). The greater the sense of self-efficacy, the more likely is an individual to expend effort to succeed and continue to persevere in attempting difficult tasks. For instance, Bandura and Cerrone (1983) found that high-efficacy subjects were more likely to exercise harder and longer than low-efficacy subjects (on an aerobic treadmill device) when their performance was revealed to be substandard. Low perceptions of self-efficacy, on the other hand, lead to an overemphasis on personal inadequacies, with the result that challenging tasks are perceived to be more difficult than they really are (Meichenbaum, 1977). How one appraises personal efficacy in successfully meeting task demands apparently exerts a powerful influence over motivational components of learning as well as performance itself.

Beliefs of personal efficacy influence our choices of activities and situations and ultimately shape our lives. We avoid environments believed to exceed our coping ability, but readily undertake challenging activities we perceive ourselves to be capable of handling (Bandura, 1993). This selective process can be observed in career choice, for instance. An individual who has strong efficacy beliefs is likely to view more career options as possible, to prepare for them more adequately through educational or vocational planning, to stay in the chosen career longer, and to be more successful in meeting its demands (Lent & Hackett, 1987).

Efficacy beliefs also determine how much stress and anxiety are experienced in threatening situations. If we believe we can exercise control over stressful events, we are less likely to avoid them; moreover, we less frequently imagine negative outcomes and are more likely to function capably in their presence (Bandura, 1993). On the other hand, low-efficacy beliefs increase feelings of stress in the presence of threat, leading to physiological side effects such as elevated blood pressure, activation of stress-related hormones, and loss of immune functions, as described in Chapter 2.

People derive information they use in forming self-efficacy judgments from a variety of sources. Bandura suggests the following: *outcomes of one's own performance, vicarious experiences, social persuasion,* and *physiological states.* Table 5.2 describes and exemplifies these four principal sources.

Development of Self-Appraisal Skill in Self-Efficacy

Information from the four sources described in Table 5.2 is weighed and compared, leading to an inference about one's perceived self-efficacy. Bandura (1986) has called the process of forming this inference *self-appraisal.* Children gradually improve their self-appraisal skills, eventually learning to make efficacy judgments that guide their actions in different situations. The development of self-appraisal seems to follow a particular pattern.

Young children lack knowledge of their own capabilities and the consequences of different types of action, as we know from having prevented them from running into traffic, climbing out windows, or stumbling down stairs. The guidance of adults is necessary until children gain sufficient knowledge of their limits and the requirements of different environmental situations. As cognitive abilities develop, judgments of self-efficacy become more in tune with reality, and adult guidance is increasingly unnecessary. We discussed in Chapter 3 how each successive cognitive stage requires new mental constructions, allowing the individual to cope with demands met at that level. The development of perceived self-efficacy follows a similar path. As new challenges and expectations are encountered, people learn to weigh diverse sources of information to make appropriate judgments.

TABLE 5.2 Sources of information used to form self-efficacy judgments

Source	Example
One's own experience	"I passed Algebra 1, I guess I can pass Algebra 2, also."
Vicarious experience	"Charlie's not very good in math but he passed. I can too."
Social persuasion	As Ramona attempted to pull herself over the bar, she heard the exhortations of her friends. "You can do it, Ramona!" "They think I can chin myself," she thought. "Maybe I can."
Physiological feedback	"This foul shot means alot to the team. I can feel myself shaking. Maybe I'd better walk away from the line for a second and calm down before I try."

A number of cognitive skills must develop to ensure accurate self-appraisal. To evaluate personal experiences, children must be able to represent and retain information derived from prior observations, which requires considerable memory skill. They must attend simultaneously to multiple sources of efficacy information, which requires monitoring of ongoing events. They must estimate the difficulty of tasks, to judge how much ability and effort are necessary to meet them and the kinds of problems they are likely to encounter. These skills require the development of *metacognition,* or the ability to examine one's own thought (Flavell, 1979). With increasing maturity, children gain a better understanding of themselves and their environment, which allows them to make more realistic judgments of efficacy in particular areas of functioning (Bandura, 1986). For instance, in examining the development of mathematical schemes, Kun (1977) found that elementary school children gradually learn that lack of ability in an area can be compensated for by increased effort and that the two do not automatically go together. Until the age of nine, children believe that persons who try harder also are more capable or that those who don't try are not very competent. Older children recognize the independence of the two factors and know that one can choose to overcome limitations by investing more effort.

Growth in cognition aids self-appraisal

The ability to use comparative information derived from observing others is also acquired through experience. Prior to age three, children do not recognize differences in ability. With increasing age, they become more accurate in appraising the abilities of others and themselves. It is not until about age six that they realize that the performance of others like themselves is the most useful comparison (Morris & Nemcek, 1982).

Enhancement of Perceived Self-Efficacy

Whether children are judging self-efficacy from their own experience or through comparative information derived from the behavior of others, educational practices can affect the accuracy of their judgments. School should provide opportunities to experience success and to develop a higher sense of efficacy for learning. Instructional procedures that clearly convey information that children are achieving will contribute to their ability to make self-judgments. Now we turn to some educational practices that serve to enhance perceived self-efficacy.

Use of Peer Models.   Peer models are particularly helpful to students who have been led by past difficulties in learning academic material or in coping with stress to doubt their performance efficacy on particular tasks. Elementary children who had met failure in earlier attempts at learning to subtract were distributed among three experimental groups: One group observed a peer learn subtraction with regrouping, another observed an adult demonstrate the operations, the third did not have a model to observe (Schunk & Hansen, 1985). Students who had observed a peer rated themselves higher in efficacy and performed better in subtraction after practice than those who had observed the adult or no model at all. In explaining the results, the authors emphasize the model–observer similarity in age. They believe that age is salient on tasks at which peers are generally less competent than adults. Watching the adult model may have led the children low in perceptions of efficacy to wonder whether they were capable of becoming as competent as the model. Schunk and Hansen recommend that academic instruction of low-achieving children be supplemented by demonstrations by peer models to enhance self-efficacy.

Children who have had difficulty in learning certain skills may also benefit from demonstrations by peer models of different kinds of behavior. Models have been categorized as demonstrating either *mastery* or *coping skills* (Meichenbaum, 1971). Mastery models demonstrate a particular skill in its proper form, as a tennis pro might demonstrate the twist service. Coping models, on the other hand, not only exemplify the correct terminal behavior, but also might illustrate how initial attempts at a skill often meet failure and how mistakes can be gradually overcome on the way to mastery. Coping models thus demonstrate how the demonstrators coped with the demands of the task as well as their eventual success. Some children view a coping model's gradual progress from lack of skill to ultimate mastery as more similar to their typical performance than the rapid learning of a mastery model. It is hypothesized that such youngsters gain enhanced feelings of efficacy from coping models.

Peer models affect self-efficacy and learning

This hypothesis has been examined in a number of studies. Schunk, Hansen, and Cox (1987) divided ten-year-olds who had experienced difficulty in solving fraction problems into four groups:

mastery model, same sex
mastery model, opposite sex
coping model, same sex
coping model, opposite sex

Observing the coping model initially make errors only to correct them led to higher self-efficacy, greater skill in solving fraction problems, and a greater rating of similarity to the observer, regardless of the sex of the model. Coping models not only improved more gradually, they made statements such as "I need to calm down and pay attention, so I can get this right."

In a later version of the experiment, observers saw either one or three same-sex models demonstrate either mastery or coping skills. Children in the single-coping model, multiple-coping model, or multiple-mastery model conditions outperformed children who observed a single-mastery model in efficacy rating and skill in doing fractions. The results suggest that coping models are more beneficial in raising self-efficacy, although observing several peers learn rapidly is also effective. With several peers to observe, it is more likely that students will find at least one model who seems to be similar in competence to themselves.

Other studies find equal benefits of learning from coping and from mastery models (Klorman, Hilpert, Michael, LaGana, & Sveen, 1980; Kornherber & Schroeder, 1975; Schunk & Hansen, 1985). The study by Klorman et al., for example, dealt with the anxiety elicited by the prospect of dental work. Subjects observed either a peer mastery model, a coping model, or a film. The two modeling conditions were equally effective with children who had not been to the dentist before, but neither had much effect on experienced dentist-goers. Differences in effects of both types of models in different studies may be due to the amount of vital information presented in the two conditions; that is, in some studies coping models present additional vital information, such as the value of hard work and concentration (Meichenbaum, 1971). Coping models can be used not only to demonstrate the steps one must go through to complete a difficult task, but also to illustrate how effort and a positive attitude can improve behavior. This approach appears most likely to enhance observers' performance and efficacy judgments.

Who makes the best peer tutor?

Peer Tutoring. Often peer models directly instruct other students. *Peer tutoring* can be implemented by assigning one student to help another or by using one student as a teacher's aide to help teach a larger group. In the one-to-one relationship, it has been found that both tutor and tutee improve academically and in attitude toward the content (Cohen, Kulik, & Kulik, 1982). For the tutor, meeting the challenge of having to present content so that someone else can acquire it results in a more meaningful understanding of the material. Anyone who has taught something to another person recognizes that the process of organizing and presenting the information often leads to new insights and a greater appreciation of the content itself.

Two factors appear to account for improvements in the performance of the tutee. One is the obvious advantage of having an instructor focus on the learning of a single student as opposed to a larger group, so that the individual's performance can be monitored directly and immediate feedback provided. The other is the effect of enhanced self-efficacy. If tutors are carefully selected to possess the characteristics of good models— similarity to the tutee, perceived competence, and capacity to demonstrate coping skills as well as mastery—then the tutees are more likely to judge themselves capable of mastering the task at hand.

Utilizing peers as aides to instruct the whole class can enhance academic learning as well as the perceived self-efficacy of observers. Again, careful selection is important. Rather than emphasize mastery models who can demonstrate the skill but do not enhance the efficacy judgments of low achievers, it may be more important to select less capable students who have nevertheless demonstrated that they can perform the task. These models are more likely to impact efficacy judgments, particularly if they model coping strategies such as effort, attention, organization, and a calm approach to a new task. Comparative information provided by the teacher while the model is demonstrating the skill ("See how Jan takes her time and checks her work.") can contribute to an improved sense of efficacy in observers who might have difficulty with the modeled skill.

Successful Group Work. Efficacy can be enhanced when students contribute to successful group work efforts. The author proudly recalls answering a single question in a college intramural quiz bowl competition, but it provided 10 points of our team's 160-point total. While the points were few, there was a feeling that they were vital to the group's performance, and my confidence that I belonged on the team was restored. Successful group efforts reduce negative social comparisons made by members of low ability. Teachers who carefully form compatible groups containing students of both high and low ability, and then select tasks easy enough to be completed successfully, will have a positive impact on the efficacy judgments of group members.

Group success contributes to individual efficacy

Encouragement of Verbalization during Performance.   Efficacy attributions can be enhanced when students are able to verbalize their thoughts and anxieties. As discussed earlier, internal verbalization can aid self-reflection and self-regulation. Overtly verbalizing our thoughts about a task facilitates learning because attention can be directed toward important task features and the resulting rehearsal can improve their retention. As a means of regulating performance, verbalization can also convey a sense of being able to control one's own learning, thus reducing anxiety about possible failure on novel or difficult tasks.

Schunk and Cox (1986) taught learning-disabled children to verbalize while learning to subtract two-digit numbers using regrouping. The children learned to recite to themselves the necessary steps ("Now, I bring down the 4") and to instruct themselves to "take it easy" or "just do one step at a time." Those who learned to continuously verbalize while solving problems rated themselves as higher in self-efficacy after training and achieved at a higher level than those who verbalized only in early stages of training or not at all. The authors believed that verbalization served to promote confidence in the students' ability to solve the problems as well as aiding in the organization of their approach to the task.

Verbalization aids feeling of control

Provision of Clear Feedback about Success.   Clear communication to students that they are achieving success is necessary to maintaining a sense of efficacy. Feedback that not only identifies successful performance but points out how partially correct responses can be improved is valuable, for the learner sees how improvement can lead to eventual mastery. For a student low in self-efficacy, it is more important to emphasize what is correct about a particular response than to focus on mistakes, because efficacy information sustains motivation for a task and strengthens confidence that success can eventually be obtained.

Helping Students Set Realistic Goals.   Positive efficacy expectations motivate students to set realistic goals leading to achievement. Bandura (1977) has identified three properties of goal setting that if properly considered by students will lead to achievement.

The first is *specificity.* The more specific one can be in setting goals, the better. Goals that incorporate detailed standards of performance are more likely to produce self-evaluative reactions and to lead to higher performance. For example, attempting to improve your typing speed by two correct words per minute is a reasonable and specific goal; "trying to do better" is too general and not capable of being evaluated.

Specific goals are easier to attain

The second property identified by Bandura is *difficulty level.* Setting goals that are unrealistically difficult to achieve leads to failure and the maintenance of low self-efficacy attributions in low-achieving students. Students who set their goals too high may have acted on the basis of an erroneous belief about their ability or inaccurate observation of models. Similarly, unrealistically easy goals may be established on the basis of lowered efficacy expectations or erroneous information about task difficulty obtained through inaccurate observation of models. Helping students to accurately appraise task difficulty and to evaluate the relative performance of others leads to realistic setting of personal goals.

The third property is *proximity.* That is, How far do goals project into the future? Pursuing proximal or short-term goals promotes self-efficacy, because progress can be more frequently observed and success can occur more often. Because progress toward distal goals is more difficult to assess and delay between the setting of distal goals and their fulfillment is greater, children receive less clear information about their ability when only distal goals are available.

In an attempt to compare the effect of proximal versus distal goals, Bandura and Schunk (1981) provided children with seven sets of training materials to aid the learning of subtraction. Some children had a proximal goal of completing one set each session for seven sessions; others had a distal goal of completing all sets by the end of the seventh session, but not necessarily one each session; and a third group worked on the lessons without an explicit goal. Those working on proximal goals reached the highest rate of problem solving; they also demonstrated greater skill in subtraction and after the sessions reported greater feelings of efficacy than those with distal goals.

As Schunk points out in a review of self-efficacy and achievement (1984), pursuing proximal goals can help develop skills and a sense of efficacy, but only if students are made to understand that the goals are attainable. Teachers who wish to promote efficacy may avoid providing comparative information about how other children performed in favor of directly telling students that they can attain the goal. Direct information should help students focus on their own improvement from proximal goal to proximal goal, which should in turn promote self-efficacy. Helping children to set their own realistic goals will help them concentrate on their own improvement, rather than the comparative performance of others.

Teacher Self-Efficacy.   Classrooms and schools in which teachers possess strong beliefs in both personal and instructional self-efficacy are most likely to help students develop their own feelings of confidence. If a teacher believes that she can promote learning, even in a difficult student, improved levels of efficacy are more probable. In a review of teacher efficacy studies, Gibson and Dembo (1984) noted that teachers with a high sense of self-efficacy for their instructional skill spent more time in working on academic learning tasks, stayed with students who did not immediately succeed, and praised low achievers when they did attain success. Teachers who doubted their ability to enhance learning spent more time on noninstructional activities, gave up quickly on students who had difficulty in learning, and were more likely to criticize low achievers for failure. The effect of low perceptions of instructional and personal efficacy is most noticeable when students are making a transition from one school or level of schooling to another. Students taught by teachers with a low sense of efficacy decrease their own perceptions of their ability to perform in the transition from elementary to middle schools, particularly if the students already doubt themselves (Midgley, Feldlaufer, & Eccles, 1989).

In addition, teachers rarely operate in isolation. They operate collectively within an interactive school system. The belief systems of school staffs can have either encouraging or discouraging effects on students' efficacy beliefs. Principals and other administrators who are able to promote a strong sense of purpose and a belief by their staff that they can collectively aid the learning of their students are invaluable. The author still recalls a principal leading an academic pep rally. The administrator ripped off his suit jacket and shirt to reveal an "I know I can do better!!!!" sign on his T-shirt. Cheers followed.

SELF-REGULATION

From our discussion so far, the critical role of self-directed behavior in attempting to explain psychological functioning is readily apparent. Bandura (1986) observed that much of our ongoing behavior occurs in the absence of immediate external reinforcement, since the consequences of our actions lie too far in the future to control behavior in the present. When we write, we may have a long-term goal in mind, but the actual writing process is guided by self-evaluation based on a personal standard of judgment, which leads to often painstakingly difficult editing and revising. Better writers become quite efficient in this practice of self-monitoring. Such *self-regulated learning* has been defined as "the process whereby students personally activate and sustain cognitions and behaviors systematically oriented toward the attainment of academic learning goals" (Zimmerman, 1986, p. 307).

Bandura (1986) identifies three subfunctions that interact during the self-regulation process: self-observation, self-judgment, and self-reaction. We must be able to observe and understand our own behavior, judge it against a personal standard, and react to it constructively. We have all completed tasks, evaluated our performance, and then mentally congratulated ourselves for a job well done, or engaged in self-criticism for poor results.

Can we practice self-observation objectively?

Self-observation provides the information necessary for setting appropriate standards and for evaluating changes in behavior. It is important that our attempts at observing our own behavior accurately reflect dimensions such as quality, quantity, speed, appropriateness, and the resulting consequences. Bandura points out that these dimensions can be observed most accurately if behavior is monitored regularly and recorded as close as possible to the time of its occurrence. If we have difficulty in learning a part for a school play, for instance, it is useful to systematically identify what flubs are made during various scenes and, immediately after each rehearsal, to record the errors that occur.

Accuracy of self-observation can be enhanced by a number of methods. One approach is to use an appropriate *recording technique.* Irwin and Bushnell (1980) describe several techniques that can be adapted for use by learners to record their own behavior. *Time sampling* is used to determine the rate of occurrence of frequent behaviors within a specified time slot. For example, during a 30-minute study period, how often do you find yourself thinking of something other than the academic material? *Event sampling* requires the counting of all events that occur across different time periods. During the school day, for example, how often do you experience failure? *Checklists* are lists of behaviors on which the user records the occurrence of particular responses, often those that are to be done in a particular sequence. Checklists are useful in making sure that you have followed all the steps in completing a chemistry experiment or operating a piece of equipment, for example. *Rating scales* are designed to quantify more subjective reactions, such as rating the quality of one's effort or ranking an event in comparison to others. Two frequently employed types of

Self-observation
is aided by
structure

scale are *numerical* ("On a scale of 1 to 10, how would you rate this text in terms of its value?") and *graphic:*

"I am precise."

| Always | Often | Sometimes | Seldom | Never |

Recording techniques are useful to the extent that the behavior being observed is clearly conceptualized and defined. Students can be trained to employ these techniques, and there is evidence that they facilitate academic skill. For example, Schunk (1983b) taught children to record the number of workbook pages completed at the end of each class session covering subtraction skills. On subsequent tests, children trained to record their own completed problems performed as well as those who were individually monitored by a teacher and better than children who did not record.

A second recording procedure consists of teaching children to *verbalize* while functioning in school. Meichenbaum and Goodman (1971) taught children judged as impulsive to verbalize, initially out loud and then to themselves, in an attempt to increase self-control. It was found that children trained to talk before responding responded less impulsively and demonstrated greater attention in completing various tasks. Meichenbaum and Asarnow (1979) suggest that statements children use to instruct themselves be succinct and to the point of what is being mastered. For example, "First estimate, then solve" can be easily recalled, and its use is directly related to success in solving math problems. Short statements may also be displayed around the classroom as reminders to children to follow appropriate steps without teacher presence. Schunk (1986) suggests that overt verbalization training be used predominantly for children who have difficulty acquiring skills requiring small steps. Rather than encourage a roomful of children to verbalize, resulting in a distracting hubbub, students likely to profit most from the technique should be selected. Teachers can make self-observation easier for students in other ways. Forms for monitoring progress can be provided for major tasks. One teacher distributes an assignment completion form with all written assignments that require several steps over a period of time. The form is presented in Figure 5.2.

Progress is easily identified if students check off each step on the form as they complete it. Self-regulation is aided because learners are more able to see where slowdowns or problems occur. In addition, feelings of self-efficacy are enhanced when proximal goals are met.

Self-observation also can be fostered by encouraging children to use *pictorial aids* to monitor their work. A teacher who assigned sets of math problems to solve had the children draw five light bulbs at different points down the side of the page, with a large bulb at the end. When a few problems had been worked, hence the first light bulb was reached, a student was to fill in the bulb with pencil, draw a star to the left of the line, and say, "Yea for me!" Each child was to work down the page until all light bulbs were "lit." Giving students the choice of where to position the light bulbs on the page allowed them control over the task as a whole, which increased interest. When the students had followed this strategy frequently, they spontaneously applied it to other academic tasks such as answering social studies questions or writing spelling word sentences (Janek, 1989).

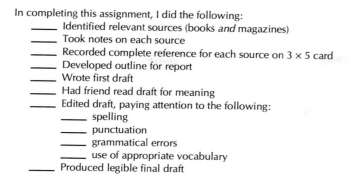

In completing this assignment, I did the following:
_____ Identified relevant sources (books *and* magazines)
_____ Took notes on each source
_____ Recorded complete reference for each source on 3 × 5 card
_____ Developed outline for report
_____ Wrote first draft
_____ Had friend read draft for meaning
_____ Edited draft, paying attention to the following:
    _____ spelling
    _____ punctuation
    _____ grammatical errors
    _____ use of appropriate vocabulary
_____ Produced legible final draft

FIGURE 5.2 Assignment completion form to aid student self-observation

Self-observation may eventually lead to *self-judgment,* or the establishment of a standard to evaluate one's behavior. As we discussed earlier, standards are acquired through receiving comparative information about the performance of similar models, as well as through personal experiences of success and failure. Comparative information is most useful in determining how well one performs in reference to others, as in the case of standardized placement tests. Scores on the Graduate Record Examination are meaningful only in terms of relative standing within a group, for example. Judging results on the basis of performance alone, without regard to normative standards, is known as *criterion-referenced* evaluation. This form of judgment requires a criterion that is fixed and widely accepted. It has been determined, for instance, that good typists should be able to type 80 correct words per minute. Performing at least at this level is much more significant than being able to type even more rapidly. Much of our self-judgment is based on meeting fixed, criterion-referenced standards that we view as goals for ourselves. One person has labored for years to run the mile in five minutes or less. Meeting this criterion will not stun the track world, but the goal is attainable for that individual, hence is worthy.

> Self-judgment is based on personal standards

Accuracy of self-judgment seems to develop progressively. The overly optimistic views evident in early elementary school students eventually become modified to the point that self-judgment is based on a correspondence between actual performance and a relevant standard. R. S. Newman and Wick (1987) examined the judgments of eight-year-olds and eleven-year-olds on a task requiring estimations of how many dots were in groups of various sizes (from 55 dots to more than 200). All children rated their confidence on a seven-point scale, but half received feedback on how they had performed and half did not. For older children, confidence was associated with how well they did on the task; that is, they appeared to use the feedback to alter their estimation of their performance. For the younger children, skill on the task and feedback were associated with lower confidence ratings. Young children who were less successful maintained their confidence despite feedback to the contrary.

Realistic self-judgments take time to acquire, as children learn how to combine external feedback and their own perceptions. Training in using feedback about one's success or failure may be required, particularly for children who are less successful in specific tasks. In a study of such training (Schunk, 1983a), fourth-graders were taught to set goals and to use comparative information about the performance of others in mathematics. Students were told in a first session that half the children like them had been able to finish 25 problems, and they might want to try at least 25 problems themselves. At the beginning of a second session, they were told that half of the other students had finished 16 problems, hence 16 might be an appropriate goal. Children given these instructions demonstrated considerably greater skill on division problems afterward and a significant increase in judgment of self-efficacy when compared to controls and children who were given only the comparative information or only the goal-setting information.

The third subprocess in self-regulation is *self-reaction* to one's performance. Self-reactions can be classified into three types: *behavioral, personal,* and *environmental* (Zimmerman, 1989). Arranging not to go with our friends for a late snack until we have finished our economics reading assignment is an example of a behavioral self-reaction. Personal self-reactions include decisions to revise our goals or to recheck our work. Environmental self-reactions, such as seeking help from a peer or teacher, represent attempts to restructure the environment to be more responsive to our efforts.

Zimmerman (1989) uses the terms *self-regulated learning strategies* to describe the types of procedures that can be used in self-reaction. He finds that the use of a variety of such strategies leads to improved test performance. Teachers were reliably able to identify many of these strategies when employed by students in high school math and English classes (Zimmerman & Martinez-Pons, 1988). Table 5.3 lists self-regulated learning strategies Zimmerman has identified and examples of student statements reflecting use of these strategies.

The list in Table 5.3 is useful because it indicates ways in which teachers can monitor students' internal self-regulatory processes through observation of critical statements and behaviors. By identifying self-regulatory references made by students, teachers can either reinforce positive ones or suggest alternatives to those that are less likely to produce effective learning or enhanced feelings of efficacy.

Which self-regulation strategies do you use?

Summary of Self-Regulated Learning and Self-Efficacy

Self-regulated students actively participate in their own learning by initiating and directing their efforts to acquire knowledge and skill, rather than relying on others (Zimmerman, 1986). To regulate personal behavior, one needs a strong sense of personal efficacy, for this will allow the individual to continue to organize and implement actions leading to selected goals. Self-regulation proceeds through three phases: (1) an observational stage, in which one's behavior should be recorded in a systematic fashion, (2) a self-judgment phase, in which standards are applied to one's behavior, and (3) a self-reaction phase, in which self-regulated learning strategies are employed to achieve academic goals. Strategies are employed to modify the behavioral consequences of one's behavior, to implement metacognitive skills (e.g., rehearsing, outlining, reviewing), and to alter environmental conditions such as requesting teacher aid. Self-regulated strategies can be learned through modeling of behaviors demonstrated by similar, competent models, or through direct instruction. Students who demonstrate self-regulation achieve at good levels, evidence increased motivation for specific tasks, and report enhanced confidence in their ability to learn.

The next time you study academic material, see if you can implement the three

TABLE 5.3 Self-regulated learning strategies

Strategies	Typical Statements
1. Self-evaluation	"I check over my work to make sure I did it right."
2. Organizing and transforming	"I make an outline before I write my paper."
3. Goal setting and planning	"First, I start studying two weeks before exams, and I pace myself."
4. Seeking information	"Before beginning to write the paper, I go to the library to get as much information as possible."
5. Keeping records and monitoring	"I kept a list of the words I got wrong."
6. Environmental structuring	"I turned off the radio so I could concentrate on what I was doing."
7. Self-consequating (providing self-determined reinforcement after performing a particular behavior)	"If I do well on a test, I treat myself to a movie."
8. Rehearsing and memorizing	"I keep writing the formula down until I memorize it."
9–11. Seeking social assistance	Statements indicating student efforts to solicit help from peers (9), teachers (10), and adults (11). ("If I have problems, I ask a friend for help.")
12–14. Reviewing records	Statements indicating student efforts to reread notes (12), tests (13), and textbooks (14). ("When preparing for a test, I review my notes.")
15. Other	Statements indicating learner behaviors initiated by others. ("I just do what the teacher says.")

SOURCE: B. J. Zimmerman, A social cognitive view of self-regulated learning. *Journal of Educational Psychology, 81*(3), 329–339 (1989). Adapted with permission of the publisher.

subfunctions of self-regulated learning. Try to employ a procedure to observe the quantity and quality of your study efforts. You might want to focus on events that interfere with learning by recording them in some way. For example, try keeping track of how many times you find yourself daydreaming.

Do you employ some standard to judge your work? If not, set a goal to be achieved in a given study session and when you are finished, determine whether the goal has been attained.

Do you identify appropriate reactions you make after having studied? Examples include providing extrinsic reinforcement for good effort or successful completions, adjusting your plans for studying next time, and attempting to alter the environment by asking for help or searching for additional explanatory material. Attending to the self-regulatory subfunctions may improve learning and is likely to enhance perceptions of personal efficacy.

EFFECTIVE TEACHING

The social learning approach has several important implications for effective teaching. We have already discussed the desirable characteristics of good adult and peer *models*, and we have described the effects models have on student learning. Effective teachers use appropriate models to demonstrate critical skills or content, to provide comparative information for students to use in setting their own goals and standards, and to communicate that it is possible to cope with and master the demands of particular tasks. The presentation of exemplary models other than the teacher adds to the diversity of the classroom and can have a positive impact on students' motivation to learn.

Many of the principles of social learning can be applied to *coaching,* a special form of instruction. Coaching traditionally refers to a direct form of teaching motor skills, including demonstrations by the instructor and the provision of immediate feedback following student attempts at imitation. Learning results from coaching in a wide variety of fields, including music, drama, the arts, and athletics, and in technical areas such as industry. Coaches must be competent in demonstrating modeled responses; in addition, they must possess appropriate prestige and, like any effective adult model, must be in control of contingent reinforcement to be effective. An interesting psychological analysis of coaching involved observation of the techniques used by John Wooden, the famous basketball coach at UCLA (Tharp & Gallimore, 1975). The researchers recorded the percentage of time Wooden spent in various coaching activities during practice sessions with his players. Fifty percent of his time was devoted to verbal descriptions of what to do or how to do it, with only 5 percent of time engaged in actual demonstration. Verbal praise and verbal reprimands were issued in equal amounts—7 percent for each. Thirteen percent of Wooden's time was spent in reviewing skills. Perhaps the most interesting aspect of Wooden's coaching was his use of "scolding" combined with prompting of forgotten behavior and descriptions of what was expected of the individual. A favorite scold was "How many times must I tell you that? More is expected of you." These comments occurred approximately 8 percent of the time, but Wooden almost never scowled, removed players from practice, or isolated them in doing repetitive exercises or calisthenics. The authors entitled this "scold–reinstruct" process a "Wooden" because of its unique occurrence in their observations of teachers and its departure from more traditional coaching punishments.

What's a "Wooden"?

It appears that Wooden established high goals for his players to attain and frequently reminded them of expected standards.

From a social learning perspective, Wooden's coaching style was characterized by less modeling and more encouragement of self-appraisal, along with the setting of high personal and team goals. His success, as defined by his extremely high winning percentage, leading to 10 national basketball championships, may have been attributable to his ability to inspire his players to regulate their own behavior in working toward a common goal. Of course, Wooden coached only athletes who were very gifted and very large. Whether his coaching approach would be useful in aiding less gifted students to achieve success in their endeavors is nevertheless worthy of study.

Peer models may be utilized to teach *social skills* as well as academic content or motor behaviors. Selected models can be reinforced for demonstrating prosocial (positive) behaviors such as initiating play appropriately or handling instructional materials in a responsible way. Observers have been reported to change their behavior based on vicarious consequences to the models. Strain, Kerr, and Ragland (1981), for example, taught elementary children to initiate social play with withdrawn children by using positive verbal requests such as "Let's play blocks" or by politely handing another child a toy. Observers were found to increase their prosocial play behavior when later opportunities arose. If selected children who are perceived as effective models by other children can be trained to demonstrate social skills, teachers may find that they spend less time in the long run having to monitor social activities themselves.

Shared curriculum goals can create increased perceptions of self-efficacy in students who work together. Salomon (1991) described an interactive science classroom approach in which students in biology, chemistry, world history, and physics classes examined the effects of deforestation on the Amazon rain forest. Each class examined the part of the topic most pertinent to its subject area, communicated its findings to the others, and shared materials and reports. The combined group developed a model of the effects of deforestation on agriculture, economics, global climate, ocean equilibrium, pollution, and extinction of species and presented their paper to a statewide conference. The most interesting finding was not that students learned significantly more about the topic, but that self-efficacy perceptions of many students increased (Hicks, 1991). The teamwork required to produce the reports apparently encouraged individuals to believe that they could effectively contribute to particular subject matter fields. Contributing to the learning of others, recognizing one's own emerging skill, and acquiring more realistic understanding of various academic fields were also positive outcomes of this interactive learning project.

Shared goals contribute to self-efficacy

SUMMARY

Social learning theory maintains that we learn by observing the behavior of others, in addition to learning via classical or operant conditioning. Bandura suggests a triadic reciprocal interaction among personal factors, the environment, and behavior as an explanation of social learning, in which the influence exerted by each set of factors can vary. Learners possess several cognitive capabilities that allow them to profit from social learning, including symbolization, forethought, vicarious capability, self-regulation, self-reflection, and self-efficacy. These capabilities allow the observation of others to result in learning that is either novel or a modification of old behavior; observation also can induce reaction to a prompt for the occurrence of old behavior, enhancement of attention, or a change in level of arousal. Four cognitive processes are necessary for any social learning event to occur: attention to relevant dimensions of a behavior, retention of verbal or visual representations of the act, production of motoric actions, and perceived motivation for performing the behavior. Motivation is derived from three possible forms of reinforcement: directly to the observer from the environment, vicariously to the model, and self-produced.

Characteristics of models are important to whether observation occurs. Effective adult models should be perceived as competent, possess status, and be in control of forthcoming reinforcement. Effective peer models are perceived as similar to the observer in terms of age, gender, competence, and background. As children develop, symbolic models presented in literature and by the media may also be effective models.

Perceived self-efficacy, or the judgment of one's capacity to attain a certain level of performance, is derived from the outcomes of our performance, vicarious experiences, social persuasion from others, and physiological feedback. If accurate perceptions of self-efficacy are to emerge, there must be self-appraisal, which requires metacognitive skills such as memory, using multiple sources of often-conflicting information, ability to determine task difficulty, and ability to use comparative information. Educational practices including the use of peer models demonstrating coping and mastery skills, the use of peers as tutors to directly instruct students in one-to-one or small-group formats, and the organization of work in small groups to allow all members to contribute to the group's goal are beneficial in enhancing judgments of personal efficacy. Children can also be helped by encouraging them to verbalize their thoughts and anxieties during performance, by providing clear feedback about their successes, and by helping them to set realistic, specific proximal and distal goals of appropriate difficulty.

Self-regulated learning, or the process of personally activating and sustaining cognitions and behaviors directed toward learning goals, is critical to school success. Bandura has identified three subfunctions of self-regulation–self-observation, self-judgment, and self-reaction. Self-observation can be improved by using appropriate recording techniques such as time sampling, event sampling, checklists, or rating scales, or through verbalization while one is completing each step of a task. Teachers can facilitate self-observation by providing forms to aid self-recording. Self-judgment entails establishing standards to judge success that are derived from external feedback and one's own criteria; it can be improved by practice in using comparative information and setting realistic goals. Self-reactions are either behavioral outcomes arranged by the learner, personal adjustments in metacognitive processes, or attempts to alter the environment. A number of learning strategies such as self-consequating, planning, reviewing, and structuring the environment can be employed to facilitate self-reaction. The three subfunctions of self-regulation are also aided by a high level of perceived self-efficacy, providing a sense that continuous self-monitoring will lead to eventual achievement and success.

A concept map for this chapter appears on page 183.

EXERCISES

1. Think of three significant people in your life, other than your parents, from whom you learned particular skills. Can you identify the personal characteristics that contributed to their being good models? Do you recall being aware of those characteristics at the time you were acquiring the skill?

2. Recall the times when your personal feelings of self-efficacy were high, when you were satisfied and confident about your performance on a particular task. What external evidence contributed to your confidence? What personal standard that you had set was met or surpassed? Did you feel more positive about the task and subsequent activities as a result of your success?

3. After rereading the strategies for self-regulation described in Table 5.3, select three statements you could utilize in regulating your own study. In what situations would you be most likely to apply them?

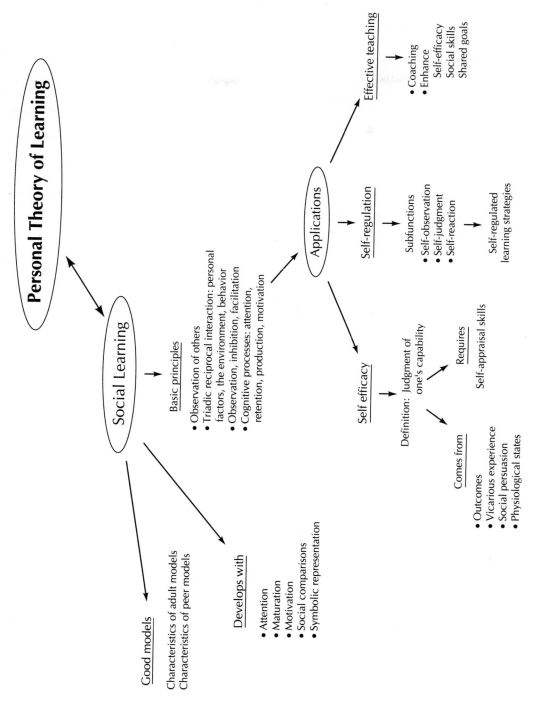

Concept Map for Chapter 5

183

SUGGESTED READINGS

Bandura, A. (1978). The self-system in reciprocal determinism. *American Psychologist, 33*(4), 344–358.

Bandura, A. (1986). *Social foundations of thought and action: A social cognitive theory.* Englewood Cliffs, NJ: Prentice-Hall.

Bandura, A. (1993). Perceived self-efficacy in cognitive development and functioning. *Educational Psychologist, 28*(2), 117–148.

Schunk, D. H. (1987). Peer models and children's behavioral change. *Review of Educational Research, 57*(2), 149–174.

Schunk, D. H., Hansen, A. R., & Cox, P. D. (1987). Peer-model attributes and children's achievement behaviors. *Journal of Educational Psychology, 79*(1), 54–61.

Zimmerman, B. J. (1989). A social cognitive view of self-regulated learning. *Journal of Educational Psychology, 81*(3), 329–339.

chapter **6**

Cognitive Information Processing

CHAPTER OUTLINE

CHAPTER OBJECTIVES

1. Analyze Bruner's and Ausubel's positions on discovery learning.
2. Differentiate Anderson's ACT model from the parallel distributed processing view of neural networks.
3. Describe the components of the cognitive information-processing theory of learning including attention, working memory, and long-term memory.
4. Explain the factors that contribute to encoding. Describe a technique you would use to aid student encoding.
5. Explain the factors that affect retrieval. Outline a technique you would use to aid learners' retrieval.

> *As Miss Flambeau rose to give the week's vocabulary test to her eighth-grade French class, Charles began to fidget. He never did very well on these tests; they always seemed too difficult. All the French words sounded alike, and there seemed to be so many of them.*
>
> *"Ecrivez la traduction en anglais, sur votre papier, s'il vous plaît," Miss Flambeau commanded. "Oh, boy, she has to say everything in French," Charles complained to himself.*
>
> *"Alors, numéro un: 'appeler.'"*
>
> *Charles groaned. ("'Appelez? Appeler?' Does she want the infinitive or the 'you' form?")*
>
> *"Deux: 'la fenêtre.'"*
> *("Oh yeah, the window.")*
> *"Trois: 'le boucher.'"*
> *("Oh no, was that the grocer or the butcher?")*
> *"Quatre: 'la salle de bains.'"*
> *("Which room is that?")*
> *"Cinq: 'la salle à manger.'"*
> *"Six: 'faire.'"*
> *"Sept: 'ouvrir.'"*
> *("Wait")*
>
> *. . .*
>
> *"Quinze, et c'est tout . . . 'la porte.'"*
> *("The door—lead me to it.")*

> *Elizabeth pulled at her hair. "The Teapot Dome scandal, when was that? If I could remember that, I might be able to recall its significance. Was it in Harding's administration? . . . Sure. My dad told me Harding never knew what was going on in his own administration. I bet that's been true for a lot of presidents. . . . Hey, maybe that's part of the significance of Teapot Dome!"*

These episodes describe two different kinds of memory tasks students are expected to do in school. The behavioral models we have considered to this point would relate Charles's difficulties to a failure to form appropriate stimulus–response connections between the French and English words. Elizabeth's efforts to recall the significance of the details of the Teapot Dome scandal would be viewed as a failure to identify generalized associations to this historical event.

Other theorists would interpret these students' "talking to themselves" as data to be analyzed in attempting to understand how learning takes place. They believe that learning occurs as a result of the individual's efforts to understand the environment. Learning is not only the acquisition of new associations, it is also a reorganization of mental structures and procedures. Recalling when the Teapot Dome scandal occurred or that *salle* means room are processes Elizabeth and Charles are using to recapture their organized knowledge of the relevant content.

Cognitive structural view = reorganization

This alternative view of learning has been traditionally described as a *cognitive structural approach* because of its emphasis on cognitive processes such as thought, memory, and judgment and their relationships. This view of learning originated in the early work of the gestaltists as described in Chapter 1. The gestaltists believed that perceptual reorganization is necessary for learning to occur and that it requires more than an accumulation of previously learned elements (Koffka, 1935). They demonstrated that learning could occur without the step-by-step shaping advocated by most behaviorists when they described learning by insight. Other theorists expanded this view.

EARLY COGNITIVE THEORIES

Jerome Bruner extended the cognitive approach by emphasizing that incoming stimuli are sorted and interpreted according to past learning, whereupon they are placed into loosely structured categories. Categories signify the process of interpreting the environment by (1) providing a place for new input to go, (2) helping us identify new objects, (3) reducing the necessity for constant learning, (4) providing a direction for subsequent instrumental activity, and (5) allowing ordering and relating of classes of events that contribute to a larger organized structure (Bruner, Goodnow, & Austin, 1956). Suppose, for example, that in studying geometry, Heather encounters a new shape—the cone. She has already formed the geometrical categories of circle and rectangle, which possess similar attributes, so the cone can be identified as similar. Much of what she has learned about the circle is likely to apply to the cone (curved lines, radius, etc.), so some old learning will apply. Processes that were useful in determining the area of the cone are likely to be similar to processes used with the other figures, so subsequent instrumental activity is affected. Finally, including the cone in her grouping of geometric shapes makes possible a new ordering and relating of categories as Heather establishes a new category of shapes that have both curved and straight sides.

Bruner was responsible for the idea that learning is most meaningful to learners when they have the opportunity to *discover* relationships among concepts on their own. Discovery entails the rearranging or transforming of evidence in such a way that one is enabled to "go beyond the evidence so reassembled to new insights" (Bruner, 1962, pp. 82–83). Bruner believed that providing learners the opportunity to make discoveries had four important benefits:

1. It increases *intellectual potency,* or the learner's ability to construct and organize what is encountered, to learn how to go about the very task of learning.

Discovery learning benefits motivation, memory

2. It facilitates a shift from *extrinsic to intrinsic rewards.* Bruner's claim expands the criticism of behavioral positions discussed in Chapter 4. He suggests that discovery learning is rewarding in itself and that it contributes to a sense of competence in the learner.

3. It contributes to the learning of certain *heuristics,* or generalized strategies that will allow the learner to continue learning well beyond the classroom.

4. It allows the *conservation of memory,* in that information learned by discovery will be remembered longer.

As a result of his emphasis on discovery learning, Bruner recommended that teachers utilize materials that generate curiosity through novelty, contrast, and incongruity. Remember the author's high school chemistry teacher, who always began a lesson with an interesting chemical reaction? The rest of the lesson was designed to allow students to re-create the reaction (two chemicals combining to change color, a compound dissolving when another element is introduced, etc.). Bruner believed that students should be able to manipulate objects, explore possibilities, and otherwise control their learning sequence. Unlike the behaviorists, he believed that errors should be examined rather than avoided at all costs. Errors have instructional value because they may reveal unanticipated misunderstandings about content. Often my old chemistry teacher spent considerable time discussing the logic and procedures followed by students who had failed to create the desired chemical effect.

Bruner (1962b) advocated a hypothetical mode of instruction, where students are free to form and test their own hypotheses. A hypothetical mode of instruction contributes to an inquiring attitude toward learning in which students not only discover new relationships, but might also recognize that not all ideas are perfectly correct or well developed. Becoming aware that knowledge is ever-changing and that learning must therefore be continual is also acquired through a hypothetical mode. Learning should therefore proceed inductively, from the specific to the general, following the steps a scientist might take in formulating hypotheses and laws. Like a scientist, students should strive to resolve the curious events they encounter by discovering generalized rules and solving related problems. In one of Bruner's descriptions of social studies curricula, for example, students are given a topographical map containing information about elevations, waterways, locations of natural resources, and so on. They are asked to project where cities, highways, and major centers of development should be placed. Their guesses can then be compared to maps of the actual development that occurred. The comparison allows students to verify or reject the principles they had used to solve the problems of economic growth. Bruner recommends the discovery approach to instruction about economic and geographical principles, rather than a more traditional teacher-centered exposition, because he believes that it results in increased long-term retention of the content, greater ability to transfer it to other situations, and increased enthusiasm for its subsequent study.

David Ausubel challenged Bruner's claims for discovery learning, arguing that not only is it less effective than promised, but it is not necessarily the correct approach for instructors to take. Ausubel also subscribed to a cognitive view of learning, but he believed that meaningful learning can result from traditional expository instruction as well as from discovery methods.

Ausubel (1964) believed that the "junior scientist" model of Bruner is not necessary, that in fact students are better off learning the same basic subject matter that the scientist did in his younger days through the expository method. Students themselves do not have to rediscover everything that has already been discovered; our culture can provide us that information much more directly. As Ausubel 1964 states:

> It is the scientist's business to formulate unifying explanatory principles in science. It is the student's business to learn these principles as meaningfully and critically as possible, and *then,* after his background is adequate, to try to improve on them if he can. If he is ever to discover, he must first learn, and he cannot learn adequately by pretending he is a junior scientist. (p. 298)

Learner as "junior scientist"?

This position led Ausubel to advocate a general-to-specific approach in teaching expository lessons. The instructor should introduce broad concepts initially, then progress to successively more specific ideas and processes. In teaching about biological reproduction, for example, a general description would precede information on more specific types, such as human reproduction. The learner can more easily assimilate incoming information because a structure has been established. Examples, applications, and illustrations also facilitate meaningful learning.

A number of studies attempted to compare reception learning to discovery, but many did not clarify whether learning by discovery is seen as a learning method at the discretion of the student or as an instructional method employed by the teacher. Moreover, the amount of guidance provided by the teacher varies considerably, so how much was discovered by the student alone and how much was provided by the teacher are often unclear in the literature. The relative effect of each approach may depend on the instructional objective of the lesson. After a review of comparative studies, Ausubel and Robinson (1969) determined that it was more efficient to use a more reception-oriented method if the intention of the lesson was comprehension of a concept or rule. When application or problem solving was the goal, less direction by the teacher appeared to be warranted, although a degree of structuring seemed to be preferable to autonomous discovery. Little advantage was found for minimally structured methods. Discovery without guidance makes the learning of concepts a terribly slow process. For young learners, on the other hand, excessive reliance on expository instructional methods appears to reduce the likelihood of recognition that one can go beyond the information given to solve problems independently. In content areas where inquiry and experimentation are critical, it would seem necessary to provide an opportunity for children to exercise their own abilities in discovering new relationships (Bruner, 1966).

Ausubel: Learn first, then discover

Discovery requires guidance

Both Bruner and Ausubel emphasized the interaction of the individual's organized learning structures with new stimuli in performing cognitive tasks such as solving problems. In that respect, both positions have much in common with Piaget's constructivist view of cognitive development. Other than noting the existence of prior structures, however, neither position provided much detail about the perception of new input, its relation to existing structures, and how it is processed so that new behaviors are possible. A model that more precisely described these processes began to emerge in the late 1960s and has become the dominant cognitive position today. It is known as the *cognitive information-processing model* of learning.

This model attempts to describe what happens to information from the moment it is perceived till the occurrence of some form of related behavior. Each step in the process is described in sufficient detail to permit simulation on a computer (André & Phye, 1986), and some forms of the model adopt terminology such as "storage" and "retrieval" from computer operations. Those advocating the cognitive information-processing approach have adopted the more rigorous techniques of the behaviorists to verify the existence of mental processes, and they employ the logical analyses and observations typically carried out by earlier cognitivists. Moreover, more contemporary versions of the model are able to make reference to neurophysiological mechanisms of learning as that field begins to yield more related information.

Several versions have been developed of a model that represents how information is processed in the human sensory and nervous systems. One of the earliest and most influential, which attempted to incorporate physiological events as well as psychological processes as they were then understood (Atkinson & Shiffrin, 1968), is presented in Figure 6.1.

Sensory register—alerting function

This three-stage model begins when stimuli activate sensitive cells in the receptor organs. As you recall, our sensory system is continually bombarded with energy impulses (light changes, sound waves, kinesthetic cues, etc.). An important phase of information processing is the discrimination of these simultaneously occurring stimuli and the determination of which should be selected for further analysis. In the model of Figure 6.1, this is the task of the *sensory register.* Its function is best illustrated by the mother who somehow sleeps through the snores of her husband as well as other night sounds, yet awakens immediately at the sound of the baby's cry. The sensory register cannot be precisely localized in the brain, but physiologists assume that the subcortical areas of the reticular formation and the hypothalamus, perhaps functioning jointly, provide this alerting function (Levinthal, 1990). Stimuli activating the sensory register may produce a sudden awareness or alertness and may result in responses such as a turning of the head, pupil dilation, or sudden movements.

Research by Sperling (1960) and others has shown that sensations are registered in their actual form for a few hundred milliseconds. If not chosen for further process-

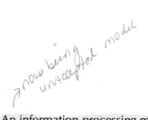

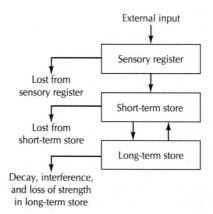

FIGURE 6.1 An information-processing model

SOURCE: Adapted from R. C. Atkinson and R. M. Shiffrin, *Human memory: A proposed system and its control processes.* In K. W. Spence and J. T. Spence (Eds.), *The psychology of learning and motivation. Vol. 2* (New York: Academic Press, 1968), pp. 90–197.

ing, sensations decay very rapidly. Rapid decay is very important to our cognitive functioning, allowing us to concentrate on one image or sound at a time. Imagine the confusion we might undergo if sensations remained for longer periods of time; we would be continually seeing double or hearing repeated echoes. For some individuals, sensations do in fact remain for unusually long periods of time. This rare phenomenon, known as eidetic imagery or, more popularly, "photographic memory," allows individuals to retain detailed images such as whole pages of text. Why eidetic imagery occurs in the few individuals who possess it, why it is more frequently found in children, and why it tends to disappear with age remain unknown (Haber, 1979).

The second part of the system illustrated in Figure 6.1 is the *short-term store*, where information currently being thought about is processed. Information in short-term memory remains for up to 15 to 20 seconds without active rehearsal, and longer if the individual repeats, analyzes, or in some way cognitively processes the content. During this initial period, information may exist both in auditory form (as in saying a to-be-dialed phone number to yourself as the operator provides it) and in visual imagery (as a mother might visualize her infant crying in pain). The next time someone provides you an amount of information, either auditorily or visually, close your eyes and rehearse it to yourself. Do you "see" the information, or "hear" it? It does not appear necessary for the information in the short-term store to be the same as the sensory input—note that we often "see" a word in our conscious thoughts even as we hear it being said.

The short-term store is limited in its capacity, usually containing about seven items of information (G. Miller, 1956). If more items are presented than can be handled, they are lost very rapidly unless rehearsed or subjected to other cognitive activity. For this reason, the short-term store was initially viewed as a bottleneck in the information-processing system, because while information in the short-term store is being processed, our capacity to think of other things is reduced.

The last major component of Atkinson and Shiffrin's model is the *long-term store*. Information that reaches it does not decay and become lost in the same moment as information in the sensory register or short-term store. Once information has reached the long-term store, it remains relatively permanently, although it may be modified or become temporarily hard to retrieve as the result of other incoming information. The long-term store has a large capacity—in fact, the prodigious amount of information we all possess in long-term storage has no practical limit. We may even possess information in long-term store that is not easily classifiable into any of the sensory modalities, such as a sense of time (Atkinson & Shiffrin, 1968).

As Atkinson and Shiffrin originally envisioned their model, the flow of information among the three systems is under the individual's control. Information is received at the sensory register, scanned and selected to be introduced into the short-term (ST) store, and then transferred to long-term (LT) store as a result of further processing. Note also that there is transfer from the long-term store to the short-term store, as indicated by the two arrows in Figure 6.1. Such transfer is presumed to occur in thinking activities in which information already permanently stored is used to process information currently being considered.

While the Atkinson–Shiffrin model provided an initial structure for understanding learning and memory, most cognitive theorists no longer employ it as the major model of information processing. There are three basic reasons for its disuse.

1. The model implies a localization of each stage that does not conform to the physiological evidence now available. While neurophysiologists have successfully described the pathways that incoming sensations take on their way to the neocortex, as depicted in Chapter 2, the point at which sensation becomes psychological meaning is by no means clear. Much of the neocortex is simultaneously activated when incoming stimuli are processed, as PET scans indicate (Haier et al., 1988). Moreover, the motor aspect of speech production is apparently separate from the comprehension aspect, suggesting that linguistic stimuli are distributed to various locations early in the process (Levinthal, 1990).

2. Research on various kinds of memory phenomenon attests to the continued interaction of the short-term and long-term store (Anderson, 1983b). Viewing them metaphorically as distinct "places" does not adequately describe their function, since information appears to move so readily between them. Most current models of cognition have substituted for the short-term store the concept of a *working memory,* in which information being processed is in constant contact with long-term memory.

Working memory supplants short-/long-term memory

3. Some cognitive functions seem to occur almost automatically, with little internal processing that can be identified based on studies of learners' thoughts and actions. For example, as reading skill increases, some identified words seem to go directly into long-term memory without being subjected to any preliminary analysis. For these reasons, cognitive psychologists have turned to *network models* of information processing, which have expanded the three-stage description of Atkinson and Shiffrin.

ANDERSON'S ACT MODEL

ACT theory — what cognitive units compose memory

J. R. Anderson (1976) provided a theory that went beyond the stage model of memory to include all the many ways in which information is processed. The adaptive control of thought (ACT) theory begins by identifying the basic *cognitive units* that compose our memory. Cognitive units can be either *propositions, images,* or *strings of words.* Propositions contain a unit *node* (the proposition) and a set of *elements* (*relations* and *arguments* of the proposition). A proposition is the "smallest unit of knowledge that can stand as a separate assertion" (Anderson, 1990, p. 123) or the smallest unit about which a true or false judgment can be made. "The river is clear" is a proposition. Anderson argues, however, that we seldom recall information as discrete propositions. In most cases, the units we recall are modified by elements such as relations (relational terms such as verbs, adjectives, adverbs, etc.) and arguments (associated nouns). The sentence "The AuSable River is clear as glass" contains the basic proposition (river–clear) as well as the relations (river is clear) and (river–clear–glass) for the relationship of clarity to glass. It also contains an argument in the form of the name (River–AuSable).

Cognitive units—associated via a network

Of what significance are cognitive units structured in this way? First, the units seem to be the material that is initially placed into long-term memory, or *encoded,* and later *retrieved.* When part of a cognitive unit is formed in long-term memory, all of it is encoded. When a unit is retrieved, it is retrieved in its entirety. For instance, when a proposition containing a subject, verb, and object is formed, all three elements will be encoded in the unit, not just one or two. When retrieval occurs, therefore, all three elements will be retrieved (Anderson, 1983b). In a sense, the propositions, relations, and arguments form a network of associated meanings that are the basic elements of learning and memory, rather than the original sentence or sentences presented.

Research evidence demonstrates that we retrieve information more in propositional form than in the form of the original input. Bransford and Franks (1971), for example, had students study 12 sentences composed of several propositions such as "The ants in the kitchen ate the jelly" and "The jelly was sweet." After practice, the students were asked to indicate whether specific sentences were among these originally presented. That is, the test sentences were either items actually studied, new sentences created from the old ones (e.g., "The ants in the kitchen ate the sweet jelly."), or sentences that could not be formed from the sentences studied (e.g., "The ants ate the jelly beside the woods."). Subjects were not able to distinguish between the first two kinds but were confident that they had not heard sentences of the third type. The results indicated to the researchers that subjects were insensitive to the actual arrangement of propositions in sentences but knew which propositions they had encountered.

Other cognitive units can be in the form of images or strings of words that have no underlying meaning (e.g., refrains from songs or chants such as "Sha na na na— good bye"). Cognitive units compose what Anderson refers to as *declarative knowledge,* or knowledge about facts and things. Knowledge about how to perform certain activities, such as solving math problems by reducing fractions, is referred to as *procedural* knowledge and requires different cognitive units called *productions* (Anderson, Kline, & Beasley, 1979).

Once propositions have been encoded in working memory, there is a probability that a *trace* linking them to long-term memory will be established. Traces have the property of strength. Repetition increases the strength of a trace, so that if a proposition is well rehearsed, the probability of retrieving it from long-term memory and the speed of its retrieval are increased. A trace, once formed, will not be lost, but its strength can decay (Anderson, 1983b). This relationship explains why we have difficulty in retrieving information we have not utilized in a long while, but with effort can eventually recall it. Of course, with no use at all over a long period of time, decay will be extensive and retrieval much more difficult.

Since working memory contains traces from long-term memory, and since new traces are continually being developed in working memory to eventually connect with long-term memory, the two systems overlap considerably. At any point in time, certain working memory elements are sources of activation of long-term memory, either because they are encodings of perceptual events (e.g., hearing a voice) or because they are internal concepts currently being processed (e.g., thinking about the meaning of what has been heard). Activation can spread from these units to associated elements in the network. Reading the word "Canada," for example, may activate stored relations and arguments such as "cold," "far away," "friendly," and "Mounties." Elizabeth's efforts to recall the significance of the Teapot Dome scandal, described earlier, took the form of an attempt to follow an associative network to retrieve infor-

[handwritten margin notes: no response to teacher asked questions — rephrase → different trial. several examples → more assoc to proposition. ACT theory summarized]

mation. As soon as the initial source drops from attention, its activation begins to decay, as does activation of the supporting network.

This *spread of activation* process has two direct implications for instruction. First, teacher-posed questions that elicit no response might be rephrased to provide alternative cues. In that way a different trace can be activated and retrieval of the desired information through the network may still be possible. Second, teachers should employ as many examples and details of important concepts as possible. The more associations to a proposition, the more likely that activation along a related network will spread, and later retrieval will be faster and more complete.

Thus Anderson's ACT model of information processing is initiated when incoming stimuli are perceived through the sensory system. Information is then encoded in an all-or-none manner into cognitive units, most frequently in the form of propositions. The strength of these units increases with practice and decays with time. Cognitive units formed during working memory become linked to those already in long-term memory, establishing a network. Retrieval occurs through spreading activation of these links or traces throughout the network. The more extensive the network, and the stronger the traces, the quicker and more probable is recall. Other stimuli may activate the network through related associations. The model is particularly useful because it can be applied to a wide variety of cognitive activities. For our purposes, it is applicable to the learning of most instructional content.

PARALLEL DISTRIBUTED PROCESSING

[handwritten margin note: ACT criticism — like computer]

In Chapter 2 we examined how neurons are connected and noted the complexity of interactions between and within the structures of the central nervous system. A major criticism of network models such as Anderson's ACT is that they employ a sequential view of cognitive processing, fostered by comparisons to how computers function. Computers rapidly execute procedures in a serial fashion. Although not nearly as quick, efficient human information processing brings together an incredible number of associations, often from diverse modalities involving different dimensions. In thinking of Canada, for example, we might also recall these propositions and sensations in a short period of time: snow, maple leaves, maple sugar, the smell of pine needles, visions of beautiful forests, the Montreal Canadiens, a member of the opposite sex met in Canada, the singers Anne Murray and Brian Adams, and so on. It is as if the human brain is able to follow several lines of thought all at once.

Parallel, not sequential processing

In considering how the brain seems to function, alternative models of information processing have recently been proposed. *Parallel distributed processing* (PDP) developed by Rumelhart, McClelland, and the PDP research group (1986) is one example. PDP does not assume that networks need to be hierarchically arranged. Like network models, memories are accessed through patterns of activation. Encoded information is recalled because of the strength of its connection with other encoded information. This model attempts to explain the complexity of cognitive processing, however, by permitting simultaneous or parallel activation distributed across several networks. When attempting to hit a baseball, for example, a batter identifies cues in the pitcher's delivery to determine whether the ball will curve, estimates its speed, and recalls how frequently the pitcher throws curve balls and where they might be aimed—all simultaneously. Such a complex act of information processing can't depend on serial or sequential processing, as a network model might suggest. In fact, the batter must integrate cues from kinesthetic, perceptual, and even emotional dimensions, as well as cognitive ones, to decide where to swing. In addition, each dimension varies in its probability of occurrence, its strength, and its importance—multiple constraints that must also be considered.

In the PDP model, each piece of knowledge is stored according to the *strength* of its *connection* to other units. The meaning of the Greek letter pi, for example, is *distributed* over connections to a potentially large number of related units. The symbols Π (uppercase) and π (lowercase) are connected to the Greek alphabet, fraternities, 3.1416, and symbolic equations. How we interpret these symbols ultimately will depend on the context in which they are presented and on the relative strengths of the various connections. Obviously the meaning must be interpreted differently when we see $c = \pi\delta$ or ΠΒΤ.

An advantage of a PDP model is that it assumes that neurological pathways can be activated in parallel, thus accounting for the speed at which many judgments are made. The connections by which units are linked are presumed to be established at the synapses of cortical neurons. This model may match more closely the physiological functioning of the brain as described by Damasio and Damasio (1992) and discussed in Chapter 2 (p. 39).

[handwritten margin note: PDP model → access many things at once, not one after another. ACT → sequential recall]

COMPONENTS OF INFORMATION PROCESSING

While the various cognitive information-processing models differ in certain assumptions and details, there is an emerging consensus about the components comprising the cognitive information-processing system.

1. Stimuli must be perceived and attended initially if learning is to take place; these processes occur at the sensory register.
2. Information is further processed into more complex cognitive units during working memory.
3. The representation of the information formed by the learner is based not only on initial input but on past learning as well. In other words, learning occurs partially in a top-down fashion in which previously acquired content determines what is learned and recalled, as well as through a bottom-up sequence in which initial stimuli influence the actual processing. Learning from instruction thus depends on what a student already knows perhaps as much as the instructional content itself.
4. Information is transferred to long-term memory, again requiring a connection to what is already stored. Previous knowledge not only facilitates transfer to long-term storage, but aids in its retrieval. The way in which the information is transferred determines how it is stored and how it can be used.

We will now examine the specific components of the cognitive information-processing model. Our analysis will emphasize implications for instruction.

Attention

Physiologists use the term *sensation* to refer to the activation of receptor muscles and the afferent pathways of the sensory system leading to the neocortex and the term *perception* to describe the activity of cells in the neocortex beyond the first synapse (Kolb & Whishaw, 1986). Sensations become perceptions when they are acted on by factors such as stored memories and contextual information. This transformation of physical energy into our subjective experience is what is continually occurring in the psychological phase referred to as the sensory register.

The sensory register is additionally important because it protects us from being overwhelmed with data. We eventually process a very small fraction of the events that impinge on us—perhaps as little as one percent according to some estimates (Schmidt, 1985). Consider the motorist who continually monitors the highway, the roadside, conversations within the car, news or music from the car radio, and so on. Hundreds of sensations are being received by the receptor muscles. Suppose a highway sign appears, announcing the proximity of the interstate route he is seeking. This sign becomes a perception as the sensory register admits it to consciousness. The driver notes the distance to the interchange and that information is processed further. All other simultaneously occurring sensations probably will be allowed to decay. Suppose, however, that the driver was reminiscing while listening to an old song on the radio or participating actively in a conversation with the passengers. When sensations from such sources are admitted to consciousness, a highway sign may very well be missed. Later the driver may report that he "never did see that darn sign." Failing to "see the sign" in this case means that the sensation did not become a perception by way of the sensory register.

Teachers can enhance the entrance of stimuli into the sensory register in three general ways. First, they can encourage alertness by ensuring that students are physically ready to receive stimulation. Sitting in the correct posture, with head up and turned toward the speaker, will increase the probability that visual and auditory stimuli enter consciousness. While physical alertness will not ensure learning, of course, it is clear that without perception learning will not occur at all. Second, teachers can vary the sensory systems that are activated during presentations. By interspersing visual signals with auditory ones, and occasionally permitting proprioceptive responses such as touch to occur, the teacher ensures that no one channel is so overworked that the learner tires and fails to monitor new information. Third, the introduction of novel stimuli or change within a sensory channel can enhance alertness. Pauses for effect, increases or decreases in volume of the voice, change in pitch, and the use of stress have long been used by skilled public speakers to keep listeners in contact with the content of their speech. Children's television shows such as *Sesame Street* utilize rapid changes of scene and camera angle to maintain viewer alertness.

Note that "attention" has not yet been used to describe the processing of information. This is because the term refers to the processing that occurs after perceptions have been formed. At that point we can say that the learner has become aware of a particular stimulus and has focused on it for a particular purpose. Attention cannot be wasted by the active learner; it is a limited resource in which concentration on specific external or internal stimuli is maintained to accomplish a goal. Attention requires selection among competing stimuli, with the chosen stimulus the one most likely to be learned and recalled. Selective focusing of receptors on a specific stimulus, followed by filtering this information to our sensory system, is referred to as *primary attention* (Norman, 1969).

Despite the best intentions of the ambivalent student, watching a favorite TV show and reading one's history assignment at the same time is a feat that cannot be sustained successfully. One set of incoming information will receive primary attention, while the other will eventually be ignored, or at best receive sporadic and therefore not very careful attention. Which one will be selected?

While it is easy to say that the less demanding and more entertaining TV show will capture our student's attention, it remains necessary to examine the variables that lead to a final choice. One factor is *novelty*; stimuli that have not been perceived at all, or have not been encountered for some time, typically take precedence over more familiar ones. A stimulus is also considered novel if it appears in an unfamiliar context, where one's expectations are violated. Thus our student's history text might be selected if the context appears to be novel or unexpected to the reader (or, coincidentally, the TV show is judged to be boring or repetitive).

Intensity is another factor that attracts attention. The loudness of a speaker's voice, the brightness of an image, the vividness of a detail—all are characteristics that demand attention. Content perceived as graphic or emotionally arousing is particularly likely to be selected.

A third factor affecting selective attention is *similarity*. It is a truism that two quite similar stimuli cannot be attended to at the same time. One will be selected, the other eventually ignored. Conversations in which two people who sound alike are talking to you will cause a good deal of discomfort, until you decide to select one and turn your back on the other. Listening to soft instrumental music on the radio while studying may not require active selection, however; the two sources of stimulation are distinct enough to be processed simultaneously.

Another way to conceptualize the simultaneous processing of soft music and reading is in terms of stimulus *complexity*, a fourth factor that affects attention. If an opera is aired that requires you to decipher the lyrics while continuing to read, you now have two sources of stimulation that are more equally complex. A selective choice at least for the short term would be necessary.

For some students, particularly those diagnosed as learning disabled, inability to maintain attention is a major impediment to learning. The term "attention deficit–hyperactivity disorder" (ADHD) has been placed in the *Diagnostic and Statistical Manual of Mental Disorders* (DSM-III-R) (American Psychiatric Association, 1987) to describe those for whom attentional problems are particularly acute. The essential features of the disorder are the consistent occurrence, before age seven, of an inability to complete tasks, impulsivity, and hyperactivity. Children so afflicted are unable to organize what they are to do and are distracted by stimuli irrelevant to the task. Following are some of the statements used in the DSM-III-R manual to describe attention deficit disorder learners:

"Often fails to finish things he or she starts."

"Has difficulty sticking to a play activity."

What factors attract attention?

"Frequent shifting from one activity to another."

"Is always on the go or always having his motor running." (American Psychiatric Association, 1987, p. 50).

Of course, all children occasionally demonstrate some or all of these behaviors. It is the intensity and frequency of the actions that lead to a diagnosis of ADHD.

Attention during learning tasks is maximized when only one important stimulus is presented and selection is not necessary. Most students eventually learn that they should listen to the teacher's voice and not to the sounds of the air conditioner, for example. But suppose two equally important events occur simultaneously. Must one be ignored? No, not necessarily. Attention can be divided, but one set of stimuli must be processed *automatically*. Automatic processing occurs when certain stimuli are recognized as containing features that are so well "coded" or understood that the learner can proceed to respond to them in a routine, systematized way, while devoting more conscious attention to another set of stimuli. One type of task that requires automatic processing is reading. In acquiring this intellectual skill, children initially detect features they have come to associate with certain letters. The process is similar to developing an internal "chart" in which each letter is defined by features such as straight lines, oblique lines, and circles (Gibson, 1965). Some letters have more common features and are easily confused: *b* with *d* for example or *p* with *q*. Others have less commonality and are more easily distinguished (e.g., *s*). Once letters and the other graphemes that are meaningful in written language (" - . ;" !, etc.) have been identified and practiced, higher-level "codes" emerge. These include combinations of graphemes and represent words or even frequently occurring groups of words. When first learning to read, the child must devote close attention to grapheme recognition by detecting key features; later on this process becomes automatic and attention is directed to meaning rather than letter or word identification (Laberge & Samuels, 1974).

Automaticity— two things at once?

As Grabe (1986) points out, automatic processing occurs only with practice, and the task must be difficult enough to require the automatization of some aspects as well. Think of your first attempts to drive a car with a standard transmission, for example. At first, you responded to each feature of the steering mechanism as a separate stimulus—the steering wheel, gear shifts, pedals, and so on. To drive successfully, however, one must respond to these components in unison, rather than in sequence. Failure in this regard leads to stalling, the grinding of gears, lurching as a new gear is selected with too little or too much gas, . . . We cannot afford to drive without reducing most of the task to an automatic level. Our conscious attention is thus reserved for monitoring traffic conditions, street lights, and so on.

Automatic processing requires confidence as well. Skillful athletes do not need to worry about the position of their feet or hands while shooting a basketball. Confident that these basic movements have been well established, they can devote their conscious attention to such practical concerns as the defense they are facing, the location of the basket or other teammates, and the time remaining on the clock. Overly critical coaching or teaching may cause learners to lose first confidence, and then automaticity, because attention is diverted to more basic matters such as "Are my feet together when I take this shot?" Beginning readers who have not developed confidence in their ability to recognize letter combinations as representing words may resort to a "sound-it-out" approach, rather than risk errors in judgment. Consequently, reading is slowed and frequently meaning is lost.

Directing Attention

Helping students focus on distinctive features is an important function of teachers in the early phases of learning. Teachers can arrange instructional activities so that primary attention is selectively directed toward critical elements of the learning task. A wide variety of techniques are available for presenting visual material through handouts, as video displays, or on blackboards. The use of underlining, bold type, capitalization, italicization, directional arrows, varying colors, changes in print size or font, circled sections, isolation of critical ideas, and using asterisks or stars next to key words all serve to direct attention. Current word-processing programs easily permit the manipulation of text to draw attention to important elements. Most modern instructional books, including this one, utilize these aids to directing visual attention.

In presenting information verbally, a number of attention-directing techniques are possible. Changes in pitch, in volume, in stress, or even in dialect can be employed. A teacher known to the author employs a Cockney or a German accent in stating key points. His students report remembering these ideas above all others! Simple directions such as "Now remember this!" or "This will be on the test!" also serve to direct auditory attention. The use of rhymes or songs to emphasize critical ideas, so charmingly presented in the 1988 film *Stand and Deliver,* can be particularly effective.

It must be emphasized that according to information-processing theory, all information processed by the learner is selected from the total available stimulation in some manner. A teacher who directs students' attention will increase the probability that the most important features are selected, but this tactic by no means ensures correct choices in every case. In fact, if attention-directing techniques are overused, students cease to take special note of their occurrence. Underlining too many key words in a paragraph, or saying "This will be on the test!" too frequently eventually may create satiation in students, who will ignore those cues and resort to less useful ways of selecting information.

Working Memory

Once information has been selected for primary attention, it enters the more overtly conscious phase of the information-processing system, that of working memory (WM). As initially described by Baddeley and Hitch (1974), WM represents a control system with limits on both its storage and processing capabilities. It is involved not only in transferring information to long-term memory, but in reasoning and understanding of new input. As such, WM corresponds to what we commonly call thinking and is a critical component of studying.

Trying to maintain information in WM has been described by Anderson (1990) as analogous to a circus act in which a juggler attempts to keep a number of plates spinning on a reed. He must continually run back to the first and respin it before it falls off

Processing needed in WM

and then respin all the others before starting a new one. If we try to keep too many items in WM, by the time we attempt to rehearse the first one, its level of activation will have declined so far that retrieval and rehearsal cannot be accomplished in a reasonable time. Anderson summarizes the properties of WM as follows:

1. Items in WM are initially highly activated.
2. If unattended, items will rapidly decay.
3. Items can be maintained if they are rehearsed.
4. The number of items that can be maintained is limited, depending on how many items can be rehearsed before they decay.
5. As items in WM decay, the speed at which they can be accessed slows.

It is clear that for learning to occur, information in WM must be processed while it is active, through rehearsal techniques such as repetition and forming an image of the material or by relating it to some other material (Baddeley, 1986).

"Should I try to remember this or write it down?"

"Is this important?"

"What do I already know about this?"

Such questions often are addressed by the learner during WM. While determining how to process incoming information is straightforward in discrete learning tasks such as remembering phone numbers or locker combinations, it is much more complicated in continuous learning activities such as reading. While reading, for example, learners must continually take new input (material from the text), relate it to what has already been read and what might be known about the topic from previous learning, and decide to attempt to recall this information, read on, or reread. It is not surprising, therefore, that inability to process information efficiently in WM and limitations in WM capacity have been related to reading difficulties. Perfetti and Lesgold (1978) hypothesized that poor readers are slow at placing new items into WM and at clearing old items out of it. Comprehension is aided by a smooth flow of information into and out of WM. Without such a smooth transition, a bottleneck is created that interferes with comprehension. Davey (1987) demonstrated that poor readers took so long to recognize words that decay occurred and performance was poor on comprehension questions asked after reading. Without availability in WM of previously read words, poor readers are forced to guess at meanings, thus raising the probability that they will make errors on more difficult items.

To overcome WM deficits, it is necessary for readers to overlearn word recognition until automaticity has been achieved. By "automatic" Samuels (1988) implies that the amount of effort or energy required to recognize a word is reduced sufficiently to permit WM to be cleared for the entry of new items. Automaticity can be obtained only through extended practice; there is no shortcut. In checking for automaticity, teachers should have students read passages aloud, checking for expression and a lack of hesitancy in their voices. Expression and smoothness in reading reflect more than dramatic ability; they are indicators of the reader's skill in moving efficiently from one set of words to the next, thus demonstrating automaticity. Samuels also recommends that teachers give novel passages to students to read orally and ask that they give back all they can remember. If a reader can read and comprehend the passage at the same time, automaticity has been established.

There is considerable evidence that WM capacity increases with age. Five-year-old children, for example, can recall four digits, ten-year-olds about six, and adults seven, on the average (Dempster, 1981). Siegler (1991) suggests that this developmental trend may reflect increasing skill in employing effective memory strategies or familiarity with the context to be remembered, as much as greater memory capacity. Nevertheless, the trend does suggest that learning tasks that place too severe a demand on WM capacity for younger children should be minimized.

Long-Term Memory

So far we have examined acquisition of content that is just being learned. What about the long-term fate of that learning? Long-term memory (LTM) is the more permanent storehouse of our memories. While it is tempting to think of LTM as a separate place, as the Atkinson–Shiffrin model suggested, recognize that it works in concert with WM, being activated by information processed in the present.

Anderson's ACT model is again useful in providing a psychological model of the structure of LTM. Recall that the model employs propositions as the main cognitive unit that is stored. When representing knowledge about various categories, it is useful to be able to determine that certain features are typical of a category while others are not. Consider what we know about "trees." They are a type of plant, often tall; they possess leaves, are frequently green, may provide homes for animals or birds, and so on. As Anderson (1990) points out, just to list the propositions that we know to be true about an object does not capture their interrelationships. "Trees" are defined by a number of attributes, each requiring specification of a value it has on some attribute. For example:

Tree
type—plant
color—green, brown
height—five feet and up
parts—branches, trunk

Anderson uses the term *schema* to describe the structure of interrelated attributes of objects that define our knowledge. Schemas contain *slots* into which are inserted the values that the object has on various attributes. Thus "type" and "color" are the attributes or slots, and "plant" and "green" are the values.

Schemas are therefore structured bodies of information that are stored in LTM and allow inferences to be made about objects and events. The assumption is that these are so linked that potentially they can activate one another. When the schema "public library" is evoked, for example, a large number of associations are almost simultaneously formed (e.g., "Be quiet," "The card catalog is probably near the front," "Where's my library card?"). It seems logical to assume that ideas relevant to the notion of a public library are stored in the brain in an interconnecting fashion, although not necessarily proximal to one another. It's entirely possible that knowledge about our library card is related to "things in wallet," and "Be quiet" is associated with "places to be quiet," including houses of worship, infant nurseries, and hospitals.

Schemas are interconnected physiologically, psychologically

Schemas are very hard to localize in either a psychological or physiological basis, but probably exist in the form described by Damasio and Damasio (1992), as noted earlier. Moreover, a great deal of research has indicated that they influence what new information will enter working memory.

The apparent dependence of the effects of schemas on a person's prior experience is important in understanding how schemas influence new learning. Without specific directions, people seem to activate particular schemas and apply an interpretation of new stimuli provided by the schema's structure. The schemas most likely to be activated are those that are the most well established within the individual. In a study of how college students interpret new text information, R. Anderson, Reynolds, Schallert, and Goetz (1977) provided short written passages to a sample of music education majors and to a sample of male students in a weight-lifting class. The passages were ambiguous in that they could be interpreted in different ways. A sample passage from that study is provided in Figure 6.2. It can be interpreted as referring to either a group of friends playing cards or a rehearsal session of a group of musicians. The music education subjects interpreted the passage in the latter sense, while the weight lifters perceived the passage as referring to card playing. In other words, the meaning we attribute to vague stimuli is likely to be influenced by what we perceive as examples of the most familiar schema available to us.

If stimuli cannot be identified or are partially misunderstood, the most familiar schema will be used, but it may be inappropriate. Perhaps the following sentences of college students can be explained by the use of misapplied schemas:

> The nineteenth century was a time of many great inventions and thoughts. The invention of the steamboat caused a network of rivers to spring up. Samuel Morse invented a code for telepathy, Louis Pasteur discovered a cure for rabbis. Charles Darwin was a naturalist who wrote the Organ of the Species. Madman Curie discovered radium. (Lederer, 1988, p. 5)

Schemas are important to learning because they provide a structure into which new content must be placed before it can be comprehended, guide our attention to

FIGURE 6.2 Passage presented to music and weight-lifting students

SOURCE: R. Anderson, R. Reynolds, D. Schallert, and E. Goetz, Frameworks for comprehending discourse. *American Educational Research Journal, 14,* 367–381 (1977). Reprinted by permission of the publisher.

Every Saturday night, four good friends get together. When Jerry, Mike, and Pat arrived, Karen was sitting in her living room writing some notes. She quickly gathered the cards and stood up to greet her friends at the door. They followed her into the living room, but as usual they couldn't agree on exactly what to play. Jerry eventually took a stand and set things up. Finally they began to play. Karen's recorder filled the room with soft and pleasant music. Early in the evening, Mike noticed Pat's hand and the many diamonds. As the night progressed the tempo of play increased. Finally, a lull in the activities occurred. Taking advantage of this, Jerry ordered the arrangement in front of him. Mike interrupted Jerry's reverie and said "Let's hear the score." They listened carefully and commented on their performance. When the comments were all heard, exhausted but happy, Karen's friends went home.

critical aspects of new input, and give us a basis for analyzing new information that is not easily processed. Effective instructors help students to activate appropriate schemas in considering new information. The beginning science student, having developed a "scientific method" schema, could be helped to approach a novel scientific phenomenon by being cued as to how the scientific method might be applied. Literature students who had formed the schema for "irony" could be directed to find ironic elements in novel pieces of literature. Essentially, the development and refinement of the schemas we possess is the major purpose of education, and instructors must continually be aware of how existing student schemas interact with new content.

Activated schemas influence new learning

Let us now consider some additional psychological processes involved in the flow of information. We have considered attention and its role in selecting information for working memory. The two other processes we must examine are *encoding* and *retrieval*.

ENCODING

Consider three students studying for a geography quiz. Martha, in attempting to remember the seven continents and their relative sizes, creates a hierarchical diagram with Australia (the smallest) on the top and Asia (the largest) on the bottom. James visualizes each continent with a number inside it referring to its relative size. Yvonne makes up a sentence in which the first letter of each word stands for a continent in descending size order: All Anteaters Need Sugar And Enormous Ants. All three students are attempting to *encode* the necessary content.

Encoding is the process of placing new information into the information-processing system so that it is capable of storage in LTM. Types of encoding include the following:

1. *Organization* or reorganizing separate instances into a single unit, as Martha was trying to do in creating her diagram.
2. *Imagery,* a visual form of organization, in which verbal content is transformed to an easily visualized image, as James did.
3. *Elaboration,* in which new information is expanded on by adding it to what one already knows, as Yvonne attempted to do in creating a sentence emphasizing the first letter of each continent.

Unfortunately, simply perceiving and rehearsing stimuli does not ensure that information is processed in such a way that it is placed in LTM. (Remember the student who writes 100 times that he will not talk in class only to talk out immediately after completing the assignment.) Much of what teachers say and present to a class or what students read and listen to is not learned because encoding has not occurred during WM. Encoding is an active process that requires the involvement of existing schemas.

Schemas assist encoding because they provide the structure to which new material can be related. For example, in a study by Kulhavy, Sherman, and Schmid (1978), high school students read short stories that were disorganized and hard to understand. One group of students was given a title for the story that related to its theme, while the control group received no title. Subjects who had been told the titles recalled more of the content. The titles, by providing a context for interpretation, served to aid the subjects in activating appropriate schema related to each story, thus facilitating encoding and eventual recall. Thinking of the title in reference to a story allowed reorganization of the content to occur and thus qualifies as an effective encoding activity.

Let us examine each of the three types of encoding in more detail. *Organization* requires the grouping of individual items to be recalled into larger units based on some similarity or relationship among the items. Suppose you are attempting to recall the items on a misplaced grocery list. Rather than attempt to remember the items in a random order, it will be more effective to group them around a common theme or function—all dairy items, cereals, vegetables, and so on. By placing items to be purchased into categories, you are effectively reorganizing your grocery list to enhance recall.

The importance of organization in memory is derived from gestaltists' work on grouping in perception, as we discussed in Chapter 1. More recently, it has become apparent that organization influences psychological processes—memory, concept formation, judgment, and problem solving, to name a few. We will encounter the effects of organization in discussing several topics in future chapters. As a general rule, any kind of organization of material to be used in these learning processes seems to be more effective than no organization at all.

Organization may be imposed by the learner (*subject-induced*) or suggested by the arrangement of the materials themselves (*material-induced*) (Ellis & Hunt, 1989). As demonstrated by a number of studies, even if material is presented randomly with no intent to provide organization in advance, learners will strive to impose order on the items when recall is required. Often the organization consists of placing items into *clusters* possessing a common characteristic (Bousfield, 1953). For example, in hearing lists of nouns, someone might cluster colors (black, yellow, orange, etc.), vegetables (peas, carrots, etc.), or animals (snake, cow, moose, etc.), so that items in these categories are recalled together. Clustering of this type seems to aid recall.

Subjective organization is imposed by learner

If long lists of random items are presented for several trials, an interesting phenomenon occurs. No matter whether the items do or do not fall into readily identifiable categories, they appear to be recalled in an increasingly consistent sequence over trials. This consistency of output order, which Tulving (1962) has called *subjective organization,* again exemplifies how existing schemas influence new tasks—in this case, by the progressive organization of incoming information according to previous learning. A similar process occurs outside experimental settings. When we find ourselves in ambiguous situations (e.g., in the middle of a large, milling crowd), we try very hard to utilize whatever we have learned about such situations to organize the present event. When called on later to explain specific events within the crowd setting, it is not surprising that individuals widely differ in their accounts. Obviously each observer has imposed his or her own subjective organization on the event. When we read varying accounts of crowd size by people of differing backgrounds in crowd estimation, we are viewing the effects of subjective organization.

How does organization affect memory more specifically? Most psychologists emphasize its effect on the retrieval of information at the time of recall. Organization, acting as an encoding process when new input is presented, serves to place separate items into new units. At recall, the new unit is retrieved. Once it has been identified, all the items within it can be retrieved also. Revisiting our grocery list example, once we have recalled that there were vegetables on the list, it is easier to remember the specific ones. The more precise and exhaustive the new unit, the better its effect on retrieval. Obviously, recalling merely that the list contained oat bran cereal does not help in selecting the specific product to be purchased. Organization is most effective in aiding memory when the new units are composed of easily identifiable elements.

Imagery, another process that contributes to encoding, consists of the transformation of verbal information to a visual form, in which the mental image includes the information to be remembered. If someone were to ask you whether there was an overhead light or a desk lamp in your childhood bedroom, you probably would attempt to visualize the room, based on your long-term memory of it. A visual representation would provide the information you needed to answer the question. Images of this type contain a good deal of detail, and consequently much interest has focused on whether images enhance memory. Research typically indicates a positive answer to that question. For example, in a study by Paivio and Foth (1970), college students were presented with 30 noun pairs, half concrete and half abstract. They were asked to link each pair of nouns with a word or phrase that they wrote down or with a picture that they subsequently drew. On immediate recall it was found that the imagery mediators produced better recall for the concrete pairs, while the verbal mediators aided recall of the abstract pairs. In another study (Perensky & Senter, 1970), subjects were instructed to form bizarre images involving the stimulus and response members of pairs of words. Word pairs were either lists of professions as the stimuli and games as the responses (Doctor–Checkers) or a random scrambling of nouns of both kinds. The results indicated that instructions to form bizarre images better facilitated performance than instructions to use any method desired merely to "link the stimulus and response members."

Imagery is a valuable coding dimension

Why does imagery enhance recall? Perhaps because concepts that can be visualized are encoded on two dimensions (visual, as well as verbal), while less easily visualized concepts are encoded only verbally. Paivio (1986) has applied this *dual coding* hypothesis to the finding that concrete information is typically remembered better than abstract information. Words such as "rooster," "piano," or "banana" are more easily remembered than "knowledge" or "justice," even though all occur frequently in our language. Can you visualize "justice"? Probably not easily, although many might symbolize it as a set of scales or a judge on a bench. It is more likely that abstract words are encoded as verbal propositions. Concrete words, since they can be encoded visually as well as verbally, should have a better chance of being recalled because two codes are better than one.

Encoding by *elaboration* involves relating new information to other facts that may be known about the new input. The learned material in the form of schemas allows the new event to acquire meaning. Suppose that in teaching children to spell the word "separate," a teacher points out that there is "a rat" in "separate." Students already know about the term "a rat," and it is assumed they can spell it. By highlighting the embedded words "a rat," the teacher has added to the word to be learned a detail that some students may not have spotted. Students exposed to this elaboration can invariably spell "separate" correctly on subsequent occasions. In essence, they have been guided to elaborate the spelling of "separate" based on their prior knowledge, and by adding information were able to make the word distinctive and thus meaningful. We can see that the teacher has helped students attend to the distinctive features of a word, has activated previously learned schemas, and, by enhancing meaning, has encouraged more effective encoding than one might ordinarily expect from a spelling lesson.

TEACHING FOR ENCODING

Since encoding is necessary for information to be placed in long-term memory, it is essential that instruction be so designed and conducted that the learner can adequately encode new material. A number of instructional techniques that reflect our understanding of the factors that influence encoding have been developed, evaluated, and revised in recent years. Kulhavy, Schwartz, and Peterson (1986) refer to these techniques as *instructional accessories*—the cues, directions, or additional material provided by the teacher that are not part of the content to be learned but influence how learning takes place. Let us now consider some instructional accessories designed to aid student encoding.

to help encoding take place

Mnemonic Devices

Mnemonics for sequential facts

More familiarly called memory tricks or aids, mnemonic devices have been used since ancient Greek orators developed techniques to help them remember speeches. The word *mnemonic* (ne-mon-ik) is derived from Mnemosyne, the name of the Greek goddess of memory. The term has come to refer to a wide variety of procedures that utilize the encoding properties of elaboration, organization, and imagery. We discuss six different kinds of mnemonics.

Method of "Loci."   *Loci* is Latin for "places," and this mnemonic requires imagining a very familiar place or object and identifying particular locations within it. You might choose your home, your room, or a well-known street. Whenever you have a list of items to remember, you simply place one item into each of the locations identified. A friend of the author imagines his favorite suit and the pockets in it. He then "places" each of the parts of the lecture he is to give into a particular pocket—the introduction in the breast pocket, the first major point and an example in the outside coat pocket, the second major point and an example in the left front pants pocket, and so on. When he gives the lecture, my friend imagines entering such pocket and taking out the appropriate part of his talk.

important info in each pocket

The loci method, which requires imagery as well as organization of the material into an appropriate sequence, can be either developed by the learner or provided by a teacher. For example, in teaching numerical place value in the second grade, a teacher might present a box in which hundreds, tens, and unit places are separated, each containing 10 empty holes. In adding two numbers, the student is provided straws to go into the empty holes. When all the holes in the units place are filled, the learner recognizes the need to go to the holes in the tens place or even the hundreds place to complete the number. In this way, the learner is visualizing the location of numbers in a sequence.

Pegword.   Rather than associate items with places, some learners like to associate items with pegwords—words that rhyme with the numbers one through ten. Since these pegwords are overlearned, the learner can use them for any kind of list or sequence of events. New items are then combined with their corresponding pegwords to form an image. Suppose that pegword one is "bun" and pegword two is "shoe." The first item to be remembered would be placed on a bun, the second on or in a shoe, and so on. Any list of items can be transformed into a series of images arranged sequentially. Entertainers often use pegwords to recall long lists of objects, people, or numbers.

First-Letter Mnemonics or Acronyms.   First-letter mnemonics or acronyms are perhaps the most commonly used mnemonic devices. They consist of taking the first letter of the name of a string of items to be recalled in sequence and creating a new word or phrase. For best results in recall, the phrase should make sense; it also should be clever and not too lengthy. Examples of frequently used first-letter mnemonics and their respective school subject areas are provided in Table 6.1.

TABLE 6.1   Examples of first-letter mnemonics used in instruction

Mnemonic	Content	Subject Matter
All Anteaters Need Sugar And Enormous Ants	The seven continents in order of descending size: Asia, Africa, North America, South America, Antarctica, Europe, Australia	Geography
Every Good Boy Does Fine	Names of lines on the G clef: E, G, B, D, F	Music
HOMES	The five Great Lakes: Huron, Ontario, Michigan, Erie, Superior	Geography
My Very Elderly Mother Just Served Us Nine Pizzas	The nine planets listed outward from the sun: Mercury, Venus, Earth, Mars, Jupiter, Saturn, Uranus, Neptune, Pluto	Astronomy
Roy G. Biv	The colors of the spectrum: red, orange, yellow, green, blue, indigo, violet	Physics
SOH CAH TOA Some Old Horse Came A-Hopping Through Our Alley	Sine = Opposite/Hypotenuse Cosine = Adjacent/Hypotenuse Tangent = Opposite/Adjacent	Trigonometry
On Old Olympus' Towering Top, A Finn And German Vend Snowy Hops	The 12 cranial nerves: olfactory, optic, oculomotor, trochlear, trigeminal, abducens, facial, auditory–vestibular, glossopharyngeal, vagus, spinal accessory, hypoglossal	Anatomy
King Henry Died Monday Drinking Chocolate Milk	Descending order of metric prefixes: kilo-, hecta-, deka-, meter-, deci-, centi-, milli-	Mathematics

short songs to remember things

Keyword.   The keyword technique is particularly useful in the learning of new words, especially foreign language vocabulary (Pressley, Levin, & Delaney, 1982). The student derives a common English word out of the word to be learned: This becomes the keyword. The next step is to associate the foreign word with the keyword. Then a visual image is formed that relates the keyword with the English translation of the foreign word. For example, to learn the German word *Hocker* ("bump"), you might select "hockey" as the keyword and rehearse hockey-Hocker until the two are strongly associated. Finally, you would produce an image that combines the keyword with the English translation, such as a hockey player with a bump on his head (Des-Rochers, Gelivas, & Wieland, 1989). In addition to its usefulness in the learning of vocabulary, the keyword technique has been effectively employed to teach botany concepts and abstract statistical information (McCormick and Levin, 1987). It seems to be most effective with associations that are concrete and can be easily visualized, in accordance with Paivio's dual coding hypothesis. Keyword should be used selectively, and the words should be presented slowly enough to allow adequate time for encoding (Hall, 1988).

Metrical Mnemonics.   The combination of rhythmic repetition with rhyming lyrics has proved to be a useful as well as enjoyable form of memory aid. Metrical mnemonics is particularly applicable to the learning of rules or procedures, as in "i before e, except after c," "Thirty days hath September, April, June, and November," or "Bottom bigger, better borrow" (subtraction). Millions of first-graders have learned the "Alphabet Song" as an aid to their recall, and many adults find themselves singing it mentally as they try to remember what letter comes after *p*. Younger elementary school children particularly enjoy metrical mnemonics because of the movement and feeling of freedom the technique stimulates. For older students, popular songs such as Billy Joel's "We Didn't Start the Fire" (Columbia Records, 1989) have aided the study of mid-twentieth century American history. In this song, names of celebrities, events, and objects of the 1950s and 1960s—for example, Syngman Rhee, hula hoops, and payola—were sung in rhyming fashion. One history teacher built an entire unit of study around this song, assigning teams of students to research the meaning and significance of selected items. In this case, the teacher was combining the use of a mnemonic device with the motivational appeal of popular music to promote learning and aid the recall of historical events.

Metrical mnemonics are particularly useful in describing sequential relationships, for when they are well constructed, a mistake in the order of recall of the items destroys the rhyme. They serve their purpose almost too well; one who relies on rhymes finds it difficult to remember a particular item without recalling the total rhyme, as in the example of adults singing the "Alphabet Song." These mnemonics also seem to be extremely resistant to extinction. The author still remembers a nonsense phrase provided in a high school biology class indicating the levels of classification of organisms: "KPC of GSV" (kingdom, phylum, class, order, family, genus, species, variety—since amended by biologists). By utilizing rhythm and rhymes in encoding, it is possible that both hemispheres of the cerebral cortex are being activated, with excitation of the "verbal" left hemisphere and the "musical" right hemisphere occurring simultaneously.

Pictorial Mnemonics.   Illustrations that serve the same role as a keyword are called pictorial mnemonics. The term to be learned is transformed into an acoustically similar concrete keyword that is then related to a pictorial representation of the associated characteristic. For example, in a study by Rosenheck, Levin, and Levin (1989), the plant group names *angiosperm, dicotyledon, rubiales, sapindales,* and *rosales* were taught to college biology students. The respective keywords were *angel, dinosaur, Rubik (cube), sap,* and *rose.* The pictorial mnemonic for angiosperm was a picture of an angel holding a bouquet of flowers. On both immediate and delayed retention tests, students utilizing the pictorial mnemonics outperformed others who were provided with figural taxonomies of plants and those who were encouraged to use their own method of study. Of particular interest in this study was the finding that pictorial mnemonics were most effective in aiding performance on problem-solving tasks where students were asked to classify unknown plant specimens based on distinguishing characteristics. Typically, mnemonic devices have been less beneficial in aiding performance on higher-level thinking (Presley, Borkowski, & O'Sullivan, 1984).

Summary of Mnemonic Devices.   A variety of mnemonic techniques are emerging as valuable instructional accessories to teaching. They appear to be applicable to diverse subject matter areas, and there is some evidence that they can facilitate higher-level thinking processes as well as recall. Teachers traditionally identify and present mnemonic aids to students. While this is desirable, it may be equally fruitful to supply information about mnemonics, how they work, and how they can aid learning at the same time that a memory device is introduced. Students who understand the nature and value of mnemonics may be encouraged to develop their own and to plan for their selective use in the future.

Spatial Representations

Some school content requires the learning of spatial relationships. Geography, geometry, and other social and natural sciences all require knowledge of the location and arrangement in space of objects, processes, and events. Understanding a map is one obvious example; others involve determining congruent triangles in trigonometry or understanding the weather cycle in an earth science class. Teachers can facilitate the learning of this type of content by utilizing spatial representations of the material.

An example of the use of spatial representation in learning is provided by Schwartz and Kulhavy (1981). While listening to a story about a fictitious group of pirates living on an island, subjects either studied a map of the island containing the geographic features mentioned in the story, studied an outline of the island with the features listed in a separate column, or saw the outline of the island but no list of features. On a test requiring application of knowledge of the map to the story, learners who studied the map showing the geographic features outperformed the other two groups. The authors concluded that the spatiality of the map facilitated understanding and application of the story.

A later study, in which fifth-graders were shown maps of a fictitious town, demonstrated that children who were asked to write a narrative story about the town incorporating 18 geographical locations recalled more of them than did children who just wrote sentences about each location (Kulhavy, Lee, & Caterino, 1985). Other subjects in the same study listened to a short story about events occurring at the map locations. Their recall of events in the story was closely related to the spatial locations they reported remembering. The authors explain these results according to a *conjoint retention* hypothesis in which both linguistic and spatial features are stored so that they can be employed together to aid recall, or separately when tasks require it. At recall, the learner is able to draw on both types of conjointly retained representation, thereby increasing the probability of remembering elements from each.

Teachers should consider displaying diagrams of narrative content that contain spatial information, particularly when attempting to aid students who are likely to have difficulty recalling verbal information presented alone.

Where would you use spatial representations?

Conceptual Models

A related instructional technique for improving students' understanding of scientific explanations is that of *conceptual models,* that is, words and/or diagrams intended to help learners build mental constructions of the system being studied. A conceptual model highlights the major objects and actions in a system as well as the relationships among them (R. E. Mayer, 1989). By using a conceptual model, a teacher can encourage a restructuring of already existing, but incomplete, schemas, and not only illustrate but explain the concepts being taught. In teaching about radar, for example, a conceptual model compared radar transmissions to the actions of a boy bouncing a ball against a wall and catching it, and pointed out the major objects involved (transmitter, receiver, pulse, remote object, etc.), the major actions (transmission, reflection, reception, etc.), and the causal relations between the two activities. Students exposed to this conceptual model recalled 57 percent more of the conceptual information associated with radar and generated 83 percent more correct answers on a problem-solving task than learners who had not received the model. In keeping with the belief that models encourage reorganization and integration of new information into a learner's existing schema, there was a 14 percent decrease in verbatim retention of the actual terms used in the radar presentation by the teacher (Mayer, 1983). In other words, learners receiving a model understand and can apply the concepts being taught and are less inclined to rely on rote recall of the teacher's words—a sign of meaningful learning.

Conceptual models = diagrams that explain

Conceptual models are ordinarily presented as printed material provided by the instructor prior to reading assignments or lecture presentations. R. E. Mayer (1989) has found them to be effective in the teaching of Ohm's law and density in physics (Mayer, Dyck, & Cook, 1984), database systems and BASIC computer programming (Bayman & Mayer, 1988), the nitrogen cycle in biology (Mayer et al., 1984), how cameras work (Bromage & Mayer, 1981), and how automobile brakes and pumps work (Mayer & Gallini, 1990). Research indicates that conceptual models are most effective when presented to students who had little prior knowledge of or low aptitude for the material in the lesson. High-aptitude students are more likely to come to the lesson with preexisting models of the process or to be able to rapidly construct them, and teacher-generated models may conflict with those the students are trying to establish. For low-knowledge/low-aptitude students, on the other hand, who possess either incomplete schemas or no relevant ones, the teacher's model provides a context for the assimilation of new concepts.

Conceptual models facilitate encoding because they enable the learner not only to organize context, but also to form a mental image of the process being described—two of the dimensions of encoding described earlier. R. E. Mayer believes that a good model portrays each major component of a system, the changes each major component undergoes in the process, and the relation between each state change (Mayer & Gallini, 1990). He cites the seven c's of a good model: complete, concise, coherent, concrete, conceptual, correct, and considerate (i.e., presented at a level appropriate to the learner in vocabulary and organization) (Mayer, 1989). It appears that any systematic process that requires explanation in a particular subject matter area can benefit from the provision of conceptual models. All that is required is effort in identifying a visual–verbal representation of a new process that can be related to concepts the student has already acquired. A conceptual model representing warm-bloodedness in animals is provided in Figure 6.3.

Analogies

In several respects, analogies function like conceptual models, in that learned relationships are compared to new ideas. For example, the action of electrons in wires can be described by comparing the particles to people dancing (Simons, 1986), or the conduction of heat through metal can be compared to particles moving through a series of Tinkertoy boxes (Royer & Cable, 1975). Analogies are more illustrative than explanative, however, and usually not as elaborate as conceptual models might be. They are nevertheless very useful in instruction because they also activate prior schemas that can then be used in encoding.

FIGURE 6.3   A conceptual model for warm-bloodedness

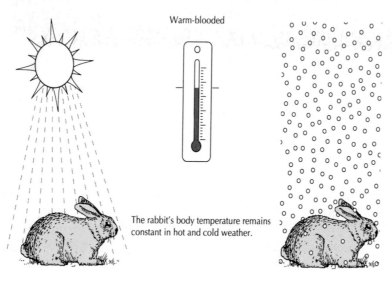

Warm-blooded

The rabbit's body temperature remains constant in hot and cold weather.

The term "analogy" or "analogical thinking" has been used somewhat loosely in the educational and psychological literature, often being confused with "metaphor" or "formal analogy." I am using *analogy* as Sternberg (1977) employs the term: "to make a decision about something new in our experience by drawing on something old." There is an inference that if two things agree in one or more respect, they will agree in others. *Metaphor* is inclusive of analogy and is meant, as in literature, to have many possible meanings to different individuals. For example, in the metaphor "A river is a snake," one person may consider the shape, another the coldness, another the danger, or yet another characteristic as central to its meaning. An analogy is thus a specific type of metaphor, a type that is more controlled, more circumscribed, more specialized, and more likely to convey a single common meaning. In terms of understanding subject matter, therefore, analogies should be more useful than metaphors in clarifying and representing new material.

You may remember standardized tests that call on you to solve formal analogy problems such as "1 is to 2 as 6 is to (. . .)." These formal analogies are used to test analogical reasoning, and performance is an important clue to an individual's capacity for higher reasoning (Sternberg, 1985). Classroom analogies are rarely formal because they do not necessarily identify each term in such a precise way. Table 6.2 presents examples of analogies that may be used in different classes to illustrate a variety of concepts and relationships.

Simons (1984) has argued that analogies are effective instructional devices because they serve three functions. In their *concretizing* function, they make abstract information more imaginable and concrete. They provide a *structurizing* function by serving as the basis for a new schema. (The formal structure of a new schema does not

TABLE 6.2 Examples of analogies used in instruction

Analogy	Content	Subject Matter
Think of the six major continents as big sausages hanging over a plate. [Antarctica]	Position of the continents	Geography
The DNA molecule is constructed like a Tinkertoy set, with the nucleus as the main circular cog and the spindles like the sticks extended out.	Cell structure	Biology
The structure of an atom is like our solar system: The sun is the nucleus, and the planets are the electrons that encircle it.	Atomic structure	Biology
Our constitutional system is like a three-pronged pitchfork—each branch has its own unique function, but like a pitchfork, no prong can function without the other.	American governmental system	Social studies
Think of a simple sentence as if it were a play: There is an actor (the subject), the action the actor does (predicate), and the thing the action affects (the object).	Grammar; parts of a sentence	English, Language arts
The lymph system is like a wet sponge, with spaces filled with water. If you squeeze it, you can force water from one end of the sponge to the other.	Endocrine system	Biology

have to be learned, since one is already in existence.) They also permit active *assimilation* by stimulating students to integrate the new information with other learned information in cognitive structure. In a series of six studies in which analogies were provided to students of various ages, Simons found evidence that supported all three functions. The analogies he provided as supplements to standard reading material about the topics consisted of 200- to 400-word descriptions of events that could be considered analogical. For example, in teaching about Piaget's developmental theory, the analogy passage compared the arrival of six new players on a football team to the qualitative/quantitative and structural/nonstructural changes that occur in cognitive development. In most of the experiments, the use of analogies improved performance on both short- and long-term recall.

Can you think of an instructional analogy?

Three issues arise when we consider the use of analogies as structural accessories. First, devising just the right analogy to achieve meaningful learning is a truly creative act. Many analogical relationships may have important dissimilarities that confuse the learner rather than provide clarification. Describing a living organism as being like a factory that takes in raw materials and puts out waste products may capture one aspect of the living organism, but the discerning student who points out that one of the defining features of factories is the production of useful goods may well ask what products living organisms produce (Royer, 1986).

In addition, analogies take instructional time that might otherwise be used for explanation or practice. Simons (1984) notes that in some experiments the extra time invested seemed rather large in relation to the performance gain. Under restricted time conditions for reading, other instructional aids may be more efficient. Simons points out, however, that the time constraints may not be as important as improved performance, particularly if long-term recall and understanding are aided.

Perhaps the most important concern in the correct use of analogies in instruction, however, is whether prerequisite schemas are in fact available to learners. For example, if a student had never played with Tinkertoys, the DNA analogy might not be effective; it would only add to what must be understood. Moreover, the use of analogies appears to follow a developmental sequence, with those used by third-graders being more literal and sometimes based on irrelevant attributes (Zook & Di-Vesta, 1991). One third-grader in their study revealed his analogical thinking with the statement: "My coat is fuzzy, therefore a seed coat is fuzzy." Instructional use of more abstract analogies may require formal operational developmental levels. Posing brief questions such as "Do you all remember playing with Tinkertoys?" and getting a quick description from the class may serve to ensure recall of pertinent past learning and help determine developmental readiness for understanding a particular analogy.

Despite these concerns, well-developed analogies that are known to the learner and are not too time-consuming can be useful instructional tools. They possess the additional advantage of creating interest and providing relevance to much of what we teach, potentially enhancing student motivation.

Questioning

Asking questions to which students are expected to formulate a response, before, during, or after reading or listening to new material, is another valuable instructional accessory. Questions of students direct attention, as we have already discussed, but they provide an organizational structure that facilitates encoding as well (Rothkopf & Bisbicos, 1967). Questions asked *before* reading or listening enhance recall of the specific information related to the question itself. They direct attention to relevant material. Questions presented *after* the content not only increase what is remembered of question-related material but have the indirect effect of aiding recall of material not specifically addressed by the question. Apparently, postquestions act to promote rehearsal of relevant content, which triggers associations to material that is contiguous to the question-specific material (Wixson, 1984). Postquestions therefore affect incidental learning as well as intentional learning. So-called *adjunct questions* can be inserted into the text that is being read or posed by teachers before, during, and after lectures and demonstrations to stimulate encoding of verbally presented content. Research on questioning has been extensive and reveals the following:

Adjunct questions direct attention

1. Questions having a low level of complexity (recall and comprehension of facts) facilitate intentional learning best. For example, asking students to tell who won the U.S. Civil War and explain why improves their long-term recall of material related to that question.

2. Low-level questions do not aid recall and understanding of unrelated material. In fact, they may encourage learners to ignore information that is not directly relevant to the question. For this reason, it may be better to ask low-level adjunct questions *after* the reading assignment has been completed, to ensure that students do not focus on any one set of facts to the exclusion of others during reading and to force them to make an active search of long-term memory for answers at the end of the assignment.

What kinds of postquestions would you ask?

3. High-level questions (application or inference questions) enhance informational and conceptual learning and aid incidental as well as intentional learning (Hamaker, 1986). For example, asking students to construct a scenario in which the Confederacy wins the Civil War requires them not only to recall and understand the facts leading to the Union victory, but to analyze the facts so that they can be used to develop a possible upset. Students are more likely to integrate different ideas that have been read (or to employ content learned previously that may be relevant) in attempting to answer such questions.

4. Because higher-level questions require readers to compose higher-level responses, these questions should be presented *before* reading. This way, readers will be looking for information that can be used in constructing an answer while they read, and more material will be intentionally processed as a result.

5. Length of material to be read seems to interact with the effectiveness of questions of different types and their location. Prequestions tend to have less effect when paired with passages that are too long (Hamaker, 1986). Postquestions seem to be most effective for long texts, perhaps because they do not divert attention from the many details of a long text, as prequestions may do.

Questions posed by teachers during class presentations have also been found to enhance encoding, as well as providing variety and perhaps a welcome break from the passive role students must often assume. Most teacher questions should be easily answerable at the knowledge or comprehension level of complexity. As learning objectives move to higher cognitive levels, more challenging and abstract questions should be asked, to permit the emergence of a coherent pattern of questions that relate to the different demands of the content. Consider the following sequence:

T: Jerome, what did Hitler do after the Munich Pact?

J: He invaded the Sudetenland.

T: Good. What do you think might have happened if the Allies had not signed that treaty agreement?

J: Hmmm, maybe Hitler wouldn't have invaded.

T: Boris, why would he have changed his mind?

Such a pattern is logical in that the teacher establishes the factual base for later questions by using the first question, in effect, to review the material. Later questions encourage thought about the implications of the event, a very important objective in the study of history. The combination of questions is most likely to facilitate elaborative encoding, since the basic facts are not only recalled but analyzed as well.

There is some indication that more higher-level questions lead to better student achievement (Brophy & Good, 1986), but lower-level questions the students can answer quickly, allowing movement to the next content area, should still predominate. As demonstrated in the questions to Jerome and Boris, teachers should stay with students, providing *probing* as well as recall questions to enhance processing of the content. Probing questions require students to construct more elaborate answers than are needed to satisfy mere recall queries and can be effective if not too difficult. The history teacher above also exemplifies the value of bringing in other students as a way of keeping all in the class on their toes, as well as serving as a source of verification. For issues or facts that may be complex, or where there may be doubt about accuracy, asking another student the same or a similar question serves to verify the initial answer. Verification questions also force students to examine their beliefs, often leading to analysis of what may only be rote knowledge.

If teachers are going to ask higher-level questions, they should be prepared to wait longer for students to process the demands of the question and produce a suitable response. It makes little sense to ask Jerome to speculate on what might have happened without the Munich Pact but allow the student no time to organize a response to a question he may not have expected. Ineffective teachers often ask such a question and jump quickly to another student (who often answers it, not because he or she understood the content any better, but because the second student had more time to prepare a response). Even worse is the teacher who, receiving no immediate reply, proceeds to provide an answer. Have you known teachers who habitually did that? During later recitations, students know that if they just delay long enough, the teacher will answer for them. This clearly does not encourage proper attention and thought.

The approach to the issue of waiting for students to formulate answers seems to separate effective from poor or inexperienced teachers (Brophy & Good, 1986). "Wait time," as it is called, should be between three and five seconds for higher-level questions, but slightly less for low-level questions intended to review previously learned material. A mix of varying levels of question complexity plus longer wait times has been associated with higher student achievement in social studies and sciences classes particularly (Tobin, 1987).

In summary, questions inserted in text, assigned as homework or in-class reading aids, or asked by teachers during recitations can aid student encoding. Care must be exercised in timing the presentation of questions, in the form and sequence chosen, and in ensuring adequate time for student response.

Advance Organizers

Advance organizers are statements that are more abstract and inclusive than the material that is to follow and serve as a vehicle for subsuming or assimilating the new material into memory (Ausubel & Fitzgerald, 1962). Remember that Ausubel believes that meaningful learning occurs only when new information is related to concepts already in existence. Advance organizers were designed to facilitate the integration of new information into established schemas.

Advance organizers are hierarchical concepts

An advance organizer is more than an outline, overview, or simple statement, such as "Here is what we are going to learn today, class." It is conceptual material that students may not have mastered in complete form. It will serve as a scaffold for what is to follow, enforcing the activation and integration of existing schemas. In an early study (Ausubel and Youssef, 1963), students read a passage on Buddhism and Christianity. Students who first read the organizer recalled more from later material on Buddhism than did students who read the Buddhism passage only. Other studies have shown that advance organizers facilitate the transfer of new information to other learning tasks (Grotelueschen & Sjogren, 1968).

Organizers seem to work best when they are developed from unitary, hierarchically organized topics. For example, Joyce and Weil (1986) describe an art museum guide who began a tour of an art museum with the following advance organizer:

> Art, although it is a personal expression, reflects in many ways the culture and times in which it was produced. . . . Within each culture, as the culture changes so art will change—and that is why we can speak of periods of art. The changes are often reflected in the artist's techniques, subject matter, colors and style. Major changes are often reflected in the forms of art that are produced. (p. 70)

During the tour, the guide pointed out various differences in art that resulted from changing times: changes in the clothes worn, muscularity of the human form, size of figures, and so on. These examples served to illustrate the central point of the advance organizer—that cultural change leads to change in artistic expression. With this organizational point or rule in mind, the students were encouraged to identify other examples as they were observed. In this way, the generalized, abstract rule provided by the advance organizer leads to the learning of more specific and subordinate concepts and rules.

Advance organizers come in different forms. The type provided above is an example of an *expository organizer*—it presents information that is more abstract than subsequent content (Ausubel & Fitzgerald, 1962). Another example of an expository organizer was used in a study by Kloster and Winne (1989) in which eighth-grade students were to learn about the prevention of computer crime. The expository organizer was the idea that new inventions give rise to new crimes, which in turn result in new methods for controlling these abuses.

Ausubel also refers to *comparative organizers,* which are ideas on a related topic that are similar in level of abstraction to the new information. In the study by Kloster and Winne, a comparative organizer was given in a description of misuses of office photocopiers and a list of efforts to control those abuses. In many respects, analogies and conceptual models are similar in function to Ausubel's comparative organizers.

Kloster and Winne found that both expository and comparative organizers aided recall and comprehension when students using them were compared with students who had received a lecture outline or a passage about computers. A key finding was that students don't automatically use advance organizers, which require additional thought and effort. A check on how well students were able to match ideas in the new material with ideas in the organizer served to identify those who used the organizer and those who did not. Merely providing advance organizers does not guarantee their use. These tools need to be clearly understood by learners, and they must be clever or unique enough to generate interest in their application.

Summary of Encoding Accessories

All the instructional accessories discussed above can be effective in aiding encoding when two conditions are met. The first is that the learner must possess in long-term memory appropriate schema, which the teacher draws on to facilitate new learning. No matter what accessory is used, the teacher is depending on the student to retrieve relevant information from long-term memory and relate it to the new content. The elaboration, organization, and imagery provided by the teacher must be based on what the learner already knows. This makes it essential that the teacher be aware of the existing schematic structure of the students. There is no easy formula for ensuring such awareness, nor is it possible to ever achieve complete understanding of what our students know. The more that is known about their interests, contemporary culture such as music and television, school events, current events outside the school, completed course work, and so on, the more likely it is that the teacher will be able to find common ideas or themes that can be used to link new content with previously acquired schemas.

The second condition is that aids to encoding are most beneficial when the student is directly instructed to use them to further understand new material. Teachers should use in advance explicit statements such as "This mnemonic device will help you to remember the sequence of the nine planets of our solar system," or "This model is very similar to the way in which a computer functions. Let us first consider the similarities, and then later identify some differences." Statements about what the instructional accessory is, what it will do, and how the student should use it to help in learning new material will increase the likelihood that students will employ these tools as encoding aids in other contexts.

RETRIEVAL PROCESSES

Once stored in long-term memory, how is information retrieved? The retrieval process starts with the presence of a cue provided by the stimulus situation. Cues vary with the nature of the memory task or type of memory being accessed; for example, the question "Where were you last Tuesday at 5:00 P.M.?" would serve as a cue to help retrieve information from episodic memory. "Can you define the psychological term *behaviorism*?" cues a specific definition located in semantic memory. Cues do not have to be verbal, nor is it necessary to provide them externally. Sometimes, merely seeing a picture may serve as a cue for past events, or smelling bread baking will stimulate recall of a pleasant kitchen in your childhood home. Retrieval is not just a passive process in which our memories are accessed by external directions alone. In fact, much of what we retrieve from memory is internally generated as a part of the active, continuous thinking that we all perform.

While the importance of retrieval cues in facilitating recall is widely accepted, the question of what accounts for the effectiveness of various cues is still open to debate. Three positions seem most explanative, although they are in conflict. The spread of activation view (Anderson, 1983b) hypothesizes that the effectiveness of a retrieval cue is directly related to the preexisting associative strength of the cue and the to-be-remembered item. If a cue has occurred frequently with an item in the past, the two become closely associated, just as our first and last names are or facts such as "Columbus—1492." One will cue the other and vice versa. If we are asked: "What does the Fifth Amendment to the Constitution protect?" the question enters WM and is broken into propositions, which activate associated networks in long-term memory. Related propositions are activated and evaluated as to whether they answer the question. If they do, a response is formed; if not, activation spreads until the answer is located. Activation spreads through long-term memory from active portions to other portions of memory, requiring a certain amount of time. Speed of retrieval is thus somewhat limited by the speed of activation of cortical pathways, but speed can be enhanced through practice and as a function of whether the information has recently been activated (Anderson, 1990). In other words, if we have practiced retrieving specific information recently, retrieval time should be lessened.

The *encoding specificity* view of Tulving (1972) offers another explanation of retrieval. A cue will be effective only if it was specifically encoded with the event at the time of input. Tulving argues that a particular event does not occur several times, allowing frequent pairings with other events; rather, it occurs only once. There can be only one "first kiss," for example. Tulving and Thomsen (1971) demonstrated this fact in a study in which different associated cues were provided during learning. Pairs of words with low associative strength, such as "black–train" were presented to all subjects initially. One group was then provided the original cues (e.g., "black"), while another was given strongly associated cues (e.g., "whistle") not seen at input. The cues initially presented with the to-be-recalled words were more effective in aiding recall, even though they were weakly associated. Tulving believes that encoding specificity most readily applies to episodic memory; it does not influence the retrieval of semantic memories, which probably have many cues associated with them.

According to a third position, retrieval is decidedly more complex. This two-

Best retrieval cues are specifically encoded

process theory requires first the activation of potential responses, then a decision-making step in which accuracy and/or appropriateness is determined. The two-process theory differentiates between recognition and recall in memory, arguing that in recognition possible responses have already been provided, while in recall both activation and decision making must occur. This position would argue that a multiple-choice item such as "The Battle of Hastings occurred in (a) 866, (b) 1066, (c) 1204, (d) 1812" is easier to respond to than "When did the Battle of Hastings occur?" because the learner does not have to generate the possible answers. Do you agree?

All three positions contribute to our understanding of the retrieval process. Some facts, events, or information in general may be so distinctive (or so well-rehearsed) that little decision making is necessary, as in recalling where we were when the *Challenger* exploded. Items to be retrieved that are less distinctive may require a two-stage process of activation followed by decision making. Items that are initially encoded with specific retrieval cues not only will possess high associative strength but will not require extensive decision making. Items not specifically encoded, or possessing low associative strength to other information, will require greater time and activation as well as selection.

Enhancing Retrieval

Just as in the facilitation of encoding, instructional procedures followed by the teacher at the time of original learning can aid students in long-term recall. In addition, students can improve their own retrieval by employing certain procedures designed to "recapture" what they have learned. The following recommendations for enhancing retrieval include both teaching strategies and student behaviors.

1. *Frequent practice and review of learned material* can enhance retrieval. Short review sessions or quizzes provide an opportunity to practice the retrieval process. Nongraded quizzes or recitation sessions can be very important in helping students get ready for major tests by allowing an opportunity for corrective feedback in a less threatening setting. Students can practice retrieval without a teacher present by pausing during reading or studying and asking themselves questions about the meaning of what they have just covered or by attempting to summarize in their own words what they have read. They can also construct their own questions to be answered as they study, or teachers can provide study questions to accompany reading assignments or as preparation for future exams. Whether teacher-generated or student-initiated, any procedure that leads to practice in retrieval is valuable. The author recalls fruitlessly scanning lecture notes during stops at traffic lights while driving to an exam, much to the displeasure of motorists behind him. The final minutes before the test should have been spent in practicing retrieval rather than in further rereading of notes.
   practice retrieval before exam
2. *Information about the nature of the learning criterion to be used in evaluations* should be provided during acquisition. Knowing that one is responsible for recalling the names and sequence of succession of the

British monarchs, but not the dates of their respective rules, will influence how the learner attends, selects, and encodes the incoming facts. Describing the learning criterion allows a better match between encoding and retrieval, so that the learner can plan how to organize material to be learned during review and study sessions. When expecting to take an essay test, for example, a student can think of related facts and examples to be used in constructing a complete answer, thus establishing a more extensive associative network. At retrieval, any one of a number of cues could successfully activate the relevant network.

3. *Developing and using distinctive retrieval cues in the form of examples and applications* can aid retrieval. Examples and applications of new material, when provided by the teacher during initial presentation, aid retrieval as well as encoding. Examples serve as additional associations to the content and, if retrieved, can activate the content itself. Retrieval cues such as examples invoke an appropriate schema, which in turn serves as an organizational structure or context in which retrieval occurs. For example, before teaching elementary school children about geometric shapes, one teacher had children bring from home objects that had three sides, four even sides, four uneven sides, and a single continuous "side." She then used the examples provided by the students to illustrate triangles, squares, rhomboids, and circles. The students' personal examples of each shape were easily recalled when they were later asked to identify new objects by shape because they could compare the new objects to "their" shapes, which were serving as retrieval cues.

4. *Questions or test items presented at retrieval should contain cues present when information was initially encoded.* A test item is really no more than a retrieval cue designed to access information from memory. Good test items (or good questions in a review session) should be stated so that cues present when the information was learned are part of the question. In assessing students' recall of pre-Civil War American history, the following question was asked: "The Kansas–Nebraska Act of 1854 provided that all questions of slavery in the new territories were to be decided by the settlers. What happened as a result of that act?" This question asks for the retrieval of specific information, and it includes a cue to the kind of answer necessary and provides a context that will aid recall of the original presentation of the information. During instruction, the teacher had named the Kansas–Nebraska Act, explained what it was designed to do, and discussed its effect. Retrieval will generally be aided by this question, because not only is the Kansas–Nebraska Act mentioned, but the additional cue of its purpose is also provided.

Context as a retrieval cue

5. *Students should use the conditions under which material is learned as retrieval cues.* Significant events occurring at the same time as original encoding ("That was the day in class when Susan said she'd go out with me."), physical conditions of the classroom ("It was hot and sticky that afternoon."), the location of the information on the text page ("That definition was right below the picture of the waterfall."), how you felt on that day, and so on can all aid retrieval if they were part of the encoding

content. Associations to the desired material may be activated by imagining the environment when the learning took place. The encoding specificity hypothesis suggests that cues present at encoding should activate episodic memory, allowing the individual to locate when or where the material was acquired. This information in turn may be used to yield other cues aiding the retrieval of meaning.

6. *Procedures such as "talking to oneself" or writing down all one can recall of a topic can serve as cues to retrieval.* By generating numerous associations, including many that are irrelevant, you increase the possibility of producing a useful one. If you are asked to write an essay on Macbeth's pride, for example, listing all you can recall about this character, down to physical details as well as personality traits, might allow a picture to emerge that would incorporate pride. At the beginning of this chapter, Elizabeth is talking to herself about the Teapot Dome scandal in an effort to generate useful associative cues. Students should be encouraged to practice "controlled" generation of possible associations to the material to be retrieved.

THE INFORMATION-PROCESSING MODEL AND EFFECTIVE TEACHING

Good chapter review

This chapter began with the development of the cognitive information-processing model of learning and its roots in earlier theories. It then described each of the structures and processes of an information-processing model, from the reception of incoming stimuli to the production of an appropriate response. Along the way, special emphasis was placed on perception, attention, encoding, and retrieval. As each process was discussed, instructional procedures and accessories that aid performance were introduced and exemplified. Table 6.3 serves as a summary of effective teaching procedures recommended for each process.

A major assumption of this view of learning is that the processes of attention, encoding, and retrieval are highly interdependent. Attention is primarily determined by retrieval of relevant past learning that aids interpretation of new stimuli. Attention determines what information is encoded in working memory. Encoding occurs most efficiently when learners retrieve additional information and procedures from long-term memory, and placement of information into long-term memory is affected by available schemas. Retrieval is determined by the form and manner in which information was initially encoded. The model suggests that it is impossible to separate any one phase or process from the others. Learning is a complex undertaking; it cannot be subdivided into components that can be isolated for separate inspection. In the same vein, the model suggests that for instruction to be effective, all structures and processes that contribute to learning must be considered.

Perhaps the most important effect on instruction of the information-processing model lies in its description of how learners function. Understanding of how people attend, encode, retrieve, and analyze information while they are engaged in learning tasks is the goal of the model. With that kind of knowledge available, educators can

TABLE 6.3 Effective teaching procedures for learning processes included in the cognitive information-processing model

Process	Procedure

Perception	Ensure physical readiness to receive stimulation.
	    Vary the sensory systems being stimulated.
	    Introduce novel stimuli.

Attention	Use visual cues such as arrows, underlines. Use auditory cues such as changes in stress, pitch, or level. Direct attention through verbal signals ("This is important!").
Encoding	Mnemonic devices: loci, pegwords, first-letter acronyms, keywords, metrical mnemonics, pictorial mnemonics Spatial representations Conceptual models Analogies Questioning Advance organizers
Retrieval	Practice and review frequently. Describe learning criteria. Develop and use distinctive retrieval cues present at original encoding. Use learning conditions as retrieval cues. "Talk to oneself" about the topic to be retrieved.

more adequately plan instructional objectives, design instructional activities, adapt learning tasks to meet differences in student abilities, improve instructional technology, develop more efficient evaluation procedures, and perhaps revise the roles in the instructional process of student and teacher alike. By emphasizing change in the cognitive structure of students as the basis of learning, this model reminds educators that active interaction between teacher and student is most crucial to effective teaching.

SUMMARY

The cognitive information-processing view of learning shares with Gestalt psychology the belief that perceptual reorganization is necessary for learning to occur. Early cognitive–structural theorists such as Bruner and Ausubel extended the cognitive approach by including internal representations in their discussion of learning, a major departure from traditional behavioral positions. Bruner believed that the formation of concepts is fundamental to learning and that concepts are best acquired through the individual's independent discovery of meaningful relationships. Ausubel believed that meaningful learning, which occurs when new information is related to what is already in cognitive structure, can result from expository instruction. Ausubel preferred a general-to-specific sequence in teaching content, as opposed to Bruner's discovery approach.

Contemporary information-processing positions began in 1968 with Atkinson and Shiffrin's three-stage model, in which information identified in the sensory register is successfully transferred from short-term to long-term storage. The implication that these three stages represent "places" to which information is sequentially sent does not conform to more recently available neurological evidence, nor does it allow for the finding that short-term and long-term processes seem to be activated simultaneously in most cognitive tasks. Anderson's ACT position extends the original model by recognizing the role of working memory in processing initial cognitive units and relating them to previously acquired schemas through the activation of a network of associations. The parallel distributed processing model suggests that associated networks are activated simultaneously, thus accounting for the diversity and complexity of thought.

The role of the sensory register and how attention is affected within it were described. Attention is a limited resource, requiring selection among competing stimuli according to factors such as novelty, intensity, and similarity. Attention can be divided only when one task has been learned to the level of automaticity. Working memory processes information selected for primary attention, but decay is rapid unless items within WM are encoded. Encoding involves organization, imagery, or elaboration of the original content so that it can be related to the schematic networks of long-term memory. Instructional accessories that enhance encoding include mnemonic devices, spatial representations, conceptual models, analogies, questions, and advance organizers.

Retrieval of information from long-term memory depends on the availability of cues, which either are highly associated with the to-be-remembered content or were encoded with the material at original learning. In recognition, memory retrieval depends on activation of the appropriate cue; in recall situations, some decision making is required. The more effective the encoding and the more distinctive the retrieval cues available, the more likely it is that retrieval will occur. Enhancement of retrieval is provided by frequent practice, examples, definitions of the required criteria, and encouragement of student use of specific cues and generation of related associations.

A concept map for this chapter appears on page 224.

EXERCISES

1. Conduct a simple experiment to determine the role of meaningful cues in retrieval. Read the passage below to eight subjects. Have them attempt to recall the story word for word immediately after hearing it and then again several days later. For four of the subjects, provide the title "Washing Clothes" before reading. Do not provide any title for the other four subjects. Write up the results of your experiment, describing the subjects, what they remembered and what they forgot at each time period, and what elaborations were added. Compare the recall of the four subjects who were given the title to the performance of the four who were not.

   The procedure is actually quite simple. First you arrange items into different groups. One pile may be sufficient depending on how much there is to do. It is better to do too few things at once than too many. A mistake can be expensive. After the procedure has been completed, one arranges the materials into different groups again. Then they can be put into their appropriate places. They will be used once more and the whole cycle will have to be repeated.

Personal Theory of Learning

Cognitive Information Processing

is
reorganization of new information based on past learning

Early theories

Gestalt "perception"

Bruner
- Categories
- Discovery learning

Ausubel
- Meaningful reception learning

Atkinson & Shiffrin Model

- Sensory register
- Short-term store
- Long-term store

Contemporary Model

is
Attention

Working memory

- Encoding
  Organization
  Imagery
  Elaboration

Long-term memory

Retrieval

or

Network Models

ACT
- Propositions
- Spread of activation

Parallel distributed processing
- Simultaneous activation

Instructional Applications

Attention
- Automaticity
- Directional cues

Encoding
- Mnemonics
- Spatial representation
- Conceptual models
- Analogies
- Questions
- Advance organizers

Retrieval
- Review
- Specific cues

Concept Map for Chapter 6

224

2. Select some instructional content you would like to present to students. Choose material that is extensive enough to require 15 minutes or so of presentation time. For the content you select, develop:

    a. A mnemonic device for factual material that must be recalled in a particular sequence.

    b. A spatial representation or concept model for material that describes arrangements of objects or how processes occur.

    c. An analogy or an advance organizer that aids in communicating the meaning of the material.

SUGGESTED READINGS

Anderson, J. R. (1990). *Cognitive psychology and its implications* (2nd ed.). New York: Freeman.

Ausubel, D. P. (1963). *The psychology of meaningful verbal learning.* New York: Ware and Stratton.

Baddeley, A. D. (1986). *Working memory.* Oxford: Oxford University Press.

Bruner, J. S. (1962). *The process of education.* Cambridge, MA: Harvard University Press.

Mayer, R. E. (1989). Models for understanding. *Review of Educational Research, 40*(1), 43–64.

Paivio, A. (1986). *Mental representations: A dual-coding approach.* New York: Oxford University Press.

Simons, P. R. J. (1984). Instructing with analogies. *Journal of Educational Psychology, 76,* 513–527.

part III
Learning and Teaching

Subject Matter Learning

CHAPTER OUTLINE

Chapter Objectives

1. Distinguish between instructional design at the system, course, and lesson levels.
2. Provide examples of instructional events described by Gagné.
3. Distinguish between whole-language and code-oriented approaches to reading.
4. Describe a content area teacher's role in aiding students to learn from reading.
5. Explain the components of the Flower and Hayes writing model.
6. Describe different approaches to writing instruction.
7. Explain the major reasons for reforming mathematics curriculum.
8. Describe different approaches to teaching mathematics.
9. List procedures to follow in teaching science.
10. List procedures to follow in teaching social studies content.

As Mr. Sawyer began to plan next year's tenth-grade social studies class, he recognized an obvious problem. There was just too much content to teach! The course normally covered units on American history, U.S. government, North American geography, economics, and cultural differences in the United States. The state board of education had recommended units on environmental education, global education, and analysis of energy use in America. Last year's students had suggested including some discussion of current U.S. politics, and since this was an election year, the recommendation made good sense.

"How am I going to organize all that content without making the class so superficial that no one can remember or apply any of it?" he moaned. "Is there anything I can possibly leave out? Can I integrate some of the content so that two areas are covered at once? Can I get a student teacher to help instruct? Maybe this is the year to go on sabbatical leave!"

Mrs. Etzlaff put down the stack of papers her Composition students had just turned in. It was the first assignment they had completed for her. "These position papers are awful," she said. "Not only are there mistakes in spelling and grammar, but the sentences and paragraphs don't make sense. There's no transition between ideas; some papers sound like Top Ten Reasons lists. These kids seem to think you can just spew out a random set of assertions about a topic and meaning will be automatically communicated. How am I ever going to teach them to write?"

Byron looked at the set of data based on the relation of the concentration of certain chemicals to their rate of reaction. He was now expected to determine the equation defining the reaction. Byron hated tasks like this. "Why doesn't Mrs. Haas just tell us the answers or give us the steps to follow?" he thought. "Chemistry would be OK if she did that, but having to solve these problems on your own is too difficult. I think you just multiply the constant times the concentrations of the reactant. Or do you? I'd better look at the numbers again."

Melinda took out her history book, intending to begin her homework. "Man, Mrs. Powell really piles it on," she thought. "How am I going to do all this reading? There's 60 pages on the American Revolution, and I have to answer a lot of questions after I'm done. It's hard to remember all the details. Why do I have so much trouble reading this stuff?"

These anecdotes represent common concerns of teachers and students as they grapple with teaching and learning the content of various school subjects. Resnick (1983) has suggested that the acquisition of school subject matter is a special form of complex leaning and should be investigated independently of other types. To that end, we now discuss how students go about learning specific academic material and some appropriate instructional techniques. Most of our attention is directed toward the learning of reading, writing, and math skills and the mastery of social studies and science, but application to other areas is included where relevant. First, we need to examine how content can be organized to enhance classroom learning.

Subject matter learning is unique

PLANNING AND ORGANIZING CLASSROOM CONTENT

In Chapter 4 we discussed the concept of task analysis and the need for identifying the sequence of learned responses that eventually results in the acquisition of an instructional objective. In planning and organizing the presentation of instructional content, we must consider three factors: the sequence in which content should logically occur, the prerequisite knowledge or skills (i.e., what is required for new learning to occur), and the cognitive subtasks a learner must complete on the way to mastering the material. The content to be taught is thus affected by the kinds of thinking required of the learner and by what is already known about the material, as well as by the natural progression of the material itself. In some cases limitations in cognitive development may affect not only what content is taught but what cognitive operations are likely to be required because of the material. For example, early instruction in mathematics must await the development of number conservation and number magnitude, as we discussed in Chapter 3. In other cases, where cognitive skills are relatively advanced, it still may be necessary to prompt required thinking, perhaps through modeling or direct instruction.

What factors must be considered in designing instruction?

Ease of learning is thus maximized when the design of subject matter instruction reflects consideration of issues of content and of learner cognitive level and prerequisite skills in initial planning. Gagné and Briggs (1979) and Gagné and Driscoll (1988) have developed an *instructional system* that integrates these components and will serve as a model for our examination of subject matter organization and instruction in this chapter.

Gagné's Instructional System

Instruction is most effective when it is designed systematically. In Gagné's instructional systems approach, planning is presumed to occur at three levels: *systems, courses,* and *lessons* (Gagné & Briggs, 1979). At the systems level, a broad subject matter area such as secondary social studies is organized, often through the cooperation of several teachers. For example, high school teachers of history, U.S. government, and geography would consider what content should be taught in social studies, which material fits best in each course, and what sequence the courses should follow. Ideally, issues of prerequisite knowledge and skills, the amount of review necessary to relate one course to another, and what material should be eliminated or repeated for emphasis are considered at the initial stage. At the course level, individual courses are planned, and the group addresses issues raised during the system level analysis—for example, the concerns expressed by Mr. Sawyer at the opening of this chapter. The *infusion* issue is a particularly demanding one in social studies, as advocates recommend new content to include while rarely suggesting topics that can be eliminated. Finally, planning at the lesson level focuses on individual lessons organized within specific courses. Lessons are designed to fit into the total course.

Problems of infusion in your area?

The course level of instructional design deserves additional attention. In determining course structure and sequence, an important role of the instructor is to arrange *enabling* and *terminal* objectives. Terminal objectives describe student behaviors to be attained at the end of the course, such as "Interpret the major theme of the novel *Moby Dick*." Enabling objectives are prerequisites. Identifying the major characters in *Moby Dick* and explaining the symbolism of the white whale are examples of enabling objectives; that is, students would need to complete them before they could interpret the novel's theme. In some cases, objectives can be sequenced for reasons of convenience or logical placement. In content areas with an inherent organization, such as mathematics, it is essential that content be mastered according to an orderly progression, with one skill leading to another. Designing course structures and sequence is an important instructional skill because it can increase the probability that students will be able to represent new learning so that it can be related to existing schemes.

Enabling objectives lead to terminal objective

Course objectives must be considered in terms of the demands they make on the learner, as well as their sequence. Gagné and Briggs described three kinds of analysis of objective: *learning task analysis, task classification,* and *information processing.* Learning task analysis is similar to that described in Chapter 4. Content the learner must either know from earlier courses or learn early in the current one is identified; many of the course's enabling objectives are composed of such material.

Task classification consists of categorizing objectives into one of five *varieties of learning* (Gagné, 1985). These are:

1. *Intellectual skills,* or capabilities to use symbols to perform certain tasks such as reading or solving math problems. Intellectual skills can be thought of as procedural knowledge.
2. *Verbal information* of facts such as names, dates, and events. Being able to state verbal information is an example of declarative knowledge.
3. *Cognitive strategies,* or skills used in managing one's own learning, such as note taking or skim reading.
4. *Motor skills,* or organized psychomotor movements such as typing.
5. *Attitudes,* or mental states that influence personal choices, such as preferring classical music to rock or electing to avoid fatty foods.

The purpose of classifying objectives is to help in identifying the optimum conditions for learning. Gagné believes that different instructional events or operations are most applicable to each variety. For example, the learning of verbal information may require practice in encoding or retrieval, while motor skills necessitate demonstrations by a model and feedback, and the learning of attitudes might be best facilitated by role-playing or simulations. If promoting awareness about pollution is a course objective, for instance, the instructional strategies required will differ from these needed to achieve a narrower objective (e.g., to ensure students' recall of information about pollution). The belief that different instruction is necessary for each variety of learning is central to Gagné's instructional system.

Information-processing analysis of course objectives requires identification of the sequence of decisions and actions the learner performs in completing the terminal objective. Information-processing analysis is more complicated than merely identifying the overt behaviors comprising a task, since it includes consideration of the cognitive processes an individual must employ during learning. It thus entails observing and listening to learners as they solve a problem or perform an operation. By analyzing how individuals make judgments, a teacher can identify common student errors and gain insight into how best to teach a procedure.

When the three different forms of analysis are completed, teachers can design the actual instructional plan. Instruction will be organized to ensure that the appropriate varieties of learning are identified and necessary content prerequisites met in the interest of enhancing the sequence of students' information-processing decisions. The instructional plan will include a series of *instructional events,* under the control of the teacher, designed to enable learners to achieve the desired objective. Although specific forms of instructional events vary for different learning objectives, Gagné and Briggs (1979) have proposed an order in which these events are most likely to occur. Their proposal is particularly relevant to us because the events correspond well to the internal processes of learning described in both behavioral and cognitive information-processing theory. Table 7.1 depicts these instructional events, shows their relation to learning processes involved in a verbal information task, and suggests possible applications to a lesson on environmental pollution.

The nine instructional events given in Table 7.1 can be applied to all five varieties of learning described by Gagné, although the introductions used may vary. Suppose the instructional objective is to acquire motor skills necessary to measure the level of a pollutant. "Presenting the stimulus material" would require a model to demonstrate the correct procedure for calibrating a measuring instrument and to give verbal instructions. If use of an intellectual skill such as being able to analyze arguments critically were an objective, "Providing guidance" might consist of cuing students to employ various facets of critical thinking, such as identifying opinion statements when reading descriptions of pollution control practices. Gagné's major contention is that although specific instructional events may differ for the five learning varieties, they can be presented according to an organized sequence.

This instructional model, including the three types of analysis of objectives and the design of lessons incorporating the nine instructional events, provides an organized approach to lesson planning in different content areas for different varieties of learning. We will draw on this model as we examine the learning and teaching of specific content areas.

[handwritten margin note: Can be applied to Gagné's 5 varieties of learning on P. 232 + includes analysis of objective.]

TABLE 7.1 Instructional events, their relation to learning processes, and an instructional example

Instructional Event	Learning Process	Example
1. Gaining attention	Reception of stimuli *[handwritten: Receptors]*	Teacher says: "Did you know East River is so polluted that no fish can live in it?"
2. Informing learner of objective	Establishing expectancy	"Today we are going to identify five causes of pollution in our rivers."
3. Stimulating recall of prerequisites	Encouraging retrieval	"Remember the pollutants that are emitted by industrial factories?"
4. Presenting the stimulus material	Emphasizing features	"These are additional pollutants that get into our water supply."
5. Providing guidance	Facilitating encoding	"Think of water pollution as coming from three sources: the air, the land and the water itself: A-L-W."
6. Eliciting performance	Activating an organized response	"Now you think of three additional pollutants that come in from land."
7. Providing feedback	Reinforcing correct responses	"Good, Samantha, insecticides is correct."
8. Assessing performance	Activating retrieval and reinforcing organized responses	"Bill, please review all the forms of pollution we have discussed."
9. Enhancing retention and transfer	Providing cues and strategies for retrieval	"Now let's apply what we have learned to our analysis of industries."

SOURCE: Adapted from R. Gagné and L. Briggs, *Principles of instructional design*, 2nd ed. (New York: Holt, Rinehart & Winston, 1979).

LEARNING TO READ

No cognitive skill is more central to our learning than reading. In fact, it is by reading that we learn the majority of the curricular content encountered in school and beyond. Therefore we consider in this section not only the initial acquisition of reading skill but the utilization of reading to comprehend academic content.

[handwritten margin note: reading defn]

Defining reading is no easy task. While a simple definition consists of "examining and grasping the meaning of written or printed characters" (American Heritage Dictionary, 1985), reading is obviously more complex. Crowder and Wagner (1992) note that reading may include a wide range of different activities about which experts might disagree. Are we reading when we attempt to translate an assembly manual to put together an appliance? When we solve a mathematical statement such as $3x = 30 - (3 \times 5)$ or when we pronounce the words *noli me tangere*? Crowder and Wagner contend that we need two words for reading—one that refers to the initial translation of print into speech and another to cover determination of meaning. Otherwise, there is confusion between how language gets into the mind and what goes on in the mind when the language is available. As we shall see, different factors seem to influence these two distinct components of reading.

Early instruction in learning to read therefore requires the learner to translate print into internal speech; comprehension becomes a more dominant concern later in the educational process. A major instructional issue, however, is the magnitude of the role played by comprehension in the initial development of reading skill. Should reading be taught by emphasizing the decoding of printed symbols into corresponding sounds, to induce students to perceive *grapheme-phoneme correspondence*? Or should the meaning of words and phrases be the central concern, as in *whole-language* approaches?

Reading has two phases: recognition and comprehension

Whole-Language (Meaning Emphasis) Approach

Whole-language advocates believe that there is a natural parallel between how we learn to speak and how we learn to read. Early reading instruction should include exposure to a rich linguistic environment, featuring integrated experiences in speaking, listening, and writing as well as reading. This holistic method has been advocated by theorists (Goodman, 1965, 1968, 1986; F. Smith, 1971) who believe that the derivation of meaning is paramount at all stages of reading instruction.

The whole-language approach shares many of the beliefs held by those studying language acquisition, as discussed in Chapter 3. Children are sensitive to patterns in the linguistic material they encounter and are capable of forming and evaluating hypotheses about them. Whole-language adherents believe, in addition, that readers depend on context cues to generate predictions about a word. Goodman (1986) describes skilled readers as sampling words from text, rather than processing them all. Words that are processed are recognized by the distinctive features of their letters. With experience, readers also inductively acquire rules about redundancy and word construction, such as "*tio-* is often followed by *-n*" or "*u* always follows a *q*." Instruction, therefore, should help children view reading as hypothesis testing, making use of contextual information to facilitate word identification as well as grapheme-phoneme correspondences. Thus words never should be presented out of context, as in studying reading lists or doing worksheets that emphasize the internal structure of words only. Goodman (1968) fears that an emphasis on phonic cues or word attack skills will distract the child from the real purpose of reading: to acquire *meaning*.

Whole-language method— part of other language skills

Whole-language instruction typically (1) begins lessons with the sharing of a whole story, poem, or song, (2) surrounds children with printed materials (on the walls on, their desks, etc.), (3) uses all forms of communication to discuss stories (writing, speaking, art, music, drama, etc.), (4) encourages understanding and use of ideas and patterns in stories, (5) uses "big" books that can be viewed, shared, and enjoyed by a large group, (6) develops particular reading skills naturally as the opportunities occur in the text, and (7) allows time for sustained, silent reading of material the individual child finds interesting (Polette, 1990). Basal readers produced by text companies for use at a particular grade or reading level are supplemented or even replaced by storybooks. Workbooks are replaced by student-maintained journals, logs, and specific writing assignments, and children are encouraged to "read" their journals to peers and teachers in group discussions. Materials to be read are often linked to central themes such as the sea or animals, which are explored through all the various forms of communication (O'Brochta & Weaver, 1991). With such an approach, reading develops naturally as a part of other linguistic skills.

Research supporting the whole-language approach is not extensive, although some studies support its value. Goodman (1965) asked beginning readers to identify words on lists taken from beginning texts and then to read the same words presented in their original context. Performance improved between 60 and 80 percent when words were identified in their original context. In a review of whole-language experience studies, Stahl and Miller (1989) found that whole-language approaches were generally more effective than traditional techniques of reading readiness when employed at the kindergarten level. At later grade levels, techniques such as phonics and basal readers were more effective. The authors suggest that kindergarten children learned about books, about printed words in books, and about the value of reading as a result of whole-language training. Effects were strongest on word recognition measures.

Code-Oriented (Sound-Based) Approach

Those who advocate a code-oriented approach to early reading instruction believe that decoding the relation between the printed symbols that appear in text (graphemes) and the sounds in speech they represent (phonemes) is fundamental. When the relationship between graphemes and phonemes has been mastered, with the result that letter and word recognition becomes routine and automatic, more time can be spent in searching for contextual cues that may add to meaning. Activities that lead to automaticity in word identification should be the central component of a child's instructional program; the role of context cues needs to be diminished. Typical lessons introduce various phonemes (/s/, /t/, /i/, etc.) and use drill and practice techniques to ensure that children acquire *phonemic awareness*—the abilities to break words into phonemic segments (e.g., "s-i-t") and to recognize phonemic identity ("sit" and "sun" start with the same sound). A young reader who has achieved phonemic awareness is able to transfer this skill to new words with similar sounds (e.g., "s-a-t" or "s-u-b"). When this skill has been demonstrated, it is assumed that the child understands the *alphabetic principle* (Byrne & Fielding-Barnsley, 1990). After the alphabetic principle has been learned, instruction can focus on letter and phoneme combinations (-ed, -ing, etc.) and then move to irregular words that require unique rules (through, enough; child, children, etc.). In terms of Gagné's instructional system, code-oriented techniques seem to emphasize task analysis of prerequisites in their determination of instructional sequence, while whole-language approaches rely more on analysis of the kinds of information processing students perform to obtain meaning.

Research comparing the two approaches appears to favor an emphasis on code. Phonemic awareness appears to be necessary for skilled reading from early grades into adulthood. In a longitudinal study of children from first to fourth grade, Juel (1988) found that children who entered first grade with little phonemic awareness

Code emphasis and rules of grapheme–phoneme correspondence

were poor readers. By the end of fourth grade, poor readers still had not achieved the level of decoding exhibited by good readers and were reading well below grade level in comprehension. Pratt and Brady (1988) found that differences in phonemic awareness accounted for much of the difference between good and poor readers for not only third-graders but also for adults who read poorly. The tasks these these investigators used to assess awareness involved being able to say "smile" without the -s, or using colored blocks to represent changes in number and order of phonemes in spoken words. By the same token, attempts to teach phonemes to preschoolers by substituting a gamelike format for traditional drill and practice techniques have proven successful, suggesting that the skill can be acquired in the more natural, less academic format favored by whole-language advocates. Byrne and Fielding-Barnsley (1991) had children match cards with the same beginning sounds or colored pictures of target objects on posters that began or ended with a particular phoneme. Complementing the finding that whole language is most effective at the kindergarten level, code-oriented techniques may also be utilized in early reading programs.

Training in grapheme–phoneme correspondence not only aids word identification of phonetically regular words, it permits irregular words such as "known," "comb," "sew," and "wrong" to be recognized at the same level of proficiency known to be achievable under a more meaning-oriented approach (Foorman, Francis, Novy, & Lieberman, 1991). Since basic rules of letter–sound correspondence do not apply to irregular words, whole-language approaches, which focus on the whole word, should have an advantage in fostering recognition, but this is not necessarily the case. These findings suggest that learning of basic letter–sound correspondence rules can transfer to irregularly spelled words. Developing readers are able to take irregular spellings into account, but may still require strategies other than alphabetic coding to become most proficient.

Phoneme–grapheme correspondence is a prerequisite

Research also reveals that comprehension becomes operative only when fluency in word identification has been achieved. The most common explanation for this result invokes automaticity. More cognitive resources can be allocated to determining meaning when letter and word identification is automatic. Evidence comes from studies indicating that for beginning and poor readers, identifying words out of context is a much better predictor of comprehension than other measures (Vellutino, Scanlon, Small, & Tanzman, 1991). Learning to read words out of context, which is a major part of code-oriented approaches, seems to contribute to later comprehension.

The claims of whole-language advocates to the contrary, the role of context in aiding reading performance has not been demonstrated as crucial to developing reading skill. Observing the eye movements of skilled readers suggests that they scan all the letters and words they encounter, not just some key features, as suggested by whole-language adherents (Rayner & Pollatsak, 1989). Moreover, the less skilled readers rely more on context than skilled readers because the former are much less facile in automatic word identification (Stanovich, 1980). Finally, in a replication and refinement of Goodman's (1965) study cited above, Nicholson (1991) found that the effect of learning words in context was less dramatic than originally described and occurred only in poor readers. Thus context cues, which may be important components of skilled reading that students eventually need, may be less necessary during reading acquisition.

poor readers need context skilled readers have auto word ID

Reading Instruction

What, then, can we conclude about reading instruction? Findings that phonemic awareness and alphabetic coding are deficient in both children and adults who read poorly, that training in these skills improves reading ability, and that poor performance predicts poor reading in later grades suggest that activities that foster the development of such skills should be a major part of any reading program. Instruction should not exclude the use of meaning-based activities, however; these activities not only encourage the beginning reader to see that reading is meaningful and is related to writing and speech, but also allow applied use of developing skills in decoding. The use of context to monitor and predict what is happening or will happen in stories, activities that encourage identification of synonyms and antonyms for vocabulary growth, discussions about the meaning of what one has read, and the integration of reading, writing, and spelling to clarify their interrelationship all seem necessary for effective reading instruction. Opportunities for sustained silent reading of materials chosen by the reader also seem valuable, since they allow the child to relate reading to personal goals and interests. Silent reading is important because the amount of time spent reading alone at school has been found to contribute significantly to gains in reading achievement in the intermediate grades (Taylor, Frye, & Marvyama, 1990).

Although context may not be as important in developing reading as many claim, there is evidence that cues derived from the linguistic context remain important in skilled reading. Findings that letter–sound training had a less dramatic effect on irregular words, as in the work of Foorman et al. (1991), indicate that the developing reader may need to acquire strategies other than alphabetic coding for identifying such items. Meaning-based, mnemonic strategies discussed in Chapter 6, such as key-word, imagery, or the use of context that would aid in recall of the word, may be necessary to the learning of irregular words. "There's *a rat* in the word *separate*" is a good example of how a mnemonic utilizing a context cue can contribute to word identification. While it is important to utilize "bottom-up" processing of words through use of rules of letter–sound correspondence, "top-down" approaches to reading such as encouraging students to routinely employ encoding strategies to aid in word recognition should also be included in reading instruction (Crowder & Wagner, 1992).

Knowledge of grapheme–phoneme correspondence does not guarantee that a young reader knows how those sounds are used in reading. Many phonics programs do not foster transfer from the types of training done in establishing correspondence to the use of the rule in real reading contexts (Adams, 1990). For example, recognizing that "silent *e*" after a consonant "causes the preceding vowel to say its name" as in "cake" or "bite," and practicing the skill on a series of worksheets, will not ensure the successful use of the rule when a child is reading text. Necessary practice in phonemic awareness and alphabetic relationships can be conducted within story contexts, so that the learner is not only decoding but is reading meaningfully. The books of popular children's authors such as Dr. Seuss and Richard Scarry provided this experience to my children, as well as amusing me. These books employ artistic representations, humor, interesting characters, and compelling stories as a backdrop for the practice of basic decoding skills.

It is clear that effective reading instruction can utilize what each model of teaching reading has to offer, depending on the need of the individual learner. Children who have difficulty in grasping the broader meanings of text should be exposed to more activities designed to reveal reading as a meaningful act. For those who have difficulty in decoding, code emphasis instruction may have to be taught in innovative ways that excite students rather than bore them. Both approaches have much to offer, but neither should be considered as the only "right way" to teach reading.

The value of both methods is illustrated in an interesting case study of a beginning teacher of culturally diverse children (Hollingsworth, Teel, & Minarik, 1992). Trained to use a literature-based, whole-language approach, the teacher at first had her students enthusiastic about telling stories, writing their own stories, and sharing and discussing them with others. She noted, however, that several students had difficulty in reading and writing simple words. Concerned about their decoding deficits and prompted by the school district's move to a new basal series, the teacher changed to a program incorporating a code-oriented method in her second year. Out of this change emerged a new reading program, which by her third year was successfully utilizing the best features of each type of instruction to aid the reading of all her pupils. In her words, "I have dramatically changed my views as compared to my year of student teaching and my first year on my own. First of all, the children finally taught me to watch them and listen to them. I now pick curriculum that suits their needs and interests best and am less affected by district curriculum or by the opinions of textbook publishers" (Hollingsworth et al., 1992, p. 126).

Reading to Learn

It has been said that no two people read the same book. Since existing schemas always filter and refine text material as encoding and reorganization occur during working memory, the individual is in fact constructing his or her own meaning from a common text. As subject matter knowledge accumulates during the school years, students become more capable of relating existing schemas to text information, with the result that learning from text becomes easier and more purposeful. Reading to learn eventually becomes the major source of new information for most learners.

How can teachers enhance high levels of comprehension in their students' reading from text? *Evoking prior knowledge* is one technique. Recht and Leslie (1988), for example, found that the more middle school students knew about baseball, the more they were able to recall about a description they had read of an inning of a baseball game. Teachers should also point out *text signals* that guide students' attention to important information. "Preview" sentences ("In the next section we will discuss . . .") and "Recall" sentences ("As we discussed in Chapter 2, . . . ") were found to aid comprehension and recall of social studies text material when teachers identified them for students (Glover et al., 1988). *Utilizing instructional objectives,* either those provided in the text or added by the instructor, can also enhance comprehension. Muth, Glynn, Britton, and Graves (1988) found that students increased the amount of time they spent reading material related to objectives and demonstrated improved recall when they were given specific objectives to accompany a reading passage.

Perhaps the most important role of the teacher, however, is to aid students to

Integrated approach most generalizable to all students?

Context contributes to determination of meaning

more know about something, more learn as read.

Reading to learn requires schema activation

employ effective reading strategies on their own, without direct reminders from the teacher or the text. Students who use strategies spontaneously will be able to acquire meaning even when reading independently from materials not specifically designed for instruction. Dole, Duffy, Roehler, and Pearson (1991) have identified five reading comprehension strategies that students require for learning from text: *determining importance, summarizing information, drawing inferences, generating questions,* and *monitoring comprehension.* These strategies, which are present to much greater degrees in skilled readers than in novices, appear to be teachable. For example, Stevens (1988) taught remedial reading students to determine important main ideas in texts. Training consisted of practice in identifying what topics or concepts were discussed in individual sentences, and noting how often each was referred to in a paragraph. Students were also taught to classify words under topics and to use labels to identify a class. For example, "lightning," "heavy rain," and "dark clouds" all refer to the topic "thunderstorm"; "the Rockies," "the mountains," and "giant, snow-covered peaks" all refer to a particular mountain range. Recognizing that topics can be described using different terms is critical to understanding that the same main idea is being referred to again and therefore assumes greater importance in the text.

> *Identifying main ideas is a comprehension strategy*

A more complete description of reading strategies is presented in Chapter 10. For now, it is important to realize that instruction in reading comprehension is not restricted to reading class. Rather, it is practiced by all teachers as they provide guidance in reading the particular text material their students are expected to master.

LEARNING TO WRITE

In one of our opening anecdotes, we found Mrs. Etzlaff stewing over the quality of writing demonstrated by her students. Her major concern was the clarity and coherence of the ideas presented. Unfortunately, Mrs. Etzlaff's problem is common among those who teach writing skills. In a national assessment of the writing of seventeen-year-olds, almost a third failed to show structured plots or adequate elaboration and detail in their stories (National Assessment of Educational Progress, 1986). Observed deficiencies of this type have led to increased interest in writing instruction and renewed study of how students become good writers.

> *Analysis of student thinking necessary to understanding writing*

Much of the current emphasis on student writing has evolved from a cognitive information-processing orientation. As Hayes and Flower (1986) point out, in process-oriented instruction the teacher attempts to intervene in the writing or composing process itself, rather than respond to completed student assignments in accordance with traditional practice. Instruction is determined after analysis of the thinking and decision making of students during their writing efforts, as Gagné's instructional systems model suggests. In their research Hayes and Flower rely on a technique called *protocol analysis,* which applies the "thinking aloud" procedure to students' writing efforts. It is believed that by recording what learners say to themselves as they attempt to write both short- and long-term assignments, a model of the writing process can be obtained. For instance, a sixth-grader describes his writing philosophy: "I have a whole bunch of good ideas and I start writing the major ones first because they are the ones that are in the front of my mind. Then the smaller ones start coming three quarters of the way in the page. . . . So I might write as many of these as I can. . . . It doesn't take that long" (Scardamalia & Bereiter, 1986, p. 66).

Such comments reveal the plans, strategies, and goals of young writers. If we are to improve their writing skills, we must be able to understand their thoughts about writing as they move from the relative novice phase to being fluent communicators. A description of the cognitive processes involved in mature writing has been developed by Flower and Hayes (Flower & Hayes, 1980, 1981; Hayes & Flower, 1986).

Flower and Hayes Writing Model

The writing model of Flower and Hayes begins with four basic assumptions:

1. The purpose of effective writing is to *convey meaning,* and to create a product that accomplishes this goal, one must engage in a type of problem-solving activity. To convey meaning, it is necessary to consider the audience—its knowledge of the topic, its interests, and how the writer can help the audience to understand what is being communicated.

Flower & Hayes model: writing as problem solving

2. Writing is *goal-directed.* Purpose is established early in the process.
3. Writing goals are *hierarchically organized* into subgoals, which combine to form a plan that eventually leads to a finished product. A typical approach of a skilled writer in completing an essay, for instance, is to establish an outline of the final product, a series of intermediate steps necessary to complete the plan, and a timetable describing approximately when each step will be accomplished. While actual performance may depart from the original plan (as we all ruefully note as we stay up until dawn, revising a paper that was supposed to be finished yesterday), it serves as a useful, although approximate guide.
4. The writing process includes a set of *distinctive thinking processes,* which writers orchestrate during writing (Flower & Hayes, 1981). Rather than treating writing as if it occurred in stages of completion, organized in a linear sequence, this model emphasizes mental processes such as revising, which can recur at several points during composition. Revision, for example, may occur early during the process when the writer realizes that the preliminary plan needs to be changed, as well as later when a rough draft has been produced.

The Flower and Hayes model of writing presented in Figure 7.1 attempts to relate these thinking processes to writing and describes the factors that influence them.

The writing process begins with analysis of the *rhetorical problem*—that is, what the writer defines the writing task to be. Flower and Hayes believe a rhetorical problem is never a given; rather, it is a construction the writer creates. Even a simple task such as writing a thank-you note to Uncle Phil requires not only conventional thank-you note language but such additional considerations as what Uncle Phil would like to read—whether the note should end with "Love" or "As ever," and so on. People will choose to define the same rhetorical problem in widely varying ways. Three factors appear to interact. One is the *assignment* itself. Differences in analyzing an

writer defn of task

Rhetorical problem constructed by the individual

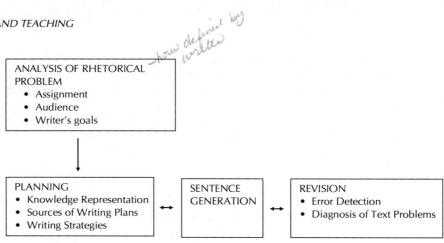

how defined by writer

FIGURE 7.1   Flower and Hayes writing model

SOURCE: Adapted with permission from J. R. Hayes and L. S. Flower, Writing research and the writer. *American Psychologist, 41*(10), 1106–1113 (1986). Copyright 1986 by the American Psychological Association.

assignment can range from the superficial ("Blech! Write another paper about Shakespeare, only this time include *Macbeth,* about two pages worth.") to the more substantial ("She wants more character analysis this time—I'll need to quote parts of *Macbeth* that refer to his personality."). Another factor is the perceived *audience* that will read the finished piece. Is the written product for a teacher, a parent, a friend, or a remote individual or institution? Will the audience be evaluating the writing in some way or is the function of the product simply to convey information? Decisions about the audience will affect the content, style, and organization of the composition. The third factor is the *writers's goals* in writing the assignment. Flower and Hayes identify four kinds of goal:

4 kinds of writing goals

1. The effect one wants to have on the reader. (Do I want to persuade people or just impress them with my knowledge?)
2. How the writer wants to project himself or herself. (Should I be authoritative? Straightforward?)
3. The meaning to be communicated. (Should I emphasize important differences in ideas, or critically evaluate specific ones?)
4. The conventions of writing to be followed. (Should I give examples or use metaphors to explain my major points?)

After comparing the protocols of good and poor writers, Flower and Hayes (1980) detected a number of differences in how the rhetorical problem was analyzed. In general, good writers responded to all three factors. They built a unique representation of the problem, including knowledge of the assignment, the audience, and personal goals. The problem representations of the poor writers, on the other hand, were concerned primarily with the surface features of the writing task, such as number of pages or words. Good writers created a rich network of goals for communicating meaning to the reader, while poor writers tended to focus more on what they knew

Poor writers focus on surface features

of the topic than on the reader's requirements. Good writers also represented the problem in depth as well as breadth, while the poorer writers established a relatively narrow view of what was to be done. Flower and Hayes summarized their analysis by stating that good writers and poor writers were simply solving different problems. The major difference is that poor writers think only of their perception of the problem; they do not attempt to project how the reader will understand what is being communicated. The situation is similar to one a teacher encountered when a third-grader wrote a short essay:

T: Randy, this essay on your dog bears a striking resemblance to the one your sister turned in last year.

R: Yes, ma'am, it should. It's the same dog.

The *planning* phase of the model involves decision making about how the rhetorical problem will be met. Writing plans are constructed by integrating information of three types: *topic knowledge* (domain-specific knowledge), *knowledge of effective writing formats,* and *knowledge of problem-solving strategies* (to support planning when known writing formats do not fit the perceived rhetorical problem). *Topic knowledge* is stored in long-term memory in the form of code words or images that can be linked to relevant schemas. Knowledge of *writing formats* consists of familiarity with procedures that are useful in accomplishing certain goals, such as "what to say in a business letter" or "what words to use when one wants to sound dramatic." *Problem-solving strategies* involve knowing how to define the writing task (e.g., how to set manageable goals, how to apply procedural knowledge to problem-solving situations, and how to monitor and direct one's own writing progress). Expert writers' planning tends to differ in several ways from that of novices (Hayes and Flower, 1986):

Planning phase utilizes topic knowledge + writing plans

1. Expert writers construct an initial task representation and a set of goals that serve to guide and constrain their efforts to write. Experts are free to set goals because they have mastered technical skills such as spelling and punctuation to the level of automatization and can concentrate on higher-level analysis of the writing problem.

2. Goals are hierarchically arranged so that one logically leads to several others. For example, in planning to write a term paper, the good writer recognizes that library research is necessary to find basic information. A preliminary outline will identify areas of the topic that may need library time. The good writer also recognizes, however, that library research may turn up information that results in a rethinking of what the paper should contain and a revision of the outline. Moreover, as writing of the paper progresses, the good writer may recognize that some component of the paper requires further research, not anticipated earlier. Back to the library. The hierarchical structure of writing goals established by the good writer during the planning phase is viewed as a temporary plan and is flexible enough to accommodate later changes. The plans of novice writers, on the other hand, are less flexible—once library research has

been completed, for example, subsequent visits are ruled out and the writer makes do with the information that has been collected.

3. The writing goals initially planned by experts may persist even if they have been modified. Good writers often return to goals they had abandoned earlier. M. Rose (1980) suggests that this ability to return to and utilize earlier goals, perhaps in a revised form, is one way good writers use to escape *writer's block*, or the temporary blankness experienced by many writers in which they are unable to continue writing according to their original plan. The author once found himself staring at a blinking cursor for 15 minutes before deciding that writer's block really exists.

4. Poor writers have difficulty organizing their knowledge around a problem and developing a focus. Their goal networks are less elaborate and less interconnected. When asked to reveal his writing plan for completing his master's thesis, one student said: "First, I'll do Chapter 1 the introduction, then Chapter 2 the review of literature, then Chapters 3, 4, and 5." When asked to be more specific, he replied, "Well, I could do the review of literature first."

How do you counteract writer's block?

*figure 7.1
P. 242*

The translation of writing plans into actual prose, the *sentence generation* phase of the model (Hayes and Flower, 1986), involves a substantial amount of work. Among other things, the writer must expand sketchy ideas into a meaningful framework ("How do I explain transcendentalism, anyway?"), interpret nonverbal material into a verbal form ("I can see the lake in my mind. How can I describe it?"), and carry out instructions ("What was I supposed to include in the summary?"). Kaufer, Flower, and Hayes (1988) found that going from an outline to an essay involved an average of eight times more words for expert writers.

Writers generate sentences in parts, between 7 and 12 words long, with experts generating longer ones. Parts of sentences are assembled in left-to-right fashion, with new parts added to the right of the last completed one or designed to replace it entirely. A writer trying to explain why he liked baseball, for instance, might generate the following:

> I like baseball because . . . the pace, it's steady and comforting. No, "comforting" is the wrong word. I like baseball because it's never predictable and never seems to be in a hurry. No, I like baseball because each game evolves at its own pace. That's it.

The longer the units one manipulates, the more fluent and rapid the writing becomes.

The more expert the writer, the greater the proportion of writing time devoted to the *revision phase* of the model. Revision occurs as a final review during sentence generation, when what should be written is seen more clearly. It has already occurred in the planning phase as the writer modified the writing plan to be employed and during sentence generation when words, sentences, and paragraphs were revised. In other words, revision is inherent in the process of transforming ideas into print; it should not be viewed as merely a final phase of writing devoted to refinement and correction of spelling and grammatical errors. The two-way arrows between planning and sentence generation and between sentence generation and revision in Figure 7.1 suggest the interactive nature of the three phases of the model.

Revision is not easy. Apparently, knowledge of what we have written makes it difficult for even the best writers among us to detect faults in our own writing. Our familiarity with what we believe we wrote, after having mulled it over, interferes with our perception of what is actually on the paper. You have probably experienced the feeling of rereading an assignment well after it has been turned in, only to find a glaring and obvious error. Why hadn't you detected it? Detecting errors in written work is easier when the writing is someone else's. Bartlett (1981), for example, found that fifth-graders could detect only 10 percent of the errors in their own written work, but 50 percent of the errors in the texts of their peers. Could it also be that we derive pleasure from observing the errors of others?

Although experts may be relatively oblivious to their own errors, they are more capable of detecting mistakes in texts than are novices. They are also more able to diagnose the problems underlying errors (Hayes & Flower, 1986). The ability to diagnose faults in writing provides an advantage over merely detecting them because it suggests a revision strategy: "I used a passive voice in this sentence. I'd better switch to a more active style to give my sentences more emphasis." Detecting an error without diagnosing its cause can prompt the writer to rewrite the material; but if the nature of the error is not understood, it may be necessary to abandon an entire thought or phrase: "I know that's not the right word, but I don't know what to put in its place." Learning how to diagnose errors as opposed to merely detecting them may be critical to improving one's skill in revision.

The Flower and Hayes model provides a detailed analysis of the information processing that occurs during writing. We shall now examine instructional procedures designed to aid poor writers in acquiring the skills necessary to improve their work.

Writing Instruction

Traditional writing instruction emphasized student practice of the technical conventions of good writing—punctuation, grammatical rules, and so on. If any effect on the actual writing of students was obtained from this approach, it was that students tended to overextend technical rules and writing became stilted (Beaugrade, 1984). In fact, research suggests that the major differences between expert and novice writers lie not so much in mechanics or technical skills as in the planning and conduct of the writing process. In the Flower and Hayes model, identifying and communicating meaning to the audience is the major purpose of good writing. Effective writing instruction therefore should be composed of activities that enhance the transmission of information from the writer to the audience via the written word. The following procedures offer promise in that regard: strategy instruction, procedural facilitation, product-oriented instruction, and inquiry learning.

Strategy Instruction.   Strategy instruction consists of direct teaching of strategies found to contribute to good writing (setting goals, generating ideas, determining information needed, analyzing the problem, etc.). For example, DeBono (1989) has developed an instructional program in writing for middle school students that provides practice in 18 thinking skills such as "deciding priorities" and "generating alternatives." The program includes graphic outlines such as a "problem-solving box" in which to "place" writing ideas. Programs of this kind show promise, but typically little positive transfer has been found in pre–post comparisons of writing occurring outside the experimental setting. As an example, Scardamalia, Bereiter, and Steinbach (1984) found little evidence of actual planning in the writing protocols of twelve-year-olds who had been trained to plan before they wrote. The problem appears to lie in converting declarative knowledge consisting of verbalized instructions about the nature of good writing to procedural knowledge in which writing strategies are spontaneously employed by the learner when necessary. To induce transfer to unsupervised writing, it may be necessary to supplement direct instruction in the use of strategies by a teacher with materials similar to DeBono's.

Problem of transfer in strategy instruction

Procedural Facilitation.   Procedural facilitation refers to aid directed toward the student's cognitive processing, rather than toward the actual substance of what the student is writing (Scardamalia & Bereiter, 1985). The facilitation may come directly from a teacher but is often in the form of support materials such as cue cards (to remind students to follow a procedure) or a checklist (to use in recording steps taken or goals reached). The rationale for the use of procedural facilitation is that the most effective help in writing comes when students are prompted to think about what they are writing before they *begin*—that is, when appropriate strategies can be applied. Four procedural aids in this category are as follows.

1. Conferencing.   Conferencing is any type of one-to-one discussion in which the teacher directs a student's attention to decisions that must be made in planning and composing. The conference is not a teacher-dominated lecture; it is designed to help students analyze their own work. Sowers (1986) suggests that teachers ask questions they want students to ask themselves. To be useful, comments or questions by a teacher must be applied by the writer when working independently. Sowers suggests that teachers concentrate on making comments of three types: those that *reflect* their perception of the student's writing, those that help students see how they can *expand* their writing, and those that aid in the *selection* of what to write about. Consider the following example.

MRS. E.: Sean, it sounds like you had a lot of exciting things happen to you on your trip. What else did you do?

SEAN: We went swimming in the ocean and there were baby whales in the ocean.

MRS. E.: Baby whales! Now you have a lot to write about after the conference. Which topics will you choose?

SEAN: The baby whales and the eagles I saw.

This teacher's comments encourage the student to reflect on what he did; they also expand his ideas about what to include and suggest a basis for selection of content.

2. Computer Facilitation.   As discussed in Chapter 4, hypermedia technology places the writer in contact with a number of resources that can be consulted during the planning process. Computers can provide support by cuing an appropriate procedure, holding in memory information the writer might not be able to retrieve, suggesting synonyms for selected words, and aiding in subdividing the writing task into manageable components. Word-processing programs, especially software featuring Windows, can facilitate actual planning and revision by suggesting formats and styles to follow. While computers can be useful in aiding revision of mechanical errors, recent technology promises to facilitate the cognitive processes that contribute to the problem-solving dimension of writing.

3. Peer Editing.   Acquisition of writing skills appears to be enhanced when peers contribute to and edit others' work. The inevitable "What I did on my summer vacation" theme could be explored by students in pairs or in group settings, in which ideas are brainstormed and recorded. After students have worked individually to produce a first draft, peers could edit mechanical errors, suggest changes in sentence and paragraph construction, and provide feedback on whether the composition is clear and meaningful. Since as noted earlier, most writers are more capable of finding errors in the work of others than in their own, peer editing enjoys a built-in advantage. Moreover, some students may respond more attentively to the critiques of peers than to those of teachers, who provide criticism on an all-too-regular basis.

Peers can help
in planning

4. Sentence Combining.   A writing exercise that has been found to facilitate sentence generation and improve syntactical construction is sentence combining. Scrambled sentences are presented and students are asked to combine them in a way that makes sense. This procedure does not correspond to the way writers normally compose sentences; but the act of arranging sentences to convey meaning, which is necessary to writing good prose, apparently activates the cognitive processes that control the formation of meaningful sentences. Sentence-combining materials are found in many writing workbooks. To add humor or drama to the activity, teachers can scramble the written components of favorite cartoon strips, the monologues of comedians, or dialogue from television shows. Students number the scrambled sentences in what they believe to be the correct order, compare their numbering with the schemes of others, and then construct an additional sentence to expand or improve the sequence. Material that is relatively novel works best, since students cannot rely on memory but must rearrange the sentences based only on their analysis of the topic.

Product-Oriented Instruction.   Product-oriented instruction is designed to help learners become aware of the product characteristics they should strive to incorporate in their writing. The approach utilizes many examples of good writing, and students are asked to create their own compositions by copying the modeled product or editing their work to conform to the model. Research indicates that students at first attend to content rather than the literary characteristics of the material they encounter, but with practice they can learn to focus on features that contribute to a particular style of writing (Church & Bereiter, 1983).

A component of good written products is word choice. One teacher provides examples of how the choice of one word in a sentence can create a positive, negative, or neutral impression, then has students attempt to choose words that create the three effects. She reports that students can readily see how meaning is subtly affected by word choice and enjoy practicing the skill. Table 7.2 contains examples of word choices that create different impressions.

Inquiry Learning. Other approaches to writing instruction place students in independent learning activities, where they are free to experiment in the writing of their own materials. The technique known as *inquiry learning* shares with the whole-language reading approach the belief that language activities must provide meaningful goals for students to attain. By offering students a selection of materials to write about (e.g., stories they are to tell, results of scientific experiments to report, information derived from research in investigating their family tree), a meaningful context for writing can be created. Stories can be kept in writing folders, and students can review them periodically.

Bingham (1986) reports that writing folders can be used to help students understand the writing process. She tells of an eight-year-old who said after reviewing his folder: "It's easier to start . . . now that I know it doesn't have to be perfect to begin with." A review of this boy's work for the year revealed that he had written about his dog three times, with each story more elaborate than the last. Bingham observes that if all the writing activities, including rough drafts, notes, and outlines, are kept in one folder, students are more likely to recognize the many steps and stages that comprise the writing process.

Evaluation of Writing

If writing instruction is to emphasize the cognitive processes that characterize expert writers, what sort of evaluation will most effectively provide the feedback needed for learning to occur? As already indicated, traditional evaluation of written products fails to provide students information that is transferred to later writing. Much of the feedback teachers typically provide is directed toward spelling, grammar, and other mechanical components. Evaluation should respond to the processes of effective writing as well as the product.

One recent format was developed by teachers in Oregon after an analysis of their own evaluations of student writing (Spandel & Stiggins, 1990). The *six-trait analysis* method is designed as a formative evaluation procedure for all grade levels. It can be used by teachers, by peers, and by writers themselves to review their own work. The

Six-trait analysis provides structured evaluation

TABLE 7.2 Word choice continua

Phrase	Neutral	Positive	Negative
Someone crying	"Weeping"	"Mourning"	"Blubbering"
A unique person	"Individual"	"Original"	"Freakish"
Not very talkative	"Quiet"	"Concise"	"Terse"

analysis requires the evaluator to assess six dimensions of a piece of writing by rating each dimension on a scale of 1 to 5. The dimensions are as follows:

1. *Ideas and content*—the extent to which ideas are clearly stated, interesting and rich with detail.
2. *Organization*—the sequence of ideas effectively moves the reader through the piece.
3. *Voice*—the writer speaks directly to the reader and seems sincere, candid, and committed to the topic; the overall effect is individualistic and expressive.
4. *Word choice*—the writer selects words that convey the intended message in a precise and natural way.
5. *Sentence structure*—sentences have a rhetorically effective, fluid structure that makes reading enjoyable.
6. *Conventions*—standard writing conventions (grammar, capitalization, spelling, punctuation, usage, paragraphing) are accurate and enhance readability.

These six characteristics all contribute to the communication of meaning in writing. The six-trait model of evaluation is a useful tool for assessing how well a person analyzes, plans, and executes a written assignment. It can be particularly helpful as the basis for discussing student writing in teacher–student conferences.

LEARNING MATHEMATICS

Curriculum Reform

In 1989 the National Council of Teachers of Mathematics (NCTM) proposed a major revision to the content and emphasis of the mathematics curriculum followed in schools in the United States. The revision included a statement of standards that all students at all grade levels are expected to meet. The standards fall into five categories: (1) learning to value mathematics, (2) becoming confident in one's ability to do mathematics, (3) becoming a mathematical problem solver, (4) learning to communicate mathematically, and (5) learning to reason mathematically. These goals are presumed to help students become mathematically literate or able to "explore, to conjecture and to reason logically, as well as to use a variety of mathematical methods effectively to solve problems" (NCTM, 1989, p. 8).

New curriculum emphasis on problem solving

One might ask why it was necessary to impose these new standards. Were these areas not covered earlier? Has mathematics changed in ways that eliminate the need for some content while introducing new areas? Has understanding of how and when children learn mathematical concepts and operations changed so greatly in recent years that a new organization is required? These are all good questions. Let us examine the reasons for the change.

Levels of achievement are low.   The famous report entitled *A Nation at Risk* (National Commission on Excellence in Education, 1983) made public the low levels of math achievement attained by American school children. While many newspaper accounts tend to exaggerate perceived levels of incompetence, research does show that performance in mathematics at most grade levels is frequently below expectations (Lindquist, 1989). In one study, for instance, fewer than half the seventh- and eleventh-grade students knew that $5\frac{1}{4}$ and $5 + \frac{1}{4}$ have the same value; 17 out of 20 fourth-graders thought that $\frac{1}{2}$ was the largest fraction less than 1; and 65 percent of a class of sixth-graders selected 0.39 as a decimal that is larger than 0.6 (Leutzinger & Bentheau, 1989). While many students may be able to make basic calculations, they appear to lack "number sense" or the ability to make sound judgments about the approximate quantities numbers represent. Carpenter (1985) believes that students often are unable to make simple judgments about the numbers they are manipulating because traditional instruction treats mathematics as the mechanical application of rote skills.

New goals for mathematics are needed.   The NCTM maintains that the educational system of the past does not meet the needs of contemporary society. The availability of handheld calculators, computers, and other technology has reduced the need for individuals to perform tedious calculations. Now, however, there is a need for students to be able to utilize these tools to obtain and communicate information. Society requires mathematically literate workers who can contribute to a rapidly changing workplace. There is a demand for people who can solve problems, often as members of a team.

Low achievement, changing goals prompt revision

Coburn (1989) has recommended that educators expand their definition of mathematical computation to include the use of calculators along with written and mental calculations. Different problem situations require different methods of computation. A component of mental computation is the ability to estimate, in which one can arrive at approximate answers without determining exact quantities. People should not need a pencil or a calculator to determine that if an item costs $12.49 and is subject to a sales tax of 6 percent, a clerk who attempts to charge $1.75 for the tax has made a mistake. Calculators should be employed as a method of computation in work calling for redundant and time-consuming calculations. When determining averages, for example, why take the time to add up the heights of 30 classmates by hand, when a calculator can accomplish the task much more rapidly? Calculators have been found to help students to focus attention on math procedures, develop explanations of math topics, present many positive and negative examples of particular concepts, and make problems less tedious and more interesting. Rather than viewing calculators as crutches or as substitutes for learning computation, some educators have found that these devices, if used appropriately, facilitate the acquisition of computational skills (Comstock & DeMarc, 1987).

Results of information-processing analyses are available.   Information-processing approaches to task analysis have produced new insights. Two information-processing phases seem to be most critical in mathematics learning: the manner in which individuals *represent* the given information in a mathematical problem and the *solution plan* they develop (R. E. Mayer, 1986).

Analysis reveals how learners construct understanding

"Representation" refers to how individuals select, categorize, and integrate the given verbal information to make the words of the problem internally meaningful. For example, consider the following problem:

The ratio of boys to girls in a class is 3 to 8. If there are nine boys, how many girls are in the class?

(a) 17   (b) 14   (c) 24   (d) not given   (e) don't know

To answer this problem correctly, it is necessary to first construct a ratio or proportion problem and form the ratio $\frac{3}{8} = \frac{9}{x}$. Post, Wachsmith, Lesh, and Behr (1985) analyzed the choices selected by fourth- through eighth-graders. Twenty-nine percent of the group correctly answered choice (c), while 17 percent selected choice (b). This wrong choice suggests that some students might have represented the problem not as a ratio, but as some type of addition problem (e.g., "Five more girls than boys, therefore I'll add 5 to 9, to get 14."). The students who chose (b) probably erred because they failed to represent the problem appropriately. That is, their error was made *before* the solution phase of the problem had begun. To assist these students, teachers must emphasize identifying problem type, to ensure accurate representation. Increased practice in calculation will not necessarily be required.

Learning mathematics is a constructive rather than a passive activity.   The cognitive information-processing view stresses that learning does not occur solely by passive absorption (i.e., receiving, practicing, and storing information). In most situations learners approach a new task with prior knowledge organized according to schemas; then they assimilate new information and construct their own meaning (Resnick, 1983).

Consider, for example, the way children learn to add. Four stages have been identified: counting-all, counting-on, derived facts, and known facts (Mayer, 1986). *Counting-all* entails the child adding 2 + 3 by counting "1, 2" and pausing, then counting "3, 4, 5—the answer is 5." All objects are represented and counted. With time and as the numbers to be added grow larger, the *counting-on* strategy emerges: The child might start with 2 and then count "3, 4, 5" or with the larger number (3) and count "4, 5." In the *derived-facts* stage, knowledge of some addition facts is used to discover answers for related problems: "I know 4 + 4 = 8, so 4 + 5 must be 1 more than 8. I count 8, 9—and 9 is the answer." *Known facts* are sums that have been memorized through practice ("8 + 8 = 16, 8 + 9 = 17," etc.). Adults are more likely to use known and derived facts to add larger numbers (Ashcroft & Battaglia, 1978).

The four stages of adding indicate that learners indeed construct their own way of adding numbers, which they revise as their knowledge grows and new problems arise. The NCTM (1989) believes that the constructive view of how mathematics is learned must be reflected in how the subject is taught, through active experience in using numbers in class projects, group work, discussions, and games.

Knowledge in mathematics should be closely connected and related to knowledge of other content.   Lindquist (1989) argues that learning mathematics only as sets of rules or as declarative knowledge eventually causes difficulty because there are so many isolated rules to learn and remember. Learning is made easier when we are able to connect rules to procedural knowledge. For this reason, connecting concrete examples of a rule or fact (adding 2 pencils and 2 pencils) allows the formation of a bridge to the symbolic dimension of mathematics (2 + 2 = 4). Topics within mathematics also should be connected. Pointing out that rounding a number is like measuring to the nearest centimeter and noting that forming five equal groups is like determining an average are examples of making connections between topics. Connections between mathematics and other subject matter areas should be made, as well. Those who teach biology, for instance, can use a statistical procedure borrowed from a math class to show how genetic traits are inherited and distributed in a population. Mastery of computer applications that permit the use of mathematical procedures such as graphing and determination of functions is another form of connection.

Representation of Mathematical Problems

The cognitive processes of representation and solution planning appear to best describe what happens when an individual engages in the learning of mathematics, and they will serve as our main constructs. It should be noted that mathematics educators have traditionally defined mathematics learning as consisting of computational skills and problem solving, with an underlying assumption that acquisition of computational skill must precede application of mathematics content to problems. Most now recognize, however, that even learning the most basic counting skill constitutes a "problem" for young children. The knowledge facts of mathematics eventually become overlearned to the point of automaticity, but this does not mean that the acquisition of those facts did not require significant cognitive effort and a procedure resembling the problem-solving activities of experts. The processes of representation and solution planning seem to characterize all mathematics learning, whether of the preschooler or the advanced mathematician.

Representation is problematic in computation and word problems

Clearly, representations differ as the symbolic nature of mathematics progresses. We describe next representation in three of the major types of mathematical skill, focusing particularly on representations that are problematic for learners.

Counting. The ability of young learners to recite numbers in a sequence does not necessarily indicate that counting has been established as a fully operational method of representing quantity. Three-year-olds who can count single digits still have difficulty in representing the relative magnitudes of numbers (Murray and Mayer, 1988) and fail to relate counting to transformations in arrangement (Kamii, 1985). Gelman and Gallistel (1978) have identified five principles that are required before counting can be considered to be a completely accurate technique of representing number quantity: (1) *one-to-one correspondence,* in which each object is represented by a counting name, (2) *stable order,* in which the counting names are consistently recited in correct order, (3) *abstraction,* in which counting can be applied to any display of objects, (4) *order irrelevance,* in which objects can be counted in any order, and (5) *cardinality,* in which the last object counted is understood to determine the value of the group. These principles are identifiable in the counting of young children prior to kindergarten (Gelman, 1980), but they require further practice and review.

Computation.   Representation is accomplished by identifying an arithmetic task as requiring one or the other of the four basic mathematical operations. Once identified, computational problems are solved by applying an *algorithm,* or iterative procedure that guides the action necessary to complete the task. The count-all, count-on rules described earlier are examples of simple algorithms for addition. Competence in mathematics computation is acquired as the learner practices using algorithms and observes their success or failure in solving computation problems (Riley, Greeno, & Heller, 1983).

Solutions depend on available rules and analysis

Utilization of algorithms appears to depend on the development of memory in children. Adequate short-term memory is necessary to keep all the terms of a mathematical problem in mind. For instance, the addition problem "How much is 3 + 2 + 1?" requires maintaining not only three numbers in short-term memory, but also the + signs and the cue "How much?" Romberg and Collins (1987) found that memory capacity directly increases with grade level; indeed, many kindergarteners and first-graders are unable to retain all the items of the foregoing problem. When additional steps and terms are present, older students also may exhibit a memory deficiency. Short-term memory failures may inhibit mathematical performance, requiring teachers to present terms at a slower pace and in a more concrete form, to make available time for algorithms to be activated.

When students can represent a math problem and identify the algorithm required for its solution, computation is relatively straightforward and success is highly probable. Difficulties arise when the problem is misrepresented, with the result that faulty algorithms are applied. A "faulty algorithm" is correct when applied to some problems, but not to others. Remember the description of misacquisitions or *bugs* in Chapter 3 (J. S. Brown and Burton, 1978)? Bugs in computation often are revealed when students consistently apply the same algorithm for them, failing to recognize that certain problems call for modification of the use of a given algorithm. Teachers need to be on the lookout for such consistent error patterns, which can reveal serious problems of representation, as opposed to tendencies to make careless errors.

Word Problems.   Achievement on math tests suffers most from poor student performance in solving word or story problems, those verbal applications of mathematical facts that have bedeviled students over the years. A student once said, "If there's a library in hell, all it has on its shelves are books filled with word problems." The difficulty here appears to lie not in students' command of math facts or in solution strategies but in the initial representation of problems. Somehow the translation of the sentences that make up a given problem are not adequately related to the mathematical algorithms needed for solution.

Several types of problem have been examined in the hope of identifying and remediating difficulties in student representation. One problem type that has received considerable research attention is the *relational* problem ("Joe runs 6 miles a week. He runs $\frac{1}{3}$ as many miles a week as Ken. How many miles does Ken run in 4 weeks?") Both elementary school and college students encounter difficulties with relational problems, primarily because they are unable to rephrase the questions in their own words. In the Ken and Joe problem, the students may be misled by the language: Since the problem says "$\frac{1}{3}$ as many," implying division, they mail fail to see that multiplication is in fact required. Lewis and Mayer (1987) demonstrated that students are more likely to miscomprehend such problems, which contain inconsistent language.

Students approach word problems possessing established sets of schemas, in which information is arranged in a preferred order. When a problem is presented in a form that conflicts with a student's preferred order, he or she mentally reorganizes the relational sentence, perhaps committing an error in the process. Other relational inconsistencies include using the relational term "less than" in a problem that requires the learner to add, using "more than" when subtraction is called for, and choosing the phrase "as many" for a problem that must be solved by division.

Other word problems types have been analyzed in terms of the errors in misrepresentation that frequently accompany them. For example, Judd and Bilski (1989) examined *change/join* problems ("Ginny had 9 pens. Barbara gave her 4 pens. How many does Ginny have?") and *change/separate* problems ("Travis had 16 pens. He gave 6 to May and 4 to Chris. How many pens does Travis now have?") Both mentally retarded ten-year-olds and non–mentally retarded (same-age) controls solved more of these kinds of problems when cues such as "altogether" (for addition problems) and "less than" (for subtraction problems) were provided as aids.

Multiplication of fractions problems ("It takes Bill $\frac{2}{3}$ of an hour to paint a car. If he painted 4 cars, how long did he work?") were presented to college students in a remedial mathematics class (Hardiman & Mestre, 1989). The difficulty inherent in these problems is recognizing that although multiplication consists of repeated addition, it is also the inverse of division. Remedial subjects did not recognize that a fractional equation with a division sign could be mathematically equivalent to one with a multiplication sign (e.g., the answer to the operation $\frac{2}{3} \times 4$ is spoken as "two and two-thirds"). The authors note that it is how fractions are used in problems that causes difficulty in representation, not the number of fractions in a given problem.

It appears that different problem types present unique difficulties for students in representation. Identifying the problem type by recognizing cue words or relating the problem to physical referents may be an important first step in solution. Appropriate algorithms, once identified, can be activated. We will consider some specific ways of enhancing students' ability to represent word problems in a later section.

Solution Phase of Mathematical Problems

Once problem statements have been accurately represented, it is necessary to pursue a solution plan. Research clearly indicates that if basic algorithms have become automatized, more attention is paid to the planning and testing of solutions, and problem-solving performance is improved. For example, research by Cooper and Sweller (1987) demonstrated that students who received an extended practice time on applying algebraic transformations in word problems (e.g., "A car travels at 30 kph for 2.5 hours. How far has it gone?") were better able to solve similar transfer problems. The authors argue that schema acquisition and rule automation are necessary for skilled problem solving. Practice must be guided by knowledgeable instructors who model the correct sequence of procedures, direct attention to critical features of particular problems, and work many examples to illustrate the difficult dimensions of particular problems. By having worked examples to refer to, students are able to reduce the cognitive overload that often occurs when novices observe the work of experts (Sweller, 1989). Slow, precise demonstration of exactly what the math instructor does in solving each step of the problem, followed by practice of each step on related problems, seems most effective.

A second factor that needs to be considered in relation to the solution phase is whether students can analyze the steps they take when solving a specific problem. Such reflection leads to a less hurried and more careful consideration of several solution strategies and a reduced tendency to jump at the first possibility that occurs to the individual. The "talking aloud" strategy, discussed earlier, aids students to reflect on their solution strategies and serves to slow down those who tend to answer carelessly and abruptly.

Analyze their own steps)

Another technique for demonstrating to students the value of analyzing the steps they take in solving problems is direct evaluation of the steps. As part of the following problem, children were asked to list two important conditions that should be kept in mind when solving it: "A sporting goods store has only three groups of iron-on digits to make numerals on shirts—numbers 4, 2, and 8. How many different two-digit numerals can they make if digits can be repeated?" Thus two conditions are (1) that there are only three digits to use and (2) that digits can be repeated. Learners who begin by reminding themselves that digits can be repeated should immediately include 44, 22, and 88 as possible combinations. Including test items that assess the planning and decisions made by students prior to solution attempts will serve to communicate to dubious students the importance of problem analysis.

keep in mind when solving W.P. → important facts given

Mathematics Instruction

If mathematical learning is a constructive process, then the role of the mathematics teacher is to help students build more complex structures, not to merely transmit information. This departure from the traditional role suggests that teachers must be aware of students' concepts about mathematics, their emerging beliefs and attitudes about the value of the subject, and their utilization of strategies, as well as the more conventional acquisition of algorithms and skills. Cobb and Merkel (1989) believe that teachers should be knowledgeable about the course of conceptual development in specific areas of mathematics, such as the evolution of stages in adding single digits. Moreover, teachers should continually look for indications that students might have constructed unanticipated, alternative meanings. Peterson, Carpenter, and Fennema (1989) found a positive correlation between what first-grade teachers knew about their students' concepts and the children's math achievement. Teachers who attended to their students' conceptual understanding asked more questions about problem-solving processes and spent more time listening to the responses.

Students need to explain their problem solving processes.

Not only is the knowledge teachers possess about their students important to mathematics instruction, but several instructional strategies show promise of contributing to improved student performance.

Teaching via Problem Solving.   Schroeder and Lester (1989) recommend problem solving as the basic format for instruction in mathematics, rather than teaching "about" problem solving. Teaching about problem solving implies direct instruction in typical problem-solving models or strategies. Students learn the steps involved in a particular model and are encouraged to become aware of their own progression through those steps when they are solving problems. Such techniques are occasionally effective, especially for students who do not spontaneously apply any type of problem-solving strategy. The danger of these approaches, as Schroeder and Lester point out, is that problem solving may become just another topic in the curriculum, likely to be taught in isolation from the rest of the content and relationships of mathematics.

Teaching via problem solving, on the other hand, encourages the learning of concepts and skills within the context of inquiry and experimentation. For example, a teacher gives each student a set of 24 one-inch-square tiles to be thought of as two dozen small tables. Students are asked to determine the number of small tables needed to make banquet tables of different sizes (area) and the number of people that could be seated at them (perimeter). The real-world situation serves as a context in which students explore area and perimeter and the relationships between them. At first no formulas are used; only after manipulation of the tiles and the development of relationships between new arrangements of squares are formulas introduced.

Another example was derived from the interest of a fourth-grade class in determining the foods that should be served in the school cafeteria. After listing a number of questions to be resolved, plans were made for finding the preferences of students who ate in the cafeteria. Students constructed a list of survey questions to be asked, chose a sample of lunchroom patrons, and agreed on procedures for asking them questions about their preferences. When the data had been collected, pairs of students worked together to organize the material and present it through a graphic display. Calculators were used to compute preferences for foods by grade, by gender, and by total school. Results of the survey were then discussed, with possible explanations and implications considered.

Based on the data and their analysis, the students were able to make a set of recommendations to the school dietitian, and changes were made in the lunchroom offerings. The results were displayed through graphs throughout the building. In this way, children were applying the techniques of statistics and experimentation to a real-world situation of importance to them. The value of employing mathematics to solve a problem that at first seemed nonmathematical became evident. By assuming the role of facilitator, rather than dispenser of information, the teacher created a climate for problem solving to occur with mathematics as the vehicle (Claus, 1989).

Student Invention of Strategies.   Studies have shown that when given the opportunity to develop their own strategies to solve problems, students can be extremely inventive. Cobb and Merkel (1989) have used a number of activities to help second-graders generate strategies to solve addition problems. In one case, students were asked to find numbers that balanced a scale as follows:

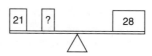

Margin notes:

Teaching via problem solving is best

when direct taught

I agree!

area + perimeter combined

Student strategies enhance learning

The activity provided an applied situation that led to a discussion of arithmetic equality. Development of individual strategies for representing the givens of simple computational problems results in increased understanding of the structure of number relationships.

Cooperative Groups. The instructional approach known as *cooperative learning* has been linked to several improvements in affective and cognitive behavior, including performance in mathematics (Sherman & Thomas, 1986; Slavin & Karweit, 1984). Cooperative learning is discussed more fully in Chapter 9 when we consider affective learning. Students working with peers in cooperative ways on math assignments have been found to achieve at higher levels on standardized math achievement tests, use better reasoning strategies, generate new ideas and solutions, and successfully transfer mathematical strategies and facts to subsequent problems (Johnson, Murayama, Johnson, Nelson, & Skor, 1981). These differences are observed only when certain key conditions are present, however.

1. Teachers clearly promote positive interdependence (the perception that one is linked with others so that one cannot succeed unless others do, and vice versa) in each learning group.
2. Students engage in face-to-face interaction while completing mathematics assignments.
3. Teachers ensure that each student is individually accountable to complete math assignments and students can promote the learning of other group members.
4. Students must learn and frequently use interpersonal and small-group skills. Such skills include leadership, decision making, trust building, and communication.
5. Teachers ensure that the learning groups engage in periodic group processing. Group processing in this sense refers to thought about the functioning of the group (Johnson & Johnson, 1989).

Cooperative learning is effective if all students are accountable

Schematic Drawings. A recently developed approach to aiding students' representation of word problems involves the use of schematic drawings, serving as conceptual models of the problem structure. Fuson and Willis (1989) used schematic drawings for "put together," "change," and "compare" word problems in teaching addition and subtraction to second-graders. A "put together" problem, like "Jan and Bill have 814 toys altogether. Jan has 342 toys. How many toys does Bill have?" would be represented schematically as follows:

Schematic drawings aid which phase of mathematical problem solving?

The drawing illustrates the relationships implied by the problem. Fuson and Willis found that second-graders could use the drawings to conceptualize the problem and

improve their performance, although a few employed the technique to indicate the solution procedure. It was believed that the drawings gave students and teacher a common vocabulary with which to discuss problems of this type, and it was the discussion rather than the diagram itself that was most helpful.

Lewis (1989) used a similar diagrammatic approach to improve college students' representation skills for "compare" problems. Here are a sample problem and the related diagram:

"Megan has saved $420 for vacation. She has saved one-fifth as much as James, who has been putting away the same amount of money every month for six months. How much has he saved each month?"

$$\text{\$420} \longrightarrow \text{Increase}$$
$$\underset{\text{Megan}}{\rule{0pt}{0pt}} \qquad \underset{\text{James}}{\rule{0pt}{0pt}}$$

The student places the known variable and its value in the center of a line. Next the unknown variable is inserted according to whether the correct operation is an increase (addition, multiplication) or a decrease (subtraction, division)—to the right if an increase, to the left if a decrease. The student must compare information in the problem statement with the diagram. In this way, students form an image of the problem's quantities and can check this representation with the text. With this approach, students are likely to avoid errors due to confusion about the direction of arithmetic change. Lewis found that training in diagramming produced greater gains on both similar and transfer problems than were found in controls. These studies indicate the potential value of utilizing schematics as aids to problem representation, which appears to transfer to improved solutions.

Cue Words. Judd and Bilski (1989) found that instructor emphasis on cue words such as "altogether" and "left" facilitated the addition and subtraction skills of both mentally retarded and non–mentally retarded learners. Apparently, problem statements are easier to represent if cue words are available. A potential danger associated with the use of this strategy is overreliance on the meaning of the cue word. Some learners assume that the presence of the cue word indicates that only one operation is possible (Schoenfeld, 1988). In pointing out cue words, teachers should always stress that the learner should verify how the word is used in a particular problem. For instance, both subtraction and addition are necessary in the problem "Lisa had $6.20 but gave $2.00 to Carrie and received $2.25 from Ruth. How much did Lisa have altogether?" Associating the cue word "altogether" with only one operation would lead to an error in this case. The focus of any strategic approach is to seek understanding, rather than to encourage students to plug values into an algorithm by rote. Teachers must communicate this warning. The example also points out how difficulties in reading comprehension influence mathematical representation.

Danger of rote learning of cue words

Appropriate Evaluation Techniques. Evaluation and feedback to students must focus on evidence concerning their representations and solution plans as well as the final answers. In assessing students' math competence, teachers should use both problems that directly test knowledge of the concept or operation involved and transfer problems, which determine whether the content can be applied to external situations. Schoenfeld (1988) observed that learners saw no relationship between prior knowledge of a geometry proof about tangents to a circle and the actual construction of that circle using a compass and straightedge. The two situations were viewed as entirely separate activities. Test items that require the student to move directly from one to the other in their thinking will reveal whether transfer has occurred.

Such items will serve an educational purpose for students responding to them, as well as an evaluative purpose. To that end, mathematics educators are experimenting with *superitems.* These items can be used on achievement and placement tests to reveal the hierarchies represented in a student's understanding of a mathematical concept. Items might initially assess awareness of an algorithm, then require recognition of conditions under which the algorithm would not apply, and then assess more abstract and peripheral applications of it. A superitem developed by Collins, Romberg, and Jurdak (1986) asks the student to imagine a machine that changes numbers. It adds the number you put in three times and then adds 2: If you put in 4, the machine puts out 14. The item then requires the student to answer three questions:

Superitems test deeper understanding

good technique to test understanding of concept.

1. If 14 is put out, what number was put in? (a check for understanding)
2. If we put in a 5, what number will be put out? (practice)
3. If x is the number that comes out when the number y is put in, write a formula that will give the value of y for any value of x. (development of an abstraction)

Items like this provide much more information about the representational and solution processes of learners than can be obtained from standard test items.

LEARNING SCIENCE

Ask yourself which of these statements is true.

Sugar ceases to exist when put into water.
Styrofoam is weightless.
Light from a candle goes farther at night than in the day.
Heavier objects fall faster than lighter ones.
Electric current is used up in a light bulb.
Gravity requires the presence of air.

Obviously none of these statements is true. They reflect, however, some of the *naive conceptions* that children entertain with respect to scientific phenomena (Driver, Guesne, & Tibarghien, 1985).

Children enter school with a number of well-established ideas about their environment, acquired through their random and uncontrolled experience of objects and events. These beliefs provide the basis for their understanding of how the world operates. In many cases, these naive conceptions seem logical to the learner and are resistant to change (McCloskey, 1983). Yet surprisingly, many of us continue to maintain naive conceptions of science based on our intuition, not on a consideration of the science we have formally been taught. McCloskey (1983), for example, found that one-third of high school physics students who had been taught Newton's law of inertia nevertheless believed that a ball traveling through a circular, coiled tube would continue to go around its outer edges after the tube ended. Newton's law states that an object will continue in a straight line motion when not being acted upon by another force. Teachers, too, possess naive beliefs about science. In a survey of elementary teachers' knowledge about physical science concepts, Lawrenz (1986) asked the following question: "What would be the final weight of a mixture of 20 pounds of water and one pound of salt?" Only 54 percent answered correctly! Twenty-eight percent did not think that adding the salt would change the weight, 15 percent thought the final weight was unpredictable and 3 percent didn't answer. Perhaps the teachers knew that since adding the salt would not change the volume (because the salt would dissolve and disappear), the mass would not change. Nevertheless, a widespread misconception about the nature of substances is obvious. The existence of naive intuitive conceptions about science, despite educational efforts, is one of the factors that have

led to suggested reforms in science education in recent years.

Linn (1986) has identified other cognitive factors that seem to determine how students learn science. Success in mastering scientific concepts depends on the learners' *processing capacity,* their use of *metacognitive strategies,* and their *depth of subject matter knowledge.* Processing capacity refers to limits on how much information can be processed simultaneously, as defined by working memory capacity. Increasing the number of variables in an experiment increases the processing-capacity demands of a task and results in age-related changes in ability to solve problems. Younger children are less capable of solving scientific tasks that require manipulation of more than two variables, for example (Scardamalia, 1977). Metacognitive strategies include being able to revise one's understanding upon realizing that revision is required, as well as representational and problem-solving abilities. Strategies to enhance

reading comprehension of scientific material presented in texts are particularly important to science learning (Waller, 1987). Depth of subject matter knowledge is also critical, because the more one knows of a science domain, the easier it is to organize the material and the more likely it is that naive conceptions will be recognized. Given adequate subject matter knowledge, the learner is more likely to retrieve information that facilitates representing and solving scientific problems.

Other factors, such as the limited amount of time allocated for science instruction, the disjointed nature of what is taught, and the inadequate scientific background of many teachers of science, are problems as well (American Association for the Advancement of Science, 1989). Even frequent instruction by well-prepared teachers is likely to be inadequate, however, unless the following factors are considered: (1) what students already know of scientific content, (2) any limitations they may have in processing information, (3) the strategies they employ in reasoning about science, and (4) any naive conceptions they hold about scientific phenomena.

Instruction in Science

The four factors just enumerated are not likely to be addressed satisfactorily unless students are *actively engaged* in confronting scientific phenomena, problems, and questions. Teachers must help students to commit themselves to the cognitive struggle of thinking about scientific content. Creating such a commitment to change is made easier when the learning of science is presented as the intriguing, challenging, and important process that it is. A number of classroom activities, laboratory experiments, and discussion questions can be used to foster this active engagement at both the elementary and secondary levels. Table 7.3 describes activities that expose students' naive beliefs and foster scientific thinking.

Each of the activities described in Table 7.3 will generate discussion, reports that can be debated, and further questions about the experiences. In many cases, students will have to be debriefed to identify some of the finer points of what has been observed. The activities are designed, however, for student investigation, not teacher explanation, so debriefing should occur only after experimentation and attempts to make inferences have been exhausted (Hyde & Bizar, 1989).

Not only must students be actively engaged to learn science. but teachers must provide adequate guidance, support, and encouragement while work with scientific problems is proceeding. It is important that materials be presented in ways that will facilitate encoding and organization. The following *instructional strategies* are effective in providing the appropriate intervention.

Elaboration.   Teachers may elaborate on given information by extending it with conceptual or pictorial representations such as advance organizers or conceptual models. *Graphic aids* can help students comprehend technical material. Science texts use graphic aids frequently in presenting data. Singer and Donlan (1989) caution that many students pay little attention to diagrams, graphs, charts, and tables, which they think of merely as decoration rather than attempts to communicate complex concepts and relationships. If students are to benefit from the information provided in graphic material, teachers must call their attention to it and provide practice in interpreting its implications. Graphs or tables similar to the material to be found in science texts are useful for practice.

Graphic aids need teacher explanation

Analogies.   Analogies can simplify important concepts. Johsua and Dupin (1987) used the analogy of workers pushing a railroad train between two stations to illustrate how basic electrical circuits work. The cars of the train were compared to electrons, friction from the track was compared to electrical resistance, and the workers' effort was akin to the battery or power source. Both sixth- and eighth-graders were able to use the analogy to overcome intuitive misconceptions about electricity. The misconceptions included the erroneous notions that two currents (positive and negative) "clash" to form the circuit and that the current lighting a bulb leaves part of itself and is recharged by the battery. The analogy allowed students to consider another viewpoint—namely, that a current once activated remains in force as a constant flow of electrons through a wire. The authors suggest that well-chosen analogies, structurally similar to the phenomenon in question, should aid in countering the effects of intuitive misconceptions.

Direct Examples.   To provide clarity in explaining complex concepts, teachers can use direct examples that illustrate how a specific scientific phenomenon can be generalized to the broader environment. Chemistry students who can perform chemical reaction problems in which salts increase the activation of the rate of melting of

TABLE 7.3 Scientific classroom activities for elementary and secondary students

Elementary	Secondary
1. *Objects that roll*	**1. *Displaced liquid volume***
Goal: To understand factors that affect speed and rolling.	*Goal:* To determine factors that affect displacement of liquid volume.
Materials: Round objects that students bring from home. Teacher-supplied spheres (marbles), hoops (tape rolls), disks (solid wheels); stop watch, inclined slope; tomato soup and vegetable cans.	*Materials:* Beaker or bowl with ounce markers, water, steel cube, and aluminum cube.
Preparation: Students are asked to predict which objects will roll down an inclined plane the fastest.	*Preparation:* Students are asked to predict relative amounts of liquid displaced by each cube and to justify their prediction.
Procedure: Hold "races," recording which objects win and lose. Discuss objects that won. Can students infer the factors that influenced speed? Weight, density, smoothness, and center of gravity are relevant.	*Procedure:* Students dip cubes and measure actual displaced liquid. Are asked to explain.
2. *Egg drop*	**2. *Trunks and branches***
Goal: To determine what factors protect an egg when it is dropped.	*Goal:* To find the relation between the thickness of a branch and how many times the tree has branched from the ground.
Materials: Packages (for groups of students to use as containers); one egg per team.	*Materials:* Ruler, calipers.
Preparation: Student teams select materials to pack around egg to protect it (Jell-O, bread, popcorn, Styrofoam, puffed cereal, cotton have all been tried).	*Preparation:* Students are asked to measure thickness of branches and the number of branch joints on one or several trees.
Procedure: After teams have wrapped the eggs, each package is dropped off the school roof (or from higher point if available—any parents have an airplane?). Discussion of results.	*Procedure:* Students compute thicknesses and number of joints, record observations, and form ratios. Test ratios with different trees, shrubs, etc.
3. *Blindfolded manipulation*	**3. *Changing an arrow's direction***
Goal: To rely on feel and manipulation of objects to gather information about them.	*Goal:* To understand the refraction of light.
Materials: Blindfold, mud, fine sand, Silly Putty, glue, baking soda, sugar (any similar, light materials).	*Materials:* Clear plastic cup, water, drawing of arrow on a 3 × 5 card.
Preparation: Arrange quantities of materials where they can be handled with a minimum of mess.	*Preparation:* Place card under cup that is three-quarters full of water.
Procedure: Students feel material while blindfolded, describing each one in terms of sensations.	*Procedure:* Students look through water in cup at arrow, then slowly move arrow away. Card will look disconnected and will appear to get smaller. Student is to explain and experiment with different locations of the card.

Why does a tomato soup can roll faster than a tape roll?

TABLE 7.3 (Continued)

Elementary	Secondary
4. *Releasing carbon dioxide*	4. *Evidence of "truisms"*
Goal: To study chemical reactions.	*Goal:* To verify the scientific validity of various truisms.
Materials: Clear cup $\frac{2}{3}$ filled with water, cup filled $\frac{1}{3}$ with vinegar, teaspoon of baking soda, five or six raisins.	*Materials:* None.
Preparation: Add the baking soda to the water and stir. Drop in the raisins and observe. Then pour in the vinegar.	*Preparation:* Students think of popular truisms that can be scientifically verified (e.g., "The early bird catches the worm," "Don't read in bad light, you'll ruin your eyes," "Red sky at night, sailors' delight.").
Procedure: Raisins will bounce (rise to the top, go down again, etc.). Students observe and record this activity. Other amounts of the three compounds could be used and observations recorded.	*Procedure:* Divide students into teams to determine validity of the statements. They might interview experts (biologists, optometrists, sailors, meteorologists) in addition to consulting reference texts.

ice will not necessarily be able to give an example of how this process occurs in the world outside the chemistry lab. In this case, the instructor can illustrate the applicability of chemistry to other phenomena by pointing out that icy roads become less slippery when salted. Specific examples of how science concepts relate to events outside the classroom will form a link between school learning and its application that is not directly apparent to many students.

Considering Alternatives. Considering more than one explanation for an event aids understanding and transfer. The alternatives may conflict, thus encouraging students to consider their choices more carefully. In the displacement of liquid volume problem, Bubules and Linn (1988) encouraged middle school students to generate alternative explanations and other possible variables that might account for displacement. The investigators found that the opportunity to reflect on what happens in displacement led to more rapid transfer to the displacement of other objects.

Aiding Reading. Aiding students to read science texts and documents for meaning serves to dispel the notion that science is a "foreign language" that few can understand. The learning of technical material from text does require a particular style of reading that may need to be taught directly to students, however. One skill in reading technical text is to identify the author's underlying structure as an aid in deriving meaning. In reading science texts, for example, readers have more difficulty in comprehension when they fail to recognize a pattern to the author's presentation. For physics texts, the "principle-first" pattern (in which the main theme of a lesson is stated up front) aids comprehension more than "proof-first" organization (in which the principle is not stated until the proof has been demonstrated) (Dee-Lucas & Larkin, 1990).

Cook and Mayer (1988), who identified five types of structure characteristic of scientific texts, also found that many learners were unaware of the existence of such differences. The five types are *generalization,* or the extension of main ideas through explanations or examples, *enumeration,* or the listing of facts one after another, *sequence,* or the connecting of series of events or steps, *classification,* or the grouping of materials into classes or categories, and *comparison/contrast,* or examining the relationships between two or more things.

Cook and Mayer trained students to recognize and interpret three of the structures in a chemistry text—generalization, enumeration, and sequence. In training for generalization of the main idea, students were taught to list and define key words, restate the generalization in their own words, and look for evidence to support the generalization. In training for enumeration, they were to name the topic, identify the subtopics, and list the details within each subtopic. For sequences, learners were asked to identify the topic, name each step, outline the details in each, and discuss what was different from one step to another. Trained students not only showed a pretest-to-posttest gain in chemistry knowledge but were able to apply their new skill to biology content as well. This research suggests that calling attention to text structure and training students to utilize it in reading scientific material may aid student understanding.

Another approach to helping students to comprehend scientific text is to provide *text annotations* or *glosses.* Glosses are marginal notes that explain technical terms, rephrase a passage that may be difficult for students to comprehend, provide background information, demonstrate solutions to sample problems, ask questions that will direct reader attention, or emphasize a point. The notations in the margins of this text serve as simple examples. Glosses can also be developed by the teacher, indicating the page and line numbers associated with each item. This material can be duplicated and provided to students for reference when they read the text on their own.

Establishing a "Learning Community."   C. W. Anderson and E. Smith (1987) described a learning community in which students engage in the four activities of a scientist—description, prediction, explanation, and control. In this approach to enhancing comprehension of scientific principles and processes, subgroups of students worked on similar problems, obtaining their results independently and explaining them in their own way. As a result, different conclusions were reached and debated, leading to open discussions and the opportunity to examine misconceptions in a supportive environment. Under such a model, not only are intuitive conceptions challenged and examined, but alternative strategies and procedures to solve scientific problems are compared.

Enhancing Perceptions.   Helping students to form enhanced perceptions of their efficacy in learning science leads to better performance. Many students feel that they are not capable of mastering science and social studies, which are regarded as too difficult or too abstract. As discussed in Chapter 3, females and some minority students often receive subtle messages that they are not expected to learn science, which in turn affects achievement (Linn & Peterson, 1986). To counter such views, teachers should practice the procedures designed to facilitate perceptions of self-efficacy, as described in Chapter 5. Introducing students to self-regulated learning strategies (Zimmerman, 1989) may provide the kind of aid students need to gain con-

Text structure reveals organization of content

Learning community groups generate discussion

fidence in learning scientific material. Encouragement to verbalize important steps in solving science problems also seems to be necessary. For example, students can reduce their expectations of failure by saying to themselves, "I always want to state my hypothesis" or "I begin by defining the actual goal," or otherwise reminding themselves that they have a plan of action to follow. Exposing students to successful models, both peer and symbolic, is another way of helping to establish a more positive sense of self-efficacy in mastering science content.

LEARNING SOCIAL STUDIES CONTENT

Student learning of social studies has been criticized frequently in recent years. American students have performed poorly in formal assessments of their learning. For instance, J. R. Anderson (1990) reports that only 6 percent of American twelfth-graders display broad knowledge of the various institutions of government or political processes, such as how Congress can override a veto or why primary elections are necessary. A similar lack of knowledge is revealed in less formal, anecdotal accounts, as in stories of students who believe that New Mexico is a foreign country or cannot pinpoint the century in which the Civil War occurred. These reports attract attention but, if valid, are frequently taken out of context. In a more positive evaluation of national assessments of educational achievement, Burke (1989) notes that approximately two-thirds of all American students know what educators who develop the tests want them to know, which he finds encouraging. He further points out that many items counted as missed were in fact not answered at all because tests are timed and some students fail to address all items within the time limit. For example, an item purporting to indicate how few countries American students could find on a map was number 60 of 80 similar questions, while the item was the sixth on the version of the test provided European students (Gallup Organization, 1988). Differences in performance may be attributable to the shorter time that remained for American students to concentrate on that particular question. While there may be reasonable explanations for some observed deficiencies, the fact remains that social studies achievement levels were disappointing.

Social studies achievement deficits?

Many of the learner variables found to affect performance in science learning appear to contribute to the learning of social studies as well. Voss, Tyler, and Yergo (1983) utilized the think-aloud procedure to analyze the performance of students pretending to assume the roles of different high-level governmental policy makers. Students differed in the quality of the policies they proposed based on (1) the amount of domain-specific knowledge they possessed about the topic (e.g., information about a country's economic condition), (2) the general problem-solving strategies used (e.g., representing the problem as a series of subgoals), and (3) knowledge of more specific social studies procedures (e.g., classifying economic goods and services or analyzing a country's form of government). The ability to combine relevant specific knowledge with general and specific problem-solving strategies appeared to be the key to successful performance.

Additional blame for poor levels of student achievement is laid on the nature and quality of instruction students receive in school. At least three deficiencies have been identified. First, the subject matter content that is lumped into the social studies area is so diverse and often so unrelated that there is substantial disagreement regarding what the field should and should not include. All the following courses may be found in a typical high school social studies curriculum: world history, American history, geography, government, political science, economics, environmental ecology, psychology, sociology, anthropology, law, minority studies, and women's studies. With such a wide variety of courses offered, it is no wonder that there is no common set of courses comprising a specific social studies curriculum. The most common element in American secondary education, a class in American history, is required in approximately one-third of U.S. schools (Voss, 1986). Thus it is not surprising that students do not possess in common a large store of domain-specific knowledge to aid in memory tasks or in solving problems.

Multiple goals complicate the social studies curriculum

A related problem for the social studies area is the absence of consensus on the goals toward which learning and instruction are to be directed. Course diversity hinders any attempt at building a learning hierarchy of skills or content. Early courses or units are rarely designed to contribute to the mastery of more complex skills in later courses, nor are later units or courses in social studies necessarily dependent on previous learning. Information-processing analyses of the learning of social studies objectives are fruitless when there is no clear goal or common content base from which learners may draw. The situation is partially due to traditional disagreements among educators over the guiding purpose of social studies in our educational system. Barr, Barth, and Shermis (1977) identified three competing purposes: (1) to transmit to students the appropriate values and beliefs of good citizens, (2) to convey the knowledge and principles of the social sciences, and (3) to aid students to be good decision makers, employing the techniques of reflection and inquiry. In other words, should social studies be designed to provide citizenship skills such as communication, participation, and critical analysis? Should content be taught so that mastery of the concepts, rules, and procedures underlying each of the social studies areas results? Or should the focus be on the inquiry process, in which the techniques of experimentation and decision making are paramount? Can any one purpose be achieved without the others? Without answers to such questions, more fundamental analyses of content and learning sequences cannot be resolved. Issues created by the infusion of new material cannot be addressed if there is no guiding curricular plan.

Teacher preparation is a third factor that can result in poor student achievement. Many who teach social studies have either received a smattering of training in several of the subdisciplines that compose social studies, with little depth in any, or have acquired depth in one or two but are quite unfamiliar with others. For example, a survey of teacher preparation revealed that 46 percent of the teachers of world history in one state had majored in fields other than history (Wiley, 1977). States have recently moved to remedy this situation, however. Perhaps as teacher preparation becomes more standardized, impetus toward standardization of curricular goals and content will also emerge.

Instruction in the Social Sciences

Most social studies experts and professional groups advocate a problem-solving orientation to instruction in which students acquire not only content knowledge, but skills in inquiry and critical thinking (Hyde & Bizar, 1989; Singleton, 1986). Unfortunately, problems are not easily utilized in the social studies area. Voss, Wolfe, Lawrence, and Engle (1991) distinguish between *well-structured* or single-solution problems, such as those readily encountered in science, and *ill-structured* problems that can be represented in many ways and consequently have many possible solutions. Social studies problems fall into the second category. Asking students to isolate the chemicals that produce a particular sulfate is one thing; requiring them to generate policies that might reduce poverty is another. In the chemistry example, only one set of chemicals will produce the desired reaction. In attempting to identify actions that might end poverty, a number of variables must be simultaneously considered, and responses must be evaluated on the basis of different criteria.

Ill-structured vs. well-structured problems

Experts will disagree about what a "good" solution might be or even how a problem might be represented (Voss, Greene, Post, & Penner, 1983). When considering how to reduce pollution, for example, side effects must also be considered. What economic effects would result from banning industrial air pollutants? What might happen if nuclear power is banned? If it isn't? It would appear that the solutions to such problems should be provided as alternatives, with possible advantages and disadvantages identified. One middle school class decided that the way to end poverty was to simply give everyone more money, without considering some rather severe obstacles to the implementation of their proposal. A better approach might have been to ask individuals or groups to identify the information required and used in representing the problem and to explain how the relevant variables were defined and evaluated. Then alternative problem solutions could be weighed and assessed.

Social studies activities therefore should begin with problem situations, but students should be required to engage in critical thinking and analysis of information utilized in reaching their tentative solutions. In that way, the challenges facing a social scientist will become more evident and a better appreciation for the field will emerge. Table 7.4 presents examples of activities that require such analysis.

Problem solutions should be evaluated

Another promising instructional approach is to require social studies students to participate in roles that relate to social institutions. Activities such as becoming interns in governmental agencies, helping in election campaigns, doing volunteer work for social groups, joining and participating in environmental clean-up programs, and organizing a special interest group foster student examination of social policies and practices. Of course, such an approach assumes that the role of social studies is to promote good citizenship. Teachers with additional goals in mind might supplement the activities with supportive classroom and text assignments.

Experience with social institutions also helpful

Facilitation of student reading of social science content also appears to be necessary to good instruction, since many of the best materials available may be written at levels of difficulty higher than most of the students have attained. Singer and Donlan (1989) suggest the use of *directed reading activities* prior to students' actual reading of assigned material. For instance, before reading a selection on "Explorers of the Western Hemisphere," a teacher might show pictures of exotic lands and ask "What do the pictures have in common?" or "How would you feel if you suddenly found yourself in the middle of this area? What would you do?" Student responses and the resulting discussion might serve to enhance comprehension by activating appropriate schemas for the assigned passage.

When wide differences in reading ability exist, as is often the case in high school classes, *multiple texts* can be followed. One teacher makes available to her history

TABLE 7.4   Social science problem areas and classroom activities promoting analysis and critical thinking

Problem	Activity
To identify political bias. How is political bias expressed?	Students read selected editorials, marking them with colored pens; one color indicates value judgments, the other factual statements. Discussion of each student's basis for judgment follows.
To analyze social science concepts such as "culture." What factors constitute a culture?	Students read about three cultures (e.g., French, Japanese, American). Critical features are identified and recorded on a large sheet. Commonalities and differences are noted.
To compare historical periods. In what ways do historical periods reflect change?	Students select newspaper articles, advertisements, want ads, "lonely hearts" columns, and other materials from current periodicals. They then examine available periodicals for past decades (1920s, 1940s, etc.), searching for the same types of material. Similarities and differences are noted.
To analyze patterns of immigration to and settlement in the United States. Where do people immigrate and why?	Students select an ethnic group. From U.S. census data, population atlases, and other sources, they describe the country of origin and determine where the largest new U.S. settlements occurred. Similarities and differences between the regions of origin and of settlement are discussed.

Promote analysis through classroom activities

class multiple copies of the following texts relating to World War II: Ernie Pyle's *Brave Men*, Bill Mauldin's *Up Front*, E. Schnabel's *Anne Frank: A Portrait in Courage*, and John Hersey's *Hiroshima*. The texts differ in reading difficulty. Students are free to examine all four books and select any one. All those reading the same book meet to discuss it and serve as a resource to those who did not choose it. In this way students who are at a disadvantage in reading can select texts they feel comfortable with, participate as equals with other students who read the same book, and assume an important role in class discussion.

SUMMARY

This chapter examined the learning of specific academic material and skills as well as the instructional techniques that have been found to aid their acquisition. Learning to read and write and achieve in mathematics, science, and social studies was stressed.

Gagné's instructional system was presented as a model for the identification and organization of content. As a guide to learning at the course level, the teacher should develop instructional objectives based on a learning task analysis of prerequisite content, determination of the variety of learning expected, and an information-processing analysis of the kinds of decision and action the learner performs in reaching the terminal objective. When analysis of instructional content is complete, teachers can design instructional events that consider both content and learning processes, such as gaining attention or facilitating encoding and organization.

Our discussion of early reading acquisition compared the whole-language or meaning approach to instruction to the decoding approach. Whole-language advocates view reading as a search for meaning in which the entire linguistic context is used to comprehend text. Instruction thus incorporates reading into other language activities such as writing, listening, and storytelling. Decoding methods, on the other hand, emphasize breaking the code, which allows graphemes to be converted to phonemes and the acquisition of automatic recognition of larger and larger phonemic and morphemic combinations. Research supports the importance of teaching decoding skills in the early grades, with context-based activities serving as additional aids to the development of comprehension and interest in the reading process. The approach that is more effective depends on the individual student.

Learning from reading requires students to assimilate text information into cognitive structures and to construct revised schemas that extend beyond the knowledge provided. Teachers can enhance learning from text by encouraging the recall of relevant prior knowledge, drawing attention to text signals, and utilizing instructional objectives to direct reading effort. In addition, learners need to develop efficient reading strategies, such as finding the main idea, summarizing, drawing inferences, generating questions, and monitoring personal comprehension.

The Flower and Hayes writing model was used to illustrate the components of mature writing, which is a planned, goal-directed attempt to convey meaning in an organized manner. The model includes analysis of the writing problem (in which relevant schemas are activated), a planning stage (in which knowledge of the topic and writing strategies are identified), a sentence generation phase, and a revision stage. The teaching of writing skills includes (1) direct instruction in writing strategies, such as goal setting and idea generation, (2) the suggestion of appropriate procedures through conferences, computer feedback, and peer editing, (3) assistance to students in focusing on their written products through activities such as word choice, and (4) use of inquiry activities that stimulate writing of journals and logs. Evaluation of writing should include both product and process-oriented assessment, as in the six-trait model.

Mathematics learning requires both accurate representation of mathematical information and utilization of appropriate solution strategies. Instruction in mathematics should be concerned with student acquisition of appropriate algorithms, teacher identification and remediation of "bugs" in student understanding, employment of linguistic cues and schematic drawings to aid in representation, and the introduction of math concepts by means of a problem-solving orientation. Evaluation of math performance should emphasize equally how mathematical concepts are represented by the learner and whether correct solutions are obtained.

Science learning is difficult because of naive, intuitive conceptions students often have acquired about the content. Amount of subject matter knowledge, processing capacity, and availability of cognitive strategies also influence learning, as well as such instructional variables as the amount of time devoted to the topic. Teachers can improve instruction by (1) challenging students' intuitive conceptions as part of a lesson, (2) utilizing a problem-solving orientation, (3) employing grouping procedures such as the learning community, (4) including instructional strategies such as elaboration, cuing, and providing examples and analogies, and (5) enhancing students' efficacy attribution. A particularly important part of instruction in the social sciences is the development of critical thinking and the ability to justify one's solutions to ill-structured problems. Recognition of text structures and utilization of alternative reading materials can help teachers to provide assistance in reading both science and social science material.

A concept map for this chapter appears on page 271.

EXERCISES

1. Design a plan for a lesson in a topic of interest to you, including a list of instructional objectives, an outline of the content you would cover, a description of key learner characteristics, beliefs, or skills you would take into account in your conduct of the lesson, a discussion of the specific strategies and materials you would use to ensure learning, and a description of how student learning would be assessed. If a small number of prospective students who are appropriate for the lesson's objectives are available, you might conduct it and evaluate student learning and your instruction.

2. Much of this chapter described instructional strategies, policies, or materials teachers might use to aid learning of specific course content. Try your hand at developing *three* such strategies, policies, or materials for a content area of your choice. Start with a careful description of the instructional objective or goal you would like students to attain, and consider the information-processing steps necessary for students to reach it. What cues, directions, areas of special practice, or examples would you employ to aid students in acquiring the desired behavior?

SUGGESTED READINGS

Dole, J. A., Duffy, G. G., Roehler, L. R., & Pearson, P. D. (1991). Moving from the old to the new: Research on reading comprehension instruction. *Review of Educational Research, 61*(2), 239–264.

Gagné, R. M., & Briggs, L. J. (1979). *Principles of instructional design* (2nd ed.). New York: Holt, Rinehart & Winston.

Goodman, K. S. (1986). *What's whole in whole language: A parent–teacher guide.* Portsmouth, NH: Heinemann.

Hayes, J. R., & Flower, L. S. (1986). Writing research and the writer. *American Psychologist, 41*(10), 1106–1113.

Hyde, A. A., & Bizar, M. (1989). *Thinking in context: Teaching cognitive processes across the elementary school curriculum.* White Plains, NY: Longman.

Singleton, L. R. (1986). *Tips for social studies teachers.* Boulder, CO: Social Studies Education Consortium.

Trafton, T. R., & Shulte, A. P. (Eds.). *New directions for elementary school mathematics. 1989 yearbook.* Reston, VA: National Council of Teachers of Mathematics.

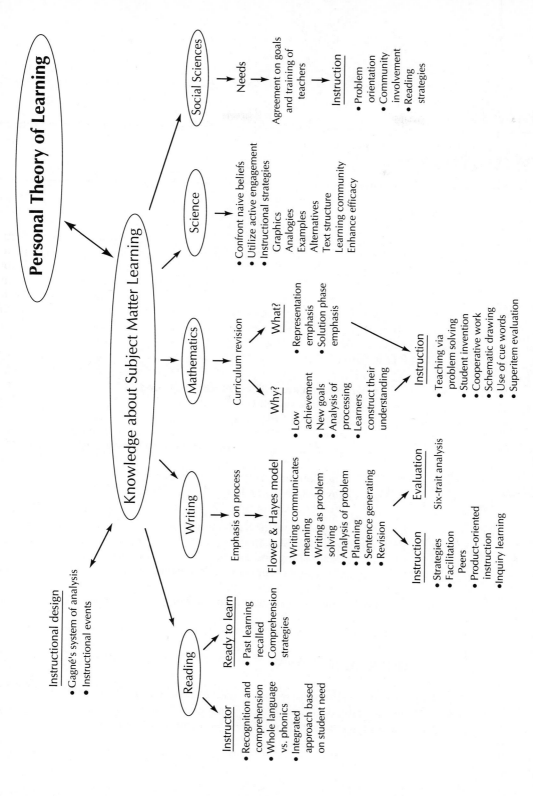

Personal Theory of Learning

Knowledge about Subject Matter Learning

Instructional design
• Gagné's system of analysis
• Instructional events

Reading

Instructor
• Recognition and comprehension
• Whole language vs. phonics
• Integrated approach based on student need

Ready to learn
• Past learning recalled
• Comprehension strategies

Writing

Emphasis on process

Flower & Hayes model
• Writing communicates meaning
• Writing as problem solving
• Analysis of problem
• Planning
• Sentence generating
• Revision

Instruction
• Strategies
• Facilitation
  Peers
• Product-oriented instruction
• Inquiry learning

Evaluation   Six-trait analysis

Mathematics

Curriculum revision

Why?
• Low achievement
• New goals
• Analysis of processing
• Learners construct their understanding

What?
• Representation emphasis
• Solution phase emphasis

Instruction
• Teaching via problem solving
• Student invention
• Cooperative work
• Schematic drawing
• Use of cue words
• Superitem evaluation

Science

• Confront naive beliefs
• Utilize active engagement
• Instructional strategies
  Graphics
  Analogies
  Examples
  Alternatives
  Text structure
  Learning community
  Enhance efficacy

Social Sciences

Needs

Agreement on goals and training of teachers

Instruction
• Problem orientation
• Community involvement
• Reading strategies

Concept Map for Chapter 7

chapter 8

Motivation

CHAPTER OUTLINE

CHAPTER OBJECTIVES

1. Discuss instinct, homeostatic, and need interpretations of motivation.
2. Explain the value of utilizing Maslow's hierarchy of needs.
3. Distinguish between extrinsic and self-determined reinforcers.

4. Describe Atkinson's expectancy × value position and distinguish between those who approach a goal and those who avoid failure.
5. Describe how the classroom can be structured to enhance expectancy of attainment of learning goals.
6. Identify the factors that enhance efficacy for classroom achievement.
7. Explain the success and failure attributions of Weiner's model, including discussion of the dimensions of internality, stability, and controllability.
8. Clarify the relationship of the four components of the ARCS model to the enhancement of motivation.
9. Provide examples of how teachers can facilitate each of the four components of the ARCS model.

Candace had been taking piano lessons for about a year. Now she was to play Beethoven's Minuet in G for her parents and friends at the school recital. As she began to play to the hushed audience, Candace's fingers suddenly seemed to go numb. She couldn't feel the keys. In addition, she couldn't see the notes in her head, as she did in practice. Forced to stop, Candace rose, bowed to the murmuring audience, and somehow managed to exit the stage.

The next afternoon, Mrs. Lippert, the music teacher, was surprised to see Candace, ready for her practice session to begin. "Why, Candace, how nice to see you here so early," she said.

"Hi, Mrs. Lippert. I just couldn't wait to come to rehearsal. I did so rotten last night that I knew I had to practice some more. I want to play the Minuet in G again."

Alex hung his head. The graded booklets for the sample state exam in U.S. history had just been passed back; the last practice exam session before Saturday's "make or break" state test was over. Students had to pass the exam with a score of 65 or better to receive state certification, and also to pass the high school class. Alex needed to pass this course to get his high school diploma the following week.

"Forty-six!" he moaned. "How could I do so rotten? I really studied this stuff, and this is what I get. Dang it!"

Alex got up and left the room, despite the surprised looks of the teacher and his classmates. When Saturday rolled around, Alex was not to be found at the testing center.

Mindy listlessly picked up her literature book. With a heavy sigh, she turned to the short story assigned for that day. "Is this boring or what?" she said. "Who wants to do this junk, anyway?" Frowning in disgust, she replaced the book in her desk and surreptitiously began reading the text for her next hour's social studies class.

Observing her from the front of the room, Mr. Corliss looked away puzzled. "Mindy's not doing her assignment, either. What's wrong with these kids? I give them class time to start on their homework assignment and they do something else. She's even reading an economics text, for Pete's sake! Why don't my students want to read good literature?"

These vignettes reveal how difficult it can be to explain why individuals behave as they do. Candace, Alex, and Mindy all act in ways that apparently seem reasonable to them, yet confound their teachers. Understanding why people behave in certain ways requires knowledge of the construct known as *motivation.* Teachers require knowledge of motivation to aid student learning because the motivational state of learners determines not only what is learned, but how much effort is likely to be expended in acquiring new learning. If teachers understand the motives that activate and direct student behavior, they will be in a better position to design and conduct instruction. This chapter examines the principles and theories that attempt to explain human motivation and explores how motivational states can be improved for successful classroom learning.

Motivation deals with why we do what we do

CHARACTERISTICS AND THEORIES OF MOTIVATION

Explanations of why individuals do what they do has been an integral part of psychology from its earliest days. Numerous hypotheses and theories designed to account for human motivation have been proposed, only to be rejected, or revised and subsequently incorporated into later positions. While one or two viewpoints have recently achieved relatively widespread acceptance, there is no one account of motivation that explains all relevant phenomena to the satisfaction of all interested parties.

Early psychological positions relied on biological reasons to account for motivated behavior. For example, William James (1890) attributed common human behaviors for which no learning was apparent to *instincts,* or innate biological predispositions. He believed that people had many such predispositions, which resulted in predetermined behavioral patterns. Examples included the "maternal instinct," the "herd instinct" (affiliating with others in groups), and "survival instincts" (e.g., eating, seeking protection, and engaging in sexual activity). The idea of the existence of genetic predispositions to act in a certain way may be defensible in some areas (see the discussion of language acquisition in Chapter 3), but many of the large number of "instincts" listed by James have since been found to depend significantly on learning. Maternal and affiliative behaviors for instance have been observed to be lacking in some individuals and are considered modifiable due to environmental factors.

Other "instincts"?

An influential biological theory of motivation in the early part of this century was that of homeostasis. States of biological deprivation are accompanied by persistent and unpleasant stimuli such as pain. This is the body's way of ensuring that its need to survive is observed and, if possible, satisfied. For example, the pain of hunger is relieved when food is ingested, and the body returns to a state of balance. The term *homeostasis* refers to this tendency of the body to strive for a constant state of equilibrium in its many physiological systems (Cannon, 1932). Homeostatic conditions are only temporary, however; because of the cyclical nature of biological needs, tensions arise again and behaviors must be reinitiated to reduce them. Biological imperatives leading to such actions became known as primary *drives,* because they were believed to drive or energize behavior designed to relieve them. According to homeostatic theory, primary drives initiate behavior that is directed toward the goal of reducing the drive; reducing the drive is satisfying, and behaviors that tend to produce satisfaction are repeated. For instance, a hungry child seeks out food. If food is located in the cookie jar, then seeking and finding the cookie jar are said to be instrumental in reducing drive tension and are expected to occur again when hunger is experienced. Learning thus accompanies drive reduction (Miller & Dollard, 1941).

What about motivation to perform behaviors other than those directly responsible for reducing biological tension? Remember our discussion of *functionally autonomous* behavior in connection with the role of operant conditioning in the classroom, back in Chapter 4? Allport (1937) argued that certain behaviors that originally were instrumental in gaining satisfaction for primary drives acquire autonomy and generalize to new situations as they are continually performed. They become independent of the original antecedent stimulus that led to their occurrence, but are maintained because some new form of satisfaction is obtained. The child looking for the cookie jar, for example, might find that walking around the house is enjoyable because new objects are encountered. Exploration thus becomes a new drive that may direct subsequent behavior. Drives acquired as a result of resolving primary ones became known as *secondary drives* and were exemplified by exploration, curiosity, gregariousness, and others (Tolman, 1932).

Secondary drives acquired while striving to satisfy primary ones

Later theories began to de-emphasize the role of homeostasis as a foundation for understanding human motivation. Striving to maintain biological balance may characterize the behavior of animals, but much human behavior falls outside the range of homeostatic explanations. In fact, people often purposely seek disequilibrium. A friend of the author's advocates the joys of skydiving; that is, he intentionally hurls himself out of a plane and delays pulling the rip cord of his parachute! Others climb mountains, ride roller-coasters, attend horror movies, and occasionally give up good jobs for new occupational challenges. Primary drives are routinely ignored in pursuit of other goals when we stay up all night to study for an exam or refrain from eating to protest a social issue or pursue spiritual goals.

For this reason, theories of motivation began to identify basic *needs* as the causes of human behavior, differentiating between needs required for survival and those that are acquired through learning. Abraham Maslow (1954, 1962) attempted to organize the various needs systematically. His *hierarchy of needs* is presented in Figure 8.1.

Maslow's hierarchy attempts to explain the relationships and priorities among the many needs psychologists have identified. *Deficiency needs,* at the bottom of the pyramid, are those that are critical to physiological and psychological well-being. The lower needs must be satisfied before higher ones are attended to. The physiological need of hunger, for example, must be resolved before it becomes critical to maintain self-esteem or gain love or recognition from others. Children who come to school hungry or from an abusive environment, for example, would not be expected to expend much energy on gaining a high grade in mathematics. Deficiency needs must be met for an individual to adapt successfully. When this is occurring on a regular basis, higher-level or *growth needs* can be pursued. The growth needs of knowledge and understanding, aesthetic beauty, and self-actualization can never be satisfied completely. They provide what Maslow believes to be the major challenges that make life worth living. *Self-actualization,* or the desire to fulfill one's potential, is at the top of the pyramid not only because it requires the satisfaction of more basic needs below it, but because it is achieved by only a very small percentage of the population (Maslow, 1968). Self-actualization requires an acceptance of one's abilities, an open-

Growth needs = challenges and life goals

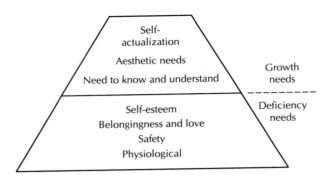

FIGURE 8.1 Maslow's hierarchy of needs

SOURCE: A. H. Maslow, *Motivation and personality* (New York: Harper & Brothers, 1954).

ness to change, creativity, and independence, and a respectful and supportive relationship with others. Those seeking self-actualization are never content with past accomplishments but strive to improve and grow, sometimes giving up what appears to be a highly satisfying life to achieve new goals.

Maslow's position suggests that no one is truly "unmotivated." All people possess goals, which they actively seek to accomplish. Some goals may not be directly related to the academic and social purposes of schools, and the routes students take to satisfy them may conflict. Resolving the tensions that result from such discrepancies should be viewed by educators as part of their instructional role. Perhaps the student who does not seem interested in academic work is affected by deficiency needs such as food, shelter, and safety. In that case, it may be necessary to collaborate with other professionals such as school social workers and counselors to ensure maintenance of physiological and safety needs. If a student seems preoccupied with gaining the attention of peers by clowning, it may be necessary to find ways to channel this behavior into academically acceptable activities such as participation in class skits or school-wide dramatics. Rather than address higher goals prematurely, teachers may have to provide security, aid students in forming positive social relationships with peers, and help them to gain self-esteem through experiencing success in basic academic tasks. Pursuit of growth needs requiring self-direction and autonomy may have to await satisfactory fulfillment of these more basic student concerns.

Can we identify students' deficits as well as growth needs?

Maslow's concept of growth motivation and the research of other theorists led to a reexamination of the assumptions underlying earlier motivational theories. One assumption was that individuals strive to gain pleasure and avoid pain—the so-called *hedonistic principle.* Drive reduction theories in which a return to homeostasis is presumed to produce pleasure are predicated on this quite obvious assumption. What constitutes pleasure or pain for many individuals is not so easily determined, however, as my skydiving friend will attest. Moreover, in some cases a pleasurable event may not act as a positive reinforcer, nor does pain or failure necessarily serve as a punishment. For example, failure to achieve a goal (which ordinarily would be perceived as punishing) has been observed to lead to increased efforts to attain the goal by high-ability students (Atkinson, 1964).

The Role of Self-Determination

In considering other factors that might explain motivation, it is important to remember the distinction between *extrinsic* and *intrinsic* incentives, introduced in Chapter 4. Extrinsic incentives involve rewards that are external to the learner: positive reinforcers such as social approval and recognition, or tangible objects such as food or money. Intrinsic incentive refers to satisfaction derived from merely engaging in a particular activity, or doing something because one wants to, rather than because one must (Stipek, 1993). Candace, in the opening anecdote, demonstrates intrinsic interest in music and is willing to exert effort to succeed at it, despite her recent failure. Unfortunately, offering extrinsic rewards under certain circumstances may undermine intrinsic motivation. Research by Lepper, Greene, and Nisbett (1973), for example, demonstrated that providing rewards such as recognition for activities children already enjoy doing (e.g., playing with Magic Markers) actually decreased participation in the same activity later, when the reward was removed. It is as if children came to *discount* the enjoyment derived from the activity when an external reward became salient (Stipek, 1993).

Analysis of the difference between intrinsic and extrinsic incentives reveals a critical variable in their composition, however. This is the degree of *self-determination* or *control* that is exerted by the reinforcer (Deci & Ryan, 1985; Deci, Vallerand, Pelletier, & Ryan, 1991; Ryan & Connell, 1989). Intrinsically motivated behaviors such as liking to read are fully self-determined; that is, they are based solely on the individual's preferences. Extrinsic reinforcement conditions, on the other hand, can fall into four categories (Deci et al., 1991):

> Extrinsic reinforcers may undermine intrinsic interests

1. *Externally regulated,* or completely under the control of an external agent. If a student is doing his homework only because he gets to see a favorite television program when it is completed, then the behavior is externally regulated.
2. *Regulated by introjection,* as in recognizing rules or demands that pressure one to behave without a full understanding of the rationale for them. The individual would rather not follow the rule, but feels guilty if she violates it. Striving to get to class on time in order not to feel like a lazy student would be an example. There is still external control in this case, but it has become partially internalized.
3. *Regulated by identification,* when the person values the behavior and accepts the regulatory control that accompanies it. An example is the student who does extra homework because he believes it is necessary for further success in the subject. The homework is done for its utility, not its inherent interest. The behavior is self-determined however because the student does it for personal reasons, rather than external ones.
4. *Regulated by integration,* where the individual has fully accepted the desirability of the reinforced behavior and has integrated it with her other values. Integrated regulation of extrinsic rewards is similar to intrinsic motivation in that both are autonomous, but intrinsic motivation is characterized by interest in the activity itself, while integrated regulation contributes to a valued outcome.

Not all extrinsic reinforcements are coercive

Thus, Deci and his colleagues have described an important dimension of extrinsic reinforcement, namely, that it ranges from coercive and external to autonomous and self-determined. It is the kind of reinforcement that allows more autonomy, control, and regulation of one's behavior that is most desirable for educational purposes, according to Deci. He believes that educators should value children's autonomy and support self-determination by offering choices, minimizing controls, acknowledging students' feelings, and making available information that is needed for decision making and task performance. Teachers who provide structure, support students' autonomy, and demonstrate involvement with students through affection, enjoyment, and availability have been found to contribute substantially to engagement and motivation level in the elementary grades (E. A. Skinner & Belmont, 1993).

The Role of Expectancy

In addition to self-determination in reinforcement, the principle of *expectancy of goal attainment* has become incorporated into modern theories of motivation. This position maintains that individuals estimate the probability of attaining their preferred goals and employ this expectancy to control future actions.

Motivation is a function of success probabilities and incentive value

An early expectancy theory was that of Atkinson (1964), who believed that people's motivation to act depended on (1) their estimation of the probability of being successful and (2) the incentive value they placed on success in the activity. This belief can be expressed according to the formula:

$$M = P \times I$$

where M = motivation, P = probability of success, and I = incentive value.

For example, the student who believes that it is highly possible to get an A in a particular course and that it is very important to earn that grade will be highly motivated to perform well. On the other hand, if the student places high value on the A but believes it too difficult to obtain, or believes that earning an A would be easy but doesn't care what grade is received, motivation will be low. The key to the formula is the multiplication sign, which reminds us that each factor affects the other; thus if one factor is particularly low, the overall level of motivation will also be low. A perceived probability of success of zero for any task will result in zero motivation, no matter what the incentive value.

What three factors comprise achievement motivation?

Atkinson applied his expectancy theory to a specific kind of motivation of particular interest to education: *achievement motivation,* or the general tendency to strive for success (McClelland, Atkinson, Clark, & Lowell, 1953). He added achievement motivation to his expectancy × value principle to explain why people appear to differ in their striving to achieve. He believed that differences in striving for a particular goal are determined by the relative strength of two competing tendencies—the tendency to *approach a goal* and the tendency to *avoid failure* in reaching it. Approaching a goal is determined by three factors: one's need for achievement or motive for success (M_s), the probability of success (P_s), and the incentive value of success (I_s). Avoiding failure is determined by the motive to avoid failure (M_{af}), the probability of failure (P_{af}), and the incentive value of failure (I_{af}). Atkinson related M_s to pride in achievement derived from past experience and M_{af} to the embarrassment of failing, also derived from past experience. A person's motivation to achieve a specific goal would be determined by the relative strengths of the approach and avoidance tendencies. People who generally approach success rather than avoid failure are said to be high in achievement motivation.

As an example, let us contrast Sally and Fiona, two eighth-graders of equal ability in a social studies class. A $100 prize has just been announced for writing the best essay on "Why we should preserve our environment." Both girls are quite capable and interested in the topic, and both would like to do well in social studies. Sally has entered similar contests in the past and has placed, but never been first. Although the probability of winning is low, the incentive is considerable, and Sally views the possibility of winning as contributing to her desire to do well in social studies. She enters the contest. Fiona, on the other hand, would like to win the prize and achieve in social studies but recognizes that winning is improbable. She does not like to be identified as someone who tries and fails. She does not enter the contest. For Fiona, the aspects of the situation that contribute to avoidance of failure outweigh those that contribute to achieving success.

Goal Attainment

Research by Atkinson and others implies that individuals can approach the same task with different goals. Dweck (1986) has suggested that the type of *goal* a student hopes to attain in attempting various tasks must be considered in understanding that person's achievement motivation. She distinguishes between *learning* or *mastery* goals, in which people seek to increase their competence or master some new skill, and *performance* goals, in which they seek to gain favorable judgment, avoid unfavorable judgment, or outperform others.

learning or performance goal?

Most achievement situations permit a choice of goals, and the one adopted determines the achievement pattern that will be displayed. Achievement patterns can be either *adaptive,* in which the learner seeks personally challenging goals, or *maladaptive,* in which challenges are avoided and persistence in the face of adversity is low. Alex, in our opening anecdote, displays the characteristics of a maladaptive and ultimately self-defeating pattern. Table 8.1 describes the relation between goal orientation and achievement pattern. Note the role of *confidence* in one's ability in mediating between goals and behavior. If level of confidence is high, an adaptive pattern will be chosen regardless of whether learning or performance goals are chosen. A low level of confidence converts a performance goal into a maladaptive pattern in which avoidance and low persistence are most likely, but it does not alter the pattern for a learning goal. Dweck attributes these effects to students' perceptions of their abilities: Those who select performance goals typically believe that ability is fixed and are constantly concerned about their own demonstration of it.

Confidence interacts with type of goal

Research reviewed by Stipek (1993) indicates that students who set mastery goals for themselves are more likely to demonstrate behaviors that lead to high achievement. These students seek challenging tasks and view their teacher as a resource in the learning process, rather than as an evaluator. For example, in one study mastery goal setters were more likely to select a task described to them as difficult

TABLE 8.1 Achievement goals, confidence, and behavior patterns

Achievement Goals	Confidence	Behavior Patterns
Performance (gain positive judgment or avoid negative judgment)	High	Mastery-oriented (seeks challenge and maintains persistence)
Performance	Low	Helpless-oriented (avoids challenge and fails to persist)
Learning (mastery)	High	Mastery-oriented
	Low	Mastery-oriented

SOURCE: C. S. Dweck, Motivational processes affecting learning. *American Psychologist, 41*(10), 1040–1048 (1986). Copyright 1986 by the American Psychological Association. Adapted by permission.

Can you name a mastery goal you are working toward?

although it would help them later on than were children pursuing performance goals (Elliot & Dweck, 1988). When they encounter difficulty, these students assume that their current strategy is not working and needs to be changed or that they are not working hard enough. This is particularly true of students who believe that their classroom and their school emphasize a mastery orientation. For example, the more students perceived their middle school classroom to support mastery rather than performance goals, the more they attributed their success to effort and effective learning strategies such as planning or organizing material (Ames & Archer, 1988). These students optimistically believe that success is caused by their interest and efforts, even as early as the second grade (Nicholls, Cobb, Wood, Yackel, & Potashnick, 1990). The author vividly recalls a mastery-oriented third-grader proudly saying, "My teacher told me I could do it [solve a math problem] and I did it!"

Mastery-oriented students use good learning technique

In addition to beliefs about their ability to achieve high goals, mastery-oriented students tend to use more deep processing strategies, such as reviewing material not understood, asking questions, and relating information to past learning (Meece, Blumenfeld, & Hoyle, 1988), or trying to discriminate important information from unimportant in studying science (Nolen, 1988). In summary, students who view learning from a mastery perspective demonstrate the qualities all teachers would love to observe in their students. How can we establish classrooms that maximize the likelihood of a mastery orientation to student goals?

Structuring the Classroom to Raise Expectancies for Goal Attainment

Ames (1992) has attempted to describe a classroom structure that will aid students in adopting a mastery orientation toward achievement goals. Three dimensions contribute to the classroom structure: the learning *tasks* employed, the *authority* or role assumed by the instructor during teaching, and the *evaluation/recognition* that follows the students' efforts. The suggested structure leads to the possible use of a number of instructional strategies, which may in turn produce an adaptive motivational pattern. Figure 8.2, which summarizes Ames's model, lists strategies teachers can use to enhance expectancy for the attainment of learning goals. Note the emphasis on the intrinsic value and practical utility of the material that is to be learned, and the de-

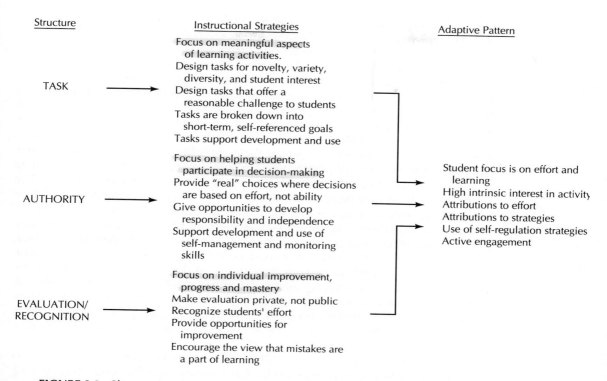

FIGURE 8.2 Classroom structure and instructional strategies supporting an adaptive motivational pattern

SOURCE: C. Ames, Classrooms, goal structures and student motivation. *Journal of Educational Psychology, 84* (3), 261–271 (1992). Copyright 1992 by the American Psychological Association. Adapted by permission.

emphasis on grades and other rewards. Personal improvement in learning based on individual effort is supported over surpassing the performance of others.

Preliminary evaluations of programs incorporating such a classroom structure indicate that teachers can implement these strategies to create a task-focused classroom environment to influence the motivational orientations of students, particularly those at risk (Ames, 1990; Tracey, Ames, & Maehr, 1990).

Teacher can alter tasks, authority, and evaluation

The Role of Perceived Self-Efficacy

As we discussed in Chapter 5, Bandura's (1986) social learning model identified expectancy as critical to learning and indicated that expectations about the probability of reinforcement were particularly important. Bandura believed that expectancies are not sufficient to account for motivated behavior alone, however. People must also believe themselves to be effective at what they intend to do. Individuals will not typically engage in a behavior if they do not perceive themselves as possessing *self-efficacy.* Emphasis on students' beliefs about their ability to acquire and employ the knowledge and skills necessary to obtain valued outcomes differentiates Bandura's self-efficacy explanation of motivation from the expectancy–value position.

Self-efficacy is affected by setting and attaining one's goals

Information about efficacy is acquired from personal experience, vicarious observations of others, social persuasion, and physiological states. People sift and evaluate this information in making judgments about efficacy for specific tasks. Factors such as pattern of previous successes and failures, perceived similarity to the observed model, credibility of the persuader, and difficulty and effort required to perform the present task are all considered (Schunk, 1989a). For example, think of a group of high school students preparing to take their first class in physics. Students will differ initially in their beliefs about their capabilities to acquire the knowledge and skills associated with physics content, perhaps based on a past history of learning in other scientific classes. Many will have had specific experiences with physics-like content as well. As they begin to work, the students will note the success and failure of peers perceived as similar in skill and experience. The credibility and skill of their instructor in explaining content, as well as the kind of feedback and rewards provided, would affect them as they continued through the course. Physiological cues, such as the amount of anxiety they experienced during tests and feelings of malaise or comfort occurring while studying or working on the material, also would be noticed. From these factors, efficacy for future learning would be determined by individual students. Motivation to continue to learn physics would be enhanced by the perception that one was making progress. In addition, as each person became more competent in the tasks composing physics, a sense of self-efficacy would be maintained (Schunk, 1989b).

Schunk (1991) identified five variables that determine how self-efficacy affects motivation for academic learning in school and summarized the research pertaining to them. The variables are (1) goal setting, (2) using cognitive strategies, (3) using classroom models, (4) receiving feedback, and (5) teacher-provided rewards. Table 8.2 describes the variables, their effects, and representative research findings.

The Role of Causality

A third critical factor in understanding motivation is determining the causal chain of reasoning individuals employ prior to behaving in a certain way. Weiner (1992) has criticized the expectancy theories of Atkinson and Bandura because those positions attend only to the immediate determinants of action, specifying only how they influence behavior at a given moment in time. Weiner argues that knowledge of antecedent historical conditions, or why an individual has come to perceive the present situation in a given way, is necessary to predict behavior. He believes that people are motivated to find out why an event has occurred or to attain a causal understanding of their world. This in turn influences their present behavior as much as current conditions.

Our attributions determine how we explain success or failure

An important set of historical conditions are grouped under the name of *attributions:* explanations, excuses, or rationales that people use to explain or justify their behavior. Consider the teacher who reminds her class that "A fool can ask more questions than a wise man can ever answer." The clever (and daring) student who says, "So that's why we all failed our last test" is attributing failure to a factor beyond his con-

TABLE 8.2 Variables affecting self-efficacy and motivation, their effects and research findings

Variable	Effect	Research Findings
Goal setting	Self-efficacy enhanced when students set and attain their own goals. Proximal goals are better than distal ones, and specific better than general (because progress can be more easily observed). Easy goals enhance motivation early, but difficult ones are better at later stages of learning (because they provide more information).	Sixth-grade students with learning disabilities who set their own math goals demonstrated better motivation than those who had goals assigned (Schunk, 1985). Bandura and Schunk (1981) found that providing proximal goals ("Do the next three problems.") improved problem-solving rate and accuracy and enhanced self-efficacy more than providing a general, distal one ("Do your best.").
Use of cognitive strategies	Belief that an acquired strategy aids achievement results in a sense of control, enhances self-efficacy, and leads to more frequent use of the strategy. Students who believe they are capable are more likely to use strategies.	Zimmerman and Martinez-Pons (1990) assessed students' use of learning strategies and found that perceptions of verbal and mathematical efficacy were related to strategy use for all age groups studied (fifth, eighth, and eleventh grades).
Classroom models	Observing similar others succeed enhances efficacy perceptions. Observed failure may lower perceptions and reduces subsequent effort.	Zimmerman and Ringle (1981) presented to first- or second-graders different models who were verbalizing either confidence or pessimism while attempting to separate two rings of a wire puzzle. Those observing high-confidence models persisted in their own attempts to solve an insoluble puzzle. Those observing low-pessimism models gave up easily.
Receiving feedback	Feedback linking effort to success sustains motivation and enhances efficacy, particularly when it is provided for early successes. Ability feedback is better at later stages of learning. Effort feedback in later stages might actually lower efficacy, because students wonder why they have to work so hard to succeed.	Schunk and Cox (1986) provided effort feedback ("You've been trying hard.") to middle school students during the first or second half of a math unit, or provided no feedback. Early feedback enhanced later efficacy attributions better than later or no feedback.
Teacher-provided rewards	Rewards are informative and enhance efficacy when they are linked to success and indicate student progress. Rewards are best for achievement; they are not as effective as recognition for mere participation. Rewards are most appropriate to develop interest in tasks with low appeal.	Schunk (1983b) offered prizes for math problems solved or for just participating in a math activity. Rewards for problem completion enhanced motivation and skill. Rewards for participation had no effect.

trol. The attributions individuals make are in essence attempts to explain the causal relationships that govern their own behavior. *Attribution theory* assumes that those who seek to influence motivation must understand the attributions students utilize to explain their successes and failures. Determining the source of student attributions is therefore a valuable goal.

Rotter (1966) differentiated among individuals according to whether they believe that reinforcement occurs contingent on their own behavior or view reinforcement as occurring by chance. He believed that people acquire generalized expectancies for *internal versus external* control of reinforcement and that these expectancies contribute to how they perform. Students who attribute their success to internal factors earn better grades and score higher on achievement tests than do students of the same ability who relate success to external, chance factors such as luck or a teacher's whim (Crandall, Katovsky, & Crandall, 1965; Messer, 1972). This is because students who believe success is due to their own efforts are likely to work hard, while those who attribute school success to external factors are prone to let events take their course.

Rotter's internal–external explanation of causality, which has become known as *locus of control,* is considered an important personality characteristic in understanding human behavior. It has been related to a number of other traits such as risk taking, tolerance for ambiguity, and preference for structured (vs. unstructured) environments (Lefcourt, 1976). DeCharms (1968) classified people who fell at the extremes of this dimension as *origins* (internally directed) or *pawns* (externally directed). Origins assume *personal causation* in which they act to produce change, assume responsibility for the outcomes and effects of their behavior, and feel capable of changing their future. Pawns, on the other hand, rely on others to determine their fate; they also avoid responsibility for their own actions and assume a dependent, inhibited role in most endeavors. DeCharms believed that pawns are unlikely to help others change their perceived locus of control because they themselves adopt that particular way of viewing the world. For teachers to alter the perceptions of their students, they must first view themselves as origins and act to cause change for themselves and others. DeCharms (1976) successfully trained teachers to become more like origins by having them participate in activities that stressed the teacher's power to change things in their own lives and the lives of their students. One component stressed the value of having students assume autonomous roles in which they took responsibility for tasks such as classroom monitoring and management. Enhanced intrinsic motivation and increased achievement were observed in the inner-city students described in this report; these results were attributed to changes in student beliefs in personal causation, which had been induced by the teachers.

Weiner's Attribution Theory

Weiner (1980) argued that in addition to understanding the *locus* of perceived causality of individuals, we must consider two other dimensions: *stability* and *controllability.* Some causes of behavior fluctuate over time, while others remain relatively constant, or stable. Whereas most people believe their ability or aptitude for a particular task remains constant despite environmental changes, causal factors such as effort or

Sidenotes (left margin):

Can you describe your locus of control?

"Origins" assume personal causation for events

Must assume personal causation to aid others

luck tend to be more variable. Most of us have at one time or another attributed success or failure on exams to such variable conditions as whether we were lucky in guessing or whether we were "really up for it" (implying high motivation and effort). The dimension of controllability reflects not only the instability of many causes of behavior, such as effort, but also their status as subject to internal control. We can increase or decrease the amount of effort we put forth on a particular undertaking. Our musical aptitude or physical coordination, although stable, cannot be altered through our volition. Luck, on the other hand, is not only unstable and unpredictable but is also beyond our control, as are many environmental events such as the difficulty of a test or the criterion used to assess our behavior. Weiner of course is referring to controllability from the point of view of the learner.

This three-dimensional analysis of causality explains the variety of attributions of success and failure that individuals make in achievement-related situations. According to Weiner (1992), five causal attributions primarily explain success and failure situations. These are *ability, effort, task difficulty, luck,* and *help or hindrance from others.* Ability and effort attributions are internal, while task difficulty, luck, and help from others are external. Attributions to ability and task difficulty are based on stable characteristics, while effort, luck, and help attributions are more variable. Effort attributions are controllable, while ability, task difficulty, luck, and help are out of the control of the individual.

> Ability attributions are stable; effort is unstable

Based on these dimensions, students can potentially make a number of different attributions to explain their achievement. Listed below are several causal attributions you might have heard students make for success or failure, classified according to the interaction of the three dimensions.

Attributions	*Classification*
"I never study. I don't need to."	Internal-controllable-stable
"I really put in the hours for that test."	Internal-controllable-unstable
"I never can do math problems."	Internal-uncontrollable-stable
"I was sick the day of the exam."	Internal-uncontrollable-unstable
"Mrs. Craig always rewards her favorites."	External-controllable-stable
"I had nobody to study with."	External-controllable-unstable
"Physics is just hard to learn."	External-uncontrollable-stable
"It just wasn't my day."	External-uncontrollable-unstable

> Why are effort attributions desirable?

Weiner (1992) argued that the stability of a perceived cause is particularly important to an individual's attributions because it influences expectancy for future outcomes. If causes are expected to remain the same, the outcomes experienced in the past will be expected to recur. Success or failure under stable conditions would ordinarily lead to anticipation of future success or failure. Causal conditions that are perceived as likely to change, on the other hand, will be less affected by present success or failure because the present outcome is not expected to be repeated.

Stability is critical to understanding *learned helplessness* (Abramson, Seligman, & Teasdale, 1978), a condition in which individuals believe that they are unable to control their lives, that no matter what they do, failure is inevitable. It develops when individuals first perceive noncontingency between their responses and reinforce-

> Stability is most important to expectancy

ment; that is, rewards occur rarely and are independent of one's behavior. The more stable the perceived cause of noncontingency ("It's just me; I'm just too stupid to learn."), the more likely it is that noncontingency will be expected in the future. With time, more related cues from the environment will suggest possible noncontingency, so that the individual in effect feels helpless in more and more similar situations. Thus Karla, who experiences helplessness when attempting to solve problems in math class, is likely to believe that tasks requiring mathematical applications in science will also lead to failure no matter what she does. Learned helplessness is accompanied by negative statements about self, a lack of effort on new tasks, and attributions to uncontrollable factors such as ability (Diener & Dweck, 1978). It contributes to poorer scores on achievement tests and lower grades in school (Stipek & Weisz, 1981) and is often characteristic of students with learning disabilities.

Learned helplessness is based on perceptions of inefficacy

Children classified as helpless respond to success and failure very differently from other children, as demonstrated in a study by Diener and Dweck (1980). Fourth-, fifth-, and sixth-graders classified as either helpless or mastery-oriented received eight success problems (easily solved) and four failure problems (no correct answer) on a task requiring visual discrimination of common shapes. They were interviewed after success and after failure. Helpless children underestimated the number of successful responses they had made and overestimated their failures. They did not view their successes as indicative of ability and did not expect the successes to continue. Subsequent failure led them to devalue their performance; for example, only two-thirds of the group believed they could re-solve the problems they had already successfully answered, while all the mastery-oriented children believed they could solve previously completed problems again.

Weiner emphasizes the role of *affect,* or internal emotional experiences, when success or failure is attributed to different causal factors. Affective reactions depend on the meaning attached to a given situation. Feelings therefore have cognitive antecedents: How we think influences how we feel (Weiner, 1986). Thinking is believed to give rise to qualitative distinctions between feelings and therefore is responsible for the diversity of emotions. Emotions are assumed to occur after the cause of an event has been attributed and prior to subsequent action. Each causal attribution of success or failure is believed to be uniquely related to a specific emotion. Weiner gives the example of earning an A from a teacher who is considered to be an easy marker. Pride is not likely to be felt if success was attributed mainly to external factors such as how easy the class was or the teacher's generosity, not to internal factors such as ability or effort. An A from a teacher who gives few high grades, on the other hand, generates a great deal of pride because attribution will be internal. In this case, the locus dimension of perceived causality and its perceived contribution to success have led to an affective reaction of pride. Do you recall grades you earned that produced strong feelings of pride? The expectations established by the teacher and your own efforts to meet them no doubt led to that feeling, not the grade itself.

Emotions follow cognition

We can now summarize Weiner's attributional theory of motivation. Figure 8.3 describes the sequences of events that lead to motivated behavior.

As an example of how the complete theory explains motivation, let us reconsider the cases of Candace and Alex from the beginning of this chapter. Candace performed poorly during a piano recital, but came early to rehearsal the next day. We might describe Candace as attributing her poor performance to lack of practice and an in-

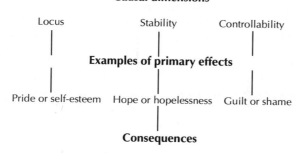

Antecedent conditions

(Information about one's personal history, the performance of others)

Perceived causes

[ability, effort, luck, others (teacher, peers, etc.)]

Causal dimensions

Locus   Stability   Controllability

Examples of primary effects

Pride or self-esteem   Hope or hopelessness   Guilt or shame

Consequences

(behavioral choices, persistence, withdrawal, etc.)

FIGURE 8.3   Sequence of events in Weiner's attributional theory of motivation

SOURCE: B. Weiner, *Human motivation: Metaphors, theories and research* (Newbury, CA: Sage, 1992), p. 278. Adapted with permission of the publisher.

ability to concentrate during the concert. These causes are perceived as internal, unstable, and controllable. Because they are unstable, Candace hopes that she will do better in the future; because they are internal and controllable, Candace may feel guilty that she didn't play well. Information about her past successes in other areas, in combination with feelings of guilt and hope for the future, can overcome the embarrassment experienced at the concert. Consequently, Candace vows to try harder and shows up early to practice.

Alex behaves differently in the face of failure. On the basis of a history of poor performance on similar tests, comparison to other students' performance, and the considerable effort he had exerted in attempting to pass, Alex probably has attributed the exam results to insufficient personal ability. Since ability is perceived as internal, stable, and uncontrollable, Alex has reason to believe that future efforts also will lead to failure. He is ashamed of himself as a result of the internal, uncontrollable attribution. Given his low expectancy for future success and feelings of low self-esteem and shame, efforts to achieve in the future are likely to decrease and withdrawal or avoidance is likely.

Weiner contends that a main value of the attributional approach to motivation is that it requires us to consider a greater number of both cognitive and affective determinants of the actions of others. In addition, it provides a clearer link between the many factors that have been found to affect motivation, such as rewards, expectancies, efficacy judgments, and perceptions of causality.

THE ENHANCEMENT OF MOTIVATION

How to enhance motivation.

Now that we have reviewed the basic concepts and theories attempting to explain motivation, we are ready to discuss the instructional procedures that will enhance motivation in students. To keep track of the multitude of dimensions and sources of motivated behavior described to this point, we employ a synthesized model that will help us relate various instructional procedures to the theoretical components of motivation. One model that serves that purpose is the *ARCS* model (Keller, 1984).

Keller's ARCS Model

The acronym ARCS stands for the four conditions that must exist in a motivated learner:

  A = attention
  R = relevance
  C = confidence
  S = satisfaction

These conditions are related to events that occur within the learning situation, although they may be traced to a learner's past experiences in similar environments.

Attention to achievement-related stimuli is critical

In the ARCS model, *attention* refers to the state of responding to achievement-related stimuli. For learning to occur, attention must be initially gained, and often sustained over long periods of time. Procedures that are particularly useful in gaining attention include sudden changes in stimulation, the use of cues within instructional material, and the introduction of incongruity and humor (see Chapter 6). In addition, sustaining long-term attention to academic tasks calls for appeals to learners' interests and curiosity.

Relevance refers to learners' perceptions that the content to be learned will have significance and value to them. Students must be convinced that mastery of the material will allow them to achieve an important instructional or personal goal. Knowledge of the intended outcome and awareness of how it contributes to goals of learning or performance goals (Dweck, 1986) are components of relevance.

Confidence is the belief that one can perform successfully in a particular learning situation. Perceived self-efficacy is a related quality, as is the belief that success is controllable and can be attributed to internal causes. Keller (1984) believes that confidence is established as a result of many successful achievement experiences over a period of years. The "management" of students' successes becomes an important role of the teacher, who must understand how important it is that students perceive these triumphs as attributable to their own efforts.

Satisfaction results from the successful completion of tasks, whether for intrinsic or extrinsic reasons. Reinforcement occurs when learners are provided information that allows confirmation or rejection of their expectancies regarding the outcome of learning. Satisfaction occurs when a student achieves or meets some related personal goal.

All the ARCS conditions should exist in a good learning environment, although they may have been established earlier in the lives of some learners as well. Let us now consider some specific ways of bringing about these conditions, either by direct communications delivered to students or through classroom activities.

Establishing and Maintaining Attention to Tasks

Table 8.3 reviews several procedures for gaining student attention and provides classroom examples for each.

Gaining initial attention to ongoing classroom activities is not enough to ensure motivation to continue to learn material outside the classroom, particularly when long periods of sustained effort are required. To maintain student attention to unit- or course-length content, a more continuous and integrated series of procedures and practices is necessary. Assigning *class projects* is one useful technique for instilling long-term attention to learning.

Projects can be defined as problem-focused, meaningful units of instruction that integrate concepts from a number of disciplines (Blumenfeld et al., 1991). Projects

TABLE 8.3   Gaining student attention to tasks and content

Procedure	Example
1. Vary the sensory nature of instructional stimuli (from verbal to visual, soft to loud, etc.).	In a geography unit, Mr. Burgess shows a picture of the ocean, then plays a recording of ocean waves crashing on a beach. "What makes the ocean appear to move and sound like this?" he asks.
2. Change the distinctive features of the instructional material.	Mrs. Sinclair underlines key words in her handouts and leaves every tenth word of the notes she provides blank.
3. Utilize novel stimuli to introduce new content.	Miss Sanchez talks to her first-graders in the voice of Manuel, a hand puppet, whenever she instructs them in a new class rule.
4. Provide examples and analogies to illustrate key points.	"Our body temperature is regulated just like the heat or air-conditioning in a house. It is adjusted by a kind of thermostat activated in our brain."
5. Introduce the conflict of differing opinions.	"The Bill of Rights never needed to be adopted. These rights are implied in our Constitution. "Do you agree or disagree?" said Mr. Hamilton.
6. Employ relevant humor to explain important concepts or to aid differentiation of key terms.	The following limerick is useful in an introductory chemistry class: There was a young student named Bell Who always used NaCl A mistake made him pour H_2SO_4 On his food—now he don't feel so well.

require a question or problem that serves to organize and direct activities. These activities result in a series of preliminary products that culminate in a final product that addresses the original question. Teachers or students themselves can create the question and the activities. The question should not be so constrained or trivial that the outcome is predetermined. Students need to develop their own approach, and it is assumed that they will be best motivated to test their ideas and deepen their understanding of content when the questions they are to pursue are authentic, unanswered questions comparable to those encountered in out-of-school settings (Blumenfeld et al., 1991). Projects have been found to enhance motivation to learn (C. W. Anderson & E. Smith, 1987; Brophy & Alleman, 1991; Marx & Walsh, 1988).

Good projects have subgoals, no predetermined outcome

As we observed in Chapter 6, a similar form of educational structure was fundamental to the discovery approach advocated by Bruner (1966). Blumenfeld et al. (1991) argue that discovery approaches were implemented without sufficient consideration for student interest in selected topics, nor concern for the knowledge prerequisites for this kind of schoolwork. Furthermore, questions were not considered from the point of view of students' and teachers' knowledge of the topic, and awareness of related instructional materials was ignored.

The use of projects can allow students to exercise choice and control of topics to work on, how to work, and what products to generate. To assume effective responsibility for controlling and choosing what and how they will study, however, students need to possess certain characteristics. Four prerequisites have been identified as critical to successful learning from projects. These are:

1. Sufficient knowledge of the content and the specific skills needed to permit exploration of pertinent information.
2. Skill in using cognitive tools (reference listings in libraries, computers and software, etc.).
3. Proficiency in planning, testing hypotheses, interpreting evidence, monitoring progress toward goals, and translating information from one form of representation to another (e.g., visual to verbal or mathematical to linguistic).
4. Perceiving errors as the inevitable by-products of attempting to solve difficult and demanding problems. As we have already discussed, errors are more likely to be viewed in such a way when classroom emphasis is on mastery-oriented learning goals, rather than performance goals (Dweck, 1986).

Teachers should be committed to allocating the time and effort required to yield desired products and should have available resources and technological equipment to support their students' engagement in project activities. Technology can enhance challenge, variety, and choice of question and solutions by providing multiple levels of tasks to match student knowledge, by allowing access to diverse sources of information, and by offering unique possibilities for products such as videotapes or computer-generated reports, tables, and graphs. Videodisc technology and teleconferencing networks are particularly useful in providing alternative sources of information, such as electronic encyclopedias and even live transmissions from weather satellites. For example, students can gather local data on the pH values of rainwater using the National Geographic Society's Kidsnet network (Tinker & Papert, 1989).

What topics and questions can be used as the basis for long-term projects? The following are some that have been carried out in classrooms:

1. Assessing local levels of acid rain and suggesting a plan to reduce it (high school class on the environment).
2. Determining availability of rooms and beds for elderly patients in a community and projecting needs for the year 2000, based on demographic data (high school social studies).
3. Developing graphs representing consumer purchases of various popular products by age, gender, and income level (middle school social studies).
4. Producing a videotape depicting the calculations required to go from American to metric measurement for liquid volume, distance, weight, speed, and temperature (sixth-grade math class).

Can you think of additional projects for course content that you might teach to maintain student attention and contribute to enhanced motivation to learn?

Creating Perceptions of Relevance

One of the most demanding problems facing teachers is helping students see the significance of what they are studying, particularly content that is a prerequisite for remote skills and ideas that not all students aspire to learn. The typical complaint is "Why do I have to learn that? I'm never going to use it again." For instruction to be perceived as relevant, learners must relate what is being learned to their *past* experience, to something they want to accomplish in the *present,* or to whatever they consider important to their *future.* Gagné and Driscoll (1988) have identified three important messages teachers should communicate to students to establish past, present, and future relevance. The first is *making new content familiar.* This can be done by employing examples or analogies that relate new information to what students already know. One teacher describes to her high school biology students how the heart works by relating its functioning to the highway system around the nearest city, with main avenues, collectors, and feeder streets compared to arteries and capillaries. To adolescents entranced with driving, the analogy not only aids recall but provides a familiar way of viewing the heart's action.

The second message consists of a *description of present worth.* Statistical procedures such as determining averages and ratings can be related to current sports interests of students, such as computing batting averages or free throw percentages. Measurement in cubic inches or liters can be based on automobile engine sizes or gas tank capacity.

The third message is *informing about future value.* Relating current material to career goals is one technique: Pointing out how mathematical procedures relate to engineering, banking, investing, or buying a home serves to connect abstract mathematical principles with adult functions students plan to assume someday.

[handwritten margin:] use Analogies when presenting new....

[handwritten marginal note:] relate to real world use.

Relevance is important to individual goals

[handwritten marginal note:] relate to career goals

Another way to establish the relevancy of school activities is to *assign students to positions of authority,* from hall monitor to head of ticket sales to club president. Many teachers have been heard to make comments like "Charles sure rose to the occasion when he took over the —— (school paper editorship, lead in the class play, etc.). I never knew he had it in him." Such statements not only reflect the power of expectations, but indicate the positive effects of satisfying needs for responsibility in some students.

Another intervention is the use of *simulation* as part of instruction. Simulations require the establishment of artificial environments in which students assume specific roles and participate according to the behavior expected of that role. In mechanical simulations, the student performs desired responses on specially designed apparatus such as a driving simulator used in driver education; or students can act out the roles of characters in a social situation. In "Exchange City," a popular dramatic simulation of a town's economy, students learn about economic principles and mathematical applications by assuming the roles of merchants, consumers, and service personnel. Many simulations are commercially available. In the American Government Simulation Series, students take the roles of government officials and participate in political interactions such as "vote swapping" to get legislation passed. Others are designed for microcomputer use. Oregon Trail and Where in the World Is Carmen Sandiego? are examples of computer simulations in which students assume the roles of early pioneer travelers or more modern tourists.

Teachers can develop in-class simulations, such as creating a product and establishing a business to market it or producing a literary magazine, which permits students to report on school events, write articles, solicit advertisements, and sell copies. The reason for devoting time and effort to such extensive activities is primarily that students acquire renewed interest in the operations being simulated (Dukes & Seidner, 1978). They are more likely to see the relevance of academic content when the concepts and skills of the classroom are actually used to solve problems and permit participation in social events. We will examine the effects of simulations in greater detail in Chapter 9, particularly their impact on the development and change of attitudes and values. For now, it is important to recognize that simulations can be quite effective in illustrating the significance of much educational content.

A second intervention that is particularly useful in aiding students to see the relevance of their learning entails *setting realistic goals,* both proximal and distal. We examined the effect of goal setting on efficacy attributions in Chapter 5. At this point, it is important to recognize that relating school content to students' goals is another way to enhance perceptions of relevance. While most students possess a long-term goal of some sort (even if it consists of leaving school, so they never have to study again), the linking of long-range plans to proximal goals that can be achieved in the short run is critical. Such large school projects as term papers are more likely to be completed by recalcitrant students if short-term tasks (writing an initial outline, developing possible sources of information, writing a first draft, etc.) are identified and planned. It is not enough for teachers to assume that students will complete these preliminary steps. In many cases, it will be necessary to provide specific guidance in accomplishing each step, to aid in establishing timelines, and to offer preliminary evaluations that will communicate to students that they are progressing toward the long-term objective.

Once goals have been set, it is important for students to develop *commitment* to

Simulations relate content to real world

Link short-term goals to long-term ones

them. This is more likely to occur when students see how a specific task relates to their personal short- and long-term goals. Eliciting commitment can be facilitated by providing *options* to students wherever appropriate. Some college teachers, for example, permit *negotiated contracts* for grades; that is, students assume responsibility for determining the type and amount of effort they are willing to put forth, and the type of performance necessary to reach the desired grade level is determined in consultation with the instructor (e.g., three term papers of a certain quality for a B, four for an A). The rationale underlying such an approach is that students are more likely to commit themselves to goals they not only value but also believe are realistically within their level of ability and are related to their interest in pursuing the content. Research has demonstrated that this approach encourages the selection and completion of more challenging goals than might ordinarily be expected, with students responding positively to the experience and exerting considerable effort to learn (DesLauriers, Hohn, & Clark, 1980).

A vivid example of how teachers can encourage long-term goal setting, foster the necessary proximal goals, and secure goal commitment is Project Choice, a program sponsored by the Ewing Marion Kauffman Foundation (E. M. Kauffman Foundation, 1992). Entire classes of several inner-city high schools have the opportunity to attend the college or vocational school of their choice after graduation, all expenses paid. To participate, students entering ninth grade sign an agreement in which they promise to attend school regularly, pass all courses attempted, graduate from high school with their class, avoid drugs and alcohol, and avoid parenthood. The program thus offers opportunity to acquire education after high school as a consequence of students' assumption of personal and academic responsibility. Parents and guardians must make a commitment as well—they must monitor student progress, participate in PTA, and attend periodic meetings with school counselors and foundation staff. The project offers extra instruction, counseling, and support to students in planning their high school program, choosing a college, and selecting a career. The first high school classes completing the program demonstrated graduation rates significantly above rates at other inner-city high schools and substantially lower rates of drug abuse and dropout. The program's results suggest that remote incentives can change short-term behavior if help is provided in meeting immediate goals and identifying obstacles to be overcome.

Instilling Confidence

Confidence is highly correlated to successful academic achievement. Teachers can contribute to emerging levels of confidence in a number of ways. Specific techniques include enhancing perceived control, de-emphasizing social comparisons, communicating clear expectations, encouraging risk taking, and fostering appropriate acceptance of help. Table 8.4 summarizes the rationales and research bases for these suggestions and describes how they can be implemented.

ways teachers can build confidence

Generating Learner Satisfaction

Satisfaction from learning can be derived both from gaining external rewards and from reaching personal goals. External rewards must be of value to learners, thus serving as incentives in the expectancy × value view of motivation. Verbal and written

TABLE 8.4 Instilling confidence in learners

Technique	Implementation
Enhancing perceived control: when learners are given some control over the events of instruction, their confidence is supported and maintained (Lepper, 1985). Learner control of choice and sequence of activities in CAI has been found to improve motivation and achievement (Burwell, 1991; Merrill, 1987). E. A. Skinner, Wellborn, and Connell (1990) found that elementary students who believed they could influence their success and failure in school were more likely to be actively engaged in learning activities, as reported by teacher's observations.	Provide choices of activities or tasks, as in "learning center" requirements or topics for term papers. Allow selection among different sample problems to be solved for practice. Permit student evaluation of quizzes and homework where appropriate. Point out how success on academic tasks indicates that students "have what it takes" to do well in school.
De-emphasis of social comparison: Ames (1992) has argued that social comparison appears to be especially powerful in affecting students' judgments about themselves, others, and tasks. Social comparison includes announcements of highest and lowest scores, public charts and displays of papers and progress, and the formation of ability groups. Children who compare unfavorably tend to rate their ability lower, to avoid taking risks, and to use less effective learning strategies. Maehr and Midgley (1991) argue that the entire school climate as well as the individual classroom contributes to social comparisons and in many cases must also change.	In the classroom, Ames (1992) recommends making evaluation private, focusing on individual improvement, recognizing a student's effort, and encouraging a view of mistakes as a natural part of learning. At the school level, Maehr and Midgley (1991) recommend fostering *personal best awards*, recognizing and publicizing a wide variety of school-related activities (not just academic or athletic), minimizing public reference to normative standards such as grades and test scores, and establishing opportunities for students to improve their performance as in instituting study skills classes.
Communicating clear expectations: Confidence is enhanced when students know what they are supposed to learn and what they will be expected to be able to do when learning is completed. Clear, specific statements in language that is easily understandable should be used by teachers to convey not only the final objective, but the sequence of steps to be followed in attaining it. Structuring the task to facilitate success on early steps will also increase confidence (Gagné & Driscoll, 1988).	Provide instructional objectives that specify the goal in terms of student behavior (e.g., "Compute the sums of two-digit numbers" or "Perform the four phases of CPR accurately in appropriate sequence."). Ensure mastery of subordinate skills before requiring the student to perform advanced skills. For example, checking that students can successfully add single-digit numbers should precede instruction in two-digit addition.
Encouraging risk taking: While building success experiences establishes confidence, we have also noted that succeeding at moderately difficult tasks in which failure may occur enhances motivation to achieve (Atkinson, 1958; Bandura, 1986; Weiner, 1992). For risk taking to emerge, learners must first have experienced a history of success. Once basic confidence in their ability has been established, learners should experience the rewards that accompany successful risk taking. Clifford (1991) has shown that exposure to risk-taking activities can increase students' subse-	Clifford (1991) employs a *variable-payoff* approach to encourage risk taking. Students are given risk-taking "quizzes" containing six easy 1-point questions and four more difficult 2-point items. They may complete only six items. Feedback is immediate. Larger unit exams are similar, with the addition of "bonus" risk items that can either add to or subtract from one's overall score. While initial reactions to these quizzes are conservative (few 2-pointers attempted), with time and the effect of feedback, more

Student control over content enhances confidence

TABLE 8.4   (Continued)

Technique	Implementation
quent willingness to tackle more difficult problems and enhance interest in the associated content.	difficult items are chosen. Students report satisfaction in solving the more difficult items and confess that they study more frequently and more efficiently in preparing for these quizzes.
Fostering appropriate acceptance of help: Ironically, children who possess the least confidence in their academic ability are the least likely to seek help from those who can provide it (Newman, 1990). Asking for help appears to function as an internal attribution of low ability and a cue to others that the help-seeker is incompetent (Graham and Parker, 1990).	To provide help before students have had adequate opportunity to work on a difficult task by themselves communicates that the teacher expects the student to fail because of low ability. A better procedure is to ask specific questions about the task after adequate time has elapsed. "Did you get that tricky third step?" (which you know is difficult) suggests that the student is capable, but the material is a challenge to all who try it.

Help-seeking seen as cue of low ability

praise and symbolic indications of teacher approval (smiling faces on papers, physical proximity and gentle touches, extra privileges, special trips and parties, positive letters to parents, tokens to be earned toward prizes, etc.) all serve as rewards to some students, but not to others. Carefully selecting among extrinsic reinforcers to find those that possess incentive value for individual learners is an important instructional task of teachers. Rewards should be provided frequently, daily, weekly, and monthly, to maintain motivation and interest in academic tasks. As Deci et al. (1991) suggest, however, reinforcement that allows autonomy, control, and self-regulation by learners should be emphasized. In all instances, rewards should be closely accompanied by informative and specific *feedback* about the nature of the behavior that is being rewarded and what can be done to improve.

Grades are a particular kind of external reward that provide a considerable amount of satisfaction to most learners. In most classrooms, however, grades are based on ability rather than effort and may contribute to the formation of performance goals that depend on a student's normative ranking (Ames, 1992). To foster mastery goals, grades should be provided frequently and should be tied directly to feedback about specific performance. They should be modifiable (i.e., students should be able to improve them by rectifying their errors). Providing students the opportunity to raise their grades by exerting additional effort—whether by repeating exams until mastery levels are reached, completing supplementary products such as essays or reports, or choosing more complex tasks as substitutes for required work—is more likely to promote enhanced achievement motivation. Research by Graham and Golen (1991) demonstrated that when students consider self-improvement as a goal, rather than comparison with others, they achieved at higher levels. By ensuring that grades reflect effort and improvement, a teacher will allow all students to gain satisfaction, rather than high-ability students only, who secure scarce rewards on ability alone.

Rewards can be student determined

Intrinsic satisfaction can be realized for students who have the opportunity to meet personal goals and to pursue content and topics that interest them, and when subject matter is presented in such a way that curiosity is piqued. Students who can see how material learned in the classroom can be generalized to external situations will also derive enjoyment from learning. Instruction that raises questions, supplies a challenge, and illuminates issues related to contexts external to the classroom will go far in maximizing students' motivation to learn.

SUMMARY

Early attempts to explain why people behave as they do included biological constructs such as instincts and homeostatic drive reduction. Maslow organized various physiological and psychological needs into a hierarchy, distinguishing between deficiency needs and growth needs. The concept of growth motivation led to a redefinition of the hedonistic principle, extending the concepts of pleasure and pain to include intrinsic, cognitive goals such as mastery and achievement.

Extrinsic reinforcement ranges from purely external to self-determined, where individuals have some autonomy in choosing reinforcing activities. Motivation is also influenced by expectancy of goal attainment; that is, learners estimate how likely they are to succeed, and choose tasks accordingly. Classroom motivation is aided when students seek adaptive learning goals emphasizing mastery of material to be learned rather than maladaptive goals that stress gaining favorable judgment in comparison to others. The tasks assigned, the authority role assumed by the teacher, and the type of evaluation and recognition that follows students' efforts all contribute to the adoption of mastery goals.

Perceptions of self-efficacy are also crucial to achievement motivation in that individuals must believe that they are effective in what they intend to accomplish. Efficacy is maximized when students can set and attain their own goals, believe they can use relevant cognitive strategies to succeed, observe successful models, receive feedback linked to effort, and obtain rewards for progress and improvement.

Attributions of causality of success or failure define one's locus of control. Weiner classifies attributions according to three dimensions: internality–externality, controllable–uncontrollable, and stable–unstable. Five attributions primarily define success in achievement: ability, effort, luck, task difficulty, and help from others. These attributions vary according to the three dimensions (e.g., effort attributions are internal, unstable, and controllable). Attributions of failure to external, stable, and uncontrollable factors define the condition known as learned helplessness, which leads to depressed achievement and failure to attempt to learn. Attributions are believed to give rise to emotional feelings such as pride or shame, which further affect behavior.

Motivation can be enhanced by focusing on four conditions that exist in the motivated learner: attention, relevance, confidence, and satisfaction. Attention can initially be captured by varying stimulation, employing humor, providing good examples, and introducing incongruity and cognitive conflict. Unit-length activities such as class or group projects are effective in sustaining attention. Perceptions of relevance can be created by relating new content to old, stressing the relationship of content to long-term student goals and needs, allowing choice among optional tasks, and utilizing simulation activities. Instilling confidence occurs as a result of increased student perceptions of control, de-emphasis on social comparisons through grading and other practices, clear expectations, support in risk taking, and learning to accept help. Learner satisfaction can be established not only by providing extrinsic rewards and feedback about achievement, but also by aiding the realization of intrinsic goals.

A concept map for this chapter appears on page 298.

EXERCISES

1. Recall when you had the opportunity to select a task or topic to be studied in a particular class. What kind of choice did you make? Did the perceived difficulty level of the assignment affect your choice? Under what conditions do intrinsic motives affect your academic or social choices, and when do external factors play a part?

2. Have you ever experienced the effect of having peers achieve while you could not, or vice versa? How did you feel? How was the situation handled by the teacher? How should it have been handled? How can tasks be assigned and structured so that both high and low achievers experience some success?

3. Prepare two lists: situations or tasks at which you would ordinarily expect to succeed and those at which you would ordinarily expect to fail. Include social as well as academic situations. What commonalities underlie these sets of situations? To alter your expectations, which of your beliefs about the tasks would have to change? What new information might you need to alter your expectations? Are there any expectancies you could reasonably change by acquiring new information or modifying the way you respond to related situations?

SUGGESTED READINGS

Ames, C. (1992). Classrooms, goal structures and student motivation. *Journal of Educational Psychology, 84*(3), 261–271.

DeCharms, R. (1976). *Enhancing motivation change in the classroom.* New York: Irvington.

Deci, E. L., Vallerand, R. J., Pelletier, L. G., & Ryan, R. M. (1991). Motivation and education: The self-determination perspective. *Educational Psychologist, 26*(3&4), 325–346.

Dweck, C. S. (1986). Motivational processes affecting learning. *American Psychologist, 41*(10), 1040–1048.

Maehr, M. L., & Midgley, C. (1991). Enhancing student motivation: A schoolwide approach. *Educational Psychologist, 26*(3&4), 399–427.

Stipek, D. J. (1993). *Motivation to learn: From theory to practice* (2nd. ed.). Boston: Allyn & Bacon.

Weiner, B. (1992). *Human motivation: Metaphors, theories and research.* Newbury Park, CA: Sage.

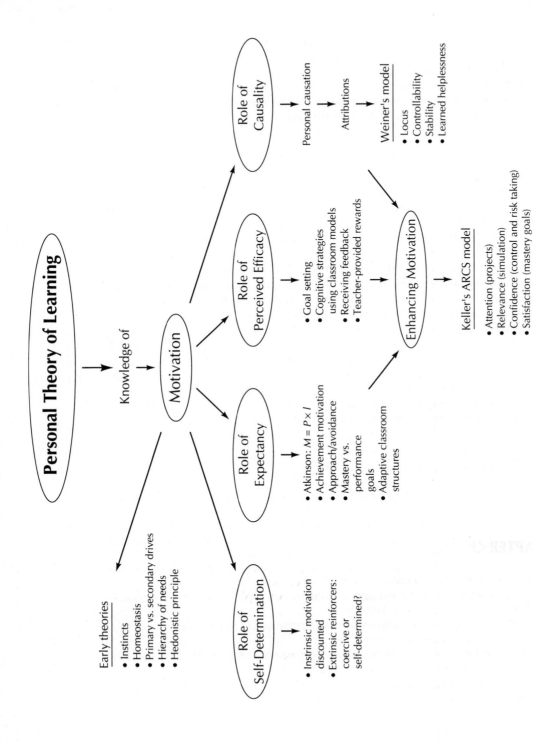

Personal Theory of Learning

Knowledge of → **Motivation**

Early theories
- Instincts
- Homeostasis
- Primary vs. secondary drives
- Hierarchy of needs
- Hedonistic principle

Role of Self-Determination
- Instrinsic motivation discounted
- Extrinsic reinforcers: coercive or self-determined?

Role of Expectancy
- Atkinson: $M = P \times I$
- Achievement motivation
- Approach/avoidance
- Mastery vs. performance goals
- Adaptive classroom structures

Role of Perceived Efficacy
- Goal setting
- Cognitive strategies using classroom models
- Receiving feedback
- Teacher-provided rewards

Role of Causality

Personal causation → Attributions → **Weiner's model**
- Locus
- Controllability
- Stability
- Learned helplessness

Enhancing Motivation

Keller's ARCS model
- Attention (projects)
- Relevance (simulation)
- Confidence (control and risk taking)
- Satisfaction (mastery goals)

Concept Map for Chapter 8

298

chapter **9**

Learning Values

CHAPTER OUTLINE

CHAPTER OBJECTIVES

1. Explain the rationale and structure of the taxonomy of the affective domain.
2. Define prosocial behavior and provide three examples that might occur in schools.
3. Distinguish among the identification, social learning, and cognitive development views of the acquisition of prosocial behavior.
4. Differentiate the general instructional approaches of character education, moral education, and an integrated approach.
5. Provide five examples of how teachers can influence discussions of moral issues through questioning.

6. Explain the components of a just community.
7. Describe Lickona's components of good character.
8. Summarize the four instructional strategies incorporated into Lickona's integrated approach to prosocial learning.
9. Explain how cooperative learning techniques can influence affective goals.
10. Differentiate between the cooperative learning techniques of jigsaw, STAD, TGT, and CIRC.
11. Summarize the underlying rationale of conflict management training programs.

Carl entered Mr. Odell's office, carefully looking up and down the hall before coming through the door. He quickly took a seat.

"I don't want anyone to know that I came to see you," he said to the principal.

"No problem, Carl. What goes on in here is strictly confidential," replied Mr. Odell.

"Yeah, but if it ever gets out that I was here, I'm dead."

"OK, no one will know. Now suppose you tell me what has you so upset."

"Well, I was in the boy's john a few minutes ago and I heard some of the guys in my history class talking. They had a copy of Mrs. Craig's test that we have to take tomorrow. They were discussing the questions and who they should let in on it."

"Hmm. . . . I should let Mrs. Craig know about this. Who were the boys?"

"Mr. Odell, I don't think I can tell you that. They're my friends."

"You really should, Carl. That way we can stop this from happening again."

"I know, but I don't want to be a squealer."

Mrs. Hostetler was down with the flu. The substitute was Mr. Downs, a young teacher waiting to join the school system.

Feeling anonymous and eager to have some fun, the eighth-grade class jumped at the opportunity. First was roll call. Charlie answered "Present" for Todd, Kent pretended to be Duncan, and Marcia took Kathleen's place. Then it was the coughing. One student, then another, began to cough violently despite Mr. Downs's warnings. Finally, it was time to roll things down the aisles—pencils, marbles, even lipsticks. Frustrated, angry, and saddened, Mr. Downs felt himself losing control.

Meg couldn't wait to get to her adult education class that evening. After a long day of playing "telephone tag" with clients, bank officials, college admissions staff, and loan agencies, she was ready for a change from her job as a college loan officer.

Tonight would be particularly enjoyable. Her sculptured figurine of a boy on a horse was all set to be fired and glazed. It had been fun using the soft clay and forming it with her hands. Now it was time to begin to see what her "creation" would really look like. Art, particularly sculpturing, was so fulfilling. Although it was hard work, you had the pleasure of seeing your efforts through to a finished product all your own. You never got to savor an accomplishment on the job. As soon as you finished one chore, there was another hassle waiting.

THE AFFECTIVE DOMAIN

What do these three anecdotes have in common? They all relate to the attitudes, feelings, and values students learn as part of their education. Carl is confused about a moral dilemma: Should he act against cheating, which he believes to be wrong, or respect a bond of friendship? Mrs. Hostetler's class is clearly valuing fun at someone else's expense ahead of responsible behavior, while Meg's enthusiasm for art class demonstrates her feeling about creative, productive work vs. office drudgery. Most educators would argue that it is not enough for students to recall the definition of a vocabulary word or be able to conjugate verbs. It is just as important for students to acquire attitudes and values that will guide their behavior as adults. Thus it is generally believed that a major reason for studying American history and government is to promote feelings of patriotism and civic pride or that reading *The Adventures of Huckleberry Finn* is as important in contributing to a sense of right and wrong as it is in learning about life on the Mississippi. For these educators, helping students to love learning, to possess confidence in their ability to learn, and to develop cooperative and responsible behavior are important objectives.

All three anecdotes illustrate *affective learning,* or learning that primarily relates to or arises from feelings or emotions. When affective learning occurs, there is noticeable physiological activity indicating an emotional reaction, as we discussed in Chapter 2. Of course, all learning requires thought as well as emotion, and this means that affective learning does not occur independently from cognition. Since, in addition, responses of some sort must follow thinking and feeling, there is a behavioral component as well. For example, the initiation of behavior reflecting patriotism, such as deciding to salute the flag, would require perception and analysis of the environment leading to a decision that saluting would be appropriate (cognition), as well as knowledge of how to form a salute (psychomotor). There also would be an emotional response invoked at the sight of the flag (affective) and the actual response itself (behavioral). From an instructional standpoint, therefore, affective learning objectives are not taught in isolation from the cognitive and psychomotor areas. The instructor must recognize teaching–learning situations that incorporate important affective components and select appropriate instructional procedures that enhance affective learning as well.

Affective learning = emotions, cognition, behavior

The relationship among cognition, behavior, and affect is perhaps best expressed in the *taxonomy of the affective domain* (Krathwohl, Bloom, & Masia, 1964), a construct that classifies different levels of affective learning according to the cognitions and behaviors that accompany each level. The acquisition of affective outcomes, for example, is said to follow a sequential process. Attitudes and values are believed to be initially *external* to the individual; that is, they have not been learned to the point of becoming part of the individual's habitual repertoire of behavioral patterns. In information-processing terms, learning in the early stages of the taxonomy is not yet

Taxonomy proceeds from external to internal

based on an interconnected network of schemas. As additional experience is integrated into cognitive structure, however, affective learning at the later stages of the taxonomy is considered to be *internal*, or part of the individual's habitual way of perceiving and responding to the environment.

The taxonomy of Krathwohl et al. is summarized in Table 9.1; each level is explained, and an example of a pattern of behavior that reflects the increasing internalization of the attitudes is provided.

Educational focus at first three levels

The taxonomy of the affective domain serves as a reminder that affective learning is a continuous process that extends well beyond the classroom. Commitment to a set of values that might guide a person's future occupation or determine a long-term hobby is established through a great number of experiences, only some of which occur in school. In most cases, the contribution educators can make to the affective learning of students will be at the first three levels. If students can become aware of the attitudes they hold, practice responding in appropriate ways, and begin to demonstrate a voluntary pattern of commitment, affective learning is well on its way. Teachers should plan instruction to foster affective responses at the early levels of the domain. Questions remain about what specific affective outcomes should be addressed and how they are learned, however. That issue is considered in the next section.

AFFECTIVE OUTCOMES

What educational goals fall into the category of affective learning? Terms such as *values, attitudes, appreciations, beliefs, morals, interests, feelings,* and *character traits* have all been used to refer to different kinds of affective outcome. In many cases these terms overlap in meaning or subsume one another. It is therefore often difficult to determine what behavior is actually being acquired when affective learning programs are studied.

Affective outcomes overlap in definition

TABLE 9.1 Taxonomy of the affective domain, with behavioral examples

Level	Explanation	Example
Receiving	Learner is aware of and willing to receive information or other stimuli about certain phenomena.	"I'll attend the diversity lecture to earn activity points for my civics class."
Responding	Learner goes beyond mere perception of a phenomenon to actively attend to it or participate in it.	Learner attends lecture on cultural diversity and takes notes.
Valuing	Learner voluntarily expresses commitment to an idea or activity.	Learner joints a local club devoted to working for increased appreciation of cultural diversity in the community.
Organization	Learner arranges and reconciles differing values to form a system.	Learner decides to drop membership at an exclusive swimming pool as a result of commitment to diversity.
Characterization by a value	Learner establishes a value hierarchy that guides action throughout life.	Learner becomes known as someone who is committed to the support of cultural diversity.

I have classified various affective outcomes into two categories that are most related to instruction in school and have been analyzed extensively in the research literature. These categories, prosocial behavior and interest in school content, seem to reflect appropriate educational goals that can be attained as part of a general curriculum. In some cases their acquisition enhances learning in other areas.

Staub (1979) distinguished between *prosocial behavior* (i.e., behavior that benefits other people) that is truly altruistic or done solely to benefit another and that which is aimed at fulfilling an obligation or gaining benefits for oneself. In other words, all voluntary acts that benefit others can be regarded as prosocial but the motivation for acting prosocially varies.

Prosocial behavior is thought to be guided by moral values and principles defining what we should or should not do. In many situations, however, values and principles are in conflict, particularly those that pit the interests of the individual against those of others. Frequently, the performance of prosocial acts forces us to engage in behavior that may bring us harm, even threaten our lives, as in undertaking extreme acts of heroism. Carl, in our earlier example, is weighing the alternatives of doing what is right by exposing the cheaters, which could net him the reputation as a "snitch" or even physical retaliation, and declining to name his friends, which Mr. Odell suggests would be wrong. In some cases, ways of accommodating conflict can be developed, as in cooperative neighborhood groups that pitch in to clean up the streets or work against crime. Both personal and group interests are advanced through these forms of prosocial behavior. In other situations, group values can suppress the expression of individual behavior. Students who thought it wrong to taunt and deceive Mr. Downs, for example, apparently went along with the group's behavior. Finally, some conflicting values lead only to confusion and a failure to take any action at all. In all these instances, prosocial behavior is determined by the interaction of cultural or social factors and personal values and beliefs. Helping students determine not only what decisions to make but how to practice prosocial behavior in the face of competing values is a major educational task.

The preferences and priorities students establish for different components of their education constitute their interest in school content. It is assumed that when interest is aroused, attention, encoding, retrieval, and motivation are all enhanced. Hidi (1990) differentiates between *individual interest* (I happen to enjoy astronomy so I attend to content that contains astronomical references) and *situational interest,* where content is generally appealing to all learners (stories about effects of the sun exploding will arouse interest in all learners, not just those interested in astronomy). As you know, arousing interest in school content is an important component of enhancing motivation to learn, and we discussed this area in Chapter 8.

Prosocial behavior benefits others but motivation can vary

Prosocial values may conflict with other values

PROSOCIAL BEHAVIOR

How Is Prosocial Behavior Acquired?

A number of theoretical explanations of how prosocial behavior is learned have been advanced over the years. Three dominant ones are identification, social learning, and cognitive development.

Identification.   The use of identification to explain prosocial behavior was derived from the psychoanalytic theory of Sigmund Freud (1938), who believed that children desire to reproduce the gratifications provided by the parents. Attributes of the parents (how they walk, talk, act, etc.) become desirable to a child because they are associated with gratification of needs such as love. Rehearsing parental roles and adopting the characteristics of the parents reassure the child that love will not be lost. Behaviorists, on the other hand, interpret identification by emphasizing the positive reinforcement derived from being like one's parents and the negative reinforcement obtained from a reduction in anxiety that accompanies what the child perceives as performance of the parental role (Sears, Rau, & Alpert, 1965).

> Identification = reduction in anxiety or obtaining positive reinforcement?

The author fondly recalls overhearing one of his sons lecture his young playmates, using the exact words of fatherly advice provided half an hour earlier: "Be nice, don't hit, and smile!" In many instances, limited cognitive skills prevent children from accurately inferring their parents' values or evaluating moral events. Parents who teach their children not only what they believe but why they believe it may enhance their children's identification with parental values.

Other psychologists have extended identification to include more generalized imitation of people other than parents. Kagan (1958), for example, notes that individuals with desirable attributes and motives that are perceived as similar to those of the child can serve as models. We often speak of "identifying" with someone in the sense that we observe in ourselves similarities to characteristics of another person, the situation being confronted, and the possible consequences.

Social Learning.   Social learning was discussed extensively in Chapter 5. Recall that Bandura (1978, 1986) and other social learning theorists departed from traditional views of how we learn from others by including the role of learners themselves in adapting personal behavior. Rather than imitate the exact behavior of a model, observers are capable of constructing their own responses based on cognitive capabilities such as symbolization, forethought, vicarious capability, self-regulation, self-reflection, and judgments of self-efficacy (see Table 5.1 for a review). People use these capabilities to adopt standards of behavior from which self-rewarding or self-punishing consequences can be determined. The development of social learning ability depends on (1) acquired skill in attending to relevant dimensions of a task or situation, (2) the development of symbolic representation and retention skill, (3) physical maturation, (4) the ability to delay gratification, (5) the acquisition of intrinsic motives such as mastery, and (6) skill in the use of comparative information about others' successes or failures. It is presumed that the acquisition of prosocial behaviors is dependent on these skills, just as we rely on them in developing cognitive functions.

> Social learning factors influence acquisition of prosocial behavior

Much is known about the short-term effects of social learning on prosocial or antisocial behaviors (e.g., cooperation, aggression). Recall Bandura's early research on the disinhibition or inhibition of preschoolers' learned responses in the "doll abuse" experiment (Bandura et al., 1963b). Vicarious punishment or reinforcement administered to a model was found to affect the behavior of observers when they were placed in a similar situation immediately afterward. If the conditions under which the observer must respond differ significantly, however, or if the model is removed, prosocial or antisocial behavior may not be demonstrated in the same form. For the social learning model to be an adequate explanation of how prosocial behavior is maintained and performed when not in the presence of a model, it is necessary to account for situational differences.

Staub (1979) has described a number of factors that appear to be responsible for altering situations in ways that potentially affect prosocial behavior. Table 9.2 summarizes these factors and applies them to the example of helping someone in trouble.

Cognitive Development. Unlike the identification and social learning approaches, the cognitive development approach does not assume that prosocial values and behaviors are learned predominantly from experiences with socializing agents. Developmental psychologists, as you recall from Chapter 3, believe that mental structures are not merely products of the environment; they develop as a result of the interaction between the individual and external influences. This interaction leads to a restructuring of the child's cognitive organization. Children therefore do not receive societal values such as respect of property as if they were blank slates. Rather, these values are assimilated in accordance with a personal, internal logic about the nature of property. Thus children and adults interpret society's moral views in a qualitatively different manner. With increased social interaction, for example, they develop the perspective that respect for property is necessary or there will be nothing left to play with. Society

Prosocial behavior constructed as result of cognitive development

TABLE 9.2 Social determinants of prosocial behavior and examples

Factor	Example
Ambiguity of stimulus (The less ambiguous the stimulus, the greater likelihood of help.)	"Does the situation really require my assistance? Will I look foolish if I offer to help that girl in the water and she really isn't drowning?"
Degree of need (The greater the need, the more likely help will follow.)	"Randy needs my help. If he fails this test, he'll flunk the course."
Extent to which help is focused on one person	"I'm the only one who knows enough math to help Randy on this test."
Degree of impact of instigating stimuli	"Suddenly, there he was, lying in the middle of the road. I didn't have time to think."
Extent to which self-initiation is required (The more decision making is required, the more likelihood of help decreases.)	"He was under the water in the pool. The rescue pole was right there."
Cost of helping	"If I had gone into that burning car to pull her out, I would have been killed, too."
Action required may be socially unacceptable	"I knew Amanda needed help on her homework, but teacher has a rule against helping others do their assignments."
Existence of a relationship to the person in need	"It was my brother who needed the kidney transplant. I had to help!"
Positive or negative events concurrent with or prior to the need for help (Psychological states or moods enhance likelihood of helping.)	"I was feeling so good about my own A in calculus that I figured even Danny deserved some tutoring."

does not impose this perspective; children construct it naturally to accommodate increasingly complex social experiences (R. H. Hersh, Miller, & Fielding, 1980).

Piaget (1932) proposed that children move through discrete stages of moral development similar to those encountered in cognitive growth. He interviewed children about their feelings about the rules of games, their evaluations of stories, and their reactions to the actions of others. On the basis of these observations, he described two stages of morality: *heteronomous* and *autonomous.* Piaget presumed that during the heteronomous morality stage, children characterize right and wrong on the basis of the consequences of an action. For example, it is wrong to drop cups if they break, regardless of whether the dropping is accidental or intentional. The amount of broken cups would determine the amount of appropriate punishment, not whether the act was or was not intentional. In autonomous morality, on the other hand, intentions do determine the evaluation of an act, and punishment is dependent on the circumstances surrounding the event. While this developmental sequence has been observed in some children, subsequent research indicated that when information about both intentions and consequences was equally available, both variables affected judgment for some kindergarten children as well as adults (Surber, 1977). Change appeared to follow a more progressive, continuous pattern than one characterized by stages.

Kohlberg (1958, 1964, 1969) and others modified Piaget's ideas, maintaining the interactionist emphasis and expanding the stage concept. In addition, Kohlberg stressed the role of *moral judgment* in prosocial behavior. He believed that morality is best explained in terms of the logical processes through which people analyze moral conflict and justify their choices of action. In referring to the three components of affective learning described earlier—feelings, cognition, and behavior—Kohlberg focused on the cognitive dimension. One may profess a certain feeling about an issue, and respond in a certain way, but without understanding the justification for the behavior, a full evaluation of the morality of the position is impossible. In the opening anecdote, Carl may elect to tell the names of the cheaters as a result of reasoning that honesty requires it or from fear that he will be punished if he does not. He may also choose not to tell out of loyalty to friends, out of fear of reprisal, from concern about acquiring a reputation as a "snitch," or for other reasons. The quality of Carl's moral judgment is revealed not by his choice of action per se, but by the pattern of reasoning with which he justifies his choice.

By emphasizing the cognitive dimension of morality, Kohlberg sought to separate the process of forming moral judgments from the nature of the judgment itself—the how to think from the what to think. He argued that it is more important for educators to attend to how individuals form moral judgments than to attempt to inculcate specific values or character traits. So many character traits might be deemed desirable that any list would be arbitrary. Moreover, the meaning of many of these traits or "virtues" is relative to conventional cultural standards. One person's "integrity" may be another's "stubbornness" (Kohlberg, Levine, & Hewer, 1983). Consider the great debates about national issues: Was moving to Canada to avoid the draft in 1968 an act of moral principle or an act of cowardice? For Kohlberg, the critical issue in affective learning is whether individuals are rational and principled in justifying their decisions.

Rational moral decision making progresses through a series of stages. Kohlberg's stages are organized systems of thought in which individuals make consistent judgments. They follow an invariant sequence, observed in all cultures, from being less inclusive of facts and the views of others to being more inclusive, and from being less socially adaptive to more adaptive. Stages are never skipped, and movement is always to the next stage. The impetus for change from one stage to the higher one is the learner's perceived inadequacy of applying his or her existing logic or system of reasoning to new experiences.

Kohlberg derived his stages by analyzing the reasoning people use to explain their choice of responses to *moral dilemmas*—stories that require the main character to decide on a course of action when faced with conflicting moral norms. The most famous of Kohlberg's dilemmas is that of Heinz and the druggist.

> In Europe, a woman was near death from a rare form of cancer. There was one drug that the doctors thought might save her, a form of radium that a druggist in the same town had recently discovered. The drug was expensive to make, but the druggist was charging ten times what the drug cost him to make. He paid $200 for the radium and charged $2000 for a small dose of the drug. The sick woman's husband, Heinz, went to everyone he knew to borrow the money, but he could only get together about $1000, which is half of what it cost. He told the druggist that his wife was dying and asked him to sell the drug cheaper or let him pay later. But the druggist said "No, I discovered the drug and I'm going to make money from it." So Heinz gets desperate and considers breaking into the man's store to steal the drug for his wife.
>
> Should the husband have done that? (Kohlberg, 1958, pp. 41–42)

Remember that Kohlberg was interested not so much in the decision the respondent made, but the reasoning behind the judgment. The same decision could be reached via different rational paths. Heinz might have considered stealing the drug because he wanted to keep his wife alive to tend to his needs or because he believed that human life is sacred. Kohlberg was able to categorize responses into three major levels of development of moral judgment: *preconventional,* or *level I* (most common with children under ten years); *conventional,* or *level II* (more likely between ten and sixteen years); and *postconventional,* or *level III* (rare until age sixteen). In level I, people approach moral issues from personal, concrete interests. At level II, they assume the perspective of members of society. Level III requires a "prior to society" perspective in which people see beyond the given laws of their respective social groups and respond according to principles they believe that any good society would advocate. Each level is further divided into two stages in which the development of the perspective of that stage is further differentiated. Table 9.3 describes each level and stage of Kohlberg's moral development sequence and provides an example of rationales at each stage.

Kohlberg's stages describe an individual moving from an egocentric orientation through a societal perspective to one that is universal. Moral judgment becomes less and less dependent on personal preferences and at the higher stages is determined more by universal principles. The highest stages, which are best able to handle moral complexity, may still be inadequate for the resolution of many true dilemmas. In those

Kohlberg's stages: reorganizations of thought about moral questions

TABLE 9.3   Kohlberg's six stages of moral judgment

Level and Stage	Description	Rationale
I. Preconventional (0–10 years)		
Stage 1: punishment and obedience	Avoidance of breaking rules; physical consequences determine right or wrong.	"I'll be spanked if I go in the street."
Stage 2: instrumental relativist orientation	Right action instrumental in satisfying self needs and those of others.	"I won't tell if you don't."
II. Conventional (10–16 years)		
Stage 3: interpersonal conformity	Orientation toward pleasing others and doing what is expected by the majority.	"A good boy doesn't spit on the floor."
Stage 4: law and order orientation	Orientation toward maintaining the social order and doing one's duty.	"What would it be like if everyone did that?"
III. Postconventional (16 and over)		
Stage 5: social contract orientation	Right action determined by broad individual rights and commonly accepted standards. Laws should change to reflect welfare of majority.	"We need to work to change that law—it violates the principle of free speech."
Stage 6: universal ethical principles	Right is defined by decisions of conscience according to self-chosen, ethical principles such as truth or justice.	"Truth is what I stand for. I have to turn in Billy although he will suffer for it."

situations, either higher-level principles of equal merit are pitted against each other (e.g., rights of the victim vs. rights of the accused in criminal cases) or there is disagreement as to whether a principle is truly universal ("Is the taking of a human life always wrong?").

What causes movement from stage to stage or from a lower to higher level of judgment? For Kohlberg, change in stage is a natural process brought about through opportunity to think through one's experiences in increasingly complex ways. Exposure to more adequate patterns of moral reasoning, at home, at school, or through social institutions such as the religious community or the peer group will suffice. When learners must consider approaches to moral conflicts that are more comprehensive and consistent than those they are used to employing, disequilibrium is created that stimulates the autonomous development of a more advanced stage.

Transitions result from exposure to more consistent values

The cognitive developmental approach to prosocial behavior has received considerable research attention. If the position is to be considered a valid explanation of the acquisition of prosocial behavior, four basic questions need to be answered. We explore these questions in the remainder of this section.

Does moral judgment change over time from less advanced forms of thought to more advanced forms?

The answer to this question is strongly affirmative. Rest (1979) reviewed cross-sectional (large groups of students at different ages) and longitudinal (same students evaluated from year to year) studies and also conducted a number on his own. All studies employed the Defining Issues Test (DIT) as the dependent variable. The DIT presents several dilemmas, then asks respondents to answer several questions, rating and ranking them in terms of their importance in helping to decide what ought to be done. For example, one question asks whether Heinz should respect the druggist's rights to his discovery.

Rest's review indicated that both number of years in school and age are related to the way subjects judge moral issues. Students moving through high school and into college show the most dramatic change. Adults are slow to change in their twenties and after leaving school; however, those who continue their education in specialties that emphasize moral thinking attain much higher DIT scores than the average adult. Decreases in lower-stage responses and increases in higher-stage judgment were observed for most individual subjects over time.

Judgment changes with age + educational level

Instead of attributing age changes to cognitive development, social learning theorists such as Bandura would attribute them to the influence of new external socialization agents at different times in life. As children move from the home to school and to the larger society, the standards of each become dominant. Social learning theorists would argue that it is not cognitive development that is critical but the environment that influences moral judgment. For this reason, it is necessary to ask a second question of the cognitive development position:

What is the relation of moral judgment to cognitive development?

While it is clear that moral judgment is related to cognitive factors such as general intelligence, reading comprehension, and general knowledge, Rest (1979) and Kohlberg (1964, 1969) report only moderate correlations between measures of these variables and DIT scores. Other factors seem to contribute. McGeorge (1975) asked adolescent subjects to take the DIT as someone "with no sense of justice" and as someone "with the highest principles of justice." Subjects could willingly decrease their scores when asked to be less just, but could *not* fake being more just. Such findings suggest that prior reinforcement of a particular value judgment will not suffice to instill it; rather, a difference in understanding, which must be developed, is necessary for moral judgment.

Moral judgment not learned through reinforcement alone

Are advances in moral judgment related to demonstrations of actual prosocial behavior?

Some might suggest that moral judgments as reflected in movement through Kohlberg's stages are not necessarily correlated with behavior because situations and values influence decision making. Sometimes moral values can be compromised. Take the case of Watergate figure John Dean, the special counsel to Richard Nixon. Dean

(1976) said that he constantly put aside larger questions of morality to pursue the practical and personal concern of gaining the president's reelection. Knowing and saying what one ought to do is no guarantee that the right thing will be done.

Research reveals relationships between scores on measures of moral judgment and on behaviors that are logically representative of an individual's moral stage, however. For example, interviews of college protesters disclosed different reasons for protesting depending on moral stage. Protesters classified as postconventional protested on the basis of inequality and unfairness, while preconventional protesters were more concerned with issues that affected their own situation (Hahn, Smith, & Block, 1968). Conformity was found to be a more frequent trait in persons classified at the conventional level than in the other two (Salzstein, Diamond, & Belenky, 1972).

Research has demonstrated that behavior characteristic of school-related situations is also related to moral judgment as defined by Kohlberg's stages. Masterman (1980) observed 120 high school students, interviewed their teachers, and obtained moral stage ratings based on Kohlberg's Moral Maturity Score to identify patterns of in-school behavior and their relation to moral judgment. Preconventional students were found to be judged by teachers and peers as most hostile and least willing to support the norms of the classroom. These students' own perceptions did not correlate with those of their classmates, suggesting the absence of one prerequisite for more advanced judgment—namely, an ability to share perspective. Conventional students were perceived as more friendly and positive, more task oriented, likely to support the norms of the group, and more likely to dominate in class discussions than preconventional students. Postconventional students received the highest teacher and peer ratings on these variables. Masterman concluded that "a high school student's moral development stage was clearly related to his mode of social behavior in a classroom" (Masterman, 1980, p. 201).

Can moral judgment be improved by deliberate intervention?

Lockwood (1978), who reviewed the forms of educational intervention that have been employed in attempting to modify level of moral judgment, identified two kinds: direct discussion and psychological education. Discussion of moral dilemmas and ethical issues was part of the ongoing classroom activity in the *direct discussion* method. Teachers monitored and intervened in the discussions when necessary, providing reasoning one stage above that being expressed by a student or group. This technique is called *plus-one matching.* Lockwood noted considerable variation in the actual arguments teachers used in plus-one matching, both from study to study and within studies. At times, teachers introduced arguments that may have been too advanced for some students or raised issues that students did not see as relevant. Lockwood (1978) found that the majority of studies employing the direct discussion method produced positive increments in moral judgment, but change did not occur in all subjects. The largest changes were found for students who were originally functioning at a stage 2 level. Change at higher levels was less frequent.

Psychological education consists of a variety of activities in addition to discussion: role-playing, counseling, empathy training, and the practice of listening skills and logical thought. Based on his overall review, Lockwood concluded that the psychological education approach is so diverse that it is difficult to determine which

[margin note] Stages of judgment relatively consistent with behavior

[margin note] Direct discussion effective at lower levels

aspects of an intervention contribute to improvement and which do not. Some aspects of the treatment may not be directly related to improved moral judgment, while others may be quite critical. Lockwood summarized his review by suggesting that intervention in moral judgment can be effective, particularly at the lower levels and when direct discussions are the focus of training.

The cognitive development position has received more attention in this section than the others because in the literature it has been applied to prosocial behavior in educational settings more frequently than identification and social learning. All three positions offer a unique interpretation of affective learning, however, and none can be ignored. The identification position seems to describe the parent–child interactions necessary to the initial acquisition of attitudes and values, while the social learning model more completely analyzes learning resulting from other situations encountered by the learner. The cognitive developmental position appears to have the most to say about the role of the learner in the development of personal values and behaviors. Next, we examine implications for the teaching of prosocial behavior derived from these positions.

How Is Prosocial Behavior Taught?

Character Education.   Just as there are a number of differing views of how prosocial behavior is learned, there are several approaches to teaching prosocial behavior in educational settings. *Character education* is a term reflecting the view that certain character traits should be directly taught and insisted on as goals of the school. As early as the nineteenth century, sociologists such as Emile Durkheim began to see the school as vital to children's eventual understanding of the rules of society. As Durkheim (1903) said:

> The purpose of education is far from merely having to develop man just as he comes out of nature's hands. The aim of education is rather to superimpose thereon an entirely new man, to create in him a new being who was not there before, to teach us to dominate ourselves, to restrain ourselves. . . . (translated by Y. Nandan, 1980, p. 38)

More recently, Ryan (1989) has argued that to stop teaching values in the school because there is disagreement about what values are useful in a pluralistic society is an abdication of the school's responsibility. Former Secretary of Education William J. Bennett (1991) also believes that there are values we can all agree on and that these can be taught directly to students as issues of right and wrong. Character educators such as Ryan and Bennett emphasize direct instruction of values because they feel recent increases in the disorderly behavior of young people are related to a decrease in attention paid to traditional values in the classroom. Wynne (1989), for example, cited rapid rises in suicide, homicides, out-of-wedlock birthrates, and drug usage among adolescents from the late 1960s to the mid-1980s. The latest statistics available support the trend toward more dysfunctional behavior in our society. For example, in 1989 there were approximately one million out-of-wedlock births, or 27 percent of all births, vs. 11 percent in 1970. Rape has tripled since 1970, and aggravated assault has

Character education = direct transmission of agreed-upon values

doubled since 1980. Arrests for drug offenses have increased 20 times since 1980 (U.S. Census, 1992). While some of these increases can be attributed to more accurate reporting, the data still seem to support the character education position, according to which traditional values are on the decline. This position advocates a return to the frequent and consistent transmission of traditional values in school to remedy these disturbing trends, although it is not clear what relation exists between these events and the school.

Most character education advocates emphasize an authoritative approach to the control and modification of student behavior. Ryan (1989) believes that values should be taught through the six Es: *Example, Explanation, Exhortation, Expectation, Experience,* and *Evaluation* (by the student). Teachers and schools should exemplify the desired value, explain its necessity to society, and exhort students to acquire the value themselves ("Just say no to drugs."). They should maintain high expectations for behavior, provide discussions and other experiences in which rules of conduct are considered, and allow students to observe and evaluate the outcomes of their efforts. The establishment of a system of recognition is recommended. Walberg and Wynne (1989) believe that schools can contribute to the character development of their students as well as to their scholastic achievement by treating their academic programs seriously. Both areas require a degree of self-discipline, which they feel is a key to the development of character.

Moral literacy = knowledge of "great books"?

Bennett (1991) commends *moral literacy,* or the presentation of basic values through great works of literature, as a means to character education. He believes curricular materials should be drawn from classic stories, the lives of famous people, or the lessons of historical events that illustrate prosocial behavior. Stories and real events are not only interesting but serve as specific reference points from which learners can determine right from wrong. Some of the materials Bennett would use to teach basic values include *The Diary of Anne Frank* (kindness and compassion), stories of Rosa Parks and Jonas Salk (how one person makes a difference), *The Little Engine That Could* (persistence), *Letter from Birmingham City Jail* (respect for the rights of others), and such Bible stories as Joseph and his brothers and David and Goliath. Bennett believes we should teach these accounts of character to our children because they "reveal the common world we all live in and the principles and ideals that bind it together" (1991, p. 137). If values are presented repeatedly in various formats, students will acquire them as general habits of thought and actions.

For Bennett, teaching these basic values should precede instruction in the great controversies (abortion, euthanasia, the role of government, etc.). He does not believe, however, that the complexity or controversial nature of many moral and ethical questions should prevent them from being discussed in school. If learners become morally literate, they will be better equipped to consider the tougher issues later on.

In summary, character education advocates support the integration of instruction of prosocial beliefs and behavior directly into the school's curriculum. Basic values of right and wrong require no debate or discussion because there is little to discuss or debate—the values are universally upheld by a society. All values including morality are treated as matters of custom and convention to be inculcated in children as a part of character education. Teachers should exemplify and exhort students to incorporate these values into their own lives.

Moral Education.   An alternative to character education is *moral education,* which is rooted primarily in the cognitive development approach. Rather than desiring to transmit a list of virtues or character traits to students, moral educators believe that virtue is synonymous with principles of postconventional judgment and should be taught by the "asking of questions and pointing the way, not the giving of answers" (Kohlberg, 1976, p. 58). Because of this focus, moral education has developed in two directions: (1) incorporating moral reasoning into the general curriculum and (2) restructuring the school environment to allow for greater student involvement in the justice structure of the school (Kohlberg, 1976).

Incorporating Moral Reasoning.   Kohlberg argued that moral issues occur in most curricular areas: in social studies as one reviews historical events, in English classes as literary works are read, and in science or health classes as issues of human behavior are encountered. Based on a review of the intervention studies discussed earlier, Kohlberg and his colleagues recommend employing two types of instructional strategy as issues of right and wrong arise in the curriculum. One is the use of *in-depth discussion techniques;* the other is *role-playing exercises.* Unlike the character education position, the teacher's role is *not* to insist on a particular answer to a question of moral judgment, but to create opportunities for students to think through their beliefs. As a result, students not only will be motivated to acquire higher levels of judgment, but will be more likely to extend their reasoning to their own behavioral choices.

> Moral education requires in-depth discussions and role-playing

In-depth discussions follow the introduction of hypothetical, content-specific and practical dilemmas. *Hypothetical dilemmas* like the Heinz story are theoretical and removed from students' lives; therefore they may generate more public discussion because of a lack of personal involvement. *Content-based dilemmas,* which are found in a particular field of study, such as an examination of President Truman's decision to use the atomic bomb in World War II, demonstrate the generalizability of moral dimensions to the lives of real people. *Practical dilemmas* relate students' personal concerns about issues they encounter in school or at home. Personal dilemmas, such as Carl's situation presented earlier, are likely to maximize emotional involvement and interest in the topic but must be carefully introduced to maintain anonymity. Teachers are encouraged to use dilemmas of all three types as the curriculum and current events might dictate (Hersh et al., 1980).

Having selected a dilemma, the teacher moves through two phases of questioning to facilitate the discussion. In the initial phase, the goal is to ensure that students understand the moral question involved; this is accomplished by eliciting students' rationales for their judgments. The second phase of a moral discussion involves in-depth examination of claims and rival rationales. The teacher's goal in this phase is to be sure that all sides are aired and that students include the alternative positions in their thinking.

Hersh et al. (1980) have identified a number of types of question for teachers to use to facilitate discussion during these phases. Table 9.4 lists these, explains their purpose, and provides an example of each.

In-depth questioning strategies generate cognitive conflict. While particular questions may induce the thinking necessary for the restructuring of moral reasoning,

TABLE 9.4 Teacher questions and examples for encouraging in-depth discussions of moral issues

In-depth discussions require highlighting alternative arguments

Question Type	Explanation	Example
Initial Phase		
1. Highlighting the moral issue	Questions that ask students to take a stand.	"Is it wrong to steal to save another person's life?"
2. Asking "Why?" questions	Asks students to explain their stand on an issue.	"Why do you think your solution is a good one?"
3. Complicating the circumstances	Adds new information to the original problem to increase complexity or to help students confront the "real" issue.	"Suppose Japan had already sent an envoy to a peace conference. Should Truman still have ordered the bomb dropped?"
In-Depth Discussion Phase		
1. Refining questions	Probing questions, which reveal the many sides of complex issues.	
Clarifying probe		"What kind of trouble might he get into?"
Issue-specific probe		"Why do people have a responsibility to obey legal authority?"
Interissue probe		"Which is more important, loyalty to a friend or obeying the law?"
Universal consequence probe		"What would happen if everyone cheated on tests?"
Role-switch probe		"Would a friend think you were wrong to tell in this situation?"
2. Highlighting arguments in contiguous stages	Encouraging students who reflect elements of a higher stage to share that perspective on a new issue.	"Monica, you gave us an interesting answer to yesterday's issue when you talked about what's good. How might that apply to today's question?"
3. Clarifying and summarizing	Rephrasing what students have said to ensure understanding and focus on a key issue.	"So you're saying a person has to want to die and someone close has to agree that that's the best thing?"
4. Role-taking questions	Asking questions that stimulate students' ability to take another perspective.	"Larry, what if the person who had to turn you in was your brother?"

SOURCE: R. H. Hersh, J. P. Miller, and G. D. Fielding, *Models of moral education* (White Plains, NY: Longman, 1980). Adapted with permission of the publisher.

the ongoing discussion itself may have the same effect. Teachers should reserve questions for times that call for further reflection by the group.

Moral educators believe that *role-playing* contributes to the development of moral reasoning by aiding in understanding the affective as well as cognitive perspectives of others. Social learning theorists also view role-playing as valuable to the acquisition of vicarious learning skills and role-taking ability, two major components of self-regulated behavior. Role-playing contributes to the rehearsal of prosocial acts, both verbally and motorically, by providing the opportunity to experience a particular role and to be forced to consider the viewpoint of someone in that role.

A large body of research indicates that role-taking skill increases with age (Kurdock & Rodgon, 1975; Selman & Byrne, 1974; Yussen, 1976). Therefore, it is important instructionally to utilize role-playing activities in accordance with the cognitive level, interests, and concerns of students. Younger children will best learn from role-playing exercises directed at behaviors and beliefs that are relevant to their immediate environment, while older students will be more capable of applying the learning from role-playing activities to more remote situations. For example, Staub (1971) had pairs of kindergarten children enact situations in which one child needed help and another provided help; then they exchanged roles. Immediately after training and a week later, girls who had the role-playing experience attempted to help in response to sounds of distress coming from a girl in another room, while boys shared significantly more candy with another boy whose parents (they were told) were unable to buy him a birthday present. Staub attributes the sex difference in the mode of help to the differences in the sex of the child needing help, with the same-sex child eliciting more empathic responses in the helper.

> Role-playing facilitates taking another's point of view

With older children, role-playing exercises may have to be more dramatic and to include reinforcing consequences. Chandler (1973) trained delinquent boys aged eleven to thirteen to make films about life situations in which prosocial values were at issue (e.g., should a student do what his gang was doing even though he knew it was wrong?). All participants had to play each role, and students took turns in all phases of film production. A group of delinquent boys received no training and a placebo group helped make films but did not assume character roles. Police reports for an 18-month period revealed that offenses decreased more significantly for the role-playing group after training than for the others. Chandler explains the improvement by suggesting that training provided new strategies for dealing with life situations, greater ease in interacting with others, and the opportunity to participate in the construction of a role for oneself. For role-playing to be effective with older children, the activity must be similar to the situations they normally face.

Restructuring the Curriculum.   Kohlberg (1976) spoke of the "hidden curriculum" of the school (remember our old friend *incidental learning,* from Chapter 1?), from which skills and attitudes are acquired without direct instruction. Moral educators believe that the hidden curriculum offers a rich opportunity for educators to involve students in moral learning. Although much can be learned from discussing dilemmas, there is no substitute for participating in the actual decision making and implementation of real prosocial policies. Classroom discussions do not lead to immediate moral action, nor do they relate to the environment outside the classroom. For these reasons, Kohlberg embarked on a series of experiments in restructuring schools to permit the establishment of connections between moral action and moral judgment.

Kohlberg's major attempt at restructuring school programs has taken the form of a *just community* (Kohlberg, 1985). His goal was to build a moral culture through the creation of shared norms within a secondary school unit. Such a moral atmosphere is necessary for conditions of cooperation and dialogue to be established (Kohlberg & Higgins, 1987). Just communities function as schools within schools, providing a core curriculum and a homeroom while allowing students to take courses from the general school program. The major program activity is the community meeting, in which issues related to life and discipline in the school are discussed and democratically decided; all students and teachers vote, and all votes are equal. Although the rules of the larger school are in effect, the community exercises the right to interpret and enforce them in its own way. The rules of the larger schools are adopted by the community only after intensive discussion and a majority vote to support them. Disciplinary infractions are presented as problems for the group to resolve democratically. Initially students are reluctant to make and enforce rules, but do so after a few community meetings (Power, Higgins, & Kohlberg, 1989). Once established, the rules tend to be quite effective; for example, in two of the communities established, stealing virtually ended when it was decided that the group would make restitution for thefts.

Power et al. (1989) noted that not only are norms of responsibility established, the norms of helping, trust, and participation are created as the community develops. Members not only pursue personal educational goals but value their common life in the community as an end in itself. For instance, when students in the community are compared to peers from the same school on whether they agree with the statement "Skipping class without an excuse is wrong because it hurts the spirit of the class," community members are significantly more likely to support the statement than are peers.

Just community programs offer students an opportunity to function more autonomously, free from the decision-making authority of teachers and principals. A teacher's role is that of member of the community, not arbiter or judge. Teachers may help to focus discussions in establishing rules, penalties, and procedures of the community, employing in-depth discussion techniques where necessary, but it is the majority (i.e., the students) that makes final decisions. While not all decisions emerge as teachers might like, the decisions produced are more consistently followed and, if found to be unfair or unworkable, are soon reviewed (Power et al., 1989).

AN INTEGRATED APPROACH

In recent years, other educators have developed alternative instructional approaches to both moral and character education. These alternatives have arisen from dissatisfaction with existing programs.

Criticism of character education arises because of its emphasis on having children do right without necessarily understanding why the desired behavior *is* the right thing. Lickona (1991a) makes this point in comparing current character education programs to the ideas of Aristotle, who wrote that we become just by practicing just

Participation in a just community leads to prosocial behavior?

Character education assumes that doing right is sufficient

actions, and virtuous by doing virtuous deeds. Character educators believe that prosocial behavior is acquired through practice to the point of automaticity. Character education programs that focus only on behaving correctly without understanding why such behavior is desirable run the risk of producing outward conformity without inner conviction. Moreover, the behaviors deemed to be correct may reflect the values of a particular segment of society.

Criticism of moral education arises when Plato's view of virtue is contrasted to Aristotle's. Plato believed that if only we "knew the good," we would be good. Moral education programs that stress moral reasoning and judgment are descendants of Plato's view. According to Lickona (1991a), however, the Platonic emphasis runs the risk of producing moral reasoning that does not carry over into moral action. In fact, this is one of the reasons for the development of action-oriented approaches to moral education, such as the just community (Kohlberg & Higgins, 1987).

> Moral education assumes that knowing what is right is sufficient

A number of more empirically grounded criticisms have also emerged; the four positions summarized below come from moral educators themselves and are related to practical issues.

1. Teachers are inclined to misuse the stages of development by labeling their students. Preconventional thought is not inferior; it is merely a developmental phase. Moreover, since people use different kinds of judgment in response to various dilemmas, there is considerable potential for error in rating individuals.

> Moral education leads to labeling

2. Evaluation of change in moral judgment is inexact and time-consuming. Although studies have shown group changes on instruments such as the Defining Issues Test and the Moral Maturity Score, these tests require considerable time for administration and scoring. Moreover, developmental changes in moral judgment, like other progressive changes, are unlikely to occur rapidly. The emphasis in many schools on looking for substantial change as a sign of academic success is not applicable to moral development.

3. The role of the teacher as "conflict inducer"—that is, asker of provocative questions to stimulate thought—is not a comfortable one for those who prefer instruction with content that has right or wrong answers. Kohlberg and Higgins (1987) found in addition that some students resist responding to moral situations, preferring instead content that is more easily defined and assessed.

4. The concept of morality does not consider gender differences in defining what is moral. In addition to justice considerations, Gilligan (1977, 1982) detected another set of concerns in listening to the reasoning of women. Females responded to some dilemmas by noting the friction created in the relationships between people or by expressing concerns that someone was excluded or rejected. Such conflicts were resolved by considering situations in their contexts and through the restoration of relationships or attention to needs. Gilligan called this a *morality of care or response* and suggested that the domain of morality should include care as well as justice. Subsequent research supported this difference between men and women, with men more frequently focusing on justice and women more

Caring is another dimension of morality

often on issues of care and responsibility (Lyons, 1989). A morality of justice implies relationships of equality, while a morality of care implies relationships of interdependence. Gilligan (1982) argues that both orientations are necessary in describing moral judgment.

Based on the foregoing criticisms of the moral education and character education positions, one recent effort in the teaching of prosocial behavior has attempted to integrate the action and cognition components of good character. Lickona (1991c) has added a third dimension as an important outcome of affective learning, that of *moral feeling* or emotion. He thus extends the Aristotelian–Platonic views of virtue to include "desiring the good" as well as "knowing the good" and "doing the good," or *moral feeling, moral knowing,* and *moral action.* Lickona believes moral feeling should be added to conceptions of character because it serves as a motivational bridge between knowing what is right and actually doing it. Instruction must focus on all three dimensions to be effective in advancing prosocial goals. Figure 9.1 describes the three dimensions and their components.

Moral feeling added to knowledge and action

The three main components of good character could stand as the affective curriculum of a school. They are the cognitive dimension of moral reasoning, the action component stressed by character educators, and moral feelings such as empathy and loving the good, which Gilligan and others believe are also a part of morality. Lickona suggests the development of educational experiences that include these components as objectives. His integrated program is not advanced enough at present to describe exactly how each subcomponent can be enhanced, but he believes they are more likely to be acquired if four types of instruction are consistently practiced. These are (1) building self-worth and moral community, (2) cooperative learning, (3) moral reflection, and (4) participatory decision making.

FIGURE 9.1 A graphic representation of the relationships among the components of good character

SOURCE: T. Lickona, *What is good character? and how can we develop it in our children?* (Bloomington: The Poynter Center, Indiana University, 1991), p. 4. Adapted with permission of the publisher.

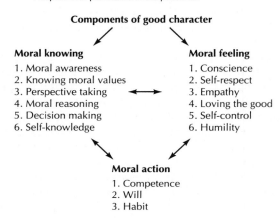

Components of good character

Moral knowing
1. Moral awareness
2. Knowing moral values
3. Perspective taking
4. Moral reasoning
5. Decision making
6. Self-knowledge

Moral feeling
1. Conscience
2. Self-respect
3. Empathy
4. Loving the good
5. Self-control
6. Humility

Moral action
1. Competence
2. Will
3. Habit

Building Self-Worth and Moral Community.   Instruction in Lickona's first area includes activities such as "partners" (in which two students learn about each other and then tell the class about the partner), "appreciation time" (in which students tell the class something that someone else did that they appreciated), "traditions" (in which each class develops its own unique functions, such as creating a class T-shirt or beginning each day with a meeting), and "problems" (in which students are encouraged to pose personal problems that other students can help to solve). These activities serve to activate a sense of caring for one another and to stimulate a sense of collective responsibility for all class members.

Cooperative Learning.   A variety of forms of cooperative learning have been developed and are reviewed in a later section of the chapter. Techniques in this area entail the creation of groups, which must work together to achieve shared goals. Lickona believes that through cooperative learning, students can acquire skills in perspective taking and decision making, gain empathy and self-respect, and develop the habit of working with and for others.

Moral Reflection.   Many intellectual activities increase children's awareness of their world and the values that govern it. The category of moral reflection includes not only the discussions of abstract or real-life dilemmas that moral educators advocate but the reading, writing about, and explaining of curricular content that character educators emphasize. The focus is on the union of cognition and affect; it is intended that students learn to value what they read about and discuss as well as acquire understanding.

Participatory Decision Making (class meetings).   In the class meeting, students discuss goals, rules, and consequences. Class meetings may be a part of a just community organizational system, or they may exist independent of other structures. The main purposes are to deepen students' sense of shared ownership in the classroom, develop self-worth by providing a forum where views are valued, aid perspective-taking skills, and create a support structure that maintains a moral atmosphere. In addition, better understanding and willingness to follow rules that are constructed by the group may lead to improved classroom behavior.

Dreikurs and Grey (1968) believe that class meetings that lead to decisions about rule breaking and then to certain, immediate enforcement of penalties will help students learn to deal with the logical consequences of their actions. Learning in this area helps students understand that certain behaviors are punished or reinforced for reasons other than the whim of authorities. From the cognitive developmental point of view, participation in class meetings should aid the transition from the preconventional to the conventional level of moral judgment. Students who discuss rules in advance of their imposition, as well as their importance, likely consequences if violated, and requirements for following them, may acquire more respect for their value.

Lickona (1991c) believes these four processes are mutually reinforcing, with each being needed for the full success of the others. He argues that discussion of moral issues is difficult when the sense of community is weak or when students don't know or like their classmates. Class discussion is "all talk" if children never work together to implement decisions made in a group. Cooperative learning fails to realize its potential if children neither plan nor evaluate their joint endeavors. Without group spirit and a moral community, participatory decision making turns into a debating forum in which students argue for their "rights" with little thought of their obligations or the common good.

One project that utilizes many of the components advocated by Lickona was described by Watson, Solomon, Battistich, Schaps, and Solomon (1989). The Child Development Project involved children in classroom meetings to plan discipline policies and procedures, established cooperative learning groups to complete learning tasks, provided opportunities for students to participate in helping activities such as cross-age tutoring, and discussed prosocial values in the context of reading assignments. The study was conducted by following two cohort groups of students through the elementary grades; one received the program while the other did not. Observations, questionnaire responses, and other test data indicated that program students became more helpful and cooperative and more frequently displayed affection and concern for others than did comparison students. Perspective-taking skills, consideration of other persons' needs in hypothetical problem situations, and use of prosocial and cooperation strategies (discussing the problem, compromising, etc.) were also found to be higher for program students. While these findings were encouraging, the individual effects of each of the program components were not isolated from the total package. For example, we do not know whether cross-age tutoring contributed to the overall effects. The study does reveal the benefit of integrating all Lickona's elements of instruction to produce improvement in character and prosocial behavior, however.

How can Lickona's curriculum be implemented?

The programs reviewed in the previous sections have as their primary focus the acquisition of values and prosocial behaviors. Two other school restructuring efforts, while not designed originally to foster affective goals, have demonstrated the potential to influence them. These are *cooperative learning* and *conflict management,* which we now discuss in turn.

COOPERATIVE LEARNING

Classroom methods designed to promote cooperative learning are effective in enhancing the achievement of students at different grade levels in a variety of subject matter areas, particularly if the cooperative groups are rewarded based on the average learning scores of group members (Johnson & Johnson, 1987; Slavin, 1990a). Apparently, cooperative learning activities improve prosocial behaviors such as commitment, helpfulness, and caring for one another regardless of differences in ability level, ethnic background, gender, social class, or physical disability (Sharan, 1980; Slavin, 1985). Students in cooperative groups develop more skill in perspective taking and display fewer hostile reactions to others, greater self-esteem, and more of the skills and attitudes that contribute to effective collaboration (Johnson & Johnson, 1989a; Sharan, 1980; Slavin, 1990b).

Cooperative learning also aids value acquisition

Cooperative learning proceeds in groups of four to six students drawn from different achievement levels. They are to work together so that all members achieve mastery of a particular learning objective. Johnson, Johnson, and Holubec (1986) have identified five requirements for the successful functioning of cooperative groups:

1. *Positive interdependence*—members must know that it is to their advantage that others learn. This perception can be achieved by establishing mutual goals, dividing the task into parts for all, dividing resources, materials or information among group members, and providing rewards for joint completion of the task.
2. *Direct interaction*—members must work closely together.
3. *Individual accountability*—each member must master the material to be learned, and each is responsible for providing support to others. It should not be possible for more capable students to do the work of others.
4. *Training in small-group skills*—students must acquire the interpersonal skills necessary to work together effectively, such as questioning, sharing, and planning.
5. *Time for processing*—time must be available during the group's meetings to assess how well the group is functioning.

Several different forms of cooperative learning have been developed. They share these common components but are designed to accomplish unique objectives. The major approaches are described below.

Jigsaw.   In the jigsaw technique, group members are all provided with the same amount of information, but each member is given one part that is unique. When a member masters his or her part, it is taught to the other members of the group. Since each member possesses a piece vital to the comprehension of the complete "jigsaw," members must cooperate to understand the whole. To assess understanding afterward, either a test is given to the entire group or a report is required (Aronson, Blaney, Stephan, Sikes, & Snapp, 1978). For example, if a report on George Washington had been assigned, research material might be broken into the first president's early life, his military accomplishments, his two terms in office, and his later life. A block of material would be made available to one member of each group. If several groups are involved, "experts" on each section meet to discuss their area and how to teach it to others. Individual groups then meet to have each member reveal his or her section. In a modified version of the jigsaw technique (Slavin, 1983), students have a common set of readings to use as a base for their understanding, but each member is assigned a separate supplementary topic that also must be reported on to the group. Grading of the modified version is based on the team's group score, so it benefits the group to help all members to master the common material.

Aronson et al. (1978) reported that children in jigsaw classes performed as well or better than students in traditional classroom arrangements. Children of different ethnic or socioeconomic background were randomly assigned to both types of classroom; therefore, differences in performance were not attributable to those variables. Preference for other group members increased as a result of jigsaw learning, without a decrease in preference for other members of the larger class. Children were observed to cooperate more frequently afterward and were more likely to see others as learning resources as a result of their experience.

Teams–Games–Tournaments (TGT).   TGT is designed to prepare students to master content and compete in tournaments against other heterogeneous groups.

After teacher instruction, students meet to help one another study and answer questions about the material. Once teams have had a chance to practice, members compete as individuals against students of similar ability levels. Each individual's performance in the weekly tournament contributes to the team's score, no matter what the ability level. The roster of the competitive group may change each week, as winners at each of the three levels are moved up to a higher level and losers at higher levels are moved down.

Research indicates that members of successful teams learn more, value their efforts more, and rate their ability more highly than members of unsuccessful teams. Those on losing teams do not rate their experience very highly and fail to learn as well as the winners. Chambers and Abrami (1991) point out that such a difference may be to the disadvantage of low-achieving or failure-avoiding students. They recommend providing cooperation both within and *between* teams by providing a reward for an entire class if all teams reach a specified learning criterion.

Student Teams–Achievement Divisions (STAD).   STAD is an adaptation of TGT in which each student's performance is compared to his or her base score. Rather than employing a head-to-head tournament, there are weekly quizzes, and teams gain points when individuals surpass their base. The competitive element is thus reduced and the identities of those who place in the lower ability levels are not made known. Slavin (1990b) believes that these changes correct the disadvantages of TGT noted above.

Cooperative Integrated Reading and Composition (CIRC).   The CIRC technique is directed toward language arts skills in the upper elementary grades (Madden, Slavin, & Stevens, 1986). Cooperative teams are formed of two pairs of students from two reading groups. After the class has read a common story, the teams work in their pairs to discuss it, reread it, ask each other questions about it, go over new spelling and vocabulary words, and summarize and write about it. Teams help each other study for tests, analyze the plot and character of more advanced stories, and edit one another's writing about the stories. The average performance of the group on the reading and writing assignments is used to determine the team grade. Not only do reading scores improve as a result of this approach, but indices of cooperation also increase (Stevens, Madden, Slavin, & Farnish, 1987).

While cooperative learning has many adherents, others are resistant to its implementation. Johnson et al. (1986) identified several myths that they believed hamper the implementation of cooperative learning programs. The myths are presented below accompanied by the analyses of the issues preferred by Johnson et al. (1986).

1. The "competitive world" myth, according to which the adult world is highly competitive and cooperative learning does not prepare children for it. In fact, cooperation is important to most human endeavors, and even if the myth were true, schools still provide much experience with individual and group competition. All that is recommended is a greater balance.
2. The "penalty to high-achieving students" myth, which suggests that working in heterogeneous groups might limit the performance of high

achievers. The evidence suggests that the better students learn at least as much in cooperative activities and often acquire more skills through having to teach others and work collaboratively (Johnson & Johnson, 1989a). Moreover, most cooperative learning activities provide opportunities for high achievers to work at their own pace as well as with the group.

3. The "unfair grading" myth, which implies that having one's grade depend on group performance is inappropriate. Johnson et al. argue that often how well we do in life is determined by how a group performs, as in the scoring for most team sports. It is also possible to utilize individual grades with improvement from one's base.

4. The "free ride" myth, which suggests that lazy students will be carried by harder-working students. Cooperative learning should be designed so that all are accountable for their efforts. For the technique to be effective, there must be established mechanisms for the group to monitor the participation of all its members.

Are all these positions myths?

CONFLICT MANAGEMENT

Encountering conflict seems to be an inevitable aspect of social situations. Managing conflict so that it serves a constructive purpose is an important skill that contributes to prosocial behavior. Training programs have begun in a number of places in recent years to aid people to manage conflict, hence reducing stress and enhancing cooperation.

The training programs that have been initiated are considerably different in their orientations, and little systematic research on their relative effectiveness has been completed. Deutsch (1993), however, has attempted to identify their common elements. As a general focus, most programs view conflict as a problem to be solved by the parties affected. Positive resolution results from everyone acting cooperatively to solve the problem, while negative resolutions are similar to competitive struggles in which one side wins while the other(s) loses (Deutsch, 1973). Attitudes and skills that contribute to cooperative problem solving are, therefore, the content that all agree should be taught. Deutsch (1993) has abstracted 13 specific beliefs or skills that individuals need to be able to resolve conflicts in a positive fashion. These beliefs, which are listed below, appear to be the goals of most programs, whether directed toward children or adults.

Beliefs
1. *Know what type of conflict you are involved in:* zero-sum (for every winner there is a loser), mixed (both can win, both can lose, or either can win or lose), or cooperative (both can win or both can lose only).
2. *Become aware of the causes and consequences of violence.* Learn what makes you angry and the healthy and unhealthy ways you use to express anger.
3. *Face conflict rather than avoid it.* Learn the typical strategies you use to avoid conflict and the negative consequences that occur when you succeed.

4. *Respect yourself and your interests, and respect others and their interests.*
5. *Avoid ethnocentrism; understand the reality of cultural difference.* Expect cultural misunderstandings and use them as opportunities to learn rather than as a basis of argument.
6. *Distinguish between* "interests" *and* "positions." Positions may be opposed, but interests may not be.
7. *Explore your interests and those of the other to identify common interests.*
8. *Define the conflicting interests between yourself and the other as a problem to be solved mutually.*
9. *Listen attentively and speak to be understood when communicating.* The feeling of being understood facilitates constructive resolution.
10. *Be alert to natural tendencies of bias, misperception, misjudgments, and stereotyped thinking.*
11. *Develop skills for dealing with those who are more powerful or have greater authority.* Knowing when you have a choice to break off the relationship and when you must stand your ground is important.
12. *Know yourself and how you typically respond in conflict situations of different sorts.*
13. *Throughout conflict, remain a moral person who is caring and just and considers the other as entitled to care and justice.*

Wouldn't it be a peaceful world if everyone followed the principles given above? Unfortunately, most of us have learned to respond to conflict as a threat rather than as a problem that often can be resolved. If we are going to educate others in these principles, we shall need to value and practice as many of them as possible. Assuming that we possess those beliefs ourselves, how do we aid students to acquire them? A number of activities designed to provide conflict management skills have been attempted in various programs around the country.

Conflict management provides alternative to responding with anger

Johnson and Johnson (1992) recommend that teachers stimulate *constructive controversy* in the classroom by dividing students into groups of four, further divided into pairs who are assigned positions of controversial topics to discuss. Each group is required to reach a consensus on the issue and complete a report on which all members are evaluated. After each pair has presented its initial position, open discussion takes place. Then pairs present the opposing pairs' position in a reversal of perspective. In the last phase of the activity, advocacy of assigned positions is abandoned and the group seeks to reach a consensus based on the evidence. Groups are encouraged to follow many rules in their deliberations, such as being critical of ideas, not people; listening to others' ideas even if one doesn't agree; and bringing out ideas and facts supporting both sides before developing a sensible position. After the groups have submitted their reports, the entire class discusses the issues and the processes used to arrive at the final position. Johnson and Johnson (1992) believe this approach contributes to the development of perspective taking, critical thinking, and other skills involved in constructive conflict management.

Principles can also be introduced through a series of written exercises. Scenarios describing various conflicts are presented in notebooks. One example features two students fighting because they have called each other names. Students are asked to complete a table indicating the possible consequences of fighting and whether they think a particular consequence is good or bad. After filling in the table, students are asked to give alternatives to fighting that the two students might consider. They then are asked to rewrite the scenario in a way that does not end in a fight. Lickona (1991b) reports that teachers have observed a decline in the number of students fighting in schools that used this program, as well as an improvement in students' ability to discuss alternatives and see the viewpoint of someone else.

Another approach is to directly train elementary school children to be "conflict managers" who work in pairs to resolve disputes without the help of adult authorities. Students selected are representative of the student body and receive training in communication skills, dealing with emotion, brainstorming solutions, and practicing teamwork. After training they monitor the playground and halls for disputes (monitors wear a badge to be recognized) and intervening when necessary. Anecdotal reports of school officials indicate that the conflict managers are of major help in managing and diminishing disputes, and the monitors themselves improve in self-esteem and in communication skills (Lickona, 1991b).

The positive reports from these preliminary studies suggest an effective set of strategies for advancing this type of prosocial behavior in children. A sequence of providing initial training in conflict management principles, followed by an opportunity to reflect on how the principles apply to real situations, then placing participants in situations that allow them to exercise responsibility for resolving conflicts appears to be a successful pattern of intervention. Such approaches merit further consideration and more extensive implementation and evaluation.

> Discussion of principles must be followed by opportunities to apply them

SUMMARY

Affective learning is an important component of education. Affective outcomes arise from feelings or emotions, but cognitive and behavioral components are required for their complete expression. The taxonomy of the affective domain attempts to classify affective learning into five different phases, moving from the externally determined receiving and responding levels to the more internal levels of valuing, organization, and characterization. Most instructional efforts have their impact at the first three levels of the hierarchy.

Affective outcomes can be categorized into two types—prosocial behavior and interests. Prosocial behavior benefits other people and is guided by values and principles of good conduct. It is also a product of competing values and the pressures of group standards. Three major explanations of how prosocial behavior is learned have emerged: identification, social learning, and cognitive development. The identification position holds that prosocial behaviors are acquired through imitation of others, particularly parents. Social learning explanations emphasize the learner's observation of the behavior of models and the application of self-regulatory capabilities to the construction of personal behavior. Generalization of prosocial behavior to other situations is determined in part by such situational differences as ambiguity of the stimulus and personal cost.

On the cognitive development view, prosocial values are thought to be interpreted according to a developmental sequence as cognitive organization is restructured. The level of reasoning of the individual determines moral judgment in conflict situations. A model describing the development of moral judgment is Kohlberg's delineation of preconventional, conventional, and postconventional morality. Preconventional judgments are characterized by personal interest and benefit; conventional thought reflects society's interests; and postconventional judgments are based on universal principles of justice and fairness. Research has indicated that moral judgment changes over time, is moderately related to cognitive development, predicts prosocial behavior in a variety of settings, and can be affected by environmental interventions. Discussions of moral dilemmas in which arguments are slightly ahead of the learner's stage are most likely to provoke cognitive conflict and eventual development in moral judgment.

Instruction designed to foster prosocial behavior has taken three forms: character education, moral education, and an integrated view combining the first two. Character education stresses direct instruction and modeling of desired traits, with curricular materials selected to illustrate them. Moral education employs discussions of moral dilemmas or experiences such as restructuring the class or school to reflect a just community. Teachers utilize in-depth questioning strategies to facilitate discussion of moral dilemmas and role-playing exercises to aid in student acquisition of perspective taking. Integrated views believe that both doing what is right and knowing what is right should be addressed in educational programs and that prosocial values should be expanded to include a morality of care as well as justice. Lickona's program contains three components: moral knowing, moral feeling, and moral action. Activities designed to build a moral community, practice cooperation, encourage moral reflection, and allow students to participate in decision making compose Lickona's program.

Two other approaches that are effective in fostering prosocial behaviors are cooperative learning and conflict management. A number of cooperative learning activities such as jigsaw, STAD, TGT, and CIRC have been found not only to advance cognitive skills but to aid in students' acceptance of others and assumption of responsibility. Conflict management techniques view conflict as a problem situation shared by all parties, which requires mutual respect and analysis of the problem. Group discussion of controversial topics, written exercises, and actual experience in managing conflict are some useful strategies.

A concept map for this chapter appears on page 327.

EXERCISES

1. The following story has been used with elementary school children to generate interest in discussing how our prejudices and expectations can hurt others. After reading it, write down three questions you would ask if you had read this story to fourth-graders and wanted to start a discussion about it. For each question, think of a possible answer students might give and plan a follow-up question.

   Vernon had a new box of pencils, each bearing the name and logo of a professional football team, which he kept in his desk. One day he noticed that his Chicago Bears pencil was missing. While looking for his pencil, he saw Ben using one just like it. Vernon knew that Ben's family didn't have much money and assumed that Ben would

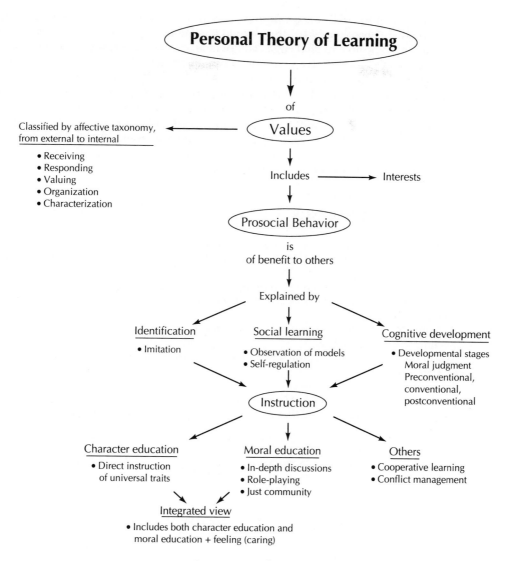

Personal Theory of Learning

of

Values

Classified by affective taxonomy, from external to internal

- Receiving
- Responding
- Valuing
- Organization
- Characterization

Includes → Interests

Prosocial Behavior

is
of benefit to others

Explained by

Identification
- Imitation

Social learning
- Observation of models
- Self-regulation

Cognitive development
- Developmental stages
  Moral judgment
  Preconventional,
  conventional,
  postconventional

Instruction

Character education
- Direct instruction
  of universal traits

Moral education
- In-depth discussions
- Role-playing
- Just community

Others
- Cooperative learning
- Conflict management

Integrated view
- Includes both character education and
  moral education + feeling (caring)

Concept Map for Chapter 9

not have his own set of football pencils. On the way to the lunchroom, Vernon knocked Ben down and threatened him: "If you ever take my pencils again, you'll be sorry."

Later that day, Vernon complained to the teacher that Ben had taken his pencil. The teacher had Ben open his desk. Inside was a complete box of pencils with Ben's name on it; it was just like Vernon's.

2. Identify a moral dilemma faced by a real or imaginary character in a content area of interest to you. Examples are Truman's decision to use the atomic bomb, Huckleberry Finn's decision to get Jim out of jail, and Galileo's confrontation with the Roman Catholic Church over the movement of the earth around the

sun. Then select three or four people of different ages, backgrounds, gender, and so on and ask them what they would have done in the place of the chosen character. To be able to challenge each person's answer, be ready with questions that highlight an alternative position. What differences do you find in individual responses? Are people certain of what they would do, or do they have reservations?

3. Think of a situation in which you and others were confronted with apparently unfair rules. Was there a conflict? What steps were taken to resolve it? Were principles of positive conflict resolution invoked and followed, or was the conflict resolved through a more negative method? How could the situation have been resolved more amicably? Were the rules changed as a result of the disagreement or did your perception of them change?

SUGGESTED READINGS

Deutsch, M. (1993). Educating for a peaceful world. *American Psychologist, 48*(5), 510–517.

Hersh, R. M., Miller, J. P., & Fielding, G. D. (1980). *Models of moral education.* White Plains, NY: Longman.

Kohlberg, L. (1985). A just community approach to moral education in theory and practice. In M. W. Berkowitz & F. Oser (Eds.), *Moral education: Theory and application.* Hillsdale, NJ: Erlbaum.

Lickona, T. (1991). *Educating for character: How our schools can teach respect and responsibility.* New York: Bantam.

Nucci, L. (Ed.). (1989). *Moral development and character education.* Berkeley, CA: McCutchan.

Ryan, K. (1989). In defense of character education. In L. Nucci (Ed.), *Moral development and character education* (pp. 3–18). Berkeley, CA: McCutchan.

Staub, E. (1979). *Positive social behavior and morality. Vol. Two.* New York: Academic Press.

chapter 10

Learning Strategies and Problem Solving

CHAPTER OUTLINE

CHAPTER OBJECTIVES

1. Explain the components of metacognition.
2. Differentiate among the eight types of learning strategy.

3. Create an example for each of the eight learning strategies.
4. Discuss basic guidelines for the teaching of learning strategies.
5. Define problem solving and explain why clarity in both givens and goals of problems is critical.
6. Describe the problem-solving processes of representation, search, and solution.
7. Explain restrictions on problem representation that must be overcome.
8. Distinguish between algorithms and heuristics and describe common heuristic search strategies.
9. Summarize the major differences between novices and experts in problem solving.
10. Describe how you would promote student problem solving in a particular area of academic interest.

Sam looked at the homework assignment and the questions Mr. Hernandez had provided. He was supposed to read the chapter "The Blue and the Gray" and answer the following questions: 1. What factors led to the secession from the Union by the southern states? 2. Was President Lincoln willing to compromise on the issue of slavery? State your reasons for your position. 3. Why did the South feel confident of victory? 4. What might the southern states have done before seceding to improve their chances of eventual victory?

"Boy, these are going to be hard to answer. Usually, Mr. Hernandez asks us questions like what were the dates of the Civil War. These are different," thought Sam. "I guess I could look at the headings in the chapter to see if they relate to these questions. If that doesn't work I could just take notes as I read and see if I can figure out the answers from my notes. Maybe I could put stick-ems on the places in the text that seem to relate to the questions, then go back to those pages after I finish reading. Hmm . . . what else could I do?"

Kelly's heart sank as she read the physics problem: "If a runaway truck weighing 12,000 lb is going 69 miles per hour and a Ford Escort weighing 4,000 lb is sitting in its path, how far will the truck push the Escort back after impact?" "Oh, oh, I'd rather figure out how much the insurance claim is going to be for the owner of the Escort," she thought. "How am I going to do this? I know there's some formula you have to use, but I can't remember it. It's not just the truck's weight times the speed—I have to include the Escort's weight somehow. How do you do that? . . . Oh, dear!"

These two anecdotes illustrate two kinds of thinking used by people as they attempt to perform various tasks. Sam is considering *learning strategies* he might use to complete his homework assignment. Kelly, faced with a difficult content area question, is struggling to perform *problem solving*. In this chapter, we examine the factors that influence the development and use of learning strategies and the solving of academic problems. We also address what teachers and others can do to enhance effective use of learning strategies and problem-solving skills.

METACOGNITIVE PREREQUISITES

The active thinking demonstrated by Sam and Kelly exemplifies *metacognition,* or the self-monitoring process that occurs in working memory as information is analyzed prior to further action. The ability and willingness to engage in metacognitive activity is crucial to the utilization of learning strategies and problem-solving skills. We encountered metacognitive processes in Chapter 5 when we reviewed Bandura's concepts of self-reflection and self-judgment and in Chapter 6 in our analysis of the cognitive information-processing model. Our purpose here is to define and examine the concept more closely, so that we may understand how it influences effective learning and problem solving.

Metacognition is thinking about thinking

Metacognition consists of awareness not only of *what* to do to perform a task effectively, but *when* and *how* various cognitive processes can be employed so that successful learning occurs. We thus possess (1) declarative knowledge of the existence of our cognitive processes and (2) the ability to regulate their use or procedural knowledge. Once acquired, knowledge about our cognitive processes remains relatively stable and can be stated overtly ("I make up a word out of the first letters of each term I'm trying to remember"), although our statement of what we do is not always entirely accurate. Declarative knowledge takes time to develop, with older learners demonstrating more awareness of the processes they employ (Flavell, 1979). Our procedural knowledge of metacognition is unstable even in adulthood, however. For instance, the author is constantly forgetting things to buy at the grocery store, despite awareness of all sorts of strategies that might be used to aid memory. Moreover, people engage in many activities in which metacognition is activated without awareness or ability to verbalize the rule being followed. For example, have you ever caught yourself listening more intently to one speaker than another during a discussion, or reading a particular section of a difficult text more carefully? Other examples of metacognitive regulation include planning what to do next, allocating time and effort, checking the outcome of mental activity, monitoring the effectiveness of attempted actions and testing, revising and evaluating strategies for learning (A. L. Brown, 1981).

Other examples of metacognition?

procedure knowledge - ability to regulate cognitive processes

Flavell (1971) identified two components of metacognition—*metacomprehension* and *metamemory.* Metacomprehension refers to knowledge about and regulation of our understanding, while metamemory refers to memory knowledge and regulation. Thinking about how we come to know a certain procedure, such as how to operate a computer, illustrates metacomprehension, while realizing that we need to apply a technique in memorizing a long list of facts exemplifies metamemory.

How do we acquire metacognition? Flavell (1979) believes it is a product of four sources: (1) knowledge of our own or others' success on cognitive tasks, such as noticing that you can balance your checkbook better than your husband, (2) experiences that accompany attempts at metacognition, such as feeling frustrated when you can't understand an instructor's comments, (3) analysis of the goals and objectives of a cognitive task, and (4) analysis of the actions or strategies employed in performing those tasks. Metacognition seems to increase in scope and accuracy the more we attempt to employ it. For example, in a study of metamemory by Andreasen and Waters (1989), first- and fourth-graders were asked before and after a memory task how they remembered pictures of common objects such as a shirt or an apple. Only the fourth-graders modified their behavior during the task as a result of pretask questioning, indicating their

ways acquire metacognition

induced awareness of procedural knowledge. First-graders reported using some sort of grouping in attempting to recall the pictures but did not coordinate what they first said about grouping in memory to what they subsequently did. The study indicated that there is a developmental pattern to the acquisition of metamemory. It begins with knowledge of strategies and ends with intentional planning of how to use them to remember. Apparently children of early elementary school age do not spontaneously plan a metacognitive approach, but they can profit from prompts provided by others.

Awareness and regulation of metacognitive processes continue to develop throughout the school years, but these forms of thought are not consistent even among older students and adults (Glenberg & Epstein, 1987; Zabrucky & Ratner, 1986). Have you ever listened carefully to someone discuss a complex topic only to realize later that you hadn't understood a word that was said? Lack of prior knowledge of the subject may of course account for some of your confusion. In many cases, however, the difficulty may be more attributable to inability to monitor the ongoing presentation, with the result that clarification cannot be requested at an appropriate time. The author experiences this frustrating condition whenever an automobile mechanic explains why a gasket has to be replaced and why it will cost only $300. Aiding students and adults to utilize metacognitive processes (e.g., detecting failures to understand, picking the right time to ask useful questions) is an important instructional goal.

LEARNING STRATEGIES

Numerous learning strategies have been described as researchers have studied metacognitive processes. Weinstein and Mayer (1986) have organized student strategies into eight categories. Each category includes procedures designed to influence certain aspects of the encoding process so that one or more learning outcome can be attained. As we discussed in Chapter 6, encoding involves the formation of connections between new information and existing schemas so that the material can be integrated into long-term memory. Remember that encoding includes elaboration (in which details are added to the content), organization (in which the material is rearranged into a single unit), and imagery (in which verbal content is transformed to a visual representation). Table 10.1 summarizes the categories of learning strategies and provides examples of how they are employed in the acquisition of specific learning content.

All these strategies can be adapted to student learning of various content areas and grade levels. In many cases, educators and researchers have combined instruction in several of these categories into a learning strategy training program. Next we review some studies of attempts to aid students to adopt learning strategies according to these eight categories.

Basic Rehearsal Strategies

Procedures one follows to attend to and memorize units and lists of items are called basic rehearsal strategies (Weinstein & Mayer, 1986). They often entail repeating material over and over to oneself to increase familiarity, as in rehearsing a new telephone number or someone's name. While basic rehearsal is generally not as efficient in aid-

TABLE 10.1. Categories of learning strategies and related subject matter content examples

Category	Example
1. *Basic rehearsal strategies:* repeating items in an ordered list	Saying the names of the Middle Atlantic States over and over again to yourself.
2. *Complex rehearsal strategies:* identifying and recording main ideas presented in class or in text	Underlining and noting on the side of the text page the main ideas in a chapter on economic theory.
3. *Basic elaboration strategies:* forming mental images of objects or associations to be recalled	Visualizing a wheatfield in the middle of a map of Kansas or an automobile in Michigan to remember states and their major products.
4. *Complex elaboration strategies:* summarizing or rephrasing in your own words how new ideas relate to existing knowledge	Forming the analogy of a three-pronged pitchfork to link the functions of the three branches of the federal government.
5. *Basic organizational strategies:* regrouping events or items to form a new sequence	Revising your notes to form a chronological listing of events that led to the Civil War.
6. *Complex organizational strategies:* reorganizing material to form a hierarchy or system	Creating a conceptual model or diagram to represent an ecological food chain.
7. *Comprehension-monitoring strategies:* checking for failure to understand what is being heard or read	Using questions provided at the beginning of a chapter on psychology to guide your reading.
8. *Affective strategies:* placing oneself in a relaxed, alert or motivated state	Employing internal attributions, such as "I can do it, it just takes time," when beginning to respond to a difficult exam.

Which types of strategy do you employ?

ing recall as more elaborate strategies, it can be useful, particularly for young children or elderly learners, and it requires minimal effort.

Basic rehearsal seems to require the development of metamemory awareness. Children do not spontaneously rehearse until approximately ten years of age, although they may be observed moving their lips while learning at age five (Kenney, Cannizzo, & Flavell, 1967). Flavell and Wellman (1977) found that training to use rehearsal was limited to immediate recall for first-graders. On later recall tasks the children failed to transfer the rehearsal strategy they had learned. Although rehearsal strategies seem to be available to young children, they seldom apply such tricks spontaneously to later tasks.

Rehearsal strategy frequently used

Learners must differentially *select* items to be rehearsed and *concentrate* on their acquisition (Dansereau, 1978). Selection is important because we cannot rehearse every set of stimuli we encounter, particularly under conditions in which information is being presented rapidly, such as during a lecture or while trying to discern a telephone number during a television spot advertisement. For this strategy to be effective, we must select only the most important groups of items under such conditions. Concentration allows us to resist distractions and focus exclusively on the intended set of items. Attempts to improve concentration typically involve teaching students to talk to themselves in a calm, positive manner to reduce anxiety, as in saying "If I just repeat the doctor's directions over to myself, I'll be okay" (Patterson & Mischel,

1975). Operant techniques to direct attention to critical items have also been employed to enhance rehearsal and recall (Alabiso, 1975).

Complex Rehearsal Strategies

Rehearsal strategies for more complex material such as textbook prose involve repetition, copying, and underlining important points. The learner is actively attempting to pay attention to the important parts of the material and transfer them into working memory. Since the content is meaningful and requires a connection to existing schema if it is to be stored in long-term memory, repetition or merely underlining main ideas without deeper processing may not be adequate to ensure later recall or understanding. In a study by Mayer and Cook (1980), students who were instructed to repeat the words they heard while listening to a passage on how radar works remembered less of the conceptual information and performed more poorly on applied problem-solving tasks related to the radar information than did students who were instructed just to listen to the passage. Apparently, the act of repeating the words heard prevented the construction of meaningful connections between ideas within the passage and existing schema. Students who just listened, however, were able to consider the meaning and implications of the content.

Have you ever underlined or highlighted key ideas in a text, only to find to your dismay, upon rereading the material later, that you have no recollection of having read it before? The author certainly has and has regretted it at 2 A.M. when studying for a history quiz. Snowman (1986) believes that to be effective, underlining must be directed toward specific objectives, perhaps suggested by the instructor. Knowledge of the criterion to be used in later assessment, such as knowing that a multiple-choice test stressing names and dates will follow, also enhances the value of underlining (Kulhavy, Dyer, & Silver, 1975). If one is left to guess at what is important, it is more likely that irrelevant facts or ideas will be underlined. The use of bold print or underlined terms in text and the accentuation of words during lectures are ways of directing attention toward the content students should rehearse.

Underlining based on knowledge of objectives

Basic Elaboration Strategies

Elaboration strategies are constructed by thinking of elements that can be added to material, thereby making the new arrangement more complete or more structured. Elaborated material is believed to be more amenable to being connected to existing schemas (Dansereau, 1978). Many elaboration strategies for the learning of basic associations and facts have been developed, including the various mnemonic devices described in the section on Teaching for Encoding in Chapter 6. Do you remember the techniques discussed then, such as *first-letter mnemonics, loci,* and *pegword*? Instructions to use mnemonic devices, accompanied by examples, have generally been found to enhance learning and retention of related content more than repetition strategies (Pressley, Symons, Snyder, & Cariglia-Bull, 1989; Rohwer, Raines, Eoff, & Wagner, 1977).

Elaboration strategies require additional details

An important component of many elaboration strategies is their utilization of visual *imagery* as well as verbal elaboration, so that the to-be-remembered content is a vital part of the new structure. The *keyword* technique is a good example of combining verbal and visual elaboration to learn new factual content such as vocabulary or basic definitions (Atkinson & Raugh, 1975; Pressley, Levin, & Delaney, 1982). In a number of studies, Pressley, Levin, and their colleagues have found keyword to be more effective than alternative methods of teaching vocabulary, such as suggesting context cues in paragraphs to help identify the new word (Pressley and Associates, 1990). Pressley, Levin, and McDaniel (1987) have developed a specific procedure for using keyword to teach important new vocabulary words. Figure 10.1 describes the steps they employ in implementing the keyword strategy in teaching a vocabulary word from an economics lesson.

Another elaboration strategy for the learning of facts from text is *elaborative interrogation.* This technique consists of inserting "*why*" *questions* after simple descriptive passages. For example, the sentence "The Western spotted skunk lives in a hole in the ground" is followed by the question "Why would that animal do that?" Wood, Pressley, and Winne (1990) found that the insertion of such questions enhanced long-term recall more effectively for middle school students than did providing the answer itself (as in adding the phrase "to protect its family" to the critical sentence). They explain such a surprising result thus:

> When children are presented with unembellished facts to learn, they must not be thinking through the relationships specified in those facts to the degree that students do when they are attempting to answer why questions; they must not be attempting to determine why the factual relation holds . . . they are not spontaneously making complete use of their knowledge base to understand the material. (p. 747)

The "why" questions apparently serve to require the reader to pause and add personal elaborations to what is being read, thus serving as a cue to later recall of the basic facts. Students who pause to ask "why" questions of themselves as they read are engaging in the same activity.

Value of stopping to ask "why" questions

FIGURE 10.1   Steps of the keyword method

SOURCE: M. Pressley and Associates, *Cognitive strategy instruction that really improves children's academic performance* (Cambridge, MA: Brookline Books, 1990).

---

1. Select an unfamiliar word.

At the fourth grade level, a vocabulary term such as "surplus" is an important word students should know in their study of economics.

↓

2. Identify a familiar English word that not only is similar to the unfamiliar word acoustically but is easily visualizable.

"Syrup" meets these criteria and serves as the keyword for surplus.

↓

3. Form a visual link between the keyword and the meaning of the new one.

The student is instructed to visualize the two words interacting in some way, as in a girl pouring a lot of syrup on pancakes with an abundant supply of syrup available behind her. The image thus clarifies the meaning, as well as relating it to the keyword.

Keyword requires visualization

Complex Elaboration Strategies

Three types
1. summarize + paraphrasing
2. note taking
3. reasoning by analogy

Complex elaboration strategies require new information be combined with prior knowledge to obtain more meaningful understanding. These strategies may involve considerable transformation of the to-be-learned content. There are three types of complex elaboration strategy that relate to improved learning and recall: (1) *summarizing and paraphrasing,* (2) *note taking,* and (3) *reasoning by analogy.*

Summarizing and Paraphrasing. Few people can recall all they hear or read in one session. Most of us are more likely to abstract the gist or macrostructure of the content presented (Kintsch & van Dijk, 1978). Evidence suggests that summarizing can be an effective strategy if students consciously attempt to paraphrase what they have read or heard, understand the criterion that is to be used to assess their recall, and know the best way to construct summaries from particular types of information (Bretzing & Kulhavy, 1979). A. L. Brown and Day (1983) have identified six rules to be followed when summarizing from text:

summarizing
from text
rules

1. Delete trivial information.
2. Delete redundant information.
3. Substitute superordinate terms for lists of terms ("Georgia products" for all the goods produced in Georgia).
4. Integrate a series of events with a superordinate action term ("There are four major Georgia products.").
5. Select a topic sentence.
6. Invent a topic sentence if there is none.

Several studies have examined the effects of training students to summarize using these or related rules. Beach and Steenwyk (1984), who taught sixth-graders to summarize single paragraphs, reported improvement on a standardized test of reading comprehension. Taylor and Beach (1984) taught seventh-graders to apply summarization rules to long passages about social studies. Students were first instructed to summarize each subsection by constructing thesis or main idea statements; then they were asked to integrate their statements to produce a hierarchical summary of the entire passage. Summaries were linked to better recall of the passage content. Rinehart, Stahl, and Erickson (1986) applied similar techniques to train elementary school children, stressing how readers should "talk through" to themselves, noting the most important information and deciding what information is redundant and can be eliminated. Recall of main ideas was enhanced for students receiving this training.

Summarization skills can be taught

Several components of instruction appear to be critical in attempting to train students to employ summarization strategies based on these studies. First, basic summarization rules must be presented and explained. The teacher as well as students should talk through and illustrate each rule for best results. Materials that have already been summarized in a scripted form should be employed. Students should first practice on single paragraphs, then move to summaries of more extensive passages. Feedback and discussion involving both the teacher and peers should accompany initial attempts. Finally, special techniques, such as using spatial maps to represent summary statements, should be presented after students have grasped the general purpose and procedures of summarizing.

Note Taking.   Note taking utilizes some of the same principles as summarizing but attempts to capture more of the content to be learned than just the main idea. Note-taking strategies are organizational as well as elaborative, so we deal with them later in this section as well. As an elaboration strategy, the main function of note taking is to encode incoming information more efficiently by adding structural details stored in long-term memory.

> Note taking provides organization and elaboration

As a general rule, if the criterion to be used in assessment is known, note taking improves recall of material compared to not taking notes or simply rereading. Without knowing what is important and how learning will be assessed, students will find no advantage in note taking (Snowman, 1986). For example, if you know you are to take an exam assessing recall of the names of the early Western explorers, recording individual's names and their accomplishments as you read will improve your performance on the test. Without such advance information, however, you are likely to take notes on other details, some of which will be irrelevant to the criterion task. In effect, you will have elaborated on information that was not needed.

Student note taking is often inaccurate or simplistic. Examination of student notes often reveals a simple paraphrased listing of information rather than a more conceptual integration of ideas (Kiewra & Fletcher, 1984). If the content to be learned is more abstract, or if the learning criterion requires higher levels of thought, then listing or paraphrasing may not be an adequate note-taking procedure.

> *Note taking has to be more than listing or paraphrasing*

Two options appear to be available to overcome these problems in students' notes. First, the instructor can supply notes, which capture more accurately the content to be read or covered directly in lecture. This has been a frequent practice for some time. I recall with shame having offered large sums to fellow college students for such notes after losing mine just prior to an exam, in the hope that the instructor's notes would somehow make up for my failure to take notes of my own. Unfortunately, research indicates that instructor-supplied notes, although sometimes helpful on later exams, may actually interfere with short-term recall. If notes are available, students may be tempted to stop encoding incoming lecture information on the belief that the instructor's notes are all they need. Reviewing both personal notes and instructor-supplied notes produces the highest level of achievement, as one serves as to complement the other (Kiewra, 1985). If instructors are to supply notes, these materials should be made available only after students have had an opportunity to form their own.

> Combination of own and instructor's notes is best

Another option is to instruct students in note-taking strategies. For example, Carrier and Titus (1981) trained high school students to distinguish between superordinate and subordinate information, to abbreviate words, to paraphrase, and to use outlines. After observation and practice in using this note-taking format, trained students outperformed those who took notes following their own style.

Reasoning by Analogy.   Thinking of an original analogy or utilizing one provided by an instructor to represent new information is another type of elaboration strategy. We discussed analogies in Chapter 6 as ways of aiding encoding in which relationships known to exist in similar content are extended to new material. Analogies have proven useful in clarifying a variety of concepts in different content areas (Royer, 1986).

Forming an analogy requires prior knowledge that can be linked to the new information. While great insight often leads to useful analogies between widely diverse areas as in the famous "DNA–Tinkertoy" example, the knowledge base of most students will not permit them to easily generate their own. Others, when provided an analogy, will be unable to use the comparison or will transfer all the information they perceive as important, both the relevant and irrelevant (Zook & DiVesta, 1991). For this reason, analogy strategies are best employed in areas of instruction containing easily observed, structural similarities between new and old material. Students who are having difficulty with new content can more readily see the analogical relationship if linkage is more obvious. One subject matter area in which similarity is high is spelling. Englert, Hiebert, and Stewart (1985) found that children with mild learning disabilities who were taught to use analogy strategies were able to increase the number of words they correctly spelled. Analogies were formed using a "rhyming rule" in which children learned that when two words rhyme, the last parts of the words are often spelled the same. After practice in identifying rhyming words and noting the letters the two words shared, students were also taught to use an imagery strategy to visualize each new word. The authors believe that word analysis and classification activities such as identifying common letters and rhyming components will aid children to generate and spell correctly new words according to orthographic patterns of those they know.

Hayes (1981) advocates a similar *context* strategy in learning the meaning of new vocabulary. Many English words have Latin or Greek roots, which if known can be used to define new words containing the same root; knowing that *spectare* means "to look at," for example, tips one off to the meanings of words such as "spectacle," "spectator," "retrospect," "introspect," and "circumspect." As Hayes observes, one does not have to be a Latin scholar to note these similarities; all that is needed is a good English dictionary. When using a similar strategy in learning second-language vocabulary, one can guess the meaning of words like "café" and "vin" by noticing their relations to the English words "coffee" and "vine."

Basic Organizational Strategies

Creating lists is a form of organization

Basic organizational strategies involve reorganizing lists of items to recall into a new and often larger framework. A *clustering* strategy in which one groups items to be purchased at a grocery store into produce (potatoes, oranges, celery), dairy products (cheese, milk, eggs), and staples (tomato sauce, flour, candy bars?), to be able to recall them more easily, is a practical example. Learning and recall are likely to be most efficient when items are organized into meaningful categories or clusters, rather than relying on serial order. Teachers can arrange lists in various ways and point this truism out to students or encourage them to form their own categories where possible (Bower, Clark, Lesgold, & Winzerz, 1969). For example, in recalling American history dates, students can separate dates of battles or wars (1779, 1812, 1861, 1914, etc.) from dates of treaties (1783, 1814, 1865, 1918).

In the area of reading, one basic organizational strategy is that of forming *lists*. A series of reports (Kirsch & Mosenthal, 1989a, 1989b, 1990a, 1990b; Mosenthal &

Kirsch, 1989a, 1989b, 1990a, 1990b) describes the formation of lists to represent information found in a variety of *documents*. Documents include such materials as forms, schedules, indices, tables, charts, graphs, labels, TV listings, bills, box scores, and Top Ten rankings. As you might guess, the average person spends more time daily reading documents than any other reading material (Guthrie, Seifert, & Kirsch, 1986). Being able to organize the information presented in documents is therefore a critical goal of reading literacy.

Mosenthal and Kirsch (1989a) believe that if students can learn to identify the structures contained in various documents, they will more easily understand and recall the inherent information and will be able to deduce relevant implications. Most documents consist of information organized by some type of matrix format, such as rows and columns, which these authors call a list. Simple lists are comparable to a list of things to do at the office, while combined lists are similar to tables with two dimensions. Reading becomes more complex when we must interpret documents that contain *intersecting lists* (Mosenthal & Kirsch, 1989b), such as TV listings that give the name of a show, its time, channel, and other information that might be relevant. A telephone rate schedule listing discounts for different days and times is another example. *Nested lists,* such as research summary tables (Kirsch & Mosenthal, 1990a) and some charts and graphs (Mosenthal & Kirsch, 1990b), are even more complex, and several variables containing subdivisions are incorporated in each variable.

> What lists do you read regularly?

The authors suggest that instruction be devoted to developing strategies for reading documents. An initial phase is determining the basic document sentence (e.g., "Ice cream flavors are being ranked" or "Magazines have a particular circulation") for combined lists. Document sentences summarize the main idea that is being expressed in the document. Intersecting and nested lists as well as charts and graphs may contain several document sentences. Practice in collecting information, summarizing lists of data with a title or label, ordering information to form a list according to some hierarchy, noting redundancy in existing lists, analyzing existing documents containing nested lists to find more basic document sentences, and analyzing charts or graphs to find lists of different kinds within them are recommended activities that will aid students to acquire strategies for interpreting most forms of documents.

Complex Organizational Strategies

Attempting to reorganize sets of ideas to form a hierarchical system requires more complex strategies. Students who construct their own organizational system improve their learning efficiency. Chan, Burtis, Scardamalia, and Bereiter (1992) found that as elementary grade students moved from simple retelling of information they heard about dinosaurs to restating it in their own words, and then to posing and solving problems with the information, their recall and expression of the main ideas in the material improved. The organizational strategies used by students enabled them to activate prior ideas about dinosaurs, suggesting that strategic knowledge contributes to the application of domain-specific knowledge (Perkins & Solomon, 1989).

This strategy helps to tell story in own words.

One widely accepted strategy of this type is that of *concept mapping.* A concept map has been defined as a "schematic device for representing a set of concept meanings embedded in a framework of propositions" (Novak & Gowin, 1984, p. 15). A good concept map shows how concepts are represented hierarchically. Recall from the discussion of meaningful learning in Chapter 6 that Ausubel (1963) proposed that our cognitive structure is hierarchically arranged, with superordinate concepts encompassing more subordinate concepts. New concept meanings are acquired through assimilation into existing frameworks.

Concept maps were originally developed by Novak (1977, 1979) as visual displays of the organized set of concepts an individual possesses. Symington and Novak (1982) observed that with practice, students in the elementary grades were capable of developing organized concept maps, which they could explain intelligently to others. In a longitudinal study of students' progress from second to twelfth grade, concept maps were found to accurately describe changes in understanding of science concepts (Novak & Musonda, 1991).

The main construction rule is that superordinate concepts at the top are connected by lines to subordinate concepts below. All the lines connecting concepts must be accompanied by linking words, to permit each branch of the map to be read from the top down. Broken lines can be used to link different branches, and examples of the concept are found at the end of each branch. Students typically take between 8 and 10 weeks of practice to construct easily understood maps (Wandersee, 1990), but once learned, the strategy is applied readily to a wide variety of content areas. A concept map accompanies each chapter in this text. Figure 10.2 is an example of a concept map developed by second-grader Amy, who has attempted to map her understanding of molecules.

Amy may not have captured all the dimensions of molecules accurately, but she does recognize that substances of different kinds are composed of them and is beginning to understand their many properties. Novak and Musonda found in examining concept maps at the eighth- and twelfth-grade levels that basic misconceptions such as the squeezability of the air, water, and solid molecules became more accurate. They recommend that concept maps be taught to students not only as ways of aiding

This book has concept map for each chapter

FIGURE 10.2 Concept map of the science concept "molecule" by Amy, a second-grader

SOURCE: J. D. Novak and D. Musonda, A twelve-year longitudinal study of science concept learning. *American Educational Research Journal, 28*(1), 117–153 (1991). Copyright 1991 by the American Educational Research Association. Adapted by permission of the publisher.

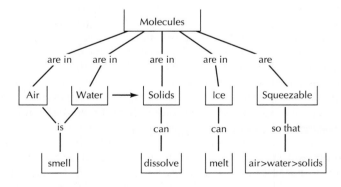

their understanding of concepts but as a means to identifying the misconceptions that hinder further comprehension of the content area.

Other complex organizational strategies require that the learner seek relations in the material being read or heard, such as locating categories, hierarchies, networks, and systems. Relations can be identified by analyzing text structure into basic components. For example, Bartlett (1978) described the *rhetorical structure* of text, or how a writer organizes information to achieve a particular purpose. Four common rhetorical structures are:

Description—to describe an event

Covariance—to indicate a causal relationship between two events

Problem solution—stating a problem and providing a solution

Favored view versus opposite view—relating alternative positions

[handwritten note: rhetorical structures of text]

Bartlett trained ninth-graders to identify these structures as clues to a writer's meaning. Students who learned to look for these structures recalled twice as much about selected passages as did controls. Can you identify the rhetorical structure used in the following item?

[margin note: What text structure does this text follow?]

Despite the argument that smoking is harmful, many claim it is not so. Smoking has been related to lung cancer, high blood pressure, and loss of appetite. But for some people, smoking may relieve tension.

(a) Description   (b) Covariance   (c) Problem solution
(d) Favored view vs. opposite

Items such as these were used to provide practice and feedback for learners in identifying text structure.

Students can be taught to identify other text structures such as *intact headings* (an outline at the beginning of a passage) or *embedded headings* (headings dispersed throughout the passage). The headings essentially serve as cues to aid encoding and retrieval. Brooks, Dansereau, Holley, and Spurlin (1983) taught one group of students how to construct good headings and provided a passage with embedded headings but without instructions; students in a second group were provided a passage without embedded headings or instructions. The trained students were told that good headings reveal the hierarchical organization of the text. Students who generated their own headings surpassed the other groups on recall measures and performed similarly on comprehension, suggesting that skill in constructing one's own organization and appropriate labels for it is highly desirable.

Strategies such as concept mapping and identifying text structure are apparently useful in assisting the learning and recall of complex information. As Snowman (1986) observes, however, strategies are useful only to the extent that learners know when, where, and why they might be employed. Metacognitive awareness of the value of available tactics and strategies and the willingness to utilize them are as important as the procedural knowledge of how to apply them to specific situations. Students also require comprehension-monitoring strategies to determine when, where, and why others may be used.

Comprehension-Monitoring Strategies

Comprehension-monitoring strategies require critical thinking processes such as observation, planning, evaluating, and modification of what one is doing to achieve a particular learning goal. Monitoring how well we are comprehending content that is being presented is crucial to our determination of whether we actually need to employ many of the strategies already discussed. Those who use comprehension-monitoring strategies achieve at higher levels on most academic tasks. Unfortunately, low-achieving students who most require them are least likely to do so. For example, Garner, Hare, Alexander, Haynes, and Winograd (1984) found that poor readers in the upper elementary grades do not look back to earlier passages they have read when they have trouble answering questions about material.

Which strategy are marginal notes designed to aid?

For this reason, training children to *ask questions* about what they have read or will read and teaching them to formulate answers to their own or adjunct questions have long been considered important strategies in the area of reading. Robinson (1946) developed a strategic approach to reading known as *SQ3R* (study, question, read, recite, and review). In SQ3R, readers are taught to glance over the headings in the chapter to see the major points that will be developed, to ask a question based on the first reading, and then to read with the question in mind. After reading, learners try to recite an answer with the book closed. Each section is then read following this sequence. Finally, a review of the entire chapter is encouraged. While studies of SQ3R typically revealed an improvement in grade-point average for students employing this approach (Whitehill, 1972), investigators have not determined the role of each component and its contribution to the overall effect. More recent research has attempted to examine the more specific effects of forming and answering questions as we read.

When students generate their own questions, it is presumed that they must notice and think meaningfully about specific aspects of the text. If we ask ourselves low-level questions, we need merely attend to relevant factual information (e.g., "Who won the presidential election in 1892?"). Questions that require us to analyze or evaluate the text, however, are more likely to call for more extensive studying. Answering questions such as "What is the author's bias?" or "Can I think of a counterargument?" demands that we not only review greater amounts of the text, but relate it to previous knowledge. Did you formulate and are you attempting to answer similar questions while reading this material?

Davey and McBride (1986) trained sixth-graders to generate questions while reading. Training consisted of an introductory phase in which the value of asking oneself questions was stressed, followed by description of "locate" (literal) and "think-type" (inferential) questions. Later lessons stressed how to generate question stems to relate one section of a passage to another and how to relate questions to main ideas. Students also were given monitoring questions they could use to evaluate question-generating strategies (e.g., "How well did I link important pieces of information together?"). Davey and McBride tested each component of their training independently and found that a complete lesson-by-lesson format is essential if students are to adopt the strategy for future use. The format must explain why it is good to self-question while reading, describe strategy components, and offer practice in using the strategy, with feedback and information on how to monitor one's use of the strategy.

Affective Strategies

Affective strategies are employed to maintain motivation, to manage anxiety, to utilize one's time effectively, and to continue concentration on the learning task at hand. Hayes (1981) notes that failure to learn often occurs not because one failed to employ the correct strategy but because adequate time was not devoted to studying. Managing our study efforts by setting aside solid blocks of uninterrupted time, utilizing a quiet work place, planning ahead to schedule study time, eliminating daydreaming or other avoidance behaviors will all maximize learning time. Hayes suggests that *attention management* tactics such as setting and resetting a timer to mark study periods (and to interrupt daydreaming if necessary) and scheduling study for times during the day when one is most efficient can improve concentration.

Affective strategies alter motivation

Dansereau (1985) has suggested *support strategies* for dealing with affective issues in studying. These include techniques for developing a positive attitude toward learning, for coping with distractions, and for monitoring (when learning is not efficient). The strategy recommended for developing a positive attitude utilizes many of the self-regulation tactics discussed in Chapter 5. Students are first given practice to make them aware of their negative and positive emotions, as well as the "self-talk" and images they create in facing a learning task. They are then asked to consider the logical conclusion of such impressions (e.g., "What will really happen if I fail the test?"). It may well be that emotional reactions to the task have been blown out of proportion. Then students practice "clearing their minds" by counting breaths and imagining a period of successful studying, as well as becoming distracted and successfully coping with the distraction. Students also are encouraged to replace negative talk and images with more positive thoughts.

There are similar desensitization techniques for approaching distractions and monitoring one's efficacy in learning. The emphasis is on determining when and where distractions or instances of inefficient learning occur, relaxing rather than responding with anxiety when unfavorable events do occur, substituting positive self-talk and images, and then taking action to remedy the situation through comprehension-monitoring, organizational, or elaboration strategies. Dansereau (1985) reported that such affective strategies improve concentration, reduce anxiety, and result in higher achievement for secondary school and college students.

ACQUIRING STRATEGIC KNOWLEDGE

Studies of the utilization of learning strategies have generally been encouraging: Students as young as six or seven are able to implement and monitor simple strategies, maintain them over time, and apply them to similar tasks. Older students who are considered strategic learners activate their prior knowledge of a topic before reading or listening, generate predictions about what is to come, identify the main idea and structure of the material being presented, construct mental images or mnemonically encode more difficult content, develop hierarchical concept maps or other note-taking techniques to organize information, and generate questions to monitor their understanding. Strategic learners also evaluate their learning, engaging in processes such as looking back in reading, managing their attention, and employing positive self-talk, imagery, and other support strategies to reduce anxiety and enhance motivation.

Direct instruction of strategic skills appears necessary for students to acquire a coherent set of strategies to apply to their learning. Strategies are rarely used in isolation. They are most often integrated into metacognitive sequences designed to acquire complex cognitive goals. Therefore, instruction must not occur in bits and pieces, with individual techniques introduced out of context. The following guidelines for teaching learning strategies to students reflect the thinking of Pressley & Associates (1990).

Strategic knowledge needs to be directly taught

1. *Use powerful models of teaching.* There should be demonstration of the strategy by the teacher, extensive explanations of its use, application to different areas of a curriculum (not just in language arts classes, for example), encouragement of students' use of strategies outside the classroom, and considerable student practice with feedback.

2. *Select a few related strategies to teach that fit well together.* If students appear to be having difficulty in reading comprehension, for example, instruction in concept mapping, question generating, and summarizing material might be taught together in the context of reading lessons.

3. *Motivate students to use strategies.* Emphasizing the effectiveness of various strategies in the long term or as investments in future learning success is important to strategy instruction. The acquisition of a strategy should be viewed by learners as a way to enhance self-efficacy and as an internally controlled approach to improving performance.

4. *Encourage students to believe that they can become effective learners.* Students should learn that becoming a good strategy user is within their power. As Pressley & Associates (1990, p. 185) state: "Acquisition of academic strategies can reduce the distance between their current selves and the possible selves to which they aspire."

5. *Extend the approach in the curriculum.* Strategies should be taught in a way that makes them applicable to different areas of students' school experience. Strategies appropriate for reading, writing, or listening obviously can be employed in different subject areas. Teachers in several areas should be involved in strategy instruction, pointing out how specific techniques might be applied to academic content. Research by Pressley, Schuder, Bergman, and El-Dinary (1992), for instance, indicated that a programmatic effort in which several teachers in a school are involved in strategy instruction is most effective.

PROBLEM SOLVING

Take a few minutes to solve the following problems, noting how they are similar or different. Solutions will be provided later in the chapter.

1. "Given a human being with an inoperable stomach tumor, and rays which destroy organic tissue at sufficient intensity, by what procedure can one free him of the tumor by these rays and at the same time avoid destroying the healthy tissue which surrounds it?" (Duncker, 1945)
2. "Dickens, Einstein, Freud, and Kant are professors of English, physics, psychology, and philosophy (though not necessarily respectively).
   a. Dickens and Freud were in the audience when the psychologist delivered his first lecture.
   b. Both Einstein and the philosopher were friends of the physicist.
   c. The philosopher has attended lectures by both Kant and Dickens.
   d. Dickens has never heard of Freud.
   Match the professors to their fields." (Hayes, 1981)
3. "A car traveling at 30 miles per/hour (mph) left a certain place at 10:00 A.M. At 11:30 A.M., another car departed from the same place at 40 mph and traveled the same route. In how many hours will the second car overtake the first car?" (Reed, Dempster, & Ettinger, 1985).

If we define a *problem* broadly as a "situation in which an individual wants to do something, but does not know the course of action to follow to get what she wants" (Newell & Simon, 1972), then *problem solving* consists of the cognitions, affective responses, and behavioral activities that are utilized in dealing with problems. Problems begin with certain conditions or pieces of information known as *givens,* a desired terminal state or *goal,* and *obstacles,* or conditions that impede movement from the givens to the goal. Both the givens and the goals can be well defined or poorly defined, contributing to the ease or difficulty of a problem. Reitman (1965) thus distinguishes among four problem possibilities, to which we have appended examples.

1. Well-defined givens and well-defined goals, as in the car problem above, in which both the given information and the form of the answer are specifically described.
2. Well-defined givens and poorly defined goals (e.g., "How can computer-assisted instruction be used to aid student learning?"), in which the givens are well known but the goal is open to interpretation.
3. Poorly defined givens and well-defined goals: "The disassembled parts of a high-powered rifle have been placed on your desk. You will also find an instructional manual for its assembly, printed in Latin. In 10 minutes, a hungry tiger will be admitted to the room. Take whatever action you deem necessary."

   Is it always easy to identify the givens?

4. Poorly defined givens and poorly defined goals: "Describe the history of the papacy from its origins to the present day, concentrating especially, but not exclusively on its social, political, economic, religious, and philosophical impact on Europe and America."

Clearly, problem types 3 and 4, even when not as outrageous as these examples, are very difficult to resolve. Type 2 problems will also require further specificity for the solver to perform successfully. Clarity in both the givens and the goal appears essential to problem solving.

Greeno and Simon (1988) have developed a more process-oriented classification system of problems, which emphasizes the types of cognitive operations necessary to solve a problem.

1. *Problems of transformation* require the solver to find a sequence of transformations leading from the givens to the goal. An example is the car/speed problem above.
2. *Problems of arrangement* ask the solver to rearrange the givens to solve the problem. An anagram problem such as "Form a word from the letters HRNGETTS" is an example.
3. *Problems of inducing structure* provide examples of an event as the givens and ask solvers to determine a general rule that explains their relationship. Series completion problems such as "Find the missing number: 1, 5, 8, 12, . . . " require induction of structure.
4. *Evaluation of deductive arguments problems* require logical deduction for solution. Analysis of syllogisms to determine whether a particular conclusion logically follows from a set of premises is necessary. The "four professors" problem above is an example.

While most problems fall into one of these categories, Greeno and Simon point out that some of the most interesting and challenging problems may contain elements of more than one type.

Processes in Problem Solving

The complexity of moving from a set of givens to a goal suggests that problem solving occurs in a series of steps or cognitive processes. One of the earliest attempts at describing the steps of problem solving arose from the Gestalt view of intuitive thinking. Wallas (1926) suggested that problem solving follows four stages: *preparation, incubation, illumination,* and *verification.* After initially examining the problem (preparation) and analyzing and reflecting on it (incubation), illumination, the famous "Aha" experience of sudden insight, occurs and reveals a possible solution. Verification or testing of the proposed solution would follow. More recently, the *IDEAL* method of problem solving instructs students to *identify* the problem, *define* it, *explore* possible strategies for solving it, *act* on those strategies, and then *look* at the effects of one's attempts at solution (Bransford & Stein, 1985).

While these approaches are useful in developing an organized technique of problem solving, they do not completely describe the steps most expert problem solvers actually follow. For example, experts rapidly generate fewer hypotheses than novices, since the former are more capable of discriminating at the outset among relevant hypotheses to apply (Chi, Glaser, & Farr, 1988). We shall discuss differences between expert and novice problem solvers in a later section. For now, it is important to recognize that recent attempts to describe effective problem solving focus more on solvers' actual behavior than on what they logically should do.

See if you can solve the following problem:

A jeweler possessed a valuable old clock, with its numerals etched into the glass face. One day, the clock face fell out and broke into four pieces. In gathering the pieces, the jeweler noticed that the numerals on each piece added to 15. Can you break the clock face into four pieces, each adding to exactly 15?

As you attempted to solve this problem, you probably read and reread it, perhaps pausing to consider some of the givens. Past experiences with glass and clocks may have been recalled. You might have imagined a clock face with numbers or looked at your own watch. Some of you might have talked or thought to yourself, describing what you believed the problem involved. Others might have drawn small clock faces to aid in memory of their appearance.

These efforts are all designed to understand the problem or *represent* it. In representing a problem, the solver considers the givens in the problem situation, the goal, the actions that can be performed, and the obstacles or constraints that must be overcome. People create different internal representations of the same problem because of differences in ability to encode one or more aspects of the problem into the representation. Representation is considered the most critical phase of the problem-solving process (Greeno & Simon, 1988).

Representation: the key to problem solving

In some cases, problems cannot be represented because relevant prior knowledge has not been acquired. Most models of learning and instruction, it will be recalled, suggest that domain-specific knowledge is necessary prior to problem solving (Gagné & Briggs, 1984). In other cases, problems cannot be represented adequately because one cannot retrieve information previously learned. A review of relevant past learning, such as reading old math notes on distance/time formulas, may be necessary for solving the car problem, for instance.

Existing beliefs that serve as obstacles also may make problem representation difficult. Gestalt psychologists such as Maier (1931) found that the common, earlier uses of objects could interfere with their being used in novel ways to solve a specific problem. In the "two-string problem," solvers must tie together two strings suspended from the ceiling that are too far apart to both be held at once by the solver. The solution is to find a heavy object from a variety of items presented, tie it to one of the strings, put it in motion like a pendulum and then, while holding onto the other string, grab the pendulum at its nearest point in its arc. When subjects had used a pliers in an electrical wiring activity just prior to the two-string problem, they were less likely to use the pliers later as a pendulum weight, even though it was the best choice among objects available. When a similar, yet different, pair of pliers was available, more subjects were likely to choose the pliers. Scissors, similar to the original pliers, were the most likely to be chosen to weight the string. If the pliers had been used a considerable time before the problem-solving session, its probability of being chosen was increased considerably. Maier described as *functional fixedness* the phenomenon whereby an object becomes associated with a particular role and cannot be viewed as functioning in a different context. The functional fixedness effect can apparently be overcome by cuing solvers to recall objects and their relevant characteristics during problem solving. It appears that most students need such aid to be able to spontaneously overcome past functional associations (Lockhart, Lamon, & Gick, 1988).

Accurately representing the problem to induce understanding of what it entails is necessary for solving difficult problems. In the clock example, we must recognize that since all the intact numbers on a clock face add to 78, simply finding combinations of unbroken numbers is not going to work ($4 \times 15 = 60$). The solution must come from somehow breaking up the two-digit numbers (e.g., representing 10 as a one and a zero). With this clue can you now solve the problem? Check Figure 10.3 to verify your answer.

If problems are correctly represented, thus activating relevant schemas, it may be possible to go directly to problem solution. Elementary math problems, for example, once represented, are quickly solved. In other cases, however, failure may require the solver to backtrack to an additional phase of "searching" for ways to solve the problem (Gick, 1986). After you recognized that the clock numbers had to be broken up, you probably began to follow a procedure to arrive at a correct solution. The mental operations you employed to consider your representation of the givens of the clock problem are known as the *search process.*

A number of strategies used during the search process have been identified, and each is useful for problems of one kind or another. Strategies can be subdivided into two categories: *algorithms* and *heuristics.* Algorithms are strategies that guarantee solution to well-defined problems to which they apply. Multiplication is the algorithm that leads to the solution of a problem such as "I want to buy 10 candy bars and they cost 55 cents each. How much will I have to spend?" *Heuristics,* on the other hand, are shortcuts to solving problems in which an obvious algorithm either is not available or exists but is not practical. After losing the combination to a new gym locker, for example, one algorithm would be to try all possible left–right–left combinations, but this would not be satisfactory to your waiting gym instructor!

Table 10.2 describes different heuristic strategies and provides examples of their use.

Experts can more rapidly determine which strategy is most likely to reach a successful solution. This level of achievement is due to a greater store of domain-specific knowledge, amassed through experience within the domain, rather than to any special ability in general problem solving. For instance, Simon (1980) estimates that chess masters have learned as many as 50,000 chess moves and combinations of moves, which they can recall during a match. These experts are able to recognize meaningful patterns of moves during a game, which they can then compare to their mass of stored knowledge. Experience in playing chess would have occurred for such an amount of knowledge to be acquired.

Algorithms always work with the right problem

Heuristic = rule of thumb that might work

What search process did you use in the four-professors problem?

FIGURE 10.3 Solution to clock face problem

TABLE 10.2 Heuristic search strategies and examples

Type	Explanation	Example
Trial and error	Searcher does not use or possess information indicating one solution path is more likely to lead to the goal than any other (Hayes, 1981). Can be systematic if one keeps track of results of each attempt.	Unable to see which of four house keys opens the front door, the solver inserts one after the other.
Hill climbing	Taking a step that logically appears to bring you closer to a goal ("up the hill"). Does not work well when problems possess hills and valleys or require solver to move away from the goal initially in order to eventually solve it.	Allocating blocks of time for each subtask of an assignment only to find that one subtask takes an inordinate amount of time, resulting in the need to replan.
Fractionation	Breaking a problem into parts. Requires knowledge of final goals and subgoals leading to it.	Completing a master's thesis by identifying necessary chapters and what has to be written for each.
Looking for auxiliary problems	Posing a related, easier problem which, if solved, helps to solve the target problem (Hayes, 1981).	If four pieces adding to 15 can't be found in the clock problem, can six pieces? Five pieces?
Means–end analysis	Compare differences between givens and goal and systematically reduce the difference between the two until the goal is reached. A table can help.	The four-professors problem can be solved by creating a table of the 16 possible combinations of names and fields and then crossing off wrong combinations as new information is considered. For example, Dickens and Freud cannot be psychologists if they were in the psychologist's audience. (Answer: Freud = philosophy, Kant = physics, Einstein = psychology, Dickens = English).
Working backward	Changing one's point of view so that the new starting place is the original goal and solver works back to the givens (Hayes, 1981).	Mazes of the kind provided on restaurant napkins for hungry children to "find the pizza." There is only one correct path leading out of the goal, but several choices leading away from the beginning point.

Expert versus Novice: Differences in Problem Solving

Recent research has identified other differences in how experts solve a variety of problems in comparison to nonexperts or novices. The reason for this research is simple: If we can identify expert behaviors that are modifiable, perhaps instruction in those areas can improve problem solving among novices. The following are the major differences found when experts and novices are compared.

Experts possess greater amounts of domain-specific knowledge. Both representational and search processes are aided considerably by possession of a body of specific knowledge that allows experts to select and respond to the critical elements of a problem. For this reason, a well-established and rich knowledge base in subject matter facts and skills would appear fundamental to success in problem solving in any given domain. Chi, Glaser, and Farr (1988) suggested that this knowledge base is a major factor in their finding that experts in problem solving in one domain are not necessarily experts in others.

Experts spend more time at problem representation than do novices, who proceed more directly to problem solution.   This difference is particularly pronounced with relatively ill-defined problems. Voss, Tyler, and Yengo (1983) posed a problem to a group of political science professors, a group of undergraduate students in political science, and a group of chemistry professors. The chemistry professors were included to determine the effects of additional academic training and expertise in non-domain-specific areas. Here is the problem: "Assume you are the head of the Soviet Ministry of Agriculture and crop productivity has been low for several years. You are now responsible for increasing crop production. How would you go about doing this?"

Subjects were tape recorded while thinking out loud during problem solution. The political science professors spent a significant amount of time analyzing the possible causes of low crop production, while undergraduates and chemistry professors went directly to problem solutions such as "Put more land into production." The expert social scientists considered additional domain-specific constraints to their representations such as the history, climate, and political ideology of the Soviet system. The results suggested that while all subjects represented the problem, experts take more time to consider all relevant factors before searching for a solution.

Experts represent problems in more abstract terms based on underlying domain-specific principles.   In a study by Chi, Feltovich, and Glaser (1981), expert physics students (doctoral candidates) were compared to undergraduates in the task of sorting standard physics problems into categories. Novices sorted based on the characteristics of the objects and situations described in the givens of the problem, such as: "These are problems that utilize springs." Experts, on the other hand, sorted according to abstract categories related to principles of physics, such as Newton's second law. In another domain, expert computer programmers categorized programming problems according to the computer procedure needed to solve them, such as "sort problems" or "search problems." Novices categorized according to the problem context (e.g., "business application") (Weiser & Shertz, 1983). Although both groups can identify the key terms provided in the information given, apparently experts are able to activate higher-level schemas based on higher-level principles.

Experts search for underlying principles

Experts utilize both inductive and deductive thinking in analyzing the nature of problems.   Lesgold, Robinson, Feltovich, Glaser, Klopfer, and Wang (1988) studied the differences in diagnosis of novice, postnovice, and expert X-ray technicians. The subjects analyzed X-ray films of diseased lungs and drew on the film the anatomical features they referred to in making their diagnoses. The more expert technicians included more anatomical features in their diagnoses and talked more about their observations of each feature in relation to the others. As new information was discovered, it was integrated into the emerging diagnosis. Novices just listed critical characteristics with little attempt to infer their interactions. The authors concluded that the experts ended up with a more coherent model of each patient based on the inferences they made about the interrelationship of the disease characteristics they observed. Novice representations were more fragmented and superficial.

After representation, experts more frequently utilize means–end strategies in which they work forward to reduce differences between the givens and the goal.   When expert computer programmers debug software, they tend to break the problem into finer subparts and to be more systematic than novices (Jeffries, Turner, Polson, & Atwood, 1981). They are also more likely to consider alternatives. For example, one expert performed some calculations about a particular program before establishing that one way of storing page numbers was better than another. Novices rarely analyze the steps they are taking to see whether they are getting closer to the goal, preferring to "force" a particular solution strategy on the problem. The solution plans followed by experts appear to be at a more complex level, with alternatives and interacting possibilities considered in advance.

Experts use means–end search strategies

Experts tend to be less flexible than novices when the fundamental nature of tasks changes.   R. J. Sternberg and Davidson (1990) point out that experts are not always better problem solvers than novices. Experts have learned through experience a number of well-established, automatic procedures that serve them well in solving the typical problems in a domain. If tasks are radically altered, however, experts may be less likely than novices to relinquish well-founded representation and solution strategies, reflecting the experts' commitment to a particular set of procedures. In a study by Frensch and Sternberg (1989), expert and novice bridge players competed with a computer in games in which the rules and structure of bridge were radically altered. Deep-structural changes (e.g., the player who put down the *lowest* card in a trick began play in the next trick) created confusion and hindered the play of expert bridge players more than it did that of novices. Surface changes such as altering the names of the four suits (spades, hearts, etc.) to nonsense syllables had little effect. Apparently, the automatic procedures that experts relied on to solve similar problems were difficult to overcome when the task was fundamentally altered. Experts did recover to eventually surpass novices in their level of play; nevertheless, their initial loss of flexibility in viewing new problems illustrates a troublesome side effect of developing expertise. Even experts need to recognize that new approaches to problems are occasionally warranted.

Let us examine this set of differences between experts and novices in teaching. Do expert teachers function like experts in other domains? Studies indicate that novice and expert teachers attend to different stimuli in the classroom environment, with the latter ignoring stimuli that novices find distracting (Berliner, 1987). Experts also make more selective use of the information they possess in their planning and instructional interaction (Leinhardt & Greeno, 1986) and employ well-established instructional and management routines (Peterson & Comeaux, 1987). Expert teachers are more capable of improvisation or spontaneous production of examples or applica-

Expert teachers selectively use information and employ well-established routines

tions when confronted by student questions (Livingston & Borko, 1989). Berliner (1987) reported that experts are more likely to utilize their fund of domain-specific knowledge to form images or hypotheses of how a classroom should be, assessing the typicality of a current situation according to those images. Although they are able to filter out irrelevancies, experts are also more sensitive to the many forms of student activity and their meanings. In summary, it would appear that expert teachers possess a deep knowledge base, represent the teaching task according to effective instructional principles, make valid inferences about the information they receive from students, and form appropriate solution plans in accord with the changing classroom environment.

Instruction in Problem Solving

Instruction that enhances problem solving in specific content areas has become a primary objective in education, as we discussed in Chapter 7. Now we consider several instructional principles that, if appropriately implemented, promise to advance performance in various phases of problem solving.

Encourage students to generate their own explanations of why worked examples of similar problems are correct.   The most frequently utilized method for teaching problem solving for most of us during our own schooling was the *worked example.* Teachers or textbooks provided a worked sample problem, most likely in math or the sciences, and then presented a similar problem with different values. Our task was to study the worked example and then solve the new problem. In essence, we were supposed to determine the underlying rule(s) that governed solution of the initial problem and transfer our learning to the new, supposedly similar problem. The author can still remember struggling to prove the Pythagorean theorem, while the exasperated geometry teacher said, "Look back at the example! Look back at the example!"

Unfortunately, experience with worked examples frequently fails to transfer to new problems. R. E. Mayer (1992) describes two kinds of obstacle to successful transfer. First, the underlying rule or explanation of why the first problem is solved correctly may not be apparent to the learner, perhaps because of difficulty in representation. Second, even if the example is clearly understood, the learner may not know how to use the underlying rule to solve the new problem. This obstacle may reflect inability to employ appropriate solution strategies as well as inadequate representation.

If worked examples are to be useful, each of the foregoing obstacles must be addressed directly. Aiding students to understand worked examples may require more teacher involvement than the traditional technique of simply serving as a model of correct solutions. It may be necessary to prompt students to verbalize their understanding as they study the examples. In a study by Chi, Bassok, Lewis, Reimann, and Glaser (1989), students were asked to talk aloud as they read worked problems pertaining to Newtonian physics. The better students (as determined on a subsequent transfer test) were observed to produce many more explanations to themselves about the conditions in the example. They accurately monitored their own understanding

Student self-explanations of problem solutions are necessary

of the examples ("I'm having trouble with this step") and generated many paraphrases and summaries of their understanding. In general, these students gave evidence of having attained independent knowledge of the underlying structure of the worked examples. Students who performed less adequately on the transfer test, on the other hand, produced far fewer self-explanations, monitoring statements, and paraphrases on the transfer task. Monitoring was inaccurate, and worked examples were reviewed only for specific information, not for underlying principles. These results suggest the value of requiring students to overtly describe their understanding of worked examples as well as copy them, not only to permit teacher detection of errors, but to supply student practice in representation.

Obstacles in deciding how to use worked examples in transfer tasks may be overcome by ensuring that an adequate number of varied examples designed to reveal all the various complexities of a concept are provided prior to transfer. Cooper and Sweller (1987) presented eighth-grade algebra students with a planned series of four pairs of sample problems. One group was required to solve all the problems, while the other group was provided a worked example for one of each pair and had to work the others. Each example pair was structured differently (e.g., the unknown might be placed on the right-hand side of the equation, rather than the left). Results indicated no differences between the groups during the acquisition phase, but the worked-examples group displayed superior performance on the transfer problems. Apparently, students who received worked examples that progressively illustrated a new dimension of the sample problems were able to develop more extensive and automated schemas, which aided transfer to similar problems. By providing a planned series of worked examples, each of which illustrates a new key feature, and immediately requiring students to work similar examples, it may be possible to enhance students' ability to generalize from worked examples during transfer.

Provide practice in representation to facilitate domain-specific problem solving.   R. E. Mayer (1987) has identified two components of representation that require training within the context of a specific academic area. *Translation training* consists of teaching students how to transform each sentence of a problem into an internal representation. *Schema interaction training* includes teaching students how to integrate the sentences, resulting in a coherent understanding of the total problem. Translation requires linguistic knowledge about semantics and syntax as well as declarative knowledge about the objects in the problem. Schema integration requires knowledge of problem types. For example, suppose the following problem were posed:

> Floor tiles are sold in squares 30 cm on each side and weigh 10 g each. How much would it cost to tile a rectangular room 7.2 m long and 5.4 m wide if the tiles cost 72 cents each?

The translation component of representation would require the student to know what floor tiles were, that "30 cm on each side" means that 30 cm is both the length and the width of the tiles, and that 100 cm equals one meter. The schema integration phase would necessitate recognizing that this information is describing an area prob-

Translation and schematic training are directly taught

lem, where length × width is computed and cost is determined by multiplying the total number of tiles by the cost of each.

Translation training requires direct instruction in comprehending sentences. Unfortunately, students often have difficulty in translating sentences that contain mathematical information. Earlier, we noted that students will often misunderstand sentences that contain relational proportions such as: "There are six times as many students as professors at this university." The inaccurate equation $6S = P$ is frequently put forward as an algebraic equivalent of that statement. Mayer (1987) suggested that training consisting of multiple-choice questions provided for target problems allows students to better focus on the translation process. Questions might aid in restating the problem givens, restating the problem goal, representing the problem as a diagram, or representing the problem as an equation. In the tile problem, a translation training question might be provided in advance as follows:

restate for better understanding (handwritten margin note)

Which of the following sentences is not true?
(a) The room is a rectangle measuring 7.2 × 5.4 meters.
(b) Each tile costs 30 cents.
(c) Each tile is a square measuring 30 × 30 cm.
(d) The length of the long side of the room is 7.2 m.

When students lack a schema for a problem, representation is likely to be in error, as the reader might have experienced when attempting to solve the rolling car problem earlier. Schema integration training must therefore focus on aiding students to recognize problem types. Mayer suggests that this can be accomplished by having students sort problems into categories, solve a mixture of problem types rather than all problems of one type, and practice representing problems with diagrams depicting problem relationships:

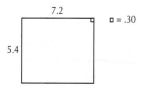

Research on translation and schema integration training indicates that students can profit in solving not only target problems, but transfer items as well. In a study also described in the section on mathematics learning in Chapter 7, Lewis (1989) taught students to identify the types of statement found in word problems and to diagram problem information. There were significant pre–post gains in performance by these students in comparison to the gains posted by those trained only in recognizing statements or to control students who received no training. It is assumed that problem solving in mathematics-related areas such as physics, chemistry, or economics could also benefit from such training.

Training in representation is perhaps even more necessary when students are confronted with ill-defined problems. Even experts will disagree about appropriate representation of ill-defined problems, as Voss et al. (1983) described. Recall the Soviet agriculture problem. Some of the experts viewed the problem from an economics vantage point, others viewed it historically, while others took a political stance. Consequently, there were at least three representations. Determining which expert representation is correct depends more on how one defines the exact nature of the problem. As with many ill-defined problems in the social sciences, however, it is not possible to directly test possible solutions that might emerge. All that can be hoped is that problem solvers will identify and consider as many of the variables that will affect the problem as they possibly can. Voss and Post (1988) believe that the likelihood of identifying these constraining factors is improved with more complete knowledge of the domain, which even the experts may not have possessed.

In addition to domain-specific knowledge, problem representation of ill-defined problems may be aided by skill in *problem finding,* or the ability to identify the many constraints and uncertainties that inhabit ill-defined problems. Problem-finding skill can be aided by instructional techniques that require students to withhold judgment about representation until all givens have been considered for their possible implications. Encouraging students, perhaps with a series of written or oral questions, to completely explore the problem situation can aid problem finding. Use of the concept map technique, in which questions of who, what, when, where, and why are asked and analyzed, may also help students to identify important constraints. If ill-defined problems are to be represented adequately, solvers must learn to take into account the factors that contribute to the vagueness and difficulty of the problem.

Consider givens before inferring your own

Instruct students in identifying analogous problem situations and in abstracting structural similarities between analogous problems. Analogical reasoning occurs when we solve a new problem by using what we know about the solution to a related problem. When we are able to form an analogous relationship between one problem and another, we have successfully made abstract information more concrete, have related the new problem to old schemas, and perhaps have integrated old schemas in a new way (Simons, 1984).

Recall the inoperable tumor problem presented earlier in the chapter. The preferred solution is that low-level rays be transmitted from different directions so that they simultaneously converge at the tumor (Duncker, 1945). No destruction of tissue will occur in this way, and the summative effect of the rays will destroy the tumor. Suppose that an analogy problem was presented to subjects before they were exposed to the tumor problem. Would these subjects benefit from the analogy? Gick and Holyoak (1980) conducted such an experiment, presenting three versions of a story about a military assault on a fortress in which all roads to the fortress are mined to explode if used by large numbers of troops. The most analogous version has the general dividing his army into small groups that attack simultaneously using different roads. This "dispersion" solution was most analogous to the preferred solution to the tumor problem and produced the most correct responses. Two other versions of the military assault (in which a tunnel was dug or an open supply route was used) generated different solutions to the tumor problem which violated the givens of Duncker's original preferred solution. Apparently, students were able to respond correctly to the new problem when the analogy presented considerable structural similarity.

Can you find analogies that help student problem solving?

R. E. Mayer (1992) believes that the learner must successfully move through three phases of thought to profit from structurally similar analogies. The first is *recog-*

nition, in which the learner must recognize that a particular event or rule is analogous to the new problem. Gick and Holyoak (1983) found that recognition could be improved if direct hints were made that a story read earlier could be applied to the transfer problem. The second is *abstraction,* in which the underlying commonality is identified and converted to a schema that can generalize to the transfer problem. According to Gick and Holyoak (1983), abstraction may require more than one analogical comparison. In their research, students were much more successful in inducing an appropriate schema in reference to the tumor problem when two similar analogues were provided. The third phase consists of a *mapping* process in which the underlying schema is directly applied to the new problem. Mapping appears to be enhanced when examples of the structural similarities of the two problems are cued.

The instructional implications for facilitating analogous transfer seem clear but somewhat depressing, based on this research. For most students, spontaneous transfer from solved problems to new ones is rare. It will be even less likely if there is a significant time delay between original learning and later problem solving (Phye, 1990). Just sequencing instructional content so that analogous material follows from earlier content will not be sufficient. Teachers must provide instructional aids to help students progress through each of the three phases of analogical reasoning. New lessons should begin with a review of recently completed tasks in the subject matter (as well as other areas) that may be analogous to the current lesson. Direct advice about how the new material may have similarities to previous content should be provided, to facilitate recognition. To aid abstraction of the underlying similarity, the teacher must model how the new problem can be solved in light of the analogous one. Explicit practice by students in analyzing the problem givens with feedback about accuracy and completeness of the identified schema will be necessary. To maximize the mapping process, practice should include a variety of analogous problems. Learning to solve problems through analogies will improve only if students are provided practice in the necessary inductive thought. With such training, they will be able to take advantage of analogous material when learning independently.

Situate instruction in problem-solving environments.   While it is important to possess a store of domain-specific knowledge to apply to problem situations, and to recognize similar problems that might be analogous, it is also necessary to be able to activate that stored knowledge. As we have already indicated, inability to call up relevant past learning spontaneously when confronted with a problem is a major obstacle for most learners. Since much that we have learned is stored as declarative knowledge, not procedural, when problems arise it is difficult to recognize that what we recall can be converted to procedures relevant to problem solution. Sherwood, Kinzer, Hasselbring, and Bransford (1987) illustrated this difficulty in their study of entering college students' knowledge of logarithms. The vast majority of students surveyed recalled logarithms only as mathematics exercises they were forced to perform. Students did not remember them as helpful tools to be used as aids to rapid multiplication.

One instructional approach designed to help students use their "inert knowledge" in a problem-solving context is *anchored instruction* (Cognition and Technology Group at Vanderbilt, 1990). This is an attempt to create a learning environment in which students and teachers explore the problems and opportunities that experts in various areas encounter and the knowledge and skills they use as tools. If novices can be immersed for extended periods in content that is anchored in real problem situations, they may learn new skills that are more easily transferable to problem-solving applications.

Anchored instruction makes heavy use of visual materials such as videodiscs to create a more dynamic context that is easily accessed. One example is a series of videodisc adventures of Jasper Woodberry. One Jasper disc poses a complex mathematical problem containing approximately 15 subgoals. Students have to generate the subproblems to be solved and then find relevant information that was presented throughout the video story. In one adventure Jasper sets out in a motorboat to buy an old cruiser. He consults a map, listens to his marine radio, checks his instruments, and stops to buy gas. Later in his trip he damages his boat and must stop for repairs. Jasper ultimately reaches his destination, test-drives the cruiser, and buys it. At the end of the video, Jasper is asking himself when he should leave for home to make it before dark and whether he has an adequate supply of fuel in the new boat. At that point, students are placed in problem-finding and problem-solving activities such as identifying Jasper's major goals, generating subproblems that reflect obstacles (running out of gas, finding the way home, etc.), and devising strategies to deal with various subproblems. Throughout the adventure, students are exposed to information relevant to Jasper's problems, such as a map indicating river distances and a radio announcement of sunset time. Students can attempt to retrieve the data from memory and scan back on the video to check their accuracy.

Videodiscs in the Jasper series are still being created, and the project continues. Initial results suggested that fifth-grade students improved their skills in problem finding and problem solving on similar tasks after working with the Jasper adventures in group learning sessions. Teachers reported that students exposed to Jasper seem to be challenged to solve the problems posed. Even students who normally do not perform well in math can contribute—for example, by noticing information in the video that is relevant to Jasper's problems.

The Cognition and Technology Group believes that the episodic, storylike tasks in the Jasper series require students to make and evaluate authentic decisions similar to the kinds of judgment real problem-solving situations would call for. While visually based materials have the inherent advantage of creating the illusion of authenticity, particularly when displayed through the adaptive mode of interactive video, other problem series in a written format could be expected to be beneficial as well. The critical component is the presence of a

semantically rich, shared environment that allows students and teachers to find and understand the kinds of problems that various concepts, principles and theories were designed to solve, and that allow them to experience the effects that new knowledge has on their perception and understanding of these environments. (Cognition and Technology Group, 1990, p. 9)

Anchored instruction would appear to be most useful in aiding students to transfer skill in arithmetic computation to the nuances of many word problems.

Materials that anchor instruction in problem solving?

Allow students to work with others to facilitate problem-solving performance.

Two school custodians were struggling with the new desk. Despite their best efforts, the desk remained immobile. Finally they set it down in the doorway and looked at each other.

"That's it, Bill," said one. "I don't see any way we are going to get this desk in through that door."

"In!" exclaimed Bill. "I thought we were supposed to be taking it out."

As the anecdote illustrates, working at cross-purposes on a task leads to considerable wasted effort. Individuals working together can profit from the contribution of others. Research indicates that groups ordinarily perform better than the average individual working alone on a wide variety of problems (Stasser, Kerr, & Davis, 1990), although the best individuals might still surpass a group. There appear to be at least three reasons for this "group effect":

Group problem solving requires listening and open interaction

1. Groups are more able to recognize and adopt correct solution strategies when proposed by a group member.
2. Groups can recognize and reject errors in representation more rapidly.
3. Groups are able to process more information collectively than individuals (Loughlin, VanderStoep, & Hollingshead, 1991).

To test these hypotheses, Laughlin et al. (1991) evaluated four-person groups and four independent individuals in their attempts to induce a rule for how playing cards were being sorted from a standard deck. A typical rule was "Even diamonds and odd clubs go together." Each time a card was sorted into a pile, the subject would be told whether it was a positive example of the rule. Subjects were to hypothesize and evaluate their induced rules as new arrays of cards were presented. Results indicated that groups performed at the level of the second-best individual in recognizing the best solution strategy and at the level of the best individual in rejecting wrong hypotheses; they were equivalent to the best and second-best individuals in processing more competing information.

Working in a group does not automatically improve problem-solving performance, however. For groups to function effectively, individuals must be willing to ask questions and verbalize their input out loud, and other members must provide explanations and positive reinforcement for good ideas. Webb, Ender, and Lewis (1986), for instance, found that randomly formed pairs of middle school students were able to aid one another's learning of BASIC programming language so that they could successfully debug sample programs. Students positively influenced the behavior of their respective partners by asking and answering each other's questions and serving as models for programming procedures. The authors suggested that teachers can take advantage of this tendency of students to serve as a resource by assigning pairs of students who communicate well with each other to common problem-solving activities.

Whimbey and Lochhead (1986) have developed a structured approach for pairs of students to practice problem-solving skills. The technique calls for students to alternate roles as *problem solver* and *listener.* The problem solver thinks aloud, explaining each step taken in her attempt to represent the problem and select a solution strategy. This might entail identifying givens and goals, recalling relevant information or formulas, thinking of analogous problems, breaking the problem into parts, and testing out hypotheses. The listener is active; he checks for accuracy and determines whether any steps are being overlooked. If inconsistencies are noted, the listener asks questions or makes statements that prompt the problem solver to review her work. The listener does not directly work the problem; rather the focus is on maintaining the problem solver's verbalizations about her thinking and approach to the problem.

By the simple expedient of switching roles, both students are enabled to practice problem-solving behavior. By thinking aloud and checking each other's thinking, they learn to generate and test hypotheses about the content they are to master. These roles are difficult to assume at first and require patience by instructors willing to make such an assignment. The following example illustrates a typical exchange between students learning to function in these roles while solving the inoperable tumor problem:

P.S.   That's easy—just juice up the rays.
L.   But that will destroy his stomach before you get to the tumor.
P.S.   Oh. Hmmm.
L.   What are you thinking?
P.S.   Nothing. I'm just reading it.
L.   What are you reading?
P.S.   The part about destroying the healthy tissue.
L.   What does it mean to you?
P.S.   You have to protect it—maybe a shield or something.
L: Will the shield let the rays through to the tumor?
P.S.   I guess not. This is tough.
L.   Yeah, it is.

Problem solvers have initial difficulty in verbalizing their thoughts, and listeners must learn to monitor the other person's vocalizations without devoting attention to their own solution attempts. With practice and experience with a number of different problems, Whimbey and Lochhead report enhanced ability to assume both roles and to ultimately improve problem-solving performance. Although research evidence does not tell us how to best achieve these results, it may be necessary to begin with listeners who can solve the target problem and are prepared to ask appropriate questions. As students become comfortable in the interactive roles required, both problem solver and listener can attack problems not yet solved by either.

To prepare students to be willing to solve problems is just as important as preparing students to solve problems.   Many students cease problem-solving efforts at the first sign of difficulty. Consequently, problems that might have been solved with only moderate effort are not completed. A sense of self-efficacy must be developed if problem solving is going to be successful. Pfeiffer, Feinberg, and Gelber (1987) describe the following attitudes as necessary for effective problem solving:

1. An attitude of inquiry, in which learners are interested in finding out not only the facts but their own reaction to the facts.
2. An attitude of flexibility and open-mindedness, in which a wide range of alternative solutions are examined.
3. A positive belief in one's own ability to solve the problem at hand. The solver must believe not only that he or she possesses the requisite knowledge and skill, but that the problem itself is solvable.
4. A belief that problems are challenges or opportunities to learn, not a source of frustration.
5. A willingness to take a larger perspective—to put a particular problem in a larger context.

Effective problem solvers need positive attitudes and expectations

Instruction designed to foster these attitudes begins with teachers as models of appropriate behaviors, sharing their interest and enthusiasm for participating in problem-solving activities. Problems that are challenging, moderately difficult, and relevant to students' interests can contribute to the development of such attitudes. Pfeiffer et al. (1987) also recommend that teachers (1) employ positive reinforcement for good problem-solving performance, (2) express the expectation that students will practice to improve their problem-solving skills, and (3) utilize shaping principles to modify relevant behaviors. Many of the techniques discussed in Chapter 9 are applicable to the development of positive attitudes toward problem solving.

SUMMARY

We began this chapter with a discussion of metacognition, or the self-monitoring process that occurs during working memory. Metacognition consists of awareness of what to do to perform a task effectively (declarative knowledge) and how to regulate various cognitive processes (procedural knowledge) to achieve learning outcomes. Metacognition is basic to the acquisition and utilization of learning strategies and problem-solving skills and develops progressively into adulthood.

Eight categories of learning strategies were described, each serving to affect the encoding process so that different learning outcomes are obtained.

1. Basic rehearsal strategies such as repetition enhance memory for lists of items.
2. Complex rehearsal strategies address more complex memory units and include processes such as underlining and notation.
3. Basic elaboration strategies require the formation of associations or mental images, as in mnemonic techniques such as loci or keyword or the asking of "why" questions during the reading of text.
4. Complex elaboration strategies require that new information be combined with prior knowledge to permit the emergence of more meaningful constructions.

Summarizing, note taking, reasoning by analogy, and utilizing word or sentence context are examples of complex elaboration strategies.

5. Basic organizational strategies require that new items be re-formed into a new, often larger framework such as a cluster or that items be arranged into lists or tables.

6. Complex organizational strategies require reorganization of broader units such as ideas into systematic representations, for example, by composing concept maps, identifying text structure, or asking design questions about complex materials.

7. Comprehension-monitoring strategies, which include observing, planning, evaluating, and modifying our own learning behavior, are useful in determining whether other strategies need to be employed. Asking questions of what we are hearing or reading and applying reading strategies such as SQ3R are examples of comprehension monitoring.

8. Affective strategies are utilized to maintain motivation and attention, manage anxiety, and employ time effectively. Self-regulation and desensitization illustrate the broad category of affective strategies.

Teaching students to effectively use learning strategies requires a direct model of instruction in which teachers demonstrate the strategy, illustrate its use in different curricular areas, and provide practice with feedback. Only a few related strategies for removing a particular difficulty students are having with a specific learning task should be attempted at one time. Students should be shown how strategies contribute to long-term success in learning and should receive encouragement that the use of these tools is within their power. Strategies are more likely to be utilized independently by students when they see how they are applied to different areas of school experience.

A problem is a situation in which an individual wants to reach some goal but does not know the course of action to follow; "problem solving" refers to those cognitions, affective responses, and behavioral activities that are utilized in dealing with problems. For problems to be solved, both the givens and goal must be well defined. Recent conceptualizations of the problem-solving process focus on adequate representation or a reconstruction of the problem to ensure that the problem is understood as a critical first step. Representation will be restricted by an inadequate base of domain-specific knowledge as well as by rigid functional beliefs about events and objects that interfere with new thinking.

After representation, a search process is selected to determine a solution path. The solver may choose either an algorithm that works if applied to appropriate problems or heuristics that operate as general strategies useful in solving most problems. Trial and error, hill climbing, fractionation, looking for auxiliary problems, means-end analysis, and working backward are examples.

Compared with novices, expert problem solvers possess greater amounts of domain-specific knowledge, spend more time at problem representation, represent problems in more abstract terms based on underlying principles, utilize both inductive and deductive thinking in analyzing problems, more frequently use means-end search strategies, and are sometimes less flexible. Expert teachers, for example, possess a deep knowledge base, represent the teaching task according to effective instructional principles, make valid inferences about the information they receive, and formulate appropriate solution plans in accord with the changing classroom environment.

Instruction designed to promote problem solving requires students to generate their own explanations for why worked examples of problems are correct, provides practice in modes of problem representation (e.g., translation, schema induction, problem finding), employs analogous problems for students to practice induction of structural rules, anchors instruction in problem-solving environments, employs small groups to facilitate problem-solving performance, and facilitates the formation of positive attitudes toward one's problem-solving potential.

A concept map for this chapter appears on page 363.

EXERCISES

1. Read the following paragraph and then draw a concept map based on its contents. Remember that a good concept map asks questions of who, what, when, where, why, and how of a central idea. After drawing your map, put it away and go on to another activity. After some time, attempt to recall as much of the paragraph as you can from memory. Was your reconstruction accurate? Organized?

   Americans were on the move in 1900. The main movement was from the farms to the cities. The cities promised higher-paying jobs in industry, in offices, and in stores. There was more excitement in the bustling cities, as well as more in the way of comforts and conveniences such as electric lights, plumbing, and telephones. Women could find a husband, as there was a higher ratio of men to women. There was less money to be made on the farm, where the work was characterized by repetitive chores such as milking cows, feeding hogs, and plowing. Unfortunately, the movement led to such a rapid rise in urban populations that in only a few years, there was a whole new set of problems.

2. Sometimes we can learn from our unsuccessful attempts at solving problems, as well as from our successes. Now that you have considered the many factors that compose problem solving, you should be in a better position to analyze your own general approach to problems. Reflect on your efforts to solve the three problems introduced on page 345. You may want to reread them to refresh your memory. See if you can answer the following questions:

   a. What made this problem difficult?

   b. Why did I miss critical clues?

   c. Was it difficult to employ a search strategy?

   d. Are there other problems similar to this one that could be solved in the same way?

SUGGESTED READINGS

Chi, M. T. H., Bassok, M., Lewis, M. W., Reimann, P., & Glaser, R. (1989). Self-explanations: How students study and use examples in learning to solve problems. *Cognitive Science, 13,* 145–182.

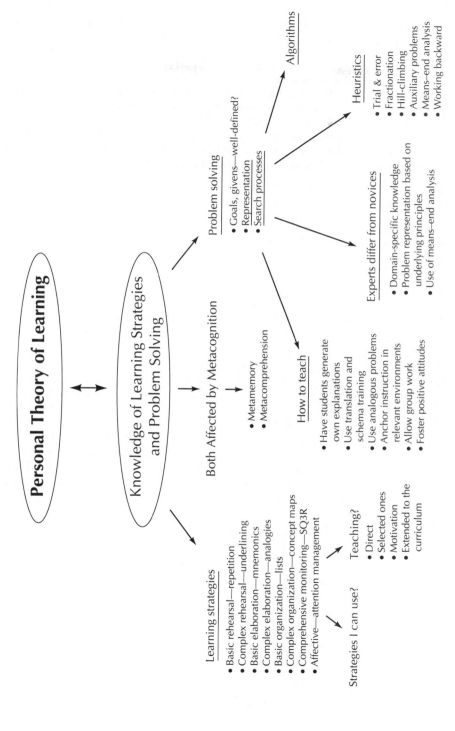

Concept map for Chapter 10

Dansereau, D. F. (1985). Learning strategy research. In J. Segal, S. Chipman, & R. Glaser (Eds.), *Thinking and learning skills: Vol. I. Relating information to research.* Hillsdale, NJ: Erlbaum.

Flavell, J. H. (1979). Metacognition and cognitive monitoring: A new era of cognitive-developmental inquiry. *American Psychologist, 34,* 906-911.

Hayes, J. R. (1981). *The Complete Problem Solver.* Philadelphia: Franklin Institute Press.

Mayer, R. E. (1992). *Thinking, problem solving and cognition* (2nd ed.). New York: Freeman.

Pressley, M., & Associates. (1990). *Cognitive strategy instruction that really improves children's academic performance.* Cambridge, MA: Brookline Books.

Weinstein, C., & Mayer, R. E. (1986). The teaching of learning strategies. In M. Wittrock (Ed.), *Handbook of research on teaching* (3rd ed.) (pp. 315-327). New York: Macmillan.

chapter 11

Disabilities and Learning

CHAPTER OUTLINE

CHAPTER OBJECTIVES

1. Tell how the terms "exceptional," "disability," and "handicap" differ.
2. Explain the sources of error in counting the number of individuals diagnosed as exceptional.

3. Discuss the purposes and components of an Individualized Educational Plan.
4. Explain the learning problems faced by students with specific learning disabilities and discuss appropriate interventions.
5. Explain how attention deficit–hyperactivity disorder affects learning and discuss appropriate interventions.
6. Describe three methods of working with students who have behavioral disorders.
7. List appropriate instructional strategies for aiding mentally retarded students to learn.
8. Discuss appropriate instructional strategies to aid the learning of visually impaired, hearing impaired, and physically impaired students.

Eight-year-old Justin wasn't getting along well with his parents and sister at home. He had difficulty in controlling his temper, complained of being sick or having a headache frequently, and rarely smiled. At school, Justin was not finishing many of his third-grade assignments, particularly those requiring him to write or complete sentences, and his teacher, Mrs. Sanchez, had written several letters home to inform his parents. Justin's parents didn't know whether school difficulties caused the physical complaints or whether an illness or medical problem accounted for their son's spotty school performance.

A checkup by Justin's doctor revealed no apparent physical, visual, or auditory problems. Talks with Mrs. Sanchez indicated that Justin's work was erratic—sometimes quite good, at other times not so good, no matter how difficult the task was. Math was a bright spot. Justin seemed to have few problems in that area. His relationships with friends appeared to be deteriorating as he fell behind in his school work, however. Mrs. Sanchez suggested that a formal assessment of Justin's school performance might be needed and that the boy could be considered for special education services. Justin's parents were dismayed; they had always considered their son to be smart. What would happen to him, and how would the school help him learn?

When Simone came to the Bleeker Street Head Start Center, she was three years old but could neither talk nor recognize herself in the mirror. Her mental development was closer to that of an 18-month-old. Now she was five and ready for kindergarten in the larger public school. She had received special training in language and speech, group play activities, and social skills and was now talking and behaving more like a four-year-old.

Simone was to be placed in an experimental school that was being restructured to make better use of teacher skills and community volunteers. Innovative curricular materials designed to enhance the learning of disadvantaged students were also to be employed. There appeared to be a good chance that the early deficits Simone encountered could be overcome.

Evan had acquired cerebral palsy, a disturbance of the motor control centers of the brain, during his mother's pregnancy. Evan was confined to a wheelchair because his condition was characterized by ataxia, or a lack of coordination, and a poor sense of balance. The condition had not affected his cognitive functioning, but he had a moderate hearing loss and did not always respond to the comments of others. Consequently, other children and some adults often believed him to be retarded as well as physically disabled.

Mrs. Casio, the school principal, met Evan at the door of his new school on the first day of class. His family had just moved to town in order to be closer to the doctor and clinic that had treated Evan for most of his eleven years. He was to be enrolled in Mr. Guinan's fifth-grade class.

"Welcome, Evan," said Mrs. Casio. "It's a great day to start school, isn't it? I just know you're going to like Woodside School. Let's go down the hall to meet your new teacher and classmates. Do you need any help with your chair?"

"Oh, no. I can handle it pretty well." Anxiously, Evan rolled himself down the hall after Mrs. Casio. As he neared his classroom, someone said, "He's coming!" With trepidation, Evan entered his new room.

These vignettes all describe children who in some way or another are disabled. In Evan's case the disability is quite apparent, since damage before his birth has left him unable to control his gross motor movements. For Justin and Simone, however, the form of disability is less obvious. Justin may suffer from a learning disability in which one of the basic psychological processes involved in understanding spoken or written language is impaired. Simone's disability probably is due to failure to receive appropriate amounts of mental stimulation and social experience prior to entering school. The presence of a disability defines a learner who is considered *exceptional*, or different from the norm on some dimension. Being different from the norm in one area does not imply that an individual is different in other respects. Evan, for instance, does not appear to differ from other students his age except with regard to his physical condition.

A *disability* can be a *handicap* to the learning of a particular skill. The two terms are not synonymous. "Disability" refers to a condition that results in an inability to perform some act, while the term "handicap" is reserved for the disadvantage resulting from the disability. Handicaps are often short-term—they exist as a result of a disability at a particular time or in a particular situation (Meyen, 1990). Rearranging the environment or learning a new skill can serve to alter the handicapping effects of a particular disability. Learning to read braille, for example, can help a person disabled by blindness to overcome the handicap of not being able to see written words. Calculators may be able to reduce the handicap imposed by a learning disability in mathematics. One of the major purposes of this chapter is to suggest some ways in which students with disabilities can overcome handicaps and learn.

Not only may disabilities lead directly to some form of handicap to learning, they may indirectly create a handicap by affecting the expectations of others. We know from our study of social learning theory that lowered perceptions of self-efficacy can result from both overt and subtle forms of social persuasion. Many people expect less of disabled persons and consequently respond to them in ways that limit such students' opportunity to learn. Oversolicitous parents or teachers may mistakenly perform tasks for disabled individuals, rather than allow them to gain the experience and

A disability is not necessarily a handicap

reward arising from personal accomplishment. Teachers who believe that retarded or learning-disabled students cannot answer particular questions in class may not direct questions to them, thereby excusing these students from participation in the cognitive activity necessary for learning. Others incorrectly assume that one form of disability implies the existence of others. The author recalls a blind friend who became irritated when strangers spoke loudly to him or even shouted. His response was to shout back: "I'm blind, darn it, not deaf!" The frustration and self-doubt created by such erroneous expectations can contribute to inadequate performance in critical areas of learning.

Expectations affect functioning of disabled

CATEGORIES OF EXCEPTIONALITY

It is difficult to determine how many children and youth have specific handicapping conditions that impede learning. Exceptional individuals are usually identified according to broad categories based on type of disability rather than by handicap. The large category of children and youth diagnosed as *learning disabled,* for example, contains students who may possess any one or a combination of disabilities in mathematical calculation or reasoning, in written language, in oral expression, or in reading or listening comprehension (Wallace & McLoughlin, 1988). The category of *behavioral disorder* may include students who suffer from anxiety, inappropriate emotional control, wide variations in mood, or frequent physical complaints (Edwards & Simpson, 1990). Students classified as having *speech/language disorders* may have difficulty in expressive or receptive language or both. The categories of exceptionality employed in schools during the identification process often fail to delineate these different handicapping conditions clearly.

In addition, a considerable amount of error may occur in the diagnosis of students with disabilities in school settings. While traditional intelligence and achievement tests are generally successful in predicting who will or will not learn well in school (Wigdor & Carver, 1982), there is sometimes bias in the manner in which these tests are administered and interpreted. Certain children obtain higher scores when tested by people they know, rather than by unfamiliar examiners (Fuchs, Fuchs, & Power, 1987). Performance of children with language handicaps, for example, may be affected by whether the student knows the test administrator (Fuchs, Fuchs, Power, & Dailey, 1983). Perhaps more critical to accurate diagnosis is the charge that students are often placed in a specific category of disability for reasons other than those that would have been indicated by valid assessment practices. In a review of the identification process, Ysseldyke et al. (1983) found that several factors were likely to influence placement:

Labels are only approximations of disabilities

1. Inconsistencies in the definitions of each exceptionality led to a variety of tests being used and a resulting lack of common assessment information. This was particularly true in identification of children in the large categories of "learning disabled" and "emotionally disturbed."
2. Decisions regarding identification were not based systematically on test results, but depended on answers to such questions as, Could the child

gain more help in the school system by being diagnosed as disabled? It should be remembered that decisions about diagnosis and placement are made for educational purposes, not as a scientific attempt to classify students as accurately as possible.

3. Once students had been referred for special education assessment, the probability was very high that they would be identified and placed; the teacher's decision to initiate a referral seemed to ensure ultimate placement.

4. Observations and ideas provided from the regular classroom teacher often were not considered in diagnosis.

As a result of this variability in assessment and decision making, some children who are not truly handicapped may be classified as disabled in some way, resulting in an overestimation of children in various categories. Nevertheless, the number of children diagnosed as possessing a disability, as indicated in national surveys, provides an estimate of the frequency of each category. Table 11.1 gives the number and percentages of handicapped children according to a recent federal report.

Table 11.1 indicates that the learning-disabled category is clearly the largest group. This high percentage may reflect the desire not to stigmatize students with labels such as mentally retarded (Singer & Butler, 1987) and attempts to obtain special instruction for children who fit no other category. The combined total of more than four million students vividly brings home the likelihood that all teachers will encounter handicapped learners at some time in their careers. It is therefore necessary to be aware of how handicapping effects associated with each disability interfere with learning and how instruction can be adapted to each type of student. This is particularly true in that the large majority of disabled students are currently *mainstreamed* into the general instructional program of the school.

Diagnosis of exceptionalities often is inconsistent

TABLE 11.1   Number and percentage of U.S. students by handicapping condition in 1989

Handicapping Condition	Number	Percentage
Learning disabled	1,941,731	47.0
Speech/language impaired	956,140	23.2
Mentally retarded	601,288	14.6
Emotionally disturbed	374,730	9.1
Multihandicapped	79,132	1.9
Hard of hearing/deaf	56,937	1.4
Orthopedically impaired	47,409	1.1
Other health impaired	45,865	1.1
Visually handicapped	22,864	0.6
Deaf–blind	1,472	0.05
All conditions	4,127,568	100.05*

*Percentages do not total 100 because of a rounding error.
SOURCE: Adapted from U.S. Department of Education, *Eleventh annual report to Congress on the implementation of the Education of the Handicapped Act* (Washington, DC: U.S. Government Printing Office, 1989), p. 15.

Historically, students diagnosed as handicapped were maintained in special classrooms, often removed from the activities of the majority. These *self-contained* special education classrooms were believed to provide the best instructional environment for exceptional students because they diminished distractions, could be slower paced and tailored to the needs of those with particular handicapping conditions, and decreased unfavorable comparisons to nonhandicapped students. The author vividly recalls a severely handicapped friend who came to school every day at the same time, then disappeared into the basement where other students were never to go, only to reemerge at the end of the day.

Self-contained
classrooms
lacked stimulation

For a number of reasons, such modes of instructional organization have been largely abandoned. Research indicated that children in segregated, self-contained classrooms actually fared worse in achievement and socialization than peers educated in the general classroom. The isolated students appeared to miss the stimulation, interaction, and opportunities provided learners in the traditional environment (Goldstein, Moss, & Jordan, 1965). At the same time, social movement for equality of educational opportunity, culminating in Public Law 94–142, the Education for All Handicapped Children Act of 1975, required a more integrated approach to the education of exceptional children. Children were to be taught wherever possible in the mainstream, being placed in the general classroom to the extent of their ability to profit from such a placement. A student with a visual handicap, for instance, might be mainstreamed in all classes except those for which the handicap called for special instruction and materials, while a student with a physical handicap might be separated only when physical therapy was being provided. The underlying principle dictating placement and special service is that of *least restrictive environment,* according to which restrictions to access to general education are imposed only for the learner's benefit. Mainstreaming provisions range from complete *inclusion,* in which all instruction is done in the regular classroom, through temporary removal for special services such as speech, to the more lengthy absences required by severely handicapped students. Fears of rejection or avoidance notwithstanding, observations of students with learning disabilities who are included in general education classrooms reveal that they are treated much like other students by teachers (McIntosh, Vaughn, Schumm, Haager, & Lee, 1993) and have a better opportunity to be accepted by peers (Madge, Affleck, & Lowenbraun, 1990).

Inclusion or
mainstreaming
is current focus

To more carefully plan, manage, and monitor the education of exceptional children, federal and state laws mandate the creation of specialized educational programs for each student diagnosed as exceptional. These *Individualized Educational Plans (IEPs)* are agreements between parents, regular and special education teachers, and school administrative personnel. They describe a particular student's handicap and give the following information: what is to be done instructionally to remediate or compensate for the handicap in the form of annual goals and short-term instructional objectives, who is responsible for the plan, the amount of time to be spent in the general educational program, and the target dates for completion/review. IEPs must be formally signed, followed, and periodically reviewed. An example of part of an IEP for a fictitious student with a learning disability is presented in Figure 11.1. The instructional objectives listed follow from the specific goal of improving the student's reading skills in the areas of word identification and comprehension. This particular

IEPs = formal
plans for disabled learners

Red Oak Public Schools—Special Services
INDIVIDUALIZED EDUCATION PROGRAM
Goals and Objectives
Joe S.

Printed: 05/17/93

Page 1

Student: Joe S.
Enrollment School: Lincoln Elem. LEA 326
Attendance School: Lincoln LEA 326
Birth Date: 07/22/84 Prim Serv/Placement: LD Dir Serv in Reg Ed Class—Int
Exceptionality: LD Related Services: SL

Grade: 2

GOAL 1: J. S. will improve his reading skills in the areas of word identification and comprehension

Obj 1.
SUB 1 BANK 2 STR 2 SET 2 OBJ 35
WHEN GIVEN A LIST OF several CVC WORDS, J. S. WILL EITHER READ OR WRITE THEM AS DESIGNATED BY THE TEACHER WITH 80 % ACCURACY.

Evaluation Procedure:
Baseline: Unmet Date 05/12/93 Provider: LD Dir Serv in Reg Ed Class—Int
Target: 80% Date 05/12/94 Status: Unmet 05/12/93

Strategies: one-to-one tutorial
Materials: CVC word lists, presented on cards or computer screen

Obj 2.
SUB 1 BANK 2 STR 2 SET 2 OBJ 38
GIVEN THE WORD FAMILIES (AN, IT, AT, EN, OT, ALL, IN) J.S. WILL FORM (ORALLY/IN WRITING) several WORDS WITH 80 % ACCURACY.

Evaluation procedure:
Baseline: Unmet Date 05/12/93 Provider: LD Dir Serv in Reg Ed Class—Int
Target: 80% Date 05/12/94 Status: Unmet 05/12/93

Strategies One-to-one tutorial
Materials: Lists of VC word families, presented on cards or computer

Obj 3.
SUB 1 BANK 2 STR 2 SET 2 OBJ 44
GIVEN A BEGINNING BLEND, J. S. WILL GIVE (ORALLY/POINT TO) THE CORRECT BLEND WITH 80 % ACCURACY.

Evaluation Procedure:
Baseline: Unmet Date 05/12/93 Provider: LD Dir Serv in Reg Ed Class—Int
Target: 80% Date 05/12/94 Status: Unmet 05/12/93

Strategies: One-to-one tutorial
Materials: Lists of blends, pointer

FIGURE 11.1 Sample Individualized Educational Plan

deficit had been identified after formal assessment. IEPs for other categories of exceptionality follow a similar format.

STUDENTS WITH LEARNING DISABILITIES

The largest category of exceptionality is also the most difficult to define. Individuals classified as learning disabled are quite diverse in the handicaps they face in learning. In effect, the term "learning disability" refers to a variety of specific disorders, and no one individual will exhibit difficulties in all areas.

Perhaps the most widely accepted definition of learning disability was incorporated into the Education for All Handicapped Children Act. The federal definition is as follows:

> Specific learning disability means a disorder in one or more of the basic psychological processes involved in understanding or in using language, spoken or written, which may manifest itself in an imperfect ability to listen, think, speak, read, write, spell, or to do mathematical calculations. The term includes such conditions as perceptual handicaps, brain injury, minimal brain dysfunction, dyslexia and developmental aphasia. The term does not include children who have learning problems which are primarily the result of visual, hearing, or motor handicaps, of mental retardation, or of environmental, cultural, or economic disadvantage. [Section 5b(4), of PL 94–142]

This definition emphasizes the academic nature of learning disabilities, rather than neurological deficits, which are presumed to be present but are not identifiable. It distinguishes learning-disabled children from those with other learning problems. The federal act also stresses the *discrepancy* between expected and actual achievement in one or more areas. Students with learning disabilities possess average or above-average intellectual ability but do not achieve at the level predicted by their age and intellectual level. Determining the amount of discrepancy is based on standardized intelligence and achievement test results, with two years below the expected level of achievement the most frequent criterion. Assessment of a significant discrepancy is inexact, unfortunately. For instance, a third-grader achieving at the first-grade level is not comparable to a ninth-grade student achieving at the seventh-grade level. Moreover, administration of different tests may yield different measures of discrepancy. Many states and local education agencies have established their own method and assessment procedures for determining discrepancy, thus contributing to a lack of standardization about who is eventually diagnosed as learning disabled (Wallace and McLoughlin, 1988).

Discrepancy in one or two areas

Some educators have criticized this definition because it does not differentiate degrees of impairment and is vague in describing the effect of the deficit on specific academic skills (Graham, Harris, & Reid, 1990). In part, these shortcomings relate to failure of all students classified as learning disabled to exhibit the same degree of handicap or the same combination of deficit areas. The category is so diverse that predictions of the kind of learning handicap to expect when meeting a child classified as learning disabled are often inaccurate. Nevertheless, some relatively common patterns of learning difficulties in specific academic areas can be identified.

Learning-disabled children differ in type of deficit

Reading Disabilities and Interventions

Reading difficulties are the most widespread and persistent problem experienced by students with learning disabilities. The term *dyslexia* is often applied to individuals with a reading disability, particularly if the condition is presumed to result from genetic or neurological involvement (D. B. Clark, 1988). A wide variety of deficits in learning have been associated with reading disability. In the early stages of reading acquisition, impaired ability to use phonological information to process written material is often observed. For example, skills in forming sound–symbol relationships (e.g., segmenting and blending the sounds within words) differentiate disabled from proficient readers (Fox and Routh, 1983). A deficit in this area impedes learning of the alphabetic principle (described in Chapter 7), which aids in the recognition of new words (Stanovich, 1986). A tendency to read certain letters or words backward or inverted is also common, with *b,d,g,q* and *m,n,u,v* as the most common reversals.

Students with reading disabilities are also slower at naming series of familiar stimuli, such as letters and objects. Rapid naming tasks are believed to reflect the ease with which sounds and meanings of written words can be accessed and thus are important to the acquisition of reading speed and fluency (D. B. Clark, 1988). Disabled younger readers also display deficits in short-term memory of verbal information such as letters or words (Mann, 1986). Rapid naming and short-term retrieval of written stimuli are crucial to the development of automaticity in word recognition (Cornwall, 1992).

Secondary level students with a reading disability have difficulty with the many independent learning tasks that are ordinarily expected in content area instruction (Zigmond, Kerr, & Schaeffer, 1988). There are problems in identifying main ideas, taking notes, and completing assignments requiring analysis of text structures. In addition, inability to read well contributes to failure to fulfill other expectations, such as meeting deadlines, showing an interest in the content area, and working without direction. Because secondary classrooms often require independent activity and selection of information among a variety of sources, reading-disabled individuals may not recognize important content to be read or may not devote adequate attention to the correct source (Spruill, 1992).

Secondary reading disabilities in comprehension

Remedial instruction designed to aid students with reading disabilities of course varies with the nature of the deficit. The most common intervention has been a *developmental* approach in which basal reading series are used to introduce a controlled vocabulary and supplementary phonics practice. Such approaches are often successful because they are frequently taught out of the regular classroom and include a wide variety of materials that can be selected for individual learners (Lerner, 1985). *Direct instruction,* a useful alternative, incorporates behavioral principles in a phonics-based approach, such as DISTAR (Engelmann & Brunner, 1984). The program is highly structured, with a specific sequence of presentations as well as statements and hand signals to be used by the teacher. In a longitudinal study of a direct instruction reading program including DISTAR, inner-city elementary students with reading disabilities improved significantly in reading achievement, particularly in letter identification and word attack skills (Kuder, 1991). Improvement was related to existing language abilities such as knowledge of phonics and syntax, suggesting that direct reading instruction programs may be most effective when coupled with training in specific language skills. For example, Cornwall (1992) found that phonological awareness significantly predicted word attack and spelling performance, rapid letter naming predicted speed in reading prose passages, and short-term memory for words added to the prediction of word recognition. Cornwall suggests that practice in basic learning skills such as remembering and identifying verbal items rapidly may be an important prerequisite for many students with reading disabilities.

Structured approach to reading instruction

Instruction of older students with reading disabilities should proceed in two directions: *compensatory accommodation,* in which students are aided to gain access to curriculum content through alternatives to reading, and *development of comprehension skill,* in which students are aided to understand the meaning of what they are to read (Spruill, 1992). Accommodations may include taping lectures for students to listen to, preparing notes to accompany lectures or having peers provide copies of their notes, finding audiotapes of text material, and pairing reading-disabled students with tutors or cooperative learning groups to prepare for tests. Assignments and testing formats may require adaptation, such as altering time limits or dictating test questions instead of requiring students to read them.

Content area teachers can aid students improve their comprehension skills by instructing them to read for a specific purpose, such as finding the main idea, studying italicized material, or skimming headings to prepare class assignments (Cheney, 1989). Small-group formats can be employed to share reading responsibility, with the teacher occasionally reading to illustrate how to find information or take notes (Stone, 1989). Some content may have to be rewritten or reorganized to reduce complexity and enhance readability. Beech (1983) makes the following suggestions for teacher simplification of text:

1. Present ideas logically, moving from generalizations to details.
2. Discuss sequences of events in chronological order.
3. Cluster related information together in paragraphs.
4. Simplify sentences by reducing sentence length through minimizing modifiers and descriptive clauses. Words that mark relationships such as "because" or "next" should be retained.
5. Choose words that occur more frequently in usage and possess high imagery content ("The amoeba is like living jelly.").
6. Avoid use of nominalizations such as "the rowing of the oarsmen." Use simple forms such as "the oarsmen row."

Writing Disabilities and Interventions

Cognitive processes are critical in writing

The Flower and Hayes model of writing (1986) discussed in Chapter 7 has served as the basis for a number of analyses of the writing difficulties of students with learning disabilities. Poor writing performance is attributed to deficits in executing and monitoring many of the cognitive processes utilized in the writing process. For example, students with a writing disability do not generate an adequate amount of content to communicate their message. Nodine, Barenbaum, and Newcomer (1985), for example, found that the compositions of students with learning disabilities are only half as long as those of normally achieving students. While time spent in planning is equivalent in both groups of students, students with learning disabilities are less likely to attend to the needs of the reader, the constraints imposed by the topic, or the organization of the text they produce (Englert, Raphael, Feer, & Anderson, 1988). Their approach to revision is characterized more by detecting production errors in the mechanics of writing than by improving clarity and organization (MacArthur & Graham, 1987). With these deficits, students have difficulty in producing coherent text and must rely on the teacher or others to monitor their writing effectiveness. An example of the work of a ten-year-old student with a writing disability appears in Figure 11.2.

If students are to produce meaningful written language, they must be aware of the various cognitive processes and must be aided to develop self-regulation of writing strategies. A number of instructional procedures designed to reach these goals have been implemented successfully. One procedure is to create *dialogues* (between student and teacher, student and student, or student with self) about the various stages of the writing process. Englert, Raphael, Anderson, Anthony, and Stevens

FIGURE 11.2   Example of written work of a ten-year-old student with a writing disability

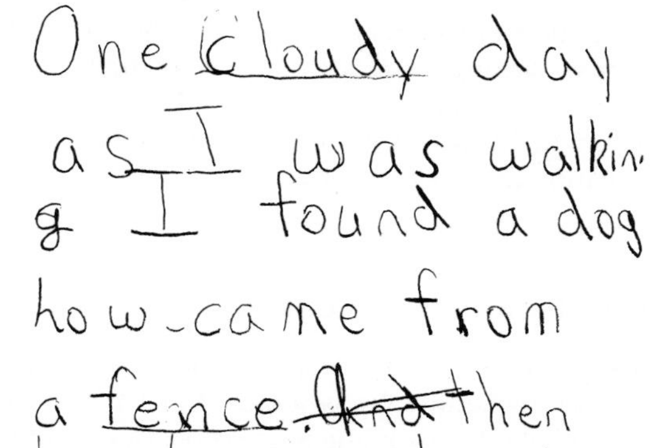

One Cloudy day as I was walking I found a dog how came from a fence. And then he chased a truck down the street and came back to me. And I took him to the Vet. Then I saw a animal and

(1991) trained students to systematically employ writing strategies to produce compositions that attempted either to explain an idea or to compare/contrast ideas. Training consisted of exposing students to a set of "think sheets," each describing one of five writing functions: *P*lanning, *O*rganizing, *W*riting, *E*diting, and *R*evising (*POWER*). Each think sheet contained self-questions or self-instructional statements to promote students' development of metacognitive control of writing strategies. For example, the think sheet for organizing asked questions such as "What is being explained?" and "What materials do I need?" These questions helped students organize their ideas into text structure categories (explanation or comparison/contrast) as a map in producing their compositions. The editing phase included consultation with a peer about how to improve the paper. Evaluation of the program indicated that dialogic instruction was effective in promoting students' expository writing abilities on the two text structures and resulted in improved performance on a transfer task requiring independent writing. Students with writing disabilities who participated in training were not significantly different from a non-learning-disabled group after instruction, despite large differences between the groups before training. The authors contend that the instruction made the writing process more visible to students by demonstrating how "self-talk" leads to successful writing. According to Sawyer, Graham, and Harris (1992), improvement of the writing skills of students with learning disabilities calls for the acquisition of all the following: (1) knowledge of effective writing strategies and the procedural know-how to employ them, (2) explicit self-regulation procedures, including goal-setting and self-monitoring skills such as self-assessment and self-recording of strategy use and effectiveness, (3) understanding of one's role as an active collaborator with peers or teachers in the process of writing, (4) direct practice in writing compositions that have different kinds of structure, and (5) experience in applying one's knowledge to new writing contexts. To ensure that all five components are acquired, teachers must function both as models of how to utilize correct strategies and as coaches who gradually withdraw direct guidance to allow students to take responsibility for regulating their own writing.

Self-regulation important in improvement of writing

Mathematics Disability and Intervention

Skill development for students with a mathematical disability does not proceed smoothly from mastery of declarative knowledge of math facts to their application in procedural knowledge to problem solving. Since most of the difficulty lies in a failure to automatize basic mathematical operations such as recognizing a division statement, less attention is available for consideration of problem demands (Goldman, Pellegrino, & Mertz, 1988). Word problems are particularly difficult for students with learning disabilities because they demand high levels of automaticity in computation as well as semantic knowledge (Kintsch & Greeno, 1985).

Many of the procedures suggested in Chapter 7 to aid students to acquire automaticity in mathematical computation are therefore relevant to the instruction of students with mathematical disabilities. In addition, Woodward (1991) recommends instructional aids such as visual diagrams of the operations involved and practice on a variety of examples to increase the chances of reaching automaticity.

ATTENTION DEFICIT–HYPERACTIVITY DISORDER

We first discussed children who have difficulty attending to tasks in Chapter 6, when we emphasized the role of attention. The term *attention deficit–hyperactivity disorder (ADHD)* is not listed in Table 11.1. Although the category has acquired considerable descriptive value among educators, physicians, psychologists, and others who work with exceptional children, it is still unclear how the classification should be included within the range of handicapping conditions. The category is defined by many behavioral descriptions overlapping those used to describe other conditions, such as learning disabilities and emotional disorders. Therefore, ADHD learners are frequently misclassified as students who possess these categories of exceptionality (Epstein, Shaywitz, Shaywitz, & Woolston, 1991). This practice only serves to raise additional questions about the validity and reliability of diagnostic labels (Cantwell & Baker, 1991). Those diagnosed as ADHD are entitled to special services, but often are accommodated under the category "Other health-impaired."

ADHD: a syndrome of possible behaviors

ADHD refers to a syndrome involving three areas of symptoms: attentional impairment, impulsivity, and hyperactivity. To be classified as ADHD according to the *Diagnostic and Statistical Manual III—Revised* (DSM-III-R) of the American Psychiatric Association (1987), it is necessary to demonstrate eight specific behaviors from a set of 14 that compose the syndrome. Behaviors include "fidgets with hands and feet," "has difficulty remaining seated," "blurts out," "can't sustain attention," and "easily distracted by extraneous stimuli." The behaviors must be observed before the age of seven and must last for at least six months. Such a diagnostic system leads to inclusion of children who are very different from one another. This wide range reflects not only the multidimensionality of the syndrome but confusion about its origin and development. The DSM-III-R definition can be criticized because it ignores possible causes and relies on potentially unreliable observations to determine the occurrence of ADHD. For example, what behavior constitutes "blurting out"? Doesn't failure to "sustain attention" have something to do with the interest level of the tasks one is to perform?

ADHD children therefore exhibit a variety of behaviors that interfere with learning. The most common symptom is an apparent lack of attention to the demands of the surroundings. Douglas and Peters (1979) identified two categories of attention deficit: failure to select the correct stimulus for the allocation of attention and inability to sustain attention after a stimulus has been selected. In the first type, important work may never begin; in the second it may never be completed. The learning of ADHD children is also affected by hyperactivity, or excessive motor activity. This characteristic not only hampers completion of the ADHD child's work, but is a source of distraction to other students. Hyperactive children are likely to fall behind their classmates in many academic areas and to receive low ratings by teachers in traits such as cooperation and interest in school (Minde et al., 1971).

Aggressive behavior is another common trait, although some ADHD children may engage in aggressive acts that appear planned and hostile, while for others, aggression seems to be more spontaneous as a result of frustration. Many of these children also have difficulty in establishing social relationships, with some initiating contact with peers in an immature, inept manner. Others remain aloof, oblivious to social stimulation, however (Whalen & Henker, 1991).

A number of interventions designed to reduce the effect of ADHD on learning have been instituted. An early approach to instruction of highly distractible children was to reduce sensory input, so that attention would be directed toward the instructional stimulus alone. Handicapped children might participate in group activities with others, but tasks requiring completion of seatwork were done in an isolated part of the room or in a specially designed cubicle. In fact, some researchers reported that off-task activity actually increased when students were in isolation (Zentall & Zentall, 1976). These results may be explained by recognizing that the problem of sustaining attention after a task had been selected, which may be more crucial to school success, was not addressed by the intervention (Douglas & Peters, 1979).

A different kind of treatment involves modification of the physical symptoms of the disorder through *psychostimulant medication.* Stimulants such as methylphenidate (MPH or Ritalin) and D-amphetamine sulfate (Dexedrine) have been used to alter the physical reactivity of ADHD children. Recall from Chapter 2 that stimulants enhance the activity of neurotransmitters by increasing the release of these substances from the synapses of neurons, thus stimulating the areas of the brain that control attention, arousal, and inhibitory processes. Drug treatment reflects the belief that ADHD is a biologically based deficiency in the child's sensitivity to environmental reinforcers that control motivation, inhibit behavior, and sustain effort. In short, "stimulants, through their effect on the nervous system, make children with ADHD more sensitive to reinforcers in the environment and thereby increase attention span or persistence of responding" (Anastapoulus, DuPaul, & Barkley, 1991, p. 210).

The effects of psychostimulants on the behavior of ADHD children have been extensively reviewed. Initial studies seemed to indicate that their use led to improvement in classroom manageability but not to improved academic performance (Barkley and Cunningham, 1978). Improvements in research design, however, produced a more recent set of studies demonstrating short-term gains on a wide variety of measures of academic productivity such as memory, sustained attention, and impulse control (Anastopoulus et al., 1991). MPH treatment has also been found to enhance on-task behavior and recall of classroom content (Douglas, Barr, O'Neill, & Britton, 1986). Increases in compliance, independent play, and responsiveness to social interaction with parents, teachers, and peers have been observed in classroom settings as a result of MPH treatment as well (Barkley, Karlsson, Strzelecki, & Murphy, 1984). ADHD does continue into adolescence and adulthood, but stimulant medications have been used to produce the same kinds of positive effect with older students (Wender, 1987).

Most of the performance improvements were found on tasks in which immediate outcomes were assessed, such as short-term memory of content in drill and practice sessions. It remains to be demonstrated whether enhanced attention during drill and practice operates to produce improvement in academic learning skills over the long term (Swanson, Cantwell, Lerner, McBurnett, & Hanna, 1991). It is also true that psychostimulants tend to wear off during a classroom day, and many teachers report a marked deterioration in behavior of medicated ADHD children in the afternoon. This "rebound effect" may involve a worsening of behavior beyond the levels observed when the child was not taking medication (Anastopoulus et al., 1991). About one-third of a large sample of boys (the large majority of ADHD students are males) treated with MPH exhibited rebound effects (Johnston, Pelham, Hozo, & Sturges, 1988). Other side effects from psychostimulant medication include decreased appetite, insomnia, somatic complaints such as headache, and a withdrawn quietness (Tannock, Schachar, Carr, & Logan, 1989). Frequency and severity of these unwanted physical effects are apparently due to a higher-than-optimal amount of dosage (Barkley, 1981) and medication of students who had not been screened for potential reactions to the drugs. Monitoring of dosage amounts and results is necessary to reduce these effects (Swanson et al., 1991).

Psychostimulant medication has a number of undesirable psychological effects as well. The on-again, off-again behavior of ADHD children who act one way while under medication and another way when medication is removed or wears off is upsetting both to the individual and to those in contact with him. While the medication is received by children and their families as a welcome relief, the pill can be perceived as a sort of "magic," working independently of the personal effort of the child. Such a view may encourage an external attribution, in which the child's contribution to his own improvement is seen as minimal. A more adaptive view that contributes to the child's perception of self-efficacy would be to think of the pill as a support to the child's developing competency (Whalen & Henker, 1991).

Pills cannot teach children to alter the cognitive and behavioral skills they need to master content and to relate to others. These skills must be taught through a form of *cognitive–behavioral training.* The main goal of such training, which should accompany psychostimulant medication, is to develop self-control and reflective problem-solving strategies, two attributes in which ADHD children tend to be deficient. This type of intervention employs many of the self-regulatory, metacognitive skills and teaching procedures that have been described elsewhere in this text, and it appears to work well in the short term. Unfortunately, review of most interventions employing cognitive–behavioral strategies fails to demonstrate transfer and generalization of these skills by ADHD children to situations outside the training setting (Abikoff, 1991). Nevertheless, it appears that a combination of psychostimulant medication and cognitive–behavioral training is the most effective intervention in the learning of ADHD children at present. In addition, it is important that parents of ADHD children be made aware of the implications of the disability and become partners in the implementation of any treatment plan.

Treatment = psychostimulants and cognitive–behavioral training

BEHAVIORAL DISORDERS

The category of exceptionality known as "behavioral disorders" includes children and youth who display a wide variety of unacceptable behaviors. Everyone occasionally acts in ways that deviate from the norm. The author knows a child who seems to constantly hum the same tune, often at inappropriate times. Another student has difficulty controlling his anger, often pounding on a desk when upset. Are these disabilities? The answer depends on the criteria used to define the condition. A widely accepted set of criteria developed by Bower (1969) classified behavior problems according to whether they are *acute* (occur to a marked extent) or *chronic* (occur

Behavior disorders defined by frequency and intensity

frequently over time). Using these two standards, Bower described five patterns that describe behavior disorders in children and youth:

1. Inability to benefit from academic instruction that is not attributable to intellectual capacity, hearing, or vision problems.
2. Inability to develop and maintain positive interpersonal relationships with peers or adults.
3. Behaviors that are highly inappropriate responses to environmental or social conditions.
4. Wide variations in mood (extreme euphoria or depression).
5. Frequent physical complaints or fatigue that have no medical basis. (Bower, 1969, p. 21)

All these characteristics may occur occasionally in any student. When they occur to a marked extent or for long periods of time, however, they indicate grounds for the diagnosis of emotional disturbance. Justin and Simone, described at the beginning of the chapter, display behaviors that are inappropriate for school, but more would need to be known about how acute and chronic these symptoms are before the children could be labeled "behavior disordered."

The first pattern described by Bower is the most critical and has the most to do with children's being placed in the behavioral disorders category. As a general rule, these students do not learn at the level one would expect from an assessment of their intellectual and physical potential. This pattern of underachievement is probably a function of the interfering effect of the problematic behavior, as the child attempts to cope with internal conflicts rather than academic tasks, and of the failure to learn itself, which may generate the problem behavior. The two factors lead to behavior patterns that are easily confused with those exhibited by learning-disabled or mentally retarded students. The major difference is the degree and frequency of the maladaptive behavior in the student with emotional disturbance (Edwards & Simpson, 1990).

Two patterns of disordered behavior emerge when one analyzes all the various characteristics that have been used to described emotionally disturbed children. One is *aggressive, acting-out behavior,* in which students exhibit disobedience, disruptiveness, tantrums, destructiveness toward their own and others' property, uncooperativeness in group situations, and negativism (Quay, 1986). A child demonstrating these behaviors is in frequent conflict with others, both in school and out. Others in turn may react to the aggressive student negatively or punitively, so that fights, verbal threats, teasing and "put-downs" typically occur when a student with this type of emotional disturbance is around. In many cases, the frequent aggression becomes socialized through gang involvement and delinquent activities.

The other behavioral pattern most commonly observed is a more internalized form of *withdrawal and immaturity.* Its characteristics are shyness, anxiety, lethargy, depression, distractibility, a preference for solitary activity, and a lack of self-confidence (Quay, 1986). *Autism* and *schizophrenia* are extreme forms of withdrawal. In autism there is inability to respond to or communicate with others, a lack of affect or emotional response, bizarre behavior, and extreme isolation from others. Schizophrenia is typified by disordered thinking, often accompanied by hallucinations or delusions, and inappropriate emotional responses (Hallahan & Kauffman,

Two patterns: aggression and withdrawal

1991). Different students vary in the severity of both dimensions of the disorder. It is easy to overlook the problems of withdrawn individuals in particular, because their behavior is not so disruptive to the classroom routine. In many cases, however, extreme withdrawal is just as destructive to the individual's ability to learn as is aggressive behavior. At times, withdrawn children who initially internalize their frustration and anxieties lose control and exhibit sudden outbursts, catching by surprise educators who had not carefully considered and monitored their behavior. These occasions often attract media attention because they result in injury or property damage.

In general, instructional *interventions* for these children involve rearranging the student's location in the classroom to reduce distractions and provide greater proximity to the teacher, the use of individualized assignments where appropriate, and closer monitoring of progress. Such students must be told gently yet honestly about the kinds of problem they create for the teacher as well as other students and themselves. Clear guidelines and firm expectations about proper behavior must also be communicated, with consequences identified and carried out surely and promptly. In addition, more specialized programs have been developed to remedy the learning problems of these children.

Three techniques that have been applied with some success are *differential reinforcement, self-management*, and *the no-lose method of problem solving*.

Differential Reinforcement

Differential reinforcement is based on operant principles involving the reinforcement of positive alternatives to the undesirable behavior. In this approach, the educator moves from an exclusive focus on what the student needs to stop doing and begins to concentrate on what the student does need to do. Punishment for inappropriate behavior is de-emphasized, and the target goals are acceptable behaviors that can be demonstrated by the student. The reinforcement schedule for alternative responses is initially continuous, then becomes progressively more variable. Differential reinforcement requires the successful implementation of six steps: (1) identification of the behavior to be reduced, (2) identification of positive alternatives, (3) selection of a system of differential reinforcement, (4) identification of reinforcers based on student preference (token systems, privileges, social activities, etc.), (5) establishment of a final criterion of success, and (6) implementation of the program and evaluation of results. Webber and Scheuermann (1991) have described a number of problem behaviors and possible positive alternatives. Examples are provided in Table 11.2.

Reinforce differentially to emphasize desirable behavior

Self-Management

Self-management can be used with students who express willingness to change behaviors they have difficulty controlling. Because monitoring one's own behavior meets adolescents' needs to control their environment and may allow them to experience a sense of competence, self-management may be less heavily resisted by that group of students than strategies relying on external control (Jones & Jones, 1990). External agents such as teachers are not always available in the immediate environment, and the goal of any intervention is to permit the individual to function autonomously.

TABLE 11.2 Problem behaviors and positive alternatives

Behavior	Alternatives

Talking back, cursing	Positive response: "I understand."
	  Acceptable questions: "May I tell you my side?"
	  Acceptable exclamations: "Dang!" "Shoot!"

Hitting, punching, kicking, pushing/shoving	Using verbal expressions of anger, pounding fist into hand, sitting next to other students without touching them.
Noncompliance	Following directions within a fixed time, following directions by second time direction is given.
Talking out	Raising hand and waiting to be called on.
Turning in messy work	No marks other than answers; no more than four erasures, nor more than three folds.
Self-injurious or self-stimulatory behavior	Sitting with hands on desk or in lap, hands not touchinhg any part of body.

SOURCE: J. Webber and B. Scheuermann, Managing behavior problems: Accentuate the positive . . . eliminate the negative! *Teaching Exceptional Children, 24*(1), 13–19 (1991). Adapted with permission of the publisher.

J. F. Carter (1993) has devised a nine-step self-management program. The steps are recorded on a planning form and are maintained by the student.

Self-management the ultimate goal?

1. Select a target behavior and its replacement—talking without raising one's hand is replaced by waiting to be recognized with hand in air.
2. Define the target behavior—hand raising is required in teacher-directed instructional activities but not necessary during nonstructured activities.
3. Design the data-recording technique—identify how the data are to be recorded (e.g., + or — marks) and when (period of day, class), and describe the recording form (e.g., index card with days and times labeled).
4. Teach the student to use the recording form—student role-plays and practices using it.
5. Choose a strategy for ensuring accuracy—student matches his or her self-recording form with the teacher's at the end of the class period.
6. Establish goals and contingencies—determine how student will be involved in setting the goal and what reinforcement will be contingent.
7. Review goal and student performance—identify when and how the plan will be modified if goal is met/not met.
8. Plan for reducing self-recording procedures.
9. Plan for generalization and maintenance—clarify how long student will self-record and how long target behavior must be demonstrated for the program to be considered a success.

No-Lose Method of Problem Solving

The no-lose method of problem solving is adapted from Gordon's Teacher Effectiveness Training (TET) model (1974). This technique stresses negotiation of "no-lose" arrangements between teacher and student. Authoritative control over students is replaced with teacher–student interdependence and the meeting of mutual needs.

Rather than assuming that teachers or other external agents know how best to remediate a particular problem, this approach involves shared decision making. Problems are initially analyzed by identifying *problem ownership*. Problems "owned" by students include poor self-control, anxiety, and inhibitions. The teacher strives for understanding of these problems by engaging in *active listening*—that is, considering the problem from the point of view of what the student is trying to communicate. In this way, responsibility for resolving the problem behavior remains with the student. Teacher-owned problems occur when student misbehavior makes teachers frustrated or angry. Teachers must communicate their standpoints through *"I-messages"* that express concern for the effect of the student's behavior on others. One message might be: "When someone starts to fight in my class, I have to stop teaching to stop the fight and then I feel bad that everyone is upset." The I-message communicates that the student is causing real problems for the teacher, which in turn can be expected to provoke undesirable feelings.

Gordon believed that through the use of active listening, problem ownership decisions, and I-messages, most problems could be understood and attempts to resolve them initiated. Problem resolution occurs through six stages, all designed to produce a mutually acceptable (no-lose) solution: (1) definition and identification of the source of ownership, (2) generation of possible solutions by both parties, (3) preliminary evaluation of solutions, (4) decisions about which solution is best, (5) determination of how to implement the solution, and (6) assessment of the effectiveness of the solution. Solution plans should lead to specified responsibilities for all parties, resulting in an agreement that all can follow and evaluate. Failure to follow through by students should not elicit retribution by the teacher; rather, the teacher should communicate a new I-message to the effect that there is now a new problem to be resolved. This approach—a deliberate attempt to help students acquire the control they need to reform their own behavior—requires patience and understanding.

In a study of teachers' attempts to resolve student problems, Brophy and Rohrkemper (1981) found that teachers rated as effective by classroom observers employed many of Gordon's recommendations. They assumed responsibility for aiding students to solve their own problems, helped them to understand the causes and consequences of their behavior, and worked to develop long-term plans, rather than resorting to attempts to control the situation immediately.

The three approaches described above present a continuum from predominant teacher control under differential reinforcement to somewhat less control under a self-management system to a more mutual interaction between teacher and student in the no-lose method. All three have their advocates, depending on one's theoretical orientation. The most useful approach in a particular situation may be a function of the amount of responsibility the student with an emotional disorder is willing and able to assume and how the teacher views his or her role in resolving student problems.

> Your example of an "I-message"?

> Why is it "No lose"?

> Which technique do you prefer?

MENTAL RETARDATION

Traditionally, mental retardation has been diagnosed on the basis of IQ scores. The American Association of Mental Retardation (AAMR) divides the IQ range into four levels: mild (IQ 55–69), moderate (IQ 40–54), severe (IQ 25–39), and profound (IQ below 25). In the schools, individuals have been classified as (1) *educable*—those with mild retardation who can learn school tasks if presented at a slower pace, (2) *trainable*—individuals with moderate retardation who cannot learn academic skills but can be taught skills that allow them to function independently (e.g., recognizing coins or reading important words such as "stop" or "go"), and (3) *severely/profoundly mentally retarded*—individuals who have serious physical impairments in addition to mental retardation and may learn only self-help skills.

Mental health professionals have become disenchanted with IQ-based criteria, however. Some people who score in the 50s are capable of working in sheltered workshops, while others with the same score cannot manage their own clothing. In addition, dissatisfaction with the validity of intelligence tests has been widespread (Sternberg & Davidson, 1990). Critics argue that intelligence tests are biased in favor of Anglo-European, middle-class students whose experience better prepares them for such tests and whose performance constitutes the norm group to which minority group students are compared (Hallahan & Kauffman, 1991; Sattler, 1988). As a result of this cultural bias, many believe, disproportionate numbers of minority group members have been labeled as mentally retarded and placed in special education programs. States such as California have in recent years declassified many students thought to have been erroneously labeled as mentally retarded by lowering the cutoff IQ score to 70. These factors led the AAMR to reconsider how mental retardation is defined and the basis for identifying levels of retardation.

The new definition, quoted below, stresses the more positive, adaptive nature of the individual and considers the relationship between the individual's capabilities and the structure and expectations of his or her environment.

> Mental retardation refers to substantial limitations in present functioning characterized by significantly subaverage intellectual functioning, existing concurrently with related limitations in two or more of the following applicable adaptive skill areas: communication, self-care, home living, social skills, community use, self-direction, health and safety, functional academics, leisure, and work. Mental retardation manifests itself before age 18. (Luckasson et al., 1992, p. 32)

Mental retardation definition emphasizes ability to adapt

In the new definition, the descriptive terms "mild," "moderate," "severe," and "profound" are replaced by four intensity levels describing the support required for the individual to function adequately: "intermittent," "limited," "extensive," and "pervasive." Thus a diagnosis of mental retardation must now reflect consideration of the individual's psychological and emotional health and well-being and the elements of his or her current environment. Although IQ is less important to the diagnosis, there is still a cutoff score of 75.

This definition promises to be more educationally relevant in that it describes the limitations and strengths of people rather than just naming a cutoff IQ score. It ties in more directly to the development of an IEP because it focuses on what the student needs in the school, at home, and in the community. By emphasizing adaptive behavior, IEPs can be designed to utilize the strengths of the individual to reach appropriate goals. For instance, a plan for a student who has demonstrated success in following directions and getting along with others might stress objectives leading to vocational independence, such as filling out applications, balancing a checkbook, and driving or using public transportation.

Appropriate *interventions* will differ depending on the intensity level of retardation, but in working with mainstreamed students, teachers should follow some general rules of instruction. Guidelines are presented here.

Guidelines for Teaching Mentally Retarded Students

1. Consider the student's strengths and weaknesses when choosing objectives.
2. State clear, precise objectives based on a task analysis of the skill to be learned.
3. Emphasize living skills (personal maintenance, homemaking, money management, job seeking, etc.).
4. Identify a manageable number of objectives that have practical application.
5. Select materials that respect the learner's interest level according to chronological age.
6. Present material in small steps with plenty of opportunity for practice.
7. Do not assume that learners will make easy inferences; be specific in describing the transition from one idea to another.
8. Review several times the steps in a multistep process.
9. Directly teach basic learning strategies involving organization and elaboration of content, such as note taking and reading for meaning.
10. Maximize the probability of success by eliminating abstract or vague content.
11. Reinforce good effort as well as mastery.
12. Monitor how successfully students work with others and be ready to defuse conflict.

SPEECH AND LANGUAGE DISORDERS

Students may exhibit speech and language disorders in a number of ways. Speech problems may involve *articulation disorders* (difficulties in the production of sounds), *fluency* (irregularity in speech rate and rhythm, as in stuttering), and *voice* (inappropriate pitch, volume, and quality of speech). Language problems may involve *syntactic structure, semantic content,* and *pragmatics* (social communication). These difficulties may affect one another. For example, children who cannot articulate sounds such as /th/, /r/, or /s/ (three of the most common articulation problems) may not be willing to speak in front of others, thereby restricting practice in and perhaps exacerbating the articulation disorders just listed. Rarely will students display these characteristics in isolation (Moran, 1990). In some cases, children with these speech disorders will receive assistance from a speech/language therapist, while in other situations short-term problems will not require special services.

Articulation difficulties, common among all children as speech develops, become problems when they continue through the elementary school years. Difficulty in articulation is the largest communicative disorder treated by speech/language therapists. It is usually explained as either a problem in discrimination (i.e., learners are unable to tell one sound from another) or as difficulty in applying phonological rules, which arises when children attempt to simplify adult pronunciations they cannot produce (McReynolds, 1988). As a result, both reading and spelling may be impaired. Reading difficulties occur because the student cannot pronounce the words presented. If phonics instruction is employed, students cannot reproduce individual sounds and blends that form the recognizable words that compose their oral vocabulary. Since children cannot spell words they cannot recognize, breakdowns in discriminating and producing individual sounds will affect the spelling of phonetically regular words. Whole-word reading methods may be less severely affected by articulation errors, particularly for words that are irregular, suggesting that whole-word or language experience reading instruction may be most appropriate for children with articulation disorders.

Articulation affects other skills

Articulation difficulties also restrict the learning of social behaviors. Although it might sound cute for preschoolers to engage in "baby talk" (e.g., substituting /th/ for /s/ or /w/ for /r/), older children may be teased or rejected for the same speech. Others may treat children with immature speech patterns as if they are younger, leading to the adoption of social patterns of behavior that are not age appropriate.

Fluency problems include interruptions in speech flow such as stuttering. All of us occasionally revise what we say or make false starts in our speech in response to threat or anxiety. Stuttering as a disorder, however, is defined by Wall (1988) as "sound or syllable repetitions that contain a minimum of two or three repetitions per unit, lasting two seconds or longer." Facial mannerisms indicating tension or struggle are also diagnostic clues. Dysfluent speakers are reluctant to enter into verbal interactions, hence miss out on learning to share in the give and take required of discussions and to organize their thoughts. Not only does this lack of opportunity for rehearsal affect the learning of verbal expression, but problems in organizing written responses on tests and other written exercises may also result.

Syntactical skill entails putting words together to form longer units of expression. Children who have difficulty in composing syntax either omit key words ("She eating" for "She is eating"), fail to match sentence parts with others ("Her go she's house" for "She goes to her house"), or put words in the wrong order ("When gym class is?"). Of course, slang terms have arisen that violate these syntactical rules (I know a student who is always asking "Where is _____ at?"), but for speech/language-disordered children, such constructions are a common occurrence. Learning is affected when comprehension of subject matter becomes difficult and oral directions in the classroom cannot be followed. The inability to understand complex structures as contained in "who" and "which" questions or subordinate terms such as "because" or "if" are particularly important to communication. Learners with syntactic disorders must devote too much of their attention to attempting to grasp what is happening in the classroom (Laughton & Hasenstab, 1986). Students who have difficulty in expressing their questions or ideas either will not be understood or will eventually cease asking for clarification.

Semantic content or meaning is expressed through concepts and the vocabulary words or phrases that express them. Children who demonstrate problems in semantic content possess a vocabulary that is inadequate to express their experience and perceptions or cannot retrieve vocabulary words they have already learned. Other problems might include persistent distortion of meaning due to inability to correctly use relational terms such as "above" or "through," or function words such as "because" or "that." For these students, mastery of any academic task that requires basic vocabulary retrieval or expression is severely limited. Without a system for classifying incoming information and expressing concepts, reading or listening for meaning is very difficult. If a child cannot distinguish between the concepts "more" and "less," for instance, mathematical or scientific operations will remain incomprehensible.

Syntactical and semantic problems affect understanding

Pragmatics relates to the social use of language as described in Chapter 3. Students who don't recognize someone else's turn to speak, stand too close when speaking, or fail to pick up subtle cues (such as the teacher who returns to class after a brief absence saying: "Why is everyone walking around the room?") are displaying poor pragmatics. The failure of an individual to grasp how words are used in a pragmatic context is illustrated in the following episode.

> The young lad was struggling out of a lake, fully clothed and dripping. A passerby stopped to give him a hand and asked, "How did you come to fall in, my boy?"
>
> The boy frowned and said, "I didn't come to fall in! I came to fish."

Classroom discourse can aggravate as well as aid in the remediation of the speech and language problems of students. Communication will be restricted rather than fostered by teachers who unduly call attention to a child's errors in speech, make demands on learners to perform publicly in ways they are not ready to meet, or expect mastery of skills requiring language competency a child has not yet acquired. On the other hand, teachers who treat dysfluent or inarticulate students with patience and courtesy can serve as models of proper verbal interaction for others. Classroom teachers can reduce the amount of verbal comprehension required by speech/language-impaired students by showing them what to do rather than telling them. During instruction, teachers may also (1) limit directions to one or two steps, (2) provide essential information in short phrases that keep the subject of the sentence close to the verb, and (3) avoid indirect commands and either/or statements, which require syntactic or semantic manipulation by the learner. Time to respond can be extended or questions can be posed that require a choice among one-word answers or perhaps a raised hand. Whole-language methods in which oral and written language activities are combined in each lesson may provide aid in the development of semantic, syntactic, and pragmatic structures.

Perhaps the most important instructional role for teachers at all grade levels is to promote generalization of new speech and language skills to the classroom. By providing brief opportunities to rehearse the new skills acquired with the help of a speech/language pathologist, the teacher is indicating that speech skills are necessary to learning in all settings. If classroom teachers work closely with speech professionals to learn which competencies are being emphasized, they will be in a position to reinforce speech behaviors that indicate generalization. For example, if relational terms (above, below, before, after, etc.) are being presented during speech therapy sessions, a math lesson might include in-class assignments that require the student to

Teacher communications reduce impact of speech disorders

indicate numbers that lie below, above, behind, before, and so on. A close relationship between the curriculum of the general classroom and the special class is important for the improvement of children's speech.

VISUAL, AUDITORY, AND PHYSICAL IMPAIRMENTS

Children with visual, auditory, or physical handicaps share a common problem in that there exists a physical condition to which a deficit in their ability to receive or communicate information can be directly linked. In other respects, however, these children are quite different from one another. They are described together in this section because the educational accommodations provided to enhance their learning are similar in focus and intent.

Visual Impairment

The definition of visual impairment included in the Education for All Handicapped Children Act emphasizes the *functional* use of vision, rather than loss of visual acuity. To receive special education services, it is sufficient that after corrections of the impairment have been implemented, the educational performance of the individual be impaired. Children with visual impairments may be able to use their vision with varying degrees of *efficiency,* depending on the type of visual impairment, the degree of loss, the age at onset of the loss, and psychological factors unique to each student (Spenciner, 1992). The type of visual impairment affects the degree of loss. If the optic nerve is impaired, light sensations may fail to reach the occipital lobe of the brain, while curvatures of the eyeball create refractive errors such as myopia (nearsightedness), hyperopia (farsightedness), or astigmatism (blurred vision at far and near distances). Refractive errors are correctable, and their effects can be reduced through classroom design. Age at onset is important because children who become visually impaired after age five may retain visual memories that can aid in learning subject matter concepts. Psychological factors enter into how students with similar levels of impairment cope with their loss—some are able to use a magnifying glass to read text successfully while others find this adaptation difficult.

Visual impairment, either through total blindness or low vision, affects all areas of learning. Because of deficits in gathering information, for example, the blind child must rely on other sense modalities to acquire perceptions and concepts. The student is not able to engage in the dual coding of image and word that is valuable to memory. Sometimes erroneous conclusions arise because other senses cannot provide information about object characteristics such as size or shape. One severely visually impaired child once suggested that "birds must be awfully big, because they make such loud noises and cats must be small, because they meow so soft." Touch is helpful in perceiving small objects that are within reach but does not aid in discriminating large objects such as mountains or little ones such as ants. Without visual information, children are delayed in acquiring concepts according to the normal progression of cognitive development, such as object permanence, causality, conservation, and classifica-

Dual coding is
reduced with
vision loss

tion (Stephens & Grabe, 1982). As a result, children with visual impairments are behind their peers in readiness for learning academic tasks in school.

Visual impairments also affect the acquisition of skills that require interaction with others such as language and social skills. Without the ability to see facial expressions or gestures, children with visual impairments are unable to use communication cues from their parents to convey messages or share information. By the same token, the parents receive little or no feedback or indication that the child understands or is interested in a particular event. Without this enriched information, children with visual impairments form less complex language patterns (Anderson, Dunlea, & Kekelis, 1984). Being unable to use visual signals (smiling, eye gazes, winks, etc.) also affects social exchanges with parents, adults, and peers. Without being able to imitate these forms of communication, the child with a visual impairment is unable to return them; hence social interactions are limited and subject to misinterpretation. Absence of facial expression and other nonverbal cues is read by others as a message of disinterest or apathy, resulting in negative attitudes and expectations. Thus the vision-impaired child may become socially isolated, failing to gain opportunities to acquire a positive self-image and the skills necessary for social competence (Sacks & Reardon, 1989).

Approximately 83 percent of children with visual impairments attend public or private schools (American Foundation for the Blind, 1988). Children are either visited by itinerant teachers who work with them individually in their neighborhood school or they are schooled partly in a resource room in a building or room designed for all students with visual impairments in a school district. In both cases, inclusion is practiced. Three general approaches designed to aid the learning of students with visual impairments are followed: (1) altering the environment to minimize specific problems of reception or expression, (2) maximizing the use of other channels of communication, to reduce the effect of the impairment on learning, and (3) remediating the particular deficit where possible. Table 11.3 summarizes the educational interventions typically applied to students with visual impairments in mainstreamed classrooms.

Hearing Impairment

The term "hearing impairment" is used to describe all degrees of hearing loss, from being slightly hard of hearing to being profoundly deaf. Hard-of-hearing individuals have difficulty hearing, but they can understand speech through listening, often with amplification. To be deaf, however, implies a hearing loss that precludes the understanding of speech through listening alone (Moores, 1987).

The most handicapping aspect of hearing loss is its effect on language and communication. The age at which hearing is lost is critical. A child who heard and acquired language skills and speech before becoming deaf has a great linguistic advantage over a child with a *congenital* hearing impairment (occurring at birth). Thus, a seven-year-old with a profound hearing loss who became handicapped at age three may have better speech, language, reading, and writing skills than a classmate with a milder deficiency that has been present since birth.

Children with hearing impairments must be taught language and speech patterns directly through repetition and corrective instruction. Their speech often contains

TABLE 11.3 Educational interventions for students with visual impairments

Intervention	Examples
Altering the environment	1. Furniture in the classroom should be so arranged that there is a clear path from the door into the room.
	2. Chairs should be pushed under tables when not being used.
	3. Location of furniture should be consistent from day to day.
	4. Materials and equipment should be identified with tactile as well as visual symbols.
	5. Classroom doors that open into the corridor should be left completely open or closed.
Using other sensory modalities	1. Interpret classroom events. This can be done by saying words as you write them on the board, spelling new words aloud, and linking new ideas to concrete experiences or objects by providing the new object to touch or using descriptive language.
	2. Employ a unit plan of instruction in which unified experiences or field trips can provide several related cues to understanding concepts.
	3. Allow students to do things for themselves. Emphasis should be on providing as little assistance as possible so they can develop confidence.
	4. Incorporate listening skills into the curriculum. Younger students need skill in identifying and localizing sounds and following directions. Older learners, who need practice in listening for the main idea, must develop auditory memory of important facts and facility in selective listening (Heinze, 1986).
	5. Permit and encourage children to use auditory and tactile aids. Auditory aids include cassette recorders and "talking books" recorded on tape. Tactile aids include braille writers, slate and stylus for writing braille, and templates and writing guides.
	6. Ensure that children have access to computer technology. Recent advances in computer-based equipment that converts printed material into synthetic speech or vibrating tactual symbols allow students to bypass visual information. Computer monitors that display large-print or high-contrast images are particularly useful for students with low vision. Word processors aid editing.
	7. Encourage independent travel. Children will receive orientation and mobility training from specialists, but others can provide practice opportunities and serve as "sighted guides" who have students touch their elbow and walk slightly behind them when mobility is needed.
Remediation or maximization of visual efficiency	1. Encourage children to use optical aids such as handheld telescopes or magnifiers. Some children resist their use because they look "weird."
	2. Locate large-print texts, felt-tip pens for better visual contrast, variable-intensity lamps, and adjustable bookstands to accommodate reading problems for low-vision students.
	3. Direct students in visual stimulation activities such as fixating on objects, tracking moving objects, shifting gaze, and reaching for objects.
	4. Rotate activities between visual and less visually dependent tasks to avoid fatigue.

omissions or substitution of some phonemes, problems with intonation and pitch, and difficulty in the rhythmic pattern of their language. Hearing loss also makes it difficult to learn vocabulary and the syntactic and morphological structure of the language. Children with hearing impairments may omit grammatical components such as plurals, articles, tenses, and little-function words ("of," "in," etc.). Short and simple kernel sentences with a subject–verb–object word order are most common. Students with hearing impairments may lack the ability to translate figurative language (M. H. Mayer, 1990). For example, phrases such as "the washing machine is running" or "he was left behind" may create confusion.

Performance in language-related subject matter therefore creates difficulties for students with hearing impairments. Their achievement scores in those areas lag considerably behind those of their hearing peers (Allen, 1986). The learning of content that relies on students' reading and integrating text material and requires written products such as essays and reports is also affected. Problem-solving skill in math and science, which depends on the use of language to represent and express concepts and relationships, may also be affected.

Hearing impairments also minimize identification of social cues important to the development of friendships with hearing peers. Incidental learning of the subtle gestures, catch phrases, and expressions that compose so much of the verbal interaction of children and youth is not likely to occur. As a result, children with hearing impairments often appear to be immature compared to their hearing peers. Communication difficulties can have negative effects on parent–child relationships as well. Not only is acceptance of the child's impairment an obstacle, but there may be feelings of guilt on the part of parents as well; and inability to communicate restricts the sharing of concerns and emotions. When children with hearing impairments begin to learn sign language as a substitute for speech, for instance, family relationships may suffer to even a greater degree because parents feel shut out of the child's world. For social-emotional development of children in these families to progress in a healthy manner, it may be necessary for mental health professionals and educators to provide support and encouragement of family members in their attempts to adapt.

Hearing deficits may impair social skills

Facilitation of speech and language skills of students with hearing impairments is a major challenge. Currently, these skills are taught by specialists following two predominant instructional techniques: the aural–oral method and total communication. *Aural–oral methods* emphasize the development of normal speech skills through direct and rigorous speech training. Amplified sounds are presented where some hearing is present. Students also learn to speech-read, by recognizing when and how sounds are revealed by the lips (Quigley & Paul, 1984). The *total communication method* arose from dissatisfaction with the aural–oral approach. Advocates of the former position believe that speech reading and oral methods provide too little information to the learner with a hearing impairment. Some sounds cannot be easily practiced without hearing them, and others cannot be read easily on the lips (e.g., /p/, /b/, /h/). This approach emphasizes manual communication, in which a combination of signs (saluting as a sign for saying "hello") and finger spelling of the English alphabet are employed.

Two competing views of communication training

Figure 11.3 presents the hand signals for spelling the alphabet in American Sign Language. Sign language differs from English in word order and in structure, but it can

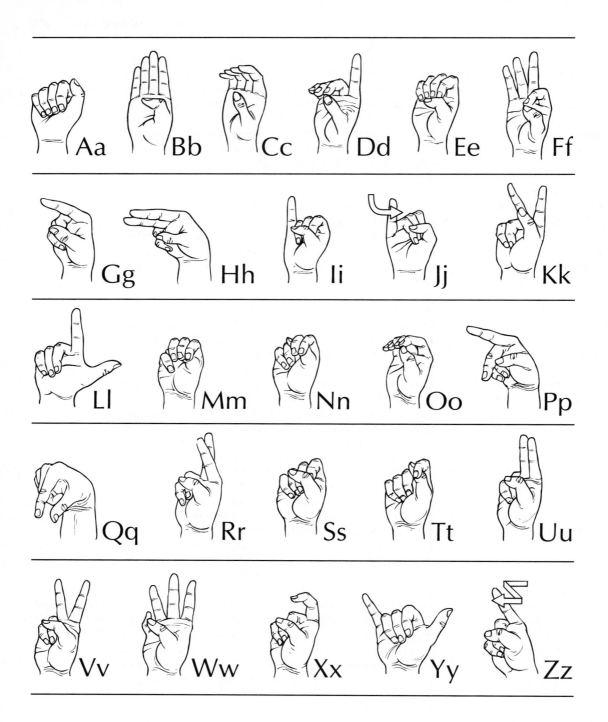

FIGURE 11.3 Manual spelling of the English alphabet in American Sign Language

be used to express ideas quite rapidly, as anyone watching people communicate through signs and finger spelling can readily attest.

Classroom interventions for mainstreamed children with hearing impairments fall roughly into the same categories designed for students with visual impairments: alteration of the environment, maximizing use of alternative sense modalities, and enhancement of the deficit. Table 11.4 presents interventions according to these three categories.

TABLE 11.4 Educational interventions for students with hearing impairments

Intervention	Examples
Altering the environment	1. Reduce distracting classroom noise, failing fluorescent lights, noisy heaters, distractions outside the class, etc.
	2. Let children select seats where hearing is the least likely to be disrupted.
	3. Utilize peers to assist students with class routines, sharing notes, etc.
Using other sensory modalities	1. Employ technological advances that translate auditory signals into other modalities. Telecommunication devices for the deaf (TDD) convert messages by telephone to visual displays. Alerting devices flash lights or even vibrate one's pillow when needed!
	2. Captioned films, overhead projections, diagrams, and conceptual models are all good alternatives to lecturing about concepts.
	3. Cooperative learning with group goals can involve the hearing-impaired student in social processes.
	4. Face student when speaking. Talk clearly in good light, and rephrase when necessary without using same words.
	5. Give assignments both orally and in writing.
	6. Provide outlines and summaries to students to accompany lectures.
	7. In class discussion, indicate which person is speaking, so student knows where to look.
	8. Use instructional materials that teach figurative knowledge directly, such as *The King Who Rained* (Gwynne, 1970).
	9. Utilize commercially available CAI programs such as The Writing Workshop to teach language skills. They enhance not only writing, but sign language as well (Kretschmer, 1985).
Remediation or maximization of auditory efficiency	1. Hearing aids, cochlear implants (electronic packages that can be surgically implanted to amplify sounds), and other devices are helpful but may require maintenance. Are extra batteries available in your desk?
	2. Devices that call attention to hearing loss are often avoided by older students, who dislike being singled out. The students affected should be consulted as to how focus on these aids should be handled.
	3. Use specific review questions to ensure understanding, not simple "yes" or "no" questions that require no expression.

Physical Impairment

Physical disabilities are most commonly classified according to their etiology: (1) *neurological conditions* caused by damage to or incomplete development of the brain or spinal cord (e.g., cerebral palsy), (2) *orthopedic conditions* caused by damage, disease, or lack of development of bones, muscles, or joints of the body, and (3) *health conditions* caused by acute or chronic disease (e.g., cystic fibrosis, diabetes) (Gleckel & Lee, 1990).

The only common element among individuals with physical disabilities is an impairment to some aspect of normal motor functioning. Cognitive functions are typically not affected unless impairment resulting from brain damage inhibits attention, memory, or thinking. The ability to receive information through the senses may be affected if vision or hearing is impaired. Students with physical disabilities are restricted in their environmental and interpersonal interactions. Being unable to move around easily, to reach out and touch, grasp, or manipulate objects, or to exert sufficient energy to participate in new tasks reduces one's opportunities to explore the environment. Possessing physical characteristics that do not conform to society's standards for physical attractiveness may affect social acceptance and the establishment of social relationships. Expectations that individuals behave according to some "normal" pattern of behavior may in addition produce conflict and frustration for

TABLE 11.5 Educational interventions for students with physical impairments

Intervention	Examples
Altering the environment	1. Adapt materials to allow use by the individual. Bookholders for texts, extended levers on tape recorder controls, keyguards for typewriters, and Velcro backing for instructional objects permit operation and utilization of learning materials.
	2. Arrange classrooms to allow easy entrance, movement, and appropriate positioning for wheelchairs.
Using other sensory modalities	1. Modify the method of student response on a particular task so that learning can be observed independent of the handicap. Allowing an individual to dictate an essay answer as opposed to writing it can be appropriate for many tasks.
	2. Encourage students to participate in a partial manner in some activities based on their interests and capacities (e.g., as a designated foul-shooter in basketball, as a batter with a substitute runner in baseball, as a narrator or voice offstage in a dramatic activity (Baumgart et al., 1982).
	3. Use cooperative learning activities in which students can perform a function useful to group goals, but within individual limitations.
Maximization of physical efficiency	1. Utilize task analysis to identify task components that can be practiced independently.
	2. Alter time requirements for performance of tasks that individuals can do adequately if not rushed.

How can we improve the physical environment for children with physical impairments?

many. A boy with a chronic heart condition could never participate in sports at the author's school. One day he defied parental and medical advice and joined in a game of kickball, only to run out of breath and collapse in the school yard. The desire to be like everyone else had overridden this boy's concern for maintaining his health, almost resulting in disaster.

Physical impairment restricts reception and expression

The development of medical and technological aids such as prostheses, input devices for individuals with limited fine motor control, and self-propelled wheelchairs, has reduced the handicapping effects of some disabilities in recent years. Nevertheless, educational intervention of some form is still necessary in most cases for students who are disabled by physical impairments. Table 11.5 suggests educational interventions involving alteration of the environment, use of alternative modalities, and maximization of physical efficiency.

SUMMARY

This chapter began with a differentiation of the frequently used terms *disability* and *handicap*. "Disability" refers to a condition that prevents some action, while "handicap" is reserved for the disadvantage resulting from the disability. Effective educational practice minimizes the handicapping effects of disabilities.

The number of children and youth identified as disabled in some way is speculative. Many children possess more than one disabling condition. Diagnosis is often inexact, and children are placed in one category or another for different reasons. More than four million children are considered to be disabled in the United States according to educational placement statistics.

In educational settings, children and youth identified as possessing a disability are mainstreamed into regular classrooms wherever desirable. Their educational progress is guided by an Individualized Educational Plan (IEP), which sets out goals, short-term objectives, the means of instruction, and the roles of educational personnel.

Students with specific learning disabilities function normally in most academic areas, although in one or two cases performance is discrepant from the norm. A learning disability is not a result of an observable deficit as in a visual or hearing impairment. The most common learning disabilities are in reading, writing, and mathematics. Common interventions follow direct instruction principles, employ prompts by teachers, and foster self-regulatory learning strategies. Learning disabilities are not to be confused with attention deficit–hyperactivity disorder, in which there is impairment of the ability to attend to stimuli, as well as impulsivity and hyperactivity. Many ADHD students benefit from psychostimulant medication to control their behavior and cognitive behavioral training.

Behaviorally disordered people suffer either acute or chronic symptoms of aggressive acting-out behavior or withdrawal and immaturity. The most effective interventions for such students are differential reinforcement of appropriate behavior, instruction in self-management skills, and a "no-lose" method of negotiating agreements between teacher and student.

The use of the term "mentally retarded" is now based on how much support is required for the individual to function, rather than on IQ score. Interventions vary with the level of retardation, but in general consist of patience, a reduction in instructional pace, and the use of more concrete, structured explanations.

Speech and language disorders include disabilities in articulation, fluency, voice, syntactic structure, semantic content, and pragmatics. Speech therapy may be able to remedy some deficits, and classroom teachers can promote generalization of new speech and language skills by working closely with speech professionals. Visual, auditory, and physical impairments produce specific disabilities, for which interventions can focus either on altering the environment, maximizing the use of other channels of communication through stimulation of other modalities, or remediating the particular deficit to the extent possible through technological and medical means.

A concept map for this chapter appears on page 397.

EXERCISES

1. Some educators have suggested that IEPs would be desirable for everyone, that all students could profit from organized attention to their personal learning needs. Reflect on your own schooling: What might such a plan have included? What strengths and weaknesses might have been identified as characteristic of your school functioning, and what long-term educational goals and short-term objectives would have been selected if an IEP had been created for you?

2. Evaluate the way in which you interact with a friend who possesses a particular disability. What beliefs do you have about his or her abilities, interests, or values? Are these beliefs ever revealed to the friend by what you do or say in the person's presence? What improvements might you make in relating to the individual so that inappropriate expectations are not communicated?

3. Readers who possess a particular disability are the focus of this exercise. How have you responded to the condition so that it is a less severe handicap in your daily functioning? Can you think of behaviors you have had to acquire to compensate for the disability? What educational, personal, or social factors aided or hampered your attempts to minimize its effect? Readers who are not disabled are asked: Can you think of practices you could follow to help disabled friends, students, or colleagues function more efficiently?

SUGGESTED READINGS

Anastopoulus, A. D., DuPaul, G. J., & Barkley, R. A. (1991). Stimulant medication and parent training therapies for attention deficit hyperactivity disorder. *Journal of Learning Disabilities, 24*(4), 210–218.

Clark, D. B. (1988). *Dyslexia: Theory and practice of remedial instruction.* Parkton, MD: York Press.

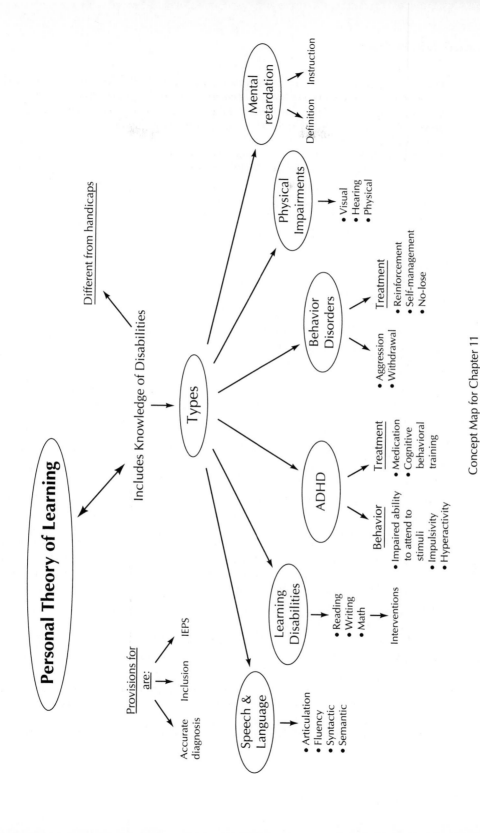

Concept Map for Chapter 11

Englert, C., Raphael, T. E., Feer, K., & Anderson, L. (1988). Students' metacognitive knowledge about how to write information text. *Learning Disability Quarterly, 11,* 18–46.

Gordon, T. (1974). *T.E.T: Teacher effectiveness training.* New York: McKay.

Meyen, E. (Ed.). (1990). *Exceptional children in today's schools* (2nd ed.). Denver, CO: Love Publishing.

Wallace, G., & McLoughlin, J. A. (1988). *Learning disabilities: Concepts and characteristics* (3rd ed.). Columbus, OH: Merrill Publishing.

part IV

Putting It All Together

A Final Word

CHAPTER OUTLINE

Final Thoughts
 Emerging Unified Theory of Educationally Relevant Learning
 Effectiveness of Instructional Techniques
 Student Characteristics That Interact with Teaching
 Value of Student Construction and Monitoring of a Strategic Approach
 Basic Learning Skills and Schematic Structures

CHAPTER OBJECTIVES

1. Summarize the evidence supporting each of the five final thoughts listed in this chapter.
2. Construct your personal theory of learning and teaching and compare it to your original version developed at the end of Chapter 1.

> *Great is the art of beginning, but greater the art is of ending; Many a poem is marred by a superfluous verse.*
>
> Henry W. Longfellow, *Elegaic Verse*

With Longfellow's caution in mind, it is hoped that this final chapter will consolidate and integrate some of the material discussed to this point, rather than prove superfluous. We also consider a few ideas about learning and instruction that have not yet been advanced and help the reader to consider the content from a more personal vantage point. This chapter should be the last step in achieving a major goal of this text as stated in Chapter 1: to aid the reader in acquiring a more complete implicit theory of learning. We will proceed by identifying and analyzing several summary statements.

FINAL THOUGHTS

Emerging Unified Theory of Educationally Relevant Learning

Historically, the study of human learning has been driven by the impact of many competing theories. We began this text with a chronological description of early learning theories, moving from the idealism/realism views of Plato and Aristotle, through the debate between the structuralists and the functionalists and the eventual establishment of the behavioral and cognitive families of theory. The behavioral orientations discussed included the classical conditioning paradigm of Pavlov and Watson, the stimulus–response connectionism of Thorndike, Skinner's operant conditioning, and the social learning position of Bandura. Cognitive positions included early Gestalt psychology, the concept-learning emphasis of Bruner, Ausubel's description of meaningful learning, and the notion of cognitive information processing. This divergence of views reflected a longstanding inability to agree on basic definitions that apply to all the different types of learning. Advocates of competing theories employed differing methodologies to validate their respective approaches and were often critical of the research procedures and assumptions of their competitors. A specific focus of disagreement was the issue of consciousness, with those favoring a behavioral tradition arguing that the contents of conscious experience, with its inherent subjectivity, could not be relied on to yield a scientific explanation of behavior.

Necessity of subjective mental states?

Two lines of research described separately in this text have merged to alter these traditional arguments. Throughout the book we have reviewed research that demonstrates the link between performance on higher-order thinking and problem-solving tasks in a variety of content areas to the conscious processing of information. We have also discussed neurological evidence that the brain does not function as a mere one-way switchboard for neural messages; rather, it may be seen as an active creator and generator of mental states that serve as intermediaries to behavior. Based on such findings, subjective mental states appear to function interactively and are necessary for a complete explanation of conscious behavior.

Determinism modified: How are we free?

Sperry (1993) has described this "cognitive revolution" as a unifying new vision of how we come to know and understand, incorporating a fresh view of mental states tempered by the determinism of traditional behavioral positions. This new model combines traditional bottom-up microdeterminism with novel principles of top-down mental causation to explain the acquisition of new behavior. Recall from Chapter 4 that the emphasis on determinism and the lack of opportunity for freedom of choice have been major criticisms of operant conditioning. In Sperry's words:

The new cognitivism retains both free will and determinism, each reconceived in modified form and integrated in a way that preserves moral responsibility. Volition remains causally determined but no longer entirely subject to the inexorable physiochemical laws of neurocellular activation. These lower level laws become supervened by higher level controls of the subjective conscious self in which they are embedded. . . . The implications become critical for a scientific treatment of personal agency and social interaction. Overall, we still inhabit a deterministic universe, but it is ruled by a large array of different types, qualities and levels of determinism. (1993, p. 879)

In clarifying this integrated position, Sperry emphasizes that the type of mentalism upheld is not dualistic as in the classic philosophical sense, in which the mind and the body function independently. In this new synthesis, mental states are dynamic *emergent* properties of brain states and so depend on acquired associations stored in memory as well as the processing continuously occurring in the active brain. Sperry believes that it is characteristic of emergent properties that they are often novel and inexplicably different from the elements from which they are built. Thus, a person's behavior may be planned, organized, and yet different from what had occurred previously.

> Behavior emerges from mental states and past associations

A good illustration of the movement to one unified learning theory is the tendency for recent remedial or training approaches to involve both cognitive and behavioral components. Those interested in remediation of most deficits in learning have devised techniques that appear to utilize the best of what each position has to offer, recognizing that the best training involves both the reinforcement of new behavior and the learner's own ability to process what is being presented toward one's own best interests. Examples described in this text include stress inoculation training (Meichenbaum, 1977), techniques designed to produce self-regulation and self-appraisal skills, and cognitive–behavioral approaches to managing classroom behavior in general and the behavior of ADHD and behaviorally disordered children.

A unified theory of learning is particularly relevant to instructional practice. Bereiter (1990) has called for the creation of a theory of learning that is designed from the beginning to ensure its relevance to educational issues. He argues that a central goal of education is the acquisition of new concepts or more complex structures that learners already possess, an objective shared with the unified theory. A good educational learning theory will account for how various external factors such as culture, personal history of reinforcement, or instructional input contribute to performance, as well as the role of internal processes such as strategy utilization or memory. In addition, the theory should explain behavior as it occurs within a particular *context*. Bereiter envisions a complete educational learning theory as being composed of many basic units called *contextual modules*. Contextual modules are the entire complex of knowledge, skills, goal structures, feelings, and standards that define a particular type of educational outcome. All these components are interdependent; if change occurs in one, all others will be affected.

> Training combines behavioral and information-processing components

Many examples of what could be construed as contextual modules have been discussed in this text. The Flower and Hayes writing model (Hayes and Flower, 1986), described in Chapter 7, includes consideration of the assigned topic and its purpose, the writer's memory of similar writing assignments and knowledge of the assigned

> Educational learning theory must examine context

TABLE 12.1 Purpose of selected instructional techniques, by chapter

Technique	Purpose
Chapter 4	
Defining instructional objectives	Learner knows what is expected
Priming initial responses	Direct attention to first steps
Prompting	Direct attention to correct stimulus or response
Chapter 5	
Use of peer models	Demonstrate mastery or coping skills
Peer tutoring	Provide one-to-one help
Self-observation	Student records own behavior
Utilizing self-regulated strategies	Student monitors own work
Chapter 6	
Using text cues, changes in voice, contrast	Direct attention to important material
Mnemonic devices	Aid encoding and memory
Spatial representations	Improve understanding
Conceptual models	Improve understanding
Analogies	Demonstrate relationships
Questioning	Review, student communication, higher-level thought
Advance organizers	Organization and integration of subsequent information
Test items as retrieval cues	Retrieval
Chapter 7	
Procedural facilitation	Aid writers to plan what they will write
Word choice	Selection of correct word to convey meaning
Teaching math via problem solving	Learn to apply concepts and skills
Using schematic drawings	Aid representation of word problems
Use cue words in math	Aid representation
Identify text structure in science and social studies	Deriving meaning from text
Chapter 8	
Providing learner control of choice of activities	Instill confidence in learners
Use variable-payoff quizzes	Encourage risk taking
Chapter 9	
Employ role-playing exercises	Development of moral judgment
Use cooperative learning activities	Enhance cooperation, acceptance of others, mastery of content
Chapter 10	
Employ basic elaboration strategies (e.g., keyword)	Memory of vocabulary terms
Help students to use concept mapping	Organization of complex ideas and relationships
Illustrate SQ3R technique	Aid reading for meaning

TABLE 12.1 Continued

Technique	Purpose
Encourage use of representation and search strategies	Facilitate problem solving
Use worked examples	Learning problem-solving skills
Translation and schema training	Representation skills
Anchored instruction	Aid learner to "situate" knowledge in problem solving
Paired learning	Practice problem-solving skills
Chapter 11	
Create student–teacher dialogues	Writing skills
Differential reinforcement	Classroom management
No-lose method of problem solving	Classroom management

topic, and the processes one follows in writing for meaning. The "situated cognition" approach of the Cognition and Technology Learning Group at Vanderbilt (1990), in which Jasper must use mathematics as part of his boating adventure, attends to the processes required for problem solving as well as the context in which the problem solving occurs (see Chapter 10). The "whole-language" method of reading instruction also appears to fit the category in its attempt to put reading into a particular context. These examples all attempt to describe learning in an educationally relevant context. They qualify as the kind of basic unit that could be combined to form a more complete theory of educationally relevant learning.

Effectiveness of Instructional Techniques

Research has established the effectiveness of many techniques that aid instruction and improve learning.   Even a brief glance at the material in this text reveals a number of procedures that have proven to be effective in facilitating learning. The complaint voiced in Chapter 1 by my student Bill—that psychological theories are not easily applied to what goes on in the classroom—just isn't valid. Effective teachers today have at their disposal a wide variety of formats or plans to follow and instructional accessories to utilize while delivering content to students. While not meant to be entirely comprehensive, Table 12.1 summarizes specific techniques discussed in the text, their purpose, and chapter where they may be found.

Student Characteristics That Interact with Teaching

A number of characteristics that differentiate students from one another interact with teaching to affect learning outcomes.   Personal differences contribute to students' learning, and even instructional events that are well planned and presented will not be effective with all students. This fact was emphasized in Chapter 11, in which we explored various disabilities and their potentially handicapping effect. Several other individual difference variables were discussed throughout this text, but have not been considered as a group. Nondisabling student characteristics that have been found to interact with instruction are:

Several critical characteristics of learners

Chapter 2
Hemispheric specialization
State–trait anxiety

Chapter 3
Age
Cognitive ability
Gender
Socioeconomic status
Culture
Conceptual tempo
Thinking style
Preferences for learning
Modalities
Locus of control
Field independence–dependence

Chapter 5
Self-efficacy

Chapter 6
Prerequisite knowledge

Chapter 8
Locus of control

Chapter 10
Prerequisite knowledge

Value of Student Construction and Monitoring of a Strategic Approach

The benefits derived from student construction and monitoring of a strategic approach to most learning tasks must be directly communicated and demonstrated. The most effective form of student processing occurs when individuals focus on the meaning of incoming information. When focusing on meaning, learners are likely to elaborate on the given information by relating it to their own experience. Furthermore, they will be inclined to construct personal examples or consider the implications of the information for their future behavior.

Learners who plan, construct, and monitor their own strategic approach to learning are engaging in a kind of deep processing. Throughout the text, we reported a variety of examples of classroom learning that were enhanced when students utilized such procedures. It seems clear that academic advantages lie with students who approach new learning tasks, assignments, tests, and related activities by considering what learning goal is required, what information is available, what techniques have worked for them before, and what procedure they should follow in advance of actual performance. Those who continue to evaluate the effectiveness of their behavior in reaching the desired goal and take steps to alter unsuccessful approaches are also likely to achieve.

Effective students construct their own learning approach

Teachers have an obligation to inform students of the benefits derived from careful analysis, planning, and monitoring of their academic work. Perhaps of more value to students, however, is the actual demonstration of such tactics by teachers as new learning objectives arise. Educators who take the time to reveal how they and other experts proceed to function on academic tasks and show how such preliminary analysis leads to success will be more likely to instill such behavior in their students.

Do you always monitor your learning?

Basic Learning Skills and Schematic Structures

Basic learning skills and schematic structures are a part of all subject matter content and should be taught within specific areas.   The effective learner acquires in the process of learning a number of skills that are widely applicable to all academic endeavors. We have discussed several. Some of the most important we have examined are reading to comprehend, writing to communicate meaning, employing mathematical algorithms, selecting and implementing learning strategies, following representational and search procedures in problem solving, establishing and testing hypotheses, setting realistic learning goals, regulating one's effort and expectations, and evaluating one's performance. Many stored schemas that we have acquired are germane to a number of areas as well. In many different contexts, it appears to be useful to be able to activate schemas for functioning according to the "scientific method" or explaining what "good teaching" is, for example.

Skills and structure in every academic area

It seems apparent therefore that to aid students to develop and maintain skills and concepts requires continued exposure and reinforcement. Research has been frequently cited to demonstrate the value of teaching to facilitate the transfer of basic skills to other areas. This goal requires that educators in all academic areas refer to, utilize, and stress basic skills and previously acquired schemas. The biology teacher in essence teaches more than biology—he or she teaches how to read biological material, how to write about biological topics, how to solve biological problems, how to conduct biological research, how and why one should value biological issues, and how biology relates to everyday life. In implementing such an approach, it is necessary to draw on and expand the concepts and skills that underlie meaningful learning.

Skills and structure taught specifically

Let us conclude this chapter by reflecting on Chapter 1, where we discussed the idea of an implicit theory of learning. As an exercise at the end of that chapter, readers were asked to attempt to identify a personal theory of how people learn. It is hoped that with study of this text, considerable transformation of that personal theory has occurred. Perhaps some of these final thoughts have been integrated into your cognitive structure. While some beliefs may have been strengthened, confirmed, and expanded, others may have been revised or eliminated. The application of your implicit theory of learning to teaching may also have changed. Your view of your role as an educator, how you should plan and conduct lessons, manage student behavior, and respond to student performance may have become modified as well.

Our implicit theories guide our actions, sometimes without very much forethought. Suppose, for example, that you were confronted with a student who had difficulty completing assignments and disrupted others' work. How would you proceed? Would you schedule a conference with the student, perhaps employing Gordon's no-lose approach to reach a mutually acceptable course of action? Would you implement some type of operant procedure to reinforce more appropriate behavior? Would you attempt to reach the student through utilization of peer models? Perhaps you would develop an alternative approach, combining some of the aforementioned procedures with others. The decision you reached would reflect your implicit theory of learning and how instruction follows.

*Implicit theory—
a guide to action*

In the course of this text, we have discussed a number of theoretical and research-based findings that have been applied to instructional issues. It is my hope that in the exploration of these ideas, many "nuggets" have been discovered by the reader, leading to the construction of a more useful and satisfying personal theory of learning and teaching.

SUMMARY

This final chapter has attempted to summarize and integrate the material discussed earlier. Five final thoughts were explained as they related to specific text content:

1. There is an emerging unified theory of educationally relevant learning.
2. Research has established the effectiveness of many techniques that aid instruction and improve learning.
3. A number of characteristics that differentiate students from one another interact with teaching to affect learning outcomes.
4. The benefits derived from students' construction and monitoring of their strategic approach to learning tasks must be directly communicated and demonstrated.
5. Basic learning skills and schematic structures are part of all subject matter content and should be taught within specific areas.

These and other ideas encountered in this text should contribute to the reader's implicit learning and teaching theory.

A FINAL EXERCISE

Write for a second time your implicit theory of learning. Include a section that reflects implications for teaching if you did not do so originally. After you have finished, search out the draft you completed at the close of Chapter 1. How has it changed?

In comparing your original and the revised version, you might consider the following components:

1. Have you now incorporated existing theories in your own position?
2. Did specific research findings contribute to your new theory?
3. Have you included greater consideration of student characteristics that contribute to different learning outcomes?
4. Has your new theory required you to analyze the instructional strategies and policies you generally employ?
5. Do you now consider the expected cognitive outcomes and the necessary student skills and abilities your teaching requires?
6. Is your teaching now directed toward a specific set of student learning objectives?

SUGGESTED READINGS

Bereiter, C. (1990). Aspects of an educational learning theory. *Review of Educational Research, 60*(4), 509–515.

Sperry, R. W. (1993). The impact and promise of the cognitive revolution. *American Psychologist, 48*(8), 878–885.

References

Abel, E. L. (1982). Consumption of alcohol during pregnancy. A review of effects on growth and development of offspring. *Human Biology, 54,* 421-453.

Abelson, H., & di Sessa, A. A. (1980). *Turtle geometry: The computer as a medium for exploring mathematics.* Cambridge, MA: MIT Press.

Abikoff, H. (1991). Cognitive training in ADHD children: Less to it than meets the eye. *Journal of Learning Disabilities, 24*(4), 205-209.

Abramson, L. Y., Seligman, M. E. S., & Teasdale, J. D. (1978). Learned helplessness in humans: Critique and reformulation. *Journal of Abnormal Psychology, 87,* 49-74.

Abramson, T., & Kagen, E. (1975). Familiarization of content and different response modes in programmed instruction. *Journal of Educational Psychology, 67*(1), 83-88.

Adams, M. J. (1990). *Beginning to read: Thinking and learning about print.* Cambridge, MA: MIT Press.

Akamatsu, T. J., & Thelen, M. H. (1974). A review of the literature on observer characteristics and imitation. *Developmental Psychology, 10,* 38-47.

Alabiso, F. (1975). Operant control of attention behavior: A treatment for hyperactivity. *Behavior Therapy, 6,* 39-42.

Allen, K. E., Hart, B., Buell, J. S., Harris, F. R., & Wolf, M. M. (1964). Effects of social reinforcement on isolate behavior of a nursery school child. *Child Development, 35,* 511-518.

Allen, T. E. (1986). Patterns of academic performance among hearing impaired students: 1974 and 1983. In A. N. Schildroth & A. M. Karchner (Eds.), *Deaf children in America* (pp. 161-206). San Diego, CA: College Hill Press.

Allport, G. W. (1937). The functional autonomy of motives. *American Journal of Psychology, 50,* 141-156.

Allport, G. W. (1961). *Pattern and growth in personality.* New York: Holt, Rinehart & Winston.

American Association for the Advancement of Science. (1989). *Science for all Americans: Project 7061.* Washington, DC: Author.

American Psychiatric Association. (1987). *DSM-III-R. Diagnostic and statistical manual of mental disorders* (3rd rev. ed.). Washington, DC: Author.

American Foundation for the Blind. (1988). *Facts about blindness.* New York: Author.

American Heritage Dictionary. (1985). Boston: Houghton- Mifflin.

Ames, C. (1990). Motivation: What teachers need to know. *Teachers College Record, 90,* 409–421.

Ames, C. (1992). Classrooms, goal structures and student motivation. *Journal of Educational Psychology, 84*(3), 261–271.

Ames, C., & Archer, J. (1988). Achievement goals in the classroom: Students' learning strategies and motivation processes. *Journal of Educational Psychology, 80,* 260–267.

Ames, C., Ames, R., & Felker, D. W. (1977). Effects of competitive reward structure and valence of outcome on children's achievement attributions. *Journal of Educational Psychology, 69,* 1–8.

Anastopoulus, A. D., DuPaul, G. J., & Barkley, R. A. (1991). Stimulant medication and parent training therapies for attention deficit–hyperactivity disorder. *Journal of Learning Disabilities, 24*(4), 210–218.

Anderson, C. W., & Smith, E. (1987). Teaching science. In V. Koehler (Ed.), *Educator's handbook: A research perspective* (pp. 84–111). White Plains, NY: Longman.

Anderson, E. S., Dunlea, A., & Kekelis, L. S. (1984). Blind children's language development: Resolving some differences. *Journal of Child Language, 11,* 645–664.

Anderson, J. R. (1976). *Language, memory and thought.* Hillsdale, NJ: Erlbaum.

Anderson, J. R. (1983a). *The architecture of cognition.* Cambridge, MA: Harvard University Press.

Anderson J. R. (1983b). A spreading activation theory of memory. *Journal of Verbal Learning and Verbal Behavior, 22,* 361–365.

Anderson, J. R. (1990). *Cognitive psychology and its implications* (2nd ed.). Hillsdale, NJ: Erlbaum.

Anderson, J. R., Kline, P. J., & Beasley, C. M. (1979). A general learning theory and its application to schema abstraction. In G. H. Bower (Ed.), *The psychology of learning and motivation: Vol. 13* (pp. 277–361). New York: Academic Press.

Anderson, L. (1990). *The civics report card.* Princeton, NJ: National Assessment of Educational Progress.

Anderson, R., Reynolds, R., Schallert, D., & Goetz, E. (1977). Frameworks for comprehending discourse. *American Educational Research Journal, 14,* 367–381.

Anderson-Inman, L. (1987). Teaching for transfer: Integrating language arts software into the curriculum. *The Computing Teacher,* (8), 24–29, 39.

Andre, T., & Phye, G. D. (1986). Cognitive learning and education. In G. D. Phye and T. Andre (Eds.), *Cognitive classroom learning: Understanding thinking and problem solving* (pp. 1–19). New York: Academic Press.

Andreasen, C., & Waters, H. S. (1989). Organization during study: Relationships between metamemory, strategy, use and performance. *Journal of Educational Psychology, 81*(2), 190–195.

Anrig, G. E., & LaPointe, A. E. (1989). What we know about what students don't know. *Educational Leadership, 47*(3), 4–9.

Aronson, E., Blaney, N., Stephan, C., Sikes, J., & Snapp, M. (1978). *The jigsaw classroom.* Beverly Hills, CA: Sage.

Ashcroft, M. H., & Battaglia, J. (1978). Cognitive arithmetic: Evidence for retrieval and decision processes in mental addition. *Journal of Experimental Psychology: Human Learning and Memory, 4,* 527–538.

Asher, S., & Markell, R. (1974). Sex differences in comprehension of high- and low-interest reading material. *Journal of Educational Psychology, 66,* 680–687.

Atkinson, J. W. (1958). Towards experimental analysis of human motivation in terms of motive, expectancies and incentives. In J. W. Atkinson (Ed.), *Motives in fantasy, action and society.* Princeton, NJ: Van Nostrand.

Atkinson, J. W. (1964). *An introduction to motivation.* Princeton, NJ: Van Nostrand.

Atkinson, J. W., & Litwin, G. H. (1960). Achievement motive and test anxiety as motives to approach success and avoid failure. *Journal of Abnormal and Social Psychology, 60,* 52-63.

Atkinson, R. C., & Raugh, M. R. (1975). An application of the mnemonic keyword method to the acquisition of a Russian vocabulary. *Journal of Experimental Psychology: Human Learning and Memory, 104,* 126-133.

Atkinson, R. C., & Shiffrin, R. M. (1968). Human memory: A proposed system and its control processes. In K. W. Spence & J. T. Spence (Eds.), *The psychology of learning and motivation, Vol. 2.* (pp. 90-197). New York: Academic Press.

Ausubel, D. P. (1954). *Theory and problems of adolescent development.* New York: Grune and Stratton.

Ausubel, D. P. (1963). *The psychology of meaningful verbal learning.* New York: Grune and Stratton.

Ausubel, D. P. (1964). Some psychological and educational limitations of learning by discovery. *The Arithmetic Teacher, 11,* 290-302.

Ausubel, D. P., & Fitzgerald, D. (1962). Organizer, general background and antecedent learning variables in sequential verbal learning. *Journal of Educational Psychology, 53,* 243-249.

Ausubel, D. P., & Robinson, F. G. (1969). *School learning: An introduction to educational psychology.* New York: Holt, Rinehart & Winston.

Ausubel, D. P., & Youssef, M. (1963). Role of discriminability in meaningful parallel learning. *Journal of Educational Psychology, 54,* 331-336.

Ausubel, D. P., Sullivan, E. V., & Ives, W. (1980). *Theory and problems of child development* (3rd ed.). New York: Grune & Stratton.

Baddeley, A. D. (1978). The trouble with levels: A reexamination of Craik and Lockhart's framework for memory research. *Psychological Review, 85,* 139-152.

Baddeley, A. D. (1986). *Working memory.* Oxford: Oxford University Press.

Baddeley, A. D., & Hitch, C. (1974). Working memory. In G. H. Bower (Ed.), *The psychology of learning and motivation: Vol. 8.* New York: Academic Press.

Bailey, S. M. (1993). The current status of gender equity research in American schools. *Educational Psychologist, 28*(4), 321-339.

Baker, D. (1986). Sex differences in classroom interactions in secondary science. *Journal of Classroom Interaction, 22,* 212-218.

Balajthy, E. (1989). *Computers and reading: Lessons from the past and the technologies of the future.* Englewood Cliffs, NJ: Prentice-Hall.

Balson, P. M., Ebner, D. G., Mahoney, J. V., Lippert, H. T., & Manning, D. T. (1986). Videodisc instructional strategies: Simple may be superior to complex. *Journal of Educational Technology Systems, 14*(4), 273-281.

Bandura, A. (1962). Social learning through imitation. In M. R. Jones (Ed.), *Nebraska symposium on motivation* (pp. 211-269). Lincoln: University of Nebraska Press.

Bandura, A. (1969). *Principles of behavior modification.* New York: Holt, Rinehart & Winston.

Bandura, A. (1971). *Social learning theory.* Englewood Cliffs, NJ: Prentice-Hall.

Bandura, A. (1977). *Social learning theory* (2nd ed.). Englewood Cliffs, NJ: Prentice-Hall.

Bandura, A. (1978). The self-system in reciprocal determinism. *American Psychologist, 33*(4), 344-358.

Bandura, A. (1982). Self-efficacy mechanism in human agency. *American Psychologist, 37,* 122-147.

Bandura, A. (1986). *Social foundations of thought and action: A social cognitive theory.* Englewood Cliffs, NJ: Prentice-Hall.

Bandura, A. (1993). Perceived self-efficacy in cognitive development and functioning. *Educational Psychologist, 28*(2), 117–148.

Bandura, A., & Cerrone, D. (1983). Self-evaluative and self-efficacy mechanisms governing the motivational effects of goal systems. *Journal of Personality and Social Psychology, 45,* 1017–1028.

Bandura, A., & Schunk, D. H. (1981). Cultivating competence, self-efficacy, and intrinsic interests through proximal self-motivation. *Journal of Personality and Social Psychology, 41,* 586–598.

Bandura, A., Ross, D., & Ross, S. A. (1963a). A comparative test of the status envy, social power and secondary reinforcement theories of identificatory learning. *Journal of Abnormal and Social Psychology, 67,* 527–534.

Bandura, A., Ross, D., & Ross, S. A. (1963b). Vicarious reinforcement and imitative learning. *Journal of Abnormal and Social Psychology, 67,* 601–607.

Bangert, R., Kulik, J., & Kulik, C. (1983). Individualized systems of instruction in secondary schools. *Review of Educational Research, 53,* 143–158.

Bangert-Downs, R. L., Kulik, J. A., & Kulik, C. L. (1985). The effectiveness of computer-based education in secondary schools. *Journal of Computer Based Instruction, 12*(3), 59–68.

Banks, J. A. (1988). *Multiethnic education: Theory and practice.* Boston: Allyn & Bacon.

Banks, J. A. (1989). Multicultural education: Characteristics and goals. In J. Banks & C. McGee Banks (Eds.), *Multicultural education: Issues and perspectives* (pp. 2–26). Boston: Allyn & Bacon.

Barbe, W., & Swassing, R. (1979). *Teaching through modality strengths: Concepts and practices.* Columbus, OH: Zaner-Bloser.

Barclay, L. K. (1985). *Infant development.* New York: Holt, Rinehart & Winston.

Barkley, R. A. (1981). *Hyperactive children: A handbook of diagnosis and treatment.* New York: Guilford.

Barkley, R. A., & Cunningham, C. F. (1978). Do stimulant drugs improve the academic performance of hyperkinetic children? *Clinical Pediatrics, 8,* 137–146.

Barkley, R. A., Karlsson, J., Strzelecki, E., & Murphy, J. (1984). Effects of age and Ritalin dosage on the mother–child interactions of hyperactive children. *Journal of Consulting and Clinical Psychology, 52,* 750–758.

Barr, R. D., Barth, J. L., & Shermis, S. S. (1977). *Defining the social studies.* Arlington, VA: National Council for the Social Studies.

Bartlett, B. J. (1978). *Top-level structure as an organizational strategy for recall of classroom text.* Doctoral dissertation, Arizona State University.

Bartlett, E. J. (1981). *Learning to write: Some cognitive and linguistic components.* Washington, DC: Center for Applied Linguistics.

Barton, P. E., & Coley, R. J. (1991). *Performance at the top from elementary through graduate school.* Princeton, NJ: Educational Testing Service.

Baumgart, D., Brown, L., Pumpian, I., Nisbet, J., Sweet, M., Messina, R., & Schroeder, J. (1982). The principle of partial participation and individualized adaptations in education programs for severely handicapped students. *Journal of the Association for the Severely Handicapped, 7*(2), 17–27.

Baumrind, D. (1973). The development of instrumental competence through socialization. In A. D. Pick (Ed.), *Minnesota Symposia on Child Psychology: Vol. 7.* Minneapolis: University of Minnesota Press.

Bayley, N. (1935). The development of motor abilities during the first three years. *Monographs of the Society for Research in Child Development:* No. 1.

Bayman, P., & Mayer, R. E. (1988). Using conceptual models to teach basic computer programming. *Journal of Educational Psychology, 80,* 291–298.

Beach, T., & Steenwyk, F. (1984). The effect of three forms of summarization instruction on sixth graders' summary writing and comprehension. *Journal of Reading Behavior, 16,* 297-306.

Beak Healthy (1991). Drugs on campus. *Watkins Health Center Bulletin-University of Kansas, 5*(2), 2-3.

Beaugrande, P. de (1984). *Text production: Toward a science of composition.* Norwood, NJ: Ablex.

Becker, H. J., & Moursund, J. (1985). The second national U.S. survey of instructional uses of school computers. In K. A. Duncan and D. I. Harris (Eds.), *Computers in education.* New York: Elsevier.

Becker, W. C., Engelmann, S., & Thomas, D. R. (1971). *Teaching: A course in applied psychology.* Chicago: Science Research Associates.

Beech, M. (1983). Simplifying text for mainstreamed students. *Journal of Learning Disabilities, 16*(7), 400-402.

Bell, M. F. (1985). The role of instructional theories in the evaluation of microcomputer software. *Educational Technology, 25*(3), 36-40.

Benbow, C. P. (1986). Physiological correlates of extreme intellectual precocity. *Neuropsychologia, 24,* 719-725.

Bennett, W. J. (1991). Moral literacy and the formation of character. In J. S. Benninga (Ed.), *Moral character and civic education in the elementary school* (pp. 131-138). New York: Teachers College Press.

Bereiter, C. (1990). Aspects of an educational learning theory. *Review of Educational Research, 60*(4), 509-515.

Berger, T. W. (1984). Long-term potentiation of hippocampal synaptic transmissions affects rates of behavioral learning. *Science, 224,* 627-630.

Berko, J. (1958). The child's learning of English morphology. *Word, 14,* 150-177.

Berkowitz, S. J. (1986). Effects of instruction in text organization on sixth grade students' memory for expository reading. *Reading Research Quarterly, 21,* 161-178.

Berliner, D. C. (1987). Ways of thinking about students and classrooms by more or less experienced teachers. In J. Calderhead (Ed.), *Exploring teachers' thinking* (pp. 60-83). London: Cassell.

Binet, A., & Simon, T. (1905). New methods for the diagnosis of the intellectual level of the abnormal. *L'Année Psychologique, 11,* 236-245.

Bingham, A. (1986). Using writing folders to document student progress. In T. Newkirk & N. Atwell (Eds.), *Understanding writing.* Portsmouth, NH: Heinemann.

Birnbauer, J. S., Wolf, M. M., Kidder, J. D., & Tague, C. E. (1965). Classroom behavior of retarded pupils with token reinforcement. *Journal of Experimental Child Psychology, 2,* 219-235.

Black, J. E., & Greenough, W. T. (1986). Induction of pattern in neural structure by experience: Implications for cognitive development. In M. E. Lamb, A. L. Brown, & B. Rogoff (Eds.), *Advances in developmental psychology: Vol. 4* (pp. 1-50). Hillsdale, NJ: Erlbaum.

Blatt, M. M., & Kohlberg, L. (1975). The effects of classroom moral discussions upon children's level of moral judgment. *Journal of Moral Education, 4*(2), 129-161.

Bloom, B. S. (Ed.). 1985. *Developing talents in young people.* New York: Ballentine.

Blumenfeld, P. C., Soloway, E., Mark, R. W., Kracjik, J. S., Guzdial, M., & Palincsar, A. (1991). Motivation project-based learning. Sustaining the doing, supporting the learning. *Educational Psychologist, 26*(3&4), 369-398.

Bosco, J. (1986). An analysis of evaluations of interactive video. *Educational Technology, 26*(5), 7-17.

Bousfield, W. A. (1953). The occurrence of clustering in randomly arranged associates. *Journal of General Psychology, 49,* 229-240.

Bower, E. M. (1969). *The early identification of emotionally-handicapped children in school.* Springfield, IL: Charles Thomas.

Bower, G., Clark, M., Lesgold, A., & Winzerz, D. (1969). Hierarchical retrieval schemes in recall of categorical word lists. *Journal of Verbal Learning and Verbal Behavior, 8,* 323-343.

Boyer, E. (1990). Civic education for responsible citizens. *Educational Leadership, 48*(3), 4-7.

Bradley, R. H., Caldwell, B. M., & Elardo, R. (1977). Home environment, social class, and mental test performance. *Journal of Educational Psychology, 69,* 697-701.

Bradshaw, J. L., & Gates, E. A. (1978). Visual field differences in verbal tasks. Effects of task familiarity and sex. *Brain and Language, 5,* 166-187.

Brainerd, C. J. (1978). Learning research and Piagetian theory. In L. L. Siegel & C. J. Brainerd (Eds.), *Alternatives to Piaget: Critical essays on the theory* (pp. 69-100). New York: Academic Press.

Bransford, J. D., & Franks, J. J. (1971). The abstraction of linguistic ideas. *Cognitive Psychology, 2,* 331-380.

Bransford, J. D., & Stein, B. S. (1984). *The IDEAL problem solver.* New York: Freeman.

Breland, K., & Breland, M. (1961). The misbehavior of organisms. *American Psychologist, 16,* 681-684.

Bretzing, B. H., & Kulhavy, R. W. (1979). Notetaking and depth of processing. *Contemporary Educational Psychology, 4,* 145-153.

Bridwell, L. S. (1980). Revising strategies in twelfth grade students' transactional writing. *Research in the Teaching of English, 14*(3), 107-122.

Brody, C. H., & Stoneman, Z. (1985). Peer imitation: An examination of status and competence hypotheses. *Journal of Genetic Psychology, 146,* 161-170.

Bromage, B. K., & Mayer, R. E. (1981). Relationship between what is remembered and creative problem-solving performance in science learning. *Journal of Educational Psychology, 73,* 451-461.

Brooks, L. W., Dansereau, D. F., Holley, C. D., & Spurlin, J. E. (1983). Generation of descriptive text readings. *Contemporary Educational Psychology, 8,* 103-108.

Brophy, J., & Alleman, J. (1991). Activities as instructional tools: A framework for instructional analysis and evaluation. *Educational Researcher, 20,* 9-23.

Brophy, J., & Good, T. (1986). Teacher behavior and student achievement. In M. Wittrock (Ed.), *Handbook of research on teaching* (3rd ed.) (pp. 328-375). New York: Macmillan.

Brophy, J., & Rohrkemper, M. (1981). The influence of problem ownership on teacher's perceptions of and strategies for coping with problem students. *Journal of Educational Psychology, 73,* 285-311.

Brown, A. L. (1981). Metacognition: The development of selective attention strategies for learning from texts. In M. L. Hamil (Ed.), *Directions in reading: Research and instruction* (pp. 21-42). Washington, DC: National Reading Conference.

Brown, A. L., & Day, J. P. (1983). Microroles for summarizing texts: The development of expertise. *Journal of Verbal Learning and Verbal Behavior, 22,* 1-14.

Brown, J. S., & Burton, R. R. (1978). Diagnostic models for procedural bugs in basic mathematical skills. *Cognitive Science, 2,* 155-192.

Bruner, J. S. (1962a). *On knowing: Essays for the left hand.* Cambridge MA: Harvard University Press.

Bruner, J. S. (1962b). *The process of education.* Cambridge, MA: Harvard University Press.

Bruner, J. S. (1966). Some elements of discovery. In L. S. Shulman & E. R. Kiesler (Eds.), *Learning by discovery: A critical appraisal* (pp. 101-114). Chicago: Rand McNally.

Bruner, J. S., Goodnow, J. J., & Austin, G. A. (1956). *A study of thinking.* New York: Wiley.

Bubules, N. C., & Linn, M. C. (1988). Response to contradiction: Scientific reasoning during adolescence. *Journal of Educational Psychology, 80*(1), 67-75.

Burke, P. E. (1989). A different interpretation of the data: Most students know a lot. *Educational Leadership, 47*(3), 6.

Burns, P. K., & Bozeman, W. C. (1981). Computer-assisted instruction and math achievement. Is there a relationship? *Educational Technology, 21*(10), 32–39.

Burwell, L. (1991). The interaction of learning styles with learner control treatments in an interactive videodisc lesson. *Educational Technology, 31*(3), 37–43.

Bushell, D., Wrobel, P., & Michaelis, M. (1968). Applying group contingencies to the classroom study behavior of preschool children. *Journal of Applied Behavior Analysis, 1,* 55–61.

Byrne, B., & Fielding-Barnsley, R. (1990). Acquiring the alphabetic principle: A case for teaching recognition of phoneme identity. *Journal of Educational Psychology, 82* (4), 805–812.

Byrne, B., & Fielding-Barnsley, R. (1991). Evaluation of a program to teach phonemic awareness to young children. *Journal of Educational Psychology, 83,* 451–455.

Caine, G., & Caine, R. N. (1991). *Making connections: Teaching and the human brain.* Alexandria, VA: Association for Supervision and Curriculum Development.

Cannon, W. B. (1932). *The wisdom of the body.* New York: Norton.

Canter, L. (1989). Assertive discipline—More than names on the board and marbles in a jar. *Phi Delta Kappan, 71,* (1), 41–56.

Canter, L. (1989). Assertive discipline: A response. *Teachers College Record, 90*(4), 631–638.

Canter, L., & Canter, M. (1976). *Assertive discipline: A take charge approach for today's educator.* Santa Monica, CA: Canter and Associates.

Cantwell, D. P., & Baker, L. (1991). Association between attention deficit hyperactivity disorder and learning disorder. *Journal of Learning Disabilities, 24*(2), 88–95.

Carbo, M., Dunn, R., & Dunn, K. (1986). *Teaching students to read through their individual learning styles.* Englewood Cliffs, NJ: Prentice-Hall.

Carlson, N. R. (1986). *Psychology of behavior* (3rd ed). Boston: Allyn & Bacon.

Carpenter, T. P. (1985). Learning to add and subtract: An exercise in problem-solving. In E. A. Silver (Ed.), *Teaching and learning mathematical problem solving: Multiple research perspectives* (pp. 123–161). Hillsdale, NJ: Erlbaum.

Carr, T. H. (1981). Building theories of reading ability: On the relation between individual differences in cognitive skills and reading comprehension. *Cognition, 9*(1), 71–114.

Carrier, C. A., & Titus, A. (1981). Effects of note-taking pretraining and test mode expectation on learning from lectures. *American Educational Research Journal, 18*(4), 385–397.

Carrow, M. A. (1957). Linguistic functioning of bilingual and monolingual children. *Journal of Speech and Hearing Disabilities, 22,* 371–377.

Carter, J. F. (1993). Self-management: Education's ultimate goal. *Teaching Exceptional Children, 25*(3), 28–32.

Cartledge, G., & Milburn, J. F. (1986). *Teaching social skills to children.* Elmsford, NY: Pergamon Press.

Casanova, U. (1987). Ethnic and cultural differences. In V. Richardson-Koehler (Ed.), *Educator's handbook: A research perspective.* New York: Longman.

Chalfant, J., & Scheffelin, M. A. (1969). *Central processing dysfunctions in children: A review of research.* Urbana, IL: Institute for Research on Exceptional Children.

Chambers, B., & Abrami, D. C. (1991). The relationship between student team learning outcomes and achievement, causal attributions, and effect. *Journal of Educational Psychology, 83,* 140–146.

Chan, C. K. K., Burtis, P. J., Scardamalia, M., & Bereiter, C. (1992). Constructive activity in learning from text. *American Educational Research Journal, 29*(1), 97–118.

Chandler, M. J. (1973). Egocentrism and antisocial behavior. The assessment and training of social perspective-taking skills. *Developmental Psychology, 9,* 326–332.

Chasnoff, I. J., Griffin, B. B., McGregor, S., Dirkes, K., & Burns, K. A. (1989). Temporal patterns of cocaine use in pregnancy. *Journal of the American Medical Association, 261*(12), 1741–1744.

Cheney, C. O. (1989). The systematic adaptation of instructional materials and techniques for problem learners. *Academic Therapy, 24*(4), 25–30.

Chi, M. T. H., Bassok, M., Lewis, M. W., Reimann, P., & Glaser, R. (1989). Self-explanations: How students study and use examples in learning to solve problems. *Cognitive Science, 13,* 145–182.

Chi, M. T. H., Feltovich, P. J., & Glaser, R. (1981). Categorization and representation of physics problems by experts and novices. *Cognitive Science, 5,* 121–152.

Chi, M. T. H., Glaser, R., & Farr, M. (Eds.). (1988). *The nature of human expertise.* Hillsdale, NJ: Erlbaum.

Chomsky, N. (1959). Verbal behavior. A review of Skinner's theory. *Language, 35,* 26–58.

Chomsky, N. (1972). *Language and mind.* New York: Harcourt Brace Jovanovich.

Chomsky, N. (1976). On the biological basis of language capacities. In R. W. Rieben (Ed.), *The neuropsychology of language.* New York: Plenum Press.

Church, E., & Bereiter, C. (1983). Reading for style. *Language Arts, 60*(4), 470–476.

Clark, D. B. (1988). *Dyslexia: Theory and practice of remedial instruction.* Parkton, MD: York Press.

Clark, E. V. (1983). Meanings and concepts. In D. H. Mussen (Ed.), *Carmichael's manual of child psychology: Vol. 3. Cognitive development* (pp. 787–889). New York: Wiley.

Clark, E. V. (1987). On the logic of contrast. *Journal of Child Language, 15,* 317–335.

Clark, R. E. (1983). Reconsidering research from media. *Review of Educational Research, 53*(4), 445–459.

Claus, A. S. (1989). Making mathematics come alive through a statistics project. In P. R. Trafton & A. P. Shulte (Eds.), *New directions for elementary school mathematics, 1989 yearbook.* Reston, VA: National Council of Teachers of Mathematics.

Clay, M. (1982). *Observing young readers.* Portsmouth, NH: Heinemann.

Clements, D. H. (1986). Effects of Logo and CAI environments on cognition and creativity. *Journal of Educational Psychology, 78,* 309–318.

Clements, D. H., & Nastasi, B. K. (1988). Social and cognitive interactions in educational computer environments. *American Educational Research Journal, 25*(1), 87–106.

Clifford, M. (1991). Risk-taking: Theoretical, empirical and educational considerations. *Educational Psychologist, 26*(3&4), 263–297.

Cobb, P., & Merkel, G. (1989). Thinking strategies: Teaching arithmetic through problem-solving. In P. R. Trafton & A. P. Shulte (Eds.), *New directions for elementary school mathematics: 1989 yearbook* (pp. 70–84). Reston, VA: National Council of Teachers of Mathematics.

Coburn, T. G. The role of computation in the changing mathematics curriculum. In P. R. Trafton & A. P. Schulte (Eds.), *New directions for elementary school mathematics: 1989 yearbook* (pp. 43–56). Reston, VA: National Council of Teachers of Mathematics.

Cockayne, S. (1991). Effects of small group sizes on learning with interactive videodisc. *Educational Technology, 31*(2), 43–45.

Cognition and Technology Group at Vanderbilt. (1990). Anchored instruction and its relationship to situated cognition. *Educational Researcher, 19*(5), 2–10.

Cohen, P. A., Kulik, J. A., & Kulik, C. C. (1982). Educational outcomes of tutoring: A meta-analysis of findings. *American Educational Research Journal, 19,* 237–248.

Coles, C. D., Platzman, K. A., Smith, I., & James, M. E. (1992). Effects of cocaine and alcohol use in pregnancy on neonatal growth and neurobehavioral status. *Neurotoxicology and Teratology, 13*(4), 22–33.

Collins, K. F., Romberg, T. A., & Jurdak, M. E. (1986). A technique for assessing mathematical problem solving ability. *Journal for Research in Mathematics Education, 17*(3), 206–221.

Comstock, M., & Demarc, E. (1987). The calculator is a problem-solving concept developer. *Arithmetic Teacher, 34*(2), 48–51.

Conger, R., Burgess, R., & Barrett, C. (1979). Child abuse related to life change and perceptions of illness: Some preliminary findings. *Family Coordinator, 20,* 73–78.

Cook, L. K., & Mayer, R. E. (1988). Teaching readers about the structure of scientific text. *Journal of Educational Psychology, 80*(4), 448–454.

Cooper, G., & Sweller, J. (1987). Effects of schema acquisition and rule automation on mathematical problem-solving transfer. *Journal of Educational Psychology, 79*(4), 347–362.

Cornwall, A. (1992). The relationship of phonological awareness, rapid naming and verbal memory to severe reading and spelling disability. *Journal of Learning Disabilities, 25*(8), 532–538.

Coyle, J. T., Price, D. L., & DeLong, M. R. (1983). Alzheimer's disease: A disorder of cortical cholinergic innervation. *Science, 219,* 1184–1190.

Crandall, V., Katovsky, W., & Crandall, V. (1965). Children's beliefs in their own control of reinforcement in intellectual academic situations. *Child Development, 36,* 91–109.

Cress, K. P., & Angelo, T. A. (1980). *Classroom assessment techniques: A handbook for faculty.* Ann Arbor: National Center for Research to Improve Postsecondary Teaching and Learning, University of Michigan.

Cronbach, L. J., & Snow, R. E. (1977). *Aptitudes and instructional methods: A handbook for research on interaction.* New York: Irvington.

Crowder, N. A. (1959). Automatic tutoring by means of intrinsic programming. In E. H. Galanter (Ed.), *Automatic teaching: The state of the art* (pp. 109–116). New York: Wiley.

Crowder, P. G., & Wagner, R. K. (1992). *The psychology of reading: An introduction.* New York: Oxford University Press.

Cuban, L. (1986). *Teachers and machines: The classroom use of technology since 1920.* New York: Teachers College Press.

Curry, L. (1990). A critique of the research on learning styles. *Educational Leadership, 48*(20), 50–56.

Cziko, G. A. (1992). The evaluation of bilingual education: From necessity and probability to possibility. *Educational Researcher, 21*(2), 10–15.

Dale, P. S. (1980). *Language development: Structure and function* (2nd ed.) New York: Holt, Rinehart & Winston.

Damasio, A., & Damasio, H. (1992). Brain and language. *Scientific American, 267*(12), 88–109.

Damasio, A. R., Bellugi, V., Damasio, H., Poizner, H., & Van Gilder, J. (1986). Sign language aphasia during left-hemisphere amytal injections. *Nature, 322,* 363–365.

Damon, W., & Hart, D. (1982). The development of self-understanding from infancy through adolescence. *Child Development, 53,* 841–864.

Dansereau, D. F. (1978). The development of a learning strategies curriculum. In H. F. O'Neil (Ed.), *Learning strategies* (pp. 1–29). New York: Academic Press.

Dansereau, D. F. (1985). Learning strategy research. In J. Segal, S. Chipman, & R. Glaser (Eds.), *Thinking and learning skills: Vol. I. Relating instruction to research.* Hillsdale, NJ: Erlbaum.

Davey, B. (1987). Postpassage questions: Task and reader effects on comprehension and metacomprehension processes. *Journal of Reading Behavior, 19*(3), 261–285.

Davey, B., & McBride, S. (1986). The effects of question generation training on reading comprehension. *Journal of Educational Psychology, 78,* 256–262.

Davidson, J. E. (1990). Intelligence recreated. *Educational Psychologist, 25*(3&4), 337–354.

Davies, I. K. (1973). *Competency based learning: Technology management design.* New York: McGraw-Hill.

Davis, K. L., & Mohs, R. C. (1986). Editorial: Cholinergic drugs in Alzheimer's disease. *New England Journal of Medicine, 315,* 1286-1287.

Davis, R., Dugdale, S., Kibbey, D., & Weaver, C. (1977). Representing knowledge about mathematics for computer-aided teaching: Part II. The diversity of roles that a computer can play in assisting learning. In E. W. Elcock & D. Michie (Eds.), *Machine representation of knowledge* (pp. 387-421). Dordrecht, The Netherlands: Reidel.

Dean, J. W. (1975). Watergate: Money talks. *Economist, 254*(Feb), 56.

de Bono, E. (1989). *Think, note write.* Logan, IA: Perfection Form Co.

DeCharms, R. (1968). *Personal causation.* New York: Academic Press.

DeCharms, R. (1976). *Enhancing motivation change in the classroom.* New York: Irvington.

De Charms, R. (1978). *Personal causation: The internal affective determinants of behavior.* New York: Academic Press.

Deci, E. L. (1975). *Intrinsic motivation.* New York: Plenum Press.

Deci, E. L., & Ryan, R. M. (1985). *Intrinsic motivation and self-determination in human behavior.* New York: Plenum Press.

Deci, E. L., Vallerand, R. J., Pelletier, L. G., & Ryan, R. M. (1991). Motivation and education: The self-determination perspective. *Educational Psychologist, 26*(3&4), 325-346.

Dee-Lucas, D., & Larkin, J. H. (1990). Organization and comprehensibilities in scientific proofs, or "consider a particle p. . . . " *Journal of Educational Psychology, 82*(4), 701-714.

Deffenbacher, J. L., & Suinn, R. M. (1988). Systematic desensitization and the reduction of anxiety. *The Counseling Psychologist, 16*(1), 9-30.

Dempster, F. N. (1981). Memory span: Sources of individual and developmental differences. *Psychological Bulletin, 89,* 63-100.

Dennis, W., & Najarian, P. (1957). Infant development under environmental handicap [Whole no. 436]. *Psychological Monographs, 71.*

DesLauriers, M., Hohn, R. L., & Clark, C. F. (1980). Learner characteristics and performance effects in self-paced instruction for community college students. *Teaching of Psychology, 7*(10), 161-165.

DesRochers, A., Gelinas, C., & Wieland, L. D. (1989). An application of the mnemonic keyword method to the acquisition of German nouns and their grammatical gender. *Journal of Educational Psychology, 81*(1), 25-32.

Deutsch, J. A. (1971). The cholinergic synapse and the site of memory. *Science, 174,* 788-794.

Deutsch, M. (1963). The disadvantaged child and the learning process. Some social, psychological and developmental considerations. In A. H. Passow (Ed.), *Education in depressed areas.* New York: Teachers College Press.

Deutsch, M. (1973). *The resolution of conflict: Cognitive and destructive processes.* New Haven, CT: Yale University Press.

Deutsch, M. (1993). Educating for a peaceful world. *American Psychologist, 48*(5), 510-517.

DeValois, R. L., & DeValois, K. K. (1980). Spatial vision. *Annual Review of Psychology, 31,* 309-341.

Dewey, B., & McBride, S. (1986). The effects of question generation training on reading comprehension. *Journal of Educational Psychology, 78,* 256-262.

Dewey, J. (1896). The reflex arc concept in psychology. *Psychological Review, 3,* 357-370.

Diener, C. I., & Dweck, C. S. (1978). An analysis of learned helplessness: Continuous changes in performance, strategy, and achievement cognitions following failure. *Journal of Personality and Social Psychology, 36*(5), 451-462.

Diener, C. I., & Dweck, C. S. (1980). An analysis of learned helplessness: II. The processing of success. *Journal of Personality and Social Psychology, 39*(5), 940-952.

Dixon, J. A., & Moore, C. R. (1990). The development of perspective-taking: Understanding differences in information and weighting. *Child Development, 61,* 1502-1513.

Dole, J. A., Duffy, G. G., Roehler, L. R., & Pearson, P. D. (1991). Moving from the old to the new: Research on reading comprehension instruction. *Review of Educational Research, 61*(2), 239-264.

Donoghue, M. R. (1969). *Foreign languages in the elementary school. Effects and instructional arrangements according to research.* New York: Modern Language Association/American Council on the Teaching of Foreign Language Materials Center. (ERIC Focus Reports on the Teaching of Foreign Languages No. 3)

Dorans, N. J., & Livingston, S. A. (1987). Male-female differences in SAT—verbal ability among students of high SAT— mathematical ability. *Journal of Educational Measurement, 24,* 65-71.

Douglas, V. I., & Peters, K. G. (1979). Toward a clearer definition of the attentional deficit of hyperactive children. In G. Hale & M. Lewis (Eds.), *Attention and the development of cognitive style* (pp. 173-247). New York: Pergamon Press.

Douglas, V. I., Barr, R. G., O'Neill, M. B., & Britton, B. G. (1986). Short term effects of methylphenidate on the peer interactions of attention deficit disordered boys. *Journal of Child Psychology and Psychiatry, 26,* 955-971.

Doyle, W. (1986). Classroom organization and management. In M. C. Wittrock (Ed.), *Handbook of research on teaching* (3rd ed.) (pp. 392-431). New York: Macmillan.

Dreikurs, R., & Grey, L. (1968). *Logical consequences: A new approach to discipline.* New York: Hawthorne Books.

Driver, R., Guese, E., & Tiberghien, A. (1985). *Children's ideas in science.* Philadelphia: Open University Press.

Dukes, R., & Seidner, C. (1978). *Learning with simulations and games.* Beverly Hills, CA: Sage.

Duncker, K. (1945). On problem solving [Whole no. 270]. *Psychological Monographs, 58,* 5.

Dunn, R., & Dunn, K. (1978). *Teaching students through their individual learning styles.* Reston, VA: Preston.

Dunn, R., Dunn, K., & Price, G. (1985). *Learning Style Inventory (LSI).* Lawrence, KS: Price Systems.

Durkheim, E. (1903). Pedagogie et sociologie. *Révue de metaphysique et de morale.* January, 37-54. In *Emile Durkheim. Contributions to L'Année Sociologique* (Y. Nandan, Trans.). New York: Free Press, 1980.

Dweck, C. (1986). Motivational processes affecting learning. *American Psychologist, 41*(10), 1040-1048.

E. M. Kauffman Foundation (1992). *Project Choice.* Kansas City, MO: Author.

Ebbinghaus, H. (1964). *Memory: A contribution to experimental psychology* (H. A. Tuger & C. E. Bussenius, Trans.). New York: Dover. (Original work published 1885)

Eccles, J. S., & Wigfield, A. (1985). Teacher expectations and student motivation. In J. Dusek (Ed.), *Teacher expectancies.* Hillsdale, NJ: Erlbaum.

Eccles, J., Adler, R., & Meece, J. L. (1984). Sex differences in achievement: A test of alternate theories. *Journal of Personality and Social Psychology, 46,* 26-43.

Edwards, L. L., & Simpson, J. (1990). Emotional disturbance. In E. Meyen (Ed.), *Exceptional children in today's schools* (2nd ed.) (pp. 223-254). Denver, CO: Love Publishing.

Eisner, E. (1969). Instructional and expression objectives: Their formulation and use in curriculum. In W. J. Popham (Ed.), *Instructional objectives.* Chicago: Rand McNally. (American Educational Research Association, Monograph on Curriculum Evaluation)

Elliott, E. S., & Dweck, C. S. (1988). Goals: An approach to motivation and achievement. *Journal of Personality and Social Psychology, 54,* 5-12.

Ellis, H. G., & Hunt, R. R. (1989). *Fundamentals of human learning and cognition* (4th ed.). Dubuque, IA: William C. Brown.

Engelmann, S., & Brunner, E. (1984). *DISTAR reading.* Chicago: Science Research Associates.

Englert, C., Hiebert, E., & Stewart, S. (1985). Spelling unfamiliar words by an analogy strategy. *Journal of Special Education, 19,* 291–306.

Englert, C. S., Raphael, T. E., Anderson, L. A., Anthony, H. M., & Stevens, D. D. (1991). Making strategies and self-talk visible. Writing instruction in regular and special education classrooms. *American Educational Research Journal, 28*(2), 337–372.

Englert, C., Raphael, T., Feer, K., & Anderson, L. (1988). Students' metacognitive knowledge about how to write information text. *Learning Disability Quarterly, 11,* 18–46.

Ennis, R. H. (1987). A taxonomy of critical thinking dispositions and abilities. In J. B. Baron & R. J. Sternberg (Eds.), *Teaching thinking skills.* New York: Freeman.

Enright, B. E. (1986). *SOLVE action problem solving.* North Billerica, MA: Curriculum Associates.

Epstein, M. A., Shaywitz, S. E., Shaywitz, P. A., & Woolston, J. L. (1991). The boundaries of attention deficit disorder. *Journal of Learning Disabilities, 24*(2), 78–87.

Erickson, F., & Schulz, J. (1982). *The counselor as gate keeper: Social interaction in interviews.* New York: Academic Press.

Erikson, E. H. (1968). *Identity: Youth and crisis.* New York: Norton.

Estrada, P., Arsenio, W. F., Hess, R. D., & Holloway, S. D. (1987). Affective quality of the mother–child relationship. Longitudinal consequences for children's school relevant cognitive functioning. *Developmental Psychology, 23,* 210–215.

Eylon, B., & Rief, R. (1984). Effects of knowledge organization on task performance. *Cognition and Instruction, 1,* 5–44.

Faigley, L., & Witte, S. (1983). Analyzing revision. *College Composition and Communication, 32,* 400–414.

Feagans, L., & Farron, D. C. (1982). *The language of children reared in poverty.* New York: Academic Press.

Feingold, A. (1992). Sex differences in variability in intellectual abilities: A new look at an old controversy. *Review of Educational Research, 62,*(1), 61–84.

Ferster, C. B., & Skinner, B. F. (1957). *Schedules of reinforcement.* Englewood Cliffs, NJ: Prentice-Hall.

Fillmore, L. W., & Valadez, C. (1986). Teaching bilingual learners. In M. Wittrock (Ed.), *Handbook of research on teaching* (3rd ed.) (pp. 648–685). New York: Macmillan.

Fishman, J. A., & Lovas, J. (1970). Bilingual education in a sociolinguistic perspective. *TESOL Quarterly, 4*(3), 215–222.

Flanagan, C. (1993). Gender and social class: Intersecting issues in women's achievement. *Educational Psychologist, 28*(4), 357–378.

Flavell, J. H. (1963). *The developmental psychology of Jean Piaget.* Princeton, NJ: Van Nostrand.

Flavell, J. H. (1971a). First discussant's comments: What is memory development the development of? *Human Development, 14,* 272–278.

Flavell, J. H. (1971b). Stage related properties of cognitive development. *Cognitive Psychology, 2,* 421–453.

Flavell, J. H. (1979). Metacognition and cognitive monitoring: A new era of cognitive-developmental inquiry. *American Psychologist, 34,* 906–911.

Flavell, J. H., Botkin, P. I., Fry, C. L., Wright, J. W., & Jarvis, R. E. (1968). *The development of role taking and communication skills in children.* New York: Wiley.

Flavell, J. H., & Wellman, H. M. (1977). Metamemory. In R. V. Hail & J. W. Hagen (Eds.), *Perspectives in the development of memory and cognition.* Hillsdale, NJ: Erlbaum.

Flower, L. S., & Hayes, J. R. (1980). The cognition of discovery: Defining a rhetorical problem. *College Composition and Communication, 31,* 21–32.

Flower, L. S., & Hayes, J. R. (1981). A cognitive process theory of writing. *College Composition and Communication, 32,* 365–387.

Flynn, J. P., Vargas, H., Foote, W., & Edwards, S. (1970). Neural mechanisms involved in a cat's attack on a rat. In R. E. Whalen, R. F. Thompson, M. Verzearo, & N. M. Weinberger (Eds.), *The neural control of behavior* (pp. 135–173). New York: Academic Press.

Folkman, S. (1984). Personal control and stress and coping processes: A theoretical analysis. *Journal of Personality and Social Psychology, 40*(4), 839–852.

Foorman, B. R., Francis, D. J., Novy, D. M., & Lieberman, D. (1991). How letter–sound instruction mediates progress in first grade reading/spelling. *Journal of Educational Psychology, 83,* 456–469.

Fox, B., & Routh, D. K. (1983). Reading disability, phonemic analysis and dysphonetic spelling: A follow-up study. *Journal of Clinical Child Psychology, 12,* 28–32.

Francis, K. T. (1979). Psychologic correlates of serum indicator of stress in man. A longitudinal study. *Psychomatic Medicine, 41,* 617–628.

Frensch, P. A., & Sternberg, R. J. (1989). Expertise and intelligent thinking: When is it worse to know better? In R. J. Sternberg (Ed.), *Advances in the psychology of human intelligence: Vol. 5* (pp. 157–188). Hillsdale, NJ: Erlbaum.

Freud, S. (1938). *The basic writings of Sigmund Freud.* New York: Modern Library.

Fried, P. A., O'Connell, C. M., & Watkinson, B. (1992). Sixty- and 72-month follow-up of children prenatally exposed to marijuana, cigarettes and alcohol: Cognitive and language assessment. *Journal of Developmental and Behavioral Pediatrics, 13*(6), 383–391.

Friedman, L. (1989).Mathematics and the gender gap: A meta-analysis of recent students on sex differences in mathematical tasks. *Review of Educational Research, 59,* 185–214.

Friend, C. L., & Cole, C. L. (1990). Learner-control in computer-based instruction: A current literature review. *Educational Technology, 30*(11), 47–49.

Fuchs, D., Fuchs, L. S., & Power, M. H. (1987). Effects of examiner familiarity with an LD and MR students' language performance. *Remedial and Special Education, 8,* 47–52.

Fuchs, D., Fuchs L. S., Power, M. H., & Dailey, B (1983). Bias in the assessment of handicapped children. *American Educational Research Journal, 22,* 185–198.

Fuson, K. C., & Willis, G. B. (1989). Second graders' use of schematic drawings in solving addition and subtraction word problems. *Journal of Educational Psychology, 81,* 514–520.

Gage, N. (Ed.). (1963). *Handbook of research on teaching.* Chicago: Rand McNally.

Gagné, R. M. (1985). *The conditions of learning* (4th ed.). New York: Holt, Rinehart & Winston.

Gagné, R. M., & Briggs, L. J. (1979). *Principles of instructional design* (2nd ed.). New York: Holt, Rinehart & Winston.

Gagné, R. M., & Briggs, L. J. (1984). *Principles of instructional design* (3rd ed.). New York: Holt, Rinehart & Winston.

Gagné, R. M., & Driscoll, M. P. (1988). *Essentials of learning for instruction* (2nd ed.). Englewood Cliffs, NJ: Prentice-Hall.

Gagné, R. M., & Merrill, M. D. (1991). In conversation. *Educational Technology, 31*(1), 34–40.

Gallup Organization. (1988). *Gallup survey questionnaire for the National Geographic.* Princeton, NJ: Author.

Garcia, R. L. (1991). *Teaching in a pluralistic society: Concepts, models, and strategies.* New York: HarperCollins.

Gardner, H. (1983). *Frames of mind: The theory of multiple intelligences.* New York: Basic Books.

Gardner, H., & Hatch, T. (1989). Multiple intelligences go to school. *Educational Researcher, 18*(8), 4–10.

Garner, R., Hare, V., Alexander, P., Haynes, J., & Winograd, P. (1984). Inducing use of a text look back strategy among unsuccessful readers. *American Educational Research Journal, 21,* 789-798.

Geffen, G., & Quinn, K. (1984). Hemispheric specialization and ear advantages in processing speech. *Psychological Bulletin, 96,* 273-291.

Gelman, R. (1980). What your children know about numbers. *Educational Psychologist, 15,* 54-68.

Gelman, R., & Gallistel, C. R. (1978). *The child's understanding of number.* Cambridge, MA: Harvard University Press.

Gelman, R., Meek, B., & Menkin, S. (1986). Young children's numerical competence. *Cognitive Development, 1,* 1-29.

Genesee, F. (1987). *Learning through two languages: Studies of immersion and bilingual education.* Cambridge, MA: Newbury House.

Gerschwind, N., & Levitsky, W. (1968). Human brain: Left-right asymmetries in temporal speech region. *Science, 161,* 186-187.

Gibson, S., & Dembo, M. H. (1984). Teacher efficacy: A construct validation. *Journal of Educational Psychology, 76,* 569-582.

Gibson, E. J. (1965). Learning to read. *Science, 148,* 1066-1072.

Gick, M. L. (1986). Problem-solving strategies. *Educational Psychologist, 21*(1&2), 99-120.

Gick, M. L., & Holyoak, K. J. (1980). Analogical problem solving. *Cognitive Psychology, 12,* 306-355.

Gick, M. L., & Holyoak, K. J. (1983). Schema induction and analogical transfer. *Cognitive Psychology, 15,* 1-38.

Gilligan, C. (1977). In a different voice: Women's conceptions of self and morality. *Harvard Educational Review, 47,* 481-517.

Gilligan, C. (1982). *In a different voice.* Cambridge, MA: Harvard University Press.

Gilligan, C., Lyons, N. & Hammer, T. (1990). *Making connections.* Cambridge, MA: Harvard University Press.

Ginsburg, H. P., & Russell, R. L. (1981). Social class and racial influences on early mathematical thinking. *Monographs of the Society for Research in Child Development, 46* (Serial no. 193).

Givner, A., & Graubard, P. S. (1974). *A handbook of behavior modification for the classroom.* New York: Holt, Rinehart & Winston.

Gleckel, L. K., & Lee, R. J. (1990). Physical disabilities. In E. Meyen (Ed.), *Exceptional children in today's schools* (2nd ed.) (pp. 359-394). Denver, CO: Love Publishing.

Glenberg, A. M., & Epstein, W. (1987). Inexpert calibration of comprehension. *Memory and Cognition, 15,* 84-93.

Glick, D. M., & Semb, G. (1978). Effects of pacing contingencies in personalized instruction: A review of the evidence. *Journal of Personalized Instruction, 3,* 36-42.

Glover, J. A., Dinnel, D. L., Halpein, D. R., McKee, T. K., Corkill, A. J., & Wise, S. L. (1988). Effects of across chapter signals on recall of text. *Journal of Educational Psychology, 80*(1), 3-15.

Goldenberg, C. (1989). Making success a more common occurrence for children at risk for failure. Lessons from Hispanic first graders learning to read. In J. B. Allen & J. M. Mason (Eds.), *Risk makers, risk takers, risk breakers. Reducing the risks for young literacy learners* (pp. 48-78). Portsmouth, NH: Heinemann.

Goldman, S. R., Pellegrino, J. W., & Mertz, D. L. (1988). Extended practice of basic addition facts: Strategy changes in learning disabled students. *Cognition and Instruction, 5,* 223-265.

Goldstein, H., Moss, J. W., & Jordan, L. (1965). *The efficacy of special class training of the development of mentally retarded children* (U.S. Office of Education, Cooperative Research Project Report No. 619). Urbana, IL: University of Illinois.

Goodlad, J. I. (1984). *A place called school.* New York: McGraw-Hill.

Goodman, K. S. (1965). A linguistic study of cues and miscues in reading. *Elementary English, 42,* 639–643.

Goodman, K. S. (1968). *The psycholinguistic nature of the reading process.* Detroit: Wayne State University Press.

Goodman, K. S. (1986). *What's whole in whole language: A parent–teacher guide.* Portsmouth, NH: Heinemann.

Gordon, E. E. (1989). *Learning sequences in music: Skill, content and patterns.* Chicago: G.I.A. Publications.

Gordon, I. J. (1970). *Parent involvement in compensatory education.* Urbana: University of Illinois Press.

Gordon, T. (1974). *T.E.T., Teacher effectiveness training.* New York: McKay.

Grabe, M. (1986). Attentional processes in education. In G. D. Phye & T. Andre (Eds.), *Cognitive classroom learning: Understanding, thinking and problem solving* (pp. 49–82). New York: Academic Press.

Graham, S. (1992). The role of production factor in learning disabled students' compositions. *Journal of Educational Psychology, 82*(4), 781–791.

Graham, S., & Golen, S. (1991). Motivational influences on cognition: Task involvement, ego involvement and depth of information processing. *Journal of Educational Psychology, 83,* 187–194.

Graham, S., & Parker, C. P. (1990). The down side of help: An attributional developmental analysis of helping behavior as a low-ability cue. *Journal of Educational Psychology, 82*(1), 7–14.

Graham, S., Harris, K. R., & Reid, R. (1990). Learning disabilities. In E. Meyen (Ed.), *Exceptional children in today's schools* (2nd ed.) (pp. 193–222). Denver, CO: Love Publishing.

Greeno, J. G., & Simon, H. A. (1988). Problem solving and reasoning. In R. C. Atkinson, R. J. Hernstein, G. Lindsey, & R. D. Luce (Eds.), *Stevens' handbook of experimental psychology.* New York: Wiley.

Greenough, W. T., Black, J. E., & Wallace, C. S. (1987). Experience and brain development. *Child Development, 58,* 539–559.

Greenwood, C. R., & Hops, H. (1981). Group contingencies and peer behavior change. In P. Strain (Ed.), *The utilization of classroom peers as behavior change assets* (pp. 189–259). New York: Plenum Press.

Greenwood, C. R., Certa, J. J., & Hall, R. V. (1988). The use of peer tutoring strategies in classroom management and educational instruction. *School Psychology Review, 17*(2), 258–275.

Greenwood, C. R., Dinwiddie, G., Terry, B., Wade, L., Stanley, S., Thibodeau, S., & Dal Quadri, G. (1984). Teacher vs. peer-mediated instruction: An eco-behavioral analysis of achievement outcomes. *Journal of Applied Behavioral Analysis, 17,* 521–538.

Gregorc, A., & Butler, K. (1984). Learning is a matter of style. *Vocational Education, 4,* 27–29.

Gross, N. B. (1958). *Living with stress.* New York: McGraw-Hill.

Grote, G. (1975). *Plato and the other companions of Socrates: Vol. II.* London: John Murray.

Grotelueschen, A, & Sjogren, D. D. (1968). Effects of differentially structured introductory materials and learning tasks on learning and transfer. *American Educational Research Journal, 5,* 191–202.

Guilford, J. P. (1959). Three faces of intellect. *American Psychologist, 14,* 469–479.

Guthrie, J. T., Siefert, M., & Kirsch, I. S. (1986). Effects of education, occupation and setting on reading practices. *American Educational Research Journal, 23,* 151–160.

Gwynne, F. (1970). *The king who rained.* New York: Windmill Books and Dutton.

Haber, R. N. (1979). Twenty years of haunting eidetic images: Where's the ghost? *Behavioral and Brain Science, 2,* 583–594.

Hahn, J., Smith, M., & Block, J. (1968). Moral reasoning of young adults: Political–social behavior, family background and personality correlates. *Journal of Personality and Social Psychology, 10,* 183–201.

Haier, J. R., Siegel, B. V., Nuechterlein, K. H., Hazlett, E. H., Wu, J. C., Peck, J., Browning, H. L., & Buchsbaum, M. S. (1988). Cortical glucose metabolic rate correlates of abstract reasoning and attention studied with positron emission tomography. *Intelligence, 12,* 199–217.

Hale, B. D. (1982). The effects of internal and external imagery on muscular and ocular concomitants. *Journal of Sport Psychology, 4,* 211–220.

Hall, J. W. (1988). On the utility of the keyword mnemonic for vocabulary learning. *Journal of Educational Psychology, 80,* 564–562.

Hall, V. C., & Kaye, D. B. (1980). Early patterns of cognitive development. *Monographs of the Society for Research in Child Development, 45* (Serial no. 184).

Hallahan, D. P., & Kauffman, J. M. (1991). *Exceptional children.* Englewood Cliffs, NJ: Prentice-Hall.

Hamaker, C. (1986). The effects of adjunct questions on prose learning. *Review of Educational Research, 56*(2), 212–242.

Hardiman, P. T., & Mestre, J. (1989). Understanding multiplicative contexts involving fractions. *Journal of Educational Psychology, 81,* 547–557.

Harris, F. R., Johnston, M. K., Kelley, C. S., & Wolf, M. M. (1964). Effects of positive social reinforcement on regressed crawling of a nursery school child. *Journal of Educational Psychology, 55,* 35–41.

Harris, L. J. (1980). Which hand is the eye of the blind? A new look at an old question. In J. Herron (Ed.), *Neuropsychology of left-handedness* (pp. 303–329). New York: Academic Press.

Harris, M. B. (1974). *Classroom uses of behavior modification.* Columbus, OH: Merrill.

Harry, B. (1992). Restructuring the participation of African-American parents in special education. *Exceptional Children, 59*(2), 123–131.

Hartmann, G. W. (1942). The field-theory of learning and its educational consequences. In *The psychology of learning: Ii. 41st yearbook of the national society for the study of education* (pp. 166–214). Chicago: University of Chicago Press.

Harvey, G. (1986). Finding reality among the myths: Why what you thought about sex equity in education isn't so. *Phi Delta Kappan, 67,* 509–512.

Haskins, R. (1989). Beyond metaphor: The efficacy of early childhood education. *American Psychologist, 44,* 274–282.

Hawkins, J. (1985). Computers and girls: Rethinking the issues. *Sex Roles, 13,* 165–180.

Hayes, J. R. (1981). *The complete problem solver.* Philadelphia: Franklin Institute Press.

Hayes, J. R., & Flower, L. S. (1986). Writing research and the writer. *American Psychologist, 41*(10), 1106–1113.

Heath, S. B. (1983). *Ways with words: Language, life, and work in communities and classrooms.* New York: Cambridge University Press.

Hebb, D. O. (1972). *A textbook of psychology* (3rd ed). Philadelphia: Saunders.

Heider, F. (1958). *The psychology of interpersonal relations.* New York: Wiley.

Heiman, M., & Slomienko, J. (1991). *Critical thinking skills.* Washington, DC: National Education Association.

Heinze, T. (1986). Communication skills. In G. T. Scholl (Ed.), *Foundations of education for blind and visually handicapped children and youth* (pp. 119-136). New York: American Foundation for the Blind.

Hersh, R. H., Miller, J. P., & Fielding, G. D. (1980). *Models of moral education.* White Plains, NY: Longman.

Hersh, R., Paolitto, D., & Reimer, J. (1979). *Promoting moral growth: From Piaget to Kohlberg.* White Plains, NY: Longman.

Hess, R. (1970). Class and ethnic influences upon socialization. In P. Mussen (Ed.), *Carmichael's manual of child psychology: Vol. 2* (3rd ed.). New York: Wiley.

Hess, R., & McDevitt, T. (1984). Some cognitive consequences of maternal intervention techniques. A longitudinal study. *Child Development, 55,* 1902-1912.

Hess, R., Holloway, S., Dickson, W., & Price, G. (1984). Maternal variables as predictors of children's school readiness and later achievement in vocabulary and mathematics in sixth grade. *Child Development, 55,* 1902-1912.

Hicks, S. J. (1991). A review of selected findings of the project. *Educational Technology, 31*(6), 54-57.

Hidi, S. (1990). Interest and its contribution as a mental resource for learning. *Review of Educational Research, 60*(4), 549-572.

Hilgard, E. R., & Bower, G. H. (1975). *Theories of learning* (2nd ed.). New York: Appleton-Century Crofts.

Hodgkinson, H. (1991). Reform vs. reality. *Phi Delta Kappan, 73*(1), 8-16.

Hodgkinson, H. (1993). American education: The good, the bad, the task. *Phi Delta Kappan, 74*(8), 617-624.

Hoffman, M. L. (1971). Identification and conscience development. *Child Development, 42,* 1071-1082.

Hoffman, M. L., & Saltzstein, H. D. (1967). Parent discipline and the child's moral development. *Journal of Personality and Social Psychology, 5,* 45-57.

Hofsten, C. Von, & Ronnqvist, L. (1988). Preparation for grasping an object: A developmental study. *Journal of Experimental Psychology: Human Perception and Performance, 14,* 610-621.

Holland, J. G., & Skinner, B. F. (1961). *The analysis of behavior.* New York: McGraw-Hill.

Hollingsworth, S., Teel, K., & Minarik, L. (1992). Learning to teach Aaron: A beginning teacher's story of literacy instruction in an urban classroom. *Journal of Teacher Education, 43*(2), 116-127.

Homme, L., Csanyi, A. P., Gonzales, M. A., & Rechs, J. R. (1970). *How to use contingency contracting in the classroom.* Champaign, IL: Research Press.

Horowitz, F. D. (1987). *Exploring developmental theories: Toward a structural/behavioral model of development.* Hillsdale, NJ: Erlbaum.

Hull, C. L. (1943). *Principles of behavior.* Englewood Cliffs, NJ: Prentice-Hall.

Humphreys, L. G. (1939). Acquisition and extinction of verbal expectations in a situation analogous to conditioning. *Journal of Experimental Psychology, 25,* 294-301.

Hutchings, D. E. (1987). Drug abuse during pregnancy: Embryopathic and neurobehavioral effects. In M. C. Broude & A. M. Zimmerman (Eds.), *Genetic and perinatal effects of abused substances.* Orlando, FL: Academic Press.

Hyde, A. A., & Bizar, M. (1989). *Thinking in context: Teaching cognitive processes across the elementary school curriculum.* White Plains, NY: Longman.

Hyde, J. S. (1986). Introduction: Meta-analysis and the psychology of gender. In J. S. Hyde & M. C. Linn (Eds.), *The psychology of gender; Advances through meta-analysis* (pp. 1-113). Baltimore, MD: Johns Hopkins University Press.

Ilg, F. L., & Ames, L. B. (1955). *Child behavior.* New York: Harper & Row.

Irwin, D. M., & Bushnell, M. M. (1980). *Observational strategies for child study.* New York: Holt.

Jacklin, C. N. (1983). Boys and girls entering school. In M. Morland (Ed.), *Sex differentiation and schooling.* London: Heinemann.

Jackson, P. (1968). *Life in classrooms.* New York: Holt, Rinehart & Winston.

Jacobs, M. K. (1977). The DIT related to behavior in an experimental setting: Promise keeping in the Prisoner's Dilemma Game. In J. Rest (Ed.), *Development in judging moral issues—A summary of research using the defining issues test,* Minnesota Moral Research Projects. (Tech. Rep. No. 3)

Jakobson, R. (1981). Can and should the Laredo experiment be duplicated elsewhere? The applicability of the concurrent approach in other communities. In P. C. Gonzalez (Ed.), *Proceedings of the Eighth Annual Bilingual Bicultural Education Conference.* Rosslyn, VA: National Clearinghouse for Bilingual Education.

James, W. (1890). *The principles of psychology* (Vols. I & II). New York: Henry Holt.

Janek, J. (1989). *The LAMPS strategy.* Unpublished manuscript, University of Kansas, Lawrence.

Jastrow, R. (1981). *The enchanted loom: Mind in the universe.* New York: Simon & Schuster.

Jeffries, R., Turner, A., Polson, P., & Atwood, M. (1981). The processes involved in designing software. In J. Anderson (Ed.), *Cognitive skills and their acquisition* (pp. 61-77). Hillsdale, NJ: Erlbaum.

Jenkins-Friedman, R., Nielsen, M. E. (1990). Gifted and talented students. In E. Meyen (Ed.), *Exceptional children in today's schools* (2nd ed.) (pp. 451-494). Denver, CO: Love Publishing.

Jensen, A. R. (1969). How much can we boost IQ and scholastic achievement? *Harvard Educational Review, 39,* 449-483.

Johnson, D. W., & Johnson, R. T. (1987). *Learning together and alone.* Englewood Cliffs, NJ: Prentice-Hall.

Johnson, D. W., & Johnson, R. T. (1989a). *Cooperation and competition: Theory and research.* Edina, MN: Interaction Books.

Johnson, D. W., & Johnson R. T. (1989b). Cooperative learning in mathematics education. In P. R. Trafton & A. P. Schulte (Eds.), *New directions for elementary school mathematics. 1989 yearbook.* Reston, VA: National Council of Teachers of Mathematics.

Johnson, D. W., & Johnson, R. T. (1992). *Creative controversy: Intellectual challenge in the classroom.* Edina, MN: Interaction Books.

Johnson, D. W., Johnson, R. J., & Holubec, E. J. (1986). *Circles of learning: Cooperation in the classroom.* Edina, MN: Interaction Books.

Johnson, D. W., Murayama, G., Johnson, R., Nelson, D., & Skor, L. (1981). Effects of cooperative, competitive and individualistic goal structures on achievement: A meta-analysis. *Psychological Bulletin, 89,* 47-62.

Johnston, C., Pelham, W. E., Hozo, J., & Sturges, J. (1988). Psychostimulant rebound in attention deficit disordered boys. *Journal of the American Academy of Child and Adolescent Psychiatry, 27,* 806-810.

Johnston, M. K., Kelley, C. S., Harris, F. R., & Wolf, M. M. (1966). An application of reinforcement principles to development of motor skills of a young child. *Child Development, 37*(2), 379-387.

Johsua, S., & Dupin, J. J. (1987). Taking into account student conceptions in instructional strategy: An example in physics. *Cognition and Instruction, 4*(2), 61-90.

Jones, K. L., & Smith, D. W. (1973). Recognition of the fetal alcohol syndrome in early infancy. *Lancet, 11,* 999-1001.

Jones, V. F., & Jones, L. S. (1990). *Comprehensive classroom management.* Needham Heights, MA: Allyn & Bacon.

Joyce, B., & Weil, M. (1986). *Models of teaching* (3rd ed.). Englewood Cliffs, NJ: Prentice-Hall.

Judd, T. P., & Bilski, L. H. (1989). Comprehension and memory in the solution of verbal arithmetic problems by mentally retarded and nonretarded individuals. *Journal of Educational Psychology, 81*(4), 541–546.

Juel, C. (1988). Learning to read and write: A longitudinal study of 54 children from first through fourth grades. *Journal of Educational Psychology, 80*(4), 437–447.

Justen, J. E., Waldrop, P. B., & Adams, T. A. (1990). Effects of paired vs. individual user CAI and type of feedback on student achievement. *Educational Technology, 30*(7), 51–53.

Kagan, J. (1958). The concept of identification. *Psychological Review, 65,* 296–305.

Kagan, J. (1971). *Understanding children.* New York: Harcourt Brace Jovanovich.

Kagan, J., Rossman, B., Day, D., Albert J., & Phillips, W. (1964). Information processing in the child: Significance of analytical and reflective attitudes. *Psychological Monographs* [Serial no. 578] 78.

Kahnemann, D., Slovic, P., & Tversky, A. (Eds.). (1982). *Judgment under uncertainty: Heuristics and biases.* Cambridge: Cambridge University Press.

Kamii, C. (1985). *Young children reinvent arithmetic: Implications of Piaget's theory.* New York: Teachers College Press.

Kamii, C., & DeVries, R. (1978). *Physical knowledge in preschool education: Implications of Piaget's theory.* Englewood Cliffs, NJ: Prentice-Hall.

Kandel, E. R., & Schwartz, J. H. (1988). Molecular biology of learning modulation of transmitter release. *Science, 218,* 433–443.

Kant, I. (1933). *Critique of pure reason* (N. K. Smith, Trans.). London: Routledge, Kegan Paul. (Original work published 1781)

Kaufer, D., Hayes, J. R., & Flower, L. S. (1988). Composing written sentences. *Research in the Teaching of English, 20,* 121–140.

Kaufman, L., Curtis, S., Wang, J. Z., & Williamson, S. J. (1992). Changes in cortical activity when subjects scan memory for tones. *Electroencephalography and Clinical Neurophysiology 82*(4), 266–284.

Keller, J. M. (1984). The use of the ARCS model of motivation in teacher training. In K. Shaw (Ed.), *Aspects of educational technology: Vol. XVII. Staff development and career updating.* New York: Nichols.

Kempler, D., & Van Laucker, D. (1987). The right turn of phrase. *Psychology Today, 21,* 20–22.

Kenney, T. J., Cannizzo, S. R., & Flavell, J. H. (1967). Spontaneous and induced verbal rehearsal in a recall task. *Child Development, 38,* 953–966.

Kiewra, K. (1985). Investigating note-taking and review: A depth of processing alternative. *Educational Psychologist, 23,* 39–56.

Kiewra, K. A., Fletcher, H. J. (1984). The relationship between levels of notetaking and achievement. *Human Learning, 3,* 273–280.

Kintsch, W., & Greeno, J. G. (1985). Understanding and solving word arithmetic problems. *Psychological Review, 92,* 109–129.

Kintsch, W., & Van Dijk, T. A. (1978). Toward a model of text comprehension and production. *Psychological Review, 85,* 363–394.

Kirby, J. R. (1988). Style, strategy and skills in reading. In R. R. Schmeck (Ed.)., *Learning strategies and learning styles* (pp. 229–274). New York: Plenum Press.

Kirsch, I. S., & Mosenthal, P. B. (1989). Building documents by combining simple lists. *Journal of Reading, 33,* 132–135.

Kirsch, I. S., & Mosenthal, P. B. (1990). Exploring document literacy: Variables underlying the performance of young adults. *Reading Research Quarterly, 25,* 5-30.

Kiser, L. (1989). Using the microcomputer as a tool to improve learning in mathematics. *Educational Technology, 29*(9), 40-43.

Kleinsmith, L. J., & Kaplan, S. (1963). Paired associate learning as a function of arousal and interpolated interval. *Journal of Experimental Psychology, 65,* 190-193.

Klorman, R., Hilbert, P. L., Michael, R., LaGana, C., & Sveen, B. (1980). Effects of coping and mastery modeling on experienced and inexperienced pedodontic patients' disruptiveness. *Behavior Therapy, 11,* 156-168.

Kloster, A. M., & Winne, P. H. (1989). The effects of different types of organizers on student's learning from text. *Journal of Educational Psychology, 81*(1), 9-15.

Koffka, K. (1935). *Principles of Gestalt psychology.* New York: Harcourt, Brace.

Kohlberg, L. (1958). *The development of modes of moral thinking in the years ten to sixteen.* Unpublished doctoral dissertation, University of Chicago, Chicago.

Kohlberg, L. (1964). Development of moral character and moral ideology. In M. Hoffman & L. Hoffman (Eds.), *Review of child development research: Vol. 1.* New York: Russell Sage Foundation.

Kohlberg, L. (1968). Montessori with the culturally disadvantaged: A cognitive-developmental interpretation and some research findings. In R. D. Hess & R. M. Bear (Eds.), *Early education* (pp. 105-118). Chicago: Aldine.

Kohlberg, L. (1969). Stage and sequence: The cognitive-developmental approach to socialization. In D. Goslin (Ed.), *Handbook of socialization theory and research.* Chicago: Rand McNally.

Kohlberg, L. (1976). Moral stages and moralization: The cognitive development approach. In T. Lickona (Ed.), *Moral development and behavior: Theory, research and social issues.* New York: Holt, Rinehart & Winston.

Kohlberg, L. (1985). A just community approach to moral education in theory and practice. In M. W. Berkowitz & F. Oser (Eds.), *Moral education: Theory and application.* Hillsdale, NJ: Erlbaum.

Kohlberg, L., & Higgins, A. (1987). School democracy and social interaction. In W. Kurtines & J. Gewirtz (Eds.), *Moral development through social interaction.* New York: Wiley.

Kohlberg, L., Levine, C., & Hewer, A. (1983). *Moral stages: A current formulation and a response to critics.* New York: Karger.

Kohler, F. W., & Greenwood, C. R. (1990). Effects of collateral peer supportive behaviors within the classwide peer tutoring program. *Journal of Applied Behavior Analysis, 23*(3), 307-322.

Kohler, W. (1925). *The mentality of apes.* London: Routledge and Kegan Paul.

Kolb, B., & Whishaw, I. Q. (1986). *Fundamentals of human neuropsychology.* San Francisco: Freeman.

Kornhaber, M., Krechevsky, M., & Gardner, H. S. (1990). Engaging intelligence. *Educational Psychologist, 25*(3&4), 177-199.

Kornherber, R. C., & Schroeder, H. E. (1975). Importance of model similarity on extinction of avoidance behavior in children. *Journal of Consulting and Clinical Psychology 43,* 601-607.

Kounin, J. (1970). *Discipline and group management in classrooms.* New York: Holt, Rinehart & Winston.

Kounin, J. S., & Gump, P. V. (1962). The ripple effect in discipline. *Elementary School Journal, 59*(3), 158-162.

Kramer, J. S. (1989). Training parents as behavior change agents: Successes, failures, and suggestions for school psychologists. In T. Gutkin & C. R. Reynolds (Eds.), *The handbook of school psychology* (2nd ed.) (pp. 683-701). New York: Wiley.

Krathwohl, D. R., Bloom, B. S., & Masia, B. (1964). *Taxonomy of educational objectives: The classification of educational goals. Handbook II: Affective domain.* New York: McKay.

Krech, D., Crutchfield, P. S., & Ballachey, E. L. (1962). *Individual in society.* New York: McGraw-Hill.

Kretschmer, R. R. (Ed.). (1985). Learning to write and writing to learn. *Volta Review, 87*(5), 5-185.

Kuczaj, S. A., Borys, R. H., & Jones, M. (1989). Some thoughts on the interaction of language and thought: Some thoughts on the developmental data. In A Gellatly, D. Rogers, & J. A. Sloboda (Eds.), *Cognition and the social world.* New York: Oxford University Press.

Kuder, S. J. (1991). Language abilities and progress in a direct instruction reading program for students with learning disabilities. *Journal of Learning Disabilities, 24*(2), 124-127.

Kulhavy, R. W., Dyer, H., & Silver, L. (1975). The effects of notetaking and test expectancy on the learning of text material. *Journal of Educational Research, 68,* 363-365.

Kulhavy, R. W., Lee, J. B., & Caterino, L. C. (1985). Conjoint retention of maps and related discourse. *Contemporary Educational Psychology, 10,* 28-37.

Kulhavy, R. W., Sherman, J. L., & Schmid, R. F. (1978). Contextual cues and depth of processing in short prose passages. *Contemporary Educational Psychology, 3,* 62-68.

Kulhavy, R. W., Schwartz, N. H., & Peterson, S. (1986). Working memory: The encoding process. In G. D. Phye & T. Andre (Eds.), *Cognitive classroom learning: Understanding thinking and problem solving.* New York: Academic Press.

Kulik, J. A., Bangert, R. L., & Williams, G. W. (1983). Effects of computer-based teaching on secondary school students. *Journal of Educational Psychology, 75*(1), 19-26.

Kun, A. (1977). Development of the magnitude-covariation and compensation schemata in ability and effort attributions of performance. *Child Development, 48,* 862-873.

Kurdock, L. A., & Rodgon, M. M. (1975). Perceptual, cognitive and affective perspective taking in kindergarten through sixth grade children. *Developmental Psychology, 11,* 643-650.

Kurland, D. M., & Pea, R. D., (1983). On the cognitive effects of learning computer programming. *New Ideas in Psychology, 2,* 137-168.

Kuypers, D. S., Becker, W. C., & O'Leary, K. D. (1968). How to make a token system fail. *Exceptional Children, 35*(2), 101-108.

Laberge, D., & Samuels, S. J. (1974). Toward a theory of automatic information on processing in reading. *Cognitive Psychology, 6,* 283-323.

Laboratory of Comparative Human Cognition. (1989). Kids and computers: A positive union of the future. *Harvard Educational Review, 19*(1), 73-86.

Lambert, L. E. (1984). An overview of issues in immersion education. In *Studies in immersion education: A collection for U.S. educators* (pp. 8-30). Sacramento: California State Department of Education.

Lang, P. J. (1964). Experimental studies of desensitization psychotherapy. In J. Wolpe, A. Solter, & L. J. Reyra (Eds.), *The conditioning therapies* (pp. 36-53). New York: Holt, Rinehart & Winston.

Laughlin, P. R., Vander Stoep, S. W., & Hollingshead, A. B. (1991). Collective vs. individual induction: Recognition of truth, rejection of error and collective information processing. *Journal of Personality and Social Psychology, 61*(1), 50-67.

Laughton, T., & Hasenstab, M. S. (1986). *The language learning process.* Rockville, MD: Aspen.

Lawler, R. W. (1981). The progressive construction of mind. *Cognitive Science, 5,* 1-30.

Lawrenz, F. (1986). Misconceptions of physical science concepts among elementary school teachers. *School Science and Mathematics, 86*(1), 654-660.

Lazar, I., Darlington, R., Murray, H., Royce, J., & Snippes, A. (1982). Lasting effects of early education: A report from the Consortium for Longitudinal Studies. *Monographs of the Society for Research in Child Development, 47*(2-3, Serial no. 195).

Lederer, R. (1988). The return of "A Plague of Boobs." *The New Yorker,* March 7, 1987.

Lee, S. S., & Lee, Y. H. K. (1991). Effects of learner-control vs. program-control strategies on computer-aided learning of chemistry problems. For acquisition or review? *Journal of Educational Psychology, 83*(4), 491–498.

Lefcourt, H. (1976). Locus of control: Current trends in research and theory. Hillsdale, NJ: Erlbaum.

Leinhardt, G., & Greeno, J. G. (1986). The cognitive skill of teaching. *Journal of Educational Psychology, 78,* 75-95.

Lent, R. W., & Hackett, G. (1987). Career self-efficacy: Empirical status and future directions. *Journal of Vocational Behavior, 30,* 349-382.

Lepper, M. R. (1985). Microcomputers in education: Motivational and social issues. *American Psychologist, 40*(1), 1-18.

Lepper, M. R. (1988). Motivational considerations in the study of instruction. *Cognition and Instruction, 5,* 289-309.

Lepper, M. R., Greene, D., & Nisbett, R. E. (1973). Undermining children's intrinsic interest with extrinsic rewards: A test of the overjustification hypothesis. *Journal of Personality and Social Psychology, 28,* 129-137.

Lerner, J. (1985). *Children with learning disabilities: Theories, diagnosis and teaching strategies* (4th ed.). Boston: Houghton Mifflin.

Lesgold, A., Robinson, H., Feltovich, P., Glaser, R., Klopfer, D, & Wang, Y. (1988). Expertise in a complex skill: Diagnosing X-ray pictures. In M. T. H. Chi, R. Glaser, & M. Farr (Eds.), *The nature of expertise* (pp. 311-342). Hillsdale, NJ: Erlbaum.

Lester, B., Corwin, M., Sepkoski, C., Seiper, R., Peucker, M., McLaughlin, S., & Golub, H. (1991). Neurobehavioral syndromes in cocaine-exposed newborns. *Child Development, 62,* 694–705.

Leutzinger, L. P., & Bentheau, M. (1989). Making sense of numbers. In P. R. Trafton & A. P. Shulte (Eds.), *New directions for elementary school mathematics: 1989 yearbook* (pp. 111–122). Reston, VA: National Council of Teachers of Mathematics.

Levinthal, C. F. (1990). *Introduction to psychological psychology* (3rd ed.). Englewood Cliffs, NJ: Prentice-Hall.

Levy, S. H., Herberman, R., Lippman, M., & D'Angelo, T. (1987). Correlation of stress factors with sustained depression of natural killer cell activity and predicted prognosis in patients with breast cancer. *Journal of Clinical Oncology, 5,* 348-353.

Lewis, A. B. (1989). Training students to represent arithmetic word problems. *Journal of Educational Psychology, 81*(4), 521-531.

Lewis, A. B., & Mayer, R. E. (1987). Students' miscomprehension of relational statements in arithmetic word problems. *Journal of Educational Psychology, 79,* 363-371.

Licht, B. G., & Dweck, C. S. (1984). Determinants of academic achievement: The interaction of children's achievement orientation with skill area. *Developmental Psychology, 20,* 628-636.

Lickona, T. (1991a). *Educating for character: How our schools can teach respect and responsibility.* New York: Bantam.

Lickona, T. (1991b). An integrated approach to character development in the elementary school classroom. In J. S. Benninga (Ed.), *Moral character and civic education in the elementary school* (pp. 67-83). New York: Teachers College Press.

Lickona, T. (1991c). *What is good character? And how can we develop it in our children?* Bloomington: Indiana University, Poynter Center.

Lindholm, K. J., & Fairchild, H. H. (1988). *Evaluation of an "exemplary" bilingual immersion program* (Tech. Rep. No. 13). Los Angeles: University of California Center for Language Education and Research.

Lindquist, M. M. (1989). It's time to change. In P. R. Trafton & A. P. Shulte (Eds.), *New direc-

tions for elementary school mathematics: 1989 yearbook (pp. 1-13). Reston, VA: National Council of Teachers of Mathematics.

Linn, M. C. (1986). Science. In R. F. Dillon & R. J. Sternberg (Eds.), *Cognition and instruction* (pp. 155-204). San Diego, CA: Academic Press.

Linn, M. C., & Hyde, J. S. (1989). Gender, mathematics and science. *Educational Researcher, 18*(8), 17-28.

Linn, M. C., & Peterson, A. C. (1986). Facts and assumptions about the nature of sex differences. In S. Klein (Ed.), *Handbook for achieving sex equity in education* (pp. 53-77). Baltimore, MD: Johns Hopkins University Press.

Livingston, C., & Borko, H. (1989). Expert-novice differences in teaching: A cognitive analysis and implications for teacher education. *Journal of Teacher Education, 40,* 136-142.

Lockhart, R. S., Lamon, M., & Gick, M. L. (1988). Conceptual transfer in simple insight problems. *Memory and Cognition, 16,* 36-44.

Lockwood, A. L. (1978). The effects of value clarification and moral development curricula on school-age subjects: A critical review of recent research. *Review of Educational Research, 48*(3), 325-364.

Luckasson, R., Coulter, D. L., Polloway, E. A., Reiss, S., Schalock, R. L., Snell, M. E., Spitalnik, D. M., & Stark, J. A. (1992). *Mental retardation: Definition. classification and systems of supports.* Washington, DC: American Association of Mental Retardation.

Lyons, N. (1989). Seeing and resolving moral conflict: Students' approaches to learning and making choices. In L. Nucci (Ed.), *Moral development and character education.* Berkeley, CA: McCutchan.

MacArthur, C., & Graham, S. (1987). Learning disabled students' composing with three methods: Handwriting, dictation, and word processing. *Journal of Special Education, 21,* 22-42.

Maccoby, E. (1990). Gender and relationships: A developmental account. *American Psychologist, 45,* 513-520.

Maccoby, E. E., & Jacklin, C. N. (1974). *The psychology of sex differences.* Stanford, CA: Stanford University Press.

Madden, N. A., Slavin, R. E., Karweit, N. L., Dolan, L. J., & Wasik, B. A. (1993). Success for all: Longitudinal effects of a restructuring program for inner-city elementary schools. *American Educational Research Journal, 30*(1), 123-148.

Madden, N. A., Slavin, R. E., & Stevens, R. J. (1986). *Cooperative integrated reading and comprehension. Teacher's manual.* Baltimore, MD: Johns Hopkins University, Center for Research on Elementary and Middle Schools.

Madge, S., Affleck, J., & Lowenbraun, S. (1990). Social effects of integrated classrooms and resource room/regular class placements on elementary students with learning disabilities. *Journal of Learning Disabilities, 23*(7), 439-445.

Maehr, M. L., & Midgley, C. (1991). Enhancing student motivation: A school-wide approach. *Educational Psychologist, 26*(3 & 4), 399-427.

Mager, R. F. (1972). *Goal analysis.* Belmont, CA: Farron.

Maier, N. R. F. (1931). Reasoning in humans: II. The solution of a problem and its appearance in consciousness. *Journal of Comparative Psychology, 12,* 181-194.

Malone, J. C. (1991). *Theories of learning: A historical approach.* Belmont, CA: Wadsworth.

Mandelbaum, L. H. (1983). Assertive discipline: An effective behavioral program. *Behavior Disorders, 8*(4), 261.

Mann, V. A. (1986). Why some children encounter reading problems. The contribution of difficulties with language processing and phonological sophistication to early reading disability. In J. K. Torgeson & B. Y. L. Wong (Eds.), *Psychological and educational perspectives on learning disabilities* (pp. 133-160). Hillsdale, NJ: Erlbaum.

Marchionini, G. (1988). Hypermedia and learning: Freedom and chaos. *Educational technology, 28,* 8–12.

Marx, M. H. (1970). *Learning theories.* New York: Macmillan.

Marx, R. W., & Walsh, J. (1988). Learning from academic tasks. *Elementary School Journal, 88,* 207–220.

Maslow, A. H. (1954). *Motivation and personality.* New York: Harper.

Maslow, A. H. (1968). *Toward a psychology of being* (2nd ed.). New York: Van Nostrand Reinhold.

Masterman, M. (1980). The social behavior of students at different stages of development. In R. L. Mosler (Ed.), *Moral education: A first generation of research and development* (pp. 188–202). New York: Praeger.

Mayer, M. H. (1990). Hearing impairment. In E. Meyen (Ed.), *Exceptional children in today's schools* (pp. 287–316). Denver, CO: Love Publishing.

Mayer, R. E. (1983). Can you repeat that? Qualitative effects of repetition and advance organizers on learning from science prose. *Journal of Educational Psychology, 75,* 40–49.

Mayer, R. E. (1986). Mathematics. In R. F. Dillon & R. J. Sternberg (Eds.), *Cognition and instruction* (pp. 127–154). San Diego, CA: Academic Press.

Mayer, R. E. (1987). Learnable aspects of problem solving: Some examples. In D. F. Berger, K. Pozdek, & W. P. Banks (Eds.), *Applications of cognitive psychology: Problem solving, education and computing* (pp. 109–122). Hillsdale, NJ: Erlbaum.

Mayer, R. E. (1989). Models for understanding. *Review of Educational Research, 40*(1), 43–64.

Mayer, R. E. (1992). *Thinking, problem solving, and cognition* (2nd ed.). New York: Freeman.

Mayer, R. E., & Cook, L. R. (1980). Effects of shadowing on prose comprehension and problem-solving. *Memory and Cognition, 8,* 101–109.

Mayer, R. E., & Gallini, J. K. (1990). When is an illustration worth ten thousand words? *Journal of Educational Psychology, 82*(4), 715–726.

Mayer, R. E., Dyck, J. L., & Cook, L. K. (1984). Techniques that help readers build mental models from scientific text: Definitions, pretraining, and signaling. *Journal of Educational Psychology, 76,* 1089–1105.

McClelland, D., Atkinson, J. W., Clark, R. W., & Lowell, E. L. (1953). *The achievement motive.* New York: Appleton-Century Crofts.

McCloskey, M. (1983). Naive theories of motion. In D. Genther & A. L. Stevens (Eds.), *Mental models* (pp. 71–94). Hillsdale, NJ: Erlbaum.

McConnell, J. V. (1974). *Understanding human behavior.* New York: Holt, Rinehart & Winston.

McCormick, C. R., & Levin, J. R. (1987). Mnemonic prose-learning strategies. In M. Pressley & S. M. McDaniel (Eds.), *Imagery and related mnemonic processes.* New York: Springer-Verlag.

McGeorge, C. (1975). The susceptibility to faking the Defining Issues Test of moral judgment. *Developmental Psychology, 11,* 108–114.

McIntosh, R., Vaughn, S., Schumm, J. S., Haager, D., & Lee, O. (1993). Observations of students with learning disabilities in general education classrooms. *Exceptional Children, 60*(3), 249–261.

McLeady, L., & Sainato, D. (1985). The effects of peer tutoring upon the social status and social interaction patterns of high and low status elementary students. *Education and Treatment of Children, 8,* 51–65.

McReynolds, L. V. (1988). Articulation disorders of unknown etiology. In N. J. Less, L. V. McReynolds., J. L. Northern, & D. E. Yoder (Eds.), *Handbook of speech–language pathology and audiology* (pp. 419–441). Toronto: Dekker.

Meece, J., Blumenfeld, P., & Hoyle, R. (1988). Students' goal orientations and cognitive engagement in classroom activities. *Journal of Educational Psychology, 80,* 514-523.

Meichenbaum, D. (1971). Examination of model characteristics in reducing avoidance behavior. *Journal of Personality and Social Psychology, 17,* 298-304.

Meichenbaum, D. H. (1977). *Cognitive-behavior modification: An integrative approach.* New York: Plenum Press.

Meichenbaum, D. H., & Asarnow, J. (1979). Cognitive-behavior modification and metacognitive development. Implications for the classroom. In P. C. Kendall & S. D. Hollon (Eds.), *Cognitive behavioral interventions: Theory, research and procedures* (pp. 11-35). New York: Academic Press.

Meichenbaum, D. H., & Goodman, J. (1971). Training impulsive children to talk to themselves. *Journal of Abnormal Psychology, 77*(2), 115-126.

Meichenbaum, D., & Turk, D. (1976). The cognitive-behavioral management of anxiety, anger and pain. In P. O. Davidson (Ed.), *The behavioral management of anxiety, depression and pain.* New York: Brunner/Mazel.

Meltzoff, A. N., & Moore, M. K. (1983). Newborn infants imitate adult facial gestures. *Child Development, 54,* 702-709.

Merrill, M. D. (1987). An expert system for instructional design. *IEEE Expert, 2*(2), 25-37.

Merrill, M. D., & Li, Z. (1989). An instructional design expert system. *Journal of Computer-Based Instruction, 16*(3), 95-101.

Messer, S. (1972). The relation of internal-external control to academic performance. *Child Development, 43,* 1456-1462.

Messick, S. (1976). *Individuality in learning,* San Francisco: Jossey-Bass.

Meyen, E. (Ed.) (1990). *Exceptional children in today's schools* (2nd ed.). Denver, CO: Love Publishing.

Meyerhoff, M. K., & White, B. L. (1986). New parents as teachers. *Educational Leadership, 44*(3), 42-46.

Midgley, C., Feldlaufer, H., & Eccles, J. (1989). Change in teacher efficacy and student self- and task-related beliefs in mathematics during the transition to junior high school. *Journal of Educational Psychology, 81,* 247-258.

Miller, A. (1981). Conceptual matching models and interactional research in education. *Review of Educational Research, 51,* 33-84.

Miller, G. A. (1956). The magical number seven, plus or minus two: Some limits on our capacity for processing information. *Psychological Review, 63,* 87-97.

Miller, N. E., & Dollard, J. (1941). *Social learning and imitation.* New Haven, CT: Yale University Press.

Miller S. C., & Cooke, N. L. (1989). Mainstreaming students with learning disabilities for videodisc math instruction. *Teaching Exceptional Children,* (1), 57-60.

Milner, B. (1985). Memory and the human brain. In M. Shafto (Ed.), *How we know* (pp. 31-59). San Francisco; Harper & Row.

Minde, K., Lewin, D., Weiss, G., Lavigneur, L., Douglas, V., & Sykes, E. (1971). The hyperactive child in elementary school: A 5-year, controlled follow-up. *Exceptional Children, 38,* 215-221.

Moore, E. G. (1986). Family socialization and the IQ test performance of traditionally and trans-racially adopted black children. *Developmental Psychology, 22,* 317-326.

Moore, O. K., & Anderson, A. R. (1968). Response environments project. In R. D. Hess & R. M. Beer (Eds.), *Early education.* Chicago: Aldine.

Moores, D. F. (1987). *Educating the deaf: Psychology, principles and practices.* Boston: Houghton Mifflin.

Moran, M. (1990). Speech and language disorders. In E. Meyen (Ed.), *Exceptional children in today's schools* (2nd ed.) (pp. 255–186). Denver, CO: Love Publishing.

Morrell, F. (1967). Electrical signs of sensory coding. In G. C. Quarton, T. Melrechuk, & F. O. Schmitt (Eds.), *The neurosciences: A study program*. New York: Rockefeller University Press.

Morris, W. N. & Nemcek, D. (1982). The development of social comparison motivation among preschoolers: Evidence of a stepwise progression. *Merrill–Palmer Quarterly of Behavior and Development, 28,* 413–425.

Mosenthal, P. B., & Kirsch, I. S. (1991). Toward an explanatory model of document literacy. *Discourse Processes, 14,* 147–180.

Mowrer, O. H. (1958). Hearing and speaking: An analysis of language learning. *Journal of Speech and Hearing Disabilities, 23,* 143–152.

Mullis, I. V. S., & Jenkins, L. B. (1990). *The reading report card, 1971–88.* Washington, DC: U.S. Department of Education.

Munn, N. L. (1954). Learning in children. In L. Carmichael (Ed.), *Manual of child psychology* (2nd ed.). New York: Wiley.

Murray, P. L., & Mayer, R. E. (1988). Preschool children's judgments of number magnitude. *Journal of Educational Psychology, 80*(2), 206–209.

Mussen, P. H., Conger, J. J., Kagan, J., & Huston, A. C. (1990). *Child development and personality* (7th ed.). New York: Harper & Row.

Muth, K. D., Glynn, S. M., Britton, B. K., & Graves, M. F. (1988). Thinking out loud while studying text: Rehearsing key ideas. *Journal of Educational Psychology, 80*(3), 315–318.

National Assessment of Educational Progress. (1986). *Writing achievement 1969–1979: Results from the third national writing assessment: Vol. I. 17-Year-olds* (Tech. Rep. No. NAEP-R-10-W-01). Denver, CO: Author.

National Commission on Excellence in Education. (1983). *A nation at risk: The imperative for educational reform.* Washington, DC: U.S. Government Printing Office.

National Council of Teachers of Mathematics. (1989). *Curriculum and evaluation standards for school mathematics.* Reston, VA: Author.

National Science Board (1987). *Science and engineering indicators—1987.* Washington, DC: U.S. Government Printing Office.

Newell, A., & Simon, H. (1972). *Human problem solving.* Englewood Cliffs, NJ: Prentice Hall.

Newman, R. S. (1990). Children's help-seeking in the classroom. The role of motivational factors and attitudes. *Journal of Educational Psychology, 82*(1), 71–80.

Newman, R. S., & Wick, S. A. (1987). Effect of age, skill and performance feedback on children's judgments of confidence. *Journal of Educational Psychology, 79*(2), 115–119.

Newman, S. B., & Roskos, K. (1993). Access to print for children of poverty. Differential effects of adult mediation and literacy-enriched play settings on environmental and functional print tasks. *American Educational Research Journal, 30*(1), 95–122.

Nicholls, J., Cobb, P., Wood, T., Yackel, E., & Potashnick, M. (1990). Assessing students' theories of success in mathematics: Individual and classroom differences. *Journal for Research in Mathematics Education, 21,* 109–122.

Nicholson, T. (1991). Do children read words better in context or in lists? A classic study revisited. *Journal of Educational Psychology, 83*(4), 444–450.

Nodine, B., Barenbaum, E., & Newcomer, P. (1985). Story composition by learning disabled, reading disabled and normal children. *Learning Disability Quarterly, 8,* 167–181.

Nolen, S. (1988). Reasons for studying: Motivational orientations and study strategies. *Cognition and Instruction, 5,* 269–287.

Norman, D. (1969). *Memory and attention.* New York: Wiley.

Novak, J. D. (1977). *A theory of education,* Ithaca, NY: Cornell University Press.

Novak, J. D. (1979). Applying psychology and philosophy to the improvement of laboratory teaching. *American Biology Teacher, 41*(8), 466–474.

Novak, J. D. (1990). Concept mapping: A useful tool for science education. *Journal of Research in Science Teaching, 27*(10), 937–949.

Novak, J. D., & Gowin, D. B. (1984). *Learning how to learn.* New York: Columbia University Press.

Novak, J. D., & Musonda, D. (1991). A twelve-year longitudinal study of science concept learning. *American Educational Research Journal, 28*(1), 117–153.

Nucci, L. (Ed.). (1989). *Moral development and character education.* Berkeley, CA: McCutchan.

Nye, R. D. (1992). *The legacy of B. F. Skinner: Concepts and perspectives, controversies and misunderstandings.* Pacific Grove, CA: Brooks-Cole.

O'Boyle, M. (1986). Hemispheric laterality as a basis of learning. What we know and don't know. In G. D. Phye & T. Andre (Eds.), *Cognitive classroom learning: Understanding thinking and problem solving* (pp. 21–48). New York: Academic Press.

O'Brochta, E. P., & Weaver, C. P. (1991). Linking reading and writing through thematic teaching in a first grade. In J. T. Feeley, D. S. Strickland, & S. B. Wepner (Eds.), *Process reading and writing: A literature-based approach* (pp. 7–21). New York: Teachers College Press.

O'Connor, M. J., Sigman, M. & Kasari, C. (1993). Interactional model for the association among maternal alcohol use, mother–infant interaction and infant cognitive development. *Infant Behavior and Development, 16,* 177–192.

Oakes, J. (1985). *Keeping track: How schools structure inequality.* New Haven, CT: Yale University Press.

Ogbu, J. U. (1987). Variability in minority school performance: A problem in search of an explanation. *Anthropology and Education Quarterly, 18*(4), 312–334.

Ogbu, J. U. (1992). Understanding cultural diversity and learning. *Educational Researcher, 21* (8), 5–14.

Olson, S. L., Bates, J. E., & Bayles, K. (1984). Mother–infant interaction and the development of individual differences in children's cognitive competence. *Developmental Psychology, 20,* 116–169.

Orestak, D. M. (1991). The effects of progressive relaxation, mental practice and hypnosis on athletic performance: A review. *Journal of Sport Behavior, 14*(4), 247–282.

Ornstein, R. (1977). *The psychology of consciousness* (2nd ed.). New York: Harcourt Brace Jovanovich.

Oser, F. K. (1986). Moral education and values education. The discourse perspective. In M. C. Wittrock (Ed.), *Third handbook of research in education* (pp. 917–941). New York: Macmillan.

Paivio, A. (1986). *Mental representations: A dual coding approach.* New York: Oxford University Press.

Paivio, A., & Foth, D. (1970). Imaginal and verbal mediators and noun concreteness in paired-associate learning. The elusive interaction. *Journal of Verbal Learning and Verbal Behavior, 9,* 384–390.

Palinscar, A. S., & Brown, A. L. (1984). Reciprocal teaching of comprehension-monitoring activities. *Cognition and Instruction, 1,* 117–175.

Papert, S. (1980). *Mindstorms: Children, computers and powerful ideas.* New York: Basic Books.

Paris, S. G., & Jacobs, J. E. (1984). The benefits of informed instruction for children's reading awareness and comprehension. *Child Development, 55,* 2083–2093.

Parsons, J. E., Meece, J. L., Adler, T. F., & Kaczala, C. M. (1982). Sex differences in attributions and learned helplessness. *Sex Roles, 8,* 421–432.

Patterson, C. J., & Mischel, W. (1975). Plans to resist distraction. *Developmental Psychology, 11*(3), 369–378.

Penn, W. Y. (1990). Teaching ethics. A direct approach. *Journal of Moral Education, 19*(2), 124–138.

Perensky, J. J., & Senter, R. J. (1970). An investigation of "bizarre" imagery as a mnemonic device. *Psychological Record, 20,* 145–150.

Perfetti, C. A. (1985). *Reading ability.* New York: Oxford University Press.

Perfetti, C. A., & Lesgold, A. M. (1978). Discourse comprehension and sources of individual differences. In M. Just & P. Carpenter (Eds.), *Cognitive processes in comprehension.* Hillsdale, NJ: Erlbaum.

Perkins, D. N. (1987). Knowledge as design: Teaching thinking through content. In J. B. Baron & R. J. Sternberg (Eds.), *Teaching thinking skills: Theory and practice* (pp. 62–85). New York: Freeman.

Perkins, D. N., & Solomon, G. (1989). Are cognitive skills context bound? *Educational Researcher, 18*(1), 16–25.

Peterson, N., & Fennema, E. (1985). Effective teaching, student engagement in classroom activities, and sex-related differences in learning mathematics. *American Educational Research Journal, 22,* 309–335.

Peterson, P. L., Carpenter, T., & Fennema, E. (1989). Teachers' knowledge of students' knowledge in mathematical problem-solving: Correlational and case analyses. *Journal of Educational Psychology, 81*(4), 558–569.

Peterson, P. L., & Comeaux, M. A. (1987). Teachers' schemata for classroom events: The mental scaffolding of teachers' thinking during classroom instruction. *Teaching and Teacher Education, 3,* 317–331.

Pfeiffer, K., Feinberg, G., & Gelber, S. (1987). Teaching productive problem solving attitudes. In D. Berger, K. Pezdek, and W. Banks (Eds.), *Applications in cognitive psychology: Problem solving education and computing* (pp. 99–108). Hillsdale, NJ: Erlbaum.

Phillips, D. (1984). The illusion of incompetence among high-achieving children. *Child Development, 55,* 2000–2016.

Phye, G. D. (1990). Inductive problem solving: Schema induction and memory-based transfer. *Journal of Educational Psychology, 82*(4), 826–831.

Phye, G. D., & Andre, T. (Eds.). (1986). *Cognitive classroom learning: Understanding thinking and problem solving.* New York: Academic Press.

Piaget, J. (1932). *The moral judgment of the child.* London: Kegan Paul.

Piaget, J. (1963). *Origins of intelligence in children.* New York: Norton.

Piaget, J. (1983). Piaget's theory. In P. Mussen (Ed.), *Handbook of child psychology: Vol. 1* (4th ed.). New York: Wiley.

Polette, N. (1990). *Whole language in action,* St. Louis, MO: Book Lures.

Pollard, D. S. (1993). Gender, achievement and African-American students' perceptions of their school experience. *Educational Psychologist, 28*(4), 341–356.

Post, T. R., Wachsmith, I., Lesh, R., & Behr, M. J. (1985). Order and equivalence in rational numbers: A cognitive analysis. *Journal for Research in Mathematics Education, 16*(1), 18–36.

Power, C., Higgins, A., & Kohlberg, L. (1989). The habit of the common life: Building character through democratic community schools. In L. Nucci (Ed.), *Moral development and character education.* Berkeley, CA: McCutchan.

Pratt, A. C., & Brady, S. (1988). Relation of phonological awareness to reading disability in children and adults. *Journal of Educational Psychology, 80*(3), 319–323.

Pratt, M., & Wickens, G. (1983). Checking it out: Cognitive style, context and problem type in children's monitoring of text comprehension. *Journal of Educational Psychology, 75,* 716–726.

Premack, D. (1959). Toward empirical behavior laws: I. Positive reinforcement. *Psychological Review, 66,* 219–233.

Pressley, M., & Associates (1990). *Cognitive strategy instruction that really improves children's academic performance.* Cambridge, MA: Brookline Books.

Pressley, M., Borkowski, J. G., & O'Sullivan, J. T. (1984). Memory strategy instruction is made of this: Metamemory and durable strategy use. *Educational Psychologist, 19,* 94–107.

Pressley, M. Levin, J. R., & Delaney, H. D. (1982). The mnemonic keyword method. *Review of Educational Research, 52,* 61–91.

Pressley, M. Levin, J. R., & McDaniel, M. A. (1987). Remembering versus inferring what a word means: Mnemonic and contextual approaches. In M. O. McKeown & M. B. Curtis (Eds.), *The nature of vocabulary acquisition.* Hillsdale, NJ: Erlbaum.

Pressley, M., Schuder, T., Bergman, J. L., & El-Dinary, P. B. (1992). A researcher–educator collaborative interview study of transactional comprehension strategies instruction. *Journal of Educational Psychology, 81*(2), 231–246.

Pressley, M., Symons, S. E., Snyder, B. L., & Cariglia-Bull, T. (1989). Strategy instruction research is coming of age. *Learning Disabilities Quarterly, 12,* 16–30.

Quay, H. C. (1986). Classification. In H. C. Quay and J. S. Wherry (Eds.), *Psychopathological Disorders of Childhood* (3rd ed.). New York: Wiley.

Quigley, S. P., & Paul, P. (1984). *Language and deafness.* San Diego, CA: College Hill Press.

Rachlin, H. (1991). *Introduction to modern behaviorism* (3rd ed.). New York: Freeman.

Rayner, K., & Polletsak, A. (1989). *The psychology of reading.* Englewood Cliffs, NJ: Prentice-Hall.

Recht, D. R., & Leslie, L. (1988). Effect of prior knowledge on good and poor reading memory of text. *Journal of Educational Psychology, 80*(1), 16–20.

Reed, S. K., Dempster, A., & Ettinger, M. (1985). Usefulness of analogous solutions for solving algebra word problems. *Journal of Experimental Psychology: Learning, Memory and Cognition, 11,* 106–125.

Reiff, J. C. (1992). *Learning styles.* Washington, DC: National Education Association.

Reimann, P., & Chi, M. T. H. (1989). Human expertise. In K. J. Gilhooly (Ed.), *Human and machine problem solving.* New York: Plenum Press.

Reinking, D., & Schreiner, R. (1985). The effects of computer-mediated text on measures of reading comprehension and reading behavior. *Reading Research Quarterly, 20*(5), 536–552.

Reitman, W. R. (1965). *Cognition and thought: An information-processing approach.* New York: Wiley.

Render, G. F., Pedilla, J. M., & Krenk, H. M. (1989). Assertive discipline: A critical review and analysis. *Teachers College Record, 90*(4), 607–630.

Resnick, L. (1983). Math and science learning: A new conception. *Science, 220,* 477–478.

Rest, J. R. (1979). *Development in judging moral issues.* Minneapolis: University of Minnesota Press.

Ribincam, F., & Olivier, W. (1985). An investigation of limited learner-control options in a CAI mathematics course. *AEDS Journal, 18*(4), 211–218.

Ricciutti, A. E., & Scarr, S. (1990). Interaction of early biological and family risk factors in predicting cognitive development. *Journal of Applied Developmental Psychology, 11*(1), 1–12.

Rice, M. L., Huston, A. C., Truglio, R., & Wright, J. (1990). Words from "Sesame Street": Learning vocabulary while viewing. *Developmental Psychology, 26*(3), 421–428.

Riley, M. S., Greeno, J. G., & Heller, J. H. (1983). Development of children's problem-solving ability in arithmetic. In H. P. Ginsburg (Ed.), *The development of mathematical thinking* (pp. 62–71). New York: Academic Press.

Rinehart, S. D., Stahl, S. A., & Erickson, L. C. (1986). Some effects of summarization training on reading and studying. *Reading Research Quarterly, 21,* 422–438.

Riordan, C. (1990). *Girls and boys in school: Together or separate?* New York: Teachers College Press.

Robinson, F. P. (1946). *Effective study.* New York: Harper.

Roblyer, M. D. (1986). Courseware: A practical revolution. *Educational Technology, 6,* 34–35, 57.

Rohwer, W. D., Raines, J. M., Eoff, T., & Wagner, M. (1977). The development of elaborative propensity in adolescence. *Journal of Experimental Child Psychology, 23,* 472–492.

Romberg, T. A., & Collins, K. F. (1987). Different ways children learn to add and subtract. *Journal for Research in Mathematics Education Monographs, 2* (Part No. 1).

Rose, M. (1980). Rigid rules, inflexible plans and the stifling of language: A cognitivist analysis of writer's block. *College Composition and Communication, 16,* 106–112.

Rose, S. A., & Blank, M. (1974). The potency of context in children's cognition: An illustration through conservation. *Child Development, 45,* 499–502.

Rosenheck, M. B., Levin, M. F., & Levin, J. R. (1989). Learning botany concepts mnemonically. Seeing the forest and the trees. *Journal of Educational Psychology, 81*(2), 196–203.

Rosenkrans, M. A. (1967). Imitation in children as a function of perceived similarity to a social model and vicarious reinforcement. *Journal of Personality and Social Psychology, 7,* 307–315.

Rosenthal, R., & Jacobson, L. (1968). *Pygmalion in the classroom. Teacher expectation and pupil's intellectual development.* New York: Holt.

Rosenzweig, M. R. (1984). Experience, memory and the brain. *American Psychologist, 39,* 365–370.

Ross, E. D., & Mesulam, M. M. (1979). Dominant language functions of the right hemisphere. Prosody and emotional gesturing. *Archives of Neurology, 36,* 144–148.

Rothkopf, E. Z., & Bisbicos, E. E. (1967). Selected facilitative effects of interspersed questions on learning from written materials. *Journal of Educational Psychology, 58,* 56–61.

Rotter, J. (1966). Generalized expectancies for internal versus external control of reinforcement. *Psychological Monographs, 80,* 1–28.

Rotter, J. B., Chance, J. E., & Phares, F. O. (1972). *Applications of a social learning theory of personality.* New York: Holt.

Royer, J. M. (1986). Designing instruction to produce understanding: An approach based on cognitive theory. In G. Phye & T. Andre (Eds.), *Cognitive classroom learning: Understanding thinking and problem solving* (pp. 83–113). New York: Academic Press.

Royer, J. M., & Cable, G. W. (1975). Facilitated learning in connected discourse. *Journal of Educational Psychology, 67,* 116–123.

Ruble, D. N., Boggiano, A. R., Feldman, N. S., & Loebl, J. H. (1980). Developmental analysis of the role of social comparison in self-evaluation. *Developmental Psychology, 16*(2), 105–115.

Rumelhart, D. E., McClelland, J. L., & PDP Research Group (Eds.). (1986). *Parallel distributed processing: Explorations in the microstructure of cognition: Vol. 1, Foundations.* Cambridge, MA: MIT Press.

Ryan, K. (1970). *Don't smile until Christmas: Accounts of the first year of teaching.* Chicago: University of Chicago Press.

Ryan, K. (1989). In defense of character education. In L. Nucci (Ed.), *Moral development and character education* (pp. 3–18). Berkeley, CA: McCutchan.

Ryan, R. M., & Connell, J. P. (1989). Perceived locus of causality and internalization: Examining reasons for acting in two domains. *Journal of Personality and Social Psychology, 57,* 749–761.

Sacks, S., & Reardon, M. (1989). Maximizing social integration for visually handicapped students: Application and practice. In R. G. Ross (Ed.), *Integration strategies for students with handicaps* (pp. 77–104). Baltimore, MD: Paul H. Brooks.

Sadker, M., & Sadker, D. (1985). Sexism in the school room of the 80's. *Psychology Today, 19,* 45–47.

Sadker, M., Sadker, D., & Steindam, J. (1989). Gender equity and educational reform. *Educational Leadership, 46,*(6), 44–47.

Salomon, G. (1991). Learning: New conceptions, new opportunities. *Educational Technology, 31*(6), 41–44.

Saltzstein, H. D., Diamond, R. M., & Belenky, M. (1972). Moral judgment level and conformity behavior. *Developmental Psychology, 7,* 327–330.

Samuels, S. J. (1988). Reading and automaticity: Helping poor readers become automatic at word recognition. *Reading Teacher, 41*(April), 756–760.

Sattler, J. M. (1988). *Assessment of children* (3rd ed.). San Diego, CA: Author.

Sawyer, R. J., Graham, S., & Harris, R. (1992). Direct teaching, strategy intervention, and strategy instruction with explicit self-regulation. Effects on the composition skills and self-efficacy of students with learning disabilities. *Journal of Educational Psychology, 84*(3), 340–352.

Sax, G. (1989). *Principles of educational and psychological measurement and evaluation* (3rd ed.). Belmont, CA: Wadsworth.

Scardamalia, M. (1977). Information processing capacity and the problem of horizontal decalage: A demonstration using combinatorial reasoning tasks. *Child Development, 48,* 28–37.

Scardamalia, M., & Bereiter, C. (1985). Research on written composition. In M. Wittrock (Ed.), *Handbook of research on teaching* (3rd ed.) (pp. 778–803). New York: Macmillan.

Scardamalia, M., & Bereiter, C. (1986). Writing. In R. F. Dillon & R. J. Sternberg (Eds.), *Cognition and instruction* (pp. 59–81). San Diego, CA: Academic Press.

Scardamalia, M., Bereiter, C. A., & Steinbach, R. (1984). Teachability of reflective processes in written composition. *Cognitive Science, 8,* 173–190.

Scarry, R. (1973). *Find your ABC's.* New York: Random House.

Schmidt, R. F. (1985). *Foundations of neurophysiology* (3rd ed.). New York: Springer-Verlag.

Schoenfeld, A. H. (1988). When good teaching leads to bad results: The disasters of "well taught" mathematics courses. *Educational psychologist, 23*(2), 145–166.

Schover, L. R., & Newsom, C. D. (1976). Overselectivity, developmental level, and overtraining in autistic and normal children. *Journal of Abnormal Child Psychology, 4,* 289–298.

Schramm, W. (1964). *The research on programmed instruction: An annotated bibliography.* Washington, DC: U.S. Office of Education.

Schroeder, T. L., & Lester, F. K. (1989). Developing understanding in mathematics via problem-solving. In P. R. Trafton & A. P. Shulte (Eds.), *New directions for elementary school mathematics: 1989 yearbook* (pp. 31–42). Reston, VA: National Council of Teachers of Mathematics.

Schunk, D. H. (1983a). Developing children's self-efficacy and skills. The roles of social comparative information and goal setting. *Contemporary Educational Psychology, 8,* 76–86.

Schunk, D. H. (1983b). Reward contingencies and the development of children's skills and self-efficacy. *Journal of Educational Psychology, 75,* 511–518.

Schunk, D. H. (1984). Self-efficacy perspective on academic behavior. *Educational Psychologist, 19*(1), 48–58.

Schunk, D. H. (1985). Participation in goal setting: Effects on self-efficacy and skills of learning disabled children. *Journal of Special Education, 19,* 307–317.

Schunk, D. H. (1986). Verbalization and children's self-regulated learning. *Contemporary Educational Psychology, 11,* 347–369.

Schunk, D. H. (1987). Peer models and children's behavioral change. *Review of Educational Research, 57*(2), 149–174.

Schunk, D. H. (1989a). Self-efficacy and achievement behaviors. *Educational Psychology Review, 1,* 173–200.

Schunk, D. H. (1989b). Self-efficacy and cognitive skill learning. In C. Ames & R. Ames (Eds.), *Research on motivation in education: Vol. 3. Goals and cognitions* (pp. 13–44). San Diego, CA: Academic Press.

Schunk, D. H. (1991). Self-efficacy and motivation. *Educational Psychologist, 26*(3 & 4), 207–232.

Schunk, D. H., & Cox, P. D. (1986). Strategy training and attributional feedback with learning disabled students. *Journal of Educational Psychology, 78*(3), 201–209.

Schunk, D. H., & Hanson, A. R. (1985). Peer models: Influence on children's self-efficacy and achievement. *Journal of Educational Psychology, 77,* 313–322.

Schunk, D. H., Hansen, A. R., & Cox, P. D. (1987). Peer-model attributes and children's achievement behaviors. *Journal of Educational Psychology, 79*(1), 54–61.

Schwartz, N. H., & Kulhavy, R. W. (1981). Map features and the recall of discourse. *Contemporary Educational Psychology, 6, 151–158.*

Schwarz, I., & Lewis, M. (1989). Basic concept microcomputer courseware: A critical evaluation system for educators. *Educational Technology, (5),* 16–21.

Sears, R. R., Rau, L., & Alpert, R. (1965). *Identification and child-rearing.* Stanford, CA: Stanford University Press.

Selman, R. L., & Byrne, D. F. (1974). A structural–developmental analysis of levels of role-taking in middle childhood. *Child Development, 48,* 924–929.

Selye, H. (1953). The general-adaptation syndrome in its relationship to neurology, psychology and psychopathology. In A. Weider (Ed.), *Contributions toward medical psychology.* New York: Ronald Press.

Selye, H. (1976). *The stress of life* (rev.). New York: McGraw-Hill.

Sharan, S. (1980). Cooperative learning in small groups: Recent methods and effects on achievement, attitudes, and ethnic relations. *Review of Educational Research, 50,* 241–249.

Sharan, Y., & Sharan, S. (1989). Group investigation expands cooperative learning. *Educational Leadership, 47*(4), 17–21.

Sherman, L. W., & Thomas, M. (1986). Mathematics achievement in cooperative versus individualistic goal-structured high school classrooms. *Journal of Educational Research, 79,* 169–172.

Sherwood, R., Kinzer, C. Hasselbring, T., & Bransford, J. (1987). Macro contexts for learning: Initial findings and issues. *Journal of Applied Cognition, 1,* 93–108.

Shipman, S., & Shipman, V. A. (1985). Cognitive styles: Some conceptual, methodological and applied issues. In E. W. Gordon (Ed.), *Review of research in education.* Washington, DC: American Educational Research Association.

Shirley, M. M. (1931). The sequential method for the study of maturing behavior patterns. *Psychology Review, 38,* 507–528.

Siegler, A. S. (1976). Three aspects of cognitive development. *Cognitive Psychology, 8,* 481–520.

Siegler, R. S. (1991). *Children's thinking* (2nd ed.). Englewood Cliffs, NJ: Prentice-Hall.

Sigel, I. (1990). What teachers need to know about human development. In D. Dill & Associates (Eds.), *What teachers need to know: The knowledge skills and values of good teaching.* San Francisco: Jossey-Bass.

Simon, H. A. (1980). Problem solving in education. In D. T. Tuma & F. Reif (Eds.), *Problem solving and education issues in teaching and research* (pp. 81–96). Hillsdale, NJ: Erlbaum.

Simons, P. R. J. (1984). Instructing with analogies. *Journal of Educational Psychology, 76,* 513–527.

Singer, D., & Butler, J. H. (1987). The Education of All Handicapped Children Act: Schools as agents of social reform. *Harvard Educational Review, 57,* 125–152.

Singer, H., & Donlan, D. (1989). *Reading and learning from text* (2nd ed.). Hillsdale, NJ: Erlbaum.

Singer, L., Farkas, K., & Kliegman, R. (1992). Childhood medical and behavioral consequences of maternal cocaine use. *Journal of Pediatric Psychology, 17*(4), 389–406.

Singleton, L. R. (1986). *Tips for social studies teachers.* Boulder, CO: Social Studies Education Consortium.

Skinner, B. F. (1948). Superstition in the pigeon. *Journal of Experimental Psychology, 38,* 168–172.

Skinner, B. F. (1950). Are theories of learning necessary? *Psychological Review, 57,* 193–216.

Skinner, B. F. (1953). *Science and human behavior.* New York: Macmillan.

Skinner, B. F. (1954). The science of learning and the art of teaching. *Harvard Educational Review, 24*(2), 86–97.

Skinner, B. F. (1957). *Verbal behavior.* New York: Appleton-Century Crofts.

Skinner, B. F. (1963). Operant behavior. *American Psychologist, 18,* 503–515.

Skinner, B. F. (1968). *The technology of teaching.* New York: Appleton-Century Crofts.

Skinner, B. F. (1986). Programmed instruction revisited. *Phi Delta Kappan,* October, 108–110.

Skinner, B. F. (1990). Can psychology be a science of the mind? *American Psychologist, 45*(11), 1206–1210.

Skinner, B. F., & Vaughan, M. E. (1983). *Enjoy old age: Living fully in your later years.* New York: Warner.

Skinner, E. A., & Belmont, M. J. (1993). Motivation in the classroom: Reciprocal effects of teacher behavior and student engagement across the school year. *Journal of Educational Psychology, 85*(4), 571–581.

Skinner, E. A., Wellborn, J. G., & Connell, J. P. (1990). What it takes to do well in school and whether I've got it: A process model of perceived control and children's engagement and achievement in school. *Journal of Educational Psychology, 82*(1), 22–32.

Slavin, R. E. (1983). *Cooperative learning.* New York: Longman.

Slavin, R. E. (1985). Cooperative learning: Applying contact theory in desegregated schools. *Journal of Social Issues, 41,* 45–62.

Slavin, R. E. (1990a). Achievement effects of ability grouping in secondary schools: A best-evidence synthesis. *Review of Educational Research, 60,* 471–500.

Slavin, R. E. (1990b). *Cooperative learning: Theory, Research and Practice.* Englewood Cliffs, NJ: Prentice-Hall.

Slavin, R. E., & Karweit, N. (1984). Mastery learning and student teams. A factorial experiment in urban general mathematics classes. *American Educational Research Association Journal, 21,* 725–736.

Slobin, D. (1964). *Some thoughts on the relation of comprehension to speech.* Paper presented at the meeting of the American Speech and Hearing Association, San Francisco.

Slobin, D. I. (1986). Cross linguistic evidence for the language-making capacity. In D. I. Slobin (Ed.), *The cross linguistic study of language acquisition.* Hillsdale, NJ: Erlbaum.

Small, M. Y. (1990). *Cognitive development.* Orlando, FL: Harcourt Brace Jovanovich.

Smith, A. (1985). *The body.* New York: Viking Press.

Smith, F. (1971). *Understanding reading: A psycholinguistic analysis of reading and learning to read.* New York: Holt, Rinehart & Winston.

Smith, J., & Alcock, A. (1990). *Revising literacy: Helping readers and writers.* Philadelphia: Open University Press.

Snowman, J. (1986). Learning tactics and strategies. In G. Phye & T. Andre (Eds.), *Cognitive classroom learning: Understanding thinking and problem solving* (pp. 243–275). New York: Academic Press.

Sokol, R. (1982). A biological perspective on substance use in pregnancy. Alcohol as paradigm for possible effects of drugs on the offspring. In D. Perron & L. Disenberg (Eds.), *Infants at risk for developmental dysfunction* (pp. 93–104). Washington, DC: Institute of Medicine. Division of Mental Health and Behavioral Medicine.

Sorenson, A. B., & Hallinan, M. T. (1986). Effects of ability grouping on growth in academic achievement. *American Educational Research Journal, 23,* 519–542.

Sowers, S. (1986). Reflect, expand, select: Three responses in the writing conference. In T. Newkirk & N. Atwell (Eds.), *Understanding writing* (pp. 76–92). Portsmouth, NH: Heinemann.

Spandel, W., & Stiggins, R. J. (1990). *Creating writers: Linking assessment and writing instruction.* New York: Longman.

Spearman, C. (1927). *The abilities of man: Their nature and measurement.* New York: Macmillan.

Spence, J. T., & Spence, K. W. (1966). The motivational components of manifest anxiety. Drive and drive stimuli. In C. D. Spielberger (Ed.), *Anxiety and behavior* (pp. 87–113). New York: Academic Press.

Spenciner, L. J. (1992). Mainstreaming the child with a visual impairment. In L. G. Cohen (Ed.), *Children with exceptional needs in regular classrooms* (pp. 82–97). Washington, DC: National Education Association Professional Library.

Sperling, G. (1960). The information available in brief visual presentations. *Psychology Monographs* [Whole no. 498], *74.*

Sperry, R. W. (1974). Lateral specialization in the surgically separated hemispheres. In F. Schmitt & F. Warder (Eds.), *The neurosciences: Third study program* (pp. 5–19). Cambridge, MA: MIT Press.

Sperry, R. W. (1993). The impact and promise of the cognitive revolution. *American Psychologist, 48*(8), 878–885.

Spielberger, C. D. (1966). Theory and research on anxiety. In C. D. Spielberger (Ed.), *Anxiety and behavior* (pp. 1–21). New York: Academic Press.

Spielberger, C. D. (1972). Conceptual and methodology issues in anxiety research. In C. D. Spielberger (Ed.), *Anxiety: Current trends in theory and research: Vol 2* (pp. 487–493). New York: Academic Press.

Spruill, J. (1992). Students with mild handicaps in secondary classrooms. In L. G. Cohen (Ed.), *Children with exceptional needs in regular classrooms* (pp. 63–81). Washington, DC: National Education Association Professional Library.

Stahl, S. A. (1988). Is there evidence to support matching reading styles and initial reading methods? *Phi Delta Kappan, 69*(4), 317–322.

Stahl, S. A., & Miller, P. D. (1989). Whole language and language experience approaches for beginning reading: A quantitative research synthesis. *Review of Educational Research, 59,* 87–116.

Stanovich, K. E. (1980). Toward an interactive-compensatory model of individual differences in the development of reading fluency. *Reading Research Quarterly, 16,* 32–71.

Stanovich, K. E. (1986). Cognitive processes and the reading problems of the learning disabled: Evaluating the assumption of specificity. In J. K. Torgeson & B. Y. Wong (Eds.), *Psychological and educational perspectives in learning disabilities* (pp. 85–131). Orlando, FL: Academic Press.

Stasser, G., Kerr, N. L., & Davis, G. H. (1990). Influence models and consensus processes in decision making groups. In P. B. Paulus (Ed.), *Psychology of Group Influence* (2nd ed.) pp. 279-326). Hillsdale, NJ: Erlbaum.

Staub, E. (1971). The use of role-playing and induction in children's level of helping and sharing behavior. *Child Development, 42,* 805-817.

Staub, E. (1979). *Positive social behavior and morality: Vol. 2. Socialization and development.* New York: Academic Press.

Stephens, B., & Grabe, C. (1982). Development of Piagetian reasoning in congenitally blind children. *Journal of Visual Impairment and Blindness, 76*(5), 133-143.

Sternberg, R. (1977). Component processes in analogical reasoning. *Psychological Review, 31,* 356-378.

Sternberg, R. (1985). *Beyond IQ: A triarchic theory of human intelligence.* Cambridge: Cambridge University Press.

Sternberg, R. (1990). T&T is an explosive combination: Technology and testing. *Educational Psychologist, 25*(3 & 4), 701-722.

Sternberg, R. J., & Davidson, J. E. (1990). Intelligence and intelligence testing [Special Issue]. *Educational Psychology, 25*(3 & 4), 173-358.

Sternberg, R. J., & Gardner, M. K. (1983). Unities in inductive reasoning. *Journal of Experimental Psychology: General, 112,* 80-116.

Stevens, R. J. (1988). Effects of strategy training on the identification of the main idea of expository passages. *Journal of Educational Psychology, 80*(1), 21-26.

Stevens, R. J., Madden, N. A., Slavin, R. E., & Farnish, A. M. (1987). *Cooperative integrated reading and composition: Two field experiments* (Tech. Rep. No. 7). Baltimore, MD: Johns Hopkins University, Center for Research on Elementary and Middle Schools.

Stevenson, H. W. (1992). Learning from Asian schools. *Scientific American, 267*(6), 70-77.

Stevenson, H. W., Lee, S., & Stigler, J. (1986). Mathematics achievement of Chinese, Japanese, and American children. *Science, 231,* 693-699.

Stipek, D. J. (1993). *Motivation to learn: From theory to practice* (2nd ed.). Boston: Allyn & Bacon.

Stipek, D. J., & Weisz, J. R. (1981). Perceived personal control and academic achievement. *Review of Educational Research, 51,* 131-137.

Stone, C. A. (1989). Improving the effectiveness of strategy training for learning disabled students: The role of communication dynamics. *Remedial and Special Education, 10*(1), 35-42.

Strain, P. S., Kerr, M. M., & Ragland, E. U. (1981). The use of peer social initiations in the treatment of social withdrawal. In P. S. Strain (Ed.), *The utilization of classroom peers as behavior change agents* (pp. 101-125). New York: Plenum Press.

Streissguth, A. P., Barr, H. M., & Martin, D. C. (1983). Maternal alcohol use and neonatal habituation assessed with the Brazelton scale. *Child Development, 54,* 1109-1118.

Stuss, D. T., & Benson, D. F. (1984). Neuropsychological studies of the frontal lobes. *Psychological Bulletin, 95,* 3-28.

Suinn, R. M. (1984). Visual motor behavior rehearsed: The basic technique. *Scandinavian Journal of Behavior Therapy, 13,* 131-142.

Surber, C. F. (1977). Development processes in social inferences: Average of intentions and consequences in moral judgment. *Developmental Psychology, 13*(6), 654-665.

Swanson, J. M., Cartwell, D., Lerner, M., McBurnett, R., & Hanna, G. (1991). Effects of stimulant medication on learning in children with ADHD. *Journal of Learning Disabilities, 24*(4), 219-230.

Sweller, J. (1989). Cognitive technology: Some procedures for facilitating learning and problem-solving in mathematics and science. *Journal of Educational Psychology, 81*(4), 457-466.

Symington, D., & Novak, J. D. (1982). Teaching children how to learn. *Educational Magazine, 39*(5), 13-16.

Tannock, R., Schachar, R. J., Carr, R. P., & Logan, G. D. (1989). Dose–response effects of methylphenidate on academic performance and overt behavior in hyperactive children. *Pediatrics, 84,* 648-657.

Taylor, B. M., & Beach, R. W. (1984). The effects of text structure instruction on middle-grade students' comprehension and production of expository text. *Reading Research Quarterly, 19*(2), 134-146.

Taylor, B. M., Frye, B., & Marvyama, C. M. (1990). Time spent reading and reading growth. *American Educational Research Journal, 27*(2), 351-362.

Teuber, H. L. (1959). Some alternations in behavior after cerebral lesions in man. In *Evolution of nervous control from primitive organisms to man* (pp. 157-194). Washington, DC: American Association for the Advancement of Science.

Teyler, T. J. (1975). *A primer of psychology: Brain and behavior.* San Francisco: Freeman.

Teyler, T. J., & Di Scenna, P. (1986). The hippocampal memory indexing theory. *Behavioral Neuroscience, 100,* 147-154.

Tharp, P. G., & Gallimore, R. (1975). What a coach can teach a teacher. *Psychology Today, 2*(1), 75-78.

Thompson, R. F. (1985). *The brain: An introduction to neuroscience.* San Francisco: Freeman.

Thorndike, E. L. (1911). *Animal intelligence: Experimental studies.* New York: Macmillan.

Thorndike, E. L. (1913). *Educational psychology: Vol. I. The original nature of man.* New York: Teachers College Press.

Thorndike, E. L. (1914). *Educational psychology: Vol. II. The psychology of learning.* New York: Teachers College Press.

Thorndike, E. L. (1924). Mental discipline in high school studies. *Journal of Educational Psychology, 15,* 1-22, 83-98.

Thorndike, E. L. (1932). *The fundamentals of learning.* New York: Teachers College Press.

Thorndike, E. L., & Woodworth, R. S. (1901). The influence of improvement in one mental function upon the efficacy of other functions. *Psychological Review, 8,* 247-261, 384-395, 553-564.

Tinker, R. F., & Papert, S. (1989). Tools for science education. In J. Ellis (Ed.), *1988 AETS yearbook: Information technology and science education.* Columbus, OH: ERIC Clearinghouse for Science, Mathematics and Environmental Education.

Tittle, B., & St. Clair, N. (1989). Promoting the healthy development of drug-exposed children through a comprehensive clinic model. *Zero to Three, 9,* 18-19.

Tobin, K. (1987). The role of wait time in higher cognitive level learning. *Review of Educational Research, 57,* 69-96.

Tobin, K., & Garnett, P. (1987). Gender related differences in science activities. *Science Education, 71,* 91-103.

Tolman, E. C. (1932). *Purpose behavior in animals and men.* New York: Appleton-Century-Crofts.

Tracey, C. B., Ames, C., & Maehr, M. L. (1990). *Attitudes and perceptions of competence across regular, at-risk, and learning disabled students.* Paper presented at the annual meeting of the American Educational Research Association, Boston.

Trafton, T. R., & Shulte, A. P. (Eds.). *New directions for elementary school mathematics: 1989 yearbook.* Reston, VA: National Council of Teachers of Mathematics.

Travers, R. M. W. (1982). *Essentials of learning. The new cognitive learning for students of education* (5th ed.). New York: Macmillan.

Treffinger, D. P. (1986). Fostering effective, independent learning through individualized programming. In J. S. Renzulli (Ed.), *Systems and models for developing programs for the gifted and talented* (pp. 429-460). Mansfield Center, CT: Creative Learning Press.

Treffinger, D. P., Feldhusen, J. F., & Hohn, R. L. (1990). *Reach each you teach.* East Aurora, NY: United Educational Services.

Trotter, A. (1989). Schools gear up for hypermedia: A quantum leap in electronic learning. *American School Board Journal,* (3), 35–37.

Tulving, E. (1962). Subjective organization in the free recall of "unrelated words." *Psychology Review, 69,* 344–354.

Tulving, E. (1972). Episodic and semantic memory. In E. Tulving & W. Donaldson (Eds.), *Organization of memory.* New York: Academic Press.

Tulving, E., & Thomsen, D. M., (1971). Retrieval processes in recognition memory: Effects of associative context. *Journal of Experimental Psychology, 87,* 116–124.

U. S. Bureau of the Census. (1992). *Statistical abstract of the U.S.: 1992* (112th edition). Washington, DC: Author.

U.S. Department of Education (1989). *Eleventh annual report to Congress on the implementation of the Education of the Handicapped Act.* Washington, DC: U.S. Government Printing Office.

Vealey, R. S. (1986). Imagery training for performance enhancement. In J. M. Williams (Ed.), *Applied sport psychology.* Ann Arbor, MI: McNaughton & Gunn.

Vellutino, F. R. (1991). Introduction to three studies on reading acquisition: Convergent findings on theoretical foundations of code-oriented vs. whole-language approaches to reading instruction. *Journal of Educational Psychology, 83*(4), 437–443.

Vellutino, F. R., Scanlon, D. M., Small, S. G., & Tanzman, M. S. (1991). The linguistic basis of reading ability: Converting written to oral language. *Text, 11,* 99–133.

Vincent, J. (1990). *The biology of emotions* (John Hughes, Trans.). Cambridge, MA: Basil Blackwell.

Voss, J. F., Greene, T. R., Post, T. A., & Penner, P. C. (1983). Problem solving skill in the social sciences. In G. H. Bower (Ed.), *The Psychology of learning and motivation: Advances in research and theory: Vol 17* (pp. 165–213). New York: Academic Press.

Voss, J. F., & Post, T. A. (1988). On the solving of ill-structured problems. In M. T. H. Chi, R. Glaser, & M. Farr (Eds.), *The nature of expertise.* Hillsdale, NJ: Erlbaum.

Voss, J. F., Tyler, S. W., & Yengo, L. A. (1983). Individual differences in the solving of social science problems. In R. F. Dillon & R. R. Schreck (Eds.), *Individual differences in cognition.* New York: Academic Press.

Voss, J. F., Wolfe, C. R., Lawrence, J. A., & Engle, R. A. (1991). From representation to decision: An analysis of problem solving in international relations. In R. J. Sternberg & P. A. Frensch (Eds.), *Complex problem solving: Principles and mechanisms* (pp. 118–149). Hillsdale, NJ: Erlbaum.

Vygotsky, L. (1962). *Thought and language.* (E. Haufman & G. Vekor, Eds. and Trans.). Cambridge, MA: MIT Press.

Wachs, T. D. (1979). Proximal experience and early cognitive intellectual development: The physical environment. *Merrill-Palmer Quarterly, 25,* 3–41.

Wade, S. (1983). A synthesis of the research for improving reading in the social studies. *Review of Educational Research, 53,* 461–497.

Walberg, H. J., & Wynne, E. A. (1989). Character education: Toward a preliminary consensus. In L. Nucci (Ed.), *Moral development and character education.* Berkeley, CA: McCutchan.

Walker, E. L., & Tarte, R. D. (1963). Memory storage as a function of arousal and time with homogeneous and heterogeneous lists. *Journal of Verbal Learning and Verbal Behavior, 2,* 113–119.

Wall, M. J. (1988). Dysfluency in the child. In N. J. Lass, L. V. McReynolds, J. L. Northern, & D. E. Yoder (Eds.), *Handbook of speech-language pathology and audiology* (pp. 622–639). Toronto: Dekker.

Wallace, G., & McLoughlin, J. A. (1988). *Learning disabilities: Concepts and characteristics* (3rd ed.). Columbus, OH: Merrill Publishing.

Wallas, G. (1926). *The art of thought.* New York: Harcourt Brace Jovanovich.

Waller, T. G. (1987). *Reading research: Advances in theory and practice: Vol. 5.* New York: Academic Press.

Walpole, B. (1988). *175 science experiments to amuse and amaze your friends.* New York: Random House.

Wander, P. (1987). *The hyperactive child, adolescent and adult.* New York: Oxford University Press.

Wandersee, J. H. (1990). Concept mapping and the cartography of cognition. *Journal of Research in Science Teaching, 27*(10), 923–936.

Watson, J. (1992). *Discovering the brain.* New York. National Academy of Sciences.

Watson, J. B. (1925). *Behaviorism.* New York: Norton.

Watson, J. B. (1926). *What the nursery has to say about instincts.* Powell Lecture in Psychological Theory. Clark University, Worcester, MA. Published in *Psychologies of 1925.* Worcester, MA: Clark University.

Watson, J. B. (1930). *Behaviorism* (3rd ed.). New York: Norton.

Watson, J. B., & Rayner, R. (1920). Conditioned emotional reactions. *Journal of Experimental Psychology, 3,* 1–14.

Watson, M., Solomon, D., Battistich, V., Schaps, E., & Solomon, J. (1989). The child development project combining traditional and developmental approaches to values education. In L. Nucci (Ed.), *Moral development and character education: A dialogue* (pp. 51–92). Berkeley, CA: McCutchan.

Webb, W. M., Ender, P., & Lewis, S. (1986). Problem solving strategies and group processes in small groups learning computer programming. *American Educational Research Journal, 23*(2), 243–261.

Webber, J., & Scheuermann, P. (1991). Managing behavior problems: Accentuate the positive . . . eliminate the negative! *Teaching Exceptional Children, 24*(1), 13–19.

Weil, T., Zinberg, E., & Nelsen, J. E. (1968). Clinical and psychological effects of marijuana in man. *Science, 162,* 1234–1242.

Weiner, B. (1980). *Human motivation.* New York: Holt, Rinehart & Winston.

Weiner, B. (1986). *An attribution theory of motivation and emotion.* New York: Springer-Verlag.

Weiner, B. (1992). *Human motivation: Metaphors, theories, and research.* Newbury Park, CA: Sage Publications.

Weinstein, C., & Mayer, R. E. (1986). The teaching of learning strategies. In M. Wittrock (Ed.), *Handbook of research on teaching* (3rd ed.) (pp. 315–327). New York: Macmillan.

Weir, S. (1989). The computer in schools: Machine as humanizer. *Harvard Educational Review, 59*(1), 61–73.

Weiser, M., & Schertz, J. (1983). Programming problem representation in novice and expert programmers. *International Journal of Man–Machine Studies, 19,* 391–398.

Wender, P. (1987). *The hyperactive child, adolescent and adult.* New York: Oxford Press.

Werner, H. (1957). The concept of development from a comparative and organismic point of view. In D. Harris (Ed.), *The concept of development.* Minneapolis: University of Minnesota Press.

Wertheimer, M. (1945). *Productive thinking.* New York: Harper & Row.

Wexler-Sherman, C., Feldman, D., & Gardner, H. (1988). A pluralistic view of intellect: The Project Spectrum approach. *Theory into Practice, 28,* 77–83.

Whalen, C. K., & Henker, B. (1991). Social impact of stimulant treatment for hyperactive children. *Journal of Learning Disabilities, 24*(4), 231–241.

Whimbey, A., & Jenkins, E. L. (1987). *Analyze, organize, write* (rev. ed.). Hillsdale, NJ: Erlbaum.

Whimbey, A., & Lochhead, J. (1986). *Problem solving and comprehension* (4th ed.). Hillsdale, NJ: Erlbaum.

White, K. R. (1982). The reaction between socioeconomic status and academic achievement. *Psychological Bulletin, 91*(3), 461–481.

White, R. W. (1959). Motivation reconsidered: The concept of competence. *Psychological Review, 66,* 297–333.

Whitehill, R. P. (1972). The development of effective learning skills programs. *Journal of Educational Research, 65*(6), 281–285.

Wigdor, A. K., & Carver, W. R. (Eds.). (1982). *Ability testing: Uses, consequences, and controversies: Part i.* Washington, DC: National Academy Press.

Wigfield, A., & Karpothian, M. (1991). Who am I and what can I do? Self concepts and motivation in achievement situations. *Educational Psychologist, 26*(3 & 4), 233–262.

Wiley, K. B. (1977). *The status of pre-college science, mathematics, and social science education. 1955–1975: Vol. 3. Social science education.* Boulder, CO: Social Science Education Consortium.

Williams, R. B., Lane, J. P., Kuhn, C. M., Melosh, W., White, A. D., & Schanberg, S. M. (1982). Type A behavior and elevated physiological and neuroendocrine responses to cognitive tasks. *Science, 218,* 483–485.

Willig, A. C. (1985). A meta-analysis of selected studies on the effectiveness of bilingual education. *Review of Educational Research, 55*(3), 269–317.

Wilson, G. S., McCreary, R., Kean, J., & Baxter, J. C. (1979). The development of preschool children of heroin-addicted mothers: A controlled study. *Pediatrics, 63,* 135–141.

Winner, E. (1986). Where pelicans kiss seals. *Psychology Today, 20*(8), 24–26, 30, 32, 35.

Witkin, H., Dyk, R., Faterson, H., Goodenough, P., & Karp, S. (1962). *Psychological differentiation.* New York: Wiley.

Witkin, H., Moore, C., Goodenough, D., & Cox, P. (1977). Field-dependent and field-independent cognitive styles and their educational implications. *Review of Educational Research, 47,* 1–64.

Wixson, K. K. (1984). Level of importance of post-questions and children's learning from text. *American Educational Research Journal, 21,* 419–433.

Wolf, T. M. (1973). Effects of live modeled sex-inappropriate play behavior in a naturalistic setting. *Developmental Psychology, 9,* 120–123.

Wolpe, J. (1958). *Psychotherapy by reciprocal inhibition.* Stanford, CA: Stanford University Press.

Wood, E., Pressley, M., & Winne, P. (1990). Elaborative interrogation effects on children's learning of factual content. *Journal of Educational Psychology, 82*(4), 741–748.

Woods, N. S., Eyler, F. D., Behnke, M., & Conlon, M. (1993). Cocaine use during pregnancy. Maternal depressive symptoms and infant neurobehavior over the first month. *Infant Behavior and Development, 16,* 83–98.

Woodward, J. (1991). Procedural knowledge in mathematics: The role of the curriculum. *Journal of Learning Disabilities, 24*(4), 242–250.

Woodward, J., Carnine, D., & Gersten, R. (1988). Teaching problem-solving through computer simulations. *American Educational Research Journal, 25*(1), 72–86.

Wynne, E. A. (1989). Transmitting traditional values in contemporary schools. In L. Nucci (Ed.), *Moral development and character education: A dialogue* (pp. 19–36). Berkeley, CA: McCutchan.

Yando, R., Seitz, V., & Zigler, E. (1978). *Imitation: A developmental perspective.* Hillsdale, NJ: Erlbaum.

Ysseldyke, J. E., Thurlow, M., Groder, J., Wesson, C., Algozzine, R., & Deno, S. (1983). Generalizations from five years of research on assessment and decision-making: University of Minnesota Institute. *Exceptional Education Quarterly, 4*(1), 75–93.

Yussen, S. R. (1976). Moral reasoning from the perspective of others. *Child Development, 47,* 551–555.

Zabrucky, K., & Ratner, H. H. (1986). Children's comprehension monitoring and recall of inconsistent stories. *Child Development, 57,* 1401–1418.

Zaidel, D., & Sperry, R. W. (1972). Functional reorganization following commissurotomy in man. *Biology Annual Report,* p. 80.

Zeigarnik, B. (1968). Über das behalter von Erkdigten und uherledington Handlurgen. *Psychologische forschung.* Abridged and translated in W. S. Sahakion (Ed.), *History of psychology. A source book in systematic psychology.* Itasca, IL: F. E. Peacock. (Original work published 1927)

Zeki, S. (1992). The visual image in mind and brain. *Scientific American, 267*(9), 69–76.

Zentall, S. S., & Zentall, T. R. (1976). Amphetamine's paradoxical effect may be predictable. *Journal of Learning Disabilities, 9*(3), 183–189.

Zigmond, N., Kerr, M. M., & Schaeffer, A. L. (1988). Behavior patterns of learning disabled adolescents in high school academic classes. *Remedial and Special Education, 9*(2), 6–11.

Zimmerman, B. J. (1986). Becoming a self-regulated learner: Which are the key subprocesses? *Contemporary Educational Psychology, 11,* 307–313.

Zimmerman, B. J. (1989). A social cognitive view of self-regulated academic learning. *Journal of Educational Psychology, 81*(3), 329–339.

Zimmerman, B. J., & Martinez-Pons, M. (1988). Construct validation of a strategy model of student self-regulated learning. *Journal of Educational Psychology, 80,* 284–290.

Zimmerman, B. J., & Martinez-Pons, M. (1990). Relating grade, sex and giftedness to self-efficacy and strategy use. *Journal of Educational Psychology, 82,* 51–59.

Zimmerman, B. J., & Ringle, J. (1981). Effects of model persistence and statements of confidence on children's self-efficacy and problem-solving. *Journal of Educational Psychology, 73,* 485–493.

Zook, K. B., & DiVesta, F. J. (1991). Instructional analogies and conceptual misrepresentations. *Journal of Educational Psychology, 83*(2), 246–252.

Author Index

Subject Index